Journals of War

Journals of War

Coming of Age with the 104th Infantry During World War II

E.J. McCully

Edited by Anne McCully Dorre

Epigraph Books
Rhinebeck, New York

Journals of War: Coming of Age with the 104th Infantry During World War II © 2017 by Anne McCully Dorre, Susan Kuwitzky, Victoria Laack

All rights reserved. No part of this book may be used or reproduced in any manner without written permission from the author except in reviews and critical articles. Contact the publisher for information.

Paperback ISBN: 978-1-944037-62-8
Hardcover ISBN: 978-1-944037-63-5
Library of Congress Control Number: TK

Book design by Colin Rolfe

Epigraph Books
22 East Market St., Suite 304
Rhinebeck, NY 12572
(845) 876-4861
www.epigraphps.com

In honor of the life of
Ernest John ("Mac") McCully
December 30, 1915–April 15, 1973

*The work of the day is done,
and I can think of no better way to relax
than to write a few lines in this "Journal of War."*

Table of Contents

Editor's Preface and Acknowledgments ... xiii
Introduction ... xvi
Relationship Charts ... xxii
    Names of Family Members and Close Friends ... xxiii
    A: Immediate Family ... xxv
    B: Mother and Extended Family ... xxvi
    C: Friends ... xxvii
Military Charts ... xxviii
    A: 104th Infantry Division Command Personnel ... xxix
    B: 415th Infantry Regiment ... xxx
    C: Operational Units—U.S. Army ... xxxi

Journal 1   1
January 1, 1937 to February 26, 1941 (Ages 21–25)
The Prewar Years: Oakland, California

Carousing and socializing with friends and women • Job at Mother's Cakes and Cookies • Marriage to Virginia • Marital difficulties • Inner turmoil about relationship with Virginia • Divorce, subsequent loneliness, and depression • Friendship with Hubert Rafferty • Friendship with Vivian and the Morgan family • Worries about bills • Bob moves in • Struggles with life's problems • Financial worries resolved • Enters Army

Journal 2 (Volume I)   85
August 4, 1941 to February 26, 1942 (Ages 25–26)
Camp Callan

Induction at the Presidio of Monterey • Arrival at Camp Callan • Assignment to Plans and Training Division • Transfer to Post Engineer's Office • Promotion to Corporal and transfer to Headquarters 11th Training Group • Application to Officer Candidate School • Vivian in contact • War is declared • Hospital stay

Journal 3 (Volume II) 139
February 27, 1942 to February 14, 1943 (Age 26)
Fort Benning, Officer Candidate School

Vivian's plans to visit • Last days of hospital stay • Frustration with office politics • Departure to Officer Candidate School (O.C.S.) at Fort Benning • Commitment, obstacles, and fears of failure during O.C.S. training • Bob enlists in Air Corps • O.C.S. graduation • Commission and assignment to Camp Adair • Daily life at Camp Adair • Relationships with women • Worries, loneliness, thoughts on life's meaninglessness • Promotion to 1st Lieutenant • Return of health condition • Expectation of promotion

Journal 4 (Volume III) 257
February 20, 1943 to February 26, 1944 (Ages 27–28)
Camp Adair and California/Arizona Maneuver Area

Life at Camp Adair • Development as an officer • Office politics • Tensions with other officers • Reflections on life, dreams, and ideals • Relationship with fatherly Colonel Smith • Visit home to see family and friends • Relationships with women • Dates with Ruth • Rise and downfall • Health challenges • Maneuvers in Oregon, Arizona, and California • Margie's interest in marriage • Concerns regarding promotion • Refusal of Advanced School • Assignment as Regimental Personnel Officer

Journal 4 (Volume IV) 323
March 2, 1944 to August 11, 1944 (Age 28)
California/Arizona Maneuver Area and Camp Carson

Final days of California/Arizona Maneuver Area (CAMA) • Arrival at Camp Carson • Vivian marries • Decides to delay leave until promotion • Worries about health conditions • Personnel records inspections • Frustration and discouragement regarding politics and delay of promotion • Complimented for best Personnel Section in Division • Phyllis • Relationships with women • Dates with "Monty" restore faith in women • Departure for European Theater

Photographs

Journal 5 (Volume IV continued) 389
September 3, 1944 to February 25, 1945 (Ages 28-29)
The War

Landing at Utah Beach in Normandy • 13 American soldiers killed • Administrative inspection and scenes of war • Nightlife • Lifeblood of mail • Marching and rail transport across France and Belgium • Scenes of destruction and impressions of the French • Promotion to Captain • Encounter with Belgian Maquis • 415th battle casualties • Move to Holland • Transport of replacements to Front • Frustrations with Army "efficiency" • Driving blackout over unknown roads • Reflections over past 5 years • Big Push • Struggles with Personnel work quotas • Vivian gives birth • Reflections on marriage • Friends KIA • Courts-martial • Opinion of 4-F civilians • German propaganda • Autobahnen • Air raids • Christmas 1944 • Thoughts on employment after the war • Update on the war • Merits of the U.S. Army • Anticipation of final breakthrough into Germany • More courts-martial • More thoughts on life after the war • Mama's Boys • GI Bill • Crossing the Roer River

Journal 5 (Volume V) 477
February 26, 1945 to June 16, 1945 (Age 29)
The War

Changes due to loss of officers • Investigation of self-inflicted wound • Bombing attack by the Boche • Transport of reinforcements • Scenes of devastation • Souvenirs • Mail • More Courts-martial • Nine men drown • Dreams of postwar life • Scenes of German countryside • Final drive of war • Prisoner of war enclosure • Scenes of devastation • Signs of liberation and German surrender • Interrogation of enemies • Nordhausen Concentration Camp • Concerns about postwar job • Bronze Star Medal • Last letter to Vivian • Travel on Autobahnen to visit Regiment • End of War • Letter to Margie nixing ideas of marriage • Preparation for leave in U.S. • Trip by boxcar through Central Europe • Staging area

JOURNAL 6 529
May 1, 1946 to August 16, 1949 (Ages 30-33)
The Postwar Years: Phoenix, Arizona

Discharge from Army • Secures VA job in Phoenix as Contact Representative • Resumes dating and socializing with friends • Revelation of Margaret *** • Louise and the Starlit Concert • Bob marries • Itinerant work in Arizona • Falls in love with Emily • Engagement to Emily • Becomes Itinerant Representative for entire state • Concerns related to job security • Marriage to Emily • Granted service connection rating due to skin disability • Passes Civil Service Test • Mistrust of women eradicated because of Emily • Granted service connection rating due to stomach ulcer • Purchases new car and a home

Appendices:
    Appendix A: Glossary of Terms   557
    Appendix B: Maps   567
        San Francisco Bay Area   567
        California   568
        Oregon   569
        Arizona   570
        France-Belgium-Holland   571
        Germany   572
        Duren-Cologne Area—Germany   573
    Appendix C: Military Awards and Commendations   574
    Appendix D: Curriculum Vitae of E. J. McCully   587
    Appendix E: Timberwolf Resources and
                 Additional Reading   596

Index   597

Editor's Preface

When I was growing up, my father spent considerable time in a den furnished with a desk, maps, a bookcase, and military memorabilia. I loved perusing the books in his library. One day, I happened upon an ammunition can behind some books in his office. Curious, I opened the lid to find a treasure trove of journals about my father's experiences during World War II as well as his subsequent meeting of my mother. Not being particularly interested in military things at the time, I discreetly replaced the books in the can, never revealing my discovery to anyone. As the years passed, however, I found myself revisiting these "secret" journals and reading sections that piqued my interest. Whether my father ever knew that I had found his journals will remain a mystery, but on one occasion he raised the subject, informing me that he had placed some "diaries" in an old "ammo can." After he died, he said, the family could do whatever it wished with them. Not long after that conversation, at the relatively young age of 57, my father departed this world. As the family historian, I kept the cherished journals, opening them only to read selected pages as the years passed by.

A decade ago, I decided to transcribe the journals into a singular manuscript. Learning about my father's life as a young man was fascinating to say the least. During the process, I came to know and understand him on an entirely different level. The more I read the journals, the more I became convinced that his writings contained an incredibly powerful and coherent story, one that I thought might be of immeasurable interest and importance to others. Ultimately, I came to the conclusion that a single volume containing all of his journals would not only serve as a treasured addition to our family history, but it would also provide a valuable contribution to the growing collection of World War II narratives, particularly those recounting the European Theater.

Journals of War is a coming of age story set in the World War II era (1937–1949). It is not so much an account of military action and combat as it is a personal narrative of my father's civilian life and military career spanning ages 21–33. The book is a compilation of six bound journals that tell a detailed story of my father's life, beginning with his time as a young man in Oakland, California, followed by his induction into the U.S. Army. It recounts his first military assignment to Camp Callan in San Diego, California, the demanding training he underwent at Officer Candidate School in Fort Benning, Georgia, and his subsequent commission as a Second Lieutenant with assignment to Camp Adair, Oregon. The journals contain descriptive accounts of bivouacs and maneuvers in the Oregon desert and the California-Arizona Maneuver Area (CAMA). They impart an extraordinary account of his experiences as a Regimental Personnel Officer in the 104th Infantry of the 415th Regiment in the European Theater and his eventual promotion to Captain. *Journals of War* describes my father's ultimate transition back into civilian life in Phoenix, Arizona, characterized by gainful employment and the culmination of a protracted yearning for a fulfilling marital relationship.

One might ask why an individual would invest so much time keeping a record of current life events. My father describes the journals as a way to keep "a record of outstanding events in my mind and certain impressions that I feel are worthy of retaining for the future." He viewed the book as a confidant of sorts, a "refuge" from worries, and a source of "comfort and solace" for expressing his thoughts and feelings. If he had married before entering the service, he might have communicated these sentiments to his wife through letters written home. However, any war correspondence would have been subject to censorship. By his own admission, my father knew the journals he was keeping would be "strictly against regulations" when overseas, but he managed to keep a record of events all the same.

One might point out that my father was part of the rear echelon and thus was not involved in battles on the front lines—the implication being that his service had not been as important as that of the combatants who saw direct action. It is true that many soldiers made the ultimate sacrifice, and this should not be marginalized. Nevertheless, my father unquestionably made sacrifices and put himself at risk as well. While performing his job as Regimental Personnel Officer, he was personally responsible for the delivery of hundreds of replacement troops through dangerous conditions to the front lines. Using inadequate maps, he navigated roads that were heavily mined and under artillery fire. He drove blackout over miles of shell-torn road. At times, he was erroneously directed into enemy territory by military police. Air raid activities, including Hitler's buzz bombs and full-scale bombing by the Germans, put his life at risk and, sadly, the War claimed many of his close friends. Then, too, as an infantry officer, he gave up five years of his life in service to our country. As did other soldiers, he endured "rain, knee-deep mud, freezing cold, and continuous marching with unbearably heavy packs." Like other GIs, he lacked the pleasant amenities of hot showers and comfortable beds. At the same time, my father was fully aware that his typing skills had played a role in his good fortune toward securing assignment to the rear echelon and attributed his transfer there to fate. In the end, however, the experiences articulated in these journals convey his own story.

This book has been a long time in the making. I wish to personally thank everyone who helped support my efforts toward the publication of *Journals of War*. I owe a special debt of gratitude to Bill Harfst (fellow Timberwolf Pup), John Pecusa, and Don DeValle for taking time out of their busy lives to read the manuscript and for offering valuable commentary and enthusiastic support. Additionally, I would like to express my appreciation to Donald Mittendorf for offering important comments in his critique of the manuscript and for sharing candid insights into his friendship with my father. I want to thank my sisters, Victoria Laack and Susan Kuwitzky, for their unwavering support throughout this project. I am also deeply grateful to Susan Kuwitzky for proofreading the manuscript, for offering useful suggestions to improve the book, and for sharing her memories and insightful perceptions about our father. Above all, I wish to thank my husband, Jim Dorre, for numerous brainstorming sessions and constructive suggestions, for all the time spent reviewing various drafts of the manuscript, and for his unfailing love and support in bringing this book to completion.

Anne McCully Dorre

Introduction

Ernest John McCully was born on December 30, 1915, in La Grande, Oregon. Because of his precarious condition, he was placed in a makeshift incubator consisting of a shoebox with a light bulb. His father died when he was two years old, and his mother remarried shortly before his fifth birthday. Growing up, he had two older sisters and two younger half-brothers. During his elementary school years, the family moved to Oakland, California. One year after graduation from high school, in the midst of the Great Depression, he was employed by Mother's Cakes and Cookies in Oakland. It was during this time that he wrote his first entry in a small diary, which ultimately led to over a decade's worth of writings about his life during the World War II era.

My father rarely spoke about his experiences during the War. This reticence seems to have been typical of many WWII veterans, or it could have been that he was reluctant to share his story with his three daughters who, at that particular time in their lives, would not have been the least bit interested in military remembrances. I once interviewed my father for a high school American History assignment on WWII, wherein he recounted a straightforward chronology of events and observations sans any personal or emotional commentary. That is not to say that he had not been affected by the War. My father was part of the 104th Infantry Division, or "Timberwolves," which liberated the Mittelbau-Dora Concentration Camp near Nordhausen, Germany. Accordingly, he had an aversion to striped fabric, which was banned in our household because it was reminiscent of the clothing worn by concentration camp prisoners. Still, this was a man who lived up to the Timberwolf motto of the 104th Infantry Divison, "NOTHING IN HELL CAN STOP THE TIMBERWOLVES," by proving himself in the military and successfully meeting the challenges of life.

Journals of War: Coming of Age with the 104th Infantry During WWII is a complete and comprehensive personal account of preto post-World War II. It is the story of the making of a soldier—the making of a man. The journals are distinctive in that they were written in the immediacy of events as they occurred and documented on an almost-daily basis. This sets them apart from after-the-fact memoirs and journal entries interspersed with commentary, both of which run the risk of embellishment and/or fading memories. They may also be distinguished from letters written to family and friends, which were restricted in their content due to censorship rules.

Throughout his writings, my father variously uses the terms, "diary," "journal," and "chronicle." Whereas some authors have attempted to argue the difference between a diary and a journal, the fact is they are the same. Both words spring from Latin roots, which connote "day" or "daily." In simplest terms, a useful definition for the word "diary" would read as "a daily personal record of events, experiences, observations, and reflections." In contrast, a chronicle merely refers to a record of events in chronological order. In deciding which of these terms to include in the title of the book, I deferred to my father's own writings. Of the three, "journal" occurs most often. Moreover, he describes one of the volumes as a "Journal of War," which I amended to *Journals of War* because there are six journals.

The journals in which my father recorded his entries span the years 1937–1949. In physical appearance, they are a varied assortment of shapes and sizes. The earliest book is a small standard five-year diary, green and leather-bound with a zipper. The diary accommodates only four square inches of writing space for each day of the year, which may explain why his initial entries appear abbreviated and somewhat choppy. Almost all of the pages are handwritten in pencil; the rest are in ink. The diary contains writings about his life up to and including entry into the U.S. Army. The second journal is a black, 6x9-inch notebook, bound with cover board and secured with a metal, two-prong fastener on the side. Most pages are typed either on blank pages or Camp Callan stationery, although the last few pages were handwritten in blue ink. This journal contains events experienced at Camp Callan. The next two three-ring notebooks are approximately 7x10 inches in size with gray, canvas-like coverings. They recount my father's experiences at Camp Callan, Fort Benning, Camp Adair, and Camp Carson. All entries are written in black or blue ink, a good number on lined pages. The most unusual book is a Remington Rand, 6x9-inch Army green notebook with canvas-like, steel-reinforced covers, connected with two strips of yellow canvas-like material. The pages are yellowed and loose and, with the exception of a few final pages, are completely typewritten on lined paper. This journal begins with an entry at sea in the North Atlantic. The final book is a 5x7-inch, small black two-ring notebook that contains only a few typed pages, most likely because by that time my father had become preoccupied with the everyday activities of postwar civilian life.

There is no doubt that my father's typing abilities were extraordinary. Indeed, that is one reason he ended up in an administrative position. As evidenced by the actual typewritten pages of the journals, his typing was impeccable, containing minimal errors. Moreover, his handwriting was clear and relatively easy to read. Among or attached to the journals were many loose papers, including extra journal pages, handwritten notes, news clippings, maps of his travels, newsletters, lists of favorite record albums and songs, portions of letters, lists of addresses, an artistic sketch ("On the Bluffs at Callan"), and even a letter of "Official Business," regarding the "Findings of court-martial." As with all aging documents and records, the condition of the journals continues to deteriorate by the day. At some point in the future these books and their contents will be donated to the Veterans History Project at the Library of Congress.

As editor of *Journals of War*, I have done everything possible to remain true to my father's words and intent. After all, this is his story. It was not difficult to edit this work, as it was very well written. Any changes were kept to an absolute minimum and relate primarily to sentence structure, punctuation, and consistency. For example, my father had a tendency to compose long sentences and his use of dashes was excessive; therefore, I made changes for clarity's sake. I also standardized some abbreviations (e.g., Lt. for Lieut.) and corrected any rare spelling mistakes. In keeping with convention, I italicized such items as book titles, operettas, and foreign words. Some names were misspelled and are so noted within brackets. I believe all changes hold true to the essence of my father's writing.

All names contained in *Journals of War* are those of real people. For a variety of reasons, and after extensive deliberation and consultation with others, I decided to remove minor portions of the text and a few selected last names. I felt that these omissions would not affect the content or intent of my father's words in any significant manner. Thus, redactions have been noted by use of the following symbol: ***. Needless to say, the original journal pages will remain unaltered and, as previously mentioned, will eventually be available in the Library of Congress.

Diaries and journals are often difficult to read and follow since significant events are interspersed with everyday mundane activities. To assist readers in this regard, I have included a brief synopsis before each section and listed these summaries in the Table of Contents as well. These summaries will allow readers to select portions of interest to them. Journals may also contain people, places, and terms unfamiliar to the reader. To aid the reader, I have added relationship charts, glossaries, maps, and indexes to promote easier comprehension. Every effort was made to identify people correctly, and anyone searching for a particular individual should find the index especially useful, as I have cross-referenced first and last names. I also researched complete names, regardless of whether both monikers appear in my father's writings, so that interested readers might readily find an individual of personal significance.

The decision to publish my father's journals was not taken lightly, as writings such as these are meant to be private. My father held strong opinions about military personnel, friends, and family. For one thing, he discussed the mistakes and bad judgments that he observed while in the Army. His journals expose private health conditions, problematic personal relationships, and a failed marriage. My father shared complicated and vulnerable emotions, ranging from intense loneliness to anxiety regarding his health to bitterness about his divorce. Beyond the candid communications found within his journals, however, stands a man who dearly loved his family, enjoyed rich friendships and social acquaintances, admired his fellow officers and other military leaders, and successfully met the challenges of his personal and professional life despite his fears and health problems.

Journals of War provides a few glimpses of my father's personality as well. A self-described romantic, my father's appreciable knowledge of the humanities demonstrates a love for classical music, literature, history, and a fascination with languages. Despite never having attended college, one might say that he was a Renaissance man to some extent. It is likely that this classical foundation influenced his writing style—richly detailed, vivid, and clear—particularly when reflecting on the beauty of Europe in the midst of destruction. Indeed, much of his writing is slightly reminiscent of the ancient historian,

Thucydides, in that it is a chronicle of lived events observed and documented from his own experiences and as an eyewitness to one of the most significant events in history. Generally speaking, however, the primary themes of the journal entries include personal and professional relationships, his military training and career, personal thoughts, feelings, and opinions, and the meaning and purpose of life.

Ever the idealist, my father held dreams of the perfect wife, home, family, and a meaningful life. An unpleasant divorce obstructed the achievement of these ideals for a time, and the War delayed his efforts to obtain them. Amid uncertainty about the future, he often struggled with feelings of loneliness, despondency, and an ever-present state of anxiety, which occasionally manifested in the form of health problems. At times, his search for meaningful relationships so eluded him that he resorted to "drinking sprees and a frenzied search for companionship." Philosophizing on life, he questioned why one generation should have to fight and struggle for existence while others remain privileged to live and die in peaceful eras.

One of the most striking aspects of my father's life during this formative time period was his indomitable drive to excel. Although initially doubtful about some of the skills necessary for Officer Candidate School, he took advantage of every opportunity to improve himself, both physically and mentally. Through hard work, diligent study, and extraordinary self-discipline, he emerged as a mature, transformed individual exhibiting self-confidence, mental toughness, and resourcefulness.

Camp Adair was the beginning of my father's development as an officer and his stellar rise to Regimental Personnel Officer. There, he found a father figure and mentor in Colonel Smith, who saw great potential in the young soldier. Through all the military training, field exercises, and job transitions, my father performed at an exceptional level. He showed a competitive side and often went head to head with other officers, vying for position. Nevertheless, it was clear that he valued his friends and that he was quick to acknowledge the accomplishments of others. When his own personal "downfall" occurred, it delayed his cherished promotion to Captain. However, whatever precipitated this mysterious event is destined to remain secret. Two months after his death in April 1973, a devastating fire at the National Personnel Records Center in St. Louis forever destroyed his military records.

The operation of any personnel office definitely has its

challenges. Imagine trying to repeatedly transport, pack, set up, and dismantle almost two tons of personnel office equipment in a field setting—during a war—and keep it running efficiently. Among his other many duties, my father was responsible for battle casualty reporting, administrative recordkeeping, reclassifications, processing replacement troops, participation in court-martial cases, and supervising a staff of 38 men. Moreover, office locations and the transport of replacement troops were often situated in dangerous locales. Indeed, my father did it all so well that he received superior ratings and a Bronze Star for "meritorious service."

As a personal life chronicle and account of one World War II soldier's experiences in the European Theater, this book would be a valuable addition to the libraries of military historians and researchers, military personnel, and those associated with the 104th Infantry Division (i.e., Timberwolves and Timberwolf Pups). Additionally, some readers will find the book important because the war it describes took place on the European soil of their homelands. As a coming of age story, the book serves as an enriching inspiration for the journeys, transitions, and challenges of life. My guess is that descendants of E. J. McCully and future generations interested in genealogical research will find this book fascinating as well.

Relationship Charts

Names of Family Members and Close Friends
Alphabetical order by first name

Name	Relationship	Chart
Bob (Westrem)	Half brother	A
Charlie (Schwab)	Lena's husband	A
Cooper	Vivian's husband	C
Don (Sainsbury)	Nephew	A
Doris	Virginia's sister	None
Ed E./Ed Erickson	Virginia's uncle	None
Elwood (Read)	1st cousin	B
Emily	2nd wife	A
Ernest (Leurquin)	Nadine's husband	B
Eunice	Vivian's sister	C
Fred (Strahl)	Friend	C
Fred, Uncle (Read)	Uncle	B
Harold (Westrem)	Half brother	A
Hubert/Hubie/Hu (Rafferty)	Friend; Virginia's ex-husband	A
Jim	Doris's husband	None
John (Strahl)	Friend	C
John, Uncle (Read)	Uncle	B
Joyce (Rafferty)	Child of Hubert and Virginia	A
Knut (Westrem)	Stepfather	A
Lena	Sister	A
Lola	Sister	A
Louie, Uncle (Harvey)	Uncle	B
Margaret (Schultens)	Elwood's wife	B
Margaret/Margie	"Girlfriend"	None
Mattie, Aunt	Aunt	B
Melanie	Mother of Fred and John	C

Name	Relationship	Chart
Morgan, Art	Vivian's father	B
Morgan, Mrs.	Vivian's mother	B
Mother	*See* Nettie Read (in Relationship Chart)	A, B
Mutt	Eunice's husband	C
Nadine	2nd cousin	B
Olive	John Strahl's girlfriend	C
Rafferty	*See* Hubert (above)	A
Raffertys [last name]	Hubert's parents	A
Ruth, Aunt	Fred's wife	B
Venita [Vineta]	Vivian's daughter	B
Veryl	Ed Erikson's wife	None
Virginia	1st wife	C
Walt (Sainsbury)	Lola's husband	A
Wavel [Waval]	1st cousin	B

Additional names and information listed in Index.

Relationship Charts xxv

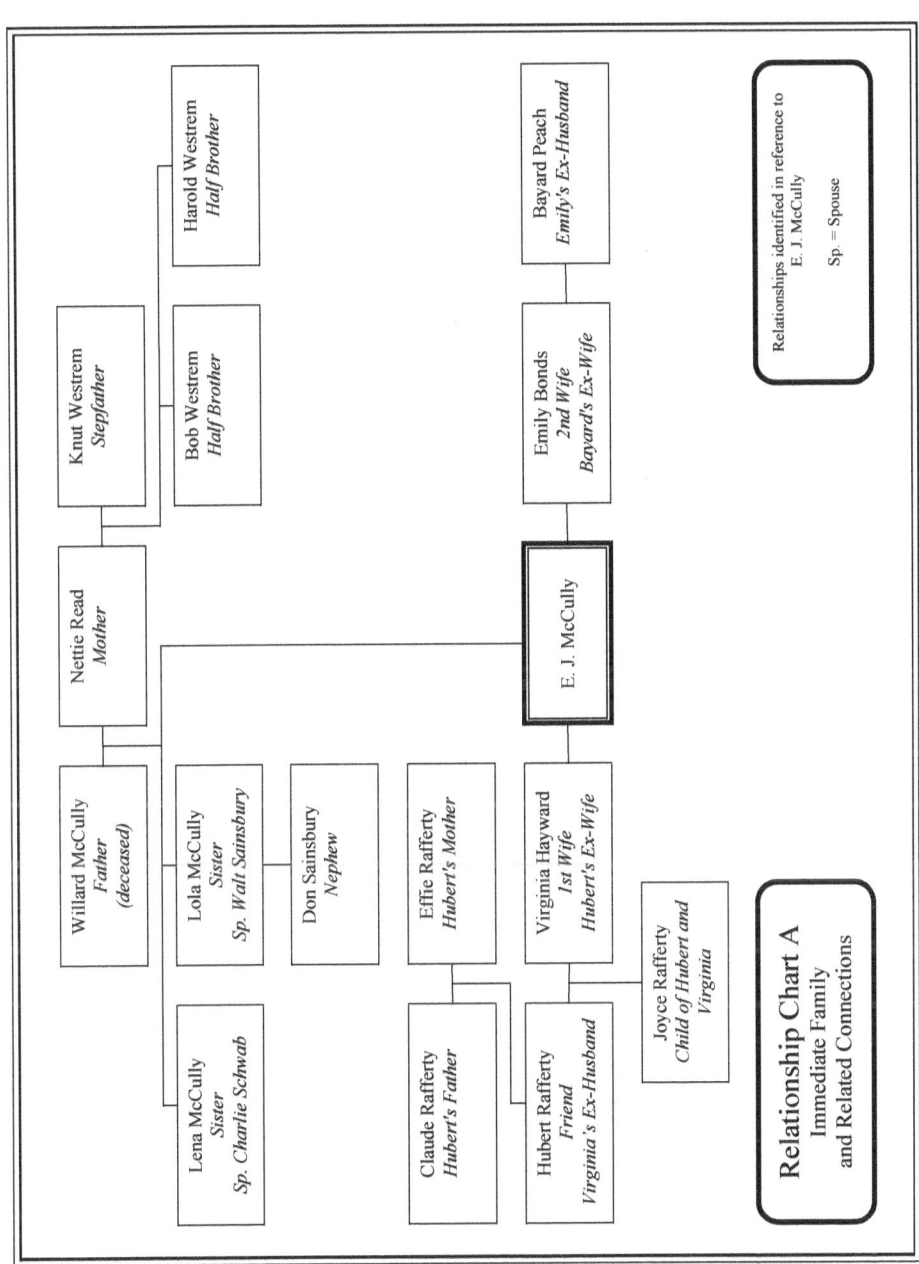

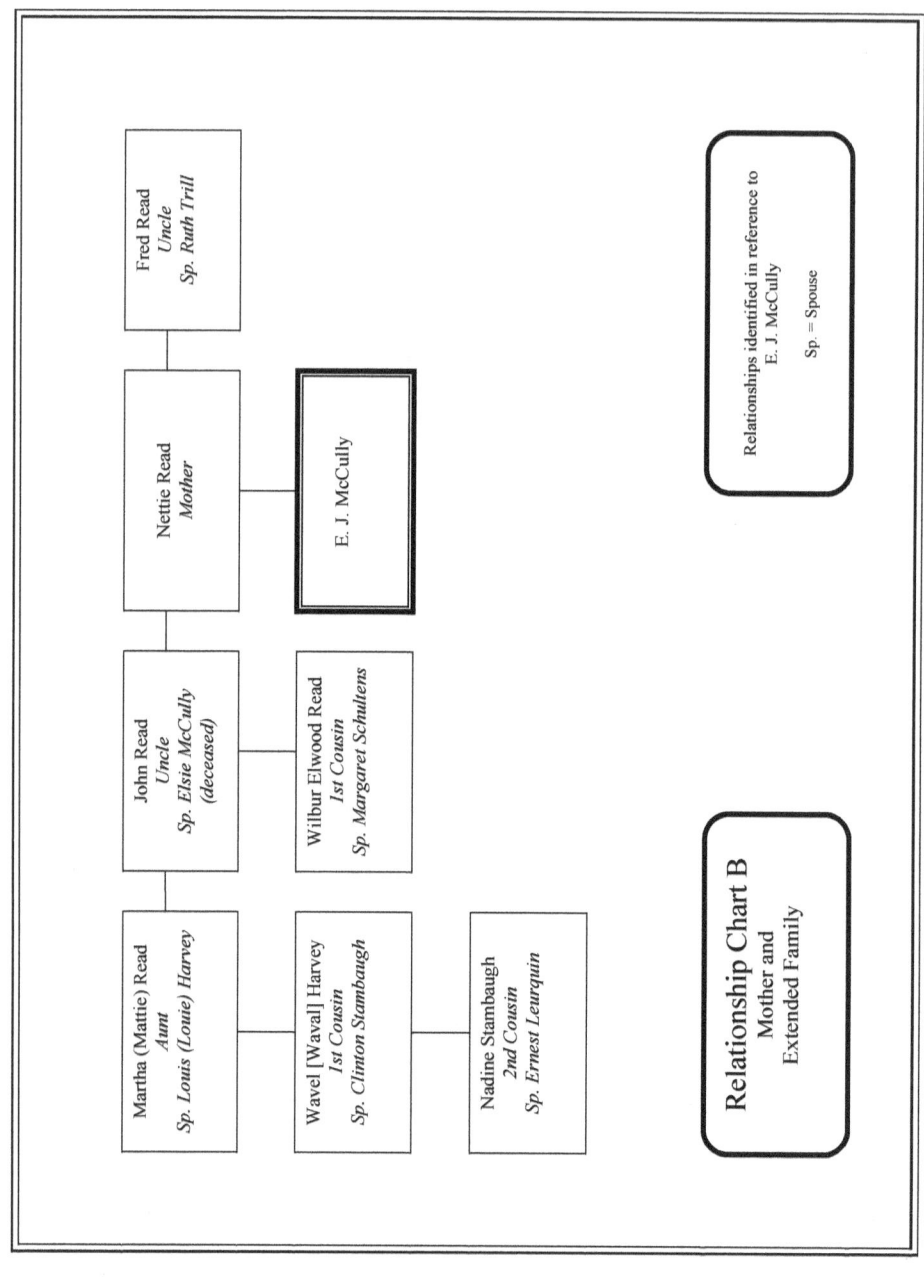

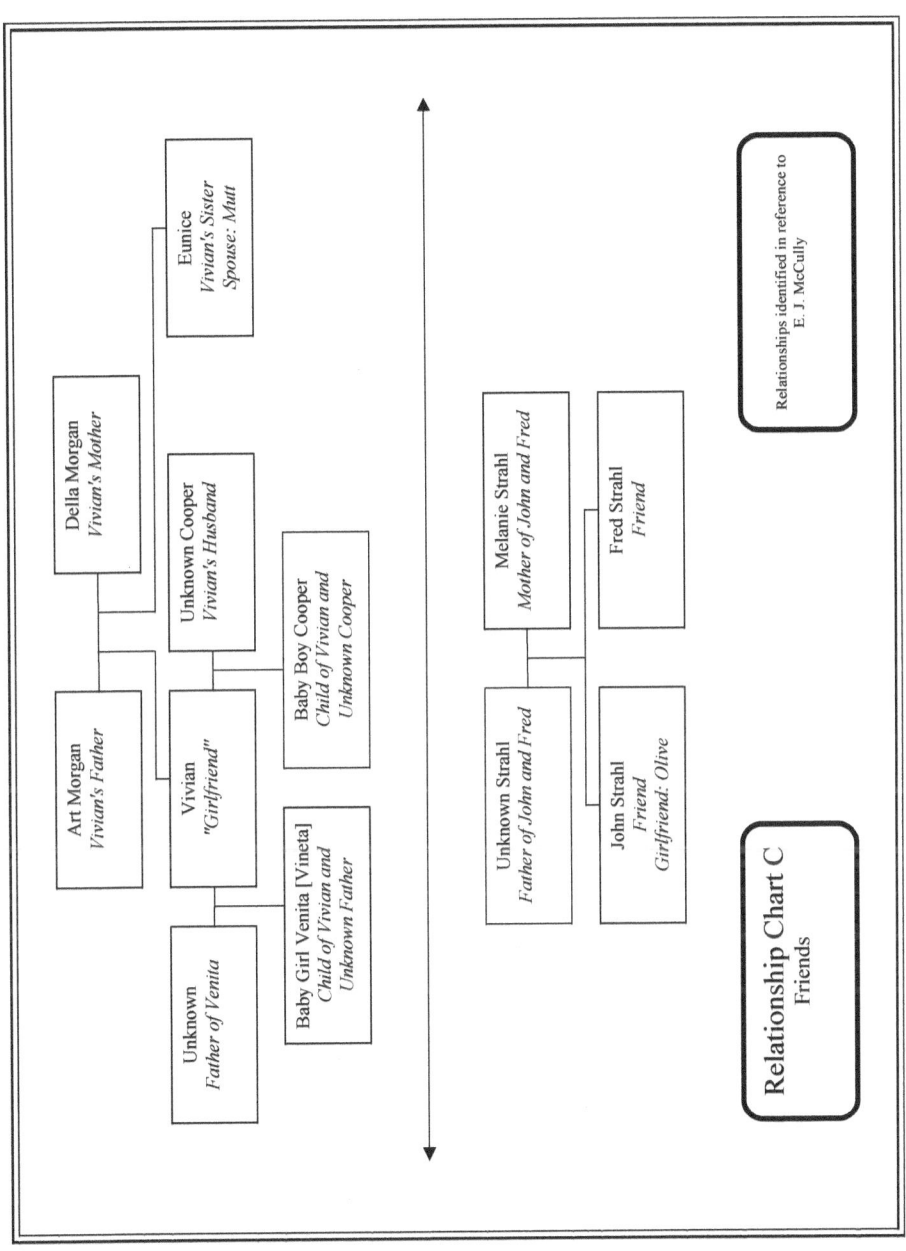

MILITARY CHARTS

Military Chart A

415TH INFANTRY REGIMENT COMMAND PERSONNEL
(23 Oct 1944 forward)
Starred names (*) appearing in *Journals of War*.

Commanding Officer
Col. John H. Cochran*

Executive Officers
Lt. Col. Gerald C. Kelleher (until 1 Mar 1945)*
Lt. Col. Peter Denisevich (after 1 Mar 1945)*

S-1 Capt. John G. Smith, Jr.*
S-2 Maj. John R. Deane, Jr. (until 1 Mar 1945)*
S-3 Maj. Hugh L. Carey*
S-4 Maj. William G. Herbert*

1ST BATTALION

Commanding Officer:
Lt. Col. John H. Elliott*

Company A Capt. Bernard F. McKerney*
Company B Capt. Russell Thomas*
Company C Capt. Herschel W. Swann*
Company D Capt. William D. Gude, Jr.
Headquarters Company Capt. Harold D. Hall*

3RD BATTALION

Commanding Officer:
Lt. Col. Gerald C. Kelleher*

Company I Capt. William W. Barnes*
Company K Capt. Raymond D. Collins*
Company L Capt. Francis J. Hallahan
Company M Capt. Leland W. Struble
Headquarters Company Capt. William D. Beard*

2ND BATTALION

Commanding Officers:
Lt. Col. Peter Denisevich (until 1 Mar 1945)*
Lt. Col. John R. Deane (1 Mar 1945)*

Company E Capt. Kenneth K. Bell
Company F Capt. Charles W. Carroll*
Company G Capt. Brown A. Craig
Company H Capt. Harold J. Strobel
Headquarters Company Capt. Ned U. Bourke*

SPECIAL UNITS

Antitank Company Captain John G. Vasilake, Jr.*
Cannon Company Captain Forrest L. Gregory*
Service Company Capt. George E. Martin*
Headquarters Company Capt. Charles H. Allwander*

Chart created from data in Hoegh, L. A., & Doyle, H. J. (Eds.). (1946). *Timberwolf Tracks*. Washington, DC: Infantry Journal, Inc.

Military Chart B

**104TH INFANTRY DIVISION
COMMAND PERSONNEL**
(23 Oct 1944 forward)
Starred names (*) appearing in *Journals of War*.

Commanding General
Maj. Gen. Terry de la Mesa Allen*

Assistant Division Commanders
Brig. Gen. Bryant E. Moore*
(until 26 Feb 1945)
Col. George A. Smith, Jr.
(26 Feb 1945 to 1 Mar 1945)
Brig. Gen. Charles T. Lanham
(5 Mar 1945 to 13 Jun 1945)
Brig. Gen. Charles K. Gailey, Jr.
(4 Aug 1945 to 20 Dec 1945)

General Staff
Chief of Staff Col. Bartholomew R. DeGraff*
Asst Chief of Staff, G-1 Lt. Col. Scott T. Rex*
Assistant G-1 Maj. Kermit R. Mason
Asst Chief of Staff, G-2 Lt. Col. Mark S. Plaisted
Asst G-2 Maj. Harold Fosnot
Asst Chief of Staff, G-3 Lt. Col. Leo A. Hoegh*
Asst G-3 Lt. Col. Donald J. Dobbs
Asst Chief of Staff, G-4 Lt. Col. Clyde L. Pennington*
Asst G-4 Maj. Alexander G. Eagle

Special Staff
Commanding General, Division Artillery Brig. Gen. William R. Woodward*
Adjutant General Lt. Col. Melvin M. Kernan*
Finance Officer Lt. Col. Luther E. Lewis
Chaplain Lt. Col. Paul C. Mussell
Inspector General Lt. Col. Russell F. Thompson
Judge Advocate Lt. Col. James O. Bass
Provost Marshal Maj. William C. Nutting
Ordnance Officer Lt. Col. James D. Williamson
Chemical Warfare Officer Lt. Col. Richard Hopelain*
Engineer Officer Lt. Col. Max E. Kahn
(to 5 Dec 1944)
Engineer Officer Lt. Col. Robert P. Tabb, Jr.
(from 5 Dec 1944)
Postal Officer Capt. Thomas E. Harrington
Quartermaster Lt. Col. Clyde M. Smith*
(until 9 Jan 1945)
Lt. Col. Robert M. Denny
(from 9 Jan 1945)
Signal Officer Lt. Col. Ralph E. Willey
Special Service Officer Major Robert C. Duffy
Surgeon Lt. Col. Hugh W. Jones
Commanding Officer Special Troops Lt. Col. Kenneth C. Haycraft

Chart created from data in Hoegh, L. A., & Doyle, H. J. (Eds.). (1946). *Timberwolf Tracks*. Washington, DC: Infantry Journal, Inc.

Military Charts xxxi

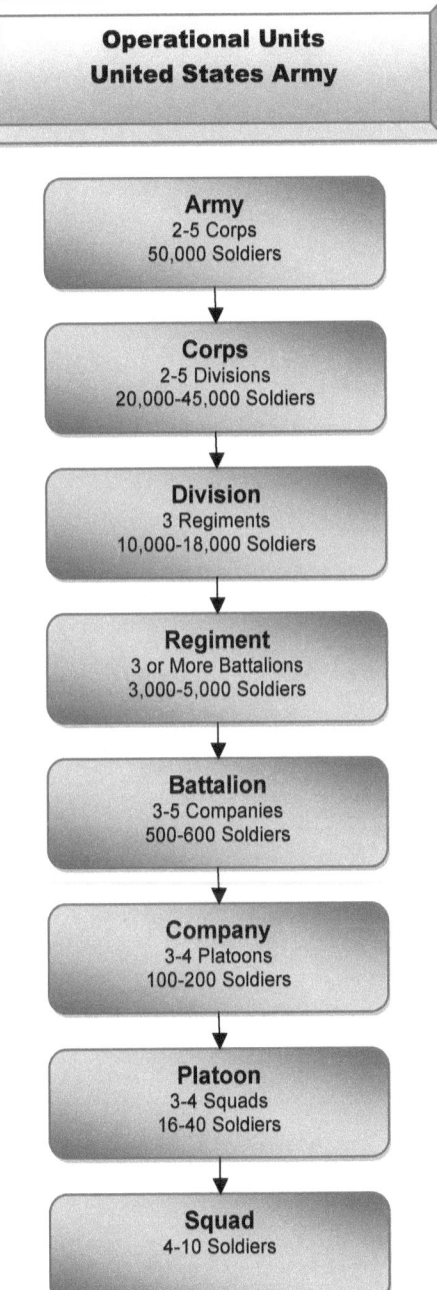

Military Chart C

Chart created by editor from data in The Official Homepage of the United States Army (www.army.mil).

JOURNAL 1

THE PREWAR YEARS
JANUARY 1, 1937 to FEBRUARY 26, 1941
Ages 21–25

So tonight, my mind is in a mad turmoil.
I know in my heart I love her
and want to give her another chance . . .
But I'm afraid because I was hurt awfully deep,
and it almost tore my heart out . . .

CAROUSING AND SOCIALIZING WITH FRIENDS AND WOMEN • JOB AT MOTHER'S CAKES AND COOKIES • MARRIAGE TO VIRGINIA • MARITAL DIFFICULTIES • INNER TURMOIL ABOUT RELATIONSHIP WITH VIRGINIA • DIVORCE, SUBSEQUENT LONELINESS, AND DEPRESSION • FRIENDSHIP WITH HUBERT RAFFERTY • FRIENDSHIP WITH VIVIAN AND THE MORGAN FAMILY • WORRIES ABOUT BILLS • BOB MOVES IN • STRUGGLES WITH LIFE'S PROBLEMS • FINANCIAL WORRIES RESOLVED • ENTERS ARMY

JANUARY 1, 1937
Recovering from effects of gala celebration of last night. Saw some relatives and had a nice turkey dinner. Went to a very dead party and got home about 1. They were mostly older people (firemen and wives).

JANUARY 2, 1937
Alarm failed to go off last night, and I was 2-1/2 hours late for work, which caused some disagreeable consequences. Working day ended swell, however. Went out on a "blind date" and met Blanche F. She is sure a wonderful girl. I think I am going to like her a lot. Made a date for Wednesday.

JANUARY 3, 1937
Sun. Got up about 1. Small breakfast. Put on riding outfit and went to a ranch out in Richmond to go horseback riding. Saw some plow horses but didn't ride. Went to a show. Small quarrel about brakes. Ended OK. Get car TUES.

JANUARY 4, 1937
Very dead day. Nothing of importance. Went to hospital with Lyle and saw his mother. Turned in about 11:15 and got up about 4.

JANUARY 5, 1937
As I said, I got up about 4 and was I <u>dead</u> this morning. So am turning in at nine tonight. Got the car about 4 this afternoon and is it a honey with its new paint job. Have date with Blanche tomorrow.

JANUARY 6, 1937
Had a tough time at work. They laid off 4 guys, and I'm a little worried. I suppose I'm foolish as we've been working 2 years steady, but I'm

worried. Took Blanche to show. Kissed her for the first time tonight. Gee, she's a sweet kid.

January 7, 1937
Got home last night at 1. Got up at 5. Felt lousy all day. One of the worst days I ever put in. Worked from 6 to 7:30. Went Jungletown [Jingletown] with Vic and had about 4 shots of whiskey and got half potted. Turned in about 11. Still worried.

January 8, 1937
Very easy day. Some unpleasant incidences at work, though. Damn! I wish I could quit worrying. Saw Blanche for a few minutes and got a date for tomorrow night. Sent all clothes to cleaners, preparatory to moving from this damn boarding house.

January 9, 1937
Saturday. Was going to work, but as it wasn't absolutely necessary, I didn't. Went downtown and broke the driveshaft in my car, which cost me 13.68 and a renewal of my worries. Went out with Blanche. Got home about 1:30. She's awfully nice, but possibly a trifle juvenile for me.

January 10, 1937
Sun. Got up about 12 and went down to get my car. Works swell. Went out and saw Lyle's folks. Lyle and I are certainly drifting apart rapidly. Caused by this damned Gilbert family. I think I was the loneliest I've ever been today. Went to the show. Then drove up in hills and thought. Came home.

January 11, 1937
Monday. Moderate day. Still worried about my job and feeling very disgusted with life in general.

January 12, 1937
Worked 11-1/2 hours today. Got through about 6:30. Went over and saw Blanche. Took a ride up in the hills and saw the snow. Stopped and had a sundae. Got home about 11.

January 13, 1937
Wednesday. Late for work about ½ an hour. Quite an uneventful day.

Beginning to be quite worried about my bills. I'll have to do some tall figuring. Expect the Gilberts' eviction any day now.

JANUARY 14, 1937
Nothing of very much interest today. Quite a big day at work.

JANUARY 15, 1937
Friday. An equally uneventful day. Although a big day, everything ran smooth.

JANUARY 16, 1937
Sat. Worked 2 hrs. today (10 to 12). Paid all bills ($37.65). Took Blanche to show.

JANUARY 17, 1937
Spent all day today looking for house or apt. in which to move. Went to show with kids.

JANUARY 18, 1937
Mon. Easy day at work. I am awfully worried about my bills. I am far behind on my car schedule. Went to Union.

JANUARY 19, 1937
Tues. As I said, I went to Union. Didn't get home till 1, so I was <u>dead tired</u> today. Too much nightlife. I think I'm coming down with the flu. I hope not, however.

JANUARY 20, 1937
Wed. Felt so lousy, I didn't go to work today. Finances are in a very critical state. Well, it looks like the final breakup of Lyle and me, a 12-year friendship. I've got to move out in order to save money. God guide me now. I surely need it.

JANUARY 21, 1937
Thurs.

MARCH 25, 1937
Have neglected to write in diary for some time. Many important things have happened. Have been betrayed by my well-loved pal, Lyle—a 12-

year friendship shattered. He moved out today, although I don't blame him entirely. I know that snake, Bob, influenced him. Am forlorn and miserable. Am more worried about my job tonight than for the last two years. It all depends on tomorrow. Am moving in with fellows I hardly know. Terribly worried by bills. I don't know where to turn. God give me guidance.

APRIL 25, 1937
First date with Virginia, my future wife, although I didn't know it then. Went to San Jose for a milkshake.

AUGUST 18, 1937
Blue and discouraged tonight. I don't know where I stand. $376 in bills. My engagement broken. The one girl in this world that I love, out with another fellow. A small check looming next week. I wonder if Virginia really loves me? I worship her. Just a fool, I guess. Always have been.

AUGUST 19, 1937
Very surprised late last night. Virginia came home and woke me up and told me she would like to become engaged again, which made me very happy. Got to work at 6. Had to go to Union meeting. I don't work tomorrow—only one oven. My bills still worry me.

AUGUST 20, 1937
Payday today. $36.32. Paid $20 on car. Still in hole on some lesser bills. Have to take Mother back to Sonora next Sunday (on a very small check). Hope V. will go with me.

AUGUST 21, 1937
Got up about 10. Didn't work. Bummed around all day. Worked on car a little. V. bought some ice cream for which I felt very much indebted. Helped Mother move over to Max's.

AUGUST 22, 1937
Got up about 9:15. Had breakfast at boarding house. Went for long ride and read books. Went to restaurant at 5:45. Saw Joe who just bought a '36 Ford Convertible Coupe.

OCTOBER 4, 1937
After months of little arguments, decisions, and heated discussions, finally broke up with V. (due to Walt's attraction, I guess). I'm a darn fool—I still love her—but I'll never see her again. Another advancement at work but now in debt to the tune of $1080.50!!!!!!!!!

NOVEMBER 1, 1937
Married today at Vancouver, Washington. 12:15 p.m.

DECEMBER 21, 1937
My so-called "married life," a complete failure. It's turned out to be everything I feared most before I wed. Sad and thoroughly disillusioned.

JANUARY 1, 1938
Firmly believe this is going to be a bad luck year. Had an awful fight last night with Virginia.

JANUARY 29, 1938
Bad luck worse yet. V. out of work today. Over $1,000 in debt. Have to move. Where? Laying men off at work right and left. Slower than it's ever been. God knows what's next.

FEBRUARY 24, 1938
Prediction made Jan. 1 has certainly proved true. Nothing but fights, quarrels. Hours cut at work. Am going to let car go back. Bills far over my head. V. and I quarrel day in and day out. I'm afraid it's no go. But I _do_ love her.

APRIL 6, 1938
It seems I never write in this book unless something terrible happens. V. very angry because I didn't get home from work when said I would. Says we're through. Well our marriage lasted 5 months, 6 days. Guess it's my fault. I try but all to no avail. Job pretty secure but $1175 in debt. ???????

APRIL 20, 1938
Can't understand V. We're head over heels in debt, but she doesn't care at all. Now thinking about going on a pleasure trip to L.A. If she'd only realize three months of work would almost see us clear of all debt.

JULY 17, 1938
Bills only down to 825.70 after 6 months' work. I can't understand it. We average $200 a month, yet in 6 months, only cut bills down $300. V. and I still quarreling and fighting over everything. Weekends are plain hell every week. I know I'm to blame for some things, but not all. Marriage is certainly "wonderful" so far.

AUGUST 29, 1938
Well it looks like it's definite this time. V. stopping out in Fruitvale to see about a divorce. The last few months have been hell. Still in debt over $1000. I'd just as soon die as live through any more of this.

OCTOBER 11, 1938
I know I've written this before, but my marriage is definitely on the rocks. V. moving out tonight. I still love her with all my heart, but she'd never believe me.

DECEMBER 11, 1938
Almost the end of the year. I made a resolution today to write in this book every day. Strained atmosphere for last three days. Marriage definitely going on rocks. Fought practically all day today because I wanted to work on the car!!! I love Virginia more than anything, but she can only see herself above all others. So I guess it's the end (what she wants). Sunday.

DECEMBER 23, 1938
Small day at work. Got a $35 check. The last for a long time. Virginia feeling swell, and we're getting along fine.

DECEMBER 24, 1938
No work today. Shopped downtown. V. and I getting along swell. Joyce was over and had her presents. Polished cars. Spent Christmas Eve with Ed and Veryl. Had a couple of bottles. Went downtown. Felt pretty good. Had a lot of fun with Ed. Virginia wahooing at 12th and Washington.

DECEMBER 25, 1938
Christmas Day. Got up about 10 from effects of last night. Saw Lena and Charlie. Left for Sonora about 12:30. Got up about 3 and had

dinner. Kids sure are swell. Got some nice presents, although couldn't afford to buy very nice ones. Mother and I talked till 11:30 p.m. Harold slept with Virginia and I.

DECEMBER 26, 1938
Up at Mother's today (Sonora). Left about 3. Had ale in Manteca and one in Dublin on way back. Not a cross word between V. and I all day!!! Folks may go to Hawaii. Sure glad for them. Got a pkg. from V.'s mother when we got home. She's sure swell. Saw Ed and Veryl. Made plans for New Year's party. He's sure swell (Ed).

DECEMBER 27, 1938
Back to work today after 4-day vacation (one day with pay). Had a wonderful Christmas. V. and I getting along swell. Small check looming. Have to put out $10 on New Year's party. So worried about bills I can't sleep. $273 in debt. Slacking up at work. Cut to 48 hours a week. Don't know what I'll do. Can only wait and see after first of year. God help us now. V. mad at Maxine, but I don't blame her—damn relatives!

DECEMBER 30, 1938
My birthday today. Received a very nice sweat shirt from mother and a nice card from my wife. Virginia strangely cold and silent today. Got through at 12:30 (one oven). Almost had a scrap with V. entering a restaurant for supper.

DECEMBER 31, 1938
New Year's Eve. Put out about 15.00 on whiskey and party essentials. Had a nice time with V. and Ed (her uncle). Everything well until we got alone. (Her good nature vanishes when we are alone.) Went to the party, which was the same as last year's—a big brawl. Accused of infidelity, etc., etc. Why go into detail. Big fight when we went home.

JANUARY 1, 1939
V. still mad. Very cool attitude all day. In the evening she said she was leaving for good. Ended OK, however. Somehow, I don't believe this year will be as bad luck-y as last year. I sure hope not anyway.

JANUARY 2, 1939
Both of us read all day. Got along pretty good until bedtime when I

suggested sleeping on the couch to prevent overcrowding. Argument—she threatened to leave again—but ended OK, and so to sleep in a good mood, finally.

JANUARY 3, 1939
Got up and V. very mad because I set clock fast so I could get to work on time. Couldn't remember how fast I set it, so was accused of being the cause of lack of trust and infidelity. Parting shot when I left for work was, "Don't forget the fountain." In other words, I was supposed to have a date with a wop by the faucet at work, etc., etc.

JANUARY 11, 1939
V. reserved, quiet, brooding over how "ill-treated" she is, I guess. Got along pretty well tho—as long as I kotow and lick feet.

JANUARY 12, 1939
Don't know why—asked Virginia to get up first this morning. Another scrap, "grounds for divorce." Came home after 10 hours' work, had a saucer full of rice for supper, although a $60 grocery bill.

JANUARY 13, 1939
Came home from work this noon. V. gone—left for L.A. Took all money in house (for grocery bill) and left for good time. She just now (8:30) phoned long distance—didn't have their address. Said she'd be back tomorrow. I wonder—this is what she wanted all along—an excuse to go.

JANUARY 14, 1939
Went to work at 6:10. Got through 11:10. I doubt if she'll come back today, promise or not. Sure "loves" me a lot—affirmations to the contrary. Didn't mind in the least leaving me stuck with $60 grocery bill and all the others. I'll always remember this day, come what may. It wasn't that "she didn't have peace of mind." I noticed she made a pleasure trip out of it—Joyce and all—OK, my day will come.

JANUARY 15, 1939
Went out last night with Bill F., Bernice, and Virginia's Aunt Georgia, down from Portland. Got home at 4 a.m. Slept till 1. Went to Ed's, then down to Best Yet and ate. Back to Ed's, read a book till 6:30, then came

home. V. not back. Promises sure mean a lot to her. Acquired certain helpful knowledge yesterday.

JANUARY 16, 1939
V. came back from L.A. last night with Joyce (about 11). Terrible row, because I went over to her relatives in her absence. Fought till about 4 a.m. I admit I listened to a lot of meddling busybodies. She's driving me crazy (V.), but I, God help me, still love her more than anything in the world.

JANUARY 17, 1939
She met me after work, and we had a talk. It (the mess) is straightened out on a new basis. I'm going to put forth every effort to do my part. I want to show her I really do love her. But I feel she's still cynical and suspicious.

JANUARY 18, 1939
New arrangement of hrs. at work. No more than 50, which means $31.40 at most. What about bills now? I'm afraid the whole situation is getting past control.

JANUARY 19, 1939
Well, it's happened. V. is pregnant. Can expect an heir in October. At a time like this! I'm thrilled, of course, but bills, treatments, and necessary preparations, meanwhile?

JANUARY 20, 1939
They had to pay me overtime, so made $37.43. Made a car payment—balance on car now $455. V. and I now getting along pretty good.

JANUARY 21, 1939
Left this morning and went up to Mother's in Sonora, regardless of gasoline bill. V. told Mother the news. I didn't say anything. Stayed all night in Sonora. V. sure is acting nice.

JANUARY 22, 1939
Kid brother helped me work on car. Left about 3 for home. V. started questioning about her relatives again on way home, which made me sore as I told her the whole truth once.

JANUARY 23, 1939
Monday. A Graham day at work. Stomach hurt all day. V. got home at 10 from Joyce's. Joyce sick.

JANUARY 24, 1939
Pretty big day at work. Got through at 6:30 and went to show. V. being very nice. I sure love her. If she'd only believe me and realize it.

JANUARY 25, 1939
Another big day. Got through at 6. Listened to fight, took a bath, and eventually to bed. But couldn't sleep for worry. $45 grocery bill, $40 gas bill, $275 other bills, and $200 to raise for the baby. <u>God</u> <u>Almighty</u>, <u>I</u> <u>can't</u> <u>stand</u> <u>it</u> <u>much</u> <u>longer</u>.

JANUARY 1939 [Memorandum]
After continual fighting since before Christmas, V. took car and all money in house. (She knew my check had to go for grocery bill.) Got Joyce and left for L.A. She says the reason she left was that "I wouldn't give her any peace of mind." I notice it was more after pleasure trip, though. She always says she wants "consideration." Yes, she sure hands it out. Leaves a filthy house with no food in it. Takes money laid aside to pay groceries and buys gas and oil on credit card that I'll have to pay for. Who said marriage was 50-50? <u>Nuts</u>. O.K. She wins this hand, but I've got one coming.

FEBRUARY 20, 1939
V. very mad this morning. Came over to work for keys to go "downtown." Went to Gilmore's and got $3 cash and 11 gals. gas and went and got an <u>abortion</u> performed on the <u>baby</u>. I got tagged for speeding while chasing after her in Sam's car.

FEBRUARY 21, 1939
V. felt awful all day today, and at 1 a.m. had to take her to hospital. She is OK but had to stay all night. I came home and to bed.

FEBRUARY 22, 1939
Got Virginia @ 9 a.m. Had a pretty nice day off. (Washington's Birthday)

MARCH 6, 1939
V.'s grandfather and grandmother from Tahoe came down. Stanley dunning us for the $41.96. I don't think he can do anything as long as I give him something each week.

MARCH 7, 1939
V. mad this morning. Worked 12 hours today. Business booming at work. V. long faced and silent when I got home. Big "discussion" tonight, talk about splitting up, etc., etc.

APRIL 7, 1939
For past few weeks have been desperately trying to get caught up on bills. Had an arrangement with V. that I was to put whole check on bills for two weeks, then $30 a week, but last two Fridays had a big beef because she didn't have any money for permanents and socks. Bills have now reached <u>danger</u> point.

APRIL 17, 1939
Well, it's happened. V. all packed, moving out. She's finally got things the way she's wanted all along. Back to Hubie. She'll never know it, but I'll always love her—and God bless her.

APRIL 18, 1939
Deadly silence all today and tonight. Had a long day at work, sure feel rotten tonight. Had the hiccoughs for 2 days now. Work getting tougher every day.

APRIL 19, 1939
Same deadly silence all day and tonight. Went to work at 9:45, through at 7:45—52 hours this week. V. pressing clothes and packing preparatory to leaving. If she only knew how I adored her.

SEPTEMBER 14, 1939
Situation and marriage worse than at first of year. The marriage has degenerated into the worst possible example of marriage. I feel like a man 40 years old. Had to sacrifice vacation. Still in debt up to our neck. What a <u>miserable</u> <u>existence</u>.

OCTOBER 8, 1939
Sunday. Ed E. came over and brought some beer. V. started bringing out the dirty linen and arguing. I asked her not to, but she kept on—till we had a tussle. Whereupon she hit me on the head with an ashtray when my back was turned. What a mess!

OCTOBER 11, 1939
V. went to work on new job at Paper Box Company. If she'd cooperate with me around the house, she wouldn't have to work. <u>I don't think it will work out</u>. Had a nice supper all fixed for her.

OCTOBER 12, 1939
V. came home from work cranky as <u>hell</u>. She expects everyone to lick her boots 'cause she's working. She doesn't count that I work, too. These lunchmeat suppers are getting me down.

OCTOBER 13, 1939
Fri. What a <u>hell</u> of a day at work. Again, V. came home cranky. She looks so darn tired, I feel sorry as hell for her, but she'd just sneer at me if I said so.

OCTOBER 14, 1939
The thought that she's making a few dollars changed V. overnight. She's on her high horse and tells me how she wants things run—so we had another beef. I told her she wasn't using the car next week, and hell will freeze over before she gets it, <u>too</u>. Going hunting tomorrow with Happy.

OCTOBER 14, 1939 [Memorandum—last page of journal]
Sat. Night. 1 a.m. (couldn't sleep). To sum it all up, the practically two years of my married life have been plain hell. Virginia seemed to change the minute we were married, from the sweetest girl I'd ever known, to something that seems incredible. She nags, curses, smokes, and keeps my nose eternally to the grindstone. Is inordinately extravagant--$60 grocery bills, $50 gasoline bills (one at $72)--and to cap it all, orders a piano delivered when we are deepest in debt, and which I begged her <u>not</u> to get. She yells continually for new clothes (she sold and cut up the $80 worth I bought before we were married), yet when she gets them, she doesn't take care of them, throws them around, walks on them, and

leaves the washing for two and three weeks at a time.

I know this sounds like I'm an angel—<u>don't misunderstand</u>. I place my blame for these quarrels at <u>50%</u>, but if she'd try being a <u>wife</u>, I <u>know</u> I could show her happiness she never <u>dreamed of</u>. You see, the hell of it is, I love her, worship her, <u>and always will</u>.

OCTOBER 15, 1939
Sun. V. had to work. Hap, Jo, and I went to Oakdale. We did some shooting but didn't get anything. V. not home when I got home at 11:10 p.m., although she was "too tired" to go with us.

OCTOBER 16, 1939
Mon. Felt pretty good today at work for change. V. staying home at my request. Acting very nice.

OCTOBER 17, 1939
Tues. Today about the same as yesterday. V. says she'd like to work till we get out of debt—that she'd apply every cent on bills.

OCTOBER 18, 1939
Wed. V. worked today. Still acting very pleasant.

OCTOBER 19, 1939
Thurs. V.'s payday. She did pay $6 food for next week but put $6 on the credit card. So what the hell is the use?

OCTOBER 20, 1939
Fri. V. worked. We are eating our meals next door. Went out to Maxine's in the evening. Had a beef about use of the car.

OCTOBER 21, 1939
Sat. Hap, Jo, and I went fishing--didn't catch anything. I came home and took a nap. Meanwhile, V. took the car and was gone about 3 <u>hours</u> (???).

OCTOBER 22, 1939
Sun. V. got Joyce, so Hap and I went fishing—didn't catch anything. V. and I <u>very</u> distant. I'm getting disgusted with her working—she thinks she's the whole support of the family.

OCTOBER 23, 1939
Mon. Well it's over—definitely and finally—the marriage I mean. V. left today. Got a message to come out to Fruitvale Station and get my car, as she left for L.A. on the train, which I have an idea is a lot of baloney. See quarterly report for details-→.

OCTOBER 23, 1939 [Memorandum]
Well my marriage lasted exactly 1 year, 357 days. V. pulled out today leaving me holding the bag in her usual loving way. $25 food bill, $72 gasoline bill, and about $200 other bills. She has never tried to be a real wife—extravagant, thoughtless, won't help—a paycheck wife. I could forgive the extravagance and thoughtlessness, but I can't forgive her running around. The fellow in the coupe, the Treasure Island phone call . . . The minute I go to work, she's in the car and gone and barely gets back in time when I get home. Suggests places for me to go on weekends, and when I go, keeps her carefully arranged rendezvous. We're definitely through, and she can have her Romeos to keep.

OCTOBER 24, 1939
Tues. Well, the puzzle finally flew together. The guy is Les ***. The one I thought was a good friend. V. has been having an affair with him for some months. That's why she suggested I go hunting and up to Sonora, etc. She is with him now, either in L.A. or in Oakland. This is absolutely the finish. I wouldn't touch her with a 10-foot pole. As soon as I get clear, I'm starting a divorce, if she doesn't first. Thank God I have some friends.

OCTOBER 25, 1939
Told the boss at work that V. threatened to make me lose my job if we ever split up. He said, "Don't you worry, you won't." Cancelled V.'s credit at Retail Credit Association. Have an appointment for an attorney at 4 tomorrow.

OCTOBER 26, 1939
Thurs. Well I saw the attorney and told him to start action on the divorce. My heart is breaking and can't sleep until 3 in the morning, but I'm sure it's for the best for both of us. I could never trust her or have any respect for her again, but I suppose I'll always love her. I'm lonely as hell tonight. No word from V. till Mon.

OCTOBER 27, 1939
Fri. Saw almost all my creditors and told them the mess I was in financially. Most of them were pretty decent, and said not to worry. Found the pawn ticket to my watch, so that's safe. Also found falsified receipts.

OCTOBER 28, 1939
Sat. Up at 7, had breakfast with the Robertses and then went out to my lawyer's. I signed the papers, and V. will be served with them in L.A. If she's decent about it, I will be, too, but if she tries to stick me, I'll <u>fight</u>. I've paid enuf.

OCTOBER 29, 1939
Sun. Up at 10:30, breakfast with Lewises, then went for ride to Oakdale and on up to Sonora and saw Mother. Told her. She's the sweetest mother in the world. Thought of V. all day. I'm going through with the divorce, but I can't tear her out of my heart. Whenever I think of her, it <u>hurts</u>, because I still love her.

OCTOBER 30, 1939
Mon. Blue Monday at work. Felt lousy all day at work. Thought of V. all day. Saw Ed and find he's an A-1 friend of mine. Also will be an A-1 witness at the divorce. Had 2 bottles of beer with him. Ate supper at Best Yet, tonight. Hap and Joe out. Piano OK. Paid loans. <u>I'm lonely tonight</u>. <u>Why</u> couldn't V. play the game?

OCTOBER 31, 1939
Tues. Thought of V. all day. Felt better today. Work going pretty good. Put out a big washing after work. Also ironed 6 shirts. Had a nice chicken dinner with Jo and Hap. I sure owe that couple a lot. Am praying I can make good on all the bills I was left with. Tomorrow is my wedding anniversary. Celebrate it with heartbreak. I don't think I can ever smile again. NOTICE IN PAPER TODAY.

NOVEMBER 1, 1939
Wed. ←SEE NEXT MEMORANDUM. My wedding anniversary, and what a tender exposé of my wife in her true colors. I found out tonight what a <u>TRAMP</u> I've been married to for 2 years. She's been going with this guy for some months. Found one of his <u>tender</u> epistles tonight. Have three good witnesses for trial.

NOVEMBER 1, 1939 [Memorandum]
Talk about filth and muck in its true colors! I found it <u>tonight</u>. My wife (I'm ashamed to admit it), whom I loved and trusted as I never can another woman, has been unfaithful to me for about 4 months. While I've been working my head off for <u>her</u>, she's been running around with Les ***. I have a letter he wrote to her. She sure must have handed him a <u>line</u>. Well one good thing, everything I ever thought of her has been <u>burned</u> <u>out</u> <u>of</u> <u>my</u> <u>soul</u> <u>for</u> <u>good</u>. All I pray for is for her to go her way, and I'll go mine. But if she tries to soak me for her attorneys' fees or alimony, I'll fight to the last ditch. What a sap I've been, but never again. From now on, it's Ernie for Ernie, for no other, and at all times.

NOVEMBER 2, 1939
Thurs. Stomach hurt all day at work. Can't say for sure how this mess will work out. I may be stuck with both attorney fees and court costs if V. fights, but Ed is going to tell her what we <u>got</u> on her, and she may drop it. She may not even come back from L.A., I hope.

NOVEMBER 3, 1939
Fri. Payday—paid some bills. Went out to some taverns and got a little swacko. Went over to Alameda with Pam, Bud, and a gal named <u>Virginia</u>. Met a gal named Charlotte (a telephone operator). She insisted on driving me home and gave me her telephone number, but—<u>nuts</u>—we ditched her.

NOVEMBER 4, 1939
Sat. Polished car all day. Went out and saw Joyce and Hubert, then went to show at Fairfax. Got home about 12. Worried as hell about bills. V.'s Gilmore bill came in today. $57.69. Wow! I don't know how I'll ever pay it.

NOVEMBER 5, 1939
Sun. Quiet Sunday. Finished work on car. Went over to Ed's. No news from V., whether she's been served or not. Went by L.P.'s station. Evidently took the night off, and so to bed at 9:45. Worried about bills.

NOVEMBER 6, 1939
Blue Monday at work. Toothache all last night and most of today. Phoned Gilmore up and stalled them off on V.'s bill. No news from

L.A. as to whether V. has been served with the summons or not. I hope it's served soon, so I can cut her out of my heart and life completely. <u>Lonely tonight</u>.

November 7, 1939
Tues. Worked till 4:30. Got a letter from Mother and Harold. No news from L.A. Ironed 6 shirts and pressed my suit pants. Had a good night's sleep. Work is slow.

November 8, 1939
Wed. Felt swell today, owing to a good night's sleep last night. Got through work at 4:30. Lola and Walt waiting for me in their new '40 Chevrolet. Went out and had a nice supper with them. Got home about 10. Worried about bills. How to pay paperboy. Need shoes, need haircut, etc. No word from L.A.

November 9, 1939
Thurs. Felt good at work. Feeling much better—physically all around. Saw Ed. Veryl received a letter from V. saying she would be decent about the divorce. I can have the divorce, all she wants is her personal belongings (!!!). It seems too good to be true, so my fingers are crossed until I get my interlocutory decree. But <u>then I never want to see her again</u>.

November 10, 1939
Fri. Got through at 4:30. Got a much-needed pair of shoes and a haircut. Dressed and went out and had a nice dinner with Rafferty's folks and Joyce. Then went out to several beer taverns and sat and thought all evening. Came home about 12.

November 11, 1939
Sat. Worked on car. Went down to pay bills but all stores closed. Hubie dropped by and we went out and proceeded to get swacko. Discussed V. a lot. Got home at 3. Hubie stayed all night at the apartment. Nice fella.

November 12, 1939
Sun. Up at 6:30 and went fishing with Jo, Hap, and Doris (Joe's niece). Caught 3 nice bass and gave them to Ed. Am invited to Ed's for dinner

tomorrow. Hap treated me to a show. A little worried about bills, as the weekend cost a little heavy.

November 13, 1939
Mon. Well the fireworks are at hand! Went over to Ed's for dinner, and who should walk in, but V. She held out her hand and said, "We can be friends, can't we?" And although I felt sorry as hell for her, I looked at her hand, and then at her, and said, "I have nothing to say," and walked out. I found out later, she phoned Hubie and wanted to see him (No. 3?).

November 14, 1939
Tues. Are the fireworks popping! V. over at 2:30 to get her stuff, and we had quite a discussion. She wants $25 to default the divorce. I wouldn't give her 25 cents. I had 2 hidden witnesses who heard her admit the charges on the divorce complaint were true. I told her I never wanted to see her again. I'm going to see George tomorrow, the <u>dirty snoop</u>.

November 15, 1939
Wed. Saw George, and he knows what I think of him. Well! It's over (I think)! V. went back to L.A. this morning and is not going to contest the divorce!!! (My fingers are crossed.) I'm going to see about a $500 loan Saturday to clear everything up.

November 16, 1939
Thurs. Got up at 4:30, went to work at 6. Easy day at work. Came home and slept for 2 hours, had supper and went out to Jo's sister's. Hap's sister went with us. I don't like her very much. Saw Doris. She's a nice kid, and I think she's a little interested in me, but <u>I'm</u> not. I'm through with women, <u>believe me</u>. Hope I get loan.

November 17, 1939
Fri. Up at 4:30 and to work at 6. Easy day. Home at 2:30—bathed, shaved, paid bills, and then went to Union meeting. Went out with Sam afterwards. Dead evening. Saw Vivian Stone at Round-up, talked and came home. Went down to Dave's Café, had two drinks, left cigarette case on table. Came back for it, and somebody had got it ($10). Got to bed at 3:30.

NOVEMBER 18, 1939
Sat. Up at 10:30. Missed chance to see Ed about loan. Came home, did my washing and ironing and pressed suits. Talked this evening. Turned down invitation to go to Oakdale on account of no finances. Figured bills and budgets till 2 in the morning. Thought of Virginia all day.

NOVEMBER 19, 1939
Sun. Up at 11:30. Had breakfast with the Robertses. Cleaned entire house. Ironed all shirts and clothes I washed yesterday. Veryl, Bernice, and May Eddy dropped by. Then Hubie and Joyce dropped by. Took a bath, shaved, wrote a letter and so to bed at 8:30. Still thinking of Virginia. I guess I'll never stop.

NOVEMBER 20, 1939
Mon. Felt good all day. Through at 4:30. Hap's sister going home (thank God). Big beef over there tonight about it. Lonely as hell tonight. Told my fortune with cards, and it looked good—I wonder. Turning in at 10:30.

NOVEMBER 21, 1939
Tues. Felt fair today. Average day at work. Came home, had supper. Rita (the girl downstairs) gave me my first piano lesson. Played Rummy till 10 p.m. and so to bed. Have made resolution to keep my big mouth shut. Received an invitation to take H. to a Thanksgiving dinner Thursday. I don't know, I'm a little skeptical.

NOVEMBER 22, 1939
Wed. Felt fair today. Came home, had supper, and went over to Ed's. While I was gone, Lola and Walt came over. Sam finally called, and we went over to SF and proceeded to get swacko and went to about 4. Had a lot of fun. Home at 12:30. Thought of V. on ferry. <u>Lonely</u>.

NOVEMBER 23, 1939
Thurs. Thanksgiving—for what? Played for a sap by the one person I <u>adored</u>? Have a date to take H. to dinner at 4:30. What a Thanksgiving—big crowd over at Hap and Joe's. Hap and Mike drank, and Jo feeling "<u>kittenish</u>." I got to feeling good but didn't get "<u>drunk</u>." Had a swell evening with Sam, Jessie, H., and Chuck.

NOVEMBER 24, 1939
Fri. Came home from work at 4:30. Changed clothes and went downstairs to a swell turkey dinner with Dot and Wally. Sat around all evening and listened to Hap and Wally reminisce over their childhood days. Came home (upstairs) and read till 1:30 a.m.

NOVEMBER 25, 1939
Sat. Slept till 10:30. Went downtown, paid all bills. Tried to get a $75 loan—no soap. They only wanted my car and $100 interest for $75. Went out to Maxine's (Lena) and gassed with them. They're a little sore 'cause I didn't come out Thanksgiving (to hell with them). Then over to Lola's and had supper. Came home and read.

NOVEMBER 26, 1939
Sun. Got up at 11 a.m. Stayed home all day. Cleaned up house. V. is back in town! I suspect dirty work. Her sister, Doris, dropped by tonight, and we had quite a talk. She was angling for a reconciliation between V. and me. But not for me.

NOVEMBER 27, 1939
Mon. The default papers are to be filed today about 5:30 p.m. Doris phoned up and wanted me to take her out, so I borrowed 50 cents and did so. I had a few qualms (suspecting trickery), but I believe it's O.K. We had a swell time. She sure is a nice girl. Too bad V. hasn't got Doris's brains.

NOVEMBER 28, 1939
Tues. Came home from work at 2:30 and cleaned house. Had a nice supper with Jo and Hap. Washed and cleaned up and finally drove over and honked for Doris. She came out, and we talked. Meanwhile a lot of strange cars kept slowing down and stopping and looking at us. Finally, V. drove up in a '39 V-8 and went in. Meanwhile, Doris and I went over to my apartment and had coffee and told fortunes. Suspicious cars in front of house????

NOVEMBER 29, 1939
Wed. Oh yes! Forgot to say yesterday when divorce trial was—it's December 18th! After work this afternoon, Doris came over while I was washing and asked me if I wanted to talk to V. I thought awhile and

said yes. We drove around in Doris's car, and V. was very nice—said she realized she'd made a sap of herself. We talked—she said she had not been intimate with Les ***. There's a <u>chance</u> for a reconciliation <u>because I still love her</u>, but I'm scared. I don't want to be hurt again.

November 29, 1939 [Memorandum]
Saw Virginia tonight, and she was very contrite and truthful. She admitted she had made a mess of things and made a sap of herself. In effect, she asked me for another chance, which I would be willing to give, but for the fact of all the gossip that has been spread by her relatives, that damn plant, and a few other reasons. So we made the arrangement that I was to go ahead and get the divorce (interlocutory) and to be faithful to each other meanwhile and when she comes up in February, we would live together for a year and see how we got along. If, in a year, we decided we couldn't, I was to go ahead and get the final divorce papers. Of course, this means I must have trust in V., because it <u>could be a trick</u>; because by living with her, I nullify my evidence and the divorce if she wanted to be vindictive. So tonight, my mind is in a mad turmoil. I know in my heart I love her and want to give her another chance because <u>I</u> would want another chance if it had been me. But I'm <u>afraid</u> because I was hurt awfully deep, and it almost tore my heart out, and some of the ideals I had built up about my Virginia came crashing down about my ears. ??????

November 30, 1939
Thurs. Thought of my talk with V. all day. So much has been said about my wife that everyone would say I'm the world's prize sap if I went back. I don't care what people think—they're not feeding me, but I've got to thrash it out in my own mind. Because even though I worship V., she destroyed practically all my faith and respect for her, and it will take time for the scar to heal.

December 1, 1939
Fri. Came home from work at 2:30, and for some strange reason (I wasn't tired), fell asleep on the Chesterfield and slept for 4 hours. Dressed and went to a special meeting in San Francisco. Had a beer and came home. Car payment this week, so I'll be flat broke. Going to work on car, clean clothes, and rearrange budget tomorrow.

DECEMBER 2, 1939
Sat. Got up about 10:30. Had breakfast. Jo and Hap not home. Paid Mrs. Roberts $3 rent. Paid car payment. Came home and cleaned entire house and scrubbed kitchen floor. Hubie phoned and wanted to know what these stories were about V. going out with him almost every night (????). Took a bath and so to bed at 10:15.

DECEMBER 3, 1939
Sun. Got up at 10:45. Cooked breakfast over at Lewises. Had dinner with the Robertses. Cleaned up house and worked out financial budget. Only item that worries me is food for last two weeks of December. If I can put $20 a week on bills till last week of May, I will be <u>all clear</u>. Wrote a letter to Mother, read, washed, and so to bed.

DECEMBER 4, 1939
Mon. Couldn't sleep last night till about 2 a.m. Thought of V. all night. What a mad turmoil my mind is in! I love her and want her back to take care of and yet I'm afraid of getting the same deal again if I take her back. I guess there is just no solution at all to the problem. Haven't heard from her since she left for L.A. Wednesday with Doris. Work is probably slow. Wonder how it will be from January to April??

DECEMBER 5, 1939
Tues. Couldn't sleep last night, either, till about 1. Small day at work. No mail at all, today. The new wrapping machine came in at work today. That was the job Bill promised me about last June. It means better pay. I hope everything works out O.K. on it. No word from V. The more I think of trying it over with V., the less I want to????

DECEMBER 6, 1939
Wed. Came home at 4:30, had supper and went to bed about 9. Another sleepless night. I can't seem to get this mess out of my mind. I live through the whole thing every night. I think of the many ways she was so sweet, and then I think of the dirt and muck she handed me.

DECEMBER 7, 1939
Thurs. Pretty hard day at work. Only one oven tomorrow. But I'll work till 12:30 anyway, and if Sam doesn't come in, I'll get a full day. Came

home at 4:30, ate, shaved, and came over to the apartment to think some more. Bills to pay tomorrow.

DECEMBER 8, 1939
Fri. Went to work at 6:30 and worked till 12:30. Came home, dressed, and paid bills. Financial budget looks pretty good. Had supper and went out to Jo's sister's and played Rummy. Came and read in bed till about 12 and so to sleep.

DECEMBER 9, 1939
Left about 10:30 for Oakdale. I went on up to Sonora and had quite a long talk with Mother. Did a lot of thinking on way up. Have made up my mind definitely. I am not going to try it again with V. I can't forget or forgive what she did.

DECEMBER 10, 1939
Sun. Rainy and stormy today. Got up about 11:45. Had breakfast over at Lewises. Went over to Ed's and had a nice turkey dinner, played cards, and then went to the Ritz and saw a fair show. Been thinking steady for two days and am resolved not to try it again with V.

DECEMBER 11, 1939
Mon. Got to work at 5:20 a.m. Had a medium-hard day but felt good. Came home at 2:30 and slept till 5:15. Had supper, read paper, talked with Robertses, washed, shaved, and so to bed at 8:30. One week from today, and I will have my divorce, unless something unforeseen shows up. Looks pretty slack at work.

DECEMBER 12, 1939
Tues. Checked in 5:50. Easy day. Felt pretty good physically—mentally terrible. Feel blue and discouraged. This whole mess (divorce) seems liked some kind of a nightmare. Why couldn't V. have been true and played the game? It's beginning to get me, I think. Dead broke week after week, thinking of V., lonely apartment (no radio now), etc. But I won't let it get me. Toothache all day. Going to bed at 8:30.

DECEMBER 13, 1939
Wed. 5:50 again today. Good day at work. Felt a lot better today. Came home, washed my clothes, cleaned house, then ate supper, took a hot

bath, and to bed at 9 p.m. No mail today. Sure wish tomorrow was Monday so the mess would be over with.

DECEMBER 14, 1939
Thurs. Got a letter from V. today. Wants me to write and let her know how I feel towards her. God, I don't know what to write. It would be so easy to try it over again, and yet, if I did, I wouldn't have any self-respect for myself for doing it. Creditors are dunning me again—blue—discouraged. I wish to hell I were dead.

DECEMBER 15, 1939
Fri. Payday. What a laugh. Came home—went out to see lawyer with Jo, then went to Union meeting. Came back to Ed's, went out with him and Veryl and got a little swacko. Ran into Helen and Jessie and "danced" with them, then came upstairs to bed.

DECEMBER 16, 1939

Sat. Dressed and went down and paid all creditors on budget. Saw Hubert and Joyce. Found out V. was telling everybody what a rat and a "tramp" I was, long before we split up. That's the final blow. I'm not even going to answer her letter. Stopped by Ed's. Saw Bernice and Bill. Came home. Had a new exhaust pipe put on car ($4.23).

DECEMBER 17, 1939
Sun. Stayed home all day. Ironed work clothes, worked on budget and fixed car heater. Took a bath and to bed at 10 p.m. Have to go to court tomorrow at 9:30 for divorce trial. I'm sure hoping everything works out O.K.

DECEMBER 18, 1939
Mon. THE DAY. Well, it's over—got my divorce today on grounds of extreme cruelty. No fuss or trouble at all. So what's that? Two years of my life wasted in the grand experiment of marriage. Never again for me. Bill schedule worked out fine, except for lawyer. He started yelling for his dough as soon as the trial was over. ?? Lonely tonight.

DECEMBER 19, 1939
Tues. Easy day at work. All time made up that was lost on trial. Toothache all last night and today. I really don't want to, but I am

going to write V. a letter explaining why a reconciliation is impossible. Three more days till I leave for Sonora for Christmas. (Broke and no presents.)

DECEMBER 20, 1939
Wed. Back hurt all day at work. Also, that damn stomachache returned. Wrote V. last night explaining why it was impossible to try it over again. Told her I never wanted to see her again and not to reply. It hurt like hell to do it, but I had to. Lonely as hell tonight. What a Merry Christmas! Divorce certainly is a wonderful thing. Why couldn't V. play the game?

DECEMBER 21, 1939
Thurs. Easy day at work. Sam and I attended the girls' Xmas party. Had a lot of fun. Gee! I'm worried sick about my bills. I can't seem to catch up on them. Don't feel so hot about my trip to Sonora. Lola and Walt going up. Half day of work tomorrow. Means small check the 29th. I don't know what the hell to do. LONELY.

DECEMBER 22, 1939
Fri. Went to work at 10:45. Half a day—got through at 4:30. Came home, cleaned up, and went down to Sam's Log Cabin. A bunch from the plant were down there, and we had quite a good time (danced, etc.). When I finally left for Sonora, I was really lit. Left 2 a.m.

DECEMBER 23, 1939
Sat. Arrived Sonora at 4 a.m. (2 hours for 118 miles). Turned in and slept till 8:30. Went down to Sonora and shopped. Bought a few Christmas presents, although I couldn't buy much, and got a haircut. Came home and cleaned car. Bob helped me.

DECEMBER 24, 1939
Sun. Stayed around house all day, resting and played with kids. Lola and Walt and family arrived. Played Rummy till 12 midnight and retired. Sure have one swell family.

DECEMBER 25, 1939
Mon. Had a very nice Christmas dinner and left with Sainsburys for Oakland about 3. Lost Sainsburys by Dublin. Stopped and saw Lyle

and his wife and wished them a Merry Christmas. Stopped and saw little Joyce and her presents. Stopped and drank a Christmas toast to V. at Sam's and came home. <u>**LONELY TONIGHT**</u>.

December 26, 1939
Tues. 45 minutes late to work today. <u>Small</u> day at work today. Work has slacked off terrible. Maybe no work Friday. Saw all my main creditors today and made arrangements to pay them according to <u>my</u> budget. (!!) Felt good today. Sure miss V. through all these damn holidays. I wish they were over.

December 27, 1939
Wed. To work at 6 a.m. today. Good day at work today. Stalled off washing machine tonight till Friday. Lewises, I believe, are becoming a trifle hostile. Well, I'm getting a little tired of the association myself. Four-day holiday coming up. Don't know what I'll do with myself, as I'll be dead broke. Lonely.

December 28, 1939
Thurs. Pretty tough day at work. Found out today that I will be able to get some time in tomorrow doing special work on platform. It will sure come in handy.

December 29, 1939
Fri. Worked 7-1/2 hours today. Came home and changed clothes and paid off all bills possible. Borrowed $1 from landlady. Went over to Bill and Ila's and saw Ed. He had a bottle, so I proceeded to get swacko.

December 30, 1939
Sat. My birthday today—24 years old and what have I accomplished? My life a wreck (thanks to V.), $500 in debt, lonely and thoroughly disillusioned. Flat broke. I'll have to stay home and stare at four walls New Year's Eve. Ironed tonight, and I guess I'll go to bed pretty soon. Lonely as hell.

December 31, 1939
Sun. New Year's Eve. <u>Happy</u> <u>New</u> <u>Year</u>! Like hell. Boy, am I low tonight. I sure wish to hell I could quietly step out of the picture. But it even takes dough to do that. Damn the day I ever met Virginia.

DECEMBER 31, 1939 [*Entry written on separate piece of paper in the journal.*]
6:50 P.M.
1235 E. 18TH ST.
This is undoubtedly the loneliest, gloomiest, most discouraging New Year's Eve I have ever spent. Flat broke, lonely, and about six months of steady paying of bills to look forward to. I am sitting listening to the radio (borrowed) all dressed up. (It doesn't cost anything to dress up.) And they say it's the woman who pays! What did I receive for 2 years of working like a dog. Playing fair and square and doing my damnedest to make my marriage a success? I received a chiseling, extravagant, thoughtless, cheap woman who never had a real thought of love in her mind at all. But someday she will pay—that I know.

JANUARY 1, 1940
Mon. Went across hall to Hap and Joe's party last night. Got swacko and came home and turned in about 10:30. Got up this morning about 10:45 and went down and had some coffee in Parkway. Thought of V. last night continuously.

JANUARY 2, 1940
Tues. Very agreeable day at work. Got through at 5. Am going to take a bath and turn in, as I am dead tired. Have made one important resolution, and I am going to keep it. I am going to improve myself physically and mentally in every way possible. Am worried about bills. Have cold in my chest.

JANUARY 3, 1940
Pretty hard day at work. Felt sick all day. Trying to come down with the flu, I think. Going to bed at 7:30. Didn't get any sleep last night. Thought of V. Received two pairs socks as birthday present from Mother. I certainly have a wonderful mother. Worried about bills. Sure hope I come out of them O.K. Lonely tonight.

JANUARY 4, 1940
Thurs. Hard day at work. Felt good today, due to 12 hours solid sleep last night. Worried about bills but will pay off what I can tomorrow. Have got to work hard on job and show them I mean business. Going

to bed early again. Tonight still lonely as hell for V. Guess I'll get over it, though. <u>Why</u> couldn't she play the game?

January 5, 1940
Fri. Friday at last! I'm sure worn out. It's raining like the devil today (tonight). Worked on bills tonight. All straightened on them, with the exception of the lawyer's. Will phone him tomorrow. Borrowed some music from Rita and will copy the words tonight (my latest hobby). Feel pretty good tonight, except <u>LONELY</u>.

January 6, 1940
Sat. Got up at 10:30. Cleaned house and went down and paid bills. Had lunch with the Robertses. Washing my kitchen sink, and Hap came over and wanted to borrow my car to go to Oakdale. I said OK but didn't like it and suggested I go, too. So I drove 160 miles in 4 hours. Got back at midnight. Read till 2:30.

January 7, 1940
Sun. Got up at 2:30. Cooked "breakfast" at Joe's, then played a game of Rummy with Annie, Rita, and George. Also talked with the Robertses. Went down to the T&D (20-cent show) and came home about 9:30. Cooked supper (Jo didn't like it, I don't think) and came home. Missed V. an awful lot today.

January 8, 1940
Mon. Bad day at work. Got a talk from "Curly." Came home at 2:30. Phoned lawyer and asked him to wait till April. He couldn't see it. Wants me to come out and see him Sat.?????. No sleep at all last night. Deadly toothache all night. Stood it till 2:30 and got up and dressed and read till 5:45. Am I dead tonight. Worried and lonely tonight.

January 9, 1940
Tues. Easy day at work. Came home and was going to wash my clothes, but it started to rain, so I cleaned house up completely. Scrubbed kitchen and bedroom floors. Got a letter from Mother and Harold today. Think I will take a bath and retire early tonight. Sure wish I could get clear of bills soon (but won't be till May).

JANUARY 10, 1940
Wed. Another easy day at work. Came home and went to library after cussing and swearing at car for half an hour (dead battery, wet distributors and spark plugs). Toots and Maud (two old hens from work) came up to see my apartment. Read book and so to bed. Worried about bills. LONELY.

JANUARY 11, 1940
Thurs. Fairly easy day at work. Felt pretty good all day. Rained almost all day. Tomorrow is payday. Means nothing as I will be flat broke again after paying bills. Awfully tired tonight, due partly to reading until midnight last night, so am going to bed at 7:30 tonight. Lonely as hell, too.

JANUARY 12, 1940
Fri. Through work at 2:30. Easy day. I don't know what's wrong with me. I'm nervous as hell and don't know what to do with myself. I guess it's this eternal sitting around the apt. Come home every night after supper, and sit and think and think and think. I can't afford it, but I'm going to go out tomorrow night, and I hope I get <u>drunk</u>—<u>anything</u> to end this monotony.

JANUARY 13, 1940
Sat. Washed clothes and ironed a shirt. Writing this at 3 a.m., feeling pretty good. Went out with Hubert and Ruby. Hubert got drunk—I drove. Lonely as hell. Damn Virginia to hell. Ruby invited me to meet her cousin??????

JANUARY 14, 1940
Sun. Got up at 1:30. Went over to Jo's and cooked dinner. Then talked with Annie and Rita. Then saw Ed and then went out and saw May and Guy. Came home and cooked supper. Am going to iron workpants and then to bed. Wonder how suggested "housewarming party" of last night will work out? <u>Worried about finances</u>!

JANUARY 15, 1940
Mon. Easy day at work. Came home at 4:30 and went to library. Al Davidson dropped by and paid a call. One of the fellows from work. Seems to be a nice fellow. Felt very good physically but am worried about bills. Also lonely as hell tonight.

JANUARY 16, 1940
Tues. Home at 4:30—supper—then home and did my ironing. Cleaned up and to bed at 8:30. Probably read a little. Feel <u>very</u> good physically but am sure worried about that lawyer and Gilmore Oil. Well, what is to be is to be.

JANUARY 17, 1940
Wed. Home at 4:30—supper, then read. Will take a bath and then to bed by (I hope) 8:30. Had a talk with Bill, and I will have to rearrange hours of Sam and me to cover full production day. I <u>realize</u> I have got to show more interest and initiative <u>in</u> my job. Tired and not quite so lonely tonight.

JANUARY 18, 1940
Thurs. Got through at 6. Ate supper, then came home and read *The Sea Wolf* till one o'clock. Don't have to go to work until 9 tomorrow.

JANUARY 19, 1940
Fri. Through at 6:30. Came home, ate, shaved, washed, and dressed and went to Union meeting. Sure getting disgusted and discouraged. I see all my friends leaving for a good time, and me? Eternally broke, clothes getting shabby, five cents over from this check. Paying and promised to pay until June or better for Virginia's damned extravagance. Sometimes I wonder, what the hell is the use. What kind of a life is this? It isn't living, it's an existence. LONELY.

JANUARY 20, 1940
Sat. Got up about 9:30 and went downtown with Jo and Hap. Hap bought a suit ($28.33) on <u>my</u> credit at Schwartz and Grodin's. I sure hope he keeps the payments up. Paid more bills. Came home and cleaned apt. Borrowed 50 cents and went to show. Lonely as <u>hell</u> tonight. Guess I'll work on car tomorrow. May go down to playground and exercise, too. It's midnight, so will turn in.

JANUARY 21, 1940
Sun. Got up about 10—breakfast at Lewises. Washed and cleaned car. Took battery out of car (after a three-hour struggle) and cleaned it up preparatory to taking it over to the plant tomorrow and having it charged. Wally (fellow downstairs) came up and visited. Had a nice

chicken dinner. Came up and read magazine till 10. Will shave and clean up and then to bed. Thought of V. an awful lot today. I face the week's work with a smile, but—

JANUARY 22, 1940
Mon. Up at 5:30. Took battery to work to have it charged. Easy day. Felt good all day. Home at 3:15. Pasted all loose pictures in photograph album, then had supper. Oh yes! Stalled off the dentist and made an appointment to see the lawyer Saturday. A guy from Gilmore dropped by to see if the bill would be cleared by February (Virginia's bill). Disconsolate and blue tonight. Clean up and turn in at 8:30.

JANUARY 23, 1940
Tues. Up at 5:30. Dressed and read magazine till 20 to 7. Pretty easy day at work. Am arranging hours satisfactorily, but it is going to be tough. Home at 3:15. Cleaned house, wrote Mother a letter, and took books to library. Feeling very good physically, but mentally discouraged.

JANUARY 24, 1940
Wed. Up at 6—to work at 6:45. Worked alone till 11:45. Came home at 1:15. borrowed Sam's car and got battery. Had to buy a new battery cable. Put battery in. Works fine. Lena came over for about 15 minutes. Had supper, shaved, washed, and to bed. May read awhile after exercises. Have been doing them since Sunday.

JANUARY 25, 1940
Thurs. Up at 6:10 and to work at 6:45. Easy day. Felt pretty good all day. Came home and dozed till 5:30. Had supper (electric atmosphere at Lewises). Talked with Robertses till 8:30. Cleanup and exercise and to bed at 9. Feel discouraged, blue, etc.(I always get this way as payday nears.)

JANUARY 26, 1940
Fri. Stalled off lawyer till April (I hope). Did something foolish tonight (I guess). Went out to see Hu, and we went out and proceeded to "gas-up." Ran into Sam, who had a bottle, and we all collected some women. Had a swell time. Met Vivian Morgan—she's <u>aces</u>. Got home at 5:30 a.m. and to bed.

January 27, 1940
Sat. Got up about 9:30 and went out to pay bills. We cruised all over town, and I did something foolish again, spent the rent money. Did a lot of drinking but not as much fun as last night. Stayed at Hu's all night. Got home about 3 a.m.

January 28, 1940
Sun. Got up about 10. Cruised all over town. Went up to Morgans about 1:30. Vivian and I went to the show. Got out about 7 and took a ride. Took her home about 9 and came home. She really is a <u>swell</u> <u>kid</u>. About 6 times more sense than V.

January 29, 1940
Mon. Am I <u>down</u> tonight. Discouraged, blue. What the hell is the use of this life? <u>Dragged</u> through work today. Got through at 5:30 Bills are in a critical state. I don't know what the hell I'll do. Always lonely as hell, always broke, always a stack of duns in the mail. If I go out, feel like a moocher or am accepting charity. Well I can fix <u>that</u>. Anyway, I absolutely won't go out again till (if ever), I'm clear.

January 29, 1940 *[Entry written on separate piece of paper in the journal.]*
9:35 P.M.
1235 E. 18th St.
Some people, I know, would say I am a chronic pessimist. I would be quite willing to agree, but I can't get it through my thick skull, why, if a fellow enters marriage with all the high ideals he is capable of, dreams of how to make <u>her</u> happy, works like a dog, sometimes as much as sixteen or eighteen hours a day, and <u>likes</u> doing it because it's for <u>her</u>. Puts all his faith and trust in <u>her</u>, thinks <u>she's</u> incapable of doing anything sordid or cheap—and then she deliberately and methodically disproves every dream and ideal and throws your love off like a dirty dishrag—<u>why</u> in the name of justice and human decency, does that fellow have to assume all responsibility for <u>her</u> mistakes, be the recipient of <u>her</u> malicious gossip, and sacrifice six months of his life to loneliness, heartache, and despair?

    Answer that satisfactorily, and I'll be the first to admit that I <u>am</u> a pessimist. The above probably sounds like the ravings of something or other, but nevertheless, that's what's in my heart.

I'm lonely, blue, discouraged, and worn out tonight. I shouldn't feel that way, I know, but what the heck, I'm the same as everyone else. I'd like to go out and have a good time, some new clothes, and a few pleasures of life. But I can't, because I'm so eternally far in debt (her debts), I don't know what I'll do next month. I can't meet them all. Well, we'll see what we shall see. Anyway, here's a toast to Virginia—I wish to hell it was strychnine.

JANUARY 30, 1940
Tues. to work at 9, through at 6:30. One hour overtime. Told Jo I was going to send piano back. OK, I guess. Fairly easy day at work with some amusing incidents (cigarette benefit). Have decided to put all overtime money in pig bank. Worried about bills and lonely, as usual, tonight. Have to get license plates Saturday ($10.10). Feel <u>fair</u> physically.

JANUARY 31, 1940
Wed. To work at 9. Felt good all day, through at 6 (half-hour overtime). Came home, had supper, and saw the Robertses for a while. Ben came up, and we had quite a talk. Well, the week is almost over, thank God. Night shift next week (pilot bread). Don't know as yet how that will affect my hours. Sure feel good (physically).

FEBRUARY 1, 1940
Thurs. Work at 9, through at 6:45. Came home and fixed my own supper. On an impulse, phoned Vivian up, and she asked me to come over and we'd go over to her sister's (Eunice). So I did, and we talked till 10:30. Drove two guests downtown. Came back, parked, and talked. Then came home without running out of gas (thank God) and to bed at 12:30.

FEBRUARY 2, 1940
Fri. To work at 9, through at 6:30. Had a hasty supper, as the Lewises were going out. Last day of the late work for a while. Went down and talked with the Robertses awhile. Came up and made out budget. Will have one cent left over. Guess I'll go out and have a good time. Like hell. I guess I've got those payday blues. Feel good physically, but mentally a wreck.

FEBRUARY 3, 1940
Sat. Got up at 10:40. Dressed, went to work, and made out worksheet, then sent money order for license plates. Then gave Rita her driving lesson. Took clothes to S&G's to be altered, cleaned, and repaired. Dropped by Ed's. He was out. Came home, phoned Vivian, and she asked me to come out. Stayed till 12:30. I think she likes me a lot, but me? A place to kill time. <u>No</u> <u>more</u> <u>women</u> <u>for</u> <u>me</u>.

FEBRUARY 4, 1940
Sun. Up at 8. Cleaned house up. Had nice dinner with the Robertses (landlady). Went over and saw Ed. Then over to Vivian's and played cards with Eunice and her, and then Hu came over and made a foursome. Hu invited me to a show at the Paramount. Got home at 11:25. We're planning a trip to L.A. I've sure got to pay Hu back for his kindness. He sure is a swell kid.

FEB. 4, 1940 *[Entry written on separate piece of paper in the journal.]*
11:25 P.M.
1235 E. 18TH ST.
I feel swell physically at this date. Except for financial conditions, I would be feeling A-1 in every way.

A lot happened today that set me thinking. Saw Vivian today, and I am quite sure she thinks a lot of me; as for me, I think she's a <u>swell</u> kid. She's kind, considerate, thoughtful, and very pleasant. <u>But</u> I will not go steady or get serious. I will see her for company, visits, a good time, and to have fun with. But if she gets <u>too</u> serious, I will skip it, because I honestly feel that I can never love, trust, or feel serious about any woman again. "Dear Virginia" tore all that out of my heart for good, I'm afraid.

Another thing I was thinking of today—Hubert (Virginia's Ex No. 1) is a swell fellow, one of the finest I know, and he has certainly been swell to me. But I'm getting so I hate myself. Every time we go out, he foots the bill, or pays for most of the drinks, or furnishes most of the smokes, etc., etc., etc.

I wish to <u>hell</u> I would be clear of debts (Virginia's), so I could have a little more respect for myself (financially) when we go out.
But no use wishing. I've got to apply myself to them and get them over with.

FEBRUARY 5, 1940
Mon. 45 minutes late to work this morning. Figured time wrong. Medium hard day at work. Home at 2:40. Slept on Chesterfield till 5:15. Had supper and came home and figured out bills. Went down and talked with the Robertses till 8:45. Am going to clean up and go to bed. May write Mother a letter first. Lonely as hell tonight.

FEBRUARY 6, 1940
Tues. Went to work at 5:50 today. Easy day. Came home at 2:30 and washed all dirty clothes. Vivian came by on way home from town. Had quite a talk about V., etc. Had supper and took a bath, shaved, and went over to her house. We went over to May's and had a piano concert, then took a ride to Lakeside Park and parked. She is becoming _too_ serious. Told me she loved me. I can't ever be serious again.

FEBRUARY 7, 1940
Wed. To work at 6. Felt tired all day, as I didn't get home till 12:30 last night. Have about 3-1/2 hours overtime in this week. Washing till 3:30. Came home and slept till 6 on the Chesterfield. Had supper, came home, folded clothes, and changed sheets on bed. Should iron, but I'm too tired. Have a date with Vivian tomorrow.

FEBRUARY 8, 1940
Thurs. Had toothache and earache all night. I finally went to sleep at 4 and was one hour late for work. Easy day at work. Home at 3. Cleaned house and cleaned inside of car. Went out to Vivian's. Played cards at Eunice's till 9. Picked up Coon and came back to Vivian's. Got home at midnight. Toothache gone.

FEBRUARY 9, 1940
Fri. To work at 6. Home at 2:30. Slept till 5:30. Dressed, had supper at restaurant, as Lewises were going out. Went over to Vivian's listened to Louis-Godoy fight. Then we came to apartment. She ironed 5 shirts for me, and we did an awful lot of talking. She sure is a swell kid. But I _can't_ let myself get _serious_. But _I_ _can_ run around and be pals with her. Pay bills tomorrow.

FEBRUARY 10, 1940
Sat. Paid what bills I could. Cost me $2.50 to get clothes altered, cleaned,

and repaired. Dressed and went over to Vivian's. Stayed till midnight. Stopped by cops in Diamond. Wanted to see my driver's license and registration card??? Vivian sure is swell. Have a date to have dinner with her and her folks tomorrow.

FEBRUARY 11, 1940
Sun. Got up about 11. Worked on car till 1. Dressed and went over to Vivian's. Went for a ride to Moraga and back. Went after Mr. Morgan. He showed us through the S.P. Commissary and then home. We had quite a talk, and then Mrs. Morgan had a swell dinner. Then played cards with Lorraine, Bill, Eunice, and Vivian. Vivian and I took Lorraine home, then parked, and I got home at 11:30.

FEBRUARY 12, 1940
Mon. to work at 9. Home at 5. Will go work at 8 tomorrow. Didn't phone Vivian up tonight. I don't want to make a pest of myself. Fairly easy day at work, although I hate the late shift. Am going to bed early tonight. The rest will do me good. Mailed Mother a letter.

FEBRUARY 13, 1940
Tues. To work at 8 today. Went to bed at 8:15 last night. Felt swell today. Got through at 5:30. Had supper, then went downstairs and had Rita play some music I had (Vivian's). Then borrowed some of Rita's. Hubert dropped by while I was at Rita's, and I missed him. To work at 8:30 tomorrow. Didn't phone Vivian tonight, either.

FEBRUARY 14, 1940
Wed. to work at 8:30. Easy day at work. Came home and cleaned apartment. Vivian phoned and said to come over at 9, then phoned again at 8:20 and said to come over right away. We went over and visited with Hubert till about 11, then parked and talked till about 1 a.m.

FEBRUARY 15, 1940
Thurs. to work at 7:30, through at 3:30. Things going pretty good at work. Came home, ate, took a bath, shaved. Loaned car to Hubert and stayed at Vivian's till 11:30. Had a swell evening. Viv made some hot chocolate, etc., etc. Hubert mentioned something about a "party" tomorrow night after Union meeting????

FEBRUARY 16, 1940
Fri. Through work at 3:30. Cleaned up, then Union meeting. Bottle of ale at Lucky 13. Home. Payday. Broke, in debt. Creditors howling. What the hell's the use? Damn Virginia.

FEBRUARY 16, 1940 [*Entry written on separate piece of paper in the journal.*]
1235 E. 18TH ST.
12:15 A.M.
Friday—payday, and again those "payday blues." I sure feel low, discouraged, and useless tonight. Came home from work, cleaned up, and went to Union meeting. Then went <u>in debt</u> for one bottle of ale at the "Lucky 13." Hubert and a bunch of the fellows out there having a good time. Me? I drink my ale (nurse it along) and nonchalantly say, "Well, I've got to be going—stay sober." They say, "Oh, have a drink before you go." Which common decency necessitates that I refuse. (It's proper to treat back.)

So, I drive home, slowly, thinking how wonderful it has been to have been married to a sweet, loving, <u>faithful</u> wife.

Yes, it has <u>not</u>. Damn her soul to hell. I hope she has to pay, someday, for the broken dreams, blasted hopes, and heartbreak that she brought, not only into my life, but into another's.

I'm so far in debt, that by going over to see Vivian and not being able to take her out or do anything for her when she's so darn swell, I'm slowly losing my self-respect. For which reason I intend to see her tomorrow and tell her that it's best that she forget we ever met, and let it go at that. I wish to hell something would happen. This life isn't even an existence. Which thought I suppose, shows, that I can't take it when the going gets tough. Yeah? Well no wonder. I "took it" for two years of <u>married</u> <u>hell</u>-no wonder I'm beginning to let go--

FEBRUARY 17, 1940
Sat. Up at 10:30. Paid off all bills possible. Then out to Vivian's. Home and fixed dinner, as Lewises were just leaving. Went out to see Lola. She's getting a divorce. I'm sure worried about the poor kid. Then went to California Hotel to "Stag Club." Stayed till 9. Then out to Vivian's. We went to May's. Nobody home. Bought 2 milkshakes and came up to apartment. Took Vivian home at 12:30. Home and to bed.

FEBRUARY 18, 1940
Sun. Up at 9:15. Worked on budget. Cleaned house and washed clothes. Dressed and went out to Vivian's. Hu, mate, and Tommy, Vivian, and I played "Hell" till 5. Had supper at Morgan's. Then Viv, Mr. Morgan, and I went through the plant. Then Viv and I went over to Eunice's. Talked to Viv till 12:30. <u>Difficulty</u>!

FEBRUARY 19, 1940
Mon. Went to bed at 3 a.m. this morning. Got up at 5:30 and to work at 6. Easy day at work. Worked till 2:30. Came home, took in washing, then worked on car (polished) till about 4:30. Slept till 6:30 on Chesterfield. Then had supper over at Lewises and came home and cleaned up. Will get to bed at about 9. Feel pretty good <u>physically</u>.

FEBRUARY 20, 1940
Tues. Up at 5:45 and to work at 6. Worked till 3. Got home at 3:30 and went to sleep on Chesterfield—slept till 6. Supper at Lewises. Message from Vivian to phone her, so I did. She said she was going to have Hubert bring her over Thursday. (I told her the other night, I wouldn't see her anymore until I was out of debt.)

FEBRUARY 21, 1940
Wed. To work at 6 and through at 3. Home and polished car till 6. Had supper and was writing Mother a letter when who should knock at the door but Sam. He made me change clothes, and we went out and proceeded to get drunk. Went over to S.F. and had a lot of fun. Felt lousy 'cause it was all on Sam.

FEBRUARY 22, 1940
Thurs. Got home at 4 this morning. Got up at 10:30, had breakfast, and Hubert came over. We proceeded to make the rounds. I spent a buck I couldn't afford but had a swell time. Again, I felt lousy because he footed most all of the bills. <u>Damn Virginia</u>.

FEBRUARY 23, 1940
Fri. Went to bed last night at 1 a.m. Got up at 5 and went to work at 6:30. Got through at 3. Watched a wreck on the corner for an hour. Came on home and cleaned house. Then fell asleep in chair till 7. Had supper. Vivian phoned and Mr. Morgan, she, and I went to a dance at the Hotel

Alameda. Got home at 1:30 a.m. Worried stiff about bills tonight. I had to spend a dollar I couldn't afford again. Hope I can hold out.

FEBRUARY 24, 1940
Sat. Got up at 9:15. Had breakfast at Lewises. Worked on car till 3. Got gas and sent money order to Local Loan. Paid on car and came home. Lola stopped by and wanted me to take her home. I did and stopped at Vivian's. Viv, Hu, I—Mutt and Eunice and Bud and Geneva and Arline played cards till 12:30. Talked to Vivian till 2:45. Home at 3.

FEBRUARY 25, 1940
Sun. Up at noon. Took a bath and fixed my own breakfast at the Lewises. Then over to Ed and Veryl's. Talked awhile and went out to Vivian's. Had a nice afternoon, and Mr. Morgan invited me to supper. Then Vivian and I went to May's and talked. Played the piano, etc., etc. Then we came up to the apartment and had toast, jam, and coffee. Took Vivian home and got home at 1 a.m.

FEBRUARY 26, 1940
Mon. Up at 7:30. Breakfast at Lewises. To work at 8:30. Easy day at work. Worried stiff about my bills. Washing machine and Gilmore are getting tough. I sure am despondent and blue tonight, and also for the first time since I met Vivian, I'm <u>lonely</u>.

MON. FEB 26, 1940 [*Entry written on separate piece of paper in the journal.*]
7:20 P.M.
1235 E. 18TH ST.
Oakland, Calif.
This certainly is a lonely, gloomy evening. It rained all day and is raining now.

The reason I feel so gloomy tonight is not because of anything special that happened today, but just a gathering together of events that have happened recently.

I'm sick of being eternally broke. Would like to go up and see the folks but can't afford it.

My bills are really getting to a serious stage, and I can't seem to catch up on them, although I never spend more than a dollar a week for pleasure.

Hell, what a life.

FEBRUARY 27, 1940
Tues. To work at 8:30. Pretty hard day at work, and to make things more "pleasant," had an argument with Lambert, the foreman, at work. He is a sneaky rat. Came home and to bed at 9:30.

FEBRUARY 28, 1940
Wed. To work at 8:30, through at 5. Hubert and Joyce dropped by, and Hu and I decided to go out. Rained and stormed all evening. Got pretty swacko and got home about 1. I slept in my car till 3:30 this morning, then came upstairs to bed.

FEBRUARY 29, 1940
Thurs. Got up at 7:30 and to work. Sure was tired at work. Got through at 5. Had supper and was going over to Vivian's, but Hubert dropped by as I was shaving and wanted me to go to the show. So he treated me to the show, and to some food after the show. I sure feel like a heel for accepting. "Always broke Ernie," thanks to that damn Virginia.

MARCH 1, 1940
Fri. Through work at 5. Had supper and changed clothes. Cashed check at "Cigar Box" and out to gas station, then to Vivian's. Talked to Mr. Morgan, and then Vivian and I went over to Eunice's and Mutt's and played cards. Then we went for a ride, stopped by the apartment, and ended up having hamburgers and coffee at the "Cigar Box." Then took her home, and I got home about 3 a.m.

MARCH 2, 1940
Sat. Up at 10:30. Washed clothes, cleaned house, paid bills, ran into Hubie, and we proceeded to have an evening. Spent about $2.50 I could "ill afford" but had fun. Stayed all night at Hubie's.

MARCH 3, 1940
Sun. Up at 10. Had a nice breakfast. Cruised around all day with Hubie. Then went over to Vivian's. Had quite a talk with her folks. Then we went for a ride. Did some high-class necking. Came home and pressed pants and to bed at 12:30.

March 4, 1940
Mon. Fairly easy day at work. To work at 6, off at 2:30. Came home, fixed my flat tire, and washed car. Then slept for an hour and a half. Cleaned up, dressed and went to Vivian's. We went over to Shirley Hines's—talked, had coffee, and home and to bed at 12:30.

March 5, 1940
Tues. Very tired all day today. Off at 2:30. Came home and slept till 5 on Chesterfield. Had supper at Lewises. Hubie phoned during supper. Came home and read paper. Am going to bed at 7:30 tonight, as I certainly am worn out. Disgusted with life in general tonight. Work is complicated.

Tuesday, March 5, 1940 [*Entry written on separate piece of paper in the journal.*]
6:45 P.M.
1235 E. 18th St.
Tired—physically and mentally tonight. I have arrived at the decision that this is a hell of an existence. What the heck the sense of it is, is more than I can figure out. It seems years that I have been working day in and day out, paying out every cent of my check on bills my "faithful" wife left me with.

The few occasions that I have gone out and had a good time, I didn't enjoy myself as I kept thinking I was robbing one of the damn creditors of the few paltry pennies I did spend. Nuts! I'm too tired to write anymore.

[*The Edgar Guest poem, "See It Through," was found on an undated separate piece of paper in the journal.*]

March 6, 1940
Wed. Felt swell today due to 12 hours sleep last night. Workday was swell. Came home at 2:30 and painted tires and polished car till 5. Had supper, ironed 3 shirts. Hubie phoned and asked me to come out to his house and talk. V. isn't coming up from L.A. for Joyce's birthday. Hu and I may go down April 5, but I won't go near V.

March 7, 1940
Thurs. To work at 6:30, through at 3. Went over and helped Mr. Morgan

polish his car. Had supper over there. Then Vivian and I went to Mutt and Eunice's and popped corn. Then went for a ride, stopped by house, and finally got home at midnight.

March 8, 1940
Fri. Through work at 3. Went down to post office to find out about income tax. Couldn't make heads or tails of what he said. Came back to house and Hu was waiting for me. He asked me if I would co-sign for him on a hundred-dollar loan. I said I would. We went out tonight and had a good time. Got home about 3:30 a.m.

March 9, 1940
Sat. Got up at 10:30 and dressed. Phoned Hu and went out to his house. We went downtown, and I paid my bills. Cruised around all day and went out tonight and had some more fun. (Hu footed the bills, which made me feel like hell.) I stayed at his house all night. He got home about 6 a.m. (Sunday). I broke a date with Vivian.

March 10, 1940
Sun. Breakfast at Hubert's, and we cruised around all day. About 7 p.m., he phoned Vivian and we all went to show. (He footed bills continuously from Friday night.) Dropped Hu off home, and I took Vivian home. I told her I couldn't see her again till May when I wouldn't be so damn broke all the time.

March 11, 1940
Mon. Felt terrible physically and depressed mentally all day. I sure am discouraged. I pay bills continuously, yet never seem to catch up on them. Meanwhile, my clothes are wearing out, and I keep feeling lower and lower. <u>Damn Virginia</u> to hell, anyway.

March 12, 1940
Tues. Felt pretty good today because I got a good night's sleep last night. My <u>eyes</u> have been bothering me a lot, lately. Still feel sort of hopeless and useless. I have made a resolution not to go out anymore until these damn bills are <u>cleared</u>, with the possible exception of the trip to L.A. that Hu wants to take. <u>To bed at</u> 9.

MARCH 13, 1940
Wed. Home at 5. Had supper, came home, ironed 3 shirts, wrote Mother a letter, and will turn in about 9. Felt pretty good physically today but still depressed mentally. Have to wash clothes Saturday and pay income tax tomorrow.

MARCH 14, 1940
Thurs. A very good day at work. Felt good all day. I have got a lot of sleep this week. Came home after supper and made out a complete budget, which will pull me out of debt by June 21. <u>If I stick to it</u>. I've got to. Felt very good physically tonight, but I sure feel hopeless when I think of the weeks of bill paying.

MARCH 15, 1940
Fri. Came home and had to wait until 7:30 for supper. Then dressed and went to Union. Got out at 10 and went out to Lucky 13 and had 1 bottle of ale. Paid for a drink for Hubert for when he gets there. Left and drove home, listening to radio in car. Gee! I sure am lonely tonight. Guess I'll turn in now—11:45 p.m.

MARCH 16, 1940
Sat. Hu stopped by at 4:30 this morning and borrowed my car for a "date." I got up at 8, cleaned up entire house. Hu finally dropped by at 2. We went out and made the rounds. Went to a dance at the Hotel Leamington, and I <u>really</u> got pie-eyed. Got home to the apartment at 5 a.m. (Hu and I).

MARCH 17, 1940
Sun. Got up about 11 a.m. and had breakfast next door. Went to Hu's house—made the rounds again—back to Hu's house and finally I took Vivian to a show. Sure felt <u>terrible</u>. Got home at 2 a.m. Sure felt awful mentally. I spent some dough I couldn't afford, etc., etc.

MARCH 18, 1940
Mon. Got up at 5:30 and to work at 6. Felt <u>dead</u> all day. Came home at 2:30. Slept on Chesterfield till 5. Had supper, and I think I'll go to bed in a few minutes. I sure feel like I am no good.

MARCH 18, 1940 [*Entry was written on a separate piece of paper found in the journal.*]
9:20 P.M.
1235 E. 18th St.
Oakland, Calif.

I certainly feel despondent, morose, washed out, and confused tonight. Had quite an eventful weekend. I very foolishly spent $8, which I certainly couldn't afford at this time. I know it was extremely foolish of me to do so. My only defense for so doing is the fact that I am now going on to the sixth month of steady paying of bills, and I mean putting out every cent.

I honestly believe, if I didn't let go once in awhile, I would go nuts sitting around this damn apartment staring at four walls night after night. I wouldn't mind that, either, I don't think, if it wasn't so damnably lonely here.

I now have my bills down to $169 at this date. I have a budget worked out whereby I will have them all paid by the middle of June, but the $8 I spent this weekend put a monkey wrench in the wheels. I'm praying I can work out of it O.K.

Hu wants to go to L.A. April 5th. I don't know. I've got to get the oil changed on the car. And I know I will be dead broke, as usual. I went to bed at 7 tonight but couldn't sleep. Don't feel very good physically, or mentally, or any other way. They say a woman can make or break a man. I guess I'm the guy that got broke.

Couldn't take it?

MARCH 19, 1940
Tues. Very pleasant day at work. Felt fair today. Came home and did a big washing. Ate supper, took a bath, shaved and went out to Vivian's. Talked with Mr. and Mrs. Morgan, and Vivian played the piano. Hu dropped by and said he got a letter from V. in which she said to ask me if I would like her to show me the town. Nuts to that.

MARCH 20, 1940
Wed. Another pleasant day at work. Got through at 2:45. Came home and ironed till 5. Hu phoned and invited me to a show with Joyce. Went to the Roxie and had a hamburger afterwards. Gee! Hu sure is a swell kid. I only pray that I'll get my bills paid, so I can repay him in full.

March 21, 1940
Thurs. Through work at 3. Hu phoned at suppertime and said to come on out. We dropped by, and I showed him through the plant. Went to Sam's and had an ale. Decided to get Peggy and Vivian and go for a ride. Went to Brooks and the Round-up and danced a lot. Had a swell time. Home about 1:30 a.m.

March 22, 1940
Fri. Sure had a pip of a hangover this morning. Through work at 3. Came home and washed car all afternoon. Dressed and went out to Hu's. Repaid the $5 I borrowed last Saturday. Met Peggy and Beverly and went the rounds. Got home at 7:30 a.m. What a night! Danced a blister on my foot.

March 23, 1940
Sat. Got up at noon. Had breakfast at Lewises. Paid Local Loan. Went over to Hu's. Bought a new pair of shoes and had my slacks cleaned. Went out and went the rounds. Met Helen and Jessie—had a couple of drinks and took them home after a meal. Home at 3:30 a.m.

March 24, 1940
Sun. Got up at 10:30 Breakfast at Hu's. Went out and had a few drinks. Went over to <u>Castro's</u> and drank some wine. Went over to Vivian's, and we went for a ride. Dropped by the apartment and had some coffee. Took her home and to bed at 12:30.

March 25, 1940
Mon. To work at 8:30. Tired all day. Got a letter from Mother. Will answer it and go to bed about 8, I guess. Kinda blue and discouraged. Hu and I are taking Helen and Jessie on a picnic Sunday.

March 26, 1940
Tues. Pretty hard day at work. Worried as hell about my bills. I'll <u>have</u> to rearrange my entire budget and stall off Monohan on the car till the 12th, I guess. I can't seem to get caught up on them. <u>Worried</u> as hell with this trip to L.A. coming up.

March 27, 1940
Wed. Another hard day at work. Looks like work is slowing up this

week. Not much stock moving out. Still worried as hell about my bills. Spending another lonely evening at home due to a flat pocketbook. Wrote some letters and guess I will turn in about 9. Looking forward to the trip to L.A. but wonder what the hell I will do for finances on it.

March 27, 1940 [*Entry was written on a separate piece of paper found in the journal.*]
8:06 P.M.
1235 E. 18th St.
Oakland, Calif.
Things seem very confusing and hopeless at this time. I only owe $160 in bills outside of the balance due on the car. I have paid off quite a few of them in full, but the smaller I cut the others down to, the more they yell for.

It certainly is discouraging. I am hoping I can hang on for another two months. But <u>I know one thing</u>, if I intend to pay them off as per schedule, I've got to absolutely stop going out. I only spend two or three dollars when I do, but even that throws my budget out of line so much I have to pay double for it. And I've <u>got</u> to be clear by June, or else. I couldn't stand it any longer than that. A six-month's sentence is <u>long enough</u> to pay for my former "faithful" wife's foolishness.

Lately, work is getting to be awfully discouraging, too.

So, as a consequence, I certainly am down in the "Mental Dumps" tonight.

March 28, 1940
Thurs. Home at 5 from a <u>hard</u> day's work. Cooked my own supper. Went over and visited with Ed. Then went over to Vivian's. Played cards till 11. Then Vivian and I went for a ride in the hills. Car got stuck in the mud. Had an anxious hour getting it out. Home at 2.

March 29, 1940
Fri. Payday. <u>Long, hard</u> day! Not enough dough to meet my creditors. God! I'm at the end of my rope as far as these damn bills are concerned. I just <u>can't</u> seem to catch up. Stayed home tonight. Raining like heck outside. <u>Lonely Lonely</u>—

March 30, 1940
Sat. Hu came in at 6 a.m. and went to bed. We got up at 10:30 and

had breakfast at the Lewises. Went downtown and made half a car payment. Roamed around town, stopped at Helen's and Jessie's. Took them out and danced a lot. Went to the 13 and saw Viv (she saw me with Helen). Got home at 4:30 a.m.

MARCH 31, 1940
Sun. Hu and I rode around town. Went out to Berkeley and saw some of the gang. Rode around practically all day. Went out last night. <u>Found out some useful information</u>. Hu and B. dropped by, and we all went over to my house and talked. Got home at 1 a.m.

APRIL 1, 1940
Mon. To work at 6 a.m. Easy day at work. Came home and washed, scrubbed all floors and cleaned house thoroughly. Took me till 9 o'clock. Tooth was starting to ache. I wonder if it's going to be one of those nights? Worried about finances and <u>lonely</u>.

APRIL 2, 1940
Tue. Fairly easy day at work. Came home, took my clothes in, and ironed till 8 o'clock. Hu and Joyce dropped by. We talked till 10 o'clock. Had some coffee. L.A. trip, Friday, is getting complicated. I've got to get out of a special Union meeting. Bills have got me worried stiff. <u>And lonely</u> tonight.

APRIL 3, 1940
Wed. Through work at 2:30. Came home and cleaned car thoroughly, that is, the <u>inside</u> of it. Washed all windows, etc. The service station guy will grease it tomorrow. Flat broke tonight, not even any cigarettes. I sure am lonely and discouraged tonight. Well, to bed, I guess, at 9 p.m.

APRIL 4, 1940
Thurs. To work at 6:15. Home at 3. Worked on car. Went down and got Joyce's locket for her birthday. She sure was thrilled. Raff and I went over to Castro's and drank a little wine. Got home at 11:30. Supposed to leave for L.A. tomorrow <u>if</u> the money comes up.

APRIL 5, 1940
Fri. Off work at 2:30. Home, cleaned up and packed. Vivian was waiting at the apartment when I got home. She was more or less sore at me, I

do believe. Paid bills and went over to Hu's. We finally left town at 6:15. Drove all night. Stopped at Fresno and Bakersfield to raise a little hell. Got into Los Angeles proper at about 6 a.m.

April 6, 1940

Sat. Took Joyce over to Virginia's. I wouldn't go in and see Virginia, although her folks tried to get me to. Had a talk with Doris and Jim. Went on over to Jack's and raised hell. About 4 p.m., Hu and I went over to see Doris and Jim. Doris assured me V. wasn't there, but I no sooner sat down then in she came and said hello. I left without saying a word.

April 7, 1940

Sun. Went out last night and got drunk. Marge drove home, and I hit the hay. Raised hell all day. About 1 p.m., we went after Joyce. Stood awhile and talked with Doris and Jim. V. stood around, but I wouldn't look at her or talk to her. Left Glendale at 6 p.m. Drove all night and got in to Hubert's at 3:45 this morning.

April 8, 1940

Mon. Had an hour's sleep and am going to work at 8:30. Seeing V. in L.A. sure gave me an awful blow. It more or less spoiled my whole weekend. Pretty as ever, but I know she's just as rotten as ever, too. Finally got through work at 5. Lonelier than I have <u>ever</u> been tonight.

April 9, 1940

Tues. To work at 8:30. Feel fairly good today. Went over and visited with Veryl (Ed's wife), then went over to Hu's. He wasn't home. Talked with Effie, then went over to Vivian's. Hu was there, and Eunice. We all went over to see Eunice's new apartment. Then Vivian and I went for a ride.

April 10, 1940

Wed. A long day at work. Home at 5. Had supper and cleaned up. Sat around apartment. Finally, Hu dropped by, and we rode around town today. Had two bottles of ale. Then Hu went home, and I went on over and talked to Ed and Veryl. Home and to bed at 10 p.m.

APRIL 11, 1940
Thurs. Home at 5. Sat home and read a book. Hu dropped by, and we went over to Jessies's and played poker with Chuck and some other guys. Came home and to bed at 11:30. Turned down a dance at the Hotel Alameda because of finances.

APRIL 12, 1940
Fri. Home and cleaned up. Went over to Morgans and told them and Viv I wouldn't go to dance at Hotel Alameda. They left for dance, and I dropped by Lucky 13 and got gassed. Met Beverly and Peggy, Sorrwine and Canifax. We all dropped by my place. Sorrwine and Canifax left. We got up about 9 a.m.

APRIL 13, 1940
Sat. Hubie, Beverly, Peggy, and I all had breakfast at Best Yet. Took them home, and Hubie and I went up to Lake Temescal and sunbathed. We went out tonight and made the rounds. Not much doing for a Saturday night. Slept at my place. Got in about 4 a.m.

APRIL 14, 1940
Sun. Woke up at 1:30. Went over to Hu's and had ham and eggs. Joyce wanted to stay with us. Went up to Ruby's for a while, then went over to Castro's, and I got gassed on four bottles of ale. Went over to Vivian's. She was mad 'cause I hadn't been over all weekend. Home at 11:30.

APRIL 15, 1940
Mon. Up at 5 and to work at 6. Fairly easy day at work. Came home at 2:30 and washed and cleaned house. Hu dropped by for a while. I read a little. Then Ed, Veryl, and Bernice dropped by with 10 bottles of beer. Bernice and I got gassed. She's a nice kid.

APRIL 16, 1940
Tues. To work at 6, home at 2:30. So tired and sleepy, I couldn't stay awake. Went to sleep in chair. Dressed and went down to 14th Avenue and took bottles back. Hu phoned—met him on 14th Avenue. Went to Piemonte's and had an ale. Then over to Castro's. Hu went home. I went up to Vivian's, and we went over and saw Eunice. Dropped by apartment and then took her home. Ran out of gas. Had to borrow 22 cents to get home on . . .

April 17, 1940
Wed. To work at 6, home at 3. Tough day. Came home and slept till 5. Had supper, came home and wrote Mother and Harold a letter. Cleaned out bill file. I won't be boarding with the Lewises after Friday, as they had some relatives move in. I'll eat in the restaurant, I guess. Sure lonely and blue tonight.

April 18, 1940
Thurs. Late half hour at work today. Home at 2:30. Cleaned car all afternoon. Dressed and went out to Hubert's. Talked till 11:30. Had a coffee and came home. Standard Oil credit card came today, so bought 5 gallons of gas. It sure was a lifesaver. Am going to see about a loan Saturday.

April 19, 1940
Fri. Home at 2:30. Washed car. Went to restaurant and had supper. Went to Vivian's. Got to talking with Art, and he suggested I let him co-sign for a loan for me! Said O.K., and I would drop by at 10 tomorrow. Went to Union. Then out to the 13. Met a gal named Betty. Took her home and went to bed at Hu's at 4 a.m. Hu got in at 6 a.m.

April 20, 1940
Sat. Up at 9 and went over to get Art. We went to the bank, and he signed for me. Practically certain of getting loan so decided to go to Sonora and see folks. Hu and I chased around town and finally left for Sonora at 2 a.m. Had some amusing incidents on way up.

April 21, 1940
Sun. Got up to Sonora at 4 a.m. Talked till 5. Got up at 9. Went to Columbia and to a fish hatchery and up to Tuolumne. Had a nice visit with Mother. Left for home at 3:30 and got home about 6:30. Talked with Hu and his folks till 10:30. Then home to bed. <u>I'm praying for loan.</u>

April 22, 1940
Mon. I got the loan! And am I happy! Paid off all small bills. All I owe now is car, lawyer, and loan. What a snap! I owe this break to Mr. Morgan. He sure is a swell guy. Took Vivian to the show and home at 12:30. <u>Happy!</u>

April 23, 1940
Tues. Fairly easy day at work. Came home at 5 and went to the restaurant. Took my clothes to the cleaners, then paid Cliff his $42.61. Bought a new radio, but I'm not worried about it, as he said I could make any kind of payments I wanted to. Sure feel happy and unworried. Maybe life is worthwhile!

April 24, 1940
Wed. To work at 7. Easy day. One unpleasant incident. Came home, went downtown and got my watch out of hock. Had it repaired. Sent some shirts to the laundry and had my boots shined. Ate at restaurant and came home. Phoned up Ed and told him to come over. We talked till 9:15.

April 24, 1940 [*Entry was written on a separate piece of paper found in the journal.*]
9:30 P.M.
1235 E. 18th St.
Very happy! I got a loan Monday for $100 through the courtesy and kindness of Vivian's dad. Paid off all bills. All I owe now is the car, the lawyer, and the loan, which I can meet very easily if I am at all sensible. I bought a new radio, but I am not worried about it, as Cliff said I could pay for it when and how I wanted to.
    I feel like a 10-ton load was lifted from my shoulders.
    Certain aspects at work are rather discouraging, but I believe they will work out O.K.
    Nevertheless, I am extremely happy tonight!

April 25, 1940
Thurs. To work at 7:30. Very busy day. One unpleasant incident again but believe I was a little "diplomatic" about it. I am a little jittery about bills. I'm all clear, but I've got so much I want to do. I need clothes, have to save for my vacation, and keep up on car loan and lawyer payments. If I'm sensible, I'll be O.K., though.

April 26, 1940
Fri. Through at 4. Home. Took a bath, changed into grey suit, went out to Meudeses and visited till 9. Then out to the 13. Hu came in at 12 in his work clothes, and we proceeded to get swacked. Hu, Peggy, and I went down to See Huy Low's and had a Chinese feed.

April 27, 1940
Sat. Home at 4:30, up at 12. Had breakfast and over to Hu's. Cruised around all day. Over to Castro's and finally out to the 13. Met Gladys and Betty as per appointment and proceeded to make a night of it. Vivian was in the 13, but I didn't see her.

April 28, 1940
Sun. Got home at 6:30 and went to bed at Hu's. Got up at 12:30. Viv phoned and reminded me of our dinner date with Eunice. Went over to get her, and she told me some <u>really bad news</u>. God help me now. I'm worried to death and don't know what the heck to do. Please God, help me.

April 29, 1940
Mon. Dead tired this morning. But to work at 6:10. Home at 2:30. Had a very bad day at work. Slept till 4 p.m. Hu dropped by, and I told him the news. He accepted half the blame, and we'll work together on the solution. He sure is a swell kid. But I'm still praying for help.

April 30, 1940
Tues. To work at 6, through at 2:30. Shined car up, brought in clothes, cleaned up, ate, and dropped by Ed's. Then out to Hu's. We rode around in the Ford. Then we dropped by and saw Ruby and Mel. Then I stopped at Crooks for lunch and had a hamburger, then home. A little worried about things.

May 1, 1940
Wed. Fifteen minutes late to work. Through at 3:45 p.m. Came home and was going to shine chrome on car but laid down and slept till 5:30. Hu dropped by and woke me up. We went to restaurant and ate. Then he went home. I dressed and went over to Vivian's. Sat around and talked. Drove Eunice home, and Viv and I had a hamburger. Talked till 11 p.m. I believe "bad news" may work out OK. <u>I hope</u>.

May 2, 1940
Thurs. To work at 6:30—dog tired. Home at 3 and shined grill on car. Then went to restaurant and had supper. Came home and did an ironing. Wrote Mother a letter. Hu dropped by, and we talked till 9:30. Washed and to bed. Bad day at work.

May 3, 1940
Fri. Big day at work. Came home, changed clothes, and had supper. Saw Bernice and bought her a drink. Met Hu and went out and raised hell. We went to the Capitol Theatre in S.F. Came back to the Lucky 13 and met Sam. We all three went over to Alameda and out to Dugan's. Raff went out with Brownie. I got home at 5:30, and he came in about 9.

May 4, 1940
Sat. Got up at 1:15 p.m. and went over to Hu's house. Killed time till 7 p.m., then dressed in cowboy outfits and went to fiesta celebration out on Hopkins. Went to a house party with two girls, Camille and Bernice. Got home at 6:30 this morning.

May 5, 1940
Sun. Up at 12 and over to Hu's. Had "breakfast," then came back and fixed the flat on Hu's car. Went to the Paramount and saw "Johnny Apollo." Well, I spent quite a bit of dough this weekend, but I'm not going to worry. Or should I?

May 6, 1940
Mon. Up at 7 and to work at 7:30. A fairly easy day with no trouble. Went down to restaurant and had supper. Stopped by and saw Veryl. Came home and cleaned home entirely. Hu dropped by, and we talked. Hu left, and I finally retired at 9:15

May 7, 1940
Tues. Up at 7 and worked till 4:15 p.m. Came home, cleaned up and went to restaurant. Stopped by and saw Ed and Veryl. Then went over to Hu's. He had gotten a little "gassed" in the afternoon. Vacation plans altered again??? Then went over and saw Vivian. Went for a ride and sat in front of her house and talked.

May 8, 1940
Wed. Fairly easy day at work. One bad instance. Came home after supper "on the cuff" at restaurant. Hu and Castro dropped by, and we went out and had 3 bottles of ale. Hu and I went out to Hopkins District and had an ale, then to Cigar Box to have a hamburger. Came home. Tentative plans for a ride tomorrow.

MAY 8, 1940 [*Entry was written on a separate piece of paper found in the journal.*]
1235 E. 18ᵀᴴ ST.
OAKLAND, CALIFORNIA
11:25 P.M.
Feeling pretty good at this precise moment due to the effects of three bottles of ale. Since the last time I wrote herein, my financial worries have lessened a great deal, due to the kindness of Art Morgan (Vivian's dad), who co-signed and thus enabled me to get a $100 loan and pay off all my creditors. However, I still have to hump somewhat if I want to get clear enough to take a nice vacation. The pain and heartbreak in my heart caused by my former wife, Virginia, is almost all gone now, or at least I hope so, although I know it isn't quite, as was proved to me quite definitely when I saw her for a moment in my L.A. trip of April 5ᵗʰ. It hurt something awful. But I believe it will eventually wear off. Vivian was getting <u>too</u> serious, and I had to tell her that I <u>never</u> intended to marry again, which I don't.

    I believe by the end of the year I will be all clear of all financial repercussions caused by my unfortunate marriage, and I can face life again with a clean slate. At any rate, I feel pretty cheerful tonight, and optimistic, too.

MAY 9, 1940
Thurs. Came home at 4. Ate and dressed and went over to Hu's. Then to Vivian's, and we all went to Brownie's house after her but no one was home. Rode around and dropped Hu at his house. Then back to my apartment. Then took Vivian home. Retired at midnight.

MAY 10, 1940
Fri. Home at 4, ate, dressed, and paid bills. Out to Hu's and went after Brownie. We all went out to Lucky 13 and got gassed. Bernice left a message at 11 for me to come after her. Did so, and we <u>all</u> got gassed. Stayed at Brownie's all night. Hu and I ate at restaurant. Didn't go to bed.

MAY 11, 1940
Sat. Went over to Hu's. Decided to dress up in cowboy outfits. Went over to Ruby's. Strolled around in Hopkins District. Took Joyce up to see parade. Took her home, and Hu and I "stagged" all evening. Got

gassed. Had close shave with another car. Got home at 4 a.m. Spent quite a bit but had fun.

May 12, 1940
Sun. Up at 10 and had breakfast at restaurant. Over to Hu's and had a wonderful turkey dinner. Stayed there all day. Then Hu, Joyce, and I went to the "Broadway." Home at 11:30. Go to work at 6 tomorrow.

May 13, 1940
Mon. Up at 5:50. Felt strangely good all day. Home at 2:30. Cleaned stove and washed clothes. Then dressed and went down to supper at restaurant. Stopped by Ed and Veryl's and talked awhile. Then came home and gave Hap a shot of whiskey. Am going to turn in about nine. Lonely tonight. Job is getting complicated.

May 14, 1940
Tues. To work at 6:15 (late). Home at 2:30. Worked on car till 6, then dressed and went to restaurant. Then to Rafferty's. Saw Effie, Joyce, and Claude. Then over to Vivian's, and we went for a ride. I certainly am dog tired tonight. Two bad instances at work (?)

May 15, 1940
Wed. To work at 6:15 and worked till 3. Tough day at work. Came home and slept till 4:15, then worked on car till 6. Went to restaurant, came home and ironed all my ironing. Worried a little about finances. May is going to be an awful tough month. Lonely tonight. Retired at 9.

May 16, 1940
Thurs. To work at 6:15. Fairly easy day. Came home at 2:30. Saw Hu for a few minutes in front of the plant. Came home and cleaned house. Drove car around back and was going to work on it but fell asleep in it. Went to restaurant and ate. Came home and will take a bath, write Mother a letter, and to bed at 7:30.

May 17, 1940
Fri. To work at 6. Seemed like a long day. Came home, cleaned up, paid all bills. Flat broke this week. Went to Union meeting. Saw Ila and Bill Vaughn and Ed and Veryl. Came home and had a couple of drinks at landlord's party. Went looking for Raff about midnight. Got home at 5:30.

MAY 18, 1940
Sat. Slept till 10:30 and then Raff, Brownie, Vivian, and I went out to Niles Canyon and went swimming. Took the gals home about 6:30, and Raff and I horsed around till about 3:30 Sunday morning. Stayed at his house, and then we got up and had breakfast.

MAY 19, 1940
Sun. After breakfast, we drove around about all day. Saw Vivian, Corine, Della, Mel and Ruby and Castro. Got a little swacko on ale and went to the T&D. Came home about 9 p.m. Lonely and disgusted with life. Especially <u>lonely</u>!

MAY 20, 1940
Mon. To work at 7:30. Sam not in—Al took his place. I go to work at 6 tomorrow. Came home, cleaned house and went to restaurant. Ran into Bill Ferguson and Seaman. Had 3 ales at "Wee Willie's." Came home and found that Vivian had phoned and said for me to phone her back, as it was very important. Went to show with Bill and forgot to phone. Raff dropped by for a while.

MAY 20, 1940 [*Entry was written on a separate piece of paper found in the journal.*]
10:35 P.M.
1235 E. 18TH ST.
OAKLAND, CALIF.
Other worries seem to have taken precedent over financial matters for the present, although financial matters are not slight by any means.

Vivian phoned tonight and left a message for me to phone her back as it was very important???? Which I neglected to do, thus complicating the affair worse yet. As soon as this "affair" is straightened out, I am going to gradually cut it off, as she (Vivian) is getting <u>too</u> damned serious to suit me.

Financial matters are fair, but I've got to hump myself to take care of that vacation. <u>Lonely</u> tonight!

MAY 21, 1940
Tues. To work at 6, through at 2:30. Came home, dressed, and went out to Vivian's. We went down and had the "important business" over with, then had dinner at my restaurant and then went to the Fairfax and saw

Of Mice and Men. Took her home, parked and talked for a while, and finally got home at 11:55. To work tomorrow at 6.

May 22, 1940
Wed. To work at 6, through at 2:45. Polished car till 6:30, then dressed and down to restaurant. Raff came in, and I went down to the Armory with him. Then gassed around. Saw Bessie and Ila. Out to Fruitvale Fiesta and home at 11:45.

May 23, 1940
Thurs. To work at 6, through at 2:30. Home and cleaned house thoroughly. Lena came over and talked. She and Lola are on the outs. Raff came over about 7:15. We went over to Alameda to the "fiesta." I was thrown in the hoosegow for not being dressed up. Came home and had bacon and eggs. Bed at 11:45.

May 24, 1940
Fri. Came home at 2:30. Dressed in outfit, went to restaurant. Then went down and got a haircut. Hu and I went downtown to the fiesta. Met Peggy and Beverly, and I lost my wristwatch--$140 gone. I guess my jinx is still following me. Saw Bernice later.

May 25, 1940
Sat. Up and over to Morgan's. Then we went over to Hu's house and slept till 7 p.m. Then Hu and I dressed, and we went out and covered the town. Hu and I got <u>drunk</u>. I did because I felt so damned disgusted at losing my watch. Slept at Brownie's.

May 26, 1940
Sun. Up at Brownie's, over to Hu's, then over to Maryann's. Got Vivian, and we all went up to Temescal and sunbathed all day. Took Vivian home and had supper at her house, then home at 8. Put an ad in *Tribune* for watch but no hope.

May 27, 1940
Mon. To work at 7:30, through at 4. Felt horrible physically all day. Someone phoned in answer to my ad. Said they would phone me later, and so far, they haven't. Maybe I stand a chance of getting my watch back. I sure hope so.

May 28, 1940
Tues. To work at 7:30. No soap on the watch. It was the *Enquirer* wanting me to put an ad in <u>their</u> paper. Mentally a wreck tonight. Worked on budget till 9 o'clock. Hu dropped by for a while. I cleaned up and so to bed at 9:30. <u>LONELY</u>.

May 29, 1940
Wed. To work at 7:30, through at 4:15. Down to restaurant and then home and took a bath. Went out to Hu's, and then we went over to Vivian's. We left and went back to Hu's and talked. I think Vivian was sore. After I left Hu's, I went over to Bill and Ila's. They had a quart, and we all got stiff. Bernice interesting. Home at 2 a.m.

May 30, 1940
Thurs. What a dreary holiday! Up at 12, dressed and sat around till 1 p.m. and read books. Hu dropped by, and we went down to Park Boulevard where I had a sandwich. Then rode around for about 2 hours. Finally, Hu left, and I went over to Vivian's. We went over and saw May. Then home and talked till 11. Then I came on home.

May 31, 1940
Fri. To work at 7, through at 3:30. Then home and cleaned up. Went downtown and bought Raff a pair of boots for his birthday. Then over to Hu's house, and we got Spud and went out for the evening. Had a lot of fun. Spud looked swell. We all got lit. Home (at Raff's) about 5 a.m.

June 1, 1940
Sat. Up at 9, and Raff and I went up to Temescal after riding all over town and going downtown. I slept about 2 hours at Raff's and about 9, we went out for the evening. Had a lot of fun and some humorous aspects turned up. Home about 4 a.m.

June 2, 1940
Sun. Up at 10 and had breakfast at Raff's, then sat around and read till about 3. Went up to Spud's and talked. About 4, had a <u>swell</u> chicken dinner. Then Raff and I took Joyce to the show. Got home to the apartment about 10. Worried and <u>lonely</u>.

JUNE 3, 1940
Mon. Disgusted with life (as usual). My teeth have been worrying me. They hurt all day—gums and all. Came home at 2:30 and washed, dressed, ate supper. Got Vivian and Joyce and went to Armory. Watched Hu march. Home at 11:30. I'm not going out anymore till clear.

JUNE 4, 1940
Tues. Worked hard today. Home at 2:30. Slept till 5:45. Went to the restaurant. Stopped by and saw Ed. Home and will do my ironing, take a bath, and to bed. I have made up my mind to get clear, and if it means staying home, I'll stay home.

JUNE 4, 1940 [*Entry was written on a separate piece of paper found in the journal.*]
9:17 P.M.
1235 E. 18TH ST.
OAKLAND, CALIF.
Well, as usual, I find myself in quite gloomy and dreary circumstances. I evidently couldn't stand prosperity (or rather, the sudden lifting of Virginia's debts, the burden of which I had been carrying for some six months). For in my exuberance, I threw all caution to the winds, and although I didn't go berserk (I did pay most all bills as they came up), I did spend foolishly far more than I should have with the subsequent consequence that I am now mildly in the same hole I was before.

It will take some desperate striving to be on board again.

It took quite a disaster to awaken me to the fact that I was drifting rapidly towards what I certainly don't want to drift to, namely, carousing every weekend and spending a lot of money for liquor.

The disaster was the loss of my watch on the night of the fiesta, which represented a total of about $140. It was quite a blow to me and quite a loss, but it certainly woke me up.

I have made up my mind to stay home until all caught up, meanwhile building my health up, and then taking a nice two-week vacation. I have two plans in mind for my vacation: (1) Going alone to Mexico; then through the Grand Canyon, Boulder Dam, Reno, Clear Lake, and home, or (2) Take Mother and tour Oregon and Washington.

Only time can tell how things will work out.

Desperately lonely tonight.

June 5, 1940
Wed. Through at 2:30. Home and worked out budget. Bill Ferguson dropped by, and we went down to Jungletown [Jingletown] and had 3 beers. I got a mild "glow" on, then to restaurant and worked on budget again. Ironed balance of shirts, will clean up and to bed. Got a letter from Mom, Bob, and Harold. Bob wants to stay with me until he gets a job. --???

June 6, 1940
Thurs. To work at 6, through at 2:30. Overtime Saturday. Came home, had oil changed and car greased. Took slacks and shirt to cleaners. Dressed and went out to Raff's (was going out to see Lola). He invited me to a show, so went to Central. Home at 11 p.m. This "Bob situation" has got me puzzled and worried. ??

June 7, 1940
Fri. Came home, took a bath. Raff came by about 5:30. Put on slacks and "hit the joints again." Ended up at the Que Tal. Raff stayed at my place, and I stayed out at Ruby and Mel's again. I spent more than I should have, but this was the last "blow-out," as Bob will be with me next week, I think.

June 8, 1940
Sat. Up at 10:30 at Ruby's and out to work at 11. Worked till 3 p.m. overtime. Home and downtown and got a haircut. Went to German House and hit the joints again.

June 9, 1940
Sun. Home and slept till 10:30. Then out to Raff's and had breakfast. Over to Ruby's, and we all went for a swim at Temescal. After Temescal, we went down to Raff's and then to the restaurant and had supper. Went to the Fairfax and got home about 10:45. Go to work at 7:30 tomorrow. Teeth have been hurting for two weeks now.

June 10, 1940
Mon. Terrible day at work. Felt awful. Got through at 4 (at last) and went down and had my bum tooth pulled. Evidently, teeth are in terrible condition. Nice bill in prospect. Worried about bills and lonely, lonely, lonely.

JUNE 11, 1940
Tues. Fairly hard day at work. Through at 4. Went to dentist and made appointment for general overhaul in two weeks. Home and cleaned house thoroughly, shaved, and so to bed about 9:30. Awfully lonely tonight and worried sick about finances.

JUNE 12, 1940
Wed. To work at 7:30. Felt good all day. Worked an hour and a quarter overtime. Down to restaurant, then home and cleaned inside of car (preparing for Sonora trip, Friday). Felt so darn lonely, I don't know what to do. Life is awfully unjust sometimes.

JUNE 13, 1940
Thurs. To work at 7:30. Felt <u>swell</u> all day???? Went down to restaurant after work, then came home and worked on car. Went to service station and had tank filled and took suit to cleaners and had it pressed. Came home and was adjusting fog lights in backyard at 9:15 p.m. Will take a bath and then to bed. I want to leave for Sonora right after work tomorrow. O.K. tonight, except lonely and blue.

JUNE 14, 1940
Fri. Through work at 2:30. Paid off all bills and left for Sonora at 4 p.m. Picked up a hitchhiker and got up to Sonora at 7:15. Had a flat on the way up. Went to high school and saw Bob graduate. Home and talked quite a bit with Mom.

JUNE 15, 1940
Sat. Got up at 10 a.m. and fooled around house. Had tire fixed. Went swimming at Sullivan's Plunge. Had a lot of fun. Came home and sat up till about 10 talking again.

JUNE 16, 1940
Sun. Got up about 8. Had a nice breakfast, and Bob and I started for Oakland about 10:30. Got back to apartment about 2. Arranged house and then went swimming out at Richmond Plunge. Then went to a 20-cent show. Home at midnight.

JUNE 17, 1940
Mon. To work at 6 and home at 2:30. Went up to Temescal and sunbathed

till about 5:30. Came home and cooked supper. Raff dropped by. About 7:30, I laid down and went to sleep—slept until 6 a.m.

June 18, 1940
Tues. Dog tired today but felt better in the afternoon. Home at 2:45, and Bob helped me wash. Took stove apart and cleaned it. Had supper and took a bath. <u>Worried as hell</u> about finances, especially as I have Bob with me now.

June 19, 1940
Wed. Home at 2:30 and ironed all afternoon. Had supper and went to bed about 10 p.m. Lonely as hell and worried about finances.

June 20, 1940
Thurs. Home at 2:30 and went swimming at Washington Park. Had supper and finally to bed about 10. Am feeling fine physically due to no more weekends.

June 21, 1940
Fri. Well, the new wrapping machine came in today (my promised promotion), and I hope it goes through. Have to go to Union tonight. Paid out every cent on bills tonight. <u>Cutting them down</u>.

June 22, 1940
Sat. After Union last night, went out and had a couple of beers. Saw Ginny. Got up this morning and went to work at 6:30. Worked till 1:45 at time and a half. Home and worked on car. Went down and had a haircut. Coon called and wanted me to take Vivian to a show. I did. Home at 12:30. Bum evening.

June 23, 1940
Sun. Up at 9:30, and Bob and I worked on the car till 1:30. Then Raff, Bob, and I went up to Temescal till 4:30. Then went to a show. After the show, went and had chow mein at See Huy Low's. Then home at 11:30. Keeping my fingers crossed for promotion.

June 24, 1940
Mon. Well, jinx is still following me. Ray Curti got the job, due to more seniority. Bill said he forgot "the talk" we had the first of last

year. However, he promised me the job on the next machine. I wonder. Discouraged. Lonely and blue tonight. Worried about finances, too. Bob is an added expense, too, although I wouldn't say anything for the world!

JUNE 25, 1940
Tues. Felt terrible all day. Cross, cranky, and worn out. Big day at work, too. Have budget figured out to be clear by August. I've got to be. I can't stand it any longer, and besides, my clothes are about worn out. Discouraged, lonely, and thoughtful tonight.

JUNE 26, 1940
Wed. Discouraged and deadly tired all day. Worried about finances. Living expenses have increased. Very hard day at work. Bob not working as yet. To bed at 10:30.

JUNE 27, 1940
Thurs. Another day of discouragement and extreme weariness. I can't figure out what makes me so dog tired at work. Stayed home all week. Read *Beau Geste* till 10:30 and then, at last, to bed. Sure feel blue and lonely tonight.

JUNE 28, 1940
Fri. Got a $38 check today—all but $1.50 on those miserable bills. Bob went to the show, and I went out and tried to find some way to end this awful loneliness. But no go. Had a few drinks (by myself) and came home at 1:50. God! I don't know—I'm lonely, lonely, lonely. About at the end of my rope.

JUNE 29, 1940
Sat. Got up about 11:30. Had breakfast and then we went downstairs and fooled around on the car. Then went swimming at Temescal. Came home, had supper, and went to the library and got the Sunday papers. I sat up and read till 3 a.m. Sure was sleepy when I went to bed.

JUNE 30, 1940
Sun. Up at 12:30. Breakfast. Cleaned house thoroughly. Then turned out a big washing. Didn't leave the house all day. Will take a bath and then to bed. Go to work at 6 a.m. tomorrow.

[*The lyrics of "The One Rose" by Del Lyon and Lani McIntire were handwritten in red pencil on the MEMORANDUM page between the months of June 1940 and July 1940.*]

JULY 1, 1940
Mon. Couldn't sleep last night due to 3 cups of coffee at 11:30 p.m., so sat up all night, and at 5:30, dressed and went to work. Dog tired all day. Came home and we went swimming at Temescal. Went to bed at 6:30 and did I sleep. <u>Wow</u>!

JULY 2, 1940
Tues. To work at 6, through at 2:30, and then up to Temescal again. Came home, listened to Baer-Galento fight. Rafferty and Joyce dropped by. He gave me $2 to pay McRaff with. I ironed ten shirts and so to bed at 11 p.m. <u>LONELY</u>.

JULY 3, 1940
Wed. To work at 6, home at 2:30. Went swimming up at Temescal, and then I went out and paid Vivian the $2 Raff gave me. Raff and I went out and had some drinks. I stayed all night at his house. Got home about 2—both of us glowing.

JULY 4, 1940
Thurs. Got up, had breakfast, and came back home and got Bob. We worked on Raff's Ford till about 2 p.m., then we all went up to Temescal till about 5 p.m. and then went to the carnival. Saw some fireworks at the lake. Home about 11.

JULY 5, 1940
Fri. To work at 6, and home at 2:30. Cleaned up and had my teeth cleaned at the dentist's and got a haircut. Raff and I went out, and I foolishly spent about 4 bucks I couldn't afford. Home about 2:30. What a night.

JULY 6, 1940
Sat. To work at 8:30, and home at 1:45. Felt lousy all day. Raff, Bob, and I then left town for Tracy. I was pinched for speeding (60) on the Tracy cutoff. Camped on the San Joaquin and cooked supper over a campfire. Rolled up in blankets and slept under the stars.

JULY 7, 1940
Sun. Up about 9 and prepared breakfast. Swam and sunbathed all day. Came home about 5:30. Bob and Raff went to the Fox Oakland, so I got Vivian and went and saw *Pinocchio*. Got home about 1:15. She's <u>still</u> too darn serious.

JULY 8, 1940
Mon. Awful tired and a little sunburned today. To work at 7:30 and through at 4. Slept on Chesterfield, had supper, and read *The Grapes of Wrath* till 11 p.m. Disgusted with life. Finances <u>critical</u>.

JULY 9, 1940
Tues. To work at 7:30. Felt pretty good. That darn Hap didn't pay for the suit he bought on my account, so the collector was at work today raising hell. Wait till I see Hap. <u>He'll pay, or else.</u>

JULY 9, 1940 [*Entry was written on a separate piece of paper found in the journal.*]
9:29 P.M.
1235 E. 18TH ST.
OAKLAND, CALIF.
I wonder why on earth, trouble seems to cling to my footsteps like a shadow. I've had nothing but bad luck since 1937. Or maybe it's just my pessimistic nature breaking loose again.

At any rate, I went on a camping trip last Saturday, and on the way up, I received a tag for speeding ($10).

Just one thing after another, and now I'm even getting dunned for someone else's bill (Hap didn't pay for his suit). On top of all my other worries, I have Bob on my hands to add to my already enormous expenses, until he can find a job. I don't mind that at all, but I'm so damned nervous and irritable from all these other worries, I'm afraid I'll blow up and let go. I realize perfectly well that it's due wholly to inexperience, but he has the idea the job is going to fall in his lap, and unfortunately, you have to look for one.

I don't know how this miserable mess, called my life, will work out. I've got to clear off about 80 or 90 dollars in bills before I can take my vacation, besides save some money for it and buy some clothes. All I can do is pray for the best and hang on. As I have said before, we shall see what we shall see.

July 10, 1940
Wed. To work at 7:30, through at 4. Saw Ed and went out to Vivian's. She was at the show. Talked to Raffertys for a while, and then came home and to bed.

July 11, 1940
Thurs. To work at 7:30, through at 4. Came home and cleaned up and got so damn lonely, I rode around town for a while. Came home about 10:30. Saw a prowler in the backyard.

July 12, 1940
Fri. Came home from work, cleaned up, and went to the dentist's. Then Rafferty and I went out. Took Ruby and Vivian out. I felt rather morose all evening, due to lack of finances.

July 13, 1940
Sat. Got up about 11. Cleaned up, and Bob and I went over to Vivian's. We all went swimming up at Temescal. Someone broke in the car and stole our wallets and my only good pair of pants. Boy, I sure have a jinx following me. Raff and I went out again, and I felt disgusted about not having any dough, so I left the El Adobe in a rush. Raff wasn't sore.

July 14, 1940
Sun. Stayed home all day. Cleaned house thoroughly and wrote Mother a letter. Sure have been down in the dumps all day. I don't believe I'll ever get the breaks. Expenses are getting too high. ???

July 15, 1940
Mon. Home at 2:30. Ruby phoned and wanted me to come out. It seems Mel had a bum on and she wanted me to drive her to work. I did. Then she wanted me to get Vivian, and we rode about 50 miles getting fried chicken for Mel. I dunno, I'm just a sucker, I guess.

July 16, 1940
Tues. Stayed home tonight. Oh yes! Forgot to mention, Vivian and I had quite a talk last night. She wanted to know if I would get serious. I told her no. She said she wanted to get married, etc., so I wished her "good hunting," and that ends that, I guess.

JULY 17, 1940
Stayed home tonight, also. Had quite a letter from Mother. She suggests that maybe Bob better come home, as my expenses are so high, but nix—he has to have his chance, too. But these damn expenses have sure got me worried.

JULY 18, 1940
Thurs. Home at 2:30. A rather miserable day, almost rainy, but Bob and I went up to Temescal for an ice-cold dip and then to bed at about 11 p.m.

JULY 19, 1940
Fri. Home at 2:30. Cleaned up and went to Union meeting. Had a couple of drinks after Union and went by Raff's house and picked him up till midnight. We went out again and got home at 2:30. I stayed at Raff's all night.

JULY 20, 1940
Sat. Up at 11. Raff suggested going up to Colusa. I objected, as I was darn near broke, but he insisted, so I went. Got to Colusa about 8 pm. (gassed). Left Colusa and went to the town of Williams to a dance. Left Williams about 2:30 and got into Sacramento about 4:30.

JULY 21, 1940
Sun. Walked around Sacramento until the restaurants opened and had breakfast. Then left for Tracy. Went to a beach and sunbathed till 10 a.m. and left for home. Got home about 2 p.m. Had supper and went to bed dog tired and $8 shyer.

JULY 22, 1940
Mon. Through at 4 p.m. Home, made supper, and read till 10:30 and then to bed. Am I worried about bills! God! I don't know if I'll pull out or not--?

JULY 23, 1940
Tues. Home at 4. Washed car and had supper. Ruby and Raff dropped by, and then Bob and I went to the library. Home and read till 11:30 and so to sleep (still worried).

July 24, 1940
Wed. Home at 4 and cleaned car. Had supper, and Ruby phoned and wanted me to drive her to Lake Chabot. I did. Then I bought her a drink, and we went for a ride. Got home at 10. Very disgusted, melancholy, and blue.

July 25, 1940
Thurs. To work at 7:30. Hard-fast day at work. Big day tomorrow, too. I am sure wondering about this compulsory military service and the effects it will have on me and my life?????

July 26, 1940
Fri. Home at 4:30. Payday. Sent lawyer $5 and went to dentist. He filled two teeth. Went out and saw Ed. Learned Virginia is living with some guy in L.A. I sure feel sorry for the guy. Rode around a little and came home.

July 27, 1940
Sat. Up at about 10. Dressed and went down and had car refinanced. I only owe $145 on it now. Got a haircut. Bob and I went out and saw the new Grahams. Bought a lot of funny papers and read them till 12:30 and then went to bed.

July 28, 1940
Sun. Up and dressed. Went over and saw Lola. Bob stayed there. I went out and saw Raff. We rode all over town. Went back to his house, and I went over and saw Vivian. Rode all over the hills. Had supper and went for another ride—quite a talk.

July 29, 1940
Mon. Home at 2:30. Went swimming, exercised, and to bed about 8 o'clock. Sure feel good physically due to swimming, etc.

July 30, 1940
Tues. Home at 2:30 and went swimming again and retired early again. Rather worried as to how vacation will work out, due to finances, C.M.S., etc.

July 31, 1940
Wed. Home at 2:30 and again went swimming. Things not going any too smoothly at work. But nevertheless, retired early.

August 1, 1940
Thurs. Home at 2:30 and swimming again. Came home and worked on budget and retired about 9:30. Had a good night's sleep.

August 2, 1940
Fri. Home at 3:30. Didn't go swimming. Paid off all bills and stayed home all night. Read magazines till 12:30. Finished paying my lawyer today. Hooray!

August 3, 1940
Sat. Up at 7. Went down and got a new driver's license. Then Hu and I gassed around all afternoon at Hu's expense. I was broke. Borrowed his car, as mine is in the garage for 3 days getting new brakes. Viv and I went out.

August 4, 1940
Sun. Up at 9 and went to Temescal with Bob and Vivian. Swam for 5 hours and got a nice sunburn. Came home, did a big washing, cleaned house, and so to bed.

August 5, 1940
Mon. Up at 5:30 and to work at 6. A very hard day. I had to break in a new kid. Bob worked 9 hours today at the plant. I went swimming by myself at Temescal. Came home and got supper and so to bed. Read till 10:30.

August 6, 1940
Tues. Up at 5:30, to work at 6. Another hard day at work. New kid. Came home and went to dentist's. Car's new brakes work swell. However, will have to take back to have him readjust them. May write Hu tonight.

August 7, 1940
Wed. To work at 6. Took car down and made them readjust the brakes. Feel hopeless and discouraged tonight. Damn grocery bill keeps me so broke I can't pay my other bills. It looks like I won't even get clear

by October to take my vacation. Meanwhile, my clothes are just about gone. God, I can't stand much more of this. Paying out every cent and nothing for myself.

August 7, 1940 [*Entry was written on a separate piece of paper found in the journal.*]
10:30 P.M.
1235 E. 18th St.
Oakland, Calif.
Bad luck seems to eternally dog my footsteps. Here is a resume of what has happened to me in the last few months:
    Lost my wristwatch ($140)
    Arrested for speeding ($5)
    Car broken into and clothes stolen ($10)
    Broke my glasses ($12.50)

    All this has happened in the space of about three short months. I had planned to take my vacation this year and forget (for at least two weeks) all the worries and troubles that have happened. It's been the only thought that has held me together for the past year. God knows, last year I did the same thing—worked and sweat all year dreaming of a nice vacation and then had to use the vacation money to pay off my "wonderful" wife's bills. And this year, I'm still paying on them after 40 weeks of denying myself clothes, haircuts, pleasure, and even necessities.

    What is complicating things at present is the damn grocery bill.

    Since I have Bob with me, it costs me, naturally enough, twice as much to live. He can't find work, for which I certainly can't blame him, but it makes it so hard just at present, after all I've gone through.
Life certainly is funny—***.

    Well, I don't know how things will work out, but I imagine the pages of this record will chronicle what happens by the end of the year. Who knows?

August 8, 1940
Thurs. To work at 6. Tough day at work. That new kid is making quite a nuisance of himself. Came home, and Bob and I went swimming up at Lake Temescal. Retired to bed quite early.

August 9, 1940
Fri. To work at 6 and finally through for the week at 2:30. Came home, cleaned up, cashed check, paid bills. Went out to Vivian's and met Fred, the guy she was telling me about. Then to Ed and Veryl's, then to Lola's, then went to a show. Retired at 12.

August 10, 1940
Sat. Up at 9:30 and polished car until noon. Then dressed and went downtown. Vivian came by in the forenoon. Got back from town about 6:30. Bought all Sunday papers, wrote Mother a letter, and read until the wee hours—thence to bed.

August 11, 1940
Sun. Bob went to work at 8. I got up about 9:30 and went over to Ed's and got buzzie and went up to Lake Temescal. We stayed till 3 p.m. I got nicely tanned and swam for about 3 hours. Came back to Ed's and drank 3 bottles of beer with him and had a lovely dinner. Bob came over about 6 and had supper. We stayed till about 9 and then came home. I sure feel good physically. All this swimming and exercise is doing me good.

August 12, 1940
Mon. To work at 6. A very easy day. Bob worked today. He is making a good impression on Riggs. We went downtown tonight to see about getting in the Union. I hope he gets in. It will help us both a lot. Still don't know what I will do about my vacation. I can't clear <u>everything</u> up before I leave. All I can do is hope.

August 13, 1940
Tues. Home at 2:30. Kind of a tough day. Pretty tired tonight for some reason or other, so am going to retire early.

August 14, 1940
Wed. Coming down with the flu, I think. At any rate, I went to bed early but don't know whether it will do any good or not. Bernice and Bill dropped by. Bill wanted me to go to a smoker Friday.

August 15, 1940
Thurs. Came home at 2:30 and went to bed awful sick. About 7:30,

Jack *** phoned and said he was coming over. He did and passed out (drunk). So I had to drive Maryl all over hell. About 2:30, they left for L.A. Got to bed at 3 a.m.

August 16, 1940
Fri. No night shift today, and the oven broke down, so I got off at 10:30. Bob and I went downtown and bought him some clothes. He worked all week. Went to Union meeting. To bed at 12.

August 17, 1940
Sat. To work at 6:30 and through at 12:30. Home and worked on car all afternoon. Then went over to Vivian's and talked till 11. We're all going up to Sonora tomorrow.

August 18, 1940
Sun. Vivian, Bob, and I left for Sonora at 6 a.m. Got up there at 9. Folks have moved. Not such a hot house, though. Left for home at 6:30. Had a nice visit. Got home about 11 p.m. Traffic!

August 19, 1940
Mon. To work at 7:30. Easy day. Dog tired tonight. Going to bed at 8:30. Bob still working. Still worried and wondering about bills.

August 20, 1940
Tues. Came home and went to bed early. Still suffering from a cold. Read a little and went to bed. My eyes seem to bother me an awful lot, lately.

August 21, 1940
Wed. Came home from work at 4 and went to the dentist's. Home and had supper. Vivian phoned and wanted me to come out, so I did. Had quite a nice evening. Rode around. Went over to Ruby's and met Butch (Jack's brother).

August 22, 1940
Thurs. Went to bed fairly early tonight. Still feel pretty bum physically.

August 23, 1940
Fri. Through work at 3:30. Home. Cleaned up and paid bills. I feel

pretty good tonight. Went over and took Vivian out, and we traveled all over town dancing, etc. Home rather late.

August 24, 1940
Sat. Got up at 12 noon. Hubie got back from Washington. I bought some clothes today!!! Hubie and I celebrated all day. Viv joined us about 2:30 a.m. I dropped off—home about 3 a.m.

August 25, 1940
Sun. Raff dropped by, and Bob and I had breakfast over at his house. We left about 2:30 and went over to Vivian's, where we enjoyed a very nice dinner at 5. Then we all went over to May's for a while and over to see Hubie again. Bob and I got home at 10:30.

August 26, 1940
Mon. To work at 6, home at 2:45. Turned out a big washing, scrubbed the kitchen floor. Bob went to the show, and I stayed home, as I was rather worn out.

August 27, 1940
Tues. Big day at work. Stayed home after work. I certainly am confused and upset about this draft bill. I'm not worried about going, but I would like a chance to pay off that loan and the car instead of losing all.

August 28, 1940
Wed. To work at 6. Dead tired tonight, with the result that I came home and went to sleep on the Chesterfield and forgot to go to the dentist's. Went to bed early.

August 29, 1940
Thurs. Came home at 2:30. Had supper and went out to Vivian's. We rode around for a while and talked for quite a bit. Went to a show at the Fairfax. Home about 11:45.

August 30, 1940
Fri. Went out and bought a set of tires for the car and paid off my radio. Hubie and I went out. Bought a bottle and went over to Peggy and Mel's house. Drove Hubie home, and we both went to sleep in the car in front of Hubie's house. Home at 6:45 a.m.

AUGUST 31, 1940
Sat. Bob worked till 5 p.m., and we dressed, and Bob, Vivian, and I went swimming out at Richmond Baths. Vivian, Bob, and I stopped and had coffee at my apartment. I took Vivian home, and we talked till 2:30 a.m.

SEPTEMBER 1, 1940
Sun. Bob and I got up at 10 a.m. and worked on the car all day (till about 5), then we rode around, stopped at Hubie's (Vivian was there), got the Sunday papers, came home, and I read till midnight.

SEPTEMBER 2, 1940
Mon. Bob and I got up at 10 a.m. and had a nice breakfast. Then we completed the work on the car. Dressed and went over and saw Lola and Walt, Ed and Veryl, the Raffertys, and Vivian. Came home, cleaned house, and had supper and to bed about 10:30.

SEPTEMBER 3, 1940
Tues. Home at 4, very tired. Slept on Chesterfield till 5. Had supper and went to bed at 6:30. Slept till 6:30 the next morning. Awoke very refreshed and feeling very good.

SEPTEMBER 4, 1940
Wed. Home at 4. Went down to service station and polished car. Had the oil changed and had the car greased. Came home, had supper, and wrote Mother a letter and then to bed at approximately 10 p.m.

SEPTEMBER 5, 1940
Thurs. Up at 6:30 and had a medium-hard day at work. Came home at 4:15 p.m. The draft bill was halted for 2 months, so I may get a chance to pay off all bills by the time I'm called. Took a bath and to bed at about 9 p.m.

SEPTEMBER 6, 1940
Fri. Through work at 3:30. Home and cleaned up. Went to the dentist's. Went out to Rafferty's, and we went out. Chased all over town. Home about 3:30. Stayed at his house all night.

SEPTEMBER 7, 1940
Sat. Got up and went downtown and paid off brakes ($19.81). Had battery charged and went over to Vivian's. She was very sarcastic, cool, and aloof. (I <u>heard</u> that she was looking for me last night.) Raff and I went to the Union dance over in S.F. Left the dance and hit the bright spots.

SEPTEMBER 8, 1940
Sun. Met two girls (Pat and Toni) in a bar, and we all made the rounds. I got tight and so did Raff. We couldn't remember driving back over the bridge, and Raff fell asleep at the wheel, and we ran up on somebody's front porch. Didn't hurt the car at all. Cruised around all day and went to the show. Came home about 9. Bob not home.

SEPTEMBER 9, 1940
Mon. (Holiday) Bob and I got up rather late. Cleaned up entire house, and I turned out a huge washing. Worked on car all day. Then we went to the show—saw *Typhoon* and *Edison the Man*. To bed about 12 a.m.

SEPTEMBER 10, 1940
Tues. To work at 6 a.m. A new man to help me. Tough day. Worked till 4 p.m. Home and stripped the car. Supper and to bed, finally, about 9 p.m.

SEPTEMBER 11, 1940
Wed. Another tough day at work. Home at 2:30. Went down to service station and bought a new battery for the car. Supper, and Hubie dropped by for a while. Bed at 11.

SEPTEMBER 12, 1940
Thurs. Still another tough day at work. Home at 2:30. Finished stripping car, and supper, and finally to bed at 9 p.m.

SEPTEMBER 13, 1940
Fri. To work at 6 a.m. We work all day tomorrow. Home at 2:30 and to dentist's. Then got a haircut. Virginia will be in town tomorrow. I don't want to see her. <u>And I won't</u>. Hubie and I hit a few rounds, and I came home at 11 p.m.

SEPTEMBER 14, 1940
Sat. To work at 6, home at 2:30 after a helluva tough day. Went out, met Ruby and Bee and her fiancé. We all got tight. Drove Ruby home, and I rode around over by San Francisco until 5:30 a.m. (lonely as hell). Came home and went to bed.

SEPTEMBER 15, 1940
Sun. Got up about 11:30. Bob and I rode around. Dropped by Ed and Veryl's, and we all went swimming. Came back to Ed's and had supper. Then Bob and I came home and went to bed at about 10:30.

SEPTEMBER 16, 1940
Mon. To work at 7:30. I heard Virginia was out with Hubie Saturday night. I guess she's trying to throw the hooks into him again. I wonder what she did with the pimp she brought up with her from L.A.?

NOVEMBER 8, 1940
Fri. It seems I never write in this book unless something terribly important happens. Nothing did. Had a lovely vacation in October. Went out tonight with Beatrice—lousy time. What a gold digger. All out of debt. More later.

DECEMBER 11, 1940
Haven't written for some time. All out of debt and actually bought a new suit. Received my draft papers today. Feel very good physically. Bob took car and went to the show.

DEC. 11, 1940[*Entry written on a separate piece of paper found in the journal.*]
OAKLAND, CALIFORNIA
1235 E. 18TH ST.
8:15 P.M.
Have hardly written in here since Sept. 16, 1940, except for one small passage Nov. 8, 1940.
    But then, that is human nature, I guess, to only pour out your troubles when things are adverse.
    Howsoever, many "stirring" events have taken place since then. I had a wonderful 2 weeks' vacation with Mother and Harold—covered over 5,000 miles. At present, I am all out of debt. Bob and I get along

swell. We bought us each a nice $38 suit. Our house is fixed up very cozily. We bought a record player and a bunch of records. Also a nice seven-way floor lamp. The apartment was completely redecorated and looks very nice. I received my draft questionnaire today.

Went up to the German House, Saturday, and met a swell girl named Myrtle. Am supposed to have a date with her Friday night. She seemed awfully nice. Think I will go to bed early tonight.

Very happy mentally. Oh yes! I'll be free and single again next Wednesday. (I have Virginia's "diploma" ready to mail.)

DECEMBER 30, 1940
Mon. Birthday again—25 years old. All out of debt—car paid for. Feel years younger. Have gained weight (7 lbs), and I most certainly do not regret the divorce.

DECEMBER 31, 1940
Tues. What a difference from last year! Took Ann S. to Hotel Oakland with ten other couples. Quite a night. Got home at 7 a.m.

JANUARY 1, 1941
Stayed home all day today. Didn't feel so good for some reason or other. Retired rather early. Go to work at 8 a.m.

JANUARY 2, 1941
Thurs. Small day at work. Laying off a few fellows. Went over to Ann's and played cards and had tea. She is 20 years old and a darn swell kid.

JANUARY 3, 1941
Fri. Another small day. Went over to Vivian's, and she had to stay home. We had quite a talk. Got home about 11:30 and turned in.

JANUARY 4, 1941
Sat. Got up at noon. Bob worked in the morning. Raff dropped by, and we had a couple at his house, then went down to "The Occidental." Took Myrtle to the German House and danced till 1 a.m.

JANUARY 5, 1941
Sun. Cleaned house thoroughly. Think I'll drop Myrtle. She's a little too ritzy for me. Bill and Bernice dropped by. Went to bed early.

January 6, 1941
Mon. Small day. Home at 3:30. Had supper and to bed about 9.

January 7, 1941
Tues. Double crew today. Home at 3:30 and to bed early again!! Rained all day.

January 8, 1941
Wed. Another big day. Things a little discouraging at work. Home at 3:30 and to bed early again. Still raining.

January 9, 1941
Thurs. Small day again. Came home at 3:30 and went out to Ruby's to see about loan "deal." Stopped by Raff's and gassed all evening. Drove by Ann's and Vivian's. Had a hamburger and came home.

January 10, 1941
Fri. Ann and I went out. Had a pretty nice time.

January 17, 1941
Fri. Union meeting. Dropped by plant and picked Annabelle up, and we went out and had a pretty good time. She certainly is a nice kid. But I am certainly far from in love with her.

January 18, 1941
Sat. Went out by myself tonight. Ran into Vivian and Raff. Got mildly tight and came home about 3 a.m.

January 24, 1941
Fri. Took Vivian out tonight. Went to the show and had something to eat later on. Had 2 (two) highballs. Then talked till 3 a.m. and home and so to bed.

January 25, 1941
Sat. Received my notice to appear for my physical examination for the draft today. So it looks as if I'll be in the Army before long. Went to a party at Ann's tonight. A lot of fun—and very interesting.

JANUARY 26, 1941
Sun. Vivian phoned up and said she wouldn't be home today??? Bob and I cleaned house, then went out and played golf and then to a show. Scalp is getting a little better.

JANUARY 27, 1941
Mon. To work at 7:30. Uproar at work owing to alterations. Am getting disgusted of that job. If it weren't for my eyes, I would join the Navy.

JANUARY 28, 1941
Tues. Received a promotion at work today. A chance to learn the trade. I wonder if I am doing the right thing by taking it?

JANUARY 29, 1941
Wed. Stayed home again tonight. Feel <u>awfully</u> discouraged, lately.

JANUARY 30, 1941
Thurs. Stayed home tonight, too, after working till 6 p.m.

JANUARY 30, 1941 [*Entry was written on a separate piece of paper found in the journal.*]
1235 E. 18TH ST.
OAKLAND, CALIF.
Eventful happenings are certainly occurring in fast and tumultuous succession. Let me record a few that have occurred since December 1940.

December 18, 1940—Obtained final divorce from that peer of all womanhood—Virginia. Did not get the papers, however, as I figure on letting her next sucker pay for those.
December 21, 1940—First date with Ann Simpson—a swell kid—nice to go out with, but that's all.
December 30th, 1940—My birthday—25 years old.
December 31, 1940—A big party (at Hotel Oakland) with Ann.
January 4, 1941—Finished paying for car.
January 17, 1941—notified by U.S. Government to appear for physical examination in regard to drafting me.
January 28, 1941—Received promotion at work with definite prospects of learning the trade.

So, it can easily be seen what is meant by "fast and tumultuous succession." There are certain aspects of the promotion that are not so appealing, but a chance has to be taken in any venture. And I very much suppose that in about 2 or 3 months, at the most, I will be drafted for a year. My financial worries are all gone, and I should be carefree, but when I let myself think of the mistakes I have made and what the future may bring, I become confused, lonely, and all jumbled up mentally.

Physical examination at 10 a.m. tomorrow.

JANUARY 31, 1941
Fri. Went down and took my physical examination. Passed as physically perfect. Worked on new job. Ann and I went to Frisco, then back to Oakland. Bad deal. I think I'll drop her, too—gradually.

FEBRUARY 1, 1941
Sat. Got up at 1 p.m. Morose and blue all day. Bought two records for my phonograph. Bob went out. Guess I'll go to the show and then home.

FEBRUARY 2, 1941
Sun. Came home after show last night. Got up today about 10:30. Played golf. Bowled some and went bicycle riding, then to the show and restaurant and home.

FEBRUARY 3, 1941
Mon. 45 minutes late to work today. Found out promotion was still going through. Developed a boil on my left foot. Went out to Vivian's and talked. Still a bad deal?

FEBRUARY 4, 1941
To work at 6. Foot awfully sore. Home at 2:30. Stayed in tonight—retired about 9 p.m.

FEBRUARY 26, 1941
Tues. Packing tonight to enter the Army for one year. Quit job tonight. Tomorrow????

The inside front cover of the journal contained a signature (Ernest J. McCully), a date ("December 25, 1936"), an entry ("21 yrs. old the 30th"), and an empty space where a picture had been placed at one time ("VIRGINIA--MY WIFE"). There was a note that "Virginia crossed out the picture." (Indeed, there was a large "x" penciled across the place where the picture had been.) A newspaper clipping contained the following announcement:

Divorces Filed
McCULLY, Ernest J. vs. Virginia

A date of "October 31, 1938" had been penciled in along the left side of the clipping with another note, "23 years old" penciled in on the right side. The facing page contained a newspaper clipping dated December 22, 1939, which contained the following announcement:

Divorces Granted
INTERLOCUTORY DECREES
McCULLY, Ernest J. from Virginia N.

The next pages begin the "FIVE YEAR DIARY."

The following list was handwritten on the last pages of the journal:

Radio Stations

S.W.

W4ETP	KNOXVILLE TENNESSEE
W5DQ	CUSHING, OKLAHOMA
W3EMR	PENNSYLVANIA
W5D1B	ROSWELL, NEW MEXICO
XFD	MEXICO CITY, MEXICO
W9AS	NEWTON, IOWA
W9FD0	KANSAS CITY, KANSAS
JYK	TOKIO, JAPAN
W9H01	DECATUR, ILLINOIS
K6NZQ	HILO, HAWAII
W1RI0	Redland, Vermont

W5DVM	Fort Smith, Arkansas
W95DQ	Indianapolis, Indiana
W9VAT	Kansas City, Kansas
W5YJ	Stillwater, OKLA.
W5AWE	ENID, OKLA.
K7FST	WRANGELL, ALASKA
W5CRQ	DALLAS, TEXAS
W9LLC	Beacon, ILL.
W9BFL	DES MOINES, IOWA

The inside back cover contained the name, "ERNEST JOHN MCCULLY," surrounded by a decorative, patterned design. All were written in ink.

Journal 2

VOLUME I
August 4, 1941 to February 26, 1942
Ages 25–26

It is here! War at last!
As I write this, an air raid is in progress
over Pearl Harbor, Hawaii...
I cannot help but wonder just what effect
this momentous news will have on my life

THIS PORTFOLIO IS THE

PROPERTY OF

Pfc. ERNEST J. McCULLY

COMPILED AND ARRANGED AT

CAMP CALLAN, SAN DIEGO, CALIF.

AUGUST 4, 1941.

COAST ARTILLERY REPLACEMENT CENTER
CAMP CALLAN, TORREY PINES
SAN DIEGO, CALIFORNIA

[*Found on insert in front of journal.*]

COAST ARTILLERY REPLACEMENT CENTER
CAMP CALLAN
TORREY PINES, SAN DIEGO CALIFORNIA

[Embossed stationery heading used for Synopsis.]

VOLUME I
(1941)

MILITARY RECORDS

HIGHLIGHTS OF 30 MONTHS
IN THE U.S. ARMY

August 19, 1941.   Pfc. E. J. McCully

INDUCTION AT THE PRESIDIO OF MONTEREY • ARRIVAL AT CAMP CALLAN • ASSIGNMENT TO PLANS AND TRAINING DIVISION • TRANSFER TO POST ENGINEER'S OFFICE • PROMOTION TO CORPORAL AND TRANSFER TO HEADQUARTERS 11TH TRAINING GROUP • APPLICATION TO OFFICER CANDIDATE SCHOOL • VIVIAN IN CONTACT • WAR IS DECLARED • HOSPITAL STAY

SYNOPSIS

From the time I had registered for the draft on October 16, 1940, until the date of my induction on February 26, 1941, I had possessed the certain premonition that I would be among the first called. Accordingly, when I received that fateful white envelope, telling me to report for induction, my financial and business affairs were all in order. I had systematically paid off every debt I owed and refrained from opening new accounts, although, at times, it took practically every cent of my weekly check to do so. To my younger brother, Bob, I owe an invaluable debt, which I can never repay, for his unselfish assistance to me at that time. All things in life have a tendency to equalize and adjust themselves, however, and I hope that my opportunity will eventually come in which I can, in some measure, repay one of the finest brothers one could wish for.

    1940, the year prior to my induction, had been a year of heartbreak and despair, loneliness, and hopeless struggling in a mire of debt, which that perfect example of womanhood, that pillar of "purity," my ex-wife, had so thoughtfully accumulated. So it was with a certain feeling of accomplishment that I held in my hands receipts entitled "paid in full," including the one from my lawyer, which had obtained my divorce for me. In looking back upon the previous year, I felt indeed, that my marriage had been "paid in full."

    It was with these thoughts in mind that I hurried about on that last week in February arranging this, arranging that, saying countless adieus, a suitcase to buy, what clothes to take, glasses to be repaired, etc.

    All too soon, however, was everything completed, and the last goodbye said. And so on a rainy February morning in 1941, I kissed my mother goodbye and boarded the interurban train at Fruitvale Station and was finally on my way—to what?

THE FIRST THREE DAYS
Day the First

With some two hundred other draftees, I left the train in San Francisco and was greeted by a small group of noncommissioned officers. We were marched to a large flight of stairs in the station where we were lined up and had our picture taken by an enterprising news photographer. (Draftees were still news at the beginning of the Selective Service Act.) We then marched to the streets where a large fleet of drab-colored Army trucks awaited us into which we were packed for all the world like a can of Monterey sardines. One more picture by the industrious photographer, and we headed for the National Guard Armory. Here we were marched up three flights of stairs and were given a lecture by a stern-voiced sergeant relative to the subject of whiskey bottles in the luggage. From what I could gather, some of the draftees were continuing their farewell parties of the night before, and some evidently needed a little more than moral courage.

The physical examination, one of the strictest I had ever experienced, given by a group of efficient doctors, took all the forenoon. After lunch at the Army's expense, we were taken before a very impressive-looking Major and took the oath of allegiance and were sworn in. We were then informed that we were going to the Reception Center at Monterey, California. About 3:30 p.m., we were driven to the station (again in the drab-colored trucks) and boarded an ancient train of doubtful vintage. It reminded me a great deal of the milk trains of the Civil War era, what with its ornate red plush upholstery and gaudy decorations.

As far as transportation was concerned, however, it performed surprisingly well, as we arrived at Monterey about 10 p.m. that night. Upon de-training, we were lined up and again crammed into the now familiar trucks. After a ride that loosened practically every vertebrae in the spinal column, we again departed the trucks in the Presidio of Monterey. Here we were lined up, given what the Army delicately refers to as a "short-arm inspection," and marched to the warehouse to receive our clothing and equipment. The less said about the uniform, the better; sufficient to say that the only item that fit me was the necktie. A slight drizzle of rain began at this time, and we were shown the correct way to make an Army bed, in a misty downpour, along with the admonition that unless our beds were made in a like manner the next morning, we would be introduced to the mysteries of "K.P." The result of this vicious-sounding warning was that no one went to bed, preferring to sit up and talk. We were assigned five men to a tent, and the business of getting acquainted kept everyone awake, although the now heavy downpour of rain on the canvas tent caused sleepiness to a certain extent. I think I dropped off to sleep about three-thirty in the morning, and so ended my first day in the Army.

The First Three Days
Day the Second

A shrill blast from the Sergeant's whistle made me raise up on the bed. (On, not in.) It was 5:30 a.m. and was still raining heavily. The company street outside the tent was a sea of viscous, ankle-deep mud. Amid much hilarity, we donned our newly issued uniforms with raincoat and lined up outside, each man holding his mess kit and tin cup. We were then marched to the mess hall and stood ankle deep in the mud amidst a terrific downpour while over four hundred men awaited their turn in a mess hall, which would only hold one hundred. The food, frankly, was terrible here at Monterey, due in part, I think, to the fact that eating out of mess kits, all the food was thrown together, and the resulting combination of stew and peach syrup, spaghetti, and jam, was far from appetizing. We had to gulp down our food as fast as we could so that those outside could get in out of the rain. Then to the end of the building and outside, where two huge tubs of boiling water awaited in which we washed out the mess kits and utensils. That is, this was finally accomplished after standing in line in the rain for an hour, awaiting your turn.

After breakfast, back to the tent where we were instructed to stay until called. The time was spent playing cards, getting better acquainted with the other fellows, and laughing at the grotesque appearance of the shapely uniforms on their various owners' bodies.

About this time, a small group of us were marched back to the mess hall again, where we heard an officer discourse for an hour on a subject known as the "Articles of War." It seemed that every man was required to hear these at least once every six months. All this time, the downpour of the rain continued, beating monotonously against the mess hall roof. This seemed to cause a great deal of sleepiness in the ranks of the ill-fated draftees, as several were admonished to stay awake and listen to the interesting "Articles of War," or else K.P., the ever present, the awful.

After lunch, we were all herded into line and taken to a large wooden-frame building where we were marched inside and given an intelligence test. The test consisted of arithmetic problems that kindergarten pupils could answer, counting blocks (many pages of these), trick questions, etc. All in all, the test was very simple and not at all difficult.

After this interesting experiment, we were made to march to still another building where we were skillfully interviewed and the very last dreg of vital information was pumped from our minds. Although we were unaware of it at this time, these tests and interviews were for the purpose of classifying us as to what arm of the service we would be best fitted for. The fact that I had taken typing in high school seemed to merit great importance, and indeed, this one factor had a great deal to do with my final disposition in the Army.

It was fairly late by now, and so we were immediately marched to the mess hall for "chow," as the Army calls it, and we were starting to do the same. After chow, most of us were too tired to do much and turned in early with the warning that there would be an inspection in the morning, along with the ever-present drumming of the rain beating in our ears. And so ended my second day.

The First Three Days
Day the Third

The howling of a high wind, interspaced by the slash of a terrific rainstorm beating against the flimsy walls of the tent, woke me at about 3 a.m. The cement floor of the tent was a lake of water, and the fire we had so carefully banked in the scrap-iron stove had been out for hours. I jumped out of bed and retrieved my suitcase, which was on the verge of floating off, at the same time placing my shoes on a dry spot. By this time, the other occupants of the tent were awake, and a flurry of moving the beds around, sweeping the water out of the tent, and rebuilding the fire, soon followed. After everything was again in order, we sat around talking of past experiences, and a more vivid cross-section of America would be hard to find than was gathered around the roaring stove in that storm-swept tent. Charlie had been a cashier in a bank in San Francisco.

Pete, a Slovak of doubtful ancestry, had been a migratory agricultural worker in the San Joaquin Valley, picking fruit and migrating from ranch to ranch during harvesting season. McGee, a Negro, had been an auto mechanic and had been in the CCC. He it was who already knew how to make beds Army style and instructed us accordingly, which factor put us one step ahead of the less fortunate draftees in the other tents. With the Negro's inherent ability to adjust himself to any unusual situation, he was completely at ease and did much to make us feel the same way. In countless small ways, he assisted us and gave us the benefit of his experience. True, his skin was black, but he was a white man for all that and a credit to his race. The remaining occupant was a 22-year-old named Henry who hailed from Arkansas, speaking with a heavy southern accent and who soon had us unconsciously imitating him in that respect. The time was thus spent until the whistle blew at 5:30. Again, we waded through the sloppy mud and lined up in the pouring rain. Breakfast consisted of the now familiar mass of assorted food. Much to our surprise, it stopped raining during breakfast, although the sky remained leaden and overcast. Upon arrival back at the tent, we were lined up and told to change to fatigue uniform or the denim jeans and blouse used for all fatigue details. A march of some three city blocks brought us to the sawmill where we were instructed to carry about two cords of logs from a nearby hill, which were to be cut and carried to our "company street" for the use of the next group of *Les Misérables*. Hard we labored for all of two hours, at the end of which time, covered with sweat, we were marched back to our tents, told to change uniforms and were again lined up. The small, but tough, corporal called us to attention and issued a pair of aluminum "dog tags," or identification discs, to each man. These are oblong, beveled squares of aluminum, heavily embossed with the draftee's name, Army serial number, and the name of his beneficiary in the event of his death. (Pleasant thought.) They are cleverly constructed with raised letters so that when they are picked up, as on the battlefield, they can be placed in a gun-like affair, which prints the actual information on the tag on certain reports. These tags represent a great improvement over the type used during the World War.

The rest of the afternoon was spent policing the area around the tents, and it was a tired and disgusted five who crawled wearily into their bunks when the lights-out whistle blew, ending my third and last day at Monterey.

Arrival at Camp Callan

The next morning was cloudy and overcast, but wonder of wonders, no rain, although a gale of no mean proportions sweeping up out of Monterey Bay howled over the tent tops playing havoc with the stovepipes and stake ropes. We had the usual breakfast and immediately after, were lined up and told that we were about to receive the cards, which told us where our next destination was to be. This caused a flurry of excitement in the ranks, and much to my amazement, mine was the first name called. With some trepidation, I looked cautiously at the all-important square of cardboard, fully expecting to read Georgia, New Jersey or some other distant Army post. All it contained, however, was the notation, "Camp Callan, San Diego, California, Station Complement." Now arose cause for worry indeed, as after some investigation, I discovered that out of four hundred men, only I and one other had cards bearing "Camp Callan" on them. The others were destined for Fort Lewis, Washington; Fort Warren, Wyoming; and other places. Why had I been thus singled out? What did "Station Complement" mean? After all, San Diego didn't sound nearly as interesting as Fort Warren, Wyoming.

I was told to pack immediately as I was leaving at 9 a.m. from the nearby Town of Salinas. Here was additional cause for worry, as none of my companions was due to leave until the following Monday. The act of my packing caused a mild sensation in my own and nearby tents, and so, with calls of "Where you going?" "Where to?" and the best wishes of my new-found friends, I walked down the company street with my duffle bag over my shoulder, my suitcase in my hand, and dressed in the huge, but warm overcoat I had been issued.

At the Quartermaster's Office I met Hutchings, the other unfortunate, and we were given our ration money and classification records, which were placed in my keeping with the instructions not to let them out of my sight. We were then placed in the back of one of the ever-present trucks and taken to the Monterey Station where the Captain bought our tickets and gave us his best wishes as he placed us on the bus, which was to take us to Salinas.

Self conscious in our bulky uniforms, we arrived at Salinas and had an hour's wait before our train, the *Daylight Limited*, pulled in. The porter was kind enough to store our embarrassing duffle bags in the luggage compartment, but although the train was air conditioned, rather than expose the Civil War-vintage shirt I had been equipped with, I rode the entire distance to Los Angeles with the bulky overcoat on. Hutchings was grandly equipped with a "choker blouse" of the 1917 era, which fact didn't seem to bother him a great deal, as I found him quite a studious chap, deeply immersed in some studies of psychology he had brought along.

The higher-ups in the Army had evidently slipped up in figuring our ration money on the streamliner, as the luncheon cost us the entire $1.50, with no tip for the waiter. We arrived in Los Angeles at 7 p.m. where I paid for our supper out of my own pocket. We had a two-hour layover here when we were transferred to the *Santa Fe Streamliner*. Here again, I suffered mental agonies as I was forced to display the horrible duffle bag to the view of the crowded station, and horror of horrors, when we did find a seat on the train, there was no baggage compartment, and I had to lug the disgraceful thing to my seat with me.

We arrived in San Diego about 11 p.m. and were again met by the Army truck. A young second lieutenant was in charge of the single truck and was assisted by his driver, a corporal. He seemed surprised that only the two of us had arrived. Hutchings and I climbed into the truck, and with the familiar noisy clashing of gears; we were off on the last lap of our journey to Camp Callan. It seemed the Camp was situated about thirteen miles from San Diego, and in no time, we had arrived and passed through the gates at which military police were stationed. My first impression of Camp Callan was of an immense cluster of finished and unfinished buildings sprawling over red-colored sandy soil through which the rain had carved huge chasms and cracks. The truck had to pick its way cautiously through the maze of cracks and small canyons, as to lose its way in one would mean, at the least, a broken axle. Eventually, we arrived at our barracks and were taken to the mess hall for coffee and doughnuts. This shiny new mess hall seemed a veritable heaven after the Monterey fiasco. When we had finished our coffee, we were conducted to our barracks. What a change from Monterey! Our beds were already made for us; the barracks themselves were sparkling new and clean and were heated by warm air. They were equipped with a warm, clean shower room, in which I took the opportunity to get rid of some of the mud of Monterey. And so it was with a grateful sigh that I sank beneath the covers, my first night in Callan, and knew no more until morning.

The First Six Months Pass

The ensuing six months were filled with many and varied experiences. The first realization I became aware of was how extraordinarily fortunate I had been as to my final disposition in the Army. Primarily, I was fortunate in being sent to Camp Callan, as it was ideally located in the great summer resort region of Southern California. Amusements of every kind were all situated in nearby cities and towns, whereas many camps were located miles from the nearest town. Numerous excellent bathing beaches were available all along the coast. Amusement parks, theatres, Scenic Balboa Park with its zoo and museums, were only a few of the many diversions that were offered.

Secondly, I was extremely fortunate as to my disposition. I learned that I had been placed in the "DEML" Detachment, or Detached Enlisted Men's List, which was regarded throughout the Army as one of the soft spots. Because of having had four years of previous military training, I was excused from the thirteen weeks of basic training, which every draftee must undergo before being assigned to a permanent station. Because of this fact, I would remain at Callan until further notice instead of again being shipped out, as in the case of the other draftees.

I was assigned to act as secretary to a Lt. Colonel Crowell and Major L. I. Cooley, who were in charge of the S-3 or Plans and Training Division at Headquarters. Here my rusty typing, which I had not used for over five years, picked up in both quality and speed. The work itself was both light and interesting, and all in all, this particular aspect of the Army was very enjoyable. We went to work at 8 a.m., had an hour for lunch, and stopped work at 4:45 p.m. We were issued special privilege passes so that our time was our own after working hours. The food was excellent, and I began to feel better, both physically and mentally. I spent about $25 and purchased a decent-appearing uniform, which I didn't have to be ashamed of, and this one factor did much to make me feel better.

About the middle of April, I was transferred to the Post Engineer's Office to help them catch up on overflow of work and remained there for two weeks. I made many friends during this time, and the first part of May, I obtained a three-day pass, and with a good friend of mine, Bob Benjamin, went home and saw my folks. We no sooner arrived back at Camp, then Benjamin was sent to the hospital with measles. Two weeks later, I came down with the same disease and likewise spent two weeks there. Upon discharge from the hospital, I came back to the detachment to find a rumor sweeping through the barracks to the effect that all draftees in the DEML were to be transferred to the 2nd Squadron of the 11th Cavalry. This prospect pleased me immensely, as I had figured my year in the Army would undoubtedly benefit me greatly physically, and to tell the truth, the monotonous office work was beginning to pall on me. It was with some disappointment then that I learned Colonel Crowell had scratched my name off the list of those destined to go. However, Benjamin and 58 others were packed off to Camp Seely some 40 miles out in the nearby desert, and from all reports, were soon undergoing quite a rugged life. I continued on in the office and soon made more friends with the new men who were sent in to take the place of those shipped out. About July 25th, I was made Private First-Class and Fifth-Class Specialist, with a resulting pay increase of up to $42 per month. Swimming became my chief diversion, and I soon obtained quite a tan. About Aug. the 11th, my two younger brothers, Bob and Harold, came down on their vacation and remained a week, during which time we were very busy enjoying all the various amusements. It was with a heavy heart I saw them leave for home, as Congress had recently extended the draftees' period of service to 2-1/2 years, and already a rumor was circulating that some of the men in the DEML would soon be transferred to Alaska and the Philippines. I have no way of knowing when or where I will see any of my friends or family again, as most of the men are resigned to the fact that we will soon be in the war. And so it is with these thoughts in mind that I finished this synopsis of my first six months in the Army. From here, where? I'm sure I don't know, but I hope I am transferred soon, as I am of the opinion that I am wasting my time here, and then, too, I really don't give a damn what <u>does</u> happen to me. Paramount above all else, I do not want this record of events to be misconstrued as a diary, for it isn't. It is merely a record of outstanding events in my mind, and certain impressions that I feel are worthy of retaining for the future.

END

August 21, 1941

Bob and Harold have been gone for two days now, and I certainly miss them. I would like to see Mother again, but I really believe it would be foolish to make the trip at present, because there are some articles of clothing I need to purchase this month, and the monthly wage doesn't go very far. Perhaps next month?

The rumors of our ultimate transfer to either Alaska or the Philippines are still persisting, but I don't credit them with much basis. I read an interesting article in the paper the other day, to the effect that the selectees may be able to obtain a discharge in 18 months, instead of the original 30 months that was scheduled heretofore.

I have been wracking my brains as to what to do this coming payday. David Davis and I had planned a double date, but he has to go to Los Angles instead, so here I am, marooned without a car, and knowing no one to visit, even if I did have one. Believe me, I refuse to remain in Camp, and so will probably end up by going in to San Diego. But perhaps it is a little early to forecast any definite happenings.

Six of us received an invitation from a Mr. T. B. Colby to spend a Sunday at his 500-acre ranch near Escondido. He sent a car down for us and drove us out to the ranch. He had also invited six young women to be his guests also, so each of us had a partner. The day was complete in every respect. Swimming in the large private pool, horseback riding, hiking, games, cocktails, dancing, and a wonderful barbecued dinner. I really enjoyed myself a lot, although I did not do very much dancing. At about midnight, he drove us all back to Camp in his station wagon, and they invited us all to come again next month. Sure feels good to get a few social invitations once in awhile.

August 28, 1941

The past few days have proven eventful indeed. The DEML Detachment is a mass of false rumors and conflicting statements. Because Congress recently approved the appropriation, soldiers acting as secretaries, clerks, and doing other types of office work are to be replaced as rapidly as possible with civilian workers. This is being done here at Headquarters with great dispatch.

Naturally, these actions cause a great many questions to arise in my mind, such as: Are we to remain at Headquarters? I think not, as with the civilian replacements now on the job, there is scarcely any work to do. Assuming that this is correct, where are we to be sent?

Alaska and the Philippines have been mentioned, as those places are situated so far away from civilization that civilian employees would be difficult to obtain. I hardly think that such good fortune could be true, however. Well, then? Are we to be reclassified as "basic soldiers" and sent down to the Battalions as cadre? Again, I think not, as the Army <u>does</u> have, despite miles of red tape, a flair for efficiency. It certainly doesn't seem to be that it would be practicable to send skilled workers, who have been given specialists' ratings in acknowledgment of that skill, to the Battalions as basics, when those skills could be put to good use elsewhere. Well, then? Where to? What? Why? Personally, I don't care. I know that in the event we are transferred, I will be greatly pleased, and the farther away, the better. As long as I have to spend 2-1/2 years in the Army, I would like to derive a little benefit from it, and I can think of no better way of doing it then to travel to far-off places, as I certainly have nothing worthwhile to hold me in this country. Then, too, to be truthful, I am bored stiff with the monotonous routine of Camp Callan, and I would welcome any hardships and rugged life, which would occur. These have been denied me on two occasions now, one on applying for the parachute troops and also on applying for admittance to the Cavalry at Camp Seely. And who knows, perhaps this is the opportunity I have been waiting for. Frankly, I believe the six months I have spent at Callan have been a total loss, with the exception of becoming more proficient in typing, secretarial work, and improving my English.

Payday will be on this forthcoming Saturday, and I have no idea what it will bring. I know I am going in to San Diego, and there may be a few social engagements, but it will probably be nothing more than the same lonely walk through town again . . .

SEPTEMBER 11, 1941

Again, a great many events have filled the interim in just the short length of time since I last wrote. As I mentioned, I had a few social engagements of negligible amusement value. I went in to San Diego by myself on payday and purchased an economically priced sport coat. The following Sunday, an ex-cavalryman, Roscoe Oglesbee, and I spent the day in La Jolla and San Diego, and had a very interesting time at the Amusement Pier in Mission Beach, and later, at the theatre in La Jolla.

Tuesday, September the 9th, I applied for a fifteen-day furlough, which to my immense surprise, was granted. The furlough is from 6 a.m., October 6th, until 6 a.m., October 21st, but I believe that I can get excused Saturday morning, October 4th, and also Friday afternoon of October 3rd, which will give me approximately 17 days in all.

I will have nearly $40 after purchasing my railroad ticket; that is, if I am successful in borrowing the sum of $10 from some one of the fellows here. If I am prudent in expenditures, I am sure that will be sufficient. Meanwhile, the necessary waiting is certainly hard to bear. Mother has no idea that I was successful in obtaining the furlough, so it will be a great surprise to her. Bob, of course, knows about it, and is, as usual, very helpful in assisting me with my plans.

Still no word of the ultimate disposition of the men in the DEML, but something is very definitely in the wind. Went swimming late last night, and it was the coldest I have yet experienced here. And the riptide was also very noticeable, being so bad that I could hardly stand my ground, at times. Went into Commander Barnes's house, night before last, with Corporal Davis and had a very pleasant evening. My weight has gone up to 150 pounds, but I am going to concentrate on getting a lot of rest during the interval before going home, so that when my folks next see me, I will be in A-1 condition. My eyes have been giving me so much trouble of late, that I am going to give up taking books out of the library, as I always overdo it, and read until all hours of the night.

SEPTEMBER 15, 1941

Today is Monday. I can't hardly call it a "Blue Monday," as there is no necessity for that—no hangover, etc. I spent a very mild weekend indeed. Slept all Saturday afternoon, then that evening went to the Camp Library and read until 10 p.m. Withdrew two books, one by James Oliver Curwood, the other by Peter B. Kyne. Both were written around 1911 and were typical examples of the sloppy sentimentality of that era. However, I enjoyed them for all of that.

Naas, Slichter, and I went to the La Jolla Shores Beach Sunday afternoon, and I spent about two hours battling the surf, diving after bottles, etc. I really think that the large amount of swimming that I have been doing is benefiting me immensely, physically. I wish I could cut down on my smoking, however, as lately, it seems to cause me quite a bit of trouble, and my overactive imagination doesn't help things, at such times. I only smoke about a pack per day, but that is too much. I was really worried about two days ago. As I have already related, we went swimming at night, and I caught a terrific cold (due to riding in the rumble seat of Naas's car with wet trunks on), and I couldn't seem to stop it. But yesterday's lying in the sun evidently helped to improve the situation, as it is about gone today.

For the last two or three evenings, I have been furbishing and repairing the equipment that I am going to take home on furlough. A little in advance to do that, perhaps, but believe me, when I <u>do</u> go home, I am going home <u>looking</u> like a soldier at least.

The "Disposal of DEML" problem is again rearing its ugly head, as recently, what little work we did have to do has disappeared, and our "jobs" have degenerated into the art of "killing time" and drinking Coca-Colas. Naturally, this condition, when once noted, will not be tolerated for long. So--? I only hope they don't get any odd ideas about this until after I take my furlough.

MONDAY, SEPTEMBER 29, 1941

3-1/2 days, not counting today, until I leave on my 17-1/2-day furlough! All is in preparation for said event, but such last-minute details as train ticket, loan of $10, haircut, and the purpose of waiting until the last minute is to help curb my ever-growing impatience. I believe from all aspects that Staff Sgt. Cook is going to loan me the very necessary $10.

Tomorrow is payday, at which time I shall get my uniform from the cleaners and purchase sundry articles that will be needed for the trip. Since last writing in this book, my <u>final</u> divorce papers arrived here from Oakland. I had applied for them September the 15th, at which time they were granted. With the arrival of them also comes the realization that, at last, that filthy episode is entirely over with. I am a free man at last, and believe me, that is the precise way that I am going to remain. It was a heartbreaking, bitter episode, but I can say this much—it is a lesson well learned! I know now that it is foolish to love a woman so completely that you can forgive anything and overlook everything. I know that it is foolish to place your complete trust in any woman. I know how foolish it is for a man to take all manner of abuse and vituperation and then to cover your hurt and take it in silence, because you could scarcely believe that the person loved was capable of such poison. But enough of that! I am free at last from all the loathsome chains of that sordid mess known as marriage, and believe me, September 15th, 1941, will always be a day emblazoned in fire to me—the fire of freedom.

It is certainly going to be great to see Hubie, Bob, Mother, Harold, and all the rest again! Five months is a long time. Of course, I have seen Bob and Harold since then, but the little time that I did see them was far too short. Colonel Crowell has been transferred to Fort Bragg, North Carolina, so evidently the S-3 Section is going to have a new boss by the time I arrive back here from my furlough. Which gives rise to the thought? I wonder what changes will be in store for me by then?

??

OCTOBER 23, 1941

Back at Camp after a thoroughly enjoyed, drained-of-the-last-vestige-of-joy, furlough. Left Oakland at 8:30 a.m., Monday, October the 20th, and arrived back in San Diego at 1 a.m. the next morning. Both streamliners were an hour late, and consequently, I missed the last bus back to Camp. Therefore, I had to wait until 2 a.m. and then catch a Los Angeles-bound bus, which went by the Camp. I walked to the entrance gate and was fortunate enough to meet an M.P. with whom I was acquainted and who gave me a ride in one of the "jeeps" to Headquarters (3-1/2 miles), as it was raining violently.

Upon arising, I was amazed to find that, in my absence, I had been promoted to the rank of Corporal and had been transferred to a different detachment, namely, the "HQ 11th Tng. Gp." Upon arriving at the office, I found that a great many changes had been made there, also. I had a new "boss," a Lt. Colonel Taliaferro, and to my surprise, my new rating evidently carries a lot more responsibility, as I was placed in direct charge of all Plans and Training communications with the Adjutant General's Office in Washington, D.C. Likewise, the receipt and disposition of all incoming training films was placed in my hands. I am quite happy in believing that the job and my future in the Army seem to hold definite promise of advancement. I will have to move to another barracks, and certain other minor adjustments will have to be made before I am satisfactorily settled again.

While on my furlough, I saw Vivian and complicated matters somewhat, as she is going to Reno, Nevada, this month to obtain her divorce and will be married about Christmas. She told me she still loved me, but I just <u>had</u> to tell her what I always told her in the past—that I was never going to marry again. I felt awful for a couple of nights, though.

I have a blind date in company with John Strahl on payday night, but I hear that my date is Italian, so I am afraid that spoils my evening before it even starts, as I have never held much enthusiasm for the Latin race. Wrote Mother and Bob today, as I haven't heard from any of them since I returned. I found out pretty definitely that I won't be able to leave here Christmas, but I hesitate to write and tell Mother this, as she was planning on my coming home then, so very much.

One extra benefit I hadn't anticipated occurred on my furlough. Evidently the love I once held for Virginia is completely dead, as she was in Oakland at the same time that I was, and I even caught a couple of glimpses of her, and not the faintest tremor of emotion bothered me. I am glad—glad. It took an awfully long time to die--.

OCTOBER 29, 1941

I have been back at Camp for approximately one week today. Have been very busy moving and getting settled. I was loath to move from the barracks where I was so well established, but despite various manipulations, I was required to do so. The difficult part of the whole situation is that practically all of the fellows in this new barracks are total strangers to me. I hope to have the place soon fixed up quite homey, though.

As far as I can learn, the problem of my future disposition in the Army (if any) is as follows: I will very probably remain at Camp Callan in the Administrative force until further orders. The noncommissioned officer rank is permanent, unless, of course, I am tried for any reason by court-martial or <u>request</u> a transfer to another organization of the Army. If however, the Government transfers me, I will still retain the rank or any higher one that I may obtain in the future.

Most of the men took their "Anti-Tetanus" shots in the arm today. I expect mine soon. Payday is this Friday, and after paying all bills and loans, I think that I will have about $21 left over, unless of course, by good fortune I receive the half a month's Corporal's pay to which I am entitled. In the event I do not receive it, however, I won't miss it too much, and it will mean a nice big check next month. The new job itself is growing quite complicated, and Major Cooley seems to be putting more and more trust and responsibility on my shoulders, but I am quite confident of being able to handle all aspects of the job.

Can't help but wonder, recently, how the "blind date" that I have this payday will turn out. But, as I have mentioned before in this little journal, only the future can disclose the outcome of that situation. I really hope that I have an enjoyable time, though, as I have felt rather discouraged and moody of late, as to just what was the damned use of existing, anyway.

November 3, 1941

Rather tired and blue tonight. The first payday after the return from my furlough is over and gone. Much to my surprise, the rather skeptical frame of mind that I had worked myself into, concerning the blind date with John Strahl, was all in vain. The girl in question, a Margaret Salerno, proved to be quite a charming little miss. However, need I say that my long atrophied heart beat never a pace faster?

The night was complete in every respect. Dinner at the U.S. Grant Hotel, cocktails in the famous "sky room" of the El Cortez Hotel, dancing at Paul's Inn and at Sherman's to the music of Sterling Young and his orchestra. It was most natural that an evening of such extensive scope would prove to be expensive, but I had a wonderful time and really feel that it was worthwhile. We saw the girls off for Los Angeles the next day at about 4 p.m. John Strahl, I believe, is one of the most likable chaps in the Detachment. Pleasant, educated, congenial, and above all, a true gentleman.

I have felt very despondent and rotten physically since my return from furlough. I like my new job very much, though; it is far more interesting than the other one and has many more educational advantages. For some reason or other, Mother, Bob, and Harold are the only persons who have written to me since my return to Camp. No letters from Art Morgan, the Raffertys, Hubie, Lola, or any of the others. Of course, a great deal of this is possibly caused by the confusion of my change of address and transfer. But at the same time, I wonder--?

Well, November 1st was the anniversary of my marriage to the peer of womanhood. If she had been faithful, this would have been my fourth wedding anniversary, but as it is, it is just a darned bitter memory, and one that I do not care to dwell too long upon. Marriage! "The Sacred Institution." I have had the most terrible cold in my chest for the past week. I have got to start getting more rest, I know, or else I am going to be in pretty bad shape before long.

November 13, 1941

Feel terrible today. I have had a terrific cold in my chest for about a month now, and it is rapidly getting to the "worry" stage. Circumstances and events seem to be rapidly building up to a climax of some sort or other. I have two bosses now—Major Cooley and a Lt. Colonel Howard. I understand Major Cooley is going to leave in about a month for the Staff School back east. I hate to see him go; he really is an A-1 person and has certainly done a lot for me. I wonder how this Colonel Howard will prove to be as a boss? He seems okay so far. Received a letter from Major Read in Eugene, Oregon (my cousin), and he stressed the fact that I should attend the Officer Training School, if at all possible. I informed him that I was out of luck in that direction, due to mathematics (or rather, my lack of same) and also the fact that my eyesight is a little below par.

I guess it will be a rather lonely Christmas for me here in Camp. It will be the first Christmas in years for me that I haven't been with my folks. The lack of mail doesn't do much to make me feel very cheerful, either. But then, I guess people on the outside are far more busy than I am in here, or else they just don't give a damn—

If they don't declare war, we are supposed to get out of here in eighteen months, which will mean that I will get discharged on August 25, 1942. But with my usual luck, they will probably declare war on August 24, 1942. I obtained a couple of passes to a dance at the Pacific Square in San Diego last Monday, so Corporal Davis and I took it in. I didn't dance a single dance, just stood around and watched. Just couldn't get in the mood for dancing, for some reason or other, but any excuse to get out of Camp for an evening makes a good evening of it. We had two days of violent rain, and for some reason or other, a rainstorm always tends to oppress me. I have been going to the Camp Theatre practically every night, and then reading until about midnight, but I am going to cut it out and concentrate on getting some sleep, as I am beginning to feel as if I am nearing the crack-up physically. Well, I can certainly concentrate on that fact in the next two or three weeks, as I am again as usual, flat, stony, and <u>dead</u> broke.

November 14, 1941
I feel in the mood for writing another episode in "The Daily Chronicle" tonight. Really turned out some work today. Was busy all morning on routine work such as supplements, training schedules, endorsements, and some letters to a Colonel Braun in San Francisco. In the afternoon, Colonel Howard, the new Assistant S-3, handed me a copy for a 30-page draft of a very confidential document, which, he assured me in a

very secretive manner, must be kept absolutely confidential. I will have to go to work about a half hour early tomorrow morning in order to get it out on time, as tomorrow is Saturday, and we only work half a day. It doesn't seem possible that Saturday is already here. I am getting so that I hate these weekends. Nothing to do, no place to go, and no money to go with, even if I had someplace to go.

Received a swell little letter from Harold the other night, and I answered it today. Imagine a little kid of twelve telling you the only gift he wants for Christmas is for you to come home! He is one of my most faithful correspondents. I am sitting here in the barracks, on my bunk, listening to the strains of some old Viennese Waltzes. Sometimes I wonder at myself. That is, at my love for this type of music. It has always fascinated me, and I guess, always will. But for some reason or other, the alluring sound of those lovely old songs always conjures up to me a mental picture of romantic old Vienna during the time of Johann Strauss—of swirling gowns, swaying couples, moonlit terraces, and starlit gardens. Perhaps some would say that I am an incurable romantic, or even a throwback to a prior generation, but at least in that generation, marriage had not attained the hideous, sordid stage to which it has degenerated today. Being of such nature, and having certain (shall I say, Dreams?) of what marriage should be, it is truly unfortunate that when I married, I was foolish enough to believe that: "Here is the one woman in the world for me—a trust that God has placed in my hands to protect, love, and cherish 'until death do us part.' To shield her from life's harder blows, to show her only tenderness, consideration, and faithfulness. To believe her incapable of deceit, unfaithfulness, or anything but good." Imagine then, the spectacle of seeing your cherished wife set out to methodically destroy your every ideal, to wipe her feet on your devotion, then throw it in your face . . . and yet there are those who say, "Oh, but the next one will be different." To that I say, true, it is only natural, as no two humans are identical. The next one would probably only have a more refined manner of doing it . . .

NOVEMBER 21, 1941

Again, sitting on my lonely bunk this night, I compose yet another episode in the life of a "draftee." Odd, isn't it, how a fellow can be lonely in a barracks that holds sixty-two men? Odd, but I can assure you that it is entirely possible.

I had a very interesting Thanksgiving this year. Commander

Barnes invited me, Corporal Davis, Corporal Schick, and Private Zane to a very nice Thanksgiving dinner at his lovely home in San Diego. It was a dinner complete in every respect—gracious company, charming hospitality, and above all, a feeling of friendliness that was hard to compare. Met Captain Eckert of the 11th U.S. Cavalry, who proved to be quite an interesting chap. We left the Commander's house about 9:30 p.m. and went to a dance at the exclusive Casa de Mañana in La Jolla, to which we had been invited. I had several dances, one with Miss Sackett, the Junior Hostess of the Camp; one with Mrs. Hopkins, the owner of the Casa; and one with a little blonde named Barbara, who seemed pleasant enough, except for her continual verbal barrage, most of which concerned "her Marine who was stationed in Iceland." Finally retired about 2:30 a.m.

Turned out a hard day's work today. And tomorrow! I dread to think of it. A huge stencil of "Inspection and Review Schedules." From certain rumors and remarks that have come my way about the office recently, I understand that I have a fairly decent chance of obtaining a Staff Sergeant's rating, probably within three or four months. It seems improbable to me, but I certainly hope that it is true.

Astounding news! I have received verbal permission to take 10 days off at Christmas! So I guess—I am going home. It will mean that I will not be able to afford very expensive presents, but just to be home at Christmas will be wonderful. I dread the long train ride, but that, too, is worth it. Tomorrow is Saturday, so I guess that I have another long, dreary weekend staring me in the face again, which, coupled with the fact that my receipt of mail has finally fallen to nothing, doesn't make me feel any too optimistic as regards a pleasant weekend.

NOVEMBER 29, 1941
Work here in the office has advanced recently to a really technical stage. A complete revision of the files (converting to the Army decimal system) has kept me quite busy of late. One aspect of all this recent industry is the fact that working continuously as I have been doing causes the time to fairly fly by. Here it is almost the end of November already!

I wonder if I will be discharged when my year of service is completed? Or, if not then, on August 25, 1942 (eighteen months service)? Somehow I doubt it, as the international situation grows worse daily. War with Japan seems imminent at this writing. Strangest of all to me, even if I do get discharged, I do not want to go back to my previous job. It was a good steady job, but as far as having any future, there was none. What then? I'm sure I don't know. I have somehow thought that there was no future for me anyway. I saw my future and happiness fade and die in the fall of 1939 when everything turned to bitter dust before my eyes.

I received a very lovely Thanksgiving gift from Margaret Salerno, the girl I met on the blind date with John Strahl. It was a large box of candy, cookies, nuts, and other confections and was most certainly deeply appreciated by me. How odd are the tricks of fate! The only person in the world who remembered me on Thanksgiving Day was a total stranger, one whom I had met just once! While from all my avowed friends, or so they loudly assert, not even a card!

Valerie, one of the secretaries here in the office, threw a veiled hint the other day about some "proposition" she was going to ask me about on January 10th. I am curious, naturally, but am certainly not in a great state of nerves about it. Heard a strange compliment today, concerning me. It seems Colonel Howard has a very high opinion of my typing. Well, that's cheerful news—too bad he still isn't in the S-3, which adds up to something I can't understand. Why the sudden influx of officers into the S-3? And then their immediate release? I also wonder what effect, if any, this will have on me?

My physical condition has improved slightly the last two or three days but still leaves much to be desired. The situation in the Far East is, as I say, growing more critical every day. I guess that is the principle motive behind the recruiting campaign here at Callan—640 men desired by December 31st—for service in the Philippines.

Colonel Hawkins is going to be appointed Assistant Camp Executive, which means, I presume, that he will soon be leaving us to be replaced by the said Colonel Knape, whom I met for a second today. He seems to be a rather crusty individual but may prove to be all right. After many long negotiations and tedious bickerings, I finally acquired a new desk and typewriter today. Not without some severe repercussions, however, as the Message Center was certainly reluctant to part with them, but nevertheless, I insisted, and got them.

SUNDAY, NOVEMBER 30, 1941

The last day of November! Last Wednesday, I completed my ninth month in the Army. Tomorrow is December 1st. In other words, nineteen days more and I will be starting for home. Again, I have an unusually large amount of preparations to make before leaving. Due to a mix-up in my recent transfer, I was "redlined" on this month's payroll and, therefore, will not be paid until the "supplementary payroll" on December the 10th. This, of course, will work a temporary hardship on me, as I had planned my stock of supplies, i.e., soap, matches, and cigarettes to last only until December 1st. I will have to arrange somehow to get in to San Diego before the 10th, as I have to take my Army overcoat in and have it taken in at the side and have some chevrons sewed on. I can then go in on the 10th and get it and then do my Christmas shopping at the same time. Gee! It doesn't seem as if I will be able to buy very many Christmas gifts this year. I think it is chiefly because of this fact that I do not feel the same enthusiasm about going home that I did on my previous furlough.

This is one of those dull, boring, mind-wracking Sundays. All there is to do is read books, write letters, listen to the radio, and as a last resort do "bunk fatigue." I guess I will go to the show this afternoon and see Bing Crosby in *The Birth of the Blues*, then tonight take a shower, and then retire early.

A thought just occurred to me. While I am home on Christmas, I will pass the 10-month mark of my service in the Army. Ordinarily, but for the extension, I would then only have two remaining months to serve.

A curious incident while at the show this afternoon. The usher called my name out in the darkened theatre, and with a certain degree of puzzlement, I responded. In the foyer, I was informed that a friend wished to see me. In some trepidation, I opened the door and there was disclosed to me—Hubie Rafferty. He had just obtained his discharge from the Army and had thought he would come down and see me before he left for home. The meeting was marked by a certain degree of embarrassment, as Virginia, the "pure," had brought him down, and with her usual "tact," had parked across the street from us while we talked. I refrained from looking across the street and most certainly did not make any inopportune suggestions, which would make necessary any movement towards the car. After a few moments' conversation, he left, and I returned to the theatre. I will see him when I go home at Christmas.

Hubie is a swell fellow and a fine chap, and at the same time, I can appreciate his position. Unfortunate enough to have been sucker number one to Virginia, except that in his case, he was left with a child to rear. I presume that is the reason he continues association with Virginia. Possibly, he will eventually remarry her for the sake of the child, although I can't see how the child could possibly benefit in view of what a "wonderful" example of motherhood that Virginia is.

As I write this, a closing bit of irony portrays itself. The radio had to play, "The One Rose," the "theme" song of my honeymoon.

December 2, 1941

I feel up to par tonight, physically, but cannot say the same about my mental viewpoint, for in that respect, I am again "down in the dumps." As I noted herein before, I did not get paid yesterday. Expect to receive my pay about December 10th and will certainly have to scurry around to make all final arrangements for going home.

Struck by a surge of ambition recently, I withdrew the necessary books from the library and am, at present, wading through Gregg's *Shorthand* book. Valerie is generously assisting me during the noon hour on this undertaking. It is far more difficult than I had imagined, but I hope that I will be able to progress satisfactorily in it, as I am sure it will be of immense value to me as long as I am in the Army, at least.

We are really having some of the Southern California weather they love to boast about so well. Here it is December, and the sky is always an azure blue, while the nearby sea gleams in a brilliant sapphire blue. The beautiful green parade ground—bordered with swaying palms and with the slender, graceful, white flagpole to set it off in contrast—it is really a wonderful sight.

Have received two letters from Mother, both of which were rather puzzling to me. The sentences were so short and rambling, I wonder if they are having trouble of any kind up there or if she is feeling all right.

Oh Damn! What is the use of all this miserable pretense? Writing all this trivial muck, when all the while this damnable loneliness is grinding and tearing away at your nerves. I wish to hell something would happen to me soon, one way or the other—I don't care what . . .

I have gotten so damned disgusted recently that I have absolutely no enthusiasm at all as regards going home at Christmas. How much more of this dreary, dull, monotonous, disgusting existence do I have to stand?????

Thursday, December 4, 1941

A beautiful sunshiny day. Only fourteen days after today until I leave for home. Still haven't obtained any enthusiasm for the trip, though. I signed the supplementary payroll today, which means that I will be paid on December 10th. Have been studying quite hard on my shorthand for the last two days and really believe that I am beginning to show signs of progress in it, although not a great deal, as it is by no means a simple subject. My physical condition has begun to worry me a great deal. I still have the cold, which I mentioned some time back, and I do not think it is natural for a cold to "hang on" for such a length of time. That, coupled with the fact that I cannot seem to obtain enough sleep, has made me determined to report on sick call sometime this weekend and find out once and for all just what seems to be the trouble. I go to bed every night at nine o'clock, sleep like a log, and have a veritable mental struggle to get up in the morning. I realize that eight hours is a normal night's sleep, but I have been sleeping like that for almost a month, now . . .

Have about made up my mind to apply for the "Officer Candidate School" (Infantry). I am almost certain that I cannot meet the necessary entrance requirements, but it will cost nothing to apply, and I will get a medical examination out of it. If, by some miracle, I am accepted, I would be sent to Fort Benning, Georgia. I also realize quite well, that in so doing, I would lengthen my period of military service considerably, as I would have to agree to a three-year period of service, if accepted. That, however, makes no difference at all to me, because I definitely do not care what happens to me, or where I may be sent, anymore.

Will probably go into San Diego, Saturday, and have the necessary tailoring done to my Army overcoat. Also have to check up on railroad schedules home. Major Cooley took the day off today, so here I am in charge of the S-3 for today. (A rather dubious honor, methinks.) Received a letter from Mother yesterday, and as I thought, she had been ill. I certainly hope she recovers quickly.

Sunday, December 7, 1941

It is here! War at last! As I write this, an air raid is in progress over Pearl Harbor, Hawaii. I have always felt, since my induction, that war was inevitable. In view of the substantiation of this belief, I cannot help but wonder just what effect this momentous news will have on my life. I know that I am going to investigate all available means of applying for Officer Candidate School. Failing that, I am certainly going to consider applying for reenlistment in the Foreign Service in the Near East.

Ted and I went to San Diego last night, and I ordered some work done on my overcoat, which amounted to $2.75. We had supper at a restaurant, and then had a few drinks at various nightclubs. Came home about 11 p.m. At 11 a.m. this morning, all Headquarters men were told to report immediately to Headquarters. It seemed that a man was needed to operate the Teletype, and as all the regular operators were in Los Angeles, I was the only man available. I had to work all the rest of Sunday night, and then continuously all the next day until about 3 p.m. Major Cooley said I had better go back to the barracks, as I looked pretty worn out.

Well, nothing but bad news in these first few days of the war. Losses, Losses, Losses, and more Losses. I sure hope that we soon start doing some blasting on our own account. One thing at least shines out in this war. At least most of the fellows have had some training. Which places me in an odd position. Although I have been in the Army almost ten months, now, I have never had a rifle in my hands and have never marched a step. So I just wonder now, what effect that will have on me, now that we are actually in the war. I hope and pray with all my heart that we get equipment in sufficient quantities to blast those damned, dirty, treacherous Japs off the face of the earth. They killed over 300 of our fellow Coast Artillery men in that sneaking raid on Oahu. I have said before, and I say it again, that I am not going through any war punching a typewriter.

Helmets and gas masks are being issued here now to all Headquarters men. That rumor that some sixty Jap planes were heading for San Francisco last night sure had me plenty worried. I sure hope that Bob and Lola and Lena will make out OK. Thank God Mother lives 130 miles away in a secluded little town in the mountains...

Thursday, December 11, 1941

Today is a day that will surely go down in history, not only for my country, but for me, too. Germany, Italy, and Hungary declared war on the United States today. Tonight, over the Teletype came official notification that all men in the armed forces would be retained in service for the duration of the war and for six months afterward. So it is quite certain that a goodly portion of my future will be in khaki clothes. I applied, yesterday, for permission to attend the Infantry Officer Candidate School, or as an alternative, the Quartermaster Officer Candidate School. The application was sent to my Battery

Commander (Lt. A. K. Mills) who, after questioning me on the extent of my education, signed it. I am hoping and praying that I will be successful on this, but my lack of mathematics seems to be quite an obstacle. I know for a fact that Major Cooley is going to do everything in his power to help me in this, or so he assured me. So after tomorrow, all that I have to pass is the very strict medical examination, and the stern interview before a Board of Officers.

Received another letter from Mother today. She certainly is worried about all this. I tried to reassure her, however. Bob sent my Schick Electric Shaver down today. He sure is a swell, thoughtful brother, and I only hope they don't draft him right away. But, of course, he is just what they need—nineteen, no dependents, etc. We have had three complete blackouts here, last night's being the longest and most complete, with unidentified planes reported in the vicinity. The Camp has been on the "Alert" here almost continuously since the war started. Steel helmets and gas masks were issued and have to be worn continuously when out of doors. (The masks are carried in a case on the hip.) During an actual blackout, all guns, including seacoast, antiaircraft, and beach lookouts are manned, as well as searchlights. Armed sentries are everywhere. Some 4,000 men have already been transferred to other posts and stations. Two men in my detachment were transferred. Insofar as I am concerned, however, I have heard nothing. The S-3 is somewhat of a puzzle. I am now working under four Lieutenant Colonels (Taliaferro, Howard, Hawkins, and Knape) and three Majors (Cooley, Robbins, and Stevenson).

I am terribly worried about my physical condition. I can only hope that the medical examination will disclose just what the trouble is. So it is with some trepidation that I look forward to the approach of the next few days. So much can happen, and so much <u>will</u> happen.

SUNDAY, DECEMBER 14, 1941
*** [*The journal included an excerpt from the December 15, 1941 edition of* LIFE *magazine. The excerpt was excluded from* Journals of War *for copyright reasons.*]
The above paragraph, taken from a popular weekly, is the most perfect example of truth I have ever seen, except that in my case, my memories are far from filled with sweetness and beauty, and I doubt very much if "tomorrow" will contain any happiness for me . . .

Ted and I obtained a pass, good until 11 p.m. last night, and went to San Diego where we earnestly endeavored to forget our troubles for a while by assiduously attempting to deplete the liquor supply of said city. Results? At 11 p.m., I was cold sober, and Ted had passed out. Cpl. Davis was in the party, too. I did notice one thing, though. The recent declaration of war has had a great psychological effect on the attitude of the civilians. We are not treated like so much dirt anymore; instead, we are quite popular and drinks are practically forced on us. My! This change in attitude is certainly "puzzling"! I wonder what could have caused it?

I packed the majority of my civilian clothes today and will send them home sometime next week. I don't know why, but I have an odd premonition that I won't be at Callan much longer, and therefore, I am making all final preparations. I have seen far too many of my "hunches" come true to ignore this one.

My application to attend the Officer Candidate School came back from Lt. Mills marked approved and with a character rating of excellent, which was rather surprising to me. However, the approval is only the first step, as I still have to pass the rigorous medical examination and the interview. Received two letters from Mother and Harold today, and they did much to cheer me up. Will have to answer them sometime today, if I get time. We should be getting our anti-tetanus shots soon, as we are all required to wear our "dog tags" continuously now.

Monday, December 15, 1941

Monday, December 15th, in the year of our Lord, one thousand nine hundred and forty one. A world in chaos, a world aflame with the devastating fire of Mars, the God of War. Thirty-two nations of this miserable planet locked in mortal combat. The age-old hates and fears, the lying propaganda, all of the customary accoutrements of war, are refurbished and again dragged into the open. A period in which the character of all men is disclosed in crystal-clear revealment. The sneaks and the cowards, the petty and small, the calm and the resolute, the brave and the weak, ad infinitum. Truly, an important page in the ledger of history is being written in these hours. Tonight, I think these things and wonder just where on the roulette table of destiny the little ball marked with my name will fall. But as to all men, only time will reveal the final disclosure of that enigma.

I took out a government insurance policy today in the amount of $10,000. Short weeks ago, when there was a possibility of this nation not being drawn into the maelstrom of war, I could not see the necessity for doing this, but with the actuality of war upon us, it is the only right thing to do, to think of the future of our loved ones.

Rifles are soon to be issued the men of the Headquarters Detachment, and I understand a review of basic infantry drill will be instigated at the same time. I packed the remainder of my civilian clothes tonight and will soon have them on their way home. My clothes rack certainly is bare, and it will be the uniform from now on for all functions, social and otherwise. I have heard nothing new on my application for the Officer Candidate School, but something should be turning up on it soon. I am as interested in seeing the results of the medical examination almost as much as I am in the whole course.

Mother and Harold are writing me quite frequently, although I received no mail from them today. Bob and I have made all emergency preparations as to our household effects in the event he is drafted, but with the passing of the bill yesterday, which stated that only men of 21 or over would be liable for military service, I believe he will be safe for at least two or three years more. That is, if I can successfully dissuade him from enlisting, which he wants to do. Should have his reply on this soon, though.

Tuesday, December 16, 1941
Work, for the last two days, has dwindled surprisingly, in view of the critical war situation. Ted and I mailed our civilian clothes home tonight for a very reasonable rate of postage. So they are gone, the last reminder and ties, which connected us with the civilian world. The sudden influx of mail, which I enjoyed following the declaration of war, has ceased, and this has a great deal to do with my attack of homesickness and loneliness tonight, I guess. However, I think the greatest reason for my constant loneliness is the fact that all about me I see fellows who have a definite future lying ahead of them after this war is fought and won. They have someone to love, someone to whom they can write and confide their thoughts, and hopes, their plans and dreams for the future. Someone who would answer every day with the full meaning of hope and cheerfulness. Someone who would be a shining star in a wilderness of loneliness, an inspiration and an added incentive for the completion of a task, so that when life finally returns to normal again, it could be said, "Well Done!" But me? Like a ship without a compass, I drift aimlessly over the sea of life, from one

course to another, without a purpose, and worse, without an anchor to moor safely in the Harbor of Contentment and Happiness. No, I guess for me, that phase of life is over and gone. All the foolish dreams and ideals, which I once held so dear, have turned to bitter mockery and an example of feminine deceit. At that, I guess I asked for it. I walked into that farce known as Marriage with my eyes wide open, and I certainly got it.

Received a letter and a nice card from Mrs. Morgan today. She certainly is a nice woman, and I am certainly proud in the realization that I have such good friends as she and Art Morgan. I had to work until nine o'clock tonight for Colonel Howard on a Manning table. But at that, I guess I don't mind—I didn't have any other way to kill any time. Received a letter from Mother today, and she is in Oakland seeing about her teeth again. I hope that she can keep busy on things like that, as I do not want her to think too much about this darn war, as she, like me, is equipped with an overactive imagination.

FRIDAY, DECEMBER 19, 1941

Evidently, the rumors I had heard recently, that men of the Headquarters Detachment were to be issued rifles, had a great deal of basis, for I read a very interesting memorandum from Ninth Corps Area today which stated definitely that all selective servicemen must have their basic training before their first year of service is completed. This may mean that quite a few of the pages in this chronicle may be written in pencil or ink hereafter, as I may not have access to a typewriter soon.

It will be hard, grueling training and hours of monotonous drilling and marching, lying on the rifle range, etc., but I am looking forward to it with some anticipation, as so far, the lack of this very necessary training has retarded me greatly in any efforts I have made for advancement. Indeed, I believe this one factor will cause my ultimate disappointment in being selected as an Officer Candidate. So I would like very much to get it over with so that I may carry out my plans, either to transfer to a more active branch of the Army, or to be sent to a school.

Bob Benjamin, my friend who was sent to the Cavalry some time ago, is here at Callan for two or three days, and we are planning a foray into San Diego for tomorrow night. We are all going to the dance, which is being held in the Service Club tonight. Valerie is going, also, and is bringing her sister, so I promised I would dance with them.

Well, if the Japs hadn't been so inconsiderate as to start the war before the holidays, I would be leaving for home today on a ten-day leave. But as it is, it will be the first Christmas in my life that I haven't spent with my folks. No letters from anyone today. I guess Mother must have just arrived back in Sonora by now from Oakland, so it will be some time before I receive any mail from them. I wrote Bill Meder, my old boss, a letter the other day, asking him some questions about my return to work when the war is over, its effect on my seniority status, etc. Not that I expect to ever return to work there, for I hereby state here and now, definitely, that due to an awfully strong "hunch," <u>I DO NOT BELIEVE THAT I WILL EVER RETURN TO WORK AT MOTHER'S</u>. As stated before, however, only the future can bear me out in this.

SATURDAY, DEC. 20, 1941

Another dreary weekend. A heavily overcast sky and a rising wind foretell that it will be a stormy one, too. Have just finished what is popularly termed "early chow" in the Army. It is now 5 p.m. on this Saturday evening, and as I can think of nothing better to do, I guess I will go to the theatre tonight. Ted went into town, but I didn't feel like going, as I need what money I have for miscellaneous purchases during the balance of the month. However, I did request him to purchase me a "spot" reading lamp, as I am ruining my eyes with these damnably inefficient barracks lights.

Received a letter from Knut this noon and will make use of some of my spare time this weekend by answering it. There are several important questions concerning my future, which I am most anxious to have answered satisfactorily. The when, why, and wherefore of all phases of the Basic training we are supposed to receive shortly and what the final disposition of my application to attend the Officer Candidate School will be. I understand the Board of Officers, which will interview all applicants, will convene shortly after Christmas. Feel rather discouraged about the latter, however, as I feel sure any chance of success that I may have had will be nullified by my lack of Basic training.

Received one letter from Mother while she was in Oakland, but since then, have had no word from her. I am rather anxious to hear from her, as I have sent her several packages, and I would like to know if she has received them all right as well as the answer to several important questions I asked her.

Talk about anyone feeling frustrated! That describes me to perfection. The utter boredom of this Camp is wearing my nerves thin. I wish to hell something would break soon that would affect me directly. If I'm not in a helluva fix! I can't go to school because of the lack of mathematics—I can't transfer to the parachute troops or any other active branch because the Army neglected to give me any basic training. So it looks very much as if I am doomed to a period of utter boredom during one of the most vivid and exciting chapters in American history. Well, I refuse to take it. I'll get transferred to a more exciting branch of the Army if I have to go in the grade of private, which will happen if I transfer at my own request.

Wednesday, December 24, 1941

Christmas Eve in the year 1941. A mental picture of the little home in Sonora presents itself. At exactly this time (5:45 p.m.), I imagine the lights are glowing and the family, having just finished the evening meal, is gathered in the living room. It is possible that the majority of the family is represented, with the exception of my oldest sister. In a few moments now, the long-awaited hour will be at hand when the presents heaped under the tree may be opened. I would cheerfully give a year of my life to be present at that gathering tonight. But as it is, here I am at work in the office. I will have to work until 8 p.m. when Colonel Knape will take over. Yes, this will undoubtedly live in my mind as one of the most lonesome and cheerless holidays that I have ever had. Even under such dreary circumstances, however, it will be a far happier Christmas than the two I enjoyed during my period of "Wedded Bliss." I remember those perfect examples of domestic harmony only too well as well as the two New Year celebrations, which followed, both of which ended in the most sordid, disgusting quarrels imaginable, usually with the "Lily of Womanhood" on the verge of passing out and her "sweet" voice uttering all the foul epithets and rotten accusations she knew of which she possessed quite an impressive collection.

I have received an unusually large number of Christmas cards to date. Practically everyone I know has sent me a nice card. Received a very nice package from Mother today. Commander and Mrs. Barnes have invited me to their home in San Diego for another nice dinner tomorrow, which I gratefully accepted. Corporal Davis and I will go in together, I presume.

My application for the Officer Candidate School is still hanging fire, although yesterday, Captain Ted E. DeTennencourt (my old Commanding Officer in the DEML) sent over a score sheet for Major Cooley to grade me on, according to his impression of my "soldierly bearing," intelligence, devotion to duty, etc. With Major Cooley doing the grading, however, my mind is at ease, because I know he will fill it out the best he can, as he did in Bradshaw's case. I find, however, that the Board of Officers at this Camp do not have anything to do with the final selecting of actual candidates, as all papers and information are forwarded to the Ninth Corps Area Headquarters, and they make the final selection up there. I hope and pray that it goes through satisfactorily, but I certainly have my doubts due to reasons, which I have stated before. My eyes have also been giving me an enormous amount of trouble, lately, although this cold, which I picked up recently, may have something to do with that. Payday is next Wednesday, and I want to send home all the money that I possibly can, so that Mother can get all of her bills out of the way. I told her that as soon as they were all out of debt that she could start putting the money that I sent home away for me as I will, in all probability, sure need it when and if I ever get out of the Army.

Closing Question of the Day: I wonder where I will be and just what I will be doing exactly one year from today?

FRIDAY, DECEMBER 26, 1941
Christmas is over for another year. I find it impossible to say that I was forgotten this year, for I wasn't. I received an avalanche of cards and quite a few very nice remembrances. No presents, however, as I made it a point to inform all my friends that I wished no presents sent, as they would prove an inconvenience if I was transferred suddenly.

Corporal Davis and I went to Commander Barnes's home in San Diego and were treated to a superlative turkey dinner again, complete in every respect. Spent a very pleasant day there, and I must admit that when we finally took our leave, burdened with cigarettes and candy by our most hospitable hosts, Davis and I were in a very convivial mood, due to the effects of a continuous round of brandies, whiskies, highballs, and dinner wine. We made our way back to Camp safely enough, however, but the many thoughts that had been going through my mind continuously all day, when joined with the depressive properties of the liquor, evidently had its usual effect on me. I couldn't get to sleep until about 2 a.m., and when I finally awoke this morning,

I had the original granddaddy of all headaches and a disposition that boded ill for all who crossed my path. By tonight, however, it has degenerated into an appalling mental condition to extreme gloom-- and the usual loneliness.

Today was, unfortunately enough for me, an extremely busy one, too. A tremendous amount of filing, telephone calls by the score, receipt of military intelligence literature from Washington, disposition and issuance of manuals, and to my horror, even stencils. Still no word of the O.C.S. and, as a matter of fact, have not seen the "score sheet" Major Cooley was supposed to have filled out for me. Oh well! There is no gain in worrying about it.

Payday will be this coming Wednesday, and I believe that I will be able to send some $20 home again this time, although it will probably run me a trifle "short." Corporal Davis and I had planned a tentative schedule for New Year's Eve, but as he may go to Los Angeles by himself, it will very probably not go through. I do know, however, that come what may, I am going to celebrate New Year's by myself, if need be.

MONDAY, DECEMBER 29, 1941
Another Blue Monday. I have no hangover, although I did a small amount of drinking yesterday with Corporal Davis. But the day is not blue for that reason. I did an awful lot of thinking yesterday, and when I think . . . I thought of many things—of this present monotonous dull and dreary existence, of the uselessness of my life, of the lack of anything to live for, the lack of any mail, and of my approaching 26th birthday (tomorrow). It doesn't seem possible that one human could have accomplished so little in 26 years.

No news of any sort concerning the O.C.S. It seems all in vain to hope for any success in that direction, but I am hoping with a grim determination that, in my heart, I fear is futile. Ted is leaving for the Master Gunner School at Fort Monroe, Va., on January 6th.

Payday will be this coming Wednesday, which is also New Year's Eve, and the way I feel at present, I think I will endeavor to get good and drunk in seeing this "Happy" New Year in. However, I suppose that I will even be cheated in this attempt, as the last few times that I have gone out, the more I drank, the more sober I got. Davis and I drove home last night in a terrific rainstorm, and it seemed the more it rained, the more I thought. It is getting so that I positively hate to go to bed anymore when taps is blown, as I know full well that I have to face the same old thoughts and memories, which seem to turn over in my mind constantly all night long. Haven't received any reply to some important letters that I mailed some time before Christmas.

I have made up my mind to one thing. If the O.C.S. fails to go through, I am going to use every means in my power to get transferred to a more active unit. In my present state of mind, I certainly wouldn't mind being at the top of the casualty list. Think of the red tape and trouble it would save. Besides, I don't like the Japs anyway. And the Germans even less.

If Davis goes to Los Angeles for New Year's, he has invited me to go along, and I believe that I will take him upon on it. God only knows what is in store for me in Los Angeles, but I hope it is something.

SUNDAY, JANUARY 4, 1942

Christmas, New Year's and my 26th birthday are over and gone. Today is again, as are most days for me, one of somber thought and melancholy. The long-awaited New Year's Eve did not come to pass, as the Camp was placed on an "Alert" status, and all passes were revoked. There was enough hilarity and celebrating in the barracks, however, to make up somewhat for the lack of freedom.

On January 2nd, I received a very unexpected letter from Lucille Anderson, whom I had met at the dance some three months ago, and after one exchange of letters had not heard from her since. She informed me that she would be present at the Service Club dance that night and said she would be expecting me. Although it was not my detachment's night to dance, I used a little influence through Miss Sackett, the Junior Hostess, and finally gained admittance to the dance. I had a wonderful evening dancing and talking. It is amazing how different things can be when you know someone is looking for you and is relying on you for a good time and a pleasant evening.

Received several letters from Vivian in which she informed me that she had obtained her divorce and had broken off her engagement to Redding, along with the ominous news that she intended to wait until the war was over and see then how I felt about the subject of matrimony. Of course, I answered immediately and explained how foolish such a move would be, in view of the uncertainty of the future and my present views on matrimony, which I feel sure will never change.

My physical condition is again worrying me, and I mean it really has me worried this time. I can only hope and pray that there is nothing seriously the matter with me, but from the way I feel at present, things do not look any too promising. This probably accounts, too, for the extremely despondent attitude that I have fallen into of late. I have lost all interest in practically everything. Whether I receive any mail or not does not seem to bother me. That situation, coupled with the fact that the new Major Stevenson and I do not "get along" any too well bodes ill for the future. Have still heard no word in regard to the O.C.S.

Ted and I went into San Diego last night and went bowling and to a few of the nightspots, but I must confess that I didn't have a good time at all. Liquor has absolutely no effect whatsoever upon me. It seems the more I drink, the more sober I get. Closing thought for tonight: I wonder what answers will be written in this book to some of the questions I have propounded herein?

THURSDAY, JANUARY 8, 1942
Worry No. 1 seems to have evaporated into thin air, as I went to the dispensary and had them check me over and—nothing wrong—whatsoever. That is the curse of having an overactive imagination. Whenever I get the slightest thing wrong with me, I immediately imagine all sorts of dire results, and the consequent strain certainly does much to impair my disposition.

I understand that we will get our first "anti-tetanus" shots this coming Saturday, and from all reports, they are very painful. No reply as yet to the letters I wrote Vivian some time ago. Camp Callan is going to be increased by some 50%, which fact will undoubtedly affect me personally in one way or another; just how, or in what way, I do not know. But I do know that work in the S-3 Office has increased at a terrific pace--spent most of the day taking inventory of training literature and military intelligence. Tomorrow will bring the task of drawing up a presentable inventory and, of course, the ever-present training schedules.

Funny thing! Last month, I was most anxious to get out of camp and forget the Army for a while but—no money. At present, I have about $20 in my wallet but absolutely no urge to go anyplace. At present, my most urgent desire is to get transferred out of this Camp into a more active unit. I don't believe that I can stand much more of this inaction. The Board of Officers for the selection of Infantry Officer

Candidates has not met as yet, but it probably will in the near future. All I can do until that time is to keep my fingers crossed and hope. Received no mail at all today.

It has been a week since Ted left for Fort Monroe to attend the Master Gunner's Course, and I rather miss him. He certainly was a fine fellow. Should be hearing from him before long, as I have his letter of recommendation from Major Cooley all ready to mail to him as soon as I receive his correct mailing address. The "Major Stevenson" problem is beginning to get a little acute. He certainly is a sarcastic old fool, and neither one of us likes the looks of the other. He gives me one supreme pain in the seat of my G.I. britches. As an officer, he would make a good plumber, sloppy uniform and all.

Tuesday, January 13, 1942

A large group of men here have left for the Coast Artillery Officer Candidate School, but still no word about the Infantry School. Have received several letters from Vivian, and matters are growing worse and worse in that direction. Despite all my protestations that I am not going to marry again, she insists that she is going to wait for me. It makes it awfully difficult, as I do not love her, although she is one of the finest girls that I have ever known. All the love in my being, I think, was burnt out of me by the "Pearl of Womanhood," and I do not think that any will ever return. I have honestly tried to tell Vivian how foolish she is being, but nothing seems to convince her.

Have also received quite a few letters from Mother, and I am certainly glad that I started to send some money home every month, as they are evidently having some tough sledding, at present. I surely hope that they make out okay. Haven't heard a word from Bob since I don't know when, but I guess he is doing all right.

We all took our first "anti-tetanus" shot last Saturday morning, and what I mean, it felt as if I had been pole-axed in the arm. All over with in about five minutes, however. Sgt. Naas and I went in to San Diego on Sunday and bowled about 10 games. Certainly had a lot of fun. We visited Sgt. Kreitz and his wife that evening, and I saw at least one woman who was extremely happy even though her husband was in the Army and was making only $84 per month. It made a great impression on me, as I thought only women of a prior generation had that certain attribute. Still, I guess she is about one out of 10,000.

On Sunday, Sgt. Strahl's girlfriend and his mother came down, and they invited me to go for a ride with them. We rode all along the Sunset Cliffs Road and out to Point Loma and really had a fine time. Came home and went to the Post Theatre and saw *Sergeant York*, which turned out to be a grand picture.

Am still having one helluva time getting rid of this damn athlete's foot that I picked up. This salve that is supposed to cure it is of no use whatsoever.

WEDNESDAY, JANUARY 14, 1942

I am becoming more and more disgusted, daily. There has been no news at all concerning the Infantry School, although I saw Major Robbins last night, and he informed me that the Board for that particular school was being "processed." Which means that it will convene soon, I presume. After noting the type of men being selected for the Coast Artillery Officer Candidate School, I am almost tempted to apply for that school, but my lack of trigonometry precludes any chance for success in that direction, as I would rather stay a corporal than to go back to one of those schools and flunk out. Master Sergeant Holder volunteered to coach me for a month in that subject. I don't know—I'm all mixed up. I want to get out of this damnable Camp—I want to advance and better myself—but as I have stated before, all I can do is to hope.

Received a letter from Bob today, and he is evidently making out just fine. I am glad, for he certainly is a good kid, and no one could wish for a finer brother. We are having truly delightful weather here for this time of the year, although we can very probably expect a great deal of rain during the next two months, that is, if it is anything like it was during February and March of last year.

I wrote letters last night and then went to the theatre and will, in all probability, do the very same thing tonight. Truly, a very exciting life, is it not? Haven't had any more trouble with Major Stevenson for two or three days. Not that I ever had any actual trouble with him, but I just don't like his looks or his attitude. He is one of the most sarcastic old fools I ever had the opportunity of meeting.

Hope I receive a letter from Mother this afternoon, as I am a little worried as to how they are making out up there. Of course, with Knut not working at present, it is only natural that times will be a little difficult for them for a while. I am going to send home just as much money as I possibly can this coming payday, and that should boost them over a few rough spots. I certainly have the world's best Mother and am glad that I realized that fact before it was too late, as some others I know are going to do.

THURSDAY, JANUARY 15, 1942
Came home from work very tired and dejected tonight. This continual worry concerning the O.C.S. is beginning to fray my nerves. Perhaps the most logical thing to do would be to forget about it until events take their course. Sent Vivian's letter off this morning in which I explained quite definitely that it was useless to "wait" for me, as I refused to take such a step, as the future is far too uncertain for that, I believe. Almost anything can happen within the next few years, and very probably, my life will be changed a great deal. In just this first year, I feel that I have matured a great deal. But that is only natural, I guess, as there is nothing like a good old Army barracks to observe human nature at its worst and at its best. Many ideas, some foolish perhaps, are changed, and some have utterly disappeared.

Received another letter from Mother today, which I promptly answered tonight. Things are evidently going along all right with the folks in Sonora, evidently. (I note that I have the evil habit of repetition in writing—possibly a subconscious manifestation of some kind?)

Evidently, some important shipments of troops to foreign stations are in the offing, as some 900 of the men in the training battalions were required to take "shots" for yellow fever. Secret orders were then issued for them to proceed to Barstow, California, from where they will probably go to the nearest Port of Embarkation, thence to either the Philippines or Panama, I imagine. I wish that it were possible for me to go with them.

I can't help but wonder just what my life will be like in the years to come. Will I ever realize my dream of a home of my own with someone to love and who would honestly return that love with all the faith and fidelity that a true, clean love really means? After seeing so much of the seamy side of life, with all its attendant cheapness and tawdry exhibitions, will I ever know a life that is clean and beautiful where all the finer sensibilities and emotions are not based on an eventual monetary remuneration? That, too, I guess, is something that only the passing of time will clarify. For none of us, during these years, can say with certainty just what lies ahead of us.

SATURDAY, JANUARY 17, 1942

Another boring, dull day of absolutely nothing to do has rolled around. This will be the last Saturday, however, in which this will be the case, as a Teletype from the War Department came through early this morning, which stated that hereafter, all military personnel working in an administrative capacity would be required to work all day on all future Saturdays. This, strange as it may seem, is not contrary to my wishes; as to be truthful, I would much rather be working than to spend the usual boring Saturday.

Received no mail at all today and was just a little disappointed. A few letters would have done much to cheer this lonely weekend. Kind fate, I note, has interceded in my behalf and has caused my little radio to give forth the loveliest music imaginable—a series of favorite Viennese strains—the lovely "Amoureuse" playing at this moment. It is truly remarkable how restful and refreshing such music can be. All the petty worries and cares of the long, hard day drift away, but unfortunately, bringing back memories of much happier days.

Have no idea what I will do tomorrow but do not think it will be much—probably the same thing I did today—lying on my bunk, reading and writing letters. Have been avidly reading Basic Field Manuals on Infantry recently. In the remote possibility that I am selected to go back east, I intend to be somewhat prepared. I took my dress uniform to the cleaners this afternoon and will probably spend part of this evening shining leather and brass, for if the Board of Officers for the O.C.S. convenes soon, I certainly want to look my best.

It's funny how this war has upset my old mental viewpoints. I haven't the slightest pang of homesickness for Oakland. Of course, I would like to return to Sonora for a while and see Mother, but I don't wish to return to my old job or even to any of the scenes of my recent civilian life. After the war is over, if it is at all possible, I am going to seek every opportunity to start life anew in some other region. "After the war is over." How filled with uncertainty, how distant, and wishful such a phrase sounds, but all things must come to an end someday, and tonight, I wonder—what then?

WEDNESDAY, JANUARY 21, 1942

No mail to speak of since Saturday, although I have haunted the mail section faithfully since then. Major Robbins stopped by the other day and assured me that my O.C.S. papers would be back soon. My physical examination will be the next thing in order, I guess. Of this latter, I am truly worried, for my eyes have been bothering me considerably of late. I just hope that they will be perfect enough to pass the requirements for officers (20/40 correctable to 20/20 with glasses). I don't know, though, as that is what they were when I first came in the Army, and I don't imagine that a year of this close office work, under inefficient lighting, has tended to improve them any.

This damnable athlete's foot that I picked up in this barracks is rapidly driving me crazy. I have been to the dispensary two or three times and obtained some of the salve they use for curing it, but it seems to be of no use whatsoever. I raised hell today, though, and they gave me some "Sulfanilamide Urea and Lanolin Paste," from the sound of which alone should be enough to cure it. I sure as hell hope so.

I surely must have caused a minor disruption up there in Oakland, as Vivian hasn't as yet answered the two letters, which I wrote to her in reply to her statement that she was going to wait until I got out of the Army. Perhaps she doesn't intend to, which all in all, would be best for all concerned, I guess.

Talk about work in the S-3 Office! Letters, memorandums, filing, stencils, inventory, and everything else. Believe me, I have really been turning it out lately. Old Major Stevenson has improved recently in his disposition but not to a great degree. However, he did break down enough to buy me a Coke the other day.

I see the Army has lowered its requirements for entrance into the Flying Cadets. Even a high school education is nonessential now, but as usual, my old familiar jinx is still on my back, as the eyesight must be perfect for that particular branch. I haven't been feeling so terribly good physically, either. Nothing definite, just a run-down feeling. I wonder what the devil I can find to do this coming payday. I certainly wish something would turn up, as I am dying from boredom.

SATURDAY, JANUARY 24, 1942

Today is the first day of a full eight-hour Saturday. The first of many, I imagine. For the past week, I have felt the lowest in spirit I think I have felt since I came into the Army. This condition is the result of a combination of many things. For one thing, my physical condition. This damnable athlete's foot that I contracted some time ago seems to be an exceptionally stubborn case. It refused to heal upon the application of several salves and is very annoying. Number two, the feeling of frustration I have in my daily work. Although I work hard and earnestly, on two separate occasions now, I have been unjustly cheated out of a higher rating "because the other fellow was married and needed the money." Number three, life has become almost unbearable with the advent of Major Stevenson, and now he has thrown a very broad hint that he would like to have a girl to take my place. His excuse, "so she could take dictation." This is extremely odd in view of the fact that my particular job has necessitated no dictation in over a year of constant work. From the wolfish look that plays continually across his silly puss, I would say that the suggestion is probably based on more personal reasons. Fourthly, and last, this O.C.S. business has me in a mental maelstrom. I was induced by my Commanding Officer, and others, to drop the Infantry course, and to apply for the Coast Artillery because appointment to the C.A. would be so much more simple from Camp Callan. I did so and started attending the refresher course in higher mathematics held in Camp, as I would have to learn Algebra, Trigonometry, and Calculus, in order to pass the entrance examinations successfully. From highly authentic sources, I now learn that 50% of those already sent back to Fort Monroe have failed in their preliminary mathematics examination. So, in my own personal estimation, this places me precisely behind the "eight ball," as unfortunately for me, the papers have already gone through, and I am to report to the hospital Tuesday for my physical examination.

Went back to work this afternoon and really turned out an enormous quota of work. At about 4:30 p.m., due to the state I had worked myself into after overhearing Stevenson's remark pertaining to the new secretary, I asked Major Cooley about what was the present status of my job. Whereupon he proceeded, in a very friendly fashion, to assure me that my work was highly satisfactory in every respect. That I had displayed initiative and high ability to learn, that my present job was entirely secure, and held high prospects of a much higher promotion. He then went on and gave me a great deal of encouragement regarding the O.C.S., told me not to become discouraged over the outcome of this particular board meeting, as there would be unlimited opportunities, which would eventually present themselves, if not just now, assuredly at a later date. Believe me, I can assure you, I felt like a million after that talk.

I went to the theatre and saw two fairly good shows tonight. John Strahl informs me that his folks are coming down tomorrow, but if so,

I don't think I will go out with them. Tomorrow, I trust, will be a day of rest and relaxation for me. A letter from Margie was the total sum of all mail received by me today.

Valerie invited me to come into La Jolla and have dinner with her, after which we attended a debate at her church. Subject: "Union Now, with Britain." I found it quite interesting. At the conclusion of the debate, I drove directly back to Camp.

Sunday, February 1, 1942

Uncertainty, and a bewildering chaos beyond all description, is again upon me. Major Cooley's talk of the other day has been nullified. Major Stevenson insisted upon obtaining a replacement for me (civilian) for, as he put it, all the men in Headquarters were applying for the Officer Candidate Schools, and he wanted to obtain an employee who would be a permanent replacement. I naturally and vehemently questioned him regarding my future disposition. Told him that it was by no means a definite fact that I was going back to the school, and in all probability, wouldn't go back, due to the mathematics angle. That I had worked hard and earnestly on this one particular job, and hated to see a year of hard effort go for naught. He assured me that I had nothing to worry about, and from the course of his later conversation with Major Cooley, learned that I was supposed to be made the "Sergeant Major" of the S-3 Section. Of this latter, though, I remain highly doubtful, as my instinctive dislike for Stevenson still remains, and I wouldn't put much of anything past him. The civilian replacement hasn't appeared as yet, and I have no idea when she will appear, and meanwhile, I am still trying to do three men's work. Only time will untangle this one particular phase of my life in the Army, and all there is to do, meanwhile, is just to wait and see how good Major Cooley's word is.

Evidently, my last letter of explanation to Vivian must have "done the trick," as I have had no further word from her since then, which was some time ago. It was a difficult thing to do, but there was no sense in kidding her or me. I just haven't any love left in me anymore.

I am still battling with this damnable athlete's foot. Nothing seems to be of any avail despite three trips to the dispensary, two salves, and one lotion. The darn stuff just refuses to heal, and runs continuously, exuding a scalding liquid that causes such a terrific itching and burning that it is impossible to sleep. I haven't had a decent night's sleep for over a week, yet when I told the doctor this, he said that it would be impossible to apply any stronger medicine until the very red soreness and inflammation had disappeared. He was, in all probability, correct in telling me this, but the present state of downright torture is very hard to bear.

The "HQ 11th Tng. Gp." is in a state of "working quarantine." One of the fellows who sleeps two beds down from me came down with a case of "American Measles," and therefore, the rest of us were placed in quarantine. This fact, of course, canceled my proposed trip to Los Angeles with John Strahl, which had been scheduled for this payday, which was yesterday. To tell the truth, though, I was satisfied that it turned out that way, as I was trying to figure out how to break the date with John, as the trip would have been pure torture for me, due to the seriousness of this athlete's foot condition.

I will celebrate the anniversary of my first year in the Army on February 26th. I wonder how many more years I must put in before I am ultimately discharged? In some ways, life seems so hopeless to me. When I am discharged from the Army, I will have no trade or even, who knows, a job to turn to. It is most natural to assume that a depression of terrible magnitude will follow the war; and by the time, if ever, that I finally get on my feet, I will be so old that it will be useless to even think of my dream of a happy home of my own. I have come to think that it would be better all around if I meet my fate during the course of this war. Please do not think this is resigning in the face of an adverse time or era, nor is it a defeatist attitude, but one might say, merely looking at something with a horribly practical eye. Look at the trouble it would save, not only me, but other people, too. After all, I have about $10,000 insurance that would certainly go far towards keeping the wolf from Mother's door. However, that is something that only destiny can decide, and most probably will.

Tuesday, February 3, 1942

Yesterday morning was the climax of something or other. After spending a sleepless night pacing the floor of the washroom in agony with this "Athlete's Foot," I was so tired, angry, and disgusted with all aspects of the Army that as soon as I reported for work, I told Major Cooley that I was going to the dispensary, which I immediately did. I really raised the devil with the lieutenant in charge. Told him I had been suffering with this condition for over a month despite his salves and lotions, and that it was folly to expect a man to continue his work while he was in almost continual agony, and that I absolutely had to have some kind of relief. He informed me that there was a medicine that he was almost certain would cure it and give instant relief, but unfortunately, there was none in stock in the hospital. Therefore, I had to go into La Jolla and buy it. It is a medicine known as Liquid Aluminii Silicate. So far, it has afforded a great deal of relief, and praise be, seems to be improving the skin condition somewhat. It seems to be a slow, painful process, however, but I am hoping for the best. The thing that worries me now, however, is the fact that some sort of a rash has broken out on my face, and whether it is this stuff spreading to my face, I do not know. According to the doctor, the disease wasn't "Athlete's Foot" at all but a condition known as "Dermatitis," caused by a tiny parasite which works under the skin and is very difficult to eliminate. What makes the whole situation so bad, however, is the fact that the Board of Officers to review Officer Candidates is going to be called soon, and I would certainly make a nice impression with my face a solid rash. Which reminds me, the Officer Candidate School situation looks as hopeless to me now as it did some time back. I just can't seem to get the darn mathematics. Probably due to the fact that I didn't even have the basic fundamentals of same in high school, which are at present so necessary in grasping the lessons as they are given in this "refresher course" I am attending. But I brought home an algebra book tonight, and if I can grasp the fundamentals of Algebra, Geometry, Logarithms, and Trigonometry, I may be able to get by the Board, which, however, I don't think would benefit me very much, as I understand the preliminary examination they give you at Fort Monroe is enough to make your hair curl. So I don't know, I most probably won't even get by the Board, in which case, I hope I can change my application back to Infantry where mathematics aren't so essential. By the way, the report on my physical examination came back today, and much to my amazement, I had passed it perfectly. Imagine that! Blood tests, X-rays, Wasserman Tests, and everything else. Of course, my eyesight was the same as when I first came into the Army, that is, 20/40 correctable to 20/20, but I had fully expected them to be worse, if anything, so that, too, was in some measure a relief.

    I wrote Mother a letter last night and enclosed twenty dollars, which should help her over the rough spots this month—at least I hope so. I am going to open a savings account in La Jolla and see how much I can accumulate as long as I remain here at Callan. Believe me, I realize the fact that after I am discharged from the Army, I am going to need that money; and as there is no way of telling how long I will be in here, I believe that if I start saving a little systematically, it will probably add up to quite a sum by the time I leave for home.

What with my physical troubles, school worries, and the many changes, which will no doubt soon take effect in the S-3 Section, I have quite a bit on my mind. Master Sergeant Holder left for the C.A. School at Fort Monroe today, which leaves me as the only original enlisted man in the entire Section. They have not as yet replaced me with a civilian, so I will undoubtedly have my hands full until she arrives, if she ever does. I don't know just what the tie-up is in that direction.

FRIDAY, FEBRUARY 6, 1942

The familiar "McCully Jinx" has struck again! The skin condition I have been raving about in the last few pages turned out to be something quite serious. None of the doctors seems to know exactly what the trouble is, and it seems very difficult to cure. I hope it is cured soon, however, as I sure don't like this hospital! I had to leave the office in an awful mess, but it couldn't be helped.

It looks very much as if the old jinx has struck in another direction, too. I believe some more grades and ratings came out, but I do not think I made Staff Sergeant, although Major Cooley had me marked for advancement. (I saw it on his memo pad.) I have a hunch that the Staff Sergeantry will go to Private Vrick, as the "poor boy" just got married, and it has been my experience that promotion in the U.S. Army is _not_ based on merit and _hard_ _work_ but on _fawning_ and _bootlicking_. This is the truth, as I have seen it in more cases than mine. So it is entirely understandable why I am disgusted with the Army, the world, and myself, too.

STATION HOSPITAL
SUNDAY, FEB. 8, 1942

No improvement at all to speak of in this terrible skin disease. Had a high fever (106 degrees) yesterday, which was induced by the typhus germs that were injected into my arm. This sort of treatment is known as fever therapy. It is impossible to sleep without sleeping tablets, and the ugly scaly rash on my arms, legs, face, and neck is a horrible sight.

I imagine, from all aspects, that I will be in here for some time, and with that fact comes the realization that this enforced stay will very probably eliminate any chance I may have had to go to the O.C.S. Also, as Major Cooley is leaving about tomorrow for the Command and General Staff School, I will—in fact I am almost certain—I will be cheated out of the long-promised promotion. And who knows, when I eventually get out of here, I may not even return to S-3. So this soldier is sick physically, low mentally, and spiritually downcast—and as far as discernible, with good reason!

TUESDAY, FEB. 10, 1942
Another day of confinement in this damnable hospital. Had an injection of 25,000,000 typhus germs in the right arm, which caused the same terrific chills and a fever of 100.6 , but it was all over in about three hours and had absolutely no effect on this damnable scaly rash. I resemble something returned from the grave—a scaly rash covers my face, neck, ears, arms, and hands.

I imagine they will give up the "fever therapy" attempt to cure this disease, as it is of no avail. What makes me so damn mad is the fact that if they had applied curative measures when I first reported this disease about a month ago, I wouldn't be in here today. I opened a savings account on the 7th of February at the Bank of America in La Jolla. <u>I wonder, tonight, about my supposed promotion and job</u>.

THURSDAY, FEB. 12, 1942
It looks very much as if some pages of this "record" will be recorded in ink, as today I learned that I am to be transferred to the Hoff General Hospital at Santa Barbara, Calif., some 250 miles distant, for special treatment. Do not know exactly when I will be returned to Camp Callan, if ever. We leave Saturday on the train, and I am loath to go, as I see all my dreams of promotion and a candidate for the O.C.S. evaporating into thin air. Well, as the Arabs say, "Kismet," it is fate, and nothing can turn aside that fact.

Valerie has been quite considerate in writing daily notes, bringing me books, etc., but I must say, I have returned sarcasm with sarcasm. No mail at all since entering the hospital.

The Lieutenant assures me that I will very probably effect a cure in about two weeks and will be returned to duty here, but I am skeptical. This damnable ailment spreads and continues to spread, and nothing seems to stop its advance. So it is a heartily disgusted Corporal who pens these lines tonight.

TUESDAY, FEBRUARY 17, 1942
Still in the hospital and have, in the interim, been shot in the arm so many times that it looks like a sieve. Received, Saturday, an injection of 50,000,000 Typhus Bacilli, which literally and figuratively "knocked me out" until Sunday noon. Seems to have dried up the majority of this rash, except for one or two very stubborn spots on my body.

Met a very interesting Jewish refugee from Nazi Germany (my next-bed neighbor), and we have been arguing continuously on the merits of matrimony for three days. He on the positive (although a divorced man!) and I on the negative side.

I am due for another 50,000,000 shot this afternoon in a wild endeavor to clear up these remaining stubborn patches, and I hope it does. We have a new captain in charge of the ward, and he seems to be a nice chap. Received my greatest record of mail yesterday—12 letters! A miracle! Vivian wrote again and is just as serious as ever. I don't know, I guess I'll just let it ride until monotony kills it.

Received news that Major Cooley had been promoted to Lt. Colonel. I am certainly glad for him; he surely deserved it, if anyone did!

HOFF GENERAL HOSPITAL, WARD 22
SANTA BARBARA, CALIF.
FEBRUARY 22, 1942
This is a dissertation on the lack of efficiency, the bungling, and the utter ignorance of the U.S. Army Medical Corps. To begin with, I first noticed this rash approximately 8 weeks ago, and, as we are required to do, made an immediate report to the dispensary. Lieut _____, in charge there, diagnosed correctly the disease at that time, but instead of taking corrective measures at once, chose to experiment with me on a total of eight salves and three lotions. Result? Due to one especially strong drug (sulfanilamide), the rashes became highly inflamed and infectious. At that point, as already noted herein, Major Cooley took me to the skin specialist at Callan's hospital, and they chose to experiment with "fever therapy," shooting a total of 150,000,000 Typhus Bacilli in me, in the attempt. It was successful to a certain extent, clearing my face, hands, and arms. But at one spot on my body, which being in such a location as to be damp and sweaty all the time, made an ideal breeding ground for this particular germ (trichophytosis) and it refused to heal. I lived several nights in agony pacing the floor of the

washroom until 3 a.m. in the morning. By this time, I learned that they had allowed the disease to reach what is known as a "Secondary Infection," which makes it quite difficult to cure.

Taking advantage of Major Cooley's absence, I was transferred here to Hoff, enduring a 225-mile ride in an Army ambulance. Expecting quick treatment at such a reputably modern hospital, I am amazed to find that in two days, the total medical treatment I have received is (1) Temperature taken, (2) Pulse taken, (3) Question: What is your trouble, son? (Captain), (4) Question: What is your trouble son? (Major), (5) An X-ray taken of my chest (where I have no infection). Wonderful medical attention! I can't see how such wonderful and truly brilliant deductions ever issued from such high-class medical men.

Needless to say, my opinion of the Medical Corps has fallen to nothing. I also suppose my chances for promotion, O.C.S., and every other thing I was working for, are nothing but memories now.

Hoff General Hospital, Ward 22
February 24, 1942

The impossible has happened! I actually received some medical attention today after being interned in this "super" hospital for three and one-half days! I received permission to take a bath in a strong solution of boric acid. (Something I had asked to do some two days ago!)

Had a complete blackout last night, with planes roaring overhead, etc. Turned out that a Jap sub shelled an oilfield some three miles from the hospital. The gunfire was easily heard here. Preparations were made to evacuate the hospital, and as I was the only Corporal in the ward, was placed in charge of the men to see that all helpless patients were carried out. Nothing came of it, however, as the sub disappeared after 25 minutes of shelling.

Have only received two letters from Mother, which had been forwarded from Callan, which makes it rather lonely and desolate here.

I can only hope that this darn rash will heal rapidly, as I feel as if I can't stand another day in this darn hospital. If they would only give me some sort of treatment, I know it would cure instantly, but instead, they are letting it spread.

HOFF GENERAL HOSPITAL
SANTA BARBARA, CALIF.
FEBRUARY 26, 1942

One year in the Army today! Little did I think a year ago today that I would be in the hospital at this time. The skin condition is improving! Yes, it is true! And by the most simple of all remedies (which I suggested), it is boric acid, bathed in three times a day. Hope to be so far recovered soon that I can return to Callan. There is no telling just when I will be discharged from here, though, as I will have to do battle with the inevitable Army Red Tape.

Had a full night's sleep last night for the first time in three weeks. I would still be lying here in bed clawing myself to death, but for the fact that I raised the devil and made them give me the boric acid. I know this factor didn't improve my popularity with the medical staff.

Hope I receive some mail today, as hardly anyone has written since I arrived here. Had quite a blackout night before last—lasted quite some time with 3" AA guns roaring over Los Angeles. It is not yet clear whether there were really any enemy planes over the area.

[*Immediately following the last entry, the journal contained the songs listed below, including their typewritten lyrics:*]

"Let's Tie the Old Forget-Me-Not"
"Serenade in Blue"
"Waiting for Ships That Never Come In"
"Song of Songs"
"One Alone"
"If I Was a Millionaire"
"It Must Be True"
"The Melody That Made You Mine"
"Sunbonnet Sue"
"Jimmy Valentine"
"When I Lost You"

[*The last page of the journal contained a typed list of songs (no lyrics), as follows:*]

"When You're a Long, Long Way from Home" - Bing Crosby
"When I Lost You" - Bing Crosby
"The Waltz You Saved for Me" - Bing Crosby
"Invitation to the Dance" - Von Weber
"The Kiss Waltz" - "Il Bacio"
"The Barcarolle from Tales of Hoffman" - Offenbach
"Narcissus" - Ethelbert Nevin
"Amaryllis" - ?
"Forget-Me-Not" - ?
"Nutcracker Suite" - Tchaikovsky
"In a Persian Market" - Ketèlbey
"In the Hall of the Mountain King" - Grieg
"Die Fledermaus" (You & You) - Strauss
"Over the Waves" - ?
"Blue Danube" - Strauss
"Tales of the Vienna Woods" - Strauss
"Nola"
"Wedding of the Winds" - ?
"Souvenir" - ?
"Danube Waves" - ?
"Poet and Peasant Overture" - Von Suppe
"Acclamations Waltz" - Lehar [Waldteufel]
"The Rainbow Waltz" - Emil Waldteufel
"Dolores Waltz" - Emil Waldteufel
"Love's Dream" - Oscar Straus
"Wine, Women, and Song" - Lehar
"Waltz of the Flowers" - Tchaikovsky
"The Honeymoon Waltz" (Viennese)[Viennese Waltz]
"My Treasure" - Waltz
"The Scarf Dance" - ?
"Indian Summer" -
"The Indian Love Call"

[*A sketch entitled, "On the Bluffs at Callan" was pasted on the inside back cover of the journal.*]

Journal 3

VOLUME II
February 27, 1942 to February 14, 1943
Age 26

*Here I sit, finally wearing the gold bars of my commission,
and I think of all the toil, work, sweat, and worry
that entered into the course,
and I know in my heart that it was <u>worth</u> it.*

VOLUME II

NOTES AND IMPRESSIONS OF HAPPENINGS AND EVENTS, WHICH OCCURRED DURING MY SECOND YEAR OF SERVICE IN THE ARMY OF THE UNITED STATES. NOTES RELATING THE EXPERIENCES ENCOUNTERED IN MY FIRST YEAR MAY BE FOUND IN VOLUME I

April 11, 1942

In the event of my death, please mail this book to

Mrs. Nettie J. Westrem
204 Shepherd Street
Sonora, California
P. O. Box 635

[The following journal pages were inserted between alphabetized index tabs (A-Z) in chronological order.]

Vivian's plans to visit • Last days of hospital stay • Frustration with office politics • Departure to Officer Candidate School (O.C.S.) at Fort Benning • Commitment, obstacles, and fears of failure during O.C.S. training • Bob enlists in Air Corps • O.C.S. graduation • Commission and assignment to Camp Adair • Daily life at Camp Adair • Relationships with women • Worries, loneliness, thoughts on life's meaninglessness • Promotion to 1st Lieutenant • Return of health condition • Expectation of promotion.

Hoff General Hospital, Ward 22
Santa Barbara, California
February 27, 1942
How events have happened within the last 48 hours! Received a letter from Vivian in which she said she was coming down to Santa Barbara to see me. I immediately sent an answer via airmail, in which I told her not to come, as I was being returned to duty. Haven't received an answer as yet, of course. The statement, "returning to duty," was true! I believe I will be returned to duty within two or three days, as this rash, due to the "boric acid" treatment, is almost completely cured! Yes! At last, after weeks of a torturing, searing, gaulding rash, I am free from it.

Today I received a letter from Margie, and she informed me that there is a rumor going around Camp Callan HQ that I have been appointed to the Officer Candidate School and will be sent to Louisiana upon my return to Callan! Perhaps I am a trifle pessimistic, but I fail to see how this can be true, as I had yet to appear before the Board of Reviewing Officers. Naturally, I hope that this miracle is true, but I certainly have my doubts. Understand that I have been "redlined" on this month's payroll due to my illness in the hospital, and it is doubtful even whether I will be able to get on the supplementary payroll on the tenth of March.

Hoff General Hospital, Ward 22
Santa Barbara, Calif.
March 1, 1942
No further news, letters, or information of any kind either concerning the O.C.S. or news from Camp HQ. However, I believe that I can expect some mail tomorrow, and perhaps that will clear up this fog of doubt concerning the O.C.S. rumor. I believe that it will be a little more

difficult than I had imagined to be discharged from Hoff at an early date. The doctor informs me that I cannot leave until all these scales have vanished. This does not bother me, as they are almost all gone, at present. But why should it take two days of red tape to get my clearance papers ready?

No answer yet from Vivian regarding the letter in which I told her it would be foolish to make the trip down here. I wish to arrive back at Callan as soon as possible, as I know from past experience in the Army that no one can look after your interests as well as I can.

I am not going to place any stock in that O.C.S. rumor until it is proven, one way or the other, in order to avoid any further disappointment.

Hoff General Hospital, Ward 22
Santa Barbara, Calif.
March 2, 1942

This will be the last notation from this hospital, thank God! The doctor, after giving me a very superficial examination, gave as his diagnosis—cured. The rash has not completely healed in one spot, but I said nothing, as even one more day in this hospital is horrible to think of. I will have to be very careful that this one particular spot does not become reinfected, but I can assure anyone that I will be the utmost in caution after witnessing some of the sights I have seen in this hospital (and the "wonderful" treatment one can expect).

Haven't heard anything from Vivian since my airmail letter in which I told her not to come down. Poor kid! I wish she could see how utterly impossible and what a horrible thing marriage really is. She is one of the finest girls I have ever known, as I have stated before, but I don't love her, and without love, no marriage can endure (or with it, either, it seems).

I hope to be able to write the next entry in dear old Camp Callan. (I certainly won't have much else to do, due to the nicely messed up payroll.) Although my clearance papers have long been signed, I still languish here, waiting for them to release the special orders.

Camp Callan, San Diego, Calif.
Barracks 2203
March 5, 1942

So much has happened since the last entry that I fear it will take a great deal of space to relate all. Even my writing in ink is related to some of the momentous happenings, which have befallen me.

To begin with, "Sneaky" Stevenson finally has things the way he wants them. It seems I am not such a bad judge of human nature, after all. It seems he obtained a soldier named Hartman, who, although he can take dictation, proves to be a very rotten typist. At any rate, he has taken over my old job, and with much unnecessary fanfare and pompous acclaim, Stevenson stated that I was to be placed in charge of the S-3 Section, taking the old Master Gunner's duties. All of which was an easy, and as he thought, smart way in which to slide me out of the job, <u>for there is no promotion</u> in this "advancement."

For some reason or other, he seems most anxious to get me entirely out of the Camp, for he again brought up his old war cry that "I would soon be leaving for the O.C.S., and he wanted me to simplify the work so a new man could take over without any trouble." I came right out with it then and told him that due to the long stay in the hospital, I was too far behind in my mathematics to think of going to the C. A. School and that I intended to change my application back to Infantry Officers School. Immediately, he started telling me the sooner I got back to school, the better "break" I would have and insisted that I see Major Robinson immediately and change my application! Whether his solicitation was all "put on" or not, I can't figure out. In fact, he is one fellow I <u>can't</u> figure out.

In a huge allotment of ratings that were issued by DEML, practically all of the fellows that I knew when Camp first opened were made sergeants or better. The 11th Group ratings have not been issued yet, and I am waiting to see just what, if any, promotion I will get. I am not going to get too worried about it, as I fully expect to be cheated out of this promotion, too, in spite of all the promises that have been made me in the past. It seems that, in the Army, the surest way to success is to get married or else to grovel at some officer's feet, and I refuse to do either. Oh well! So much for the events at Callan. Only one more thing of importance—I had to write to Castlemont High School for verification of my R.O.T.C. training in reapplying for the Infantry School.

Just before I left Hoff Hospital, I received a letter from Vivian in which she said that she was coming to San Diego in spite of all I said and that she would arrive on March 11th or 12th. I immediately answered and told her that if she was determined to come down, at least to wait until the end of the month, as I hadn't been paid and was flat broke. I have received no answer to this as yet, and whether she still insists on coming down on the 12th or not, I do not know. I <u>do</u> know one thing though, I am going to tell her once and for all that I am <u>not</u> going to get married, and there is no use of our keeping up this continual debate on the matter. The matter will have to be settled, once and for all.

So, on all these matters, there is nothing I can do but to calmly wait and see just what this mass of events and happenings will crystallize into. I am so disgusted tonight, that I don't care what happens, but I do know that I am going to get into the war in an <u>active</u> branch, if I have to go in grade of private.

CAMP CALLAN, SAN DIEGO, CALIF.
BARRACKS 2203
MARCH 9, 1942

Perhaps I was a little hasty in judging this new job of mine. It is a much easier duty, although it holds a great deal more responsibility. I have direct charge of three men, and my chief duty seems to be that of directing their efforts. Last Tuesday, however, I had to go out on the target boat and take pictures of the shell splashes as they hit near the target. As we had to go out about eight miles, and the boat is none too large, I had a bad session of seasickness (due, I think to the fact that I felt a little weak after my recent hospitalization.)

It is quite definite, now, that there will be no promotion. Same old story—S-3 last, as usual. Stevenson and I get along a little better now that I do not work directly under him.

I can expect Vivian to arrive definitely on Wednesday, according to her last letter. I am still determined to end the matter once and for all.

Bob sent my R.O.T.C. certificate down, so I will soon be all set on the Infantry application. I wonder how much good it will do me.

CAMP HEADQUARTERS (S-3)
CAMP CALLAN, CALIF.
MARCH 19, 1942
10:00 P.M.

Again, much water over the dam. Vivian came down and stayed with some friends of hers, Mr. and Mrs. Walter DuPont, until last Sunday night. We had a lot of fun and covered all the nightspots. Sure enough, Vivian had some idea about us going to Yuma, Arizona, and so, as I said I would, I ended it once and for all. I explained very carefully just why a marriage would never work out, and we parted the best of friends. I saw her off on the bus Sunday night and received a card today in which she said she had a nice trip home.

Stevenson and I <u>aren't</u> "clicking" very good. I certainly hope Major Cooley comes back soon, but I doubt if he could do much to repair the damage Stevenson has done. He certainly threw the hooks into me as far as an advancement is concerned. I feel disgusted as hell with the Army, in general, but there is nothing I can do about it.

Found out I have to take my physical examination for the O.C.S. over again. I doubt if any more bad luck can happen to me, as it has all happened. More later, tomorrow.

CAMP HEADQUARTERS (S-3)
CAMP CALLAN, CALIF.
MARCH 21, 1942
3:00 P.M.

I didn't find the expected time to write yesterday so will make up for it this afternoon. Today is Saturday, and a grand and beautiful day it is.

Stevenson left about 1:30 p.m., and as a result, I am in complete charge of the Plans and Training Office for the balance of the day. A rather empty honor, methinks, as my personal opinion of the aforementioned P&T Office has fallen, recently, to a new low. Stefanski arrived back from the Master Gunner School, and he too, is out of luck as far as obtaining a Staff-Sergeantry is concerned. However, he is assured of getting one before I do, so I fail to see why he has any cause for worry.

I have felt so terribly depressed and downcast by this "rating argument" that I have absolutely no ambition or a single spark of energy left. Frankly, I have reached the stage where I do not give a damn what happens. Whether I live or die now, or within the next five years, doesn't matter a tinker's damn to me. Which is one reason, I suppose, that the thought of being transferred to active duty in the fierce battles that are sure to come, bothers me not at all. I am really looking forward to the time when I receive that "special bullet with my name on it." After all, there comes a time in every human life when all interest in the serious business of living ceases to exist and to be so all important. It is my personal opinion that this is not necessarily the talk of "one who couldn't take it," but rather a sensible viewpoint of one who has merely discovered that he has absolutely nothing to live for. All my life, my dearest dream was to find a girl who would, perhaps, care enough for me to want to adventure down the road of life together. It can easily be seen, therefore, that if such a dream had become a reality, life at the present time, would at the present time, undoubtedly be far more worthwhile than it is.

When that horrible fiasco of my unfortunate marriage came about, it turned something in me into a solid mass of bitterness and poison. I sincerely believe that I aged twenty years at that time, if not physically, I most certainly did mentally. I have had the opportunity of meeting dozens of girls, who were, in all probability, very fine girls, but it is a simple statement of fact to say that there is absolutely no response left in my being. My heart is like a chunk of ice, and I freeze up mentally whenever I am with one.

Take Vivian, for instance. I have known her for approximately two years. She claims to be very deeply in love with me and would do anything for me. She would, without a single doubt, make a man the finest wife one could desire, in all respects, yet despite our long acquaintanceship, I haven't a spark of feeling for her. Which explains precisely just why I severed our relationship. It simply wasn't fair to her to waste some of the years of her youth on something that could never be.

Youth itself is about over for me. I am 26 years old and am certainly too far along in life to ever realize the dreams I once had. I realize that fact, and that is why I say wherever I am sent is perfectly satisfactory to me, providing there is plenty of action.

Having such a detached view of life, in general, provides me with the most wonderful opportunity to observe the amusing efforts of some of these "stalwart defenders of democracy" in their efforts to remain safely seated at a nice comfortable desk for the duration.

Camp Callan, San Diego, Calif.
Barracks 2203
7:30 P.M.
March 22, 1942
One of those dreary stay-at-"home" Sundays. Read all morning, had a chicken dinner at the mess hall and saw Olive (John Strahl's girlfriend)

and John for a few moments. Came back and read some more, and then about 3 p.m., went down and took a shower, during the course of which I discovered, to my horror, that I had contracted one of the most annoying inconveniences in the Army. I immediately went to the dispensary and took the necessary steps to rid myself of it. It sure makes me seethe with anger, however, as this and the famous "athletes foot episode" related before, were all due to this damnable dirty latrine, and I am getting sick and tired of it.

Received my bankbook back from La Jolla, and my account for "the home of my own" is growing steadily. Fifteen dollars already, and I intend to add to it substantially every month. At this time, I would like to state, that in the event I "go forth to meet my destiny" during the course of this war, please, whoever may read this book, take steps to inform my mother that I leave the bank balance in the La Jolla Branch of the Bank of America to her, together with all my other worldly goods.

Strahl leaves for QM School next week. I wonder about my school??????????

CAMP CALLAN, SAN DIEGO, CALIF.
BARRACKS 2203
7:50 P.M.
MARCH 23, 1942
Truly a busy, busy Monday! Had to work all day at the "Assistant S-3's" desk, opposite Major Stevenson, on training Schedules, film Schedules, etc. Amazing news concerning the O.C.S.! Major Robbins informs me that 9th Corps Area HQ in Utah has been asked to forward all my allied papers pertaining to the O.C.S.—that I am on the list of those destined to go; and that on Wednesday at 1 p.m., I must go to the station hospital and have my physical examination renewed. How I hope that this is not another one of those endless disappointments to which I have grown so accustomed! Even if I am so fortunate as to be one of those elected to go, the struggle is then only beginning. I realize full well just what I am letting myself in for, and there will probably be times when I will wish with all my heart that I had retained enough common sense to stay in the "soft-snap" I had in the office. Fort Benning, I understand, is very different from sunny Southern California. After three months of rigorous marching, drilling, arduous study, and intensive training, providing that I am fortunate enough to graduate, I will be granted the privilege of wearing the gold bars of a second lieutenant. From there, I

will be shipped to some field unit for hardening for an indefinite time (which I do not think will be too long a time), and from there to active duty—God knows where. In spite of all this, I know full well that it is what I really want, and I intend to put my heart and soul into the final attainment of my goal. If I fail to graduate (and in view of my typical luck, it is highly possible), at least I will be able to say that I made a good try and refused to stagnate in some office. For, once in the Infantry, I am assured of seeing action at an early date, even if I have to see it as a corporal, which is certainly no disgrace.

Ted and I may go into San Diego tomorrow and do some bowling; and Saturday, I am supposed to go to Los Angeles and stay overnight at John Strahl's house, at which time we will probably all go out (John and Olive, Margie and I). Wonder how the weekend will turn out?

Camp Callan, San Diego, Calif.
Barracks 2203
March 25, 1942
5:45 P.M.

Today I went to the station hospital and had my physical examination renewed. No trouble at all. All they did was type over all my former examination papers and forward them to Major Robbins. All I have to do now is to wait on the list until notified, which I hope will be soon.

Stevenson was out on the Artillery Range all day today, and needless to say, his presence wasn't missed! I still believe my first premonitions concerning him were correct, as the tension between us is still very noticeable. For that reason, my most fervent wish is to be appointed to the school. Otherwise, I know that I will transfer at the earliest opportunity, as it is impossible to work efficiently in that tense atmosphere. In the event the O.C.S. falls through, I would like to apply for the parachute troops but am afraid the very rigid physical requirements will probably nullify my chance of success in that direction.

It is quite certain now that I am going to L.A. this weekend. Wonder if I will be glad I went, or if I will regret it.

Camp Callan, San Diego, Calif.
Barracks 2203
March 26, 1942

Thirteen months in the Army today! Bad omens, too! From all signs and symptoms, I believe that the damnable curse of that athlete's foot is appearing again! I first noticed the symptoms last night and immediately applied the boric acid and talcum powder mixture that I have kept on hand since I was in the hospital. It seemed to stop the liquid, which had started to exude from the skin but also seemed to dry the skin until it was brittle, which results in a very painful condition. I phoned Lt. Gordon, and he said to keep applying the powder. I hope to God it doesn't get worse, just now anyway, when the school situation looks as if it may break soon.

Letter from Margie today, and they are all evidently expecting me up in Los Angeles on Saturday. Also a letter from Vivian, and I may say that her letter seemed somewhat icily remote. She also informed me that she was busy going to the Saturday night dances as per my request. So it begins to look as though she is finally on her way to eventual happiness, for which fact, I am truly glad. She really deserves the best!

CAMP CALLAN, SAN DIEGO, CALIF.
CAMP HEADQUARTERS (S-3)
MARCH 27, 1942
BARRACKS 2203

The clash of wills and sarcasm between Stevenson and me is becoming more and more potent everyday! Despite various obstacles, which were placed in my path, I am still leaving for Los Angeles tomorrow at eleven a.m.

Discovered today that my application for Infantry School will have to have the direct approval of the Adjutant General's Office in Washington. Still hoping vainly that I will be successful in this venture, but only the future can disclose that fact. Understand, too, that <u>leadership</u> is the prime requisite of graduation from the school. In other words, if I am sent, I will have to suddenly drop my timidity, or stage fright, which has always affected me when addressing a large group of people. Well, my mind is made up! It can be done and <u>will be done</u>! I can be just as tough and truculent as the next fellow, and if that is what is desired, I can certainly furnish it!

Well, I hope the L.A. trip is a success after all this planning.

CAMP CALLAN, SAN DIEGO, CALIF.
BARRACKS 2203
MARCH 30, 1942

The Los Angeles trip <u>was</u> a success! Had a very nice time, although I was none too well fixed financially. Went to the Palladium for dancing, and later the next day, to the beach at Santa Monica. Margie was quite as charming and pleasant as she was the other time, but same old story as far as I am concerned. Had to take an old sleeper bus home, and after about eight breakdowns, arrived back at Camp at about 5 a.m., then had to walk the three miles to Headquarters and arise at 6:45 a.m.

Received a letter from Bob today telling me that he had sold my car (as we had planned) for $400, which he will forward down to me. I plan to put it in my bank account and not touch, but on the contrary, to add to it for the eventual home of my own, which I <u>will</u> own. I mean it—I'll have my own home or know the reason why. No more news on the O.C.S., but I am still hoping.

Furloughs are again approved, but I would much rather have the six days en route to Fort Benning.

Stevenson almost human for a change. Can't figure it out, but it won't last.

CAMP CALLAN, SAN DIEGO, CALIF.
BARRACKS 2203
APRIL 1, 1942

Have been busy going to the show for the last few days. Received the "magnificent" sum of $57.20, after they had deducted $6.80 for insurance and 53 cents laundry. Which makes my total monthly wage $64. When the House of Representatives passes the new pay bill, I will receive $66 per month.

Some talk again of eventual ratings for Ted and I, but I feel rather discouraged about that subject.

Talked with Major Robbins about the O.C.S. again today. He tells me that he expects to receive the quota for Infantry School soon. I understand that there are so many recent applicants for this school that the applicants will be assembled before the Board of Reviewing Officers en masse, as it were, and be selected at that time.

Ted, Phil, and I intend to go into San Diego on Saturday and have a nice dinner, then an evening of bowling. I intend to put $20 in my bank account towards the purchase of my home.

Feel fairly good physically for a change, due to the two days of sleep I managed to acquire over the weekend.

Camp Callan, California
Barrack 2203
April 2, 1942
Bothered, the last two or three days, with a bad chest cold. It seemed somewhat improved today, however.

Ted and I went out to "shell mound" today, which is on the bluffs in Camp near the ocean. Later on, in the afternoon, we took a staff car and went into La Jolla and took measurements of the Civic Center playground, which is to be set up with Army materiel on Army Day. This, of course, was all S-3 work, although we did stop in La Jolla and have a cool and refreshing beer. Received a letter from Margie today in which she said she was coming to San Diego on Sunday to see her brother, Nicky (Navy), and that if I wasn't busy--. I wrote back a fictitious reply explaining that "I had to do some surveying on Sunday." No entanglements for me, thank you. In fact, I think a gradual cessation of my letters to her would be best, as I don't care to let this acquaintanceship develop into something serious.

Intend to take a shower tonight and sincerely hope that it will not cause this damnable athlete's foot to break out again, as it seems to have a tendency to do.

Camp Callan, San Diego, Calif.
Barracks 2203
April 3, 1942
Passed a moderately busy day at the office. Received a letter and a lovely knit sweater from Margaret (my cousin Elwood's wife) and also a letter from Jean Erickson, Ed Erickson's daughter. The "Free Mail" service started today. No more stamps required, except for airmail and packages. Sent Mother her two copies of the "Power of Attorney" that I had notarized today. I retained one copy myself. Also sent $20 to my bank today, so that makes a total of $35 towards the purchase of my home.

Ted and I were going into La Jolla tonight but changed our minds at the last moment and will go to the theatre instead. I think I will buy Bob a nice pen and pencil set for his birthday.

Evidently, my two extremely "formal" letters to Vivian achieved the desired results, as I have had no reply for some time, so—I guess—that is another interlude in my life that I can mark CLOSED.

Kaup and Barurby left today on their 5-day furloughs. I would take one soon, except that I am still waiting hopefully for some word from the O.C.S. How I pray that it goes through! It seems that is all I truly want.

EASTER SUNDAY
CAMP CALLAN, CALIFORNIA
BARRACKS 2203
APRIL 5, 1942

Had a very pleasant weekend with Ted and Phil. Went to the Tower Bowl and bowled about 6 games. Highest score—152. Not so good. Six of us pooled our finances and took a taxi back to Camp. Arrived back at Camp about 3 a.m.

Ted and I got up early and went to church in La Jolla. Although the services were Catholic, I enjoyed the services very much.

After church, we bowled two more games at the La Jolla Bowl and then had a nice T-bone steak dinner.

I bought Bob a nice Parker pen and will send it to him tomorrow. I hope he likes it—he's sure a swell brother.

Received my bank book back from La Jolla tonight, and I am really proud of the new $35 balance, but it looks pitifully small when compared to the $2500, which is the goal I have set for the purchase of my home.

Terribly tired tonight as we must have walked 20 miles last night and this morning. Have to write Mother <u>tomorrow</u>.

CAMP CALLAN, CALIFORNIA
BARRACKS 2203
APRIL 6, 1942

Ted and I went to the show last night. Not a great deal going at work today, so I wrote three letters, one to Mother, one to Harold, and one to Raff. Sent Bob's pen to him and also sent my Schick shaver home to see what could be done about repairing or trading it in on another one.

I think the new draftsman, Storm, is in for a "bad time," if he persists in his heavy drinking and not reporting for work on account of hangovers. Stevenson was pretty mad about it.

I felt awfully lonely this weekend, and tonight I feel the same—and tired and disgusted, too.

Received no mail at all today, which didn't help matters any. I wonder if Margie came to San Diego, yesterday, to see her brother?

Still no word on the O.C.S. Expect Major Cooley back on the first of next month, and it can't come too soon for me.

Camp Callan, California
Barracks 2203
April 8, 1942

Moving day in the S-3 today! Due to an increase in the amount of space allotted to us, we were all very busy moving desks, tables, lights, etc. It is arranged very nicely now, however.

Valerie is leaving for Chicago on Friday, and from rumors that I have heard, it looks very much as though I will have to take her place as stenographer to Colonel Taliaferro.

Received a letter from Mother, one from Margie, and one from Vivian. Vivian's was, thank goodness, just a friendly letter. Margie's was, too, and very pleasant. She evidently didn't come to San Diego on Sunday. I sent the Camp Callan *Oozlefinch* home to Mother today. Expect Kaup and Barurby back from furlough tomorrow. I am supposed to bowl on the 11th Group Bowling Team tomorrow. Only have about four bucks to last me the rest of the month. Wonder if I can make out okay?

Saw a very good show tonight, and it gave me a great deal to think about—such as <u>ideals</u>.

Camp Callan, Calif.
Barracks 2203
April 10, 1942

No mail at <u>all</u> today. I had to act as stenographer to Colonel Taliaferro all day, and imagine the same will hold true for the next two weeks until Valerie's return. Another man sent to the Infantry School today. When I questioned Major Robbins regarding this, he gave me the same old evasive stall: "You are sent upon the Adjutant General's approval—this man was sent from Ninth Corps Area."

We all went bowling last night (my score 133-93-123). Ended up at Cecil's Tavern where an amusing incident took place. The proprietor's wife had evidently had one too many, for she insisted that I bore some resemblance to Tyrone Power and insisted on buying for the entire group. The drinks were certainly appreciated, but I can't say that the drunken flattery was, because I am still undergoing a terrific amount of heckling on account of it.

Tonight I am again lonely and disgusted due to a series of happenings: (1) the O.C.S., (2) argument about ratings, (3) broke, (4) lonely, (5) to hell with it all.

Camp Callan, California
Camp Headquarters (S-3)
April 11, 1942

Saturday afternoon. I didn't have to, but as I had nothing better to do, I came over to the office and plan to write some letters. Still working for Colonel Taliaferro and am in charge of the Assistant's S-3's office this afternoon.

Major Stevenson seemed very solicitous this afternoon, inquiring as to what progress I am making on the O.C.S. application. (?)

Ted is doing a little private hell raising with Stevenson regarding his Staff-Sergeantry, which he was supposed to receive upon graduation from the Master Gunner School. Certainly don't blame him. He left this morning to spend the weekend in Los Angeles.

I guess about all the excitement that the weekend will hold for me is seeing the two "horse operas" at the Camp theatre.

Received a letter from Raff, and he tells me that the "Acme of Purity" is again working in San Francisco. So she is finally back on her old hunting grounds! Well, there should prove to be a few more ignorant saps, such as me, before she ultimately finds herself burnt out, as she suddenly will become aware of someday!

Camp Callan, California
Camp Headquarters (S-3)
April 12, 1942
1:14 P.M. (SUNDAY)

Again over at Headquarters, killing a few hours of this dreary weekend. I think I will go over to the barracks in a few moments and start my usual Sunday physical refurbishing (shave, shower, shampoo, etc., etc.). I hope the shower doesn't cause its usual effect of breaking this skin rash out, as it has done in the past.

No mail at all today. The show, last night, proved to be the height of something or other. Two of the rottenest pictures it has been my privilege to witness in some time. However, I am a glutton for punishment, as I plan to go this evening and see *The Courtship of Andy Hardy*.

I presume Kaup will arrive back from his furlough tomorrow morning.

Have heard no further word from Bob since he sold the car, and to be truthful, I am a little worried as to the final outcome of the sale. I hope he didn't have any trouble, as after all, he is rather inexperienced and of a trusting nature. Hope to hear from him soon, at any rate.

CAMP CALLAN, CALIF.
BARRACKS 2203
APRIL 13, 1942
5:35 P.M.

A terribly busy day! Worked for Colonel Taliaferro again today and had to distribute over 2,000 manuals. Had a big discussion about ratings with Major Stevenson, and from all that was said, I am still behind the eight ball. A few "interesting" facts that came to light during the discussion proved to be very bizarre. *** evidently obtained his high rating by a clever ruse—posing as a graduate of the Master Gunner School—when he has never been near the place. Far be it from me to disclose this fact, however. I prefer to obtain my rating by hard work and honest ability. Just one letter today, from Harold. Outside of that one item, no happenings of any importance, except for the fact that I am getting extremely fed-up with working as hard as I can, and then being neatly shelved when any ratings are issued. Still no word on the O.C.S., either, and yet, I don't dare take a furlough in case they assemble all candidates for interview.

The rash is okay, I guess. No repercussions from the shower.

CAMP CALLAN, CALIF.
BARRACKS 2203
APRIL 16, 1942
8:40 P.M.

Quite a few interesting events have occurred. Received a letter from Bob, which contained $350 by means of a cashier's check. He borrowed $50 with which to buy a Model A Ford. I promptly deposited the check in my account in La Jolla, which gives me a grand total of $385, at this writing, towards the purchase of my home. Felt a few pangs of regret, though, for the money represented the old 1937 Chevrolet, the thought of which brings to mind a host of memories. Some happy, some sad. I took my honeymoon in that car, and the final parting between my wife and I took place in it. Many were the happy, happy, evenings spent in its familiar interior, and many the tear that was also shed. The terribly lonely nights when I thought I couldn't go on and parked on a desolate knoll overlooking the lights of San Francisco and Oakland. I think, during those horrible nights, when a world seemed to be crashing in ruins at my feet that the old car seemed to comfort me by the very strength of its happy memories. When I first thought of selling it, it seemed as if I was selling part of myself, but then sensibly thought it was, after all, the most practical thing to do.

Perhaps the money derived from its sale may, by some miracle, provide the means of finding happiness, at last, in a home of my own. Even though I seem doomed to be forever a vagabond down the road of life, searching for something that seems to eternally elude my grasp- -that intangible, beautiful thing known as sweet contentment and a soul at peace with the world.

Don't feel so good tonight, and to tell the truth, a little despondent. Things are still sliding along at work. Still acting as secretary for Colonel Taliaferro. A little friction with Major Stevenson every now and then.

Still no word from the AGO about the O.C.S.

CAMP CALLAN, CALIF.
BARRACKS 2203
APRIL 17, 1941 [sic]

Not a great deal to do today—one or two stencils and letters for Colonel Taliaferro. He left for the summer home of Lt. Colonel John A. Scrugham, former Governor of the State of Nevada, and will not return until Monday. Meanwhile, I will have to act as secretary to Lt. Colonel Adams. Will also have to work tomorrow afternoon, as I compiled a new duty roster for the six men in the S-3 and decided to take the first turn.

Vernon Slichter made Staff Sergeant today, after being made Sergeant a month ago. So it can easily be seen that I am still "taking a beating" as far as ratings are concerned. Had a big argument with Major Stevenson about that subject and, frankly, told him that I thought it was unfair. I have more responsibility than any one of the enlisted men in Headquarters, and yet when ratings are issued, I am always left out.

Another man sent to Infantry School today (Ninth Corps Area Quota).

Ted tried vainly to get me to go to town with him tonight, but no dough, so I didn't go.

CAMP CALLAN, CALIFORNIA
BARRACKS 2203
APRIL 20, 1942
Another weekend endured. Went to town Saturday afternoon (left work about 3:30 p.m.) and did a little bowling, had four beers, and came home.

Sunday, we arose in time for breakfast (!), then played three games of volleyball, took a sunbath, and then had a nice chicken dinner. After dinner, Ted and I went over to the Signal Corps darkroom and developed a large group of pictures from some negatives we had been saving. I sent mine home immediately to have Mother put away for me. Later in the evening, we all went to the theater and saw *To the Shores of Tripoli*, a saga of the Marines—very good. And so to bed at 11:30 p.m. Passed a moderately busy day at work today—a total of eight new books arrived from Washington. Am trying to fix it up with the Range Officer so that I can fire the record course for .30-cal. Springfield and the .45 automatic pistol.

There was a rumor of a very "CONFIDENTIAL" letter, via the office grapevine, which stated that all men under 35 at Camp Callan would be shipped out by July 15, 1942, for presumably, foreign duty. If this is true, and I hope it is, it pleases me only too well. However, I find that one thing is definite. I cannot be "shipped out" until I am given a definite answer, one way or the other, on my O.C.S. application. I hope they inform me soon.

I received my bankbook back from La Jolla this morning and am now the proud possessor of $385 towards the ultimate purchase of a home of my own.

My eyes have been bothering me considerably of late—and have determined to quit smoking when my present supply is gone—to see if it will remedy this situation, and also if it will help to increase my weight (as I think it will).

I could get a furlough next month, I suppose, if I wanted it; but I just can't bear the thought of going home in the grade of corporal. I hope, when Major Cooley returns on the first, that he will do something about the ratings. It certainly makes me disgusted and angry when I think of how the S-3 has been "passed over" in this respect.

Camp Callan, San Diego, Calif.
Barracks 2203
April 21, 1942

Lying on my bunk looking out over the shimmering expanse of the blue Pacific spread in a wondrous panorama beneath my window, I think many thoughts. For today, many things occurred. The first, and of primary importance, the allotment of ratings for the HQ 11th Tng. Gp. came out today. Eventually, this afternoon, Colonel Taliaferro stated that "he thought he could make me a Technician 4th Grade"! Truly a magnanimous gesture! After <u>fourteen</u> months' service in the Army of the United States, they see fit to reward me with a "jaw-bone" sergeantry! In reality, it is a step down for me, as a Technician 4th Grade, under the old specialist ratings, was the same as a Private First Class, 1st Class Specialist.

May I state, with utmost sincerity, that it is not the money involved, it is the downright injustice of the thing. All of the men who entered Camp Callan at the same time I did are line sergeants or better, and even some men who entered four months after I did.

Take Slichter, for instance. Because of the fact that he was recently married, he was made a staff sergeant last Saturday, yet I was informed just prior to that, that the quota of staff sergeants for Camp Callan was full.

I said nothing to Colonel Taliaferro when he informed me of this "breathtaking" news, but I typed a letter stating why I would rather remain a corporal then become a jawbone sergeant. It was a frank letter stating quite accurately my viewpoint of this situation, and I gave it to Major Stevenson. He was, shall I say, "hypocritically sympathetic," but handed me the same old drivel that has been drooling from his mouth for months: "There is nothing I can do about it."

In the letter, I asked which was more important to the Army, a man's hard work and earnest endeavor to advance himself or the fact that a man "had recently married."

I do know that I don't want their damned cast-off rating, and if they make me take it, I sure as hell won't wear the damn stripe unless I have to. I don't know how this damned mess will work out. I suppose I've cooked my goose plenty by being so frank in my utterances, but I don't give a damn. I thought the Army was a man's outfit, and I find it is based on bootlicking, favoritism, and ratings go to the man who can spill the best sob story.

To hell with the whole cheap set-up!

CAMP CALLAN, CALIFORNIA
PLANS AND TRAINING OFFICE
6:15 P.M.

An eventful day, or perhaps I should say, the past two days. Due to the horrible row Ted and I raised about ratings, Kaup decided to go to the C.A. O.C.S., which would leave the Technical Sergeantry open for Ted. He is entitled to it, I guess, but I still don't see why I am supposed to be satisfied on a Technician 4th Grade. After all, Major Cooley and Stevenson promised me that I would be made a sergeant major, which carries a staff sergeant's rating.

Major Stevenson and Colonel Knape were relieved from the S-3 today and placed in the Officers Replacement Pool, which is to be shipped out on Field Duty soon. To be truthful, I rather hated to see the Major go—we had some beautiful arguments and towards the last, he really did get in there and fight for some ratings for us. (Not that it did any good.)

I really don't know whether *** sincerely intends to go to school or not. Personally, I think it is one of his famous subterfuges and think he is really gunning for a master sergeantry.

Learned also that Major Cooley had been promoted, today, to a Lieutenant Colonel. I am sincerely glad to hear it; he is a fine officer and a real man.

Received a letter from Strahl today, and his description of the O.C.S. is certainly hair raising, but nevertheless, I am determined to go if it is at all possible.

I have also made up my mind that <u>I am not going home on furlough until I have been promoted</u> to something better than a Tech. 4th Grade. I just couldn't do it, that's all. <u>Fourteen months</u> of <u>hard</u> <u>work</u>, for <u>what</u>?

Strahl's mother, Melanie, also wrote today and expressed again, her invitation for me to come to Los Angeles and visit them this coming payday. I am almost tempted to do it. It is so unbearably lonely and nerve wracking here. San Diego is composed chiefly of cheap beer halls, cheap dances, and cheaper women, so there is certainly no advantage in going to San Diego instead.

Well, much can happen before then, so I think I will bide my time for the present, and we shall see what I write in here after payday.

<u>T-H-E D-A-Y</u>!
Camp Headquarters (S-3)
Camp Callan, Calif.
April 25, 1942

It is here! My chance has finally arrived! I am leaving for Fort Benning, Georgia, this coming Monday night. It all happened yesterday. A quota for the Infantry School came in over the Teletype, and Major Robbins told me to get ready, as I "was on my way." Thrilled and excited as I am, I realize full well what faces me in the ensuing three months. But I solemnly vow, here and now, that I will study and apply myself with every atom of earnestness in my being.

April 26, 1942

Continuing from yesterday. It doesn't look as though I will have very much time in which to visit Mother. If I leave here early enough tomorrow, I will arrive home sometime Tuesday and will have to leave for Georgia, either Thursday or Friday. Well, I will have to make the best of it.

The fellows in the S-3 office all "chipped in" and bought me a beautiful $15 Parker pen as a farewell gift, and it really put a lump in my throat. They certainly are a swell bunch of fellows.

Ted, Phil, and I went out last night and celebrated the occasion "quite appropriately." Arrived back at the barracks via taxi at about 4 a.m.

In preparation for the intensive course of study that faces me at Benning, I am taking along a large group of manuals that I will need the most. On the trip back, I will have to <u>Study</u>, <u>Study</u>, <u>Study</u>, especially the I.D.R.

I really have only one fear that perturbs me—my <u>eyesight</u>. At the completion of the course, we will be given a "final-type physical examination," and it is <u>very rigid I understand</u>.

Tomorrow will tell the story. If the orders come out soon enough, I will leave shortly thereafter. Don't know when or how often I will be able to write herein but will probably find some time.

Perhaps, who knows, this may be the beginning of a change in my luck—and some of my dreams and ideals will yet materialize.

Pacific Limited
En Route to Georgia
May 1, 1942
Here I am, finally on my way after a rather hectic "4-day delay en route." Had to borrow Bob Rasmussen's car to go up to Sonora. Mother, Bob, and Harold were fine. Mother took the news fine. Came back to Oakland yesterday, and Art Morgan insisted that I remain overnight and use his Lincoln-Zephyr to escort Vivian out in.

I never knew that I had such wonderful friends. They treat me just like one of the family, and if you could have seen Baby Venita throwing kisses to me as the train left the station—it really did something to me.

As the train wound around the shores of San Francisco Bay, I passed many scenes that were familiar in my childhood and many places where Virginia and I used to go fishing. How odd is life, that I should now ride down those rails on my way to what?

My knees are shaky, and I feel just a little scared at the thought of Fort Benning, but <u>I will not fail</u>, and I pray the Good Lord that he will see fit to give me the necessary determination and—pure luck—to get through.

Vivian, herself, has changed immensely, and I guess it was fortunate that I had such a short delay, else I might have weakened on my matrimonial taboo. She was really very pretty, and God help me, I know she really loves me. Yet I can't bring myself to try again the horror of matrimony.

Didn't see Lola or Lena at all. No one seems to know where Lola is living, and Lena wouldn't give a damn where I was going anyway.

This school is really the first thing in my life that I prayed for, and that I received, so please God, help me to graduate, and I promise that I will study and work with all the intensity that I possess.

This train is no streamliner, as can be judged by the writing. [*Scribbles on the page.*]

Denver, Colorado
7:30 A.M.
May 3, 1942
It seemed to take this train forever to reach Denver. Passed through Cheyenne, Wyoming, late last night (where John Strahl is currently stationed at <u>his</u> O.C.S. course). Judging from the large amount of snow

in that city, I may state that I am well pleased to be on my way to the Sunny South.

Perhaps it is due chiefly to my usual overactive imagination, but my eyes have been bothering me so much, lately, that I am extremely worried as to the effect this would have on my eventual graduation. One consolation—I know for a fact that Strahl's eyes are much worse than mine. However, the fact that I am trying to get in a combat unit, whereas, the Quartermaster is a supply unit, may make some difference. If I fail to graduate, I can assure anyone that the sole reason will be—my eyes—but not for lack of study or intensive work. Strangely enough, however, I have a strange premonition that I will be successful. I will!

Didn't get a berth last night and did I regret it! Some old hen behind me possessed the Queen of all snores, and her inimitable mimicry of the wail of a banshee continued throughout the long night. I looked back at her once, and her mouth was so far open, I could have stuck a pair of my G.I. shoes in it.

I will have to change trains at Kansas City and again at St. Louis. Certainly hope that I arrive at Fort Benning on the 5th, as it would leave a hell of an impression, showing up late.

My nerves seem to have quieted down now, and I am not quite so shaky regarding the school.

It seems as though I am continually trying to peer into the future, but I can't help but wonder just what destiny holds in store for me in Georgia.

Another thought—Virginia's cheapness did serve a purpose. It provided me with an incentive to advance and better myself, at any cost, just to show that lying example of cheapness, if nothing else.

St. Louis, Missouri
L&N Railroad
May 4, 1942

Nearing the last stages of my journey now. I bought a Pullman in Kansas City last night and had a restful night's sleep. Woke up nearing St. Louis this morning.

I seem to be spending quite a bit more money than I anticipated, but this is unavoidable. At any rate, I shall soon make up all that this has cost me, as it will be for my home. I opened a <u>joint</u> bank account in Sonora, and Mother will make the deposits for me. Only have a balance of $235 now, but I will soon have it over $500 if I have anything to say. My nervousness over the approaching ordeal at Fort Benning has given way to a strange confidence in myself. I will do my very best and that is all I can do. At the same time, I realize how very fortunate I am in being chosen for this school. It is reliably estimated that it costs the government around $2500 to put a man through the school.

MAY 5, 1942
COMPANY 12
2ND TRAINING REGIMENT
FORT BENNING, GA.
Well, here I am, and is it hot! I was issued my blankets, a chair, pillow, etc. The issuance of books, rifle, belts, etc., will take place later on tonight or tomorrow. This is real Army life I notice—strict military courtesy and discipline. According to rumor, school will not start until Monday, but then, according to the curricula, I am definitely in for it.

Basic training—marching, bayonet drill, drill and command, and study, study, study for weeks and weeks. But I asked for it, and it is my big chance to make good, so I pray to God to give me the necessary stamina and knowledge to graduate successfully.

I am not so worried as I was about my eyes. Some of the other fellows have eyesight of 20-70 and worse and wear those heavy-lensed glasses, so I feel convinced that if they can get by, I feel sure I can.

This is an enormous fort. Camp Callan could be put in the area where the refuse cans are kept. Saw some of the parachute troops in action today, too.

FORT BENNING, GEORGIA
MAY 6, 1942
Hotter than the furnaces of Hades today. With the usual Army flair for efficiency, we had to turn in all equipment that was issued yesterday, as our group of 26 men was transferred to Company 20, which is a great deal farther out in the sticks.

Have become a little better oriented and have a good idea of exactly what is in store for me. Believe me, the curricula are really drastic. I am so nervous, I shake continually. In fact, I may as well be frank, I am scared to death! The reason is obvious—I am so far behind the other students— no basic training, don't even know how to roll a pack, know nothing at all about infantry or the weapons used, whereas most of these students are all from the Infantry and are well up on those subjects. Also, before graduation, there is the far-famed "Final Type Physical Examination," which includes a four-hour X-ray examination.

Another interesting bit of information: At times, when least expected, a man will be called out in front of 200 men and be told "to take over," which means giving commands for close order drill and setting up exercises. In fact, he is expected to take the place of the Company Commander. The reason for this is obvious, to see if you have the qualities of initiative and leadership necessary in an officer. Well, this is a very serious matter to me, as I will have to overcome, <u>almost at once</u>, my weakness of a retiring nature, or shall we say timidity and stage fright? Also, it is very necessary that all commands be issued in a stentorian tone, and I have a low-modulated tone of voice.

In about our 7th week of training, when we study field fortifications, it will be necessary for each man to dig himself a "foxhole" and then let a 13-ton tank run over him.

Finally arrived in Company 20 and was assigned to "Bed 10." Had chow in our new mess hall, and our new officers seem a great deal more pleasant than those in Company 12. From questioning older candidates, we learn that there are three dates on which a candidate can be discharged as ineligible—the fourth week, the eighth week, and the tenth week. How I hope and pray that I will graduate. I have never wanted anything so much in my life. I will make good, though, I <u>promise</u>.

Filled out five or six huge questionnaires as to my personal history today and chose Australia and South America as my choice of stations, in the event I receive my commission. All candidates are addressed as "Gentlemen." Guess school will start for sure on Monday, and then hard, man killing drill, obstacle course, maneuvers, tactical field problems, learn the Garand rifle, the .30- and .50-caliber machine guns, anti-tank guns, fortifications, map reading, social customs, and a million other items.

God, I earnestly pray for every bit of initiative, stamina, knowledge, and foresight that you can now give me, for there will be no failure on my part as to willingness, hard study and work, and the desire to be an Officer.

Fort Benning, Ga.
May 7, 1942
Torn by doubts and fears tonight. These vicious rumors are still

circulating around, and we received our maps and equipment today, and Man O Man, that Map Reading Course really has me worried, due to my famous lack of mathematics; and it also involves the use of the alidade, the protractor, and the compass—all of which are mysteries to me. Also, our first week's schedule came out today, and we have physical training tomorrow, which may mean that I, or anyone, may be called in front of the platoon to give commands, which I do not know. (No basic training, thanks to Callan.)

At times I feel that I haven't a chance, and yet I am so damn mad, now that I finally got here, that I will study like mad out of pure stubbornness. I will graduate. At any rate, all I can do is pray that they will give the recruit drill in easy stages. Lights out, now.

FORT BENNING, GA.
OFFICER CANDIDATE SCHOOL
MAY 9, 1942
In our introductory message from our Battalion Commander, he stated that the lessons would be thrown at us in such a manner that it would be the same as trying to stop the flow of water from a fire hydrant. This statement has certainly proved true! Never in my life have I had information literally thrown at me and then expected to absorb all of it.

Yesterday, we had physical training and infantry drill. Surprisingly enough, my old (10 years ago) R.O.T.C. training has stood me in good stead. So far, I have not committed any blunders, and the CO actually complimented the Company on its fine, snappy performance! (!) Today we had 2 lectures and a training film and then drill and command. This was the one item I had dreaded most, to get out in front of a bunch of men and yell commands at them. Volunteers were asked for, and after one had volunteered for a five-minute stint, one reluctant, scared-looking candidate was called forth. I knew then that it would be better for me to volunteer in order to make a better impression as to my qualities of leadership, so I did so, although my heart was in my throat. I came out fairly well, although I committed a few errors, and the most important thing, I gained a little confidence.

This school is, in fact, a second West Point. Talk about discipline! We are forced to walk at attention at all times, and when standing, must stand "at ease" with chests out and shoulders back at all times—or else—the ever-present threat of "gigs." (Too many of which will flunk a man from school.) Poker-like rigidity is demanded when at attention in the ranks, despite sweat, flies, sun, and heat. Beds must be absolutely <u>perfect</u> and shelves arranged very strictly in a set formula. Shoes must be like mirrors, haircuts 1-1/2 inches, clothes spotless, etc. We were issued Garand M1 rifles, and I know how to take one apart already. We will drill with the rifles next week.

I know that my drill and commands will have to improve 100%, and my academic work lots more, before I will stand a chance of obtaining my commission, but at least I shall do my very best.

No mail as yet, not that I will have time to answer any. Still praying that my eyes will not continue to bother me as they have. They are really getting bad, and I haven't time to get my glasses readjusted.

Fort Benning, Georgia
Sunday, May 10, 1942

Bourke and I ran the obstacle course five times last night, and as a result, I was so stiff and sore today, it was torture to move. I didn't get up for breakfast but lay in bed until about noon. I have felt awfully funny all day. My eyes seem to be getting worse from day to day, and they really have me worried now. My glasses are of no avail whatever, as they no longer "fit" my eyes.

When we have marksmanship, compass reading, etc., what then? Well, we start our map reading course tomorrow, so God help me on it. And we also have some more drill and command training. I practiced a little on that tonight, though.

Have received no mail, as yet, but I guess it takes lots longer to get all the way from California.

I hope to God my eyes get a little better tonight, as I will really need them tomorrow.

Fort Benning, Ga.
Monday, May 11, 1942

Really tired tonight! Lectures, training, films, marching, physical training, etc. I commanded a squad today, but evidently committed one blunder (standing the men in the sun too long). Don't know whether I got gigged on that or not. I did receive one gig on the inspection this morning (pillow not folded neatly). I am on the list to command the squad tomorrow, too.

Today marks my <u>second</u> day without one cigarette. I can tell now, how very much the habit had a grip on me.

I still feel rather confused about the whole course. They are throwing the lessons at us so fast that a fellow hardly knows which way to turn. It is a rather odd situation—this being at school—sometimes. I feel all pepped up, as if I could do anything they ask, and other times it is most discouraging. But I will not weaken in my resolve. At the very least, I shall do my very best.

Have not received one letter from anyone since my arrival at Fort Benning on May 5th. Certainly hope that I get some soon, as I need a little cheering up, I think.

Fort Benning, Ga.
May 12, 1942
No gigs today that I know of, although I didn't do any too good commanding the squad today. We had a really stiff course in map reading today (which was all Greek to me!). Had physical training this afternoon, and I really believe that this violent routine of physical training is starting to build me up. I was scarcely recognizable, what with a 1-1/2" haircut and my face already quite sunburned. We drill tomorrow with the new Garand rifle. (By the way, I haven't lifted a rifle for 10 years and am completely ignorant of the new manual of arms.) I worked until 9:30 p.m. on the map-reading course, and even then, didn't finish all the questions. What I have already stated previously in this manual is starting to hold true—I have become so disgusted at the way they cram totally unknown information down your throat and then expect you to know it immediately, that I almost felt like calling it quits today. But I will not be a quitter. I will see this thing through to the finish and do my best, and then if I do not pass, and it is termed a disgrace, well, I guess it will be a disgrace! But oh God, how I pray to pass!

Fort Benning, Georgia
May 13, 1942
Again no gigs today, but the map-reading course is getting to be something fierce. However, I am beginning to assimilate some of it, so I feel a little better. We had our first drill with rifles today, and was it hot! Wow! I wonder with what fortitude I will be able to withstand the terrific heat of the summer months.

I had been wondering what would happen if I managed to graduate without having much experience in leading a platoon. Well,

I won't have to worry! We are going to have lots of that experience starting tomorrow with <u>Bourke</u>, which means that I will get it the next day. Well, I've got to overcome this self-consciousness some way, and it may as well be <u>now</u>. For I can assure anyone, my determination to graduate is as strong as when I first applied to the Board.

My morale is dropping like hell. No mail at <u>all</u> since I left Oakland. Sure wish someone would write.

I had to buy $11.76 worth of suntan uniforms "to be used when we are officers" they say. Also, $20 worth of equipment to be taken out of our pay. My bank account sure took a beating on this course, but I have 2 months' pay coming, plus $63 travel pay—I hope—to make it up.

Fort Benning, Ga.
O.C. School
May 14, 1942

Tougher and more grueling, day by day, grows the map-reading course. So much of it is far over my head that I don't know what to think. We are going to have our General Test on it next week sometime, and that will tell the story. I intend to "cram" over the weekend, with Bourke's help, and can then only ask for God's assistance. We have no command training schedule for the balance of this week, so I will also have an opportunity to brush up on that subject. Despite the galling disgrace that I will feel in my own mind if I fail to graduate, one enormous benefit that I will have obtained from this training is the immense physical improvements. Despite the hard, dirty work, poor food, terrific heat, and utter weariness, I am feeling better physically than I have for years.

The administration course is a very fierce course, too. It would be astounding to an outsider to see with what rapidity and in what quantities they are shoving this information down our throats and then expect us to retain it all.

No mail as yet from home, and I certainly feel lost and lonely and sometimes wonder why in hell I am struggling so hard.

Ft. Benning, Ga.
O.C. School
May 15, 1942

Another tough day consisting of lectures and training films. We will have the General Test for Map Reading on Tuesday (after a trip to Frey

Ridge for practical use of maps on Monday). I will have to cram to an unholy extent on Sunday in order to even skim through.

So far, Thibodeaux is the only man in our barracks to whom I have taken an active dislike, although there is one other loud-mouthed Jerk who is quite annoying. As I mentioned beforehand, there was no command training scheduled until next week, but I volunteered for a little more training in that subject tomorrow afternoon (normally free.) <u>I need it</u>.

Received one card and one letter, both dated April 27th, so they meant nothing, as I had seen both parties when last home. Certainly hope that I receive some <u>current</u> mail <u>soon</u>. Or I wonder if people give a damn?

We will study the Garand rifle next week, and that will include firing it out on the range. <u>Hope</u> my eyes hold out. Big inspection tomorrow, so I cleaned, stripped, and oiled my rifle completely. Well, think I will turn in now, as these Georgia latrine flies aren't conducive to literary efforts. Tomorrow?

Fort Benning, Ga.
May 16, 1942
Lectures all morning and drill and command training in the afternoon. Today marked the third time I had been out in front of a squad, and to my amazement, my knees hardly shook at all on the ensuing drill. After drill, Bourke and I hiked far out into the woods and spent about two hours shouting vociferous and stentorian commands at each other from a distance of about 60 feet. I gained many helpful hints on this important technique by doing this, and we intend to do it tomorrow. We also intend to study <u>maps</u> in preparation for the dreaded "G.T."

Came home and found a letter from Vivian, the first letter from anyone since my arrival here, and was it welcome! Also wrote Mother and Bob. Certainly pray that I will be able to get by in the coming Map Test. I have got to study more on the 22-5 Manual, <u>too</u>.

I believe that I am gaining weight, as it is readily apparent to these men, and they are almost strangers. More tomorrow—too tired for more tonight, as we hiked about 5 miles this afternoon.

Fort Benning, Ga.
May 17, 1942
Spent all morning in the barracks waiting for our interview, but the

interviewing officer didn't get around to Bourke and me, so about 1:30 p.m., I had the Mess Sergeant fix Bourke and I a nice lunch, and we hiked out into the woods to the secluded spot we found and spent about five hours on Map Reading. I learned a great deal more about the subject, and also, I have managed to obtain a glimpse of several of the dreaded G.T.'s They are not so terribly hard, providing ours are made in the same fashion, so my mind is a little more at ease on that subject. However, I will have to study my conventional signs a little more.

I was Platoon Charge of Quarters today, so I will have to get the men up at 5:30 tomorrow morning. Felt awfully tired today, don't know why. We wear leggings, open shirts tomorrow and will board the *Chattanooga* (narrow gauge) and will go out in the field for practical map work all morning. I think that will be some fun, except for this blazing Georgia sun.

FORT BENNING, GA.
MAY 18, 1942
Another hard day done away with. Fieldwork this morning, with the compass, alidade, and all other map-reading equipment. I found it all very interesting. Then a drill period of administration followed by two hours of hasty field fortifications. Came home tonight and found three letters, one from Ted, one from Dave, and one from Margie, which had been forwarded from Camp Callan. Answered Ted and Dave in one letter, then studied maps and coordinates for four hours.

Well, tomorrow is the dreaded G.T. on Map Reading, and I can only pray that I will pass. A good portion of my eventual graduation will hinge on that factor.

Still no mail from home, and I am beginning to wonder. It seems to be that something must be wrong, or Mother would have answered the three letters that I have written.

Still feeling very good physically, and my eyes haven't bothered me for some time. Drill and command tomorrow, but I don't feel worried, at least not as much as I did at first.

FT. BENNING, GA.
MAY 19, 1942
Well, we had the long-awaited nerve-shattering General Test this afternoon. To be truthful, I don't know just how I came out on it. They pulled a fast one and used a strange map with tricky coordinates, which

threw me "off the beam" for a while. I know I got all the conventional signs, and I think, most of the coordinates, but can't say for sure. I <u>know</u> I botched up a couple of the mathematical computation questions. Can only pray that I <u>passed</u>.

Received a letter from Mother today, the first since I left. Had drill and command training this afternoon, but I had no assignment. However, of my own volition, I intend to get in quite a bit of that before I am assigned.

A show was put on in "Harmony Holler" for the benefit of Company 20 by the Negro Service Section, and I mean, they really had some talent.

Hope I get some more mail tomorrow. It seems that is about all I have to look forward to anymore.

Fort Benning, Ga.
Saturday Evening
May 23, 1942

The pace of instruction has increased at such a tremendous rate that I have not had time to write. We had another G.T. on the Garand rifle, and I think I passed, although I am not sure. We fired the range (1000") yesterday and will fire on the 200-yd. range on Monday. All next week from Tuesday on will be taken up by the .30-caliber machine gun. Everyone in the barracks received another gig today for having a dirty rifle, although I worked until 11 p.m. on mine. (Lt. Deetz said that these gigs today would not count, except the star gigs.) I haven't received a star gig as yet and earnestly pray that I don't receive any, as they are the ones that disqualify.

One man, so far, who couldn't take it. He threw up the sponge and dropped out today.

Wrote three letters tonight. I understand Gillingham is coming back to school on June 1st. He seems to be very optimistic.

Think I will let the rifle cleaning go until tomorrow and will get a good night's sleep tonight.

Fort Benning, Ga.
May 24, 1942

I worked 5 hours today on that damn rifle, and then we go out tomorrow morning and will get it all dirty again. Also put all my O.D. uniforms and fatigue clothes (blue) in my barracks bay, shined all my shoes, and cleaned out my footlocker. Received a letter from Mother today, and Bob is evidently going to enlist in the Air Corps. Well, that kid has all my blessing and best wishes, as he is the world's finest brother, and I am certainly proud of him.

I asked Mother if she would arrange to have my household goods freighted up to Sonora, as I have quite a few valuable items that I treasure quite dearly. They were all I managed to salvage out of my "great" marriage.

No other mail at all, and I sure wish I had received more. Bourke and I are going out and run the obstacle course in a few minutes to get into practice for the time when we will have to run it with a rifle and combat pack.

I may state at this time that I have never felt so good, physically, in all my life. This, in spite of the fact that I have never before had to endure such hard and arduous physical work.

Ft. Benning, Ga.
May 26, 1942

Faster and faster the tempo of instruction increases. We fired all day yesterday out on the Rifle Range, and I missed gaining the sharpshooter's qualification by only 7 points. However, I did make a marksman's rating, so that isn't so terrible. My shoulder was almost a solid black-and-blue color from the continuous kick of the Garand. To cap it all, we had to fire for four hours this morning on moving targets out on the Antiaircraft Range. It was pure torture until my shoulder finally became numb. We start on the .30-caliber machine guns tomorrow, and we will have that subject for the balance of the week. I'm sure praying to God for assistance on that course, as it is a very technical and rugged course, and one of which I know absolutely nothing at all.

Margie sent me a large picture of herself, yesterday, and it certainly is a beautiful picture. I can't imagine why she sent it, but believe me; I will certainly make sure I continue to sign my letters, "Your friend." No more of the feminine sex for me! I am going to take a shower and turn in early tonight, as that range just about exhausted me physically.

Fort Benning, Ga.
May 27, 1942

The Browning .30-caliber heavy machine gun was the *piece de resistance* today. We started out with assembly and disassembly, functioning of the parts, and then had two hours of machine gun drill, including such pleasing items as carrying the heavy tripod on your back at a dead run, lying prone on the ground, and assembling the gun. To cap it all, the drill was conducted during a pouring rain, and we had to slide in the prone position into a gooey mixture of mud and sand. I have been the squad leader of our squad (12 men) all this week. We received the grades of the G.T. on Map Reading today and am very happy to state that I passed with a grade of Satisfactory. There are only two grades—Satisfactory and Unsatisfactory. I only missed four questions out of 39 questions, so I presume I passed with an average score, at least.

Found out tonight that we will find out <u>definitely</u> if we are going to be commissioned or not, in our 10<u>th</u> week. So I will know the story in seven more weeks. In the meantime, this machine gun course seems to be very technical and difficult. The famous Lt. Winthrop Rockefeller is one of our instructors in this subject.

FT. BENNING, GA.
MAY 29, 1942

Fired the Browning machine gun today and spent all day out on the hot range. I didn't do so well in the preliminary firing, as I managed to get the traversing and elevating wheel mixed. However, that firing was not for record—that will be tomorrow, so I hope that I can qualify.

Next week's schedule arrived today and what a set-up! I will need every bit of initiative, stamina, and luck that I can possibly muster. We will have combat problems, tactics, light (air-cooled) machine-gun firing, run the obstacle course, and hours of drill and command training.

Received a check for $65 in lieu of my travel pay. This, of course, doesn't begin to repay me for what I spent on the trip out here, but I shall send that home and the majority of my two months' pay so that my bank balance will again be to its original figure and further on towards the purchase of my <u>own home</u>.

No mail at all today.

Lights out, so no more tonight.

FORT BENNING, GA.
MAY 30, 1942

Fired for record on the M.G. Range today, and I managed to qualify with nine points to spare. Should have done better, but yesterday's foolish *faux pas* on the traversing knob lowered my score so much that it was impossible to bring it much higher.

    Wrote letters all evening and sent Mother the check for $65, which I requested that she bank for me. Next week's schedule still has me worried a lot, but I <u>will</u> get by! Platoon drill by individuals is starting now, and I expect my assignment either the latter part of this week or the first of the fifth week.

    Observed a very interesting demonstration of anti-mechanized defense measures. Some of the mines, loaded with 6 pounds of T.N.T., were set off. I might add they were quite impressive.

    A letter from Ted and one from Hubie. Hubie is a good egg. Sure hope he decides to come back here.

    If I never wanted anything in my life, I want to graduate from this school. In spite of my fears, I seem to have some inner voice that assures me that I will. I will, no doubt, have cause to ascertain, on August 7th, whether this premonition was true or not.

FT. BENNING, GA.
SUNDAY MORNING
MAY 31, 1942

I have spread a blanket on the lawn at the side of the barracks and am absorbing some of this famous Dixie Sun. Most of the fellows went into Columbus last night and indulged in some form of nightlife. Funny thing, but I can gain just as much relaxation hiking around in these Georgia pinewoods and taking a sunbath. There isn't much logic in visiting Columbus, as on Saturday nights, its population is composed of 99% military personnel, and frankly, I see enough of military life during the week.

    I can't help but ponder upon the strangeness of life. Here I worry upon the possibility of my graduation almost continuously, yet according to my theory of life, would I have been sent back here in the first place if destiny had not decreed beforehand that I would be successful? I am aware, of course, that my eventual graduation depends almost wholly upon the initiative and qualities of leadership that I am to demonstrate. May I state, however (at the risk of being taken for a weak sister), that such things as commanding a platoon of men and delivering speeches in front of 200 men came awfully hard to a man who had done neither.

Another puzzling factor in my life—my greatest wish is to have a happy marriage and children, yet, although I realize both Margie and Vivian are two very fine women, the thought of marriage with either is impossible. Am I then so much of a dreamer that I will hesitate and delay until all possibility of a happy marriage is lost? In analyzing these feelings, though, I realize that my hesitancy is caused by two factors: (1) the fear, which I cannot kill, of making another horrible mistake, as I did the first time, and (2) the uncertainty of my future life. While I would have enough financial security to do so if I graduate, what of my life after the war? For this war, as all wars do, must come to an end sometime, and then, providing I come through safely, God knows I will have no job, no trade, and no profession. So then?

All these are questions only the boundless, mysterious future can answer, and I suppose they will be—in good time.

INFANTRY SCHOOL
FORT BENNING, GA.
JUNE 1, 1942
Can't say that I feel any too cheerful tonight. We fired the air-cooled Browning machine gun today, and much to my amazement, I qualified as an Expert Machine Gunner with a score of 232. This makes me feel very happy, as that is the highest qualification one can get with that weapon. But, we had a very strict General Test on the machine gun this afternoon, and I am quite sure I missed at least 6 parts of questions. My correct answers are far in the majority, but whether this will keep me from failing the test or not, I do not know.

The flies that infest our barracks are becoming simply terrible! They not only are a particularly vicious type of fly, but multiply by thousands.

Tomorrow, we start the first day on defilade fire, direct and indirect laying of the machine gun, and here again, I need all the guidance the Good Lord can extend, as that subject brings back my old nemesis—mathematics. I can only pray for success and wonder just what I will write in here two months hence. For then, I will know, one way or the other.

INFANTRY SCHOOL
FORT BENNING, GA.
JUNE 2, 1942
Still in a rather despondent mood. We had a long (4 hr.) session on

"combat tactics in supply" this afternoon, and to be frank, it was over my head. It was cheering to note, however, that it also affected the majority of the others that way. We ran the obstacle course today, plus a hard morning of physical exercises, rifle drill, and games. We have an average of two fellows a day who faint in ranks, from heat prostration.

We start the dreaded "theory of indirect and direct laying of the machine gun" tomorrow. We also understand that the really vigorous aspect of this training starts tomorrow. What we have had up to now has been only a warm-up. Tomorrow starts the real work of carrying an 80-pound M.G. tripod and gun up and down the dry, dusty hills of Benning. Had an interview with Lt. Deetz this morning, and the only thing he cautioned me on was the fact that "my voice and command were a little weak." ----?

INFANTRY SCHOOL
FT. BENNING, GA.
JUNE 3, 1942

Eight hours of the "theory of direct and indirect laying of the M.G." out on Galloway Range today. Tonight I am in an exhausted state, both mentally and physically. Besides listening to long lectures, which were, frankly, all Greek to me, we had all marching and exercises executed at the double time. During our usual 10-minute rest period, we were double timed to a point some half-mile distant and put through <u>10</u> minutes of some of the most strenuous exercises I ever experienced. All this in a broiling sun. Result? Over eight men sick in quarters tonight and the balance in a sad shape. I managed to stick it out, and frankly, I relish this phase of the training. For as one of the officers stated, "This is where the mice and men are separated."

As to my mental condition, I am afraid that things look awfully black. Due to the enormous amount of mathematical calculus, algebraic terms, and numerous formulas it is essential to know, I seem lost. I just can't seem to grasp the huge amount of information, which is thrown at us. We will, I understand, have the <u>General Test</u> on this subject next Tuesday, and even with a prodigious amount of study, which I have outlined for myself every night and over the weekend, I do not see how I can possibly assimilate enough to pass the G.T. Is this, then, the answer to all my hard work and the dream I have formulated for the past year? Is this, like all my other dreams, to go sliding into the dust of oblivion?

No matter how my friends protest to the contrary, I just couldn't stand the disgrace of "flunking out" of this school. I could never face them again. It is no consolation to me to know that many other men here are in the same boat.

Again, as so often mentioned in the past, my only hope is to pray to God with every atom of sincerity in my soul, that I will, by some miracle, be successful in this venture. God knows how, but—

Only a letter from Valerie today, but I am of a mind to discontinue my darned correspondence. To hell with it. No one seems to care enough to write me, so why should I?

OFFICERS SCHOOL
FORT BENNING, GA.
JUNE 4, 1942
Four hours this morning on the use and nomenclature of the aiming circle, the rangefinder, and the BC scope. This afternoon, four hours more of the "Theory of Indirect Laying," which, frankly, is composed of algebraic functions, calculus, and intricate angles. I think I managed to absorb a little of it today, but believe me, I will have to "bone" on this subject at a terrific pace over the weekend.

Another pleasant thought—this being our fourth week, this weekend will take place the "ceremony" of all candidates "grading" each other as to desirable characteristics, attitude, ability, drawbacks, etc. This, also, is a critical phase of the school, deciding, in many cases, the ultimate graduation of many a candidate.

Received a letter from Margie today, the total extent of my mail. I am so stiff and sore tonight that I can scarcely move, and tomorrow we have 8 solid hours out in the broiling sun on Galloway Range, which means, of course, double time, drills, exercises, and hard work.

After last night's outburst herein, I have again clenched my teeth and am determined that I will get through.

OFFICERS SCHOOL
FT. BENNING, GEORGIA
JUNE 6, 1942
Had a complete day of "indirect laying" out on Galloway Range yesterday, complete with firing of tracers at ranges up to 1500 yards. This morning we had an inspection in ranks, which I passed, fortunately, and then had an hour of command training. The rest of the

weekend is ours. Had to "grade" each other today, as I have previously mentioned. Wonder how I will come out on this? Oh Yes! Miracle of Miracles! Our first "G.T." on the machine gun came back today, and I passed satisfactorily! I only missed 5 <u>parts</u> of questions.

I certainly hope I have as much luck on the Tuesday G.T., but I seriously doubt it. However, I intend to do my best. Supposedly, a candidate is allowed to flunk <u>4</u> G.T.'s and still graduate, <u>but</u> he must have outstanding qualities of leadership, i.e., commands, drill, etc., in order to offset the 4 flunks, <u>and</u> <u>I</u> <u>am</u> <u>still</u> <u>somewhat</u> <u>nervous</u> <u>when</u> <u>in</u> <u>front</u> <u>of</u> <u>a</u> <u>platoon</u>.

No mail at all today, and I am certainly lonesome, too. I just wonder, why in hell I am back here working like a dog to advance myself, when no one really gives a damn? Life is certainly puzzling sometimes.

Fort Benning, Ga.
June 7, 1942

Stupendous news! I am actually beginning to assimilate some of these intricate mathematical formulas! At any rate, I now hold a little hope as regards the dreaded G.T. on Tuesday.

Today was a very <u>warm</u> Sunday, and Bourke and I went out in the field and studied like the very devil on "indirect laying," and its theory. No mail at all today, and I am really worried because I sent that $65 check home to Mother and have received no word from her at all in acknowledgment. Also, I know Bob must have enlisted or returned to work by now and have received no word from him, either.

I understand that upon graduation, they ask for volunteers for foreign duty, so I have made up my mind to do so, if the opportunity presents itself.

For some reason or other, I feel very optimistic today about successfully completing the course, but of course, I realize I have many hard weeks of study and drill ahead of me. I believe if I set my teeth in grim determination, that I can do it, however. <u>And</u> <u>I</u> <u>will</u>, or at least it can be said I gave them a darn good run for their money.

Fort Benning, Ga.
June 8, 1942

Another hard day done away with. It was so hot out on the Antiaircraft Range today that I believe I must have dehydrated a trifle. I drank two canteens full of water and two large cups of punch at noon and was still thirsty. The feeling of lassitude and extreme fatigue caused by this "dehydrating" process affected me very much today, so I drank copious amounts of saltwater tonight, as that restores the vitality.

No mail at all today, either, so that certainly doesn't cheer me up a great deal.

Tomorrow is the final and dreaded arrival of the "Indirect Laying" General Test. Hope that I will be able to write something encouraging in here tomorrow, in reference to this subject.

Heard a rumor today that Camp Callan had been moved out lock, stock, and barrel. If this is true, I guess it was indeed fortunate that destiny saw fit to grant me my wish and send me here. I have studied so hard and frantically for the past three days and nights that my eyes feel all burnt out.

Fort Benning, Ga.
June 9, 1942
Tonight I am in the depths of gloom and despondency. For I believe—no—I am almost certain—I <u>failed</u> on the long-dreaded Indirect-Laying General Test. I can say that I did not fail because of lack of knowledge but because of the manner in which it was given. We were allowed only <u>1 hr.</u> to work a test, which covered 2 weeks' work. The test consisted of some 49 questions, and after a demonstration of one of the problems, we had only 45 minutes to complete the test. I managed to get a total of 35 questions right, out of the 49, but do not think that is enough to pass.

Tomorrow we start on the famous B.A.R., and the day after that; we have the Bayonet and Hand Grenade. Received two letters from Mother today, and she tells me that she and Bob went to Oakland and moved all my belongings up to Sonora. Bob left for Oakland and enlisted in the Army Air Corps, and from the gist of Mother's letter, I guess he is in Monterey by now. Well, I only hope this mess will be over before he graduates from the Air School. I don't care what happens to me, but I wouldn't want anything to happen to Bob.

Fort Benning, Ga.
June 10, 1942
Put in eight hours of study for the nomenclature, functioning, and care of the Browning Automatic Rifle. Tomorrow we have 4 hours of bayonet drill (most of which is carried out at a dead run) and then the Hand Grenade.

Thought and thought and worried all day about my failing on the G.T. Guess it doesn't do me any good to worry, but I do want to graduate so darn badly, that it would just about kill me if I failed.

Of course, one cheering note is the reality that the <u>academic</u> work only counts 25% of your total grade, so if I could make an outstanding impression in the drill and command exercises, but there my damnable <u>lack</u> of <u>experience</u> precludes almost any hope of anything outstanding.

I am assigned to give my speech tomorrow night, so I do hope that I will be able to report some degree of success on it tomorrow evening.

From all reports, the bayonet drill is something really rugged and violent in the way of physical exercise. From the way the sun practically blistered us today, I hope it is cool tomorrow. No mail today.

FORT BENNING, GA.
JUNE 14, 1942
It seems that my last entry, prior to this one, was prophetic in more than one respect. Lieutenant Elliot (the CO) called me in Thursday night and told me that I would have to improve my leadership abilities a great deal. This, naturally, was quite a blow to me, but even though it did rock me back on my heels, it made me realize that I <u>will</u> have to improve tremendously, therefore, I requested Lt. Deetz, the next day, to give me every opportunity to get out in front of the platoon. He assured me that he would, so next week, it will start, and I <u>will</u> make good. I've just <u>got</u> to.

Bourke and I went into Columbus last night, and I bought quite a few essentials that I needed, i.e., pajamas, pencil, shower slippers, towels, etc. Had a steak dinner and one bottle of beer and then came home. Don't think much of Columbus. It, too, is full of cheap women, cheap liquor, and is, in fact, a typical Army town. It is much worse than San Diego in this respect, as there are over 100,000 soldiers in this vicinity.

Again, on this beautiful Sabbath morning, I earnestly pray my Lord that He will see fit to give me the necessary guidance and conviction to successfully graduate.

FORT BENNING, GA.
JUNE 18, 1942
I have utilized every opportunity in the last few days to volunteer for

command training in front of the platoon. How much good this will do me, remains to be seen. Next week, I am about certain to be assigned as platoon sergeant, or as platoon leader. I am going to study, as I have been, on those two duties. Had a night demonstration last night until 12:45 a.m., and tonight we will have scouting and patrolling deep in the woods until about 1 a.m. This morning, we had two hours of drill and command and one hour on the obstacle course.

We were paid yesterday, and I plan to send home $75. I also bought $5 worth of Defense Stamps and think I will buy that much every payday, so that, who knows, I may have a few Bonds when and if I eventually return to civilian life. Received a letter from Bob, and he has enlisted as a Flying Cadet in the Air Corps. At present, he is in the Reception Center at Monterey but will, without a doubt, be transferred at an early date. I hope the war is over by the time he finishes his training.

FORT BENNING, GA.
JUNE 20, 1942
My mind has been in a state of the utmost confusion this past week. At times, I am all enthusiasm and am sure that I will graduate, but again, at times, I am in the depths of despair, and the possibility of my graduating seems awfully remote. The past week was, I believe, the toughest I have ever put in. We had three "night problems," all of which took us through these quagmire Georgia swamps, and it rained in a terrific thunder-and-lightning storm each night. We fired the Browning Automatic Rifle, had hours of physical training (calisthenics), and more hours on the obstacle course. As I have already stated, I have seized every available opportunity to get out in front of the men in our daily command training, but whether this will be sufficient or not, I do not know. Although I requested to be assigned all possible duties in this field, my name did not appear on any duty roster this past week.

I was so exhausted last night that I laid down on the bed and didn't even get under the covers all night. The physical aspects of this course worry me not at all, as I am keeping up just fine with all competition. If I can only convince them that my voice and command will improve rapidly.

If I fail to graduate, God knows where I will be sent, and I certainly won't care a great deal. Have felt so low of late that I have neglected to write to anyone.

I sent home $80 instead of the $75 I had planned, and as a result (providing it arrives safely), I now have $380.22 in the bank towards the purchase of my home and $5 in defense stamps. Wonder if my saving will ever do me any good? I sent the $80 in <u>cash</u> in a letter to Mother, so it will be a question as to whether it will arrive safely or not.

We have another rugged week ahead of us next week—two General Tests, one on scouting and patrolling, and one on the 61- and 81-mm mortars. The last night exercise we had was a combat patrol problem, and our patrol ran into two machine guns and a squad of riflemen. If they hadn't been using blanks, I wouldn't be writing this at present. Certainly was a lot of fun, though, as well as a constructive and interesting problem.

Fort Benning, Ga.
June 21, 1942

The 21st of June and the beginning of summer! Somehow I can't help but feel that this will be a memorable summer in the story of my life. I had a restful night's sleep last night (with the exception of the usual eternal battle against beetles, bugs, and various insects). Received a letter from Mother and Harold today. Poor Mother! She feels so lonely now that Bob, too, is gone. If anyone in our family has to die, I hope it is <u>me</u>. I have nothing to lose, and it is most certainly true that my passing would scarcely be noticed. If only this war will end before Bob enters into actual combat! I did a huge laundry this morning—coveralls, leggings, canteen cover, hats, caps, pajamas, etc. I am going to devote my entire afternoon to hard and assiduous study on the dreaded G.T. we will have on the morrow. Funny thing, but my one visit to Columbus was enough for me. I don't intend to go in again until I leave here. The letters I received from the family and friends almost make me sick at heart—everyone is so positive and certain that I will graduate "with flying colors," and things are so uncertain and distant. It will tear my heart out if I don't graduate. But I will! I will! I will!

Fort Benning, Ga.
June 22, 1942

Here I am, way up in the air again on this eternal seesaw of emotions. The "G.T." that I had felt <u>sure</u> I had flunked came back today, and wonder of wonders! It was marked <u>satisfactory</u>! I very probably didn't pass it with a high score, but the main thing—I passed! Also had the long, 50-question G.T. on scouting and patrolling and technique of rifle fire, and it was a snap. So far as I can ascertain, I only missed at the most, 2 questions. With all this good news, I am all-enthusiastic and feel sure that I can improve my leadership to the point where it will be acceptable. Our group (or class) picture is being taken today.

FORT BENNING, GA.
JUNE 23, 1942
Our first day on the mortars. Today consisted of nomenclature, fire orders, and initial laying. Tomorrow we fire them out on Buchanan Range, which should prove to be fun, as the shells are loaded with appropriate amounts of T.N.T., and they say the roar and concussion is terrific.

I talked with Lt. Deetz yesterday, and he promised to see that I obtained some Drill assignments. Hope that I will be able to make good on them. Much to my horror, my eyes have again started to give me trouble. I think it is this brilliant sunshine, so I think the best thing for me to do is to get a good pair of sunglasses ($7). Have also been thinking that it would be a good idea for me to go into Columbus and have my eyes fitted for a new pair of glasses before this "FINAL TYPE PHYSICAL" falls due. No mail as yet from Mother confirming the receipt of the $80.

I have got to stop worrying, as I realize that that is one bad side of my nature that I should strive to overcome.

Ran about 2 miles last night for exercise so am a trifle stiff tonight.

FORT BENNING, GA.
JUNE 24, 1942
Well, way down on the seesaw of emotions. The B.A.R. Graded Test came back today, and I received my first "Unsatisfactory." Needless to say, this cast a pall of gloom over my feelings. I do not know whether this foretells for sure any ultimate decision regarding my success or failure, but I do know that it certainly doesn't do my record a great deal of good. It surprised me; inasmuch as that was one test I didn't worry about a great deal. In fact, I thought I had passed it with a reasonable degree of accuracy. On top of that, we have the Graded Test on the mortar tomorrow, and thanks to the extreme rapidity of the subject (3 days), and the poor instruction on the mathematical formulas, I am nicely confused. So? Two? No mail at all today, and some time ago,

I discontinued all my correspondence, except to Mother's, so I don't give a damn if anyone writes anymore or not. The laughable part of the whole thing is, we will order our uniforms next week—that on top of all the encouraging news today.

Sometimes I wonder—

Fort Benning, Ga.
June 25, 1942

About level on the seesaw today. After a rugged day of firing the mortar, sighting and laying, double time, and a lousy lunch in the field, we had a Graded Test on the mortar. As a result of frantic cramming during last night, this morning, this lunch hour, and during the 10-minute breaks, I <u>believe</u> I passed the test. However, the story is not yet completed, for tomorrow, we have the Gunner's Examination in which the mortar must be mounted, sighted, cross leveled, and aligned on the aiming stake in less than 60 seconds. The result of this test counts 25% on the final grade of the G.T. On Saturday, I have been assigned a period in drill and command, and believe me, I intend to get out there and <u>raise hell</u>. I've <u>got</u> to show 'em I can do it.

This terrible suspense of not knowing whether you are going to graduate or not is certainly nerve wracking. Here we are, almost on our 8th week, are ordering our uniforms, and "Foundation Week" is drawing nigh. "Foundation Week" is the date on which we find out definitely if we graduate or not. A total of five men on our floor of the barracks have been eliminated so far—2 because of physical unfitness and <u>3</u> dropped out at their own request.

Again today, I received no mail at all, and I am really worried (there I go again) as to the disposition of the $80 I sent home. I would sure hate to see it go down the drain.

In the event I don't graduate, I will request <u>not</u> to be sent back to Camp Callan. Have been giving the idea of joining the parachute troops some thought, but the only bad feature—I would lose my rank by so doing. If I find it necessary, I will try it and see.

Goofy as it may sound, however, I have a feeling that I will make the grade all right. Don't know why, but something seems to tell me.

Next week, we enter into actual combat and tactical training. I have been assigned to a light machine gun squad, and from all reports, we are really in for a few weeks of hell. I am really going to pour myself into this <u>heart and soul</u> and see what happens.

No word from Bob.

FORT BENNING, GA.
JUNE 27, 1942
12:30 P.M.
Passed the "Gunner's Examination" with a score of 81-1/2% out of a possible 100. This will give me an additional 20 points in the Mortar G.T. in the event it was low. Started work yesterday on the 37-mm anti-tank cannon, and I find it intensely interesting. I think I am going to like that weapon fine.

Spent all this morning watching a demonstration of "An Attack on a River Crossing." This afternoon, we sign the payroll, order our uniforms, have drill and command training, and run the obstacle course for record time.

Received my first "Star Gig" this morning on the rifle inspection (missing rear sight) but think it will be cancelled, as they took it off themselves.

10:30 p.m. Saw Deetz this afternoon as to why I hadn't received more opportunities in drill and command training. His answer was so evasive it puzzled me. I just can't figure out the score on that. Well anyway, 3 more weeks, and I will know definitely if I will graduate or not. Next week is the dreaded last rating of men by each other. This week will tell the story on whether I can make sufficient impression or not to get by. Please God, if I ever needed help and guidance, it is now. Ordered our uniforms today.

FORT BENNING, GA.
SUNDAY, JUNE 28, 1942
Well, in about 21 days, I will know definitely, one way or the other. I will undoubtedly receive my chance this week to lead the platoon, and it is going to be up to me to show them that I have what it takes. I suppose, to anyone reading this diary, that the period of my story here at Benning may be chronicled as one long series of wails and moans. However, strange as it may seem, I didn't mean these entries to sound that way. I attempted to describe my feelings honestly, and needless to say, the newness and confusion of life at the Infantry School was certainly confusing.

The spectre of failure haunts me more than most, I guess. I know there are those who say, "What if you don't make it—you will have had a wonderful experience and education." "It is better to have tried and failed, than not to have tried at all, etc., *ad nauseum*. True, perhaps, but I'm just not that way. I would never have any <u>respect</u> for myself again, if I don't make it.

Somehow, however, I still have that faith deep inside me that I will graduate. Whether it will prove true or not, I cannot tell, but if it does, I realize full well that this will be only the beginning, and I will have to study hard and diligently to improve myself to the point where I can term myself a real officer.

At any rate, come what may, this next week, I intend to put every iota of initiative, perseverance, thought, and hard work into the course.

FORT BENNING, GA.
JULY 1, 1942

Well, "old pessimistic" is at it again, for tonight I am the most discouraged that I have been since my arrival at the school. Yesterday, we fired the 37-mm anti-tank cannon and had the Graded Test on that weapon. I believe that I passed the test satisfactorily. With the completion of that weapon, we are entirely finished with the subjects of weapons and are now entering into tactics. Out of a total of 8 General Tests, I only missed one, which, according to what I hear, is above average.

<u>However</u>, here are the latest assortment of rumors, which have caused my discouragement: Our neighboring Company (the 21st) had their "Foundation Day" the other day, and <u>40</u> men were disqualified. Despite my continuous request for assignments (for in what other way can I improve myself?), I have only received <u>two</u>, besides those that I volunteer for, and on each of those two occasions, the drill was culled off before they reached my assignment.

Therefore, the possibility that they have noticed any improvement in my drill and command is indeed remote, although I have tried my utmost to show improvement, and all the fellows say that I <u>have</u> improved. It is indeed a bitter pill to swallow, but I guess it is just a fact in which I bit off more than I could chew. If I had had my basic training prior to leaving for the school, it might have been another story, but I couldn't step right into the advanced training that is given here and learn the fundamentals at the same time. I have no excuses. If I were a better man, I could have done it, I guess.

If, then, this bitter happening comes to pass, I may as well look into the future a little. Just where will I go from here? Frankly, I never felt so lost and bewildered in my life. I will request not to be sent back to Callan, for I could never face that crowd after not making it. In fact, I feel as though I could never face anyone whom I once knew. I have no idea where the Army will place me, but there are a number of factors, which will very probably have a bearing on that subject. One is the fact that with the training I have received here, I will probably be classed as of more value to the interests of the Army. If it is at all possible, I am going to get in the parachute troops, for even though it is known as the "Suicide Corps," life doesn't mean anything to me anymore.

Fort Benning, Ga.
July 3, 1942
The Mortar Graded Test came back yesterday, and I passed successfully. Spent all day yesterday on Tactics and digging a nice deep foxhole. Talk about work! We are, by now, deep in Tactics, and it is really a lot of hard, grueling work. Due to the many facts and happenings that I have recorded in past chapters, I have given up almost all hope that I will graduate. Heard today some news that I could take as cheering, I suppose, but I am not going to take it as such. I have done that before. One thing I will do, though. I shall continue to study and work just as hard as I can. This end of the week (tomorrow), we have the 8th week grading of the students by each other. Wrote Mother today and told her not to worry if she didn't hear from me for some time and explained the situation to her.

Fort Benning, Ga.
July 4, 1942
Two hours of drill and command this morning. No obstacle course today—too slippery, as it is raining violently. At the conclusion of the D&C, we were handed the papers on which we were to grade each other, accompanied by a lecture by Major King on how to fill it out. This particular grading is going to be very important, and all men who have faults to correct can expect an interview with Major King. So I fully expect an interview.

Yes, I guess McCully really bit off more than he could chew this time. I feel very deeply that I have disgraced myself by not getting out there and drilling like an old drillmaster, but I find that only one thing can bring that about—experience. I feel almost certain that I won't make it now, and as a result, I just don't care what happens to me anymore. It seems everything in life that I really wanted is out of my reach. A happy marriage? I had to marry a cheap, thoughtless chiseler. Advance myself? No soap—not enough experience.

Just in the very remote possibility that I may graduate, I am going to be interviewed Monday night as to joining the parachute troops. We have "Battalion in Attack" all afternoon.

Fort Benning, Ga.
July 5, 1942
Well, two weeks from today, or earlier, I should know definitely, one way or the other, whether I have made the grade or not. We all made out the horrible "Grading Sheets" today and a more difficult task I never performed; and believe me, there are some worried boys in this barracks. I fully expect an interview with Major King early next week as to why I have shown no improvement in drill and command, improvement that I was never able to demonstrate because I was never given the assignments!

I have felt low and depressed many times before (as witness this book!), but I can truthfully say I have never felt so completely hopeless as at present. I have stopped all correspondence to friends some time ago. I guess Margie, Cook, Ted, Hubie, Art Morgan, Vivian, and all my other friends will wonder what has happened to me, but it is better that things be severed in one sharp blow than that they find out my disgrace right away. I realize that they will find out eventually, but by the time they do, I hope to be safely overseas and in actual combat, for that is the only way in which I can erase this disgrace from my name, and erase it I will!

Fort Benning, Ga.
July 6, 1942
The climax draws near, and I can now see that my most recent premonition as to the outcome of the school is rapidly drawing near. As related recently, I had signed for an interview as to joining the parachute troops, _if_ and when I graduated from here. Today the list of names for interview was printed, and my name was missing from this. I can only assume that they didn't think my qualifications were high enough for that branch. With that realization, I can assume, with some degree of certainty, that I am marked for dismissal soon.

Truly, in utter frankness, am I then so much a failure? I have worked like a dog to accomplish the realization of this ambition. I know that my scholastic grades are well above average, for I have seen some of the others. I have only 4 delinquencies (or "gigs") to my credit, whereas some of the others have 9 and 10. My conduct in class has never been criticized, and as for hard study, I have left the area only once in almost three months. As for my personal grading of me by my fellow candidates, the only remark cast against me was the fact that I needed a little more experience in drill and command.

This fact, however, seems to tip the scales against me, yet they do not consider the fact that I learned this new type of drill and manual of arms overnight. For I never had one hour of basic training, to my credit, before coming here, as did the other candidates. Despite the fact that in almost three months my marching and manual of arms has been criticized but once—that counts for nothing. I was well aware of this weakness and volunteered at every opportunity in order to improve myself but was not given the opportunity, although I requested Lt. Deetz to give me a chance to show improvement on three different occasions. Despite his promises that he would do so, nothing ever came of it. In conclusion, then, if the Army wanted me to demonstrate improvement, why was I not given the opportunity? For in what other way can you show improvement? As I stated before, I am not making excuses--I hate them, and if I was a better man, I could have done it, but why? Why? I know for a fact there are several examples of men in the class who couldn't be trusted with a K.P. detail, and yet they seem to be getting by all right.

Am I then, so much a failure?

Fort Benning, Ga.
July 8, 1942

As I so correctly surmised, I was one of the group of men who were interviewed by the Major. Quite an interesting interview. He was quite affable and pleasant. Asked me many questions and finally came out with the reason—inexperience. He seemed quite amazed at the fact that I had never had any previous training.

Well, no use going into detail. I have two weeks in which to display my prowess at drilling a platoon, a task to which I solemnly promise to put forth every ounce of effort I can. That was the only criticism I had. My lessons and administrative work were all okay.

Whether I can make sufficient impression in those two weeks

remains in doubt, in view of the highly technical movements that I will be confronted with, but I shall certainly give it everything I have.

Fort Benning, Ga.
July 10, 1942
Exactly 12 midnight at this writing. I am Company Charge of Quarters tonight. We are now getting involved into higher tactics, and they are really <u>tough</u>. Had one Graded Test on General Tactics, and I fear that I didn't do so well on it, to say the least. Was Platoon Sergeant yesterday and today and will be tomorrow. Also have two exercises to give tomorrow during drill and command, and needless to say, I have <u>got</u> to give them everything I have.

Have only received mail from Mother, recently, but I can't answer until I find out if I am going to graduate or not, and I shall know <u>that</u> in less than two weeks.

Sometimes I get so discouraged and low, <u>but</u> I will not give up. I will keep plugging away and shall do my best until I <u>do</u> find out.

Fort Benning, Ga.
July 12, 1942
Sunday again. Had charge of drilling the platoon yesterday during command training and also believe that I managed to give my two assigned exercises in a presentable manner, especially in view of the fact that both Major King and Lt. Deetz were standing watching me. Most of the fellows say I did extremely well in it, but whether the Major thinks so is yet another matter. Foundation Day is rapidly drawing nigh, so at least I shall soon know <u>if</u>; and if not, I will then find out where I am going next. We have a terrific week facing us starting tomorrow—five days in the field and lunch in the field every day. All on tactics. I fully expect to be assigned the platoon as leader on Thursday for the balance of the week, and if so, I will need every bit of guidance that Providence can provide. Haven't written a single letter since the discouragement started and don't intend to until it is all over, one way or another. I believe, just to be sure, that I will start packing my possessions in an orderly manner so that I will have no confusion when I do leave. Sure miss mail and news from home, but it is better than having them know how I have disgraced myself.

Fort Benning, Ga.
July 14, 1942
Tuesday already! Have been working steadily, and I might say, furiously, on "Anti-Tank Platoons in the Assault and Defense." The 37-mm Graded Test came back today, and I passed with a score of 88%. Don't know for sure, but I have a hunch that I will be assigned as platoon leader for Thursday, Friday, and Saturday. If so, it means my one chance to convince them that I can drill a platoon, and rumor has it that <u>this</u> Friday is <u>Foundation Day</u>. Possibly because I am the subject, but it hardly seems fair to me to eliminate a man on the basis of <u>two</u> assignments before the platoon. However, that seems to be the case. In the event I am called before the Board, which I feel is almost a certainty, I intend to express my views on the subject, not in a snotty way, but just plain facts. In view of the fact that all my other work is satisfactory, it seems foolish to me to throw away 3 months of arduous training because of that minor technicality. After all, in the heat of battle, no one will be worrying about "Column left-Column right."

Letter from Raff today. He expects to come back here sometime next month. That makes it "nice" if I flunk out.

Fort Benning, Ga.
July 15, 1942
Lunch in the field today, out on the Tactics Range. All day on "The Heavy M.G. Platoon in Attack." And was it <u>hot</u>! Salt tablets are being furnished us at the table, now, as one candidate has died from "dehydration," or lack of salt in the system, due to excessive sweating. The rumor about Foundation Day has more or less straightened out. It is evidently on Tuesday, and the Board will meet the preceding Monday. Some of the candidates have been notified to appear before the Board already. So far, I have not, but whether this is a good omen or not, I can't say.

Spent the evening running the obstacle course and high jumping, as we have a tough session on that course this Saturday. Also did some high jumping. Have volunteered steadily on the command training every morning. I expected to be assigned the platoon for the next three days, but so far, no news. Thank God I have lost almost all my nervousness when before the platoon. I guess it's rather late in the game to pray, but nevertheless, I do pray the Lord tonight, if he sees fit, to give me a chance to graduate.

Fort Benning, Ga.
July 16, 1942

I think today was about the toughest day we have had at the school. Title of the problem, "The Battalion in Attack," all enacted out in person by us over a good 10 miles of Georgia's "lovely" terrain. Hot? Man O Man! I ran out of water about 2 in the afternoon and decided to take 2 salt tablets to alleviate the terrific sweating. Result? The extra strong solution of salt evidently didn't agree with my stomach, as I lost my entire lunch shortly thereafter.

I feel about completely worn out tonight, and we have the same problem in <u>defense</u> tomorrow. My assignment in today's problem was a Platoon Sergeant of a mortar platoon.

Oh yes! New developments in the critical graduation situation. Lt. Deetz asked me this morning what weapons I had qualified in, and I replied <u>all</u>, except the B.A.R.

Also, three men were interviewed by another major, but whether this means good or bad (my name was not included), I do not know. However, it can be taken as follows: It may be a <u>sure</u> sign that I won't make it, as Applegate and Behr's names were not included, either; and in the mind of most of the men in the barracks, they are almost <u>sure</u> to fail. So? Does this mean the end?

Fort Benning, Ga.
July 19, 1942

Today is a rather lonely, thoughtful Sunday for me, for it may well be the last Sunday, which I will spend here at Fort Benning. Tomorrow we have the long-awaited 4-1/2-hour Graded Test on Tactics, but this does not worry me. On Tuesday, it is reliably rumored that all men who were interviewed by Major King, and some who weren't, will appear before a Board of Officers who will determine whether they will graduate or not. Their decision will be final. My exact status is a puzzle to me. Some of the candidates have been notified that they will have to appear before the Board, but I have not been notified so, as yet. However, there is no gain in kidding myself. I feel sure that I will have to appear. Therefore, my only chance is to make a good impression when before the Board, and this is known to be a very difficult task, as the Board is known to use a variety of "trick" questions in their so-called grilling. At any rate, this week will tell the story, one way or another. I will either stay here for the remaining two weeks and graduate or will be on my way to

God Knows Where sometime next week. If I do not graduate, I want to either join the parachute troops or get overseas as soon as possible, for I feel that I could never return to the West Coast. It is chiefly for this reason that I have ceased all correspondence with people on the West Coast. Perhaps one would think this is unnecessarily cruel to Mother, but it is better this way than that she should know of the disgrace that I have made of myself. As for the others, evidently my letters weren't missed anyway. I can just hear my "fond" sister, Lena, saying, "I told you so." In one respect, though, my conscience is entirely clear. I had put forth serious and earnest effort throughout the entire course. Not for nothing have I endured terrific heat, sweat, hard labor, drilling, marching, and the most strenuous of physical exertion. I feel that I am a far better man physically than when I arrived here.

It is truly laughable, though, that the Government should spend some $3000 to educate me, and then eliminate me because of "inexperience," which they refused to allow me to correct.

At least I should make one helluva good frontline solider, for I have nothing to lose, and it matters not to me whether I live or die. As long as I can take 3 times as many Germans or Japs along with me.

Fort Benning, Ga.
July 20, 1942

Well, it has been confirmed at last. The Board meets all day tomorrow, and although even as yet I have not been notified that I will have to appear, I feel sure that I will have to appear. Probably in the morning. From all reports, the Board will be comprised of the Company Commander, Battalion Commander, and an as yet unknown Colonel. Evidently, any hope of eventual graduation will depend on the impression made before this Board.

We had our 4-1/2-hour Graded Test today, and to be truthful, the outcome of it has me puzzled, as I know I forgot several of the administrative details. I don't suppose it matters a lot anyway.

No mail at all today, either, which makes a total of over three weeks, now. Sure miss it, but I guess that is one of the many pleasures that I will now have to forego because of not graduating. Hottest today since I have been here. We were in open bleachers all day, simply sweltering, our water canteens so hot we couldn't touch them. No relief tonight, either, I see. As I write, the sweat is simply dripping off me, and my pants are a soggy mess.

FORT BENNING, GA.
JULY 21, 1942

It is here—60 unfortunate men are at present pacing up and down in the barracks, awaiting the dread summons to appear before the Board, including me. This interview will decide all, and there will be no appeal. By this time tomorrow, I will know very definitely, my fate.

At least the weeks of strain and worry will be over and done with, and I will be on my way—to what? My fate is in the hands of God, and He alone can decide just what destiny has in store for me.

So it seems that on this beauteous summer day, all my ambitions, and perhaps a few of the rosy dreams of my youth are crashing again into the bitter dust. If one had a tendency to believe a few of the ancient philosophies of India, I certainly must have committed horrible misdeeds in former incarnations; for it is their philosophy that one must pay in their present incarnations for sins and misdeeds committed in former incarnations.

The hardest blow to me is the necessary cutting of all contacts with friends and family.

FORT BENNING, GA.
JULY 22, 1942

Either I am the world's most fortunate individual, or else God has seen fit to give me a great deal of guidance. At about 6:30 p.m. yesterday, I was called out of the barracks and started the long "Death March to the Execution Chamber." Upon arriving at the Orderly Room, the 1st Sergeant stuck his head out the door and said, "McCully, you will not have to appear before the Board." It seems I had been mistaken—the men on the bottom of the list were the best men. They had interviewed the worst ones, first.

This morning, the final "chopping of heads" took place. All the doomed men were called out of ranks, and by the Grace of God, I remained in ranks. Happy as this makes me tonight, I realize full well that I still have 12 days before we receive our commissions, and in that time, anything can happen, as we will be under constant surveillance until the day of graduation, and as Lt. Deetz said this morning, "One slip—and we're out." Besides the fact that we still have two very tough Graded Tests ahead of us, a rigid physical examination, and the fact that I am not sure just how well I did on that 4-1/2-hour Graded Test. So?

Fort Benning, Ga.
July 26, 1942
Have been very busy for the last four days. On Friday night, or rather Saturday morning, we had the long tactical problem, "Battalion in Attack—the Dawn Attack," at the conclusion of which we had a 20-minute Graded Test, which was really a tough son of a gun. Have no idea how I made out in it, but I hope to God it was satisfactory. On Saturday morning, we were fingerprinted and filled out our Officer Qualification Cards. After a full afternoon on "umpiring," I returned to the barracks to find a letter from Hubie and found that he was here in Fort Benning—3rd S.T.R., so I hiked down the road, and there he was. Sure had a wonderful time then, and all today, talking over old times.

I am still inclined to worry a bit until I actually get that commission in my hands, because [of] (1) two G.T.'s that haven't yet been returned, (2) 3 very tough G.T.'s next week, (3) a very rigid physical examination next week, (4) my usual luck.

However, all I can do is to keep my fingers crossed and pray. I know I am certainly going to work like a maniac all next week. I sure hope that I can get a 10-day delay en route, as I certainly desire to see the folks again.

Fort Benning, Ga.
August 2, 1942
Well, it is certain now! I will graduate Tuesday morning, August 4th, at 10 a.m. The orders came out today, and "2nd Lieutenant Ernest J. McCully, AUS, Serial Number 0-1289287, was assigned to Camp Adair, Oregon." Camp Adair is near Corvallis, Oregon, and this extremely fortunate assignment makes me very happy indeed, especially in view of the fact that we were authorized 10 days' delay en route, plus six days travel time, which means that I will be able to see all of the folks for a little while.

So it is today that I see the culmination of my highest hopes and dreams, despite hours of black despair and worry. Passed my physical examination yesterday, perfectly. If nothing else, I have learned one great lesson back here—worry gains nothing, so why worry? From now on, I am going to express the utmost confidence in myself, and in every way. I do not know what lies ahead of me at Camp Adair, but I shall certainly do my best in every respect, and something tells me I shall do nothing to let down the traditions of the U.S. Army.

COLUMBUS, GA.
AUGUST 5, 1942
7:45 A.M.
Here I am, sitting in the train just before it leaves for home. I am going home the Southern route, through New Orleans, Texas, New Mexico, Arizona, and up through Southern California. Had a beautiful graduation exercise yesterday, at which time, Colonel Corcey, the speaker stated, "For many of these young men, today is the culmination of a long-held dream," and I for one can certainly underscore that statement. Here I sit, finally wearing the gold bars of my commission, and I think of all the toil, work, sweat, and worry that entered into the course, and I know in my heart that it was worth it. Passed through New Orleans last night and obtained Pullmans. Didn't think a great deal of New Orleans, but then I didn't have a great deal of time in which to judge it. Woke up on the morning of the sixth, nearing Houston, Texas, and of course, the inevitable "bad break" had to occur. Our section of the train was detached, so here we sit until 12:15 p.m. A three- or four-hour delay, which of course, comes out of my precious leave. It is supposed to make up the time before we reach Los Angeles, but I doubt if it will.

AUGUST 8, 1942
ON *THE OWL*
EN ROUTE
Just left Los Angeles after one of the most disgusting trips I ever experienced. From Houston, Texas, on—sidetracked at every siding, unbearable dust, soot, and desert heat. It took the train 8 hours to make 100 miles through the desert. Bought a Pullman in L.A. and plan to enjoy a restful night's sleep prior to arriving in Oakland. I wired the Morgans my time of arrival. I think the reason for my bad luck on the train from Houston was because they thought I was in charge of the troop train (which it really was). As a result, I played nursemaid to sick soldiers and hungover, stricken corporals practically all the way.

    For some reason, I have a strange inner feeling of calm confidence that I will make good at Camp Adair, and I have too much faith in my inner convictions to doubt it, as witness my premonition as to graduation. My most fervent desire is to become an officer and gentleman who will be a credit to the U.S. Army. I have also promised myself that I shall never worry again. My fate is in the hands of God.

August 20, 1942
On *The Beaver*
En Route
Had a wonderful 10-day leave and one that will live in my memory for a long, long time. The Morgans were so kind, it made me feel badly that I was unable to repay them in some way. I brought Mother down from Sonora, and she is to go to the doctor's and find out what is wrong and will be operated on, if necessary.

Left Oakland last night at 6:28 p.m., and now (9 a.m.) am in Southern Oregon. Expect to arrive in Albany, Oregon, about 1 p.m., thence by bus to Corvallis and Camp Adair. Of course, the old McCully characteristic—worrying—is struggling to assert itself, but as stated before, I have decided to stop that altogether, so I am paying no attention to it. I can't help but wonder, however, just what my first assignment will be.

I certainly hope that I arrive on time, as I certainly don't want to report late. All in all, I guess I am one helluva lucky fellow, and I am rather anxious to get settled and find out just what I have to do and can make appropriate preparations for it. More tonight, after arrival. As I note, it is quite a feat to write decently on the train.

Officers Quarters, Room 44
Camp Adair, Ore.
August 22, 1942
A hectic 2 days indeed, since I last wrote. Arrived, registered, signed multitudes of papers, assigned to quarters and unit, attending school, calisthenics, and drill. I was assigned as platoon leader in a rifle company, temporarily, I was told. Camp Adair will be, in time, I think, one of the largest camps on the Pacific Coast. It is now some 33,000 acres in extent and will, without a doubt, expand. The recruits will not arrive until September 15th, and much to my relief, they will be raw green recruits direct from reception centers. I would much rather train green men than more experienced men, until I can obtain some experience myself, at least. In the meantime, we have to attend school every day and have an hour and a half of calisthenics and drill every day. It was here, in that subject, that I committed my first *faux pas*. I was to explain the difference between "In Cadence" and "Ready, Exercise" and became nicely confused. No excuse, I just wasn't any too familiar with the problem. I was not unduly nervous, however, but I have got to

study like a maniac, for the enormity of what I <u>don't</u> know appalls me. <u>But I will</u>, I promise, study as never a mortal studied before.

Bed now, as I am worn out.

OFFICERS QUARTERS, RM. 44
CAMP ADAIR, OREGON
AUGUST 25, 1942

Have been so busy the last few days that I haven't had a chance to write. Found that our cadre will receive a training course of approximately 17 weeks duration in all phases of instruction, and then about March of next year, we will be shipped overseas. We have been attending school on military training, methods of instruction, etc. Today, we had a 3-hour course on the B.A.R., and I was really amazed at how well I remembered the piece. Also had an hour on squad tactics, and this morning our usual hour and a half on physical training and infantry drill. My nerves have subsided somewhat, and I am not very nervous when in front of a platoon. If I can just get a few tips on preparing a lecture now, I will feel a great deal better. No hot water or heat in our quarters, as yet, due to unfinished construction, so that makes the leisure hours a little hard to bear, but I imagine that will soon be remedied.

I studied like the very devil last night, and as a result, made out fine in the squad tactics session. The food is delicious after the Benning stew, but the enormity of the task I have ahead of me still appalls me. I intend to give it my every effort, however, and--?

OFFICERS QUARTERS, RM. 44
CAMP ADAIR
AUGUST 26, 1942

Another hard day. Had our usual session of calisthenics this morning, and believe me, they are really working us over! I am stiff and sore all over. We then had a lecture on training films and military training, on which subject we will soon have a Graded Test. This afternoon, it was 3 hrs on the B.A.R. again (examination tomorrow) and then an hour of command drill.

Wonder of wonders! I think I am slowly but surely gaining a little self-assurance! At least the thought of getting out in front of my platoon doesn't cause me to quake mentally as much as it used to. Our Battalion Commander (Lt. Colonel Smith) is very congenial, and I am fortunate in having a Company Commander as swell as Lt. Prevics. I have received no mail at all as yet, but then I only mailed my letters recently.

Guess I had best cut this short, as I have an immense amount of study to do and would like to write a letter to Lola.

OFFICERS QUARTERS, RM. 44
CAMP ADAIR, OREGON
AUGUST 27, 1942

Had an unusually strenuous session of calisthenics this morning, then a period of Infantry Drill, in which I drilled and explained movements to a platoon of officers quite successfully, considering my shortcomings. After that, two interesting training films on that subject. Then a two-hour session with the B.A.R., including an examination, and I was then excused for the balance of the day to do some work for my Company Commander. I have been assigned the task of giving an hour lecture on the nomenclature of the light machine gun, and strange to say, I wasn't sent into a spasm of fear when I received the news. Strangely enough, with the realization that I will have to do these things, my stage fright is rapidly leaving me, with the result that I gave a fairly creditable performance in drilling the platoon today. Don't mistake me—there is plenty of room for improvement, and I know it, but I am improving. No mail today. My whole body is stiff and sore as a result of these calisthenics, and here is a factor that has me a little worried--my childhood affliction of hay fever seems to be returning. Haven't been bothered with it since we left Oregon when I was 7 years of age.

CAMP ADAIR, OREGON
AUGUST 28, 1942

Usual hard day. The light machine gun lecture was changed to "Nomenclature of the Enfield Rifle," today. I gave it and wasn't afflicted with stage fright, but I did notice slight hesitancy, talked too fast, and as a result, finished the half-hour speech in half the time I had allotted myself. While the speech was not bad, I realize I have room for a large amount of improvement and will have to make a very thorough preparation. Today's errors, I think, were a little excusable in that (1) I had never seen the rifle until last night, (2) short notice, hence short preparation, (3) my first speech. However, I realize I cannot afford to make any mistakes.

Received a letter from Lola today, and Lena is letting things go just the way I figured she would—pays no attention to Mother—won't take her to the doctor's. Damn her anyway—a fine example of womanhood she is—selfish, self-centered, greedy, lazy!

Finally have acquired hot water, and so, a delicious hour-long shower tonight. We do not get Saturday afternoons off, needless to say, but I may go into Corvallis tomorrow night.

We are also paid our travel money tomorrow night, $191.25!!!

CAMP ADAIR, OREGON
AUGUST 30, 1942

I went into Corvallis last night and spent quite a bit of money but all on necessary items that I needed badly. A radio—quite reasonably priced—a reading lamp, an electric alarm clock, ashtrays, wastebasket. The alarm clock is especially nice and will be a fitting addition to my home when and if I ever acquire that. Had three bottles of beer, and then Lt. Bourke and I caught a taxi and returned to Camp.

From the gist of Lola's letter, I guess Mother is rather seriously ill and will soon be in the hospital to have an operation. While the diagnosis is as yet incomplete, it is thought to be kidney stones. I can only pray God that is what it is and not cancer as she seemed to think. It may take every cent I have saved up for the purchase of my home, but I will spend, and gladly, every cent to my name and what I can earn in the future if it will only ease Mother in her declining years.

I have a 1-hour lecture on "Marksmanship with the Light Machine Gun, Cal. 30, HB, M1919A4," and although it is still some time away, I will have to make very thorough preparation for it. So far, I haven't made a great deal of progress on said preparation. No mail at all as yet. Hope I receive some tomorrow.

Have to study now.

CAMP ADAIR, ORE.
AUGUST 31, 1942

Received a letter from Mother today, writing to me on Friday, and evidently she was to be operated on Saturday morning for removal of the kidney stones. So far, I have heard no word as to how she made out, but I pray God that she made out all right. I know her heart wasn't any too strong.

Another strenuous day, and I was completely worn out tonight.

Had a long 4-hour session on squad tactics, which meant crawling across fields on our stomachs under a blazing sun. The damn hay fever was out in full force all day today, too. Still worried as to how to put across successfully, the lecture on marksmanship.

My stomach has been terribly upset for the past three days. Received a nice letter from Melanie and Freddy, John Strahl's mother and brother. John is evidently somewhere in Australia at this time. Can't seem to think of much more to write, so may as well retire. Big day tomorrow, pictures of us drilling, etc., etc.

Camp Adair, Ore.
September 1, 1942
Had a tough morning of the usual calisthenics, drill, and then "Defense Against Chemical Attack" and "Marches and Bivouacs." Was excused this afternoon to work on my forthcoming lecture. Have it drawn up roughly now and will complete it tomorrow. The schedule was changed, and so tonight, I am Battalion Duty Officer, which means that I will have to take bed check at midnight of Company A, D, and the HQ Co. Also, I will be Bt. Duty Officer over the weekend. Subscribed to *The Oregonian* tonight and also signed my pay voucher. I will receive $196 for pay since August 4th. Certainly an improvement over my Corporal's pay.

Wish I could receive some word regarding Mother's condition soon. I am worried as hell about her, but I feel sure she will be just fine. Feel more confident about the lecture tonight, and I intend to make every effort to make it a good one. Have got to study like the very devil in the next few weeks in order to prepare myself properly to instruct my platoon in the correct manner when it arrives. Hope I receive some mail soon, as it seems I just <u>live</u> until the mail arrives.

Camp Adair, Oregon
September 2, 1942
6:45 P.M.
The customary morning of calisthenics, drill, and lectures. Am getting used to the calisthenics and am happy to say I am improving steadily in drilling and instructing a platoon. Worked all afternoon on my forthcoming lecture. I am the loneliest tonight that I have been since coming to Oregon. Must I continue forever through life like a soul adrift? Other men seem to have no trouble at all in forming new contacts, but I? No mail at all today, either, which certainly didn't help much.

To be truthful, I haven't been feeling up to par physically, either, so I intend to take a long shower, shave, and retire about 8 p.m. tonight and see if that will make any difference. Perhaps it is this bad physical condition, which makes me feel so downhearted, gloomy, and "don't give a damn whether school helps or not." That, and the fact that there is such a damnable lot to learn and so little time to learn it. At least the little radio that I purchased is proving to be a great comfort. With its harmonious melodies, my troubled soul is at peace for a little while. I am truly worried about Mother now, but it does seem to be that if anything of a serious nature had occurred, I would surely have heard about it.

CAMP ADAIR, OREGON
SEPTEMBER 4, 1942
9:20 P.M.
The last two days have been about the same as those mentioned previously—hard work, hours of instructions, and preparing training aids for my lecture, which has again been postponed until Monday. I hear that we will not work tomorrow afternoon. Of no benefit to me is this momentous news, however, for alas, I have been assigned as Company Duty Officer over the weekend, which means, of course, that I must remain in the Company Area at all times.

Oh well! I can use the time to further my studies and answer my mail, for yes! I received four letters today. Still no direct word as to Mother's condition, however, since her operation. I am also beginning to worry a great deal about the continued silence from Bob. I happened to think, he has probably finished his 3-months' school by now, and they may have sent him overseas. I certainly hope not. I don't care what happens to me, or I would never have transferred into a combat unit, but I hate to see him get into it.

Received a letter from Elwood (Major Read) congratulating me on gaining my commission. He said he would finish the Command and General Staff School on Sept. 20th and would look forward to the pleasure of seeing me in Eugene.

CAMP ADAIR, OREGON
SEPT. 5, 1942
Remaining in Camp on this weekend. Cause? I am Battalion Duty Officer for Saturday and Sunday. Had an entire morning of methods

of instruction and had this afternoon off, so I did a lot of reading and wrote seven letters.

That, and a lot of thinking, of just what a pointless life I lead. I strive to better myself continually. Despite my disgust of life, I still cling to my high ideals, which are, in reality, I suppose, outmoded. I don't care especially for the delights of liquor. I can take a drink, but it certainly doesn't bother me at all if I can't go to where it is available. Smoking, I suppose, is my big vice, and I even get tired of that, at times. Perhaps, in reading this, you might say, "painting some beautiful wings on your shoulders, aren't you"? But it isn't. I have faults—too damn many to suit me, but I am also an orderly soul who likes to work for a definite objective, and yet I have none, just living a pointless existence. Oh well! Who knows? Perhaps someday (probably when it is too late), I will have an incentive.

CAMP ADAIR, OREGON
SEPTEMBER 6, 1942
Truly a beautiful Sunday. I arose about 8:30 a.m. and went over and had a nice breakfast of bacon and eggs. Then back to quarters and read a little, then wrote some more letters. After completing the letters, walked over to Regimental HQ And mailed them. After lunch, I think I will thoroughly clean my room and refurbish some of my equipment, then a complete shave and shower, and will then put in about 2 hours on tomorrow's lecture.

I guess, when time was available, I would go into Corvallis a little more frequently, if it wasn't for the inconvenience of getting in there. There is only <u>one</u> <u>convenient</u> manner of getting in, and that is by <u>taxi</u>, which is, of course, quite formidably expensive.

Understand we are going to have a big "Activation Day" party in the Officers Club on September 15th. At least we were all required to "chip in" for the same. I do hope my lecture comes off all right tomorrow. Hope I receive some mail today, although I hardly expect it, in view of the four letters I received Friday.

CAMP ADAIR, ORE.
SEPTEMBER 7, 1942
LABOR DAY
Not a little disgusted tonight. No mail at all today and found out that I will be Duty Officer again on the night of the Activation Day Party.

Damn! All Bn. Schools have been cancelled until further notice, and we are to prepare our company areas for the occupancy by the recruits when they start to arrive on the 16th. As a result of this cancellation, I didn't get to give my long-awaited speech on the L.M.G., for the cancellation came through just as I was setting up my equipment.

Am tremendously worried about Bob, due to his long silence. They may have shipped him overseas already, so I wrote him another letter requesting him to write. Also, I have never received word from Lena or Lola as to how Mother made out on her operation on August 29th. Thoughtful of them.

Believe me, if I can't go to that party on the 15th, I am certainly going to Portland this weekend, for once those recruits get here, we'll never get off.

The little radio is now playing "My Heart At Thy Sweet Voice" from *Samson and Delilah*, and it makes me think of happier days when I used to listen to that self-same piece.

Camp Adair, Ore.
September 8, 1942
Found out that it may be possible for me to attend the dance after all, if certain angles are worked. Took part in a demonstration of rifle marksmanship all morning, and this afternoon, worked on the Company Mess Hall. At the conclusion of the day, I felt rather restless, so Bourke and I went into town and had dinner, walked around a bit, bought some stationery, stamps, etc., and came home. Was offered an introduction to a young Oregon State freshman, whom I may ask to attend the dance—and again I may not—I don't know. Have been thinking of going to Portland over the weekend, and if so, may go over to Vancouver and see Aunt Mattie and Uncle Louie and Wavel and Ernest. Received 1 letter today from Ted Stefanski back at Coast Artillery O.C.S. He graduates on the 11th of this month. He sure is a good kid. Still no news concerning Mother.

Guess I will turn in, as I presume we have a big day ahead of us. Official circles now have it that we will not receive our men until October 15th, due to lack of essential equipment.

Camp Adair, Ore.
September 9, 1942
Another long, hard day draws to a close. It is one of extreme loneliness

for me, for I received no mail at all today, and I am still uninformed as to Mother's condition or as to the whereabouts of Bob.

I wrote an answer to Ted's letter and also opened a checking account (via the mail) with the United States National Bank of Corvallis. Deposited my entire check ($195.10), and there it will remain until need for it arises.

Believe me, I have been getting more and more disgusted with life in general, of late. I really intend to go up to Portland this weekend and see if I can't do something to end this deadly, purposeless existence that life has become for me. Still don't know just how the "Activation Day" dance will turn out. I presume I will have to remain in the Company Area as Duty Officer, even though I did hear reports that such officers would be allowed to attend.

The way I feel tonight, I don't much give a damn.

CAMP ADAIR, OREGON
SEPTEMBER 10, 1942
Today about the same as yesterday. The calisthenics are starting to build me up tremendously. Worked on training aids all afternoon, so I took part of the time to build myself a very nice shelf, which gave me much more room on my table for writing.

Again no mail at all today, of any description. I am really worried now, as to Mother's condition, for it seems to me they would have informed me one way or another. If I do not receive any mail at all tomorrow, I am going to send a telegram and find out just what the situation is.

We go into woolen O.D. uniforms on the 15th and can, at last, crawl out of these untidy, hard-to-keep-clean "Bombays."

Still planning on going to Portland, day after tomorrow, although Holzmann was made Duty Officer but presume there will be some other fellows going up, so we can all share expenses to hire a taxi for said journey.

CAMP ADAIR, ORE.
SEPTEMBER 14, 1942
I went to Portland as I had planned, although I had a terrible head cold. Had a rotten time, although I visited all the relatives in and about Portland and Vancouver.

It wasn't any fun at all. Had to take a taxi every place I wanted to go, which ran into about $15 before the weekend was over. Couldn't get a room to stay overnight on Saturday night so had to make a deal with a cabdriver to use his room. The cold settled in my chest on the way home, and developed a sore throat on top of that, and thus ended my adventurous weekend in the big city. When I arrived home, found some mail from Mother, or rather, <u>about</u> Mother. She is doing fine and wanted me to wire her $180, which I couldn't do, as I am Duty Officer today and couldn't leave Camp. So I mailed the $180 to her via airmail. I think that doctor must be doing a little chiseling somewhere, as so far, the operation (removal of kidney stones) has cost some $345. Of course, this momentarily sets back my home buying dream, but believe me, we only have one Mother, and I am so happy to see her completely well again.

Life has become such a drear and vapid existence, I wish to God something would happen to end this damnable purposeless existence.

CAMP ADAIR, ORE.
SEPTEMBER 15, 1942
Had the big Activation Ceremonies this morning, complete with a formal dress parade and address. This horrible cold that I contracted last week just about has me down. Was really sick last night. We were dismissed for the rest of the day, and so, not feeling so good, I remained in quarters, wrote letters in reply to one from Mother, and drew up a lesson plan and lesson analysis for the dismounted drill I am to instruct in tomorrow and Friday. Was also assigned an hour of instruction on "Interior Guard Duty." Strange, but such assignments worry me not at all anymore, as my present state of mind is still one of sheer boredom and disgust with this miserable farce called life. I wrote another letter to Bob. He is evidently still at Sheppard Field, Texas. I guess I had best go in and shave, shower, and shine my dress uniform, as we are all required to attend the great Activation Day dance and reception at the Officers Club, which will no doubt be a "gay" and "happy" affair, what with no partner, <u>punch</u> to drink, and <u>nuts</u> to crunch on in between stages of boredom.

CAMP ADAIR, OREGON
SEPTEMBER 17, 1942
The Great Reception wasn't so hot, in my opinion. I remained about 45 minutes. It would have been all right, I guess, if I had had a partner,

but I was alone, along with about 200 other lieutenants, and it was so horribly crowded. At any rate, Lt. Green and I left and went into Corvallis, drank beer, met two girls, took them home, came back, more beer, something to eat, and finally, home. Lousy time.

The next day, I gave a period of Infantry Drill and have one assigned for tomorrow. Worked like a dawg all day today. No mail. Wrote Bob a long letter, as I received one from him, and one from Mother yesterday.

I am actively looking forward to the arrival of the men, and wonder of wonders, I continue to gain poise and control when speaking. I have a good platoon sergeant, thank goodness, and I hope to train my men both efficiently and well.

Feel better now, cold disappearing, but <u>very slowly</u>. All officers in Co. B. bawled out by Skipper tonight for improper instruction to cadre on bayonet training. ??????

Camp Adair, Ore.
September 18, 1942

Friday here already! Worked on training aids all morning and had Lesson Plans and Analysis this afternoon. Elwood and Margaret dropped by about 1:30 this afternoon. He looked fine, but to his disappointment was not assigned here, but instead, was sent to 9th Corps Area HQ in Salt Lake City.

This miserable cold seems to be terribly difficult to get rid of and is extremely annoying, to say the least. They are really pouring the lectures on us now. I seem destined to be the Chief Infantry Drill Specialist in the Company, as I have five periods of that assigned as well as one on Military Courtesy and Discipline, Extended Order, and various others.

The Skipper was in a little better mood today. Tomorrow, we have inspections of the enlisted cadre, some lectures, and then the afternoon off. I don't feel any enthusiasm for it, but I will have to go in to get my pants and laundry. May come back immediately, however, as I have an enormous amount of Lesson Plans and Analysis to get out for next week.

No reply, as yet, affirming the receipt of money I sent to Mother. ???????

Camp Adair, Ore.
September 20, 1942

Went into the great City of Corvallis yesterday (forgot to get my laundry) but I did get my pants out of the cleaners, bought some necessary supplies, and had four pictures taken at the Howell Studio. They will very probably turn out to be the monstrous creations they usually do, but Mother wanted one.

Didn't get up until 11 a.m. and then had a very nice dinner, came home and swept and mopped and industriously cleaned my entire room. I think I was never so disgusted and lonely as I was yesterday while in town. Absolutely nothing to do. Sat in a hotel lobby and read a magazine until time for dinner, had dinner, went to a lousy show, had a malted milk, and came back home at 9 p.m. Exciting Saturday night!

Well, Friday night I wrote a long letter to Margie terminating that friendship. She was beginning to get a little too serious for me, and so, as must always be the case with me, I guess—*Finis*.

Still no mail from home telling me of the receipt of the $180 or as to Mother's condition.

Had a wonderful letter from Melanie Strahl, John's Mother. Hers is certainly a beautiful character, so rare in these days of cheap life and commonness.

?← FT. BENNING, GA.
(WORRY)

Camp Adair, Oregon
Sept. 21, 1942

The usual type of Monday. Lectures all morning. Lesson Analysis and Lesson Plans all afternoon, then worked on training aids, and tonight after supper, cleaned rifles for tomorrow's show.

Received a letter from Mother today. She received the dough all okay and will soon be out of the hospital. Wrote her and Raff tonight. Now have a total of 15 letters owing me. A new man (a West Pointer) was assigned to our Company. Can't say if this will affect my disposition in the Company or not.

I have been thinking of going to Eugene on this coming weekend and seeing Uncle Fred and Ruth. Don't know for sure whether I will or not.

Signed the payroll voucher tonight--$172.75. I have to catch up on two months of my insurance, and I think I will also have a monthly deduction of an $18.75 War Bond taken from my pay every month. It will be a way of saving automatically, in addition to my other savings, for I have to save even faster now to get that home.

Camp Adair, Ore.
Sept. 22, 1942
A hard morning of extremely hard work in practical work on "Training of the Individual Soldier." Built training aids all afternoon, came home (after going to the PX and having one bottle of 3.2 beer), had supper.

Received a letter from Leo Cook and so answered it tonight. My proofs of the pictures I had taken Saturday came back today, and as I fully expected, they were monstrous. He may be able to salvage them I don't know. I ordered two grinning and two sober. All the other poses were too horrible.

Got up at 5 this morning and walked up to 1st Bn. Area and had the cadre fall out for reveille.

Am beginning to get that lonely, disgusted feeling again, so guess I will go to bed early and see if I can't mayday it. May go to Eugene Saturday. I don't know.

I rather expect to be Officer of the Day sometime next week so will have to study up on Interior Guard procedure.

I still think life is one ironic joke. Just what is the point of it?

Camp Adair, Oregon
September 24, 1942
I doubt very much if this will be a very long passage tonight.

Tomorrow is a fateful day. I have to take Company C and put it through the paces on reconnaissance patrols and then critique the operation of same before the Battalion.

No mail of any kind today. Things are not as harmonious around the Company as they could be. The latest L. rumor now has it that we will not have any men until after the first of the year. M'Gawd! Three more months of this stuff, and I will be batty. Duty Officer again tomorrow. I have a tendency to be despondent again, but I am not going to allow it to grasp me. I will, I will strive to improve myself continuously, both physically and mentally. I am not going to let this constant loneliness and despondency get me down. I seem to be denied any happiness, but believe me, at least I can strive to improve myself constantly, and who knows, perhaps happiness will take care of itself.

CAMP ADAIR, OREGON
SEPTEMBER 25, 1942
Worked on Lesson Plan and Analysis for "Practice Marches" that I thought I had to give today. (That is, I worked until late last night.) Am writing this during my lunch hour, and so far, have received no mail at all.

Tomorrow is Saturday, and as I have mentioned, I may go to Eugene and try to have a good time. So far, in all my excursions on weekends, I have had a lousy time.

We have had one Lieutenant go batty so far, although I understand he was noticeably crazy before he did so. He went A.W.O.L. over last weekend—returned Tuesday and was placed under arrest. He again left, and so far, hasn't returned, although he did phone up from Eugene (drunk) and say he would return when he felt like it. Needless to say, he will be minus a commission when he returns.

Our big Battalion Demonstration (which B Company presented) came off very well yesterday, I understand. General Kramer, who was present, was very pleased and called it excellent instruction.

CAMP ADAIR, OREGON
SEPTEMBER 29, 1942
What a day! Worked harder today than since I left Benning. Wrote some letters, took a shower, and believe me, I'm gonna turn in early!

Went to Eugene over the weekend, and as usual, had a lousy time, although it was better than the Portland weekend. Uncle Fred and Aunt Ruth weren't home. Went out on a blind date with Lt. Aronson. What a "monster" the date was! University of Oregon senior, and as appealing as a bucket of soapsuds. I don't know, maybe I'm just antagonistic to all women. Stayed at the Hotel Corvallis Saturday night and walked around town all day Sunday. Came back to Corvallis on the bus, met Lt. Green, who was driving Upham's car, and I drove him back to Camp, as he was in a decidedly "unstable" state. I am practically out of ready cash, as I don't like to use my checking account. I will be Officer of the Day on this coming weekend so will have to study up on the procedure of "formal guard mount."

Too tired to be disgusted tonight.

CAMP ADAIR, ORE.
SEPTEMBER 30, 1942
The last day of September! No mail at all today. That fact can really

make one feel well! Worked like a dawg today, too. An exceedingly tough morning of bayonet drill and calisthenics, and this afternoon, in a rehearsal for a battalion demonstration to be put on tomorrow, I crawled about 1,000 yards flat on my stomach. Tomorrow we put on the actual problem, with firecrackers added, for realism.

I guess we will get paid shortly, and I can sure use the money, as I have a great amount of things to buy in preparation for when we enter into actual training—principally, a short coat ($315) and a field jacket.

Rather lonely and blue tonight. Wish I had some incentive to live and work for. Dog tired again tonight, so I guess I will take a shower tonight and retire.

One cheering note—my stage fright is fading fast away. I find it now surprisingly easy to get out in front of the men and present a subject in a clear, concise manner.

Hallelujah!

Camp Adair, Ore.
October 1, 1942

Exhausted tonight! Put on the Battalion demonstration today, and it was mediocre, to say the least, due to insufficient preparation by Lieutenant Upham. Paid today, so I sent the check to the bank and will draw whatever is necessary via personal checks.

I have so many expenses this month; it makes me shudder, though. My pictures came back from Corvallis today—a little on the monster side, perhaps, but with my features.

Also took out an allotment (to be taken out of all future checks) for one $25 War Bond every month. Listed Harold as the beneficiary in the event of my death.

Hard labor all afternoon in the Company Area. Guess I will send one picture to Mother, one to Mr. and Mrs. Morgan, and keep the other two.

Don't think I'll write any letters tonight. I'll save that for over the weekend, for as Officer of the Day, I'll have to stay around the regimental area all weekend.

Camp Adair, Ore.
October 2, 1942

Fairly easy day, this date. Usual repetitious instruction all morning, and Lesson Plans and Analysis all afternoon. Orders came out on the

DB this morning—I am Officer of the Day and also Company Duty Officer over the entire weekend. So, a pleasant (and boring) weekend looms in the offing.

The Skipper celebrated his "railroad tracks" (Captain's bars) tonight, so I spent a half-hour shooting the bull with he and the Bn. Commander, Colonel Smith. By the way, Colonel Smith seems to be a prince of an old duffer.

No mail at all today, and I haven't answered those I have received, saving that for something to do over the weekend.

Life again seems to be continuing on its lonely path of melancholy for me. It seems cause for regret to me, in a way. Life could be so full and mean so much, especially in these times when every hour and minute must be lived to the utmost, before. And yet my life must be squandered on the interminable sands of loneliness.

Camp Adair, Ore.
October 3, 1942
Worked around Company Area all morning. At 11:30 a.m., we had formal guard mount, at which time I took over the duties of Officer of the Day for today. I have to inspect the sentries twice before midnight, and once between midnight and reveille.

Cleaned up my room this afternoon and packaged and addressed the pictures I am going to mail. No mail this morning, and I hardly expect any this afternoon. I have been busy paying my bills and must say the old bank account is dwindling at a terrific rate.

Went to the PX and had two 3.2 beers and bought some magazines and sundry articles that I needed.

Guess I will write to Harold tonight, also, as I haven't heard from him since I left San Francisco.

I was just thinking—the first of next month I would have been married 5 years, if faithfulness had still meant what it should.

As it is, on Dec. 18th, I will have been divorced for 3 years.

Camp Adair, Ore.
October 5, 1942
My duties as O.D. were successfully culminated yesterday noon. I finally got the pictures and Mother's package sent off after a hectic time getting the stamps. Spent all morning out in the cold, dank hills, which surround this cantonment, creeping, and crawling "a la infantryman,"

in preparation for the demonstration, which our Bn. will present for the benefit of the Divisional Officers on Friday afternoon, and in which I will participate.

I have been selected as the officer from my Company to attend the Camouflage School, so I spent 2 hours in school this afternoon at a long conference on said subject, at the end of which we had a Graded Test, which I feel sure I passed successfully. The last two hours were spent in clambering over Coffin Butte (the Camp's most prominent landmark). Despite the <u>rigorous</u> physical work of today, I feel <u>swell</u> tonight.

Lt. Bertram and I have laid tentative plans for a weekend in Portland, so once more I sally forth in search of a few hours of merriment and happiness. And who knows, maybe this time?

CAMP ADAIR, ORE.
OCTOBER 6, 1942
Rehearsal for Division Demonstration again all morning. My role in same has been changed somewhat. I am an umpire of the demonstration (I might add, <u>the</u> umpire) and will therefore walk about the field communicating with the officer-in-charge via one of the "Walkie-Talkie" radios. Camouflage School again all afternoon. Subject: "Choice of Positions." Tomorrow afternoon will be the final day of the school and will consist of practical work, digging in a machine-gun nest, and camouflaging the same.

The weekend in Portland seems to be certain now, as Lt. Bertram managed to get a substitute for his "Duty Officer" assignment.

Received a letter from Rafferty today, and it is certain now that he will graduate from old "Fort Benning University for Boys." Nice work, Lug!

Also a letter from Mother, who is now back in Sonora and is worried as the devil about her doctor bill. She doesn't have to worry, though; she still has my bankbook, which should allay the majority of the bill.

Somewhat despondent tonight.

CAMP ADAIR, ORE.
OCTOBER 7, 1942
Dress rehearsal for the big demonstration all morning. Spent it crouched in the bushes with the radio transmitter and a Garand slung across my back.

Finished the last day of the Camouflage School this afternoon, and our group was voted the best gun position of the lot.

Fate seems to be intervening on the proposed Portland jaunt. No rooms at all available in Portland for reservation. Received no mail at all today.

Lt. Bertram and I still intend to go to Portland, but I hope—and I hope not in vain this time—that we will have a good time this time. The last three times I went out proved to be complete flops.

I am beginning to feel quite a bit better physically, due to several nights of wonderful sleep.

Tonight, as a closing thought, I wish to hell all the weeks of preliminary training were over and I was on my way overseas.

I ask only one final thing of life. If and when I die, let me die honorably and bravely, a soldier's death.

CAMP ADAIR, ORE.
OCTOBER 8, 1942

Lesson Plans and Analysis all morning, and this afternoon, another rehearsal for the big demonstration tomorrow. Again my role has been changed somewhat. I am still the umpire, but I am also to give an exhibition as a reconnaissance scout, which consists of skulking along a patch of woods, holding a Garand at an aggressive angle, crawling under and over two barbed-wire fences, and rushing across a 5-acre field by the "simple" process of rushing 20 yards and then "hitting the dirt," then repeating this process countless times until the other side of the field is gained and then disappear into the woods. All this to the great detriment of my knees and body, as this particular portion of Oregon is famed for its unyielding earth.

Again no mail at all, but I wrote to Mother and Art Morgan. By the way, there is something puzzling in the extreme—not a word or letter from Vivian or her folks for over a month and a half. (?????)

Portland trip still pending, but I have my fingers crossed for the success of the same.

CAMP ADAIR, ORE.
OCTOBER 9, 1942

The tempo of events again increases! Was told to report to the Regimental Adjutant this afternoon, and he asked me how I would like to attend the Cannon Company School at—dear old Fort Benning!

Naturally, I told him I was very interested in that, and he said he would keep me in mind. What I said is definitely true, much as I hate Georgia and its clime. I would gladly endure it for the sake of what this school can teach me, for after all, the more schools I can go to, the more I will learn, and the more I learn, the faster I can advance. Then, too, it is imperative that I learn all I can, for if I am fortunate enough to survive this war, I intend, with all the earnestness in my being, to make the Army my life work. There is nothing I desire more. However, I hold no great hope of being one of the lucky ones selected to go (due again to my old curse of lack of experience), and so all I can do for the present is to keep my fingers crossed, and hope.

The big and long-rehearsed Divisional Demonstration came off this afternoon, and it was a tremendous success. Three generals, 8 colonels, and numerous lesser bigwigs were present, and Gen. Cook was extremely lavish in his praise. Our Bn. Commander (Colonel Smith) thanked each officer personally for his cooperation. He is one officer that truly sets an example to strive to emulate.

Feminine companionship seems to be assured for our weekend. I have a blind date for Saturday evening and a blind date with an Army nurse for Sunday. I hope neither one proves to be a monster. We leave at noon tomorrow, and I again voice the hope that <u>this</u> weekend will prove to be a different story from previous "fiascoes."

No mail at all today and for the past two days. Looks as though I have been forgotten again.

Camp Adair, Ore.
October 12, 1942
Lost out on the Cannon School deal, but I am just as well satisfied. Either way it would have worked out, I would have been satisfied. In some respects, the Portland weekend was a success, and in others, not. Spent a great deal of money. Had a date Saturday night with a "Lonnie," which I personally didn't have a very high opinion of. The Army nurses were okay, too, but nothing out of the ordinary. Along the last of Sunday evening, I met a cute little blonde named Ruth, and she wanted me to write her, and we have a date for the weekend after next. She is pretty nice, but I detect the old familiar blonde tactics, so believe me, as far as I am concerned, she is just another date. I really can't understand myself. I seem to get in arguments with all the women I meet. Or perhaps I am just allergic to them. At any rate, it's always the

same old story—nothing ever moves my pulse. They are just a bunch of women to me. I know now that it must be true, as I said before, everything was burnt out of my heart about three years ago.

Camp Adair, Oregon
October 13, 1942
Lesson Plans and Analysis all morning and attended a Battalion Demonstration and then had practical work in the same for the balance of the afternoon.

Lt. Wingenbach of our Company was transferred to C Company. We will definitely have the Landscaping Detail this weekend, so no one leaves the Camp over the weekend.

Wild rumor that the recruits will be in <u>very</u> soon. Received the shoes I requested Harold to send but no letter. Received a letter from Warrant Officer Cook, but that's all.

Think I was the most mad and disgusted with this place since I have been here today. The weather has turned bitterly cold, and it is raining softly. The patter of the rain outside my window brings anew the longing, the loneliness, and a host of memories of other, and perhaps happier days.

Finally, after such a long time, I guess Vivian and I are at last really finished. She only wrote once and failed to answer my second letter, so I never wrote again, which after all, is all for the best I guess.

Camp Adair, Ore.
October 14, 1942
Lesson Plans and Analysis all morning. Excused for a short time this afternoon to go to the hospital and see my Platoon Sgt. Took the opportunity to stop by the Officers PX and buy my necessary short coat. Cost $35.95, but it is certainly very nice. Came back and worked around the Company Area for the balance of the afternoon.

Received a letter from Vivian today, but I don't think I will answer it, as in thinking it all over, perhaps that would be the best way to end our friendship; for it can never be anything more. In that manner, it would die unnoticed, and she would feel free to go on and find someone who would return her affections.

Did not receive any mail other than that.

Lt. Miller had a birthday today, so we all gathered in his room, which gathering included Captain Farrington and Colonel Smith.

Sat around and drank Scotch until about 9 p.m., at which time I excused myself and returned to finish my refurbishing of my uniform equipment.

Feel lonely and ill at ease tonight, and again, the eternal question, "Just what is the purpose of my very purposeless life?" hovers in my mind.

CAMP ADAIR, ORE.
OCTOBER 15, 1942
Tired and worn out tonight. Was in charge of the gravel detail all day, and we shoveled and loaded 7, 2-1/2-ton loads of gravel.

Received a letter from Ruth this noon to which I sent an immediate reply stating that I would call for her this weekend, as we are not going on the "dirt detail" over the weekend. It is quite definite. Lt. Aronson, Lt. Bertram, and I are going to Portland over the weekend and have a suite reserved at the Hotel Multnomah. Don't know how it will work out, but I hope satisfactorily.

Also received a letter from Mother, and she is evidently feeling much better, for which I am very grateful. She received the picture I sent, as did the Morgans.

Another social gathering in my room tonight—Lt. Aronson, Lt. Wingenbach, Lt. Bertram, Lt. Drosman, Captain Prevics, Captain Farrington—and tonight we drank rum. I only had one drink, though. Our CO (Captain Prevics) is getting harder and harder to understand.

Recruits should arrive soon, and then we will be so busy, no more weekends.

OCTOBER 19, 1942
CAMP ADAIR, ORE.
The weekend was a huge success, albeit somewhat expensive for me. Ruth and I had a wonderful time, and it was with real regret that I left for Adair. She is an awfully nice girl, but again, my habit of icily analyzing each companion of an evening, disclosed, as it always does, each fault in painful clearness. A nice girl, but absolutely no quickening of my pulse. In many respects, she reminds me of the great V., blonde, petite, charming manners, but also, shrewish temper, jealousy. In fact, in a few more years, she would be another Virginia.

No more weekends for me. I have sated my unholy appetite for merriment and companionship for a while. My next paycheck will be awfully small, as all deductions will be taken out this month—insurance, war bond, etc.

I have reason to worry, I suppose, if I but let myself, but I'm not. Tired tonight. No sleep Saturday, no sleep Sunday, gravel detail today (9 loads), and just worn out. I owe four letters but have got to let it go. Just can't make it tonight.

OCTOBER 20, 1942
CAMP ADAIR
12:10 a.m. at this writing. Lt. Furey, Lt. Bertram, and Lt. Swerz were in for a social gathering, and we did quite nicely by a quart of bourbon. Getting to be a regular old sot, am I not? Wrote Mother, Bob, and Ruth, explaining to Ruth that I wouldn't be up to Portland again for some time.

I think the justly famed gravel deal is about completed, as the Bn. has just about a surfeit of gravel now. What we do from now on remains to be seen.

I have resolved to stay in Camp for the next two consecutive weekends, so I imagine they will be dull and tedious periods of time for me.

Received a letter from Vivian, but I do not think I will answer it in order to pursue the plan I have originally mentioned. Also, a letter from Margie, which I had best mention, but it is going to be puzzling to answer all right.

Bob's application for Flying Cadet was approved, for which I am truly glad, as it was what he wanted; but I hope to God he never gets into actual combat.

OCTOBER 21, 1942
CAMP ADAIR
Exhausted upon arising this morning. Built one sidewalk today and loaded over 15,000 rounds of ammunition into machine-gun belts, by machine, of course. Went to the PX tonight and bought some magazines. Intend to retire in a few moments and try to recuperate a little. Have had the feeling, since my return from Portland, that I am not progressing, and the usual gloomy mental aftermath, which always follows one of my weekends.

We will definitely have the "dirt-handling detail" this coming weekend. Received one letter from Lola today, and that was all.

I do not intend to let this "Gloomy Aftermath" get a grip on me this time. Instead, I think I will view the coming tedious days with a cheerful air and see if that isn't better.

Received a birth announcement card from the Fergusons, and it makes me think with regret of the home and family that could have been mine but for--. Oh well, no benefit in dwelling on that subject, I guess. Three years of bitter memories have passed, and perhaps that is enough.

October 22, 1942
Camp Adair

Another dull, dreary, boring day—of really—marking time. Sidewalks, "Company installations," etc. Lt. Aronson and Lt. Wingenbach and I finished the bourbon tonight, thank God. It appeals less and less. Received a letter from Mother Melanie in Los Angeles, which I answered as well as one to Margie. Puzzling situation there.

Still have a tendency to feel a trifle depressed but am not going to let it get me.

Latest rumor now circulating—"entire 104th Division will be moved en masse to Fort Leonard Wood, Missouri." Pure speculation methinks, due to the delayed arrival of our men.

Melanie sent me John's new address. He has been transferred to some bombardment group in Australia.

I wish, somehow, that we were on our way overseas and could get this thing over with.

I'll probably be dead again in the morning. It is now 11:40 p.m., and oh what a struggle I have to get up in the morning.

October 23, 1942

10:45 p.m. Aronson and I spent the entire day working on the Company Area, and as a result, I am really tired tonight. No mail at all today. However, I sent the picture she wanted and wrote to Lola and John Strahl as well. Shined my Sam Browne belt, and then Lt. Ereza dropped by and said to come down to his room where I partook of two slightly stiff highballs.

Tomorrow morning we again work on the Company Area, and then in the afternoon, we have the long-dreaded dirt detail.

I learned tonight that I have been selected as the Officer from Co. B. to attend the Mess Officer School, for which I shall receive a diploma (!)

One good thing—I do think all of this hard work is doing me a world of good physically. Whether I do as much to tear it all down by these occasional drinks, I don't know. I hardly think so, however, as I certainly don't drink to excess. Anyway, who is there to give a damn whether I drink or not? No One.

Sunday, Oct. 25. 1942
Camp Adair, Oregon

Dug and hauled 4 loads of dirt yesterday afternoon and did the same thing this morning. We were going to haul more this afternoon, but when we came in for lunch, the Captain had just received a telegram notifying him of his Mother's death. He immediately left on a 15-day emergency leave, so this afternoon, I spent my time cleaning my room to a spotless stage.

No mail at all today. Received a letter from Ruth, Saturday, and it had the same old line, "Why do you have to remain in Camp for 2 weekends?" "I wait so anxiously for your mail." "I can't wait to see you again." Etc., etc. She is a little young, I guess (18), or I imagine she would know better than to use such timeworn tactics. Just another Virginia, or at least she will be in a few more years. I may go up and see her again on Nov. 7-8, but—just another date to me.

Furey and Ereza's girls came down this week and had lunch at the Officers Mess.

Think I will give myself a complete physical refurbishing and relax for the balance of the day.

October 26, 1942
Camp Adair

A gloomy day. Received no mail at all. It drizzled slightly all day today, but nevertheless, we went out and rehearsed a problem, which B Company must present tomorrow morning. At 5 p.m., all companies joined in an intensive search from Coffin Butte, east, for scrap iron. We finished that at 6 p.m., had supper, cleaned up, and then attended Regimental School until 9:45 p.m. Turned down an invitation for some highballs in Bertram's room.

Have felt so disgusted with this miserable killing of time around here. It is almost a temptation to go "over the hill." Here we sit killing time when we have a completely furnished modern Army Camp and no men. Yet this country never needed trained young men before more in its history than at the present time. All of this bickering over drafting the 18 year olds! Waiting for elections. Yet the truth is, this country is being <u>licked</u> <u>right</u> <u>now</u>. Not that we won't win, eventually, for <u>we will</u>! But <u>can't</u> they see that all this senseless delay only means <u>more</u> needless sacrifice, more Pearl Harbor!

October 29, 1942

For the past two days, I was given a detail of men and was told to have them rearrange the Battalion Area. After finishing tonight, the Colonel came to my room and told me the work was performed in a <u>superior</u> manner! (!) Oh yes! Special orders came out from Div. HQ, and I was selected from Co. B. to attend the school on Mess Management from Nov. 2nd until Nov. 24th, upon graduation to receive a diploma. Tonight I was informed that I have been appointed Regimental Police and Prison Officer for the next month, which is a full-time job, but must be accomplished "in addition to my other duties."

Received one letter today from Ruth. Answered it tonight. I am Duty Officer over the weekend, which is also payday and Halloween, so I must watch the others prepare for a joyous weekend, and I remain in Camp.

Beginning to pick up weight again—152—and feel very good physically due to these rigorous days of work. I <u>think</u> after this present date with Ruth—no more. That is, if I can terminate it diplomatically. Already, she is getting a little too serious for me, and that doesn't pay.

Camp Adair, Ore.
October 31, 1942

Have been extremely busy for the past few days on my new job of Regimental P&P Officer. I find the work quite interesting. I have a detail of 14 men with which to work on the various jobs of construction, which I am assigned.

Mother Melanie sent me a pair of silver bars from Los Angeles. So darn sweet of her, and yet I fear she was a trifle optimistic, as methinks it will be many months before I earn the privilege of wearing the bars of a 1st Lieutenant.

Received a letter from Margie today, and also one from Lola, which I answered immediately. I took over Ereza's duty as Officer of the Day, as he had planned to go to Portland anyway, and I had to remain in Camp as Duty Officer.

Wrote Mother the other night and asked her if she would make me some curtains for my room. It is raining violently outside tonight, and I am in a thoughtful, but not despondent, mood.

CAMP ADAIR, OREGON
NOVEMBER 1, 1942
Woke up about 10:30 a.m., too late for breakfast. Took a refreshing shower, shaved, and dressed for the Guard Mount Ceremony. After Guard Mount, came back to quarters and went to Mess Hall and had a very nice turkey dinner. Several of the officers brought their wives and sweethearts to lunch, and it made me a trifle envious. Wish that it were possible for me to do that sometime, but I don't think I ever will, unless it is with a girl that I intend to marry, which is, of course, something that will never happen.

Have made up my mind, once and for all, to put all my resolutions into effect, and from now on, I shall strive continually to attain my goal of being an excellent, capable officer--and a gentleman.

Received a letter from Rafferty. He graduated from O.C.S. at Benning and was assigned to Camp Robinson, Arkansas. He had a 12-day leave, but that wasn't enough time for him to come home and see his folks.

Well, who knows? We may yet run into each other before this war is over.

CAMP ADAIR, ORE.
NOVEMBER 2, 1942
What a day! It poured a torrential downpour all day long, which caused the entire Regimental Area to be flooded, due to the "well-engineered" drainage system that had been installed. Being Regimental Police and Prison Officer, my faithful detail was called to the rescue, and working hard all day, I managed to stem the flood. Also had another detail of 15 men put in my charge to construct walks and scrapers around the Officers Quarters. Tomorrow, I will have an additional 10 men put under my supervision for Regimental work. I had two conferences in Colonel Cochran's Office pertaining to the work, and one with the Adjutant. Tomorrow, I also have an enormous day's work ahead of me. One thing about the job, despite the pure <u>hell</u> of it, I am in continual contact with the brass hats.

Received a nice letter from Melanie, and Bob's picture arrived. It sure is swell. He's so damn young, tho, why did he have to get in this mess? Just having his picture around decreases the loneliness around here. He's <u>swell</u>!

The boys came back from Portland—and with some interesting facts regarding Ruth. She is evidently exactly what I thought she was—a replica of Virginia. She went out with Aronson, and although she told him she thought he was repulsive and questioned him about me continually, she is pulling the old blonde tactics, even called Bertram up at the hotel and asked him for a date on Sunday. Well, it only means I'll go through with our planned date all right, for I don't go back on my word, but I'll break it off exactly as I had planned.

One amusing incident today, old Colonel Floyd, who is notorious for his crustiness, left a notice on the Regimental bulletin board that he wanted to see me. I contacted him, and he said, "One of your truck drivers drove over my planted area." In an effort to be courteous, I said, "Thank you, Sir. I'll caution him about that." Whereupon, with his usual explosive bark, he replied, "Caution, Hell—eat his Goddamn A-- out!"

Soaked to the skin all day today but no ill effects, and as a matter of fact, my physical condition is continually improving.

Camp Adair, Ore.
November 3, 1942
More difficult daily grows the Police and Prison Officer detail! Didn't receive the 10 men (extra) today but will for sure tomorrow, and I now have about 1,000 additional jobs to put them on.

Have been attending the Mess Management School for the past 2 days, and believe me, it is very inefficiently conducted.

Was invited to go skating with the crowd tonight but just didn't feel like it. Received a photo booklet of Texas from Bob, my only mail today.

Not a great deal to write about today. I feel rather "low" tonight.

The 96th Division is now receiving its new men at a rapid pace, so I think I am safe in saying that it will not be so very long until our men start arriving.

We had our pictures taken today for our identification cards.

For tonight, my mind is a mental blank, so I may as well close.

CAMP ADAIR, ORE.
NOVEMBER 4, 1942
Pure hell all day—the P&P job, I mean. "Nuff said."

No mail at all for the last two days. Wonder what happened to everybody?

Don't know how this weekend will turn out, in view of the many (so far) puzzling circumstances. I will have to attend that damn Mess School tomorrow and Friday, which interferes something terrible with the P&P Officer job.

For some reason, probably an accumulation of all the discouraging incidents that have occurred so recently, I have lost a great deal of my enthusiasm for Camp Adair, and even some of my high ambitions and ideals seem to be slipping. These, however, I hope to regain. I have been retiring early every night and have managed to get a very good night's sleep steadily, all of which has done me a great deal of good.

The P&P job is very valuable in one respect—I am learning to handle men and organize their labors. If they would just leave me <u>alone</u>!

CAMP ADAIR, ORE.
NOVEMBER 9, 1942
A wonderful weekend, albeit a trifle expensive for me, but it was indeed worth it. Told Ruth it was best that we forget our meeting, but she said she would expect a letter from me. However, I <u>can't</u> write. If I did, it would only complicate things further. She's sweet, though. I don't care. I'm afraid I have given her a raw deal. <u>Why</u> did I have to have an experience that the memory of it always spoils everything beautiful that I ever find?

P&P job functioning now with some degree of efficiency. I <u>heard</u> I was given a very good efficiency rating on the monthly efficiency report. Who knows, perhaps I will be an Officer yet.

The Grand Ball and Official opening of our Officers Club takes place this Saturday. Attendance at same is <u>compulsory</u>, and I will stag it <u>as usual</u>, I guess.

Only 2 hours' sleep last night, and it is midnight now, so perhaps had best call it a night.

<u>Rumor</u>: (Latest) Fillers <u>soon</u>!

NOVEMBER 11, 1942
Today a holiday, so I went to Salem last night with Aronson, Ereza,

Bertram. Had a perfectly <u>lousy</u> time. Was stranded at some dive and had to take a taxi back to town. Got back to Camp at 5:45 a.m. Slept till noon and then spent the day cleaning my room, etc. Wrote a few letters.

My original supposition that handling the many men and duties necessary on the P&P job would give me valuable experience in handling men is certainly proving true. About the last vestige of self-consciousness I had is rapidly crumbling.

Feel rather good physically but, mentally, I am rather despondent. It seems no matter how hard I try, happiness is denied me, and I guess that it will always be that way for me.

Have received no mail for some time. It is quite definite that no leaves will be granted on Thanksgiving, and I fear such will be the case on Christmas, too.

A night problem will be held tomorrow night, following a prearranged compass course through the trackless wilds of Camp Adair, I presume.

CAMP ADAIR, ORE.
NOVEMBER 12, 1942

Another day gone. Hauled over 12 tons of rock-fill into the area today, as I received permission to use the steam shovel up on Coffin Butte. The Chapel area, which I am busy having my crew landscape, is finally beginning to take shape. Tomorrow I must complete a sidewalk and fence near the new Officers Club in preparation for the gala celebration this coming Saturday night.

We went on the night problem (compass course) tonight—3-1/2 miles in pitch darkness. Didn't have any trouble, outside of one argument with Upham, that silly ass.

Am supposed to go to the dispensary tomorrow for an eye check, after which they will issue me some new G.I. spectacles.

No mail at all for the past three days. I guess it is really all over with Ruth, as I told her I wasn't going to write.

Think I will turn in early tonight, as I have certainly been tired the last few mornings.

CAMP ADAIR, ORE.
NOVEMBER 13, 1942

<u>Truly a Momentous Day</u>! Colonel Smith called me over to his table at

the noon mess and told me to break Lt. McLaughlin in on the P&P job as soon as possible, as he was appointing me the Battalion S-3!

Such a remarkable turn of events leaves me dumbfounded. For this is indeed a tremendous step up for me and carries a much higher rank in time. If only now that I have it in grasp, I can make good on this job. I pray, tonight, with all the sincerity in my being, that God will see fit to make this so; and so tonight, I receive my chance to show that I have what it takes.

The big gala ball tomorrow night—and I guess I will stag it, although Captain Prevics wants me to take a girl his wife is acquainted with, known as Betty Lee. ???

A letter from Bob once more, and he is now in Nashville, Tenn. as an Air Cadet, and am I proud of him!

Nice going Pal!!!!

CAMP ADAIR, ORE.
NOVEMBER 16, 1942

I went to the reception in the Officers Club, and was introduced to Major General Cook, enjoyed the dinner (although a stag), but didn't go to the dance. Instead, Lt. Aronson and I retired to my room where, with the help of a case of 7-Up and a quart of bourbon, we had a private celebration of our own. Colonel Smith dropped in and joined us, and although Aronson went to sleep (as usual), the Colonel and I had a very interesting talk. It seems Colonel Cochran was very highly impressed with the way I handled the P&P job!

Today, I officially terminated my association with the B Co. and transferred my duties as P&P Officer to Lt. McLaughlin. Effective tomorrow, I start my new duties as Battalion S-3, and on this, I pray with all my heart that I will make good on this great chance the Lord has seen fit to offer me.

Sunday, I went on a blind date with Holzmann and met a very attractive sophomore from O.S.C. She was cute; and we had dinner, a show, and a half hour of dancing at her sorority house. Helen was her name.

Deathly silence from Ruth in Portland, and also from me in Adair.

CAMP ADAIR, ORE.
NOVEMBER 17, 1942

First day as S-3. Honors! No Less. Was given Major Elliott's office and desk. The work is somewhat complicated, but I think I am beginning to get the idea and certainly hope I can get into the swing of it soon.

I think Captain Prevics was slightly piqued at my getting appointed to the Colonel's staff. I rather think he was gunning for the job himself. It isn't worrying me, however, as I only follow orders, so to hell with him. I never liked him anyway.

A letter from Chambles today, and that was all. Still going to Mess School in the afternoons and hope to finish the course.

Seem to be having some trouble with my gums. They bothered me exceedingly today. Trench mouth?

I think I will retire early tonight (10 p.m.) for a change and catch upon some much needed sleep. Received about 75 recruits today, and I imagine the balance will start pouring in soon. As it is now, no more weekends, absolutely no Christmas leaves, and work on Saturdays and Sundays.

Camp Adair, Ore.
November 18, 1942
Hard at work today on training schedules for the 1st fourteen days until the MTP schedule starts. Learned some somewhat disconcerting news today, but I am not going to let it throw me. Captain Prevics definitely was after the job I now hold, hence the bitter sarcasm on his part. Captain Hall will be advanced to Bn. Executive, Captain Crane to S-2, and I ? who am now holding a Captain's job—will I be held on permanently as S-3, or until Major Elliott's return? One factor has to be considered there. Another cadre of officers will be sent out of here in about January, so if I "cut the buck" satisfactorily on it, I think I can hold it; however, fate alone will decide that issue, and therefore, I pray the Lord above to give me guidance and help tonight.

One letter today from the *Reader's Digest* Association notifying me that I would receive a year's subscription from Major W. E. Read! No other mail at all.

It is now almost midnight, so I had best retire, for I intend to work like a fiend tomorrow.

Oh yes! As a Staff Officer, I must now attend the Advanced Course in the Divisional School, presented by General Cook and General Kramer.

CAMP ADAIR, ORE.
NOVEMBER 20, 1942
11:42 P.M.
Heartily discouraged tonight. We had that damnable Division School problem, and as a member of Colonel Smith's Staff (S-3), I had to go. We had to write (as I thought) a solution to the problem, and as it turned out, I was, acting as S-3, supposed to write out a <u>field</u> order! I remember the field orders (FO) Colonel Crowell used to turn out at Callan, but unfortunately, never connected them with this particular phase. Result? Poor Colonel Smith did 99% of the work of the S-3 function today. I feel heartily ashamed, but <u>believe me</u>, I intend to learn FO. To make it worse, old *** Prevics acted (for today) as S-4, and I certainly noticed his continual attempts to throw a knife into me, which is only natural, seeing as I have the job he wanted. All I can do on the above, I guess, is to ask the Lord for guidance. Who knows?

One letter from Mother yesterday but none today at all. My teeth and gums have been bothering me something terrible, lately.

I am having no trouble on my schedule so far, and I sent my first week's schedule to Regiment today. Whether it will be approved or not, I do not know.

CAMP ADAIR, ORE.
NOV. 22, 1942
The fillers are arriving! 44 men were assigned to the 1st Bn. today. Actual tng. starts tomorrow on the temporary two-weeks schedule. Meanwhile, this weekend was a veritable <u>hell</u> to me. I worked until almost midnight, Saturday, almost all of today, and until 8:30 p.m. tonight. I have been going crazy in all that time trying to allocate an insufficient number of instructors to cover the horribly complicated plan that the "great" Major Elliott left me confronted with. I've <u>got</u> to organize some sort of definite plan by tomorrow, and I can only <u>pray</u> that I will be successful in doing so, for I certainly don't want to pull another FO *faux pas* on <u>this</u>. I've <u>got</u> to make a good impression on Colonel Smith and <u>demonstrate the fact beyond all doubt that I can handle the job</u>.

No mail at all for several days, and I am getting so I don't care whether I get any or not. People so seldom write.

I guess there will be no more weekends at all to look forward to--week after week of hard, unrelenting work--but that is one item that never harmed anyone.

CAMP ADAIR, ORE.
NOVEMBER 23, 1942
Much has occurred in the last few days. Lots of mail. Mother, Valerie with plans I requested from Camp Callan, and one from Vivian. I finally found a workable form in which to present the schedules, so my prayers were answered. I worked until midnight on two nights to accomplish it, though. Something big is in the wind. I was told to select an <u>understudy</u> for my job as S-3, so it looks very much as though I <u>may</u> be one of those who will leave here in January to form a new cadre, which would mean a promotion, of course. I selected Lt. Aronson as my understudy. I graduated from Ninth Corps School on Mess Management today and received a very fancy diploma and hearty congratulations from General Dunckel.

I think, but Oh God, how I hope not, I have some dread disease of the gums, as they have been bleeding and hurting oh so painfully the last week. I will go to the dentist tomorrow and learn the bad news, and on this, as usual, I pray that it is not something that will interfere with work!

CAMP ADAIR, ORE.
NOVEMBER 26, 1942
THANKSGIVING DAY
It rained violently all day, and my gums ached and bled just as violently all day. Diagnosed yesterday as the start of Vincent's disease or trench mouth. Undoubtedly picked up in the Mess Hall. I have been washing my mouth out every 3 hours with Hydrogen of Peroxide, but it doesn't seem to be of much avail. I go to the dentist's again tomorrow.

Felt so lonely and depressed today that I called the Morgans long distance and wished them a happy Thanksgiving.

Due to the mix-up caused by the Regimental S-3, I do not know if <u>my</u> schedules are mixed up or not. But I <u>do</u> know that starting tomorrow, I must make out next week's schedule and then dive into the MTP breakdown, for I have <u>got</u> to convince Colonel Smith that I am worthy of his trust. Payday is next Monday, and I spent very little of last month's pay (with the exception of the Portland weekend). It is just as well, what with all these new taxes coming up.

A prayer today to the effect that <u>I will make good as S-3</u>.

CAMP ADAIR, ORE.
NOVEMBER 30, 1942
Worked like mad today, for I must make good on this job! The new MTP arrived today˙ from Division, and I must revise it completely as well as draw up plans for a new Non-Coms School and get out next week's training schedules.

Was really surprised today, though. I thought I would surely catch hell, as I was gone all afternoon to a conference with the Regimental S-3 and then to the dentist's. On returning to my office, I explained what had happened during the afternoon, and he [Colonel Smith] said, much to my supreme amazement, "Fine staff work, Mac, and by the way, you are doing just fine on the job—keep it up." So I feel rather fine tonight, but believe me, I really intend to put out on all my work and to uphold my job.

Gee! It feels good to be doing work you are interested in—and advancing, too. If only I had someone to plan with and for. One who, whatever happened, would be pulling for me. One who would make life worthwhile!

The 30th of next month will be my 27th birthday, and life so far, just a meaningless existence!

CAMP ADAIR, ORE.
DEC. 1, 1942
Worked hard today. Just about completed next week's schedule and the school for Non-Coms, so the only big item now facing me is the revision of the MTP, which is going to be pure hell.

An interesting thing today--. Today was the day when all efficiency reports on all officers must be in, and I happened, by merest chance to get a glimpse of mine that the Colonel wrote out on me. Much to my amazement, he had rated me Superior in every category but one, which was marked excellent. Superior is the highest rating attainable, so if I can only repeat that performance from month to month, I will feel that I am becoming a true officer.

Attended school tonight (Division), and Lt. Aronson, as my understudy, had to go.

Only one thing now worries me, and that is, let me do a good job on the revision of the MTP.

It is now 12:30 p.m., so I think I will turn in, as I am awfully tired. No mail today.

Camp Adair, Ore.
Dec. 3, 1942
A little puzzled and bewildered today. Colonel Smith helped me and assisted me so much on the MTP that I fear he did about 99% of the actual technical work. While he said nothing and is still (!) as nice as he has always been to me, I wonder if this will make any difference in his opinion of my abilities.

I understand recommendations went in today for certain men to be promoted to 1st Lieutenant, however, I hold no hopes for myself on this score. I expect to be a 2nd for at least a year, so no excitement wells in my breast at the news.

I yet have an enormous amount of work to accomplish before the week is over, and tomorrow is another damnable Division problem, so it looks very much as though the tentative plans I had plotted, to go to Portland with Lt. Furey, will not be cancelled.

Worked until midnight last night with the Colonel—and school every other night this week—so I haven't even had time to write any letters.

Still hoping for the Lord's assistance and help on this S-3 work.
?

Camp Adair, Ore.
December 4, 1942
What a day! Went crazy this morning trying to readjust schedules because of rain. Finally succeeded after 2 hours. Then worked like mad all the rest of the morning trying to finish the NCO School schedule and next week's schedules.

This afternoon, the Division problem--wading through swamps and muck, freezing to death. <u>Miserable</u>! I was so far behind in my work that I didn't stop to eat much.

Went back to work tonight after supper, but the Colonel ordered me to be sure and leave by 8 p.m., as he said I had been working too late. (!)

I <u>may</u> get to go to Portland tomorrow, I don't know for sure. If I do, it will be a stag affair, as far as I am concerned. I have no date, but I guess that is to be expected anyway.

Tired tonight, so guess I will shower and turn in.

CAMP ADAIR, OREGON
DECEMBER 7, 1942

A truly "blue" Monday! I really think I "enjoyed" my last trip to Portland this last weekend. Had a horrible time, and the money spent was indeed not worth it. Work didn't seem to "go" today, either. Just couldn't seem to get going. The rain complicated the schedules something terrible, too! Tonight, as usual, I guess, I am thoroughly disgusted with life. I have made up my mind once and for all—I am going to stop looking for romance, for such a thing is definitely not in the cards for me.

Colonel Smith notified me Saturday that he had recommended me for promotion to 1st Lt. Somehow, though, I can't get very excited about it, for what in hell is the use of striving, trying my best to advance myself, if there is no purpose behind it? Foo!

Had a blind date on Sunday—name Sylvia—a divorcee. Cold, taciturn, highly nervous—a negative personality.

Despite the "low" attitude, I am determined to throw myself into my job with everything I have. Still determined to "show" that witch, Virginia, I can do it!

CAMP ADAIR, ORE.
DECEMBER 10, 1942

What a week! Hectic is no word. Rain! Downpours! Complicated schedules, not enough barracks for instruction, not enough instructors (etc.). Worked until 1 a.m. almost every night this week. Finally got two separate schedules out—one in case we start MTP training, one for Battalion Control. In my estimation, Colonel Smith is still doing too much of my work, though. I've got to turn out more work!

If I get time, I've got to mail all my Christmas cards this weekend. God knows that's all I am going to have time to shop for this year.

Another 4-hr Division School tomorrow afternoon, which means a lengthy field order to write by 10 tomorrow night.

Thought I was getting the flu for a while, but it faded out. My teeth are still bothering hell out of me.

No mail for days and days now. If I get all my work done, I may go to Salem Saturday.

Guess I'll turn in, as it is now 1 a.m.

Assistance, Dear Lord, in my work. I really need it.

Camp Adair, Ore.
December 13, 1942
Went to Salem last night and met a nice girl named Ardell. Made a date for New Year's Eve, but I don't know whether I'll keep it or not.

Came home today and did all my Christmas shopping at the PX. Bought myself a nice U.S. Army ring and a lounging robe. Bought Mother a string of pearls; Harold, a ring; Bob, an identification bracelet; Vivian, a locket.

Cleaned up my room thoroughly. The MTP training starts tomorrow. I finished the program but have yet to check the Company Commanders' schedules. I will be in charge of all training in the 1st Battalion tomorrow, as the Colonel has to go to Salem.

The Colonel made quite an issue of thanking me for my hard work all last week. He surely is swell. No mail today. Think I'll take a shower and turn in, as I am dog tired.

My teeth and gums are getting worse. I've got to get time to get to the dentist's tomorrow.

Camp Adair, Ore.
December 14, 1942
One of those days when it seems impossible to accomplish anything. Finished about half of the control directive but still have the worst of the problems yet to iron out. Tomorrow morning is the big 3-hour show that I had scheduled for over a thousand men to attend. Had a great deal of trouble getting the projector to function properly, and then the sound system went haywire. Finally had all arrangements and corrections made about 10 p.m.

Have heard no more about my promotion. In some ways, Colonel Smith puzzles me greatly. 99% of the time, he is a wonderful person to work for, but the other 1%, he is quite stern, and a little sarcastic. Can't blame him, though, I guess. He certainly has a huge responsibility on his shoulders, and I certainly don't hold it against him.

Had the urge, today, to slip back into my old feeling of despondency and despair, but I am not going to give into it. This job is not too big for me. I can and will, with God's assistance, make a success out of my life in the Army.

CAMP ADAIR, ORE.
DEC. 16, 1942

Myriads of petty details today, but regardless of this, this S-3 work is <u>darned</u> interesting! It was impressed on me today, through several odd circumstances, just what a lot of authority I <u>do</u> wield. Saw my name on the Officers roster in Regt'l HQ today, and underneath in red letters, the word, Captain. Which means nothing, actually, but the fact that I am really holding down a Captain's job, and eventually, if I can learn fast enough and work diligently enough, I may attain that rating.

Had quite an interesting talk with the Colonel today, and I believe that my ideals regarding the conduct of training in this battalion are highly approved of by him, and it is evidently up to me to enforce them. He left the entire Battalion in my charge today, as he is Acting Regimental Commander in Colonel Cochran's absence.

The only thing that worries me--if I can only learn field orders and the finer points of staff work--so that when maneuvers start, I can again do all my work efficiently and as a true officer should.

CAMP ADAIR, ORE.
DECEMBER 17, 1942

Again that feeling of not having accomplished much, with the exception of having found a few more ideal training areas. In all other respects, though, the "training obstacles" are immense. Chemical warfare situation all messed up. Lost time situation all messed up, etc., etc.

I've <u>got</u> to get all that straightened out. Must start work on the 3rd week's training schedule before long.

Mail today—and lots of it. A package from Mother and Harold, cards from lots of people. Uncle John wants me to come to Portland for Christmas, Uncle Fred to Eugene. If I can, I may go to Eugene, but I'm not overly enthused.

Another damn afternoon of school tomorrow afternoon, which will be pure hell and, as usual, it comes on a day when I am swamped with work.

Almost 1 a.m., and I am worn out in body and mind. I haven't been to bed prior to midnight for over a month. Those G-D schools, not worth a plugged nickel, yet we must go 5 nights a week. Disgusted and mad tonight, chiefly with myself, because I can't do better.

CAMP ADAIR, ORE.
DECEMBER 18, 1942
Managed to straighten out quite a few of the details, but things are not quite as perfect as I would like them.

Try as I might, it is again about midnight, although I didn't work tonight. Lt. Furey and I went over to the Officers Club and had a few beers and quite a bit of talk. He is an awfully fine fellow and one for whom I have the utmost respect. Although he is a West Pointer, he never refers to it, truly an admirable quality.

A card from Wavel in Vancouver today, inviting me up for a nice Christmas dinner. Also received the same invitation from Uncle John and Aunt Ruth (as mentioned before).

Felt simply terrible this morning, as though I were coming down with the flu, but it wore off. Tomorrow will be a critical day, and I can only hope the Colonel will be satisfied with the training.

Still can't figure out how New Year's will work out. I don't feel exactly enthused about going to Eugene, and yet Salem offers much less along the line of diversion.

CAMP ADAIR, ORE.
DECEMBER 19, 1942
Again, all is a mass of confusion and turmoil. Worked until about 10 p.m. with the Colonel and then made a tour of inspection with him later on. Just as I thought I had everything straightened out, things became all messed up because some dumb @*!?! didn't read orders.

Didn't go out this weekend, deliberately, because I knew I had too damn much work to catch up on.

Had another verification today, of the rottenness and cheap characteristics of the modern woman. John Strahl, who is in the front lines in Australia and recently sent money home to Olive to buy a wedding ring, found out that his so-called "true love" had been married for some three weeks, or at least so his Mother writes. Which all goes to show the sterling qualities of this modern generation of women.

I may get off Christmas Day, I don't know. Am not worrying too much about it. I just don't give a good GD anymore. I try, but am I getting anyplace? HELL NO!

Camp Adair, Ore.
December 21, 1942
Due to the rapidly climbing sick rate, recently (198 men in the hospital out of this Regiment), tomorrow was declared a day of rest and relaxation. So I prepared an hour-and-a-half show for all the men in the 1st Battalion, composed of a lot of interesting training films. I will give the introductory talk to the men prior to the showing of the films.

Heard a satisfactorily verified report tonight that Colonel Smith was <u>very</u> well pleased at the way I am handling the S-3 work. Glad to report that my stage fright has disappeared, for I had a chance to prove it today. I was in charge of over 600 men at one time in the Battalion Quadrangle and had to order them around into our complicated Bayonet formation. Who knows, I may be an <u>Officer</u>, yet!

Training schedule somewhat balled up, but I am so happy that I feel overflowing with assurance and confidence that I can handle the job, with some semblance of efficiency.

Camp Adair, Ore.
December 24, 1942
Christmas Eve
Again, as last year, I am in an Army Camp on this holy night, and again, as last year, I am lonely and lead just as purposeless an existence. Circumstances are perhaps different this year, in that I have bettered myself perhaps, but what is the point in bettering myself if there is no goal to strive for and no one to work for? I worked until 2300 last night and all of today. Finally, about 9 p.m. tonight, I got out my "control directive" on training, plus myriads of miscellaneous memorandums. I am not satisfied with the control directive, for I fear, despite my hardest efforts, it will prove inadequate. Margie sent me a lovely box of stationery. Aronson and I are going to Eugene tomorrow to have Christmas Dinner with Aunt Ruth and Uncle Fred.

Colonel Smith is down in bed with a severe cold, and that means I have got to cut the buck on training, for as a Staff Officer, I am now second in command of the Battalion until he recovers.

Oh God! My Christmas Prayer is to allow me to run my training henceforth without a flaw!

CAMP ADAIR, ORE.
DECEMBER 27, 1942
Borrowed the Colonel's car on Christmas, and Lt. Aronson and I went to Eugene and had Christmas Dinner with my Aunt Ruth and Uncle Fred. Very nice.

Last night, Ereza, Aronson, Bertram, and I went into Salem. I had a blind date—Arleen. Fairly nice, no brains, no personality. Don't know whether I'll go out or not on New Year's Eve.

Cleaned my room out thoroughly today and caught up on all my mail, finally.

If I get through next week all right without a screwed-up training schedule, I'll be the luckiest mortal alive. The Colonel will be back at work tomorrow, I guess. He certainly has been pretty sick.

My birthday, in 3 more days. 27 years old, and what the hell have I accomplished? Not a damn thing.

Think I will turn in early tonight and get a good night's rest.

CAMP ADAIR, ORE.
DECEMBER 28, 1942
Another typical Monday! Everything went wrong. To make it worse, I have so many types of as-yet-unfinished directives to turn out—allotment of ammunition, etc., etc. Colonel Smith still pretty sick, but he came to work for a while today and was not in too happy a mood.

Regimental School tonight. Worked for an hour or so after school but gave up in despair when I saw the prodigious amount of "excavation" the fourth week will entail.

Some of the promotions for those who were recommended when I was came through today. None for me as yet, but I still have hopes, as Colonel Smith was wondering about it today, too.

I will be Bn. Staff Duty Officer on New Year's Eve. But I don't mind, as I will do my celebrating, if any, on the following Saturday evening. Am not looking forward with any great expectancy to that night, however, as it will probably be a dismal failure, as were all the rest.

I pray again for guidance in the trying days ahead.

CAMP ADAIR, ORE.
DECEMBER 29, 1942
Again, a helluva day! I did manage to get the 4th week tng. directive out, but I feel as though I am quite far behind in my work. I have got

to get to work today (tomorrow) on that ammunition allotment thing, or else. Well, all I can do is to just put everything I've got into it and see what happens.

I do not think I will go out on cadre according to a list of names I happened to see today.

A few more promotions reached here today, but so far, no news of mine, and to tell the truth, I am beginning to wonder about it.

Had to go to Division School tonight. Training all messed up today on account of this damnable rain. A steady downpour all day, and it is beating against my windows in a violent storm now.

Received no mail at all today. Guess I must have caught up with all my correspondence at last.

For now, in a rather disgusted mood. I think I will turn in.

CAMP ADAIR, ORE.
DECEMBER 30, 1942
My Birthday—<u>27</u> years old today!

Yes, another milestone in the somewhat boring and monotonous story of my life has rolled around. To be truthful, I feel much older than my years perhaps indicate.

Tonight, I reflect on the year that has just passed, and truly, it has been a momentous year for me. Although I have advanced so far, beyond my wildest dreams, <u>I am not satisfied with myself</u>. I am worried as to whether I can satisfactorily and efficiently handle my job when things become really technical, i.e., firing on the range, ammunition allotments, staff work, field orders, etc. Well, that is one huge question mark that will only be answered by the passing of time. I know that at all times, I shall do my very best, and with the Lord on my side, I <u>will</u> win through.

I think I will write Mother a long letter tonight and retire early. Had hoped to receive my promotion on my birthday but no soap. It will surely come through soon, however, as much talk is being given that subject in certain quarters.

CAMP ADAIR, ORE.
JANUARY 3, 1943
Lt. Ereza and I went to a very drab and boring social function at the Elks Club in Corvallis on New Year's Eve. Had a lousy time with a bunch of ancient chickens and bald-headed roués trying to act sweet sixteen.

Didn't go out Saturday night as I had planned—instead presented a show in the Regimental Recreation Hall for the 1st Battalion, and gave a speech to each of the four showings. After that, I worked until 12:30 a.m. over at Bn. Hqtrs.

The entire Battalion was placed under quarantine today for mumps, measles, and spinal meningitis. This dismal fact complicates the training schedules beyond measure, and in fact, all of the work is becoming rapidly technical, so much so that I wonder. But to my amazement, Colonel Smith seems to think I am doing a marvelous job, and in fact, is so lavish in his praise that I am somewhat embarrassed, especially when he does it in the presence of fellow officers.

Floods are rampant throughout the Willamette, rain continuous, and what training we <u>do</u> present is awfully inefficient.

Camp Adair, Ore.
January 5, 1943

More and more complicated grows the job, in many respects. I had to raise hell today because some of my orders weren't carried out. Made some enemies by so doing, I guess, but believe me, if some of the inefficient, sloppy training that is going on, at present, is a sample of Fort Benning, I am certainly disappointed in my Alma Mater. If I have to lose a few so-called "friends" in order to do what my job calls for, well, it will have to be done, I guess.

No mail at all today, and still no news of the promotions. I would certainly like to know what the score is in that particular angle. Signed a voucher today for an additional $100 clothing allowance. Guess it will help to pay my income tax if nothing else.

Rather hope to get away this weekend, but who knows? Received a nice letter from Melanie the other day. No news from Fred since his last letter.

Camp Adair, Ore.
January 9, 1943

Oh God, how long? How long? These miserable, abominable, horrible weekends. Didn't want to, but I was selected to be on the Welcoming Committee at the dance, so I had to go. Same old usual tripe. Stand around, have a lousy time, and watch these so-called "officers and gentlemen" make asses out of themselves.

Every weekend that I go out, I swear I will never go on another one—have a rotten time <u>every time</u>.

Physically, I am deteriorating fast, I think. I haven't been to bed before midnight in over 2 months, what with working nights—5 nights of school per week, and now the damned Army even tells us how to spend the weekend.

Have given up hope on the damned promotion. Guess I shot my mouth off too soon, as usual, but dammit, I know the recommendation went in.

What the hell anyway. If I had someone to care and plan for, it might be different, but as it is, this lonely, damnable existence means <u>nothing</u>.

Camp Adair, Ore.
January 11, 1943

One of those horrible Mondays when <u>nothing</u> can be accomplished despite superhuman efforts. Worked like mad all day. For some reason, I have the uncomfortable feeling that I am "slipping" on this job. I'm not as assured as I was for a while. Am also in an extremely nervous condition, despite a large amount of sleep over the weekend.

No mail at all for days and days now, and I seem to get lonelier by the day.

Heard a well-substantiated rumor today that the long-looked-for promotions will be held up until we have 6 months' service in because "other men are waiting who have more seniority." Oh well, I thought such a thing was too good to be true anyway.

Rumor also hath it that we may go overseas in April or May. Lots of work lies ahead tomorrow so had best get all the sleep I can, for I have got to step up my efficiency.

Lonely—Lonely—Lonely.

Camp Adair, Ore.
January 14, 1943

I think McCully is, today, at about the lowest ebb he has been in months, both physically and mentally. If I don't start to get some rest, I feel sure something will "give" someplace. I just couldn't do a damn thing in the office today—couldn't do a damn thing.

I have several major problems now confronting me, the biggest of which is <u>getting the range procedure outlined</u>. Also have a big field order to turn out tomorrow, plus the School for Illiterates to organize and supervise, for I was appointed the director thereof by G-3.

I honestly think I am cracking up physically. I look simply terrible. My teeth are continually bothering me—I sincerely believe I have sinus trouble—and this continuous cold I have.

I pray tonight again for God's assistance in the many problems that will ensue in the next few days.

CAMP ADAIR, ORE.
JANUARY 15, 1943
For some strange reason or other, things went unaccountably smooth today. The FO's on the Division problem were handled without too much difficulty, and I managed to get the placement tests given to the illiterates without too much trouble.

Felt very good physically, too! Aronson, Ereza, and I have planned to go to Portland tomorrow night but don't know just yet for sure whether I will or not.

Still no word on the long-awaited promotion—and have had no mail for several days.

One cheerful happening—several of my fellow lieutenants have remarked that they thought I was doing a remarkable job as S-3. Of course, that has to be taken with a grain of salt, but it does tend to cheer one up a little.

Tomorrow will be the first time I have been out of Camp in some time, but I hold no hopes that it will be any different from the usual, drab, boring, lonely, frustrated excursion it usually is.

CAMP ADAIR, ORE.
JANUARY 18, 1943
Amazing! Despite my morbid predictions, I had an awfully nice time in Portland. Spent a "deal" of money, I guess, but it was worth it. Met two very nice girls, as far as girls go. Managed to visit Wavel and Ernest and Nadine Sunday afternoon.

Job ran fairly smooth today, for a Monday, and in view of the fact that I didn't get home until about 3 a.m.

Bad news in a way--range firing has been upped a week, so I <u>have</u> to get that procedure ready by Wednesday, plus next week's training directive. Oh well! Somehow--. Rumor has it that this Division is destined to go to Alaska. M'Gawd! It was only 18 degrees in Portland yesterday, and I damned near froze to death.

Encouraging news occurred today when I appointed 1st Lt. ***

my range officer. The Colonel said, quote: Rather an odd situation to have a 1st Lt. as your assistant--but I can assure you that won't be for <u>long</u>!

CAMP ADAIR, ORE.
JANUARY 19, 1943
Bitterly cold today! Tonight a velvety blanket of snow covers the Camp, and I expect it to be about 4 inches deep by morning. Was out on the range all afternoon, and it made me feel somewhat sick to see those poor devils lying in the snow banging away at the targets.

Didn't progress so rapidly on the range procedure today. Tried, in vain I think, to gather information on that subject, but that damnable Regimental HQ is so damned vague about everything until the last minute. In fact, things are in such a damned turmoil at the office, <u>I wonder if I am doing an efficient job</u>. Finally got my driver's license today, so I am now driving jeeps like an old hand. Don't suppose there is much I can do on this range firing but do my best and pray to the Lord, as usual.

There is so much <u>I don't know</u>!

CAMP ADAIR, ORE.
JANUARY 21, 1943
7:00 P.M.
Woke up this morning to find over a foot of snow on the ground. It continued to snow all day, and with the fall of night, it has now started to come down with great intensity. Nevertheless, I made several reconnaissances out to various ranges, bucking snow in the little jeep until it almost stalled several times.

The range procedure is starting to clear up somewhat, but there is still an aura of inaptness on my part that I do not like.

Received a check for $100 from the Government today as clothing allowance. Will have to start worrying about Income Tax before long.

I don't think I will be going any place this weekend, as I am Battalion Staff Duty Officer and must sleep in Battalion Headquarters. We won't have one of those miserable tactical problems tomorrow but must attend five hours of Air-Ground at Division School.

Still lonely as hell—have received no mail for the past four or five days.

Range firing starts next week—<u>I think</u>.

CAMP ADAIR, ORE.
JANUARY 25, 1943
11:20 P.M. (2320)
Another typical Monday, while not too bad, it could have been smoother. Colonel Smith a trifle cool, of late. Perhaps my imagination, but then I guess he has a lot on his mind, of late, now that he is acting Regimental Commander while Colonel Cochran is gone. Methinks many and great will be the changes around here in a few short months. I only hope that I can maintain efficiency and good work on my part, but at times, it seems somewhat hopeless, as the technicality and difficulty of this job continue to grow.

My mail has fallen to a new low. It seems as though every friend I have has forgotten me.

Tomorrow, I have a lot to do--reconnaissance in all areas for materials to prepare the range for firing.

Have felt physically and mentally at a record low for the past few weeks. Hope I can snap out of it soon, or else.

CAMP ADAIR, ORE.
JANUARY 26, 1943
MIDNIGHT
One of my worst days for some time. Felt absolutely terrible, both mentally and physically. For one thing, I feel so very much that I am not doing a capable job here. It would be typical of me to attain the highest aspiration that I had hoped for and then to lose it because of lack of knowledge. Range firing starting tomorrow morning, so I must arise at 5 a.m. I am writing this in my office tonight, as I am Battalion Staff Duty Officer and must perforce remain in Headquarters overnight.

Feel as though I am coming down with the flu, and I seem to be so nervous of late that I even hate myself.

Questioned Colonel Smith about the quality of my work of late, and he assured me it was just fine, that "I was doing a fine job." So . . . ????

No mail at all today, as usual, and believe me, it certainly makes it difficult, for that is my one form of relaxation.

CAMP ADAIR, ORE.
JANUARY 27, 1943
Well, it happened—much to my amazement. As of January 22, 1943,

it is now 1ˢᵗ Lieutenant E. J. McCully, although I didn't receive official notification until today.

Happy as it makes me, I realize full well the many new responsibilities and worries that will now befall me. The question now facing me is, can I make myself capable enough to handle this new rank? Can I by sheer study and application bring myself to the point of efficiency, whereby I will really deserve the rank I now hold?

God willing, I <u>will</u>. As back at Benning when some inner voice seemed to continually tell me that I would make the grade, that same voice tells me now that I <u>will</u> make a success of my life in the Army; and anyway, it seems to me that <u>confidence in one's self</u> is half the battle.

Happy indeed am I today, but many are the hard and difficult tasks, which lie ahead.

CAMP ADAIR, ORE.
JANUARY 29, 1943

All is well and serene as regards Colonel Smith and me. Worked half a day in the office, and for the afternoon, acted as Battalion Range Officer, supervising firing on the range.

Tomorrow I act as Battalion Commander and must attend a conference with General Cook at 11 a.m. In the afternoon, I attend a four-hour Advanced Course Division School, representing Colonel Smith, the Executive Officer, S-2, and S-3.

Had a few drinks with all the officers tonight, celebrating my promotion, the final one with Colonel Smith, who said, "With all good luck, and may there be many more of them, Mac." To which I said, "To which I only have one thing to add: "May I always live up to what they represent." And he replied, "You will, never fear, my boy."

So you say, sentimental gush! But all I can say is that I <u>really meant it</u>, for my deepest desire is to be, eventually, <u>a real officer</u>, a <u>real man</u>, and a <u>gentleman—Always</u>.

JANUARY 30, 1943
CAMP ADAIR
11:40 P.M.

Somehow I knew all this very fortunate chain of circumstances could not last. My latest downfall was first noticed late last night, and it came like a bolt out of the blue. My old enemy TRICHOPHYTOSIS has returned and is firmly embedded. How I ever picked it up again, I do not know. My fingers are entirely covered with tiny, watery blisters, and of course, various other parts of my body are affected. When I think of the total hell I went through at Hoff General Hospital in Santa Barbara, I dread to think of another session like that. The only thing I can think of to cure it is to go to the hospital for a couple of days and take the hot boric acid baths that cured it previously. So I intend to go to the medics tomorrow and ask for that treatment. Suppose there will be the inevitable red tape, though.

The only procedure open for me to follow is to keep cool and collected and lick this thing in as short a time as possible. Again, only inscrutable fate knows the eventual outcome of all this.

An "interesting" episode occurred last night. For some time, I had possessed the idea that Colonel Smith had cooled somewhat in his estimation of my abilities. At any rate, acting as Regimental Commander, he had to call a Regimental Staff meeting, so it was left to me to hold the Company Commanders Meeting. Due to a previous altercation with Captain Jessen, who didn't like the idea of holding meetings on his "free" nights, I proceeded to give them hell and told them any official orders issued by Colonel Smith would be carried out whether they liked it or not. I mentioned it no further, as I considered it a private matter between the Captains and me, but it got back to the Colonel, who, to my amazement, was highly pleased. He told the person who told me that, "It's just what they needed, and if they think I won't back him up, they're crazy. Believe me, I glory in that boy's spunk."

Later, he told me personally, the same thing. So perhaps I am, after all, on the right track in handling some of these difficult diplomatic problems that arise.

God! If I didn't have to come down sick just now. I am supposed to be Battalion Range Officer tomorrow. I will be, but then I go to the dispensary.

CAMP ADAIR, ORE.
JANUARY 31, 1943
Well, here I am in the hospital again, and getting the same goddamned runaround from these <u>miserable, inefficient, damned medics</u>. I came up here voluntarily to get this damned stuff cured in the shortest possible time because it is spreading rapidly, and he [a medic] prescribes <u>calamine lotion</u>, which I have been using for two days to no avail. I may as well wash my hands with <u>water</u> for all the good it does.

It makes me so damned mad! If they would give [me] a canister of boric acid and let me soak for 2 or 3 hours, it would be gone in no time, but no! "We can't rush into this thing," and all the time one must calmly endure sleepless nights and this damned continual burning itch.

Jesus! And to think those are the halfwits we have to rely on to dress wounds in combat.

I suppose I'll be marooned in here for another damned month, and there will go my job, probably, as there were several delicately balanced diplomatic angles that were hanging fire.

CAMP ADAIR, ORE.
STATION HOSPITAL
WARD 200
FEB. 2, 1943

Another day drags by, but the condition seems to be improving far more rapidly than during my previous incarceration. Hope to be out of here in a few more days.

A few additional facts <u>and</u> worries now confront me, gleaned from the visits of several of the fellows in the last few days. *** (who is taking my place) is not making an outstanding success of it. Furey and Prevics came up and so informed me. In fact, *** came up today and had several questions puzzling him. Major Elliott will be back soon from Benning, and I just wonder what new complications and troubles this may present, if any?

I have been lying here, just thinking, for the past two days, sort of reviewing my life as it were. What I discovered was anything but a feeling of accomplishment.

Perhaps I am just downright envious, but all of these other officers have so much more to live for, so much more to spur them on to higher achievements—their wives and sweethearts arrive faithfully for the daily visiting hours—and me? Alone, as always.

CAMP ADAIR, ORE.
STATION HOSPITAL
WARD 200
FEBRUARY 3, 1943

The skin condition seems to be improving rapidly but have had trouble with one or two splotches.

No visitors at all today, no mail, and nothing to do. In one respect, I am glad to be in the hospital, for it gives me an opportunity to catch up on quite a bit of badly needed sleep. As noted on previous pages, I have been reviewing my life in its entirety, and I have come to one sincere conclusion. Namely: I <u>am not satisfied with myself or my progress</u>, and from this day forth, I shall put forth every effort to improve myself in <u>every respect</u>, so that when I am finally discharged from the Army, I shall still be a <u>man</u> in every respect, an officer and a gentleman.

I can state, with some assurance, that the next few months will prove momentous indeed, for many changes will take place. The cadre will be going out, new commanders will be going out, and new ones will be coming in. How all this will affect me personally, I cannot say, but fate alone will make the final decisions.

Camp Adair, Ore.
Station Hospital
Ward 200
Feb. 4, 1943

I feel rather fine today—about 100% better than yesterday. I honestly think I am well enough to be discharged from the hospital, at least by tomorrow, but I shall have to take exceptionally careful precautions in order to prevent this stuff striking again.

If I get out tomorrow, it will be Friday, and heaven knows what additional work has crept up on me during this "hospital interlude."

Received a letter from Lola and answered it immediately. Guess she is having rather a rough time of it, thanks to ***. Poor Kid! I feel so sorry for her. If I think <u>my</u> life has been blasted, what about hers?

Lt. Aronson phoned up and told one of the nurses to tell me he said "hello." The fellows have been swell, and I was really surprised at the number of them who called—Fox, Prevics, Ereza, Furey, Bertram, etc. I have made many friends here, at that, and think I can count myself very fortunate.

Camp Adair, Oregon
Room 44, Officers Quarters
February 5, 1943

Back "home" again! Was discharged from the hospital this morning, after the usual amount of red tape. Came back to work and found myself somewhat lost. It will take awhile, I feel sure, to catch up again, and in the meantime, what is Colonel Smith's attitude? He seemed a trifle silent and taciturn again. Perhaps Lt. *** has made a great impression on him, as to his capabilities in my absence. Well, all I can do is to continue to work hard and earnestly on the job, to my utmost ability, and show him that I intend to earn my silver bar. After that, fate--.

This eczemic condition is not entirely healed, and I am going to have to be the utmost in caution to prevent a recurrence.

Received a letter from Margie today, and she is getting a little too serious, so before very long, I guess I had best start cutting.

Lts. Ereza, Bertram, Furey, and others are going to Portland and want me to go, too. I don't know, but I think we will get Saturday afternoon and Sunday off, and if so--?

CAMP ADAIR, OREGON
FEBRUARY 13, 1943
Note the long lapse of time! And for a good reason, too—I can assure anyone—work! I have been working day and night to catch up and am, about now, just about aboveboard.

Still rather an odd situation over at Bn. HQ à la ***, but I am certainly not worried, as I have really been pouring it on, of late.

Colonel Aaron made me Director of the four special training schools in this Regiment, and so, I am busy almost every night. But at least one good thing came of it—I get out of the Division Schools.

No mail for several days but got one from John Strahl (V-Mail) today.

I did go to Portland last weekend and had a fairly good time. Went out with the same gal I went out with last time. I was in Portland but can't recall her name for the life of me.

I elected to stay in Camp this weekend and get some blessed rest!

CAMP ADAIR, ORE.
FEBRUARY 14, 1943
VALENTINE'S DAY
I didn't sleep so well last night. Physically, I am not up to par. I have a continual, terrific cold, but what man in the Regiment hasn't?

I was working in the office right after lunch today when Colonel Smith came in and asked me if I wanted to go on a reconnaissance with Colonel Cochran and a major from the Field Artillery. So we went and were gone all afternoon, riding around the hills near Monmouth.

Had quite a talk with the Colonel tonight. He thinks he is going out on cadre, which would leave Major Elliott the new Battalion Commander, and I wonder how I would get along with him?

He told me that I "could reasonably expect my Captaincy in about five months, and from there, the next logical step would be to Major as Battalion Executive." However, that is all in the future, and again, fate always takes care of such matters. Also said that I would definitely remain with the Timberwolf Division and go overseas with it.

As regards the above, *n'est-ce pas?* And who knows?

[*Section "Mc" of the journal contained the following, written on the index divider itself.*]

STATIONS ASSIGNED TO—

PRESIDIO OF MONTERY, CALIFORNIA
CAMP CALLAN, SAN DIEGO, CALIFORNIA
FORT BENNING, GEORGIA
CAMP ADAIR, CORVALLIS, OREGON

[*The following passage (author unknown) was found on the last page of Section "S" of the journal.*]

MARRIAGE

---- But the One Girl went from me: suddenly her divine face grew cruel, her eyes narrowed and their white eyelids slowly drooped. <u>She stopped only to powder my dreams to ashes</u>, and with malicious fingers to smear their blackness beneath my cheekbones and around my eyes.

"Mortal fool! Did you think to hold me forever?" Her laughter fell as the tinkle of little brass bells that chime all awry in the temple gardens of Korea. Falling, changed to little sharp and frozen teardrops that each stabbed my shuddering heart.

Thus passed the One Girl. <u>And I had only the stillness of walled space, and the places that quivered where she had been, and the ticking of a little clock</u>.

Twice empty for having once contained her, I wrapped my face in shadows and let the mortal, measured hours flow by -----------

[*Section "X" of the journal contained addresses and telephone numbers (both of which were not included in this listing) of the individuals listed below.*]

1. Lt. John A. Strahl
2. Warrant Officer Leo H. Cook
3. 1st Sgt. and Mrs. H. E. Chambles [crossed out]
4. Mr. and Mrs. Fred B. Read
5. Brechbiel
6. Lt. Colonel L. I. Cooley
7. Major W. E. Read
8. 1ˢᵗ Sgt. & Mrs. H. E. Chambles
9. Mrs. Nettie J. Westrem
10. Mrs. Melanie Strahl
11. The Morgans
12. Miss Margaret Salerno
13. Ted Stefanski
14. Commander & Mrs. G. C. Barnes
15. Mr. and Mrs. Claude Rafferty
16. Pvt. J. R. Westrem
17. The Rices
18. Maxine's Phone
19. Mrs. Lola Sainsbury
20. Lyle
21. Mr. John A. Read
22. Mr. & Mrs. Ernest Leurquin
23. Mrs. Lewis B. Harvey
24. Lt. H. R. Rafferty
25. Pvt. Fred Strahl

[*Section "X" of the journal also contained the following.*]

Records to buy—When—

1. A Kiss in the Dark—Victor Herbert
2. Vienna City of My Dreams
3. Schubert's Serenade
4. Dream of Love—Liszt
5. Amareuse
6. Fairy Tales of the Orient—Waltz--Strauss

Journal 3: Volume II 255

[*The journal contained the following loose documents, listed below:*]

1. "The Chapel News" newsletter (November 13, 1942).
2. A clipping from a handwritten letter dated April 7, 1945 from La Jolla, California, to "Dear Mac." The letter included three small stamps with photographs: a man in uniform, two children, and a woman. The reverse of the letter read: " . . . Austria, New Guinea, and the Philliphine [sic] Island. He look [sic] just fine. He said Barnhart . . . "
3. A note (in E. J. McCully's handwriting) on a small piece of paper: "A <u>built</u>-<u>in</u> radio, with switch for listening to records would be an improvement here. Also, how about one of my field telephones--<u>built in</u>?"
4. A typed "Record Catalogue" listing on Timberwolf stationery, with prices.
5. A handwritten "Albums" listing, with prices.
6. A memorandum dated 28 May 1945 to all units of the 415th Infantry from E. J. McCully, Capt., Infantry, Personnel Officer (by order of Colonel Cochran), regarding the placement of military uniform decorations and insignia.
7. A copy of a letter in an envelope to President and members of general court-martial appointed by paragraph 1, Special Orders 244, Headquarters 104th Infantry Division from William R. Woodward, Brigadier General, U.S. Army Commanding. Subject: Findings of court-martial.
8. A California-Nevada road map from Union Oil Company, marking the places E. J. McCully had lived or been stationed, was attached to the inside back cover of the journal.

JOURNAL 4

VOLUME III
FEBRUARY 20, 1943 TO FEBRUARY 26, 1944
Ages 27–28

Rest? What a laugh!
They moved us today some 75 miles east of Bend, Oregon,
and it is really DESERT. Bitterly cold at night—water freezes.
Boiling hot during the day, and a high wind constantly
fills your nose, eyes, and throat with sand.

[*A Timberwolf patch was fastened to the inside cover of the journal with the following notation printed below.*]

E. J. McCully
Personnel Officer
415th Infantry Regiment

VOLUME III
NOTES AND IMPRESSIONS
OF HAPPENINGS AND EVENTS
THAT OCCURRED DURING MY
THIRD YEAR OF SERVICE IN
THE ARMY OF THE UNITED
STATES. NOTES RELATING
THE EXPERIENCES ENCOUNTERED
IN MY FIRST AND SECOND YEARS
MAY BE FOUND IN VOLUMES I AND II.
FEBRUARY 26, 1943.

Personnel Officer

LIFE AT CAMP • ADAIR DEVELOPMENT AS AN OFFICER • OFFICE POLITICS • TENSIONS WITH OTHER OFFICERS • REFLECTIONS ON LIFE, DREAMS, AND IDEALS • RELATIONSHIP WITH FATHERLY COLONEL SMITH • VISIT HOME TO SEE FAMILY AND FRIENDS • RELATIONSHIPS WITH WOMEN • DATES WITH RUTH • RISE AND DOWNFALL • HEALTH CHALLENGES • MANEUVERS IN OREGON, ARIZONA, AND CALIFORNIA • MARGIE'S INTEREST IN MARRIAGE • CONCERNS REGARDING PROMOTION • REFUSAL OF ADVANCED SCHOOL • ASSIGNMENT AS REGIMENTAL PERSONNEL OFFICER

CAMP ADAIR, ORE.
FEBRUARY 20, 1943
What a week! And many new developments. Erstwhile "friend" *** is hard after my job, and he is licking boots like a madman to get it. I certainly am not worried, however. It takes a helluva lot better man than *** to get ahead of me. Felt kinda bad about it for three days but wised up to it when I found out what the opinion of the other officers are of ***—and it isn't very high.

Had a heck of a long talk with Colonel tonight. He suggested we go on a "fling" up to Portland some weekend! (!)

Also, he came bustling in to Bn. HQ tonight, bursting with the news of a compliment paid me by Colonel Aaron, the Regimental Executive Officer, in front of Colonel Cochran, the Regimental Commander. They were evidently talking about the progress of my 3R Schools, and Colonel Aaron said, "There is one of the best officers in the Regiment." Quite a compliment, believe me, considering the fact that Colonel Aaron is a West Pointer and a real officer in every sense of the word.

Believe me, I intend to show *** up in every way for what he really is, so watch my smoke.

CAMP ADAIR, ORE.
MARCH 12, 1943
Indeed, it has been a long time since I have written in the old logbook, and again, quite a few events have happened and are in the process of happening.

The "***" situation rather solved itself after he made quite an ass out of himself, at least in the opinion of many officers in the 1st Battalion. We went on a four-day bivouac near Sulphur Springs and had quite a bit of fun—raids, sham battles, and rugged outdoor life—and I mean rugged. Cold! We almost froze to death every night.

Major Elliott returned, and as I rather expected, he is busy making quite a nuisance out of himself. Tomorrow is the official completion of the MTP Basic Training, and a big Division Review is scheduled for tomorrow morning. Over 15,000 men in one huge parade!

<u>Big News</u>! Colonel Smith has okayed a 12-day leave for me starting on March 25<u>th</u>, and am I going home in a hurry!

March 13, 1943
Camp Adair, Ore.

Saturday. We had our big Division Review this morning—in the mud. I marched with Colonel Smith at the head of the Battalion. Quite impressive. Over 15,000 men passing in review. We had to stand at attention for over an hour while the newly made Assistant Division Commander, Brigadier General Moore, was given the Silver Star for gallantry in action on Guadalcanal. He flew here directly from Guadalcanal to take his post. As I stood at attention with my eyes glued to the front, I thought of many things. Of how, little less than a year ago, I was a corporal down in San Diego, and now, although I have perhaps advanced myself, I find that I am just as unhappy and dissatisfied with myself as I was then. Is there then to be no happiness in life for me? Must the things I want most in life—a home, a wife and children, a secure future, peace and contentment, be eternally denied me? Must I forever be a lonely soul making a never-ending pilgrimage down the road of life? Must I admit then, to my innermost self, that the heartbreak I once underwent destroyed forever all the beautiful things in life?

If that is true, would it not be a far better thing then, that I go meet my fate in the South Pacific? I feel almost certain that when we do go "over," it will be to fight the yellow men of Nippon, for that fact is continually emphasized here. Strangely enough, however, the thought of actual combat does not worry me a bit. I ask only one thing of God—and myself: When I go, let me go honorably and with courage in my heart, let me be an example to my men, let me be worthy of my heritage.

When I go home on leave the latter part of this month, I intend to dress as carefully as I can, bestow all the affection I can on Mother, and cram all of life that I possibly can into those precious 12 days, for I have a certain feeling that this will be the last time until the war is won and decided.

Camp Adair, Oregon
March 14, 1943

A quite slow, dreary and rather quiet Sunday. Cleaned my room, took a shower, had a few 3.2 beers at the Club with Sucey, Green, and Wingenbach. That really about sums up today.

Spent a little time shining up some brass, etc., etc. Can't help but wish it were a little closer to the 25th, but then I presume the time will pass fast enough.

This Major Elliott is a rather difficult guy to figure out. We don't "click" at any great rate.

I guess bootlicker *** will act as S-3 while I am on leave and presume he will continue to lick just as fast and furiously as he has in the past.

I am getting to the stage of boredom at life that it really doesn't make a hell of a lot of difference to me just what does happen.

Camp Adair, Ore.
March 15, 1943

Leave date changed to March 22nd. Official this time. I am waiting until after midnight tonight and then will phone United Airlines and try to get a reservation for Monday. Probably too late.

Have to go to the dentist first thing tomorrow morning, and once and for all, get these darn teeth fixed. Still a rather tense atmosphere around Bn. HQ. Guess old *** will have the job cinched by the time I get back, although he is now back in Co. A as Executive Officer.

Curious thing tonight. I was teaching my Illiterate School and was expostulating at full speed. Looked up and who should I see but old John Hamilton Cochran himself (the Regimental Commander). He didn't say a word but sat and listened for a while. Don't know what he thought. A little later, Captain Needham walked in, and in the course of the ensuing conversation, remarked, "You're lucky, getting such a good base in this S-3 work. If you're ever chosen as Regimental S-3, you will have something to work from." Almost immediately, he started to hedge in his customary manner, "Not that you should get such an idea, etc., etc." Which, knowing Needham as I do, makes me wonder. Evidently some such trend has been thought of. Not that I ever expect to get such a post, for I doubt if I could handle it. I am in severe doubts as to my ability as Battalion S-3.

I am madly trying to get things organized for the trip home.

Uniform is none too immaculate, and I did so want everything to be just right for this trip. Oh well, I will have to make the best of it. Will have to decide what I want to take home and all.

What a difference! From San Diego, I mean. This time I am going home with a new promotion and newly won signs of advancement. I repeat tonight, as I have on many a dark night, that <u>I will</u> make Virginia sorry she ever cheated on me.

Tonight I ask, Dear Lord, continue to give me guidance and help in all the ensuing years to come.

CAMP ADAIR
MARCH 16, 1943
Reservations for the plane have all been made. I leave Portland at 9:20 a.m., Monday morning, on the United Airlines plane unless I get "bumped," so here's keeping my fingers crossed. For if I manage to make the flight, I will be home in Oakland at 1 p.m., Monday afternoon.

Went to the dentist this morning and had <u>9</u> small cavities filled. Needless to say, my mouth feels much better, despite the 3 hours of torture this morning.

Evidently, Cochran thought my teaching was all right last night, for in asking for an officer's contribution of $100 in supplies for the conduct of my school in Regimental School he stated, "Very fine instruction is being given in this school by volunteer officers."

More mad rumors of two cadres, eventual promotions, etc., are filling the air. Haven't accomplished much towards organizing for the trip home so imagined I will do most of it over the weekend. Lt. Rebman will act as S-3 in my absence! <u>Good</u>! Colonel Smith in an exceptionally gracious mood!

CAMP ADAIR, ORE.
MARCH 20, 1943
I am in quite a state of excitement tonight, for I only have one more night to spend, and I will be on my way home. 12 days to precious freedom. I have finished all my packing and cleaning of my uniform.

I wonder just what this leave will bring in the way of changing the deadly, dull routine of my life? I hope that my plane reservation won't be cancelled, though it will only delay me a day or so if it is. At any rate, I leave tomorrow night at about midnight for Portland. I only hope that this will be one leave which will be all joy—no sadness, no tears—for I feel in my heart that this will be the last leave I shall receive before the "big show" starts and I go out to play my infinitesimal part in the scheme of life.

I shall be nothing but happy, confident, and <u>alive</u> while I am home, for I want to leave the memory of something <u>fine</u>.

CAMP ADAIR, ORE.
MARCH 21, 1943
In a little more than four hours, I shall be on my way <u>home</u>! All arrangements have been completed, and all that now remains is for my luck to hold on the plane reservation. I have a strange feeling, however, that it <u>will</u>.

I completed as much of the S-3 work in advance as I possibly could. I am very glad that Rebman is taking over the S-3 function in my absence, as he is a whale of a fine fellow, whereas that sneaking, slinky, double-faced ***!

I guess there will be no more entries in this saga of a humdrum existence until I return, and then I wonder what experiences shall be unfolded herein.

Perhaps it would be best if I managed to get a little sleep before midnight, as I must catch the 1:15 bus to Albany, and heavens alone knows how long it will be until I retire again.

CAMP ADAIR, ORE.
APRIL 5, 1943
Well, the leave, probably my last one, is a thing of the past. Had a wonderful visit with the folks, but the parting was inevitably a little sad in view of the circumstances. The Morgans were the same wonderful people they have always been, the utmost in kindness and genuine hospitality, and again, I felt so helpless and at a loss as to how to adequately ever repay them. To my dismay, Vivian still proclaims the fact that she loves me, and yet to my horror, I realize that in spite of the wonderful person she is, I don't love her. Arthur Morgan, the finest man I have ever known said, "Frankly, we had always hoped--," and yet I must hurt these fine people because the <u>thing</u> I married turned everything in me into a chaotic mass of confusion, doubt, mistrust, suspicion, and icy coldness.

People always say, "Are you going to let <u>one</u> mistake ruin your life?" And yet they don't, they <u>can't</u>, realize what it did to me. How long, O God, does this episode of doubt, bewilderment, and confusion continue? Must I always feel this way? Will the things I long for never be mine? A home, a loyal wife, children, and all that a home means? Must the things I want most be eternally denied me because of the wreckage of one attempt at happiness? And yet, daily, from coast to coast, border to border, and in every state that I have been in, I see examples of cheating wives, lying husbands, cheap womanhood. Lying, cheating, grasping, tawdry, <u>cheap</u> women.

Meanwhile, the years slip away, and all accomplishments and gains are empty—mean nothing. I will be 28 on my next birthday and even have a grey hair scattered here and there.

As for my future (the immediate, I mean, for we live on borrowed time), it is hard to say. It will take some time to get back to a state of normalcy in the S-3, for so much can happen in a few days. And then, operations in the field? Maneuvers? Cadre? Overseas? I don't give much of a damn.

The sooner I get it, the better.

CAMP ADAIR, ORE.
APRIL 6, 1943
A hard day. It is always so hard to "get your feet back on the ground" after a long absence. It was just one of those days in which it was impossible to "get going." Major Elliott is far worse than any other person I have yet encountered to get along with, just as I thought he would be. Nevertheless, I shall continue to go ahead and do my work as best I possibly can, and if it isn't good enough, to hell with them. The Colonel will be back from his leave on the 14th.

I have a great many things to wind up tomorrow, complete the FO for Monday's march, firing of stragglers, etc., etc.

I have really earnestly and seriously got to start improving my health. I have made up my mind to stop smoking, if necessary, but the main thing I have to do is to somehow obtain a lot of good restful sleep, something practically impossible around here, as schools tonight kept us until 10:30, and it is now 12.

CAMP ADAIR, ORE.
APRIL 9, 1943
More and more tension in the daily work with Elliott in command. Finished up many tasks today despite all the obstacles placed in my

path—and four schools in two days. Attended a conference tonight termed by the General, Company Commanders, and Prospective Company Commanders. ?????

The bunch wants me to go to Portland this weekend, but I don't know. I am tired, blouse has not been cleaned, etc., etc.

Still no mail from home since my return to Camp.

Hear reports that one of the new officers thinks he is excellent staff material due to his prowess with foreign languages and former profession of attorney.

Guess I will turn in, as it is now midnight, and I must be up by 7 a.m.—I hope—.

CAMP ADAIR, ORE.
APRIL 11, 1943
SUNDAY

A beautiful spring day—azure blue sky, birds singing outside my window, and all the world seems gay and worthwhile, except for me.

As is usual for me, I guess, I am today disconsolate, extremely depressed, and disheartened with life. I didn't go to Portland. I knew I needed the rest more, but I didn't get the complete relaxation that I needed. Most of the night, I turned and tossed and thought—thought of what a horrible *faux pas* I have made of my life, of the absolute lack of anything to live for—no future, no incentive to survive, nothing.

From the above, one could easily assume that I am nothing but a moral weakling of the worst sort, continually deploring my fate, when all the time I realize there are so many souls far more lost than I am. But surely, each human soul is entitled to a little of that ingredient known as happiness, and I cannot understand why I am eternally denied this. Perhaps I don't deserve it.

RAINY CAMP ADAIR
APRIL 22, 1945

Rugged, rugged days! Since I last wrote, we have been out in the woods on a weeklong bivouac, and it has rained almost continually. I did what I consider real work and performed conscientious effort on planning and arranging the bivouac, and Colonel Smith heartily approved. But Major Elliott has made himself as obnoxious and heartily disliked by all as much as he possibly can, inasmuch as he is not Battalion Commander—yet. He nags all staff members continually, and he rides the poor S-2 at all times. He and I have had several severe verbal clashes, and I know he hates my guts. What is worse, the cadre is going out soon, and I know he will remain as Bn. Commander, as Colonel Smith will assuredly go out on cadre.

When he does, that is the time when McCully puts in a transfer to the parachute troops at Fort Benning, as life and all ambition would be simply unbearable with that Arkansas buffoon in command. Truly he is a travesty of an officer, if I ever saw one.

So again, as almost always for me, life and ambition are at a low ebb. Tired out, both physically and mentally, I don't know (and don't care a helluva lot) what will happen in the near future.

Only one bright star gleams through this fog of despondency. Colonel Aaron, the second in command of the Regiment, was talking to Colonel Smith, and again my subject of 3R Schools came up, and he said, "I'll bet McCully has the best 3R School in the Division." So at least I have good graces in the eyes of one of the highest-ranking officers in the Regiment.

Only the good God above, and inscrutable fate, can foresee what my destiny may hold. But, Oh God, tonight how I pray for good judgment, guidance, and perhaps, maybe, just a little—happiness, at least before we go over. I don't mind going at all, but I hate to go, feeling that I have been cheated of so much of life by Virginia and her like.

CAMP ADAIR, ORE.
APRIL 26, 1943

To Portland this last weekend and saw and participated in the Furey-Starrett marriage. It was the most beautiful ceremony I ever saw, complete with sabers, ushers, cutting of the cake with *my* sword, etc. I guess in reality it was the kind of ceremony I always wanted myself and never had. Ah well, it was wonderful just to be a part of it! Maxine was there, and she certainly looked charming.

However, in some respects, the weekend was somewhat deteriorating, and so for that reason, I took Duty Officer this weekend and am again determined to get all the rest I can. I have so much mail to answer that I will never get caught up. Life is getting more and more rugged. We are firing the platoon proficiency test, and tomorrow starts the physical hardening tests. Colonel Smith went to Yakima with the AT Detachment, so "Joe Blow" is in charge.

Nuff sed.

Camp Adair, Ore.
April 30, 1943
Colonel Smith still up in Yakima, but wonder of wonders, Major Joe Blow is getting much easier to get along with. Wonder if it will last?

Rumors right off the griddle tonight—cadre goes out on May 15th to train 65th Division. Many and varied changes to take place in the Regiment in the next month.

I don't think I will be on the new cadre. Guess I am doomed to remain with the 104th Division. In the meantime, combat tactics and maneuvers grow more rugged every day. The next two weeks are going to be pure hell.

Mail has slacked off something terribly, probably because I haven't had time to answer any myself.

Despite my desperate efforts to think I am happy, I'm not. I'm lonely and still unhappy. I am staying in this weekend, and God knows when I will get another weekend off. Somehow, I don't care, the weekends have degenerated into drinking sprees and a frenzied search for companionship, which always ends with a feeling of utter disgust at the cheapness of life.

Camp Adair, Ore.
May 1, 1943
O Joyous Mayday! Oh yes, indeed! Worked all day long, and tonight I stopped work long enough to shave, shower, dress, and go to the buffet luncheon at the 415th Officers Club and then to the Division Officers Club for dancing (one dance with Lt. Hiner's wife). Happiness and merriment at every turn—for everyone else. Perhaps I am just jealous of the ease with which other people can attain happiness, but still the fact remains, there seems to be none for me.

At present, I seem to be stymied by a series of continuous problems needed for the tactical situations for the week that we are in the field continuously. (Week after next.)

Still the wild and assorted cadre rumors are floating around. No one seems to know where or when who is bound.

Tonight, outside my window, the wild geese are honking as they fly north once more, and my spirit is just as restless and perhaps as impatient as theirs.

CAMP ADAIR, ORE.
MAY 3, 1943
Felt fairly good today. Turned in my plan to Division HQ today on Battalion Tactical Training for next week—six tactical problems. I was highly complimented on it by Colonel Smith. I hear that my friend, Lt. Aronson, will get a Company when the cadre goes out. Good for him, he sure is a good egg. I don't think the cadre will affect me in any way. I may get my Captaincy in July or August, but the fact that Major Joe Blow may be Bn. Commander by then tends to make that possibility a little questionable.

I think I shall again go to Portland this coming weekend, for it may well be the last weekend for many long weeks to come, as Unit Training is about over, and combined Unit Training will soon start.

No mail for a long time, despite having written quite a few letters.

Lonely again, and again I wonder what the purpose of this mad millrace of life can be.

MAY 6, 1943
CAMP ADAIR, ORE.
Have been working like a fiend for the last few days on a plan for 1st Battalion Tactics, week of May 9-15. Submitted it, and G-3 told me that General Moore had said that mine was "Excellent, in fact, outstanding, the best of all three battalions in the Regiment." (!) Many changes now being made in the Regiment. Reliably reported that Aronson will get a company (Captaincy). Upham, too. Capt. Petersen to Regimental HQ, and *** finally kissed his way into Regimental HQ. What changes lie in store for me I do not know, but I hardly think there are any. I happened to get a look at my efficiency rating by Colonel Smith again for this month. Superior all the way through, including <u>Performance of duties in the field</u>.

Aronson's girl, Betty Crutchfield, informs me that she has a date for me that is a knockout this weekend. I wonder—guess it will be another weekend like all the rest.

Well, God knows I'm going, for it may well be the last for many weeks to come.

MAY 17, 1943
CAMP ADAIR, ORE.
The Battalion maneuvers are over, and a rugged, rugged week it

was--continuous rain and bitter cold. Went to Portland this weekend to forget it and had a wonderful time. I met an awfully nice girl, Maxine Williams--a nurse, 21 years old. Am supposed to have some dates with her in the near future.

Today I was Control Officer out on the tower on the Infiltration Course. Ran over 2,000 men through it. Men creeping and crawling over 100 yds. of shell-torn terrain with three heavy machine guns spitting live ammunition 18 inches over their heads, my hands pulling the switches, which set off the 18 charges of dynamite scattered throughout the course. What a laugh! Me—the guy who used to quake in front of a platoon.

I am dog-tired tonight, so guess I will turn in and try and get some sleep, for tonight may well be the last night of rest for a long time.

MAY 23, 1943

Tonight I am alone, lonely, and frightened, more so than at any other time in my life. Not from anything regarding the Army, hell no! It's me and my crazy foolhardiness. Recently, and for some time past, I have become increasingly despondent and disgusted with life, and I guess this is the inevitable climax. Perhaps if I hadn't been so alone, had had something to live for, something to return to, it wouldn't have been so bad. At any rate, all I can do now is to pray to my Lord God and ask for His guidance and help now. I very probably don't deserve it and guess I never will, but if only I could have one more chance to try again.

Went to Portland and again spent quite a bit of money. Found out that Laura Krauser had formed a lot of serious ideas about me, so I had to disillusion her. It seems all I do is cause trouble, anguish, and heartbreak to other people—nice people.

CAMP ADAIR, ORE.

JUNE 12, 1943

Still no word from Cochran regarding ----. Colonel Smith is desperately trying to work a few angles—install Captain Prevics as S-3, retain me as understudy until such time as enough confusion reigns that he can reinstall me as S-3. But I do not think it will ever work out. Colonel Cochran will force his hand on it and will continue to gun for me forever after.

Tomorrow morning at 0600, we leave on a 5-day bivouac, and I feel so terrible physically, I don't know how it will work out. I hope to God nothing happens to destroy any efficiency on my part, either mentally <u>or</u> physically, now of all times.

Of course, in view of everything that has occurred, I feel so low that it is hard to say how things will work out, but I do know I certainly need God's help and assistance, now more than ever.

Camp Adair, Ore.
June 17, 1943
Returned from the bivouac tonight. Everything worked out fairly well, but I didn't feel I was as efficient as I could have been. But how could I have been with this mess going around in my mind continually?

Still no word of any kind from Colonel Cochran, but I expect it any day now, as I have been back almost two weeks. He knows I am still S-3, however, as I have had two or three occasions to talk to him. Each night, I pray with all my heart and soul that this awful mess may "work out" in some manner, but who knows?

If nothing else, this terrible catastrophe has taught me one terrible, searing lesson. I know now, once and for all, that life holds nothing for me—no wife, no home, no children—and there is no point in my searching for them; and therefore, I shall never have any more to do with women. Like a curse to me, they bring only unhappiness and sorrow.

Colonel Smith's plan may work, <u>but I wonder, how I wonder</u>!

Camp Adair, Oregon
June 20, 1943
Returned last night from the "special" two-day, "enemy detail" bivouac. Rather rough and cold. I learned quite a bit from it all. Again today, I am at a low ebb mentally, and I feel more than ever that all of life is over for me. No future, nothing but black despair confronts me. Nevermore for me will there be the faintest glimmering of happiness.

If only Cochran would do something. However, it is part of his sadistic makeup to keep an aura of tenseness and suspense about such a situation. However, I shall know before long, for the S-3 promotions will be in effect by July 22, and I am certain that I will not be promoted. So then, all will know.

Life is indeed drear now that I have cut all communications and correspondence, except for Mother. She doesn't know, and I pray God she never does.

Besides everything else, I now have new, additional physical worries to confront me. My physical condition is far below par—and worries me.

Tomorrow starts another week of bivouacs (RCT #5, CPX, and additional problems).

How long, dear God, must this awful situation—and life—go on?

Camp Adair, Ore.
June 22, 1943
Without a doubt, the worst three days I ever spent. Left Monday morning on RCT #5. Rained continuously. No supper until midnight (cold lunch), then moved into a forward assembly area where rolls were dropped (no blankets). Sat huddled in an amphibian jeep until 0500. Night turned bitterly cold, men huddled under dripping trees, an 8-mile reconnaissance on foot. Moved to the attack at 1140. Counterattacked until 1330 over 8 miles of rugged cross-country hell. Tonight I am weary and footsore. The only ray of hope that shines through for me—Colonel Smith says it looks as though my only punishment may be loss of promotion (may not lose my S-3 work).

Guess I will turn in early tonight and try to rest, for tomorrow we have a rugged CPX confronting us, which I have a hunch, will be a mean one, and without a doubt, more rain.

Camp Adair, Ore.
June 24, 1943
Faster, more deadly, and more rigorous daily, grows the pace. The CPX wasn't bad, got through it in fair shape. My hay fever is giving me great trouble, as all the weeds and orchard grass are springing into full growth, now. We will have nothing more to do this week until the Battalion Firing Test (combat), which is a IV Corps test, and which will be held on next Monday and Tuesday.

Heard from an unauthenticated source that my only punishment may be loss of promotion and a fine. It is a puzzling situation, for it has been a month tomorrow since my downfall, and I haven't heard a word, and Cochran is not the man to tarry when meting out punishment.

All I can do, as I have said before, is to hope and pray that somehow, in some way, this catastrophe may solve itself.

I hear now that we leave for the maneuver area, Bend, Oregon, on about August 11, 1943, and will not return to Camp Adair. Hope there are less weeds in the Bend, Oregon, area.

Camp Adair, Ore.
June 27, 1943
Sunday Night—2342

Lt. Rebman and I went to Corvallis and Albany over the weekend where I bought about $10 worth of map-reading equipment and an $85 wristwatch. It is a Swiss watch and very beautiful. I thought that I might as well derive some practical benefit from my pay instead of throwing a goodly portion of it away, as heretofore. Still no news as to my disposition. A letter came to the Colonel asking if I had complied with AR 345-415 (prompt report to CO), and as I had, everything was okay. But--?

Tomorrow comes the Infantry Battalion Combat Firing Proficiency Test in which I must function as an efficient S-3 <u>as never before</u>. So God, again I ask for your guidance, as an efficient job well done, right now, would be an invaluable asset to me, God knows!

No mail at all for days and days. Guess everyone (Mother) has forgotten me. I can't expect any from anyone else, as I cut all communications.

Camp Adair, Ore.
July 2, 1943

The Bn. Test is over. We evidently passed it but not in a too outstanding fashion. Yesterday was the start of the big Division CPX, and I had to come down with the flu, of course. In bed all day yesterday and today, fever of 102 degrees last night. Despite my objections, Colonel Smith insisted I stay in bed, but I know my absence probably left them in a helluva hole on the CPX. Guess my luck has turned permanently to the bad type. Colonel Smith showed me a confidential letter in which Colonel Cochran had recommended him for promotion to the full grade of Colonel, and he said he felt that he owed much of that recommendation to me! Which I consider a very great compliment.

Still no word as to any punishment Colonel Cochran may have thought up for me, but Colonel Smith says he doesn't think he intends to do any more than to block my promotion for a while.

Camp Adair, Ore.
July 3, 1943

Finally got out of bed today. Still don't feel up to par physically but felt that I had better get up anyway. Also more complications physically--?

Things should "pop" around here before long, as they are shoving new officers in here every day. Either a cadre should go out, or overseas replacements should be taken out.

Guess I will work on a large packing case to ship my things home in tomorrow. S-3 work still functioning okay, but some sign of Cochran's vengeance should manifest itself before long. Think I will turn in and try to get some decent rest tonight. No mail except from Mother, which I shall answer tomorrow. According to Hubie, it looks as though Vivian and Jack are really "that way" at last. So it looks as though dear Vivian may find happiness at last.

I'm glad for her sake, for I realize only too well that such a thing ever happening to me—now—is forever gone and shattered.

Couldn't feel any lower tonight, I guess.

CAMP ADAIR, ORE.
JULY 4, 1943
I can remember happier Fourth of Julys! Still have a beastly cough that will not leave, occasional spells of nausea, and a sensitivity about the eyes that bodes ill for when we leave on RCT #8 on this coming Tuesday. Manufactured a wooden box today in which I shall pack the majority of my belongings and ship them home when we leave for maneuvers.

I certainly feel swell (in a pig's eye!). We have a Battalion demonstration on "Attack of a Fortified Position" tomorrow, under my supervision. Guess it will go all right. I wonder how rugged this RCT #8 and #7 are going to be. I suppose it will rain (as usual).

About all I can do is to pray for improvement in my physical condition, and if it's not asking too much, also in the set-up around here. Something is sure to pop soon, and the sooner the better for me!

CAMP ADAIR, ORE.
JULY 5, 1943
Quite an easy day! I might say I felt 1/10 of 1 degree better today. Went out to the Willamette River on a reconnaissance with the Colonel today and did the hay fever hit! Man O Man! I suffered something terrible with it. Worst ever!

Tomorrow starts RCT #8 (Defense), and if this hay fever hits as bad, with all the extensive foot reconnaissance I will have to do, I will truly be in sad shape. It only lasts until noon on Wednesday, however, so I may be able to tough it out.

No mail, as usual, today. I have only been out of Camp once since May, and believe me, I am not very anxious to get out, either.

Quite a substantial rumor came around today that the 415th Regiment would furnish 30 officers for overseas replacements. If so, I sure hope I go. My life is finished here—that I know.

CAMP ADAIR, ORE.
JULY 9, 1943
By this time, I feel quite a bit improved, physically. Still have a bad cough and a cold in my chest. Colonel Smith is gone, transferred to Regiment as Regimental Executive Officer. So—Joe Blow is now the Battalion Commander. Strangely enough, however, I seem to be getting along fairly well with him. All promotions in the Army have been "frozen" until further notice. In a way, it is possible that that might alleviate my situation, giving Cochran time to grow lenient or something, but I doubt it. We leave Sunday afternoon at 1400 for four days in the field on two very tough problems (RCT). I hope to goodness my hay fever doesn't start in again.

No mail for several days.

I do hope to God that everything will work out okay for me, and although it seems in vain, I pray the Lord tonight that some miracle might happen to make life again worthwhile.

CAMP ADAIR, ORE.
JULY 10, 1943
Saturday. Worked all day. Went on a reconnaissance with all the Regt'l and Bn Staffs this afternoon. (Preparation for RCT #7 and #8 tomorrow.)

Well, on August 10th, one month from today, I will be writing this book in Bend, Oregon, out in the field, and I do mean out! Will be out for three or four months anyway, and from there--.

You know, silly as this book may seem, it has been a great comfort to me. To a lonely person, I guess something like this is a lifesaver. Other fellows have their girl to write to. I have my book, or more properly, a log, I guess.

Received a letter from Bob, and he is now in Blytheville, Arkansas, at the Advanced School. He sure is a great kid. I only hope he keeps going to school until this thing is over.

Have got to get going and start sending some of my stuff home before it gets too late.

Major Elliott okay so far.

CAMP ADAIR, ORE.
JULY 19, 1943
The change finally came about, but in an unexpected manner—the old seniority angle. It seems that Furey must be promoted first (being a West Pointer). So, in order to bring this about, Captain Prevics is now S-3. I am on a detached basis, officially listed as Ass't S-3, but I know that will and cannot last and ultimately some other disposition will be made of me, but what? In the interim, "Joe Blow" gets more and more difficult to work with.

Still feeling far under par physically. And mentally? Well, I just feel as though life is over for me. Not a single solitary thing to live for. I am just marking time in an existence that is wearisome and holds only bitterness no matter what way I turn.

Dear God—just what is the purpose of such a life? Surely I was placed here for something more than this. At any rate, I ask for courage to carry on, from now on, with my head held high, and at least let me "go down" with all flags flying.

CAMP ADAIR, ORE.
JULY 20, 1943
Busy packing my things to send them home. I now have two footlockers and a large chest I managed to construct. Poor Mom! I don't know where she will ever find room to store all my things!

Bn. HQ all a-turmoil. I don't know, but I have an odd premonition that things are about to "break" around here before very long. We leave for maneuvers on August 7th.

Time passes so fast! It is hard to realize that I am well into my third year in the Army. Getting ancient fast, too! 27 years old, going on 28. Feel a little better physically today, and I certainly hope it continues! No mail at all from anyone for an awfully long time. The weather grows hotter daily, but I revel in it! The hotter the better after that miserable winter.

Still taking lots of our officers overseas in the replacement pool, and I certainly hope my name is on the list.

Camp Adair, Ore.
July 21, 1943
The "shake-up" has started! Lt. Ereza and Losey to Div. HQ, G-2 Section, detached basis. Lt. Richton to Washington, D.C. Thus leaving vacancies in the Company. I expect a more complete shake-up about the end of the month. Just what my eventual fate will be is hard to say. Two more officers went out on the Overseas Replacement List today. I hope my name appears on it before very long. Joe Blow is getting more and more difficult every day. Felt pretty fair, physically, today for a change.

There is talk that Prevics is, in reality, understudying Bn. Executive, and will, in the grand shake-up, be sent out as such, thus leaving the S-3 job again vacant. But in my personal opinion, that is so much bush-wah, for I fear old Colonel Cochran will be eternally "gunning" for me from now on.

Can't help but think quite a bit of Margie. She was a <u>real girl</u>.

Camp Adair, Ore.
July 25, 1943
We fired all day on the Carbine Range yesterday, and I was fortunate enough to qualify as expert with a score of 181. Had the last, and probably the most lavish, of all 415th Inf. Dances last night. I helped one of the boys out and escorted an "extra" girl, an Army nurse—name, Lucille Smith. She was nice all right, very attractive, but I'm afraid my lack of "jitterbugging" ability didn't add to the enjoyment of her evening. Had two (2) beers and a glass of champagne and called it an evening.

In the interim, things grow more and more upset every day. Rumors, rumors, and more rumors each day. Examples: "28-man cadre to go out at the end of month." "28 officers to go overseas—ditto." "We will receive Major Denisevich as a new Bn Comdr." "Joe Blow to be transferred to another Bn as Exec." "Prevics to go out on cadre as Bn Exec." "Many officers to be reclassified." Etc., etc., *ad infinitum*.

What all these can mean, as they might pertain to me, I don't know, but more and more, to me, the inevitable realization that, for me, life and any chance of happiness therein, is over.

There is nothing to look forward to.

Camp Adair, Ore.
July 26, 1943
The tense atmosphere and highly unsettled conditions increase, it seems, almost hourly. Lt. Rebman returned from his leave, and returned from it, to face this unbearable mess.

I feel lost without a definite responsibility being mine. Received another new officer today to replace some of those who went overseas, I presume. Rumor now has it that we will receive "fillers" prior to departing for maneuvers—6 Captains, 6 1st Lts., and 21 2nd Lts.—will remain behind from said maneuvers to train fillers.

I have recently grown so discouraged and weary of the seeming futility of all of life that it becomes a weary task merely to rise and meet the new day.

Meanwhile, the dissatisfaction and resulting tension caused by "Joe Blow" and his daily foolish antics causes a continual nervous strain on all members of the command. How Colonel Smith is missed! And how "Joe Blow" is hated!

Camp Adair, Ore.
July 31, 1943
The absolute dregs of despair have been attained by me today. If I felt any lower, I don't know how I could stand it. This mess around here is so damned mixed up and confusing that knowing what may happen next is well nigh impossible. Joe Blow finally realizes what is thought of him by every officer in the Battalion, and as a result, is making it as miserable as he possibly can for everyone. Understand he now wants to bring back "Sneaky ***" into the Battalion. He sold Lt. Ereza down the river into 2nd Bn in order to get Furey his Captaincy and wouldn't recommend poor hardworking Pruitt for his 1st Lieutenancy.

Why did I have to work like a maniac to advance myself and end in this mire of inefficient commanders, worry, petty intrigue, and unhappiness? Why did I believe all those dreams when I received my commission just 1 year ago next Wednesday?

Oh my God, is there no future, no happiness, nothing at all left for me? Nothing before I go overseas? It seems inevitably not, just a dreary routine of worry, hard work, and loneliness.

Camp Adair, Ore.
August 1, 1943
A dreary, dreary Sunday, as usual. Had a good night's rest, however. Packed most of my things and managed to segregate my belongings into three classes: (1) Those I am taking on maneuvers, (2) Those I am leaving here in storage, (3) Those I am sending home.

Physical condition worrying me a bit. However, those worries are as nothing compared to my mental turmoil. (1) What will be my disposition, for I know I cannot remain at Bn. HQ on an unattached basis? What does Joe Blow plan to do? Tomorrow, I am going to the station hospital and try to get a complete physical examination for two (2) purposes: (1) to find out exactly what my shortcomings, physically, are, (2) to enable me to apply for transfer to the parachute troops, if possible, when I can stand no more of this petty outfit—and as the majority of other officers are doing.

Life seems to be as utterly hopeless and unfathomable as ever.

We are evidently in for at least two months of hell at Bend—freezing at night, roasting during the day, 18 inches of dust on most roads, etc. Rumor #1143298—We may go to INDIO, CALIFORNIA, after maneuvers.

[The following entry was typewritten on a loose piece of paper in the journal.]

August 1, 1943
On this day of my life, I have never felt more discouraged and despondent. I feel sincerely, today, that life holds absolutely nothing for me. Part of this feeling, I agree, can be attributed to a naturally pessimistic nature, but not all of it. Will I never again be filled with hope, with ambition, and with the pure, unbounded zest of living? Today, I ask myself these questions: How will my future in the Army work out? How will the maneuvers in the Bend area work out? Will my one fatal error ever be erased? Will I ever know real happiness with someone by my side that I can love, work for, and make happy? Only the Good Lord above can answer these questions, and perhaps, in his infinite mercy, He will someday see fit to guide my steps into the right path. Until that time, and that time only, will I know the answers to the above.

CAMP ADAIR, OREGON
AUGUST 2, 1943

The time for the departure of the 104th Division for the Bend Maneuver Area draws closer at hand. I bought some more fatigues from the QM Warehouse today, and it really set me back a bit, financially. Also went to the hospital today and had a long talk with Captain German, who assured me that I had absolutely nothing to worry about as regards my physical mishap of recent date. I also requested a complete physical examination (Form 63) preparatory to requesting transfer to the parachute troops at Fort Benning, Georgia.

I don't intend to submit the request for transfer right away, as the physical examination is good for three months, but I intend to use it as an "Ace in the Hole" in the event that things get too damned miserable due to Joe Blow and his antics. Then, too, I have been extremely curious, for some time, as to the exact status of my health. That is, I have had an almost continuous cold since I arrived at Camp Adair, have felt almost continuously run down, especially since my recent hospitalization; that is, no pep or energy, etc. So I think it is an excellent idea to find out, once and for all, just how I stack up physically, especially just prior to the start of the summer's maneuvers. From all reports, despite the fact that the maneuvers will be extremely rugged and consist chiefly of almost continuous movement, I think they will benefit me immensely, especially in view of the fact that the high, dry climate of the Bend Area is reputed to be quite beneficial.

Oh yes! Another possession now belongs to McCully, which is bound to prove valuable at some time or other in the future—that is this portable Royal typewriter. Perhaps it was foolish to do so, but it is something that I have always wanted, and in view of the fact that it is an almost new model, I think I purchased it at quite a bargain price--$55.

Joe Blow continues to be just as miserable as ever. Some new developments did occur today, however. Sneaky *** was observed busily using his best sneaking tactics around Joe. Also, Joe called Rebman into his office and told him, quote: "Keep your nose clean out on maneuvers when umpiring, and possibly when maneuvers are over, you may be a company commander or a platoon leader." Rebman told him, "Most probably a platoon leader, don't you think, Major?"

If ever I saw a more hated man that old Joe Blow is around here, I have yet to live a long time. Intend to go up and finish my examination tomorrow, and meanwhile, have got to figure how to pack the rest of my junk.

CAMP ADAIR, OREGON
AUGUST 3, 1943
Another day of unbearable tension draws to a close. Spent the morning at the QM cutting stencils. A staff meeting was held this afternoon, and after that, I went to the hospital where I managed to complete the blood tests and X-ray and dental (during which time he filled four small cavities). Tomorrow I will finish it up with the blood pressure, heart, lungs, etc., etc.

So many of the officers of 1st Bn. are transferring out, it is causing quite some comment. The shock for which I must steel myself is here. Promotion—Furey to Captain--Buckley, Freeland, also. Pennington and McLaughlin to 1st. No use spending (or wasting) time in grieving, I guess, just what I must expect as long as Cochran remains in command.

My big worry now is my final disposition. I am not holding a T/O job, so it is reasonable to assume that the first dirty detail that comes along, I will be thrown into it.

2310 Army time, so I had best hit the hay, I guess.

CAMP ADAIR, ORE.
AUGUST 5, 1943
Two exceedingly dreary days have passed. Cloudy and rainy. Yesterday was the anniversary of receiving my commission—August 4, 1942. Little did I think, on that happy day, that future events would take such a gloomy turn.

Joe grows continually more and more miserable to serve under. *** will be returned to Co. A, as Executive Officer. Pennington *** to be promoted to 1st Lt.!

Received a letter from Bob yesterday, and he continues to do swell! Guess he will graduate either on the 28th or 29th as a Flight Officer or as a 2nd Lt. He is not yet sure which it will be.

I mailed 107 pounds of belongings home by railway express, including my saber, typewriter, radio lamp, etc.

It seems hard for me to look forward to the maneuvers with any degree of anticipation, for there is nothing to look forward to except various and sundry details, and almost perpetual disfavor, it seems.

I passed the physical exam for paratroops, <u>I believe</u>. At least I will find out for sure later this afternoon or early tomorrow morning. This will be the last entry from a civilized abode.

In Bivouac, Sisters, Oregon
August 9, 1943
Much has occurred in these four days. I passed the parachute troops physical examination 100% perfect. All I have to do now is to submit my application for transfer. We moved here à la convoy at 0100 Saturday morning, during which time I almost froze to death, being overly optimistic and storing my short coat in Camp Adair. I wrote Mom today and asked her to send me my G.I. overcoat from home. It is warm and should be all right for out here. We are now in base camp at the foot of the "Three Sisters," three 10,000-foot, snowcapped peaks of the Cascade Range. The "D" series maneuvers start day after tomorrow and will be plenty rough from all reports. Fairly warm during the day, but it turns bitterly cold at night, hence my bedding is composed of three G.I. blankets and a 100% wool sleeping bag, all encased in the regular Army officers' bedding roll, and it still is uncomfortably cold!

Still wandering around as "Ass't S-3," but no other disposition, and it sure gripes me. The parachute troops are beginning to look plenty good.

In Bivouac in the desert near Redmond, Ore.
August 16, 1943
Again, much water over the dam. Pulled one of my justly famous "*Faux Pas,*" and while acting as lifeguard at Suttle Lake, was sunburned so severely with 2nd degree burns on both legs that it destroyed some of the nerves, and I couldn't walk. Result? Three days in the Field Hospital. The Bn. is approaching a stage of near mutiny with "Joe" in command, due to his numerous boners and ignorance. Latest rumor has it that Colonel Smith will return to assume command, but this I doubt very much.

Rugged and more rugged grow the problems! Dust, endless marching, one canteen of water per day, filth, weariness, and utter fatigue, cold, insects, scorpions. *C'est la guerre!* How true!

As for me, a sense of utter frustration besets me. There lies no future for me with the 415th. The transfer to the parachute troops looks better and better to me, and so, for tonight, on a note of absolute despondency, I close.

In Bivouac—30 miles E of Brothers, Oregon—<u>Desert</u>
August 29, 1943
By flashlight.

The first sentence of the last entry holds true again. Have been working like a fiend on all the three weeks of the "D" series. At last, they are over, and we are now supposed to be on a two week's "rest period" before the Corps maneuvers start. Rest? What a laugh! They moved us today some 75 miles east of Bend, Oregon, and it is really DESERT. Bitterly cold at night—water freezes. Boiling hot during the day, and a high wind constantly fills your nose, eyes, and throat with sand.

Prevics was sent to the Advanced Course at Benning, so at present, I am again the S-3, but I feel sure "Joe" will make some changes, as he is making life so damned miserable for everyone in the Bn. that it is dangerously near a stage of revolt. I will be able to write a bit oftener, at least during this rest period.

Bivouac Area
Desert
Sept. 1, 1943
By Flashlight

Although 24-hours VOCO and 3-day leaves are available, I turned them down. I feel so disgusted and fed up with life, I'd just as soon rot in this desert.

Lt. Thomas was transferred to Bn HQ as Ass't S-3. I am S-3, but I feel sure that by this action, "Joe" is carefully greasing the skids under me. When Thomas is "broken in" enough, I will be eliminated. I questioned Joe on all this, and he assured me that (1) I was S-3, (2) MY work was efficient and satisfactory, (3) His usual hour-long harangue of pure "bull," but <u>I don't trust him</u>. He is the "knife in the back" type.

My God, how long, how long must this miserable existence continue? Must I always feel that there is no hope, no salvation? Even a criminal has <u>some</u> hope of redemption.

Bivouac Area
Desert—Hampton, Ore.
Sept. 2, 1943
By Candlelight

Another day ticked away. Received a letter from Bob, or rather his graduation announcement. So it is now Lt. Robert J. Westrem! Nice going fella! Although I can't be there to personally congratulate him, I know he certainly deserves it.

As for me, still "plodding" along in the Infantry! Somehow, though, I like the Infantry. It still remains "the Queen of Battles," and without it, nothing could be consolidated. From the present aspect of things, however, I shall, without a doubt, become famous as Uncle Sam's oldest 1st Lieutenant. Some of the new batch of promotions have come in, and without a doubt, the other S-3's will soon have their captaincies. Whereas, for me, I can see the "Thomas, Ass't S-3" angle of Major "Joe" beginning to clarify itself. Oh well, I have nothing anyway, no future, no girl, <u>nothing</u>! Indeed, it becomes a task to face the coming day.

Bivouac—Desert
East of Hampton, Oregon
September 4, 1943

Am sitting in the sun outside my tent, writing this. Methinks something is in the wind as per organization of this Battalion, as Colonel Cochran is at present in close conclave with "Joe" in the CP tent, and they are talking over all personnel in the Bn. It has become evident during the past few days that some sort of reorganization was necessary, as so many officers had left—Prevics to Ft. Benning, Smerz and Capt. Farrington to the hospital at Camp Adair—the latter probably will be reclassified. Also Rebman went to the hospital, etc.

I imagine, in my heart, this is the long-dreaded blow I have been awaiting, and perhaps today will mark the day that McCully "hit the skids." Colonel Cochran is evidently an implacable and remorseless enemy once an individual steps out of line. So perhaps, today, more of my ambitions and dreams will go crashing down into the dust. It is indeed fortunate, if that is the case, that I have severed all correspondence, with the exception of Mother, for I can never hold my head up again if things work out as I think they probably will. Another confirmation of the present situation. Lt. Smith, of Regiment, has returned to duty, so Lt. *** (Sneaky) has returned to the 1st Battalion. In view of the fact that he is about a month senior to me, has excellent suction with the Major and Cochran, it is highly evident that he may replace me as S-3. About all I can do now is (as so often in the past) ask the Good Lord for guidance out of this mire of petty human weaknesses, for only He can show me the right path and correct actions for me to follow.

It was bitterly cold last night; I couldn't sleep because of its intensity. We killed a rattler about two feet long in the vicinity of the CP tent yesterday, one of the common "Prairie Rattlers," a particularly vicious-looking thing. Dear Mother sent my overcoat, which arrived last night, and I think I will have opportunity to thank her a million times over before the maneuvers are over.

At least that is one thing that nothing can rob me of—I have the finest Mother in the entire world.

Desert
Hampton Oregon
Sept. 7, 1943
By Candlelight.

Nothing new to clarify the aura of suspense, which continues to hang over the 1st Bn. That is, except for small bits of conversation, which evidently confirm my theory ***. Odd, isn't it, how one person can go A.W.O.L. and not give a damn about anything but getting away on pass, and he will get all the breaks, whereas, the other can honestly work to perfect himself and because of <u>one</u> misstep, curtains.

Perhaps it is the moral weakling in me that causes me to wail thusly, but it <u>doesn't</u> seem just.

Enough for tonight! I am <u>tired</u> more mentally than physically if the truth be known.

No mail at all today, but then, who would write to me anyway!

Desert
Vicinity, Hampton, Ore.
September 11, 1943

Thunder, lightning, and violent rains—by candlelight

Tired tonight—body and mind. Our first desert storm finally broke tonight. It is raining violently, but Lt. Pruitt and I are quite snug in our "double igloo." I have 3 candles going, affording some degree of warmth.

We finished the Corps "CPX" this morning at 0800, and from an S-3/S-2 point of view, it was highly successful. I really learned how to order arty [artillery] fire. Major Denisevich seemed pleased, at any rate.

Had a talk with the Regimental Adjutant recently and learned that maybe in a few <u>years</u>, Cochran may relent. <u>At least</u>, I learned that <u>Major Denisevich</u> considers me the best Bn. S-3 in the Regiment (although the others are being promoted).

Had a big argument with Lt. Neill today, in which "Joe" had to intervene. Possibly bad results for me, as Lt. Neill is a great pet of Joe's, but the Maje had to agree that I was in the right.

Will this damnable tension and discontent never cease?

Only time, etc.

Bivouac—Desert
Sept. 18, 1943

The Corps maneuver (1st problem) is over. We have been resting for two days, and today we become tactical at 1800 and then enter the 2nd problem. I believe my S-3 work was creditable to some extent.

The miserable and continual tension still hangs over the 1st Bn, and I still argue interminably with "The Desert Fox." Oh My God, how I pray for some change for the better to occur soon.

Bob was home and visited the folks for a few days, and I am certainly proud of the kid. It is now <u>Lieutenant</u> Robert J. Westrem!

Quite a definite rumor now has it that we will go to Camp White (Medford, Oregon) upon the conclusion of maneuvers, and I understand it is a horribly desolate hole in comparison to Camp Adair.

I don't know, all of life and its joys seem to be over for me, and all I can do is to wait and see what will occur.

Bivouac—Desert
Near Silver Lake (Dry) Ore.
October 9, 1943

Just enough time for a few lines before Problem No. <u>5</u> turns tactical. Many things have happened. We have a new Division Comdr, General Terry Allen, who recently fought in Sicily. The past days with the "Desert Fox" have been miserable, indeed, but I have made out pretty fair in the critiques, according to the umpires. "Joe" has "goofed off" plenty in the last few problems, and now I hear we will get (temporarily) a new Bn. Comdr., a Colonel Rex, who all reports say is a pretty square fellow. Joe will still be exec, however, so there won't be much cessation of misery. Buckley (3rd Bn S-3) got his captaincy and Freeland's is on the way I hear. Colonel Cochran has been treating me very nicely, of late, so who knows, maybe in a few years--. Furey was ordered to the Parachute School and left last night. *** (Sneaky) is now Personnel Officer, as Tufts "goofed off," so he is out of the way.

More later.

BIVOUAC—LAVA BEDS
NEAR HORSE RIDGE, ORE.
OCTOBER 27, 1943

The Summer Maneuvers are rapidly drawing to a close. We have just finished Problem No. 7, and tomorrow at 1500 the situation becomes tactical for the start of M-8, the last problem. Of course, thousands of rumors have been circulating as to our ultimate disposition; but lately, that rumor stating that we would proceed by train to Indio, California, for two months of desert training and maneuvers, seems to be the most accurate of them all. Well, so be it. *KISMET* as the Mohammedans say.

I had the faintest ray of hope, lately, that perhaps old man Cochran had relented somewhat in his attitude towards me, as a very strong rumor came out that the three Bn. S-3's and two other officers were to be sent to Fort Benning to attend the Advanced Course, which would mean in a short time, my promotion to Captain. But I learned tonight from the Regimental Adjutant that the plan had been cancelled. However, the start of the rumor served its purpose—to show the true attitude of "Joe Blow' towards me. I learned, with some degree of authenticity, that he intended to send his latest *** and pet, Lt. Thomas, instead of me, when the privilege of going rightfully belonged to me. So it did me quite some good when it was cancelled. Lt. Pruitt and I (the other underdog of the 1st Bn Staff) teamed up together during the entire conduct of these maneuvers, and if I do say it myself (with a pardonable blush of modesty), we obtained a very good record throughout all the problems. We were commended right and left, and so Joe will find it extremely difficult to get rid of me on the grounds of inefficiency, at least, but he is certainly making a determined effort along that line.

Physically, I feel very well, despite the utmost rigors of this type of terrain and the extremely terrible weather, which we have encountered out here. Mentally, I remain with the same attitude, which had become almost normal for me since May in 1943. Lonely, depressed, and disgusted with life in general but determined to work like a damned dog in order to prove to the world and to myself that because a man slips once, there is no reason that he cannot yet prove himself to be a man in every sense of the word.

Forward Assembly Area
Near Long Butte, Ore.
29 October 1943

Physically tired tonight. Problem became tactical yesterday at 1500, and I have had no sleep yet and probably won't be getting any, either, as we eat an "early" breakfast at 0130 this morning and will very probably leave this area to cross the Deschutes River by assault boat around 0300.

Surprise of all surprises! The news came through last night that Freeland had obtained his captaincy, and the Major must have thought I looked a little despondent or something, for he called me over and said, "Colonel Cochran gave some indication the other day that you were not permanently removed from his promotion list but that there will probably be a little unavoidable delay." He also talked up this latest WD circular regarding sending of young officers to the Command and General Staff School at Fort Leavenworth, Kansas. That is something that would really be beyond my wildest dreams, and I entertain no false hope of going, but at the least, all of the above happenings give me reason to think that perhaps all is not in vain, after all. There are some indications that this particular problem (the last one of the summer's maneuvers, thank God!) may be over earlier than we think. Leaves and furloughs have been granted all men, but I did not apply for any, because I will not take one until I can go home with promotion, no matter how far off that may be.

It looks very much as though the 104th Division will be going overseas before very long, because of the outstanding record this Division made during the maneuvers, and whereas the other two divisions, the 91st and 96th, are returning to camps to continue training, we are probably going to Indio, California, for winter maneuvers (desert training). All we will need upon the completion of those maneuvers will be some additional 13-week, basically trained men, and we will be about ready to board ship to fight either the Nips or Nazis.

Don't believe that I have mentioned the fact that my friend Rafferty went overseas with the 2nd Division. At least his address is now APO #2, c/o Postmaster NY, NY. He certainly was a fine fellow, and I wish him all of the luck in the world, for he certainly deserves it.

The Major was his usual miserable self all through today's work, and I guess it will never be any different.

3 November 1943
In Bivouac
9 miles S of Bend, Ore.
2335 P.M.
A stormy, rainy night.

A howling wind, driving sheets of icy rain before it skirls around the CP (Command Post) tent this night, sweeping off those lonely mountain peaks, the Three Sisters. It is indeed icy, for they are almost covered with winter snow now. Indeed, we are leaving this area none too soon.

Inside the tent it is quite cheerful, an industrious fire snaps and crackles in the little stove, and with such a combination, how can I help but be in a reflective mood tonight?

Only two nights ago was my "wedding anniversary." Six years ago, I was married. It hardly seems possible! Six years in which the intervening years have passed like a series of kaleidoscopic events. Four years since my divorce—years of heartache at first, but then my eventual recovery, my struggle to get out of debt, my first years in the Army, my gradual rise, my downfall, and now the months of hard work in which I have strived to prove myself.

All of the above has served a purpose, I guess, for I am fully matured now. I will be 28 the 30th of next month, practically an old man. Indeed, it is a different me from the scared "2nd Looie" who departed Fort Benning with so many qualms. Today I am sure of myself, hardened, both physically and mentally, and able to command troops. For there have been times when I have commanded this entire Battalion, due to the inefficiency of our milk-soft Adjutant and his cohorts.

My dreams and ideals, once so lofty, are now taken for what they are—impractical daydreams. For the bitter truth is, that which comes so naturally and easy to other men—a wife, a home, and happiness—for me can never be. We have our orders now. We proceed to Hyder, Arizona, to set up and train in the desert (California-Arizona Maneuver Area). General Allen stated that it was a "staging area," preparatory to going overseas. So before too long a time, we play for the big stakes. We will leave here about November 11th on troop trains from Camp Abbott.

Leaves will be in order when we arrive down there, but I will not take a leave until I get my promotion, if ever. I couldn't for my own self-respect.

When my checking account is finally transferred and consolidated in Sonora, I will have around $1168.72 in the bank plus about $250 in War Bonds that I have sent home, and I, today, increased my War Bond allotment to two (2) War Bonds per month. Not bad for a guy that was eternally in debt when married and all his own fault, so his wife said. Well, nuff sed for tonight.

Bivouac near Bend, Ore.
5 November 1943
2345
A bitterly cold night, although the prevailing high winds, rain, and sleet of the last two days have finally ceased. Bitterly cold—identical with the turmoil in my mind. For tonight, the tension of the last few days burst. The S-3's of the battalions were sent to the Advanced Course at Fort Benning, that is, all of them except the S-3 from the 1st Bn., in whose place was substituted the name of Lt. Thomas, otherwise known throughout the Battalion as "the fair-haired boy" and "the Major's pet." I determined to have it out once and for all with the Major, and in questioning him about it said, "He was sent from the S-3 quota that was talked about recently, wasn't he, Major?" At first, he denied knowledge of such a battalion commanders meeting, but when I told him that Major Beistel had already told his S-3 about it, who in turn told me, he rather hastily reconstructed his story. He said that he had nothing to do with recommending Thomas, but knowing his sneaky tactics as I do, I doubt it. I then questioned him outright as to what effect this would have on me upon Thomas's return, and he said he didn't know, that perhaps the Colonel had different plans for Lt. Thomas upon his return (as Captain). I then stated that I felt my work had at least been up to par during the recent maneuvers, in view of the fact that the majority of my critique notes had been extremely commendable. He said that the Colonel felt so too, in questioning him about my status the other day, for he asked the Colonel if I was to be permanently denied a promotion and the Colonel replied, "Of course not, but he will have to wait awhile." During the entire talk, the Major kept insinuating that perhaps the Colonel had sent my name to Corps, as one of those younger officers to be sent to the Command and General Staff School at Fort Leavenworth, Kansas. This, however, I believe, was a subterfuge on his part, to cover up his sending Thomas to the other school. He stated that my work was entirely efficient and satisfactory and that he

had no complaint on that score. So there is the entire dreary mess as it stands tonight. When Captain Prevics returns from Fort Benning during the early part of next month, he will automatically replace me as S-3, due to his rank, and when (Captain Thomas) returns from there, I will no doubt be relegated to the Assistant to the Assistant S-3. The only straw of hope to which I may cling now (for hard work and attention to duty mean nothing), is the fact that we have acquired seven (7) new officers within the past two days, thus padding the officer strength of the Battalion out of all normal proportion and pointing to one very definite indication (especially in view of the fact that the Commanding General was purported to have stated so) that an officers cadre would soon be going out to activate another division. If I am sent out on that, I may have a chance to start anew (away from old Joe Blow, thank God), but in what capacity, I can't say, as S-3's are not sent out on cadre, as a general rule.

So tonight, again, just as I stand on the threshold of vindication (or so I thought), fate steps up and bludgeons me down. So again, it is *KISMET*, as fate ordains, so be it.

Much to my surprise, I received a letter from Vivian tonight, the first in six months, stating that she would like to come and see me on her vacation. I wrote a nice friendly letter to her and told her that we were leaving Oregon in a few days and could not tell her where I was going.

The transfer of my funds to the bank in Sonora is now just about complete, for I received my new checkbook today. I requested that it be made "joint tenancy" account, one in which Mother can draw checks on it at any time, so my mind is relieved on that score. Mother will never be in need again, at least while I live, and when I finally "get mine," the $10,000 insurance will take care of her for the rest of her life I feel sure.

Again tonight, as so often in the dreary annals of this log, I will creep into an icy sleeping bag, tired, both mentally and physically, dejected, and entirely convinced that life holds nothing at all for me and very probably never will.

BIVOUAC 9 MI S OF BEND, ORE.
7 NOVEMBER 1943
2100

A typical "Gloomy Sunday" for me. Didn't do much at all today but remain in the CP and catch up on a bit of the administrative work. Joe was his usual "pleasant" self all during the day, snapping everyone's head off, bawling everyone out, from private on up. Sometimes I sincerely think that he wakes up in the morning hating himself.

New worries, in addition to those already filling my mind. My old nemesis seems to have had a recurrence for some unknown reason, as I wasn't bothered at all during the maneuvers. Fate never seems to tire of buffeting me around, or am I just unduly sensitive? The only time in my life when I was really happy was when I was first appointed S-3 and all the time that Colonel Smith had the Battalion, but that happiness was short lived when Old Joe Blow took over. Again it seems as though my premonitions have an uncanny habit of working out, for just about every situation that I forecasted when he took over has worked out to the letter.

There is but one shining star in all the sea of despair that engulfs me. I determined to see Colonel Cochran and determine exactly where I stood, so I had my opportunity the other day when they called a battalion commanders meeting, and I asked him, "Sir, I would like to know if, in your opinion, my work as been efficient and satisfactory, especially during the recent maneuvers." He answered, "Excellent work, it was extremely satisfactory." Short and to the point, but that was all I could get out of him. So what is the score? The Bn. Commander states that my work is highly efficient, the Regimental Commander says the same, and all of the officers in my Battalion are of the opinion that the Battalion would have folded up many times during the past maneuvers if it hadn't been for me. The Regimental S-3 says I am the best Bn S-3 in the Regiment, and of course, Colonel Smith has told several people the same, and yet it seems that if anyone is to be passed over when it comes to advancement, it is me.

As I have stated before, my only hope is to go out on the cadre as a Battalion S-3 (MOS 2160), but I believe that my chance for this is extremely slim. So what then is to be my fate? I can only, once again, as so often in the past, call on the Good Lord to put an end to this present miserable set-up and end this horrible existence that has been in effect since the first part of this year. I do not think that I can stand much more of it physically or mentally, either. I seem to be able to stand about anything physically. As God knows, I have continued to work on some of these maneuver problems when everyone else was out on their feet. But human flesh and blood can stand only so much.

ON TROOP TRAIN
EN ROUTE TO ARIZONA
12 NOVEMBER 1943
1417

Once again on a train, in California. This time, a troop train en route to Arizona. Memories engulf me, for I am somewhat familiar with all this terrain. Sometime tonight I will pass within 60 miles of home and Mother, "trains that pass in the night." How different it all is from previous trips, for then I had the limitless future to look forward to, and now I have nothing.

I have but one consolation. Out of all the discouraging events of the past few months, one thing is manifest: <u>I have won the high regard and the esteem of my fellow officers</u>. Just what my future will be, I cannot say. Without a doubt, I will remain an S-3 until Prevics's or Thomas's return. There are rumors that a cadre is definitely going out, but whether I will go, remains to be seen.

Physical worries are again adding to my despondency and have determined to settle it once and for all upon arrival in Arizona.

ON TROOP TRAIN
"SOMEWHERE IN ARIZONA"
14 NOVEMBER 1943
1450

Passed thru L.A. about 1800 last night, so I phoned the Strahls. John was home (released from the Army), and Melanie was very excited—made me promise to write. Guess I will have to—should have left well enough alone.

All the gang "played hooky" from the train during the 2-hour stopover in Los Angeles and got mildly stinko on beer. Fun while it lasted but felt miserable this morning. Everyone is planning to take a leave as soon as we hit Hyder, but I cannot and will not go home in my present status.

I <u>know</u> in my heart that I have earned a promotion, but as long as it remains unattainable, I shall stay where I am.

I certainly hope that things start to break for me soon, as I am about at my rope's end. In reference to the cadre, I hope this is particularly true.

CAMP HORN, ARIZONA
70 MILES E OF YUMA
DEC. 6, 1943
So much has happened recently that it is hard to know just where to start in. To begin with, upon arrival at Camp Hyder, I found that the present leaves being granted would probably be the last, so against my will, I applied for and was granted a 15-day leave (Nov 19-Dec 4). Followed a wonderful two weeks. The Morgans, as usual, were kindness itself. Art loaned me his car when I was in Oakland, and Vivian and I renewed acquaintanceship with Lyle and Carol. Visited Lola and Walt. Rented a car ($77) and made 2 trips to Sonora and saw Mother and Harold. Saw the Raffertys and, of course, about everyone else. It was wonderful! Vivian still has a lot of funny ideas about marriage.

I left 3 days early and visited John Strahl and his family in L.A. Perhaps I should say Margie, instead, as we were together almost continually during my stay in L.A. To my horror, I find that she, too, has wild ideas about marriage. I tried to talk her out of it but wasn't any too successful.

Left L.A. at 8:30 a.m. Saturday morning, reported to the Casual Company in Yuma, Arizona, that night and rode out to Camp Horn the following day. Now here is where my "psychological intuition" came into play again. I felt horribly depressed at the thought of returning to Joe Blow and all attendant horrors again, but <u>something</u> seemed to tell me that important changes were in the wind, <u>and sure enough</u>, the moment I signed in, I was informed that I had been placed on SD with Special Troops at <u>Division Headquarters</u>. I couldn't imagine why until I finished the last of my investigating today. My friend, dear old <u>Colonel Smith</u>, took advantage of the time he was temporarily commanding the Regiment and saw Colonel Aaron (another good friend), who told me today, quote: "I know what the set-up was down in 1st Bn. I asked G-1 to send you up here. I always did say you were one of the best S-3's in the Regiment. I want you to be my S-3 and take over all of this training up here. I can't offer you any promotion, right away, but when we finish the 13 weeks' training here, I have arranged with G-3 to put you up there for a while and then send you to Fort Leavenworth, Kansas."

Well, you can imagine how I felt and what a tremendous load is off my shoulders now that I am away from J. Blow. I have unlimited opportunities now and a chance to prove myself. At the same time, though, I realize full well the heavy responsibilities and the many difficulties that now face me. Oh God above, give me thy fullest help and assistance now, for like a reprieve to a doomed man, this is my one chance to make good. Help me, O Lord, in the heavy days that are to come, and let me meet them all with assurance, judgment, and the poise of a true officer and a gentlemen.

Camp Horn, Arizona
Dec. 8, 1943

Work, work, and more work! Finished a huge Training Memorandum today on range firing, which contained a thousand and one details. Colonel Aaron's comment? <u>Fine</u> <u>work</u>! So different from working with J. Blow. He just gives you the job and lets you do it. From now on, it is up to me. Everything seems to be going so swell, I am almost afraid it can't be true, but O Lord, how I pray for it to be so. Please let this be a turning point in my fortunes. I worked so damned hard throughout maneuvers, and all for naught, it seemed. I guess when the great Martin Prevics returns, he will find out how much he <u>don't</u> know about S-3 work. Likewise, Thomas, because I sure didn't "break him in" as old Elliott wanted me to. Perhaps I am a bit vindictive, but he was <u>such</u> a downright <u>heel</u>.

So tonight, I vow to throw myself into this work with everything I have got, to show Colonel Aaron I appreciate the chance he has given me—for he is a <u>man</u>!

Camp Horn, Arizona
Dec. 9, 1943

Another day of hard, unrelenting work. But I enjoyed it! Firing all arranged for. I hope to goodness it goes off smoothly. Don't know if I goofed off on "Mine Training," or not, but will clinch it tomorrow. Colonel Aaron told me today, "You should learn a lot on this job—your responsibilities are much heavier than on your former job."

I bought a trench coat, a gabardine officer's shirt, and 5 sets of badly needed insignia, today ($32.25), but I needed the stuff.

It may be my imagination, but the majority of the unit commanders seem a trifle hostile about my highly authoritative position. Well t'hell with'm. I intend to do a complete job whether they like it or not!

So again, I reiterate, let me make an outstanding success of this job, if nothing else.

Wonder what Lt. Cox will be like?

104TH DIVISION
HEADQUARTERS COMMANDANT'S OFFICE
12 DECEMBER 1943

My first week in the new job completed! I am so happy on this job now, if it will only last, and if I can only make good on it! But I will, I vow it, if hard work and diligence mean anything (and I am certainly accustomed to hard work, without any credit for it, I might add). If at all possible, I want to get this Mine School deal straightened out tomorrow, and I intend to see G-3 about sidetracking (if necessary) Cochran's proposal to send me to the Advanced Course at Fort Benning. For frankly, I think the present opportunities available to me now are much greater than if I ever returned to the 415th Regiment. That is my greatest wish, right now—to be assigned permanently to some organization <u>other</u> than the 415th. Lt. Pruitt returned from his special detail up at Camp Ibis today, and he, too, is happy beyond all measure at this SD order detailing him to Division (away from the horrors of Joe Blow). He sure is a good kid and a real friend. I might say he was the only friend I had out on maneuvers, and we really worked together, and as a result, turned in a good job all the way through, much to Joe Blow's disappointment.

My God, how I pray that this is not another scurvy trick of fate's, to seemingly give me all the breaks again and then only to bludgeon me down to my knees later on as has been the case so often in the past. I even feel better physically because I am not working under the continual strain and tension that was always normal down in the Battalion. By the way, much to my satisfaction, I hear that Joe is having one helluva time down there now, what with both Pruitt and I gone, who were the only men in the Bn that were really trained for those jobs. He has two men holding down the job of S-3 and no replacement for Pruitt at all. Well, let him find out just how nice it is. He thought Thomas and Prevics were such efficient men. Let him find out now.

I only hope that Cochran doesn't get another quota to go to the Advanced Course for he, too, suddenly doesn't want me to leave the Regiment and told G-3 that I was to go on the next quota. Well, the hell with him, too. I am perfectly satisfied where I am, and if I never see the 415th again, it will be too soon.

Wrote a few letters today and ordered four books from the

Infantry Association, things that will look nice in a home of my own. But there I go again dreaming a lot of impossible and perhaps impractical dreams. Hope that I will be able to write a few encouraging excerpts in here within the coming week.

CAMP HORN, ARIZONA
15 DECEMBER 1943
Things aren't <u>too</u> encouraging. The pressure of work has increased greatly, and the range firing seems to be going exceptionally well. A great many of the Special Troops seem to be bucking the instruction on Mine Training, however. Well, this is only a passing phase and will pass, in time. Then, too, none of these units has ever had anyone coordinate their training before, and it seems to cause, naturally, some resentment.

Have received no mail at all for several days and can't imagine what the tie-up can be, unless it is just the usual notoriously slow delivery of mail.

Colonel Aaron seems extremely reticent of late, but this could be caused by some sore teeth that he has been battling, of late.

I hope that the Good Lord will see fit to give me guidance, now, as never before, especially during the months of January and February.

I am getting well rested, what with nearly 12 hours sleep per night.

Aronson, Pruitt, and I talking of going to Phoenix this coming weekend--?

CAMP HORN, ARIZONA
18 DECEMBER 1943
I <u>was</u> going into Phoenix today, had a ride all arranged for, a hotel room with Lt. Aronson, and even a quart of bourbon—in cahoots with Aronson—but that damned Lt. Robbins failed to show up at noon, and under the regulation of one officer being present at all times, I could not leave. Well, believe me, I am certainly going to raise hell until I get off next weekend (Christmas Day included).

The big "mess" finally occurred. Colonel Cochran submitted my name as one of those officers to leave for Fort Benning to attend the Advanced Course early in January, but I refused it. I told Colonel Aaron that I preferred to remain here and see what my chances would be on going to the Command and General Staff School at Fort Leavenworth.

For if I went to the Advanced Course that would again put me under obligation to Colonel Cochran to the 415th Infantry Regiment and under the jurisdiction of Joe Blow, which I could not stand in any event and never will. I guess I was about the first officer in the history of the Division who ever turned down a school, according to the fuss that was raised. Colonel Aaron and the Chief of Staff were arguing about it at the breakfast table, etc. At any rate, Colonel Aaron had to go down and see Colonel Cochran about taking my name off of the list, and so I told him, "Sir, if you see Colonel Cochran about this, be as diplomatic as you can, for I will be blackballed in the 415th Inf. Regiment forever, if he ever finds out that I refused this school." To which he replied, "Don't you worry, I will, and anyway, I think I can get you transferred out of that Regiment entirely, before long." He certainly is a fine man, a West Pointer, and he has enough "pull" up here that he can very possibly do me a lot of good, if fate so dictates.

Meanwhile, along other lines, Margie is growing absolutely fanatical about the subject of marriage. She is, without a doubt, one of the finest girls that I have ever known and would make a man an A-1 wife, but as always, there are the eternal obstacles. What if I were shot up before the war is over? What about after the war? What security could I offer anyone, and all the thousand-and-one complications that go to make up that great institution, MARRIAGE? Plus the fact that I can't even understand myself. You can take a girl who has about everything that a normal man would desire in a wife, put her in my arms, and it is the same as always—I am as cold as ice, no respondent love stirs in my being. As always, I am so afraid of the thought of marriage that I hate myself for being a heel to such a swell girl, but the awful truth remains—I can never marry, and I guess I never will. That is why that I am convinced that the best thing that can ever happen to me is to go overseas as rapidly as possible, get mine, and forget this goddamn life. I don't think I ever realized it quite so much as with Margie. For a while, I thought I was kidding myself until the "right girl" came along, but now, I don't know. Even if the so-called "right girl" came along, I would very probably tell her the same thing that I have told Vivian and Margie—it's a rum go. Meanwhile, the inherent difficulties of talking myself out of such a situation is decidedly hard. I hate to hurt either of them, and yet, I know in my heart it would never work out in either case. Why in hell can't these women just be friends, and let _me_ do the proposing, when and if it is necessary?

It's a foolish thing to think that the thoughts of my former marriage still affect my actions now, but I guess I have become so accustomed to thinking of what a horrible thing that marriage really is, that I will never think otherwise.

When visiting the Raffertys on my recent leave, I saw some snapshots of my former wife taken recently, and I must say that her years of dissipation are finally catching up with her. She looks about 35 years old, blowsy, and on her last promise of what once was beauty. I thank the Good Lord above that I got out from under that mess, even at the horrible price I had to pay.

Well, it is about time for supper so had best go and get ready for it.

Camp Horn, Arizona
21 December 1943

Here it is Tuesday already. Work has been going along satisfactorily. Everyone in Division HQ circle is out or around. Sometimes I feel almost in a mood of despondency again. Everything seems so hopeless. Will the Leavenworth deal go through, and if not, what will my ultimate disposition be? For I have seemingly burnt all of my bridges behind me as far as the 415th Infantry is concerned.

Lt. Collins and I, Danny Strelnick (Red Cross) and Colonel Mulcahy put on a mild stinkeroo at the Division Officers Club last night. Had a good time. Collins talking about me going home for Christmas with him (to San Diego) but am undecided as yet.

Colonel Aaron extremely affable. No mail of a personal nature for some time. Wonder what Margie's reaction was to my last letter in which I explained as best I could, the utter futility of marriage?

Camp Horn, Arizona
22 December 1943

Tonight I sit here in a quandary, a violent mental turmoil, for no one is able to advise me, and I wonder, how I wonder, if I have done the right thing. For this evening, Colonel Cochran played his highest card. He phoned me and asked me personally whether I wanted to go to the Advanced School, or not. I stuck to my guns, however, and told him NO. By this single act, I have forever blackened any chance I may have had for promotion in the 415th Infantry Regiment. I am blackballed for life as far as Colonel Cochran is concerned. But I do not care. I would rather remain a First Lieutenant up here than to be a Major in that damned Regiment. At least I will have peace of mind and no Joe Blow. At any rate, I could not let Colonel Aaron and Colonel Smith down, after all they had done to get me out of that hole, and I had already told Colonel Aaron that I preferred to remain up here with him and strive for the Fort Leavenworth School. If that school goes through, I will stand to gain much; and if not, at least I am away from such vindictive characters as Joe Blow and Colonel Cochran.

Meanwhile, the internal strife in that Regiment increases daily. Capt. Lilienstern to Division under the stormy protests of Cochran, Major "Pipsqueak" Haggard alerted for overseas duty, Major Beistel relieved of his command for applying for the Military Occupational Government and sent down to Joe Blow as Executive Officer, 1st Bn. Rumors of an impending investigation of the 415th by General Moore, because so many officers of that Regiment are applying for transfers, and also because of its low training accomplishments.

More on this later.

CAMP HORN, ARIZONA
27 DECEMBER 1943

Had a <u>nice</u> Christmas weekend! Went to San Diego with Lt. Collins and met his folks who, incidentally, are really fine people. Had not one, but <u>two</u> Christmas dinners, listened to hours of good music and, all in all, it was wonderful! Arrived back here via a third Lieutenant's "car" at about 0600 this morning, and as a result, I am physically exhausted. Phoned Commander Barnes up, but they evidently were out.

I worried and thought a great deal over the weekend about my turning down the Advanced Course but finally arrived at the conclusion--what will be will be.

Meanwhile, no new developments have occurred along that line. All is calm and quiet. Colonel Aaron hasn't had much to say, of late.

I investigated my Classification Card quite thoroughly today, with the following results: I am <u>classed</u> as a <u>staff</u> officer (not <u>line</u>)— my official classification—"Plans and Training Officer." Two 6-months' ratings of <u>superior</u> (highest obtainable) by Colonel Smith. As to what J. Blow and Colonel Aaron will grade me remains to be seen, but I will know by the end of the month.

Fingers crossed for G-3 or Leavenworth!

Camp Horn, Arizona
28 December 1943

Slept like a log last night, although it turned bitterly cold. Cold all day today, too. I wish it would warm up. I always feel miserable when cold.

The mail is again messed up, I guess. Haven't received hardly any for several days. Colonel Aaron in quite good spirits today. Am fairly well caught up in all the work, but that is one of the vagaries of S-3 work, rushed one moment, all quiet the next.

Still keeping my fingers crossed in the hope that everything will work out okay up here.

Have been feeling rather blue and glum since my return from San Diego, but that may just be an aftereffect of the fatigue caused by the journey (hardly any sleep), etc.

Have got to diplomatically sever relations with Margie, but it is going to require a great amount of tact in order to avoid hurting her feelings. To my horror, her letters grow increasingly fervent with each new one. She is an awfully sweet girl, and I wouldn't hurt her for anything, but I can never marry anyone.

Camp Horn, Arizona
1 January 1944

Last night was New Year's Eve, and what an evening! Had a couple of drinks with Lt. Cox and Colonel Aaron and retired about 2230. The night before was my birthday, and Lt. Cox and Lt. Collins presented me with a carton of Camels (the only birthday gift I received from anyone). Colonel Aaron offered a toast in honor of the occasion in some special brandy of his that was of ancient vintage. He has been in exceptionally fine spirits of late, and my work has been progressing quite smoothly. I only hope it continues in that manner.

It seems there is an additional ten weeks on my efficiency rating that Colonel Smith will have to initial, and so I went down to see him today and found that he was going overseas! I told him, "I certainly wish that I was going with you, Sir," to which he replied, "Don't worry, if the opportunity presents itself, you will be the first officer that I will ask for." All of which made me feel mighty good, for there is no other officer that I would rather serve under when I go overseas. He sure is a grand old man, and a real soldier.

I wrote Margaret last night and tried to explain, as diplomatically as possible, the difficulties involved, and my many shortcomings as a husband. I only hope that she will take this in the spirit intended and will realize the hopelessness of the entire situation.

We definitely start maneuvers on the 13th of February, and they will last for three weeks, at the end of which time no one knows for sure just where we will go or what our disposition will be. It is a terribly puzzling situation, for they are taking men out of the Division and sending them overseas at the rate of some 200 men per week. That includes many officers, too, and many of my best friends have already left. Which leaves me again thinking, I guess I pulled one of my usual famous *faux pas* when I turned down the Advanced Course, but I still think it was worthwhile, as long as I don't have to go back to the tender mercies of JOE BLOW.

When I think of the latter subject, I always get terribly down in the dumps, but only fate can tell whether my decision was a wise one or not.

Think I will go to Phoenix on the next weekend and see what I shall see.

CAMP HORN, ARIZONA
JANUARY 3, 1944
Had a moderately quiet weekend. Lt. Cox, Collins, Robbins, and I bought a case of beer and played poker until about midnight on Saturday night. Didn't do much on Sunday except read magazines, as I received very little mail. The weather has been getting progressively colder, and I hope it doesn't get much colder.

As regards my future up here, I do not know, and a black pall of depression affects me when I think of it too deeply.

If my cleaning arrives back today, I feel sure that I shall plan on going into Phoenix this coming weekend, for what reason I don't know, for nothing interesting ever happens to me. I guess that phase of life is over for me anyway, though, so what the hell.

Colonel Aaron still in exceptionally fine fettle, and I certainly enjoy working for him. He's a real soldier.

CAMP HORN, ARIZONA
JANUARY 7, 1944
Many incidents have occurred, recently, that indeed merit notation! My 66-1 was sent to Joe Blow for his entry of "manner of performance" rating and, wonder of wonders, he marked two separate ratings of

SUPERIOR! I was truly amazed, for I honestly thought he would vent his anger in the last glorious burst of vindictiveness. Therefore, for the benefit of my record as an officer, I now have 5 separate ratings, given by 3 different Colonels, all marked Superior, which is the highest rating of efficiency possible to be given an officer. Whether this dubious accomplishment means anything or not, remains to be seen.

A talk was given today by a Major Powell of the Royal Air Force, and at this meeting, I met Major Needham, the 415th Regimental S-3, who said, quote: "I certainly wish you were back in the 1st Battalion—the S-3 work down there is in one god-awful mess." Evidently the gold brick Captain Prevics isn't doing so well.

Now for the bad news. For some time, a well-founded rumor has been circulating to the effect that Colonel Aaron was to be transferred to the 413th Infantry as Regimental Executive Officer, and it seems to be becoming quite definite. Yesterday, we learned that Colonel Aaron was going to the hospital on Monday for an indefinite stay, as his health is run down.

The above events leave me hanging on a rather precarious limb, as I have most efficiently cut my own throat in the 415th (not that I want to return in any event), and as to what my disposition will be up here, God only knows. For there will, without a doubt, be a new HQ Commandant appointed to take Col Aaron's place. My SD terminates at the end of the 13 weeks, and then?

I have only one shred of hope, depending entirely on the amount of "drag" Colonel Aaron has in higher headquarters, for he made the remark today, "There are a lot of things I have got to attend to around here before I leave for the hospital."
?

CAMP HORN, ARIZONA
10 JAN. 1944
Had an interesting weekend. I didn't go to Phoenix. Lt. Cox and I borrowed a trailer from Co. D and went down into the creek bed east of camp and scooped up a load of gravel, which we hauled home and spread on the floor of our tent, which up to that time, had consisted of about 3 inches of flour-like dust. Big improvement! We decided to go hunting on Sunday, and so, the next morning we loaded two .30-cal. carbines, two .45-cal. pistols, field glasses, K-rations, compass, etc., and took off into the desert. Traveled due north for about 35 miles over

some of the wildest, most barren and desolate terrain I have ever seen. Not a living thing did we sight but had a great amount of fun firing off about 100 rounds of ammunition at various targets. Took some pictures.

Colonel Aaron is going to the hospital tomorrow afternoon. <u>100</u> lieutenants, infantry, are going to be shipped overseas and will leave by this coming Thursday. No one knows who has been selected, as yet.

How I wonder, how I wonder, just how this ungodly mess is going to work out!

I am <u>definitely</u> going to Phoenix this weekend with Aronson.

Camp Horn, Arizona
January 13, 1944

Today is a beautiful sunny day. All the ranges seem to be extremely active this morning—machine guns of all calibers are chattering viciously, the long familiar <u>ka-rumph</u> of the 60- and 81-mm mortars echo from those ranges.

The order came out—100 lieutenants were sent overseas. My name wasn't on it, but many of my old friends were sent—Bertram, Upham, Pennington, and many others. Bertram came up to tell me good-bye. He was a swell little kid. I wish I had gone. Things seem, again, to be so terribly messed up around here. Colonel Aaron has gone to the hospital. No one knows when he will return. My throat is hopelessly cut, at least in the 415th, etc., etc.

I intend to go to Phoenix this weekend, but I know in my heart it will be the same old dreary ordeal. No mail has come from anyone for a long time. I have removed all Oakland friends from my mailing list anyway. Vivian was becoming a bit serious again.

We leave for maneuvers in 4-1/2 weeks, <u>and</u> we are definitely <u>not</u> coming back to Horn. From there, no one knows, but what with POM Schools (Preparation Overseas Movement) so frequent, we are a cinch to take to the transports before long.

<u>Good</u>!

Camp Horn, Arizona
January 18, 1944

Don't feel exactly up to par tonight. I did go to Phoenix this past weekend and had a fair time but am not overly enthused about going again. Spent a lot of money and, all in all, it wasn't worth it. Arrived back at Horn at 0700 Monday morning, and as a result, slept like a dead man. Have been told by many friends that Colonel Cochran and Joe Blow are instituting a formal request that all officers on Special Duty (SD) and Detached Service (DS) be returned to their organizations. This means, of course, back to the salt mines, if it is approved. I intend to fight it in every way possible but, of course, am handicapped by Colonel Aaron's absence.

My mail has been flooding in at a prodigious rate, but I have lost all enthusiasm for writing. Received a telegram from Bob that he was home in Sonora on his last leave and wanted to know if I could make it home. I sent a return wire stating that it was impossible to obtain a leave and asking if it was possible for him to obtain a ride via AAF flights to Phoenix, Yuma, or Dateland, Arizona, and to advise me; but so far, I have not received an answer. He seems to think he is headed overseas, doggone it, and I have never seen him since he went into the Service. I hope he can make it down.

Received four letters and my "Military Review" this morning. I certainly am far behind in my correspondence now.

The way things are going now, however, I guess it doesn't make a great deal of difference.

Camp Horn, Arizona
20 January 1944

Not a great deal new to write about, except that the rugged life out in the field starts again soon, and we will very probably end up at Camp Granite (50 miles from the nearest highway), where we will spend approximately 8 weeks (rumor).

Still have that rather hopeless outlook on my future in the Army. With Colonel Aaron gone, I don't stand a chance of realizing the initial hopes I had when I first came up here so will probably inevitably end up back with J. Blow, doomed for the duration of my tenure in the Army.

Had an argument with Lt. Collins yesterday. In many respects, he is an insufferable, conceited ass. Well, he'll just have to get over it—I'm certainly not going out of my way.

Lt. Cox's promotion should be here in a few days—to Captain. He's a swell kid. Just to show you how extremely "fair" the Army is, however, I am senior to him by six months, have an efficiency rating of straight superior, and yet?

I expect more dirty work by Colonel Cochran within the next two days, but I don't give a damn!

CAMP HORN, ARIZONA
21 JANUARY 1944
Quite a busy day. Wound up several pesky details that had been hanging fire for over a week. An incident with Colonel Cochran occurred today. I went to the Commissary to buy a field jacket, and he was just coming out, whereupon he glared at me and quoth blithely, "Hello, McCullough" and stalked off at my polite rejoinder of "Good afternoon, Sir." Indicative?

Received a letter from the girl I met in Phoenix, and she wants me to write and "be sure and come to Phoenix on the weekend of 29-30." No thanks! No entanglements for me, thank you. I've had quite enough.

50 of the "chosen few" of the Division Staff are going to a dance in Wellton, a little town 30 miles from here, tonight. Our hostesses to be 40 nurses from the 32nd Evacuation Hospital. I may as well go and have another rotten evening.

Still feel discouraged as to what my ultimate disposition may be.
?

CAMP HORN, ARIZONA
21 JANUARY 1944
1957—AFTER IT HAPPENED
No, I didn't go to the dance at Wellton after all, and the last question was answered most completely. Colonel Cochran had a talk with General Allen and convinced him that I was needed back in the 415th Infantry, and so, on Monday the 24th of January, after a few months of freedom, I return to the salt mines to the petty tyranny of JOE BLOW and to the unending, petty politics of that wondrous organization. In my desperation, inasmuch as there was an S-3 meeting tonight in the tent of the Division G-3, I talked with Major Hoegh, the top "3" man of the Division, and he told me many things that I had not known before, that in his estimation, the work I had performed while acting as S-3 of the Special Troops deserved nothing more than a rating of "SUPERIOR" all the way through. For as he said, and I quote, "You have performed a job that was difficult in the extreme in coordinating the activities of the Special Troops when all of the advantages had been

given to the infantry regiments, as was their right. There is no other man than you that I would rather have with me in the G-3 Section, but I had a long talk with Cochran and told him that if you don't want this man, let me have him; but Cochran told him, "NO, that man is going to be one of my S-3's and I want him back." At any rate, Hoegh is going to talk to the Chief of Staff and see if I cannot gain a reprieve of sorts to finish the work that is, at present, confronting me; and so, in my own heart, I will know that I have finished the job that Colonel Aaron laid out for me. But after that, I must return to the First Battalion under the "gentle mercies" of J. Blow, and so ends all my dreams of any further advancement or betterment in the U.S. Army. I shall write Margie tonight and cut off all of the deep entanglements and final bonds that should have been cut before now. For this happening tonight is the final blow, the end of all hope, the end of all human living, the end of all my once proud ideals, crashing into the dust where all of the others went some years ago. Perhaps then, this is the final tale in the saga of a defeated man, licked before he started some may say, and yet, if human gain were measured by the striving, the aching heart, the bitter mind, the broken dreams and shattered ideals, t'would have been different, perchance, but not now.

Camp Horn, Arizona
22 January 1944
ONE YEAR A 1ST LT. TODAY

The week's extension, or more aptly, "reprieve," was granted this morning, thus giving me time to prepare my clothing (excess) for shipment home, and also, all other excess equipment that I will not need from hereon out. I am still somewhat dazed by the sudden happenings, which occurred yesterday, but am determined to make the best of it. I am convinced that something must be in the wind if Colonel Cochran wants me back as badly as he has fought to get me back. There has been a continual battle on that subject ever since I first came up here, climaxed by his direct request to General Allen that I be returned to the Regiment. Well, I have made up my mind on one aspect. When I go back, I am going to be aggressive as hell, and let J. Blow and all the others know just where I stand, and if no promotion is forthcoming, I will make life so goddamn miserable for the Personnel Section with applications for parachute troops, overseas duty, and every other type of special duty, that they will be glad to get rid of me. I am especially glad of one thing. I have had the very great opportunity, in the time that I have been up here at Division, to make some mighty fine contacts, which may well stand me in good stead later on.

One sad incident occurred today—Colonel Smith, the best friend that I ever had in the Army, and I mean that literally—he couldn't have treated me better if I had been his own son, left for Fort Meade, Maryland, to go overseas. I imagine he will be given some staff job in the now forming invasion staff, for he was a very brilliant man, even if the damn fools in this Division didn't realize it. He came to see me before he left, and I told him of the catastrophe that had happened to me, and he said, and I quote: "I don't know whether they will let me ask for an officer by name or not where I am going, but if it is at all possible, I am going to send for you." I could ask for nothing better, and it was with real sadness that brought a lump to my throat, that I shook hands with him. So here's all the luck in the world to you, Colonel Smith. You were a grand guy, a real officer in every sense of the word, and a man who was very kind to a green, scared 2nd looie, just out of the O.C.S..

I wrote Margie THE final letter tonight, once again severing all connections with her, for there is no sense in continuing a relationship that can never be. Truly I can never hope to meet a girl with finer sensibilities or ideals than hers, but for me, the question of marriage is most definitely OUT, so why clutter up her life?

The female sex caused me additional difficulty today, too, for the girl I met in Phoenix phoned me up and wanted to know if I was going to come in on the 29th or not. When I hedged a bit, she became exceedingly angry, so I hung up. To hell with her and her kind. She didn't tell me until the last part of the evening that she was married and had two kids. Well, I've certainly had my share of trouble with that type of woman, and believe me, they can all go to hell, and it gives me great pleasure to tell them so. Cheap, sordid, chiseling, damned women. That's all you ever meet, and I thought of her poor husband, very probably going through the same mental hell that I went through with "the Gem of Virtue" that I married.

I wrote a letter to Colonel Aaron tonight explaining the status of training in the Special Troops now that I would soon be leaving, thanked him for the opportunity he gave me by asking for me, told him that it had been a pleasure and a privilege to have served under him, etc. This may well prove to be another "ace in the hole" for me later on. For he and Cochran are deadly enemies, and Aaron will be exceedingly scorched when he finds that Cochran has pulled a fast one in his absence; and besides, Aaron knows how very far out on a limb I put myself when I turned down the Advanced Officers School, and diplomatically speaking, this will prey on this mind, if I know Colonel Aaron. "'Tis well to plant your seeds where they will do the most good."

As for the future, it is again, *KISMET*!

Camp Horn, Arizona
25 January 1944

Willy-nilly, it seems that I am again doomed to become embroiled in the many nefarious intrigues common to the 415th Infantry. As witness these latest developments:

By investigating quite thoroughly, I discovered today just what my fate was to be when I returned to the 1st Battalion, and here is what the military travesty, the one and only J. Blow, had mapped out for me: Captain Prevics to remain as S-3 until "fair-haired boy" Thomas returned from school, Lt. Koonrod to return to a company as a platoon leader, and I to take his place as Bn. S-2. Upon Thomas' return, he would be made the S-3 (which is what J. Blow had been industriously working on since he became Battalion Commander). You can see the damnable cleverness of this whole set-up, as I would be neatly shelved for the duration of the War in a job for which I cared nothing and has a permanent T/O rating of 1st Lt. However, Captain Smith, the Regimental Adjutant, phoned me up today, and proposed the following set-up. That I take the job of Regimental Personnel Officer (T/O rating of Captain), and he said that he had talked to Colonel Cochran, and Cochran had said that he would approve my promotion to Captain in that job. Now, however, this is all not so simple as it may sound. Admittedly, the good Captain Smith has his own chestnuts roasting in the fire, and he harbors a mighty enmity towards my old enemy, Lt. ***, who was the Personnel Officer before he went to the AG School, and this is Smith's way of getting revenge on *** for sneaking the school away from him. Therefore, the whole problem, as it now stands, is this—I would be accepting a job and a type of work about which I know absolutely nothing. *** returns from the school in a short time, and without a doubt, will be of mighty wrath when he discovers these moves, not that he worries me in the least, but I will be at somewhat of a disadvantage working in a job of which I know nothing. Nevertheless, I intend to take it, rather than go back to the 1st Battalion and the tyranny of J. Blow.

What still remains unfathomable to me, <u>WHY</u> did Cochran raise such a mighty furor to get me back in the Regiment if he did not know what to do with me when I came back? Dear God, tonight I am bewildered by this mass of confusion and the uncertain events, which lie before me; and so, once again, as so often in the past, I ask your help and guidance in the trying days that are sure to come.

CAMP HORN, ARIZONA
26 JANUARY 1944
Finished my investigation down in the 415th Infantry today, and evidently, the military travesty, Joe Blow, had really intended to "show me" once and for all. For it seems I was destined to return to Co. B, my original starting point, but it seems his plans miscarried a bit, thanks to Captain Smith, for I went down and saw Smith today, and he assured me that he had talked it over with Colonel Cochran and that my return order would read, "assigned to Regimental HQ Co., in the role of Regimental Personnel Officer." He really wants me to take the job, and assured me that it was not so difficult, that Mr. Lauck would give me a hand for the first month or so, and that Colonel Cochran really wants me in that job. Why, I don't know. I still fail to understand why the Army spends over a year training a man on one specific type of duty and then blithely puts him on a job of which he knows nothing. However, with me, it is a case of looking into the future, too. For a man who becomes sufficiently skilled in personnel work has an unlimited future after the War is over; and then, too, there are certain advantages as far as the more rugged aspects of Army life are concerned, i.e., when in garrison, it is all indoor office work, and on maneuvers, we remain in the "rear echelon." However, it is a job of heavy responsibility, for all of the records of a regiment are my responsibility, and I am responsible for many statements to which I sign my name. Well, so be it. Fate so decrees, and I must humbly bow my head. I do, however, intend to apply myself with every atom of work in my being and, God willing, I will make a success of this assignment. As to the disposition of my erstwhile enemy, ***, I do not know, but it looks now as though he will be turned over to the tender mercies of Joe Blow upon his return and, of course, his resentment and wrath at my appointment to his job will be mighty, which does not worry me at all; for after all, I am not too crazy about the job, and certainly had nothing to do with the events leading up to my return to the 415th Infantry. It seems hard to take,

even now, for Major Hoegh had a job for me in the S-3 Section, which would have led, eventually, to better things; and old Cochran had to destroy it, and for what clear purpose, I still cannot understand.

Have received no mail for several days, and indeed, it looks very much as though my final letters to Margie had taken great effect. Well so be it, for I have ceased all correspondence to friends in Oakland, San Francisco, and indeed, all except my immediate family. For, as usual, I had to get most enthusiastic and shoot my mouth off about the Leavenworth deal that Colonel Aaron was fixing up for me. Which reminds me, I wonder just what Colonel Aaron's reaction will be when he finds out that I have been returned to the 415th and that I sacrificed the Advanced Course in vain?

CAMP HORN, ARIZONA
28 JANUARY 1944

Nothing new, à la 415th. All has been silent from that quarter since my talk with Smitty. I, however, have been pondering deeply the many aspects of personnel work that I <u>don't</u> know. As to this, however, only the future will disclose just what will occur.

The Division moves out into the field on the 1st, but all Personnel Sections will remain in camp and move out with the rear echelon on the 2nd. It will only be a two- or three-day problem at the most, but almost immediately thereafter, we start packing up for the move to Camp Granite, our new base camp. The actual "concentration area," however, I understand is some 217 miles NW of here near Blythe, California. The Corps maneuvers, themselves, I do not think will be so rugged as they may sound. They will last, at the most, for about the last 20 days of February, and I certainly won't mind that, after the horrible rigors of the Oregon maneuvers.

I wonder what the Great ***'s reaction will be when he finds that I have taken the position, which he licked boots so madly to obtain?

The gal in Phoenix sent another letter today, even after the Sunday incident. Nothing seems to discourage her. I wrote her a letter today, explaining just why that any furtherance of our acquaintanceship was impossible and, needless to say, I hardly expect an answer.

I can think of no other period of time during which I have felt so horribly depressed and moody as I have for the last few days— thinking, thinking, thinking—of all the hard work, worry, and striving to perfect myself that has gone for naught and still the interminable enigma. WHY did Cochran strive so mightily to return me to the 415th when the work, sweat, and endeavor that went into my training in S-3 work must be ruthlessly scrapped? I sat in the Officers Club last night, drinking numberless beers, and sought in vain for a satisfactory solution to this question, but all in vain. There is none. Except for the powerful enmity of Joe Blow, who evidently wanted to ensure my "proper relegation to deepest disgrace."

Latest communiqué via latrine channels—at the conclusion of training in the Blythe area, this Division leaves for a staging area near Indiantown Gap, Pennsylvania, prior to movement overseas.

Only the one letter today, but then I can't expect too much anymore, for I have determined to cease the most of my correspondence. I think the Margaret affair is about over, although she still insists that she is going to continue writing, even after the receipt of my last letter. It was a hard decision to make, but without a doubt, it is best for her. I am rather a sad bet for any sort of a life after this mess is over with.

GUIDANCE NEEDED!

HEADQUARTERS COMMANDANT'S TENT
CAMP HORN, ARIZONA
30 JANUARY 1944
In the terse terminology of the Army, be it known:
"4. 1ST LT ERNEST J. McCULLY, 01289287, 415th Inf, is reld of SD with HQ Sp Trs effective 1 Feb 44, and will report to CO, 415th Inf for dy." What a world of striving, of working, what a sense of frustration, what visions of intrigue, the usual political machinations, gossip, and bickerings, that little paragraph portends! Yes, the order came out today, and so tomorrow morning, I shall return to the 415th Inf and perhaps soon, I shall know only too well, just why Colonel Cochran wanted me returned to the Regiment.

Captain Cox, Lt. Robbins, and I went to the little desert hamlet of Sentinel yesterday afternoon and had a wonderful steak dinner, which in comparison to the horrible meals we have been getting at the Officers Mess, made the 60-mile roundtrip worthwhile. Came home last night and drank upwards of a half case of beer and played poker, a game which by now, I should know enough to leave alone, as I never win. It is merely a case of handing my money across the table. I didn't lose too much, however, and after a period spent listening to Eddie Cantor's War Bond Drive, I dropped to sleep at approximately 0200.

Woke up about 1030 this morning and went up and took a refreshing shower and shave. Had the usual horrible Sunday dinner and came back to the office determined to straighten out my personal records, equipment, and other necessary details, preparatory to returning to the salt mines.

Received one letter in the mail today from John Strahl's mother. It was quite pleasant, as all of her letters are, but I don't think that I will answer it for some time until I find out how things are going to work out down in the 415th.

Well, I had best get busy on packing my somewhat scattered equipment, and I doubt if I will find time to write in the old journal for some time.

Personnel Office
415th Infantry
31 January 1944

On the contrary, I find I have time tonight, after a somewhat eventful day, to write a few lines in this possibly humdrum, if not downright boring, chronicle. I spent the morning assembling my equipment, and right after lunch, went to the showers and shaved. About 1500, I obtained a command car and returned to the 415th, bag and baggage. Reported to the Adjutant, and after such preliminaries as being assigned a tent, storing my bedroll and baggage, etc., I reported to Colonel Cochran, who had the following remarks to say: "McCullough, I want you to take over the job of Personnel Officer, as our Personnel Section is in terrible shape. It will be up to you to straighten it out, and this is a great opportunity for advancement for you." At any rate, he was most congenial and affable, in fact, the most that I have ever seen him. For at the supper table (I am now counted as one of the Regimental Staff Officers), he looked up suddenly and said, "Glad to have you back with us," to which I replied, "Glad to be back with you, Sir." All this delicate repartee after the verbal clashes Cochran and I had over my SD at Division! Truly, I have stepped into a hotbed of political intrigue, however, and I am going to have to watch my step. *** is due back here on about the 9th of February, and from what I hear, he pulled so many fast ones up here that he is heartily disliked (even as he was in the 1st Battalion) and, as a result, is slated to go to a rifle company. If I know Master *** as well as I think I do, however, he will continue to cause an endless amount of trouble and will be certain to make it. There is even some wild talk of my being put in for promotion ahead of schedule in order to clinch the job, but this I think, is mostly theory, for Army Regulations so state that a person must hold a job for three months to which he is being promoted, and I do not think an exception will be made in this case.

Well God help me now. I am so woefully green on this job that it is pitiful, and I only hope now that I can make good on this job. For truly, its postwar advantages are tremendous, and in fact, if I can master this type of work, it will undoubtedly have a tremendous effect on my life after the War.

Of one thing I am certain and have therefore made a vow to myself—I have got to learn to keep my big mouth shut, and this I intend to do, come hell or high water.

In my tent
415th Infantry
1 February 1944
The Division moved out en masse today, with the exception of the Personnel Sections. We leave tomorrow morning at 0800 and will return Thursday afternoon. We will go with the rear echelon, out only about 18 miles. I put in my 1st day of personnel work today, and I certainly felt like a novice. The immensity of things I don't know appalls me.

Many rumors now: "This Division will never go overseas as a unit." "100 more officers will go overseas soon." "We have had too much desert training," etc., etc., *ad infinitum*!

I'm getting so I don't care a helluva lot, but I would like to get my "railroad tracks" before I go over, as "no promotion over the ocean" is the watchword overseas I understand.

I think I will turn in early tonight, for I have to get up at no later than 0630, roll my bedroll, and I have a nice blinding, splitting headache, too!

"Guidance needed."

Horn, Arizona
3 February 1944
Well, the big (and first) Division Exercise is over. I moved out with the rear echelon yesterday morning and we didn't do a damn thing all the time we were out! I was appointed "Officer of the Guard" upon arrival

in the area and had to post the necessary guards. Went to bed at 1900 and had a good night's sleep. Moved into camp today at 0800. Took a shower at Division with Danny Strelnick, the Red Cross representative, and the rest of the afternoon was just spent (by myself) in trying to become oriented. The work is all so new and strange to me that I feel somewhat self-conscious, but I pray to God that I can soon become adjusted and fit in, and above all, turn out an efficient job.

One gleam of hope—talking to Woodman, Captain Smith, Pruitt, and Captain Deane tonight (over a glass of Tequila), and Smith seems confident that I will be okay on the job, as it seems the Personnel Section seems to like to work with me.

How I hope everything works out. Have ceased correspondence with Margie.

No more contact with Cochran.

Prevics seems to be making an ass out of himself.

Horn, Arizona
6 February 1944

Well, here it is Sunday. So far, no furor in the Personnel Section. I have been exceedingly busy trying to assimilate this new type of work and becoming acquainted with the new circle of fellow officers who now surround me. Captains Smith, Deane, Vick, Luthi, and I all went into the little town of Aztec, Arizona, the other night and had a nice steak dinner. I seem to be quite well liked up here, but then, of course, one can never definitely determine that until something happens. Captain Vick, Luthi, and I went to the popular desert resort known as Agua Caliente yesterday, went swimming in the large outdoor pool, had one of the famous hot mineral baths, and another nice steak dinner. We arrived back at Camp about 2300 last night.

I spent today finishing up some work that I had left over from the day before and writing letters. We will move out on this coming Thursday (Feb. 11th) and will ride some 273 miles to the NW to the new "concentration area," and the situation becomes tactical for the first Corps maneuver at 0600, Feb. 15th. The entire Corps maneuvers will only last approximately 21 days, so we should be able to take them in a breeze.

The "*** political situation" proved to really be something after investigating. As I had so clearly defined his repulsive personality in earlier excerpts in this journal, he has proven to be one of the most hated officers in this Regiment, most of which was due to his ruthless, throat-slitting tactics he uses to advance himself at any cost. He will undoubtedly raise a most god-awful stink when he returns and finds that he has been relegated to a rifle company, and the job he slit so many throats to get is now in the hands of his most hated rival (me). As I have stated before, however, that repugnant piece of humanity bothers me not at all, for it takes a far better example of manhood to beat me than the erstwhile brother ***. Even the chaplain hates him, which should prove something or other.

Old Joe Blow came in the office the other morning, probably to see if it were true or not that I was up here, and he had the same stagnant smile on his silly puss that he usually uses when in the vicinity of the Commanding Officer. I didn't pay any attention to him, and he soon stalked out. Well that baby is in my power now, to a certain extent, and at every opportunity I shall see that he is appropriately "chewed" by Colonel Cochran whenever he slips on his records in the slightest.

Desert—somewhere
Near Blythe, California
February 12, 1944

Well, here we are out in the desert again! Problem becomes tactical at 0600, 15 February 1944. I have been working like hell in order to familiarize myself with this work. We left Camp Horn at 0300 yesterday morning and rode until 1500 yesterday afternoon. Immediately after arrival, we reported to AG and set up our present, very comfortable bivouac. Colonel Cochran has been very cordial, and I learned that he was madly trying to promote me on my S-3 service, and it would have gone through, too, but CAMA came out with a directive that all promotion of officers was frozen until further notice! Typical of my luck. I guess I am just doomed to never again be promoted. *** should be back in a few days (he has been reassigned to Co. A). The chaos that struck when HQ received that fateful letter re: "the assignment and attachment" of officers is still in progress. Five of the worthless "deadwood," excess captains are being reclassified ***. The Army is evidently bearing down on inefficiency, and this is also reputed to be a sign that the 104th Division will be broken up. The only part of the letter than can affect me is the paragraph stating that an assigned Captain must fill a T/O vacancy; and I, a 1st Lt., am holding a Captain's job (as I have done since holding my commission).

Rumors are rife re: our ultimate destination after these 3 weeks' maneuvers, but the truth is, no one knows where we are going.

What lies before me now?

Desert—near
Blythe, California
February 14, 1944

The time for the problem to become tactical draws near! Meanwhile, the shuffling of the Regiment was momentous, indeed. Such changes as Needham to Exec O 1st Bn, Carey to Rgt'l S-3, Fox to Company A, Southern, Mills, Bochterle and many others to "attached only" status. Meanwhile, we have received about 14 new officers, many of them 1st Lts., which places our Regiment far over its authorized T/O strength and forecasts another overseas shipment of officers soon. My personal situation remains somewhat precarious, for if one more Captain is assigned to the 415, he must be assigned the duties of Personnel Officer, and I will be relegated to God knows where!

Mail has fallen off considerably, and the biggest question preying on my mind: Can I make a success of this job, especially throughout the 3 weeks of these maneuvers? I have been appointed a "Section Commander" with some 300 men under me, and in the event of enemy attack, will defend my sector of the rear echelon. The responsibility is mine.

*** should be back in about two days, and what a stink there will be then!

It was a War Department order, which froze all promotions until further notice. I cannot help but wonder where we will go after the 6th of March. Cochran and Smith (Capt.) still cordial and pleasant, but ?

Feel fairly good at present, that is, physically, but I haven't written in a long time.

Somewhere in the
Desert—Feb. 16, 1944

The internal reorganization of the Regiment continues! Many and varied are the changes. Bochterle to 95th Division. Went to Regt'l HQ today to obtain some data, and old Cochran was nicer than pie! Heard thru rumor that I "was doing a nice job."

We move to a new location tonight, approximately 8 miles distant. This is certainly a soft life in comparison to S-3ing under the Desert

Fox. Which reminds me, *** was due back today but haven't heard a word from him. The work tends to be difficult, at times, but I hope to master it. It was terrifically cold last night. The old sleeping bag really felt good.

According to "latrine rumor," Fort Devens, Mass., appears to be our next destination—staging area.

Another letter from the gal in Phoenix, one from Harold, one from Mother. I haven't had much time for correspondence.

Twenty more days of this, and then?

I seem to be getting along with my men (30) and assistant (WOJG Lauck) just fine. He is a nice fellow.

If we move late tonight, probably no sleep.

More later—meanwhile—

Guidance needed.
"The situation is somewhat delicate."

Somewhere in the Desert
February 18, 1944

The first phase of the problem is supposed to end at 1200 today, but so far, have received no verification on this. On the move, which took place the other night, we in this Section experienced quite a bit of confusion, and as a result, I had a meeting the next morning and told the men just what to expect from now on and just where I stood on certain matters of discipline. Have heard no untoward results of this meeting, but I think it cleared the atmosphere somewhat, for this Personnel Section had been accustomed to quite a bit of friction and confusion under the former jurisdiction of ***. By the way, he has not reported back for duty yet, but should, at the latest, be back within the next two days.

It was bitterly cold the night that we made the move, and the "flight jacket" that Bob sent me really proved itself. (Riding in an open jeep with the windshield down, à la combat, certainly isn't conducive to comfort, to say the least.)

At any rate, life back here in the rear echelon is a great improvement. The AG informed me that my work up here, so far, has proved entirely satisfactory, which gives me reason to hope that eventually I may make a somewhat satisfactory personnel officer.

My mail has consisted entirely of magazines for the last two days, and I hope that I will receive some letters this afternoon, but I suppose not. Gee, I haven't heard from any of the old gang in Oakland for so long—the Morgans (and Vivian), the Raffertys, Jessie and Frank, Lyle and Kay, etc. In respect to Vivian, though, I guess it is better that I don't. I certainly hope that she finds happiness with someone. She was such a fine girl and a wonderful person to know. Without a doubt, Margaret thinks of me as an unspeakable beast, and probably she is right, for it is a cruel thing to do to abruptly stop an acquaintanceship almost without a word of explanation, but I had to. Why keep something up that could never be?

Wish I had some inkling of what lies in store for me in the next 6 months but, as with everything else that is just something that will have to wait, and wait, and wait.

Dry Streambed—Desert
Sunday, 20 February 1944

I had to leave some of my men behind yesterday when we moved, and due to inadequate explanations from AG, I rode over 10 miles in a jeep rounding them up. Then Mr. Lauck and I rode over 60 miles last night <u>blackout</u>. Got into the enemy lines at one time but weren't captured.

Oh yes! <u>The</u> News! *** came back and, of course, was exceedingly scorched. His mighty tail feathers were somewhat droopy after he was informed. He stated that "he was going to see Cochran" and evidently did, but from what I hear, he had a rather cold reception and went back to Company A.

It is raining violently at the present time, and high winds are moaning and echoing down these countless streambeds. I don't expect any sleep and am looking forward to a miserable night, for I am Officer of the Guard and must check the posts hourly (no raincoat).

No mail recently, and it has been very scarce the entire week. Maneuvers will be over by March 4th, and there are countless rumors as to our ultimate destination.

On this last problem, Captain Prevics and my old operations sergeant were captured with our complete Division orders, overlays, and SOI's, the sin is cardinal for an S-3!

Sandy desert—cactus
Rain and cold
February 23, 1944

It rained all night and is continuing today. Leaden skies and the melancholy downpour make the day and this existence seem gloomy and depressing beyond all measure. It is on days such as this that I wonder if ever again I will know the joys of the many privileges that are part of a civilian's taken-for-granted life. Such things as dawdling over a complete breakfast on a lazy Sunday morning, driving your own car to the theater, coming home to someone you love (and who loves you), having a party with a few good friends, working and puttering around your car on Saturday afternoons. All this, however, I know too well, lies in the far, dim, distant future, if at all.

We will probably move late tonight, as we are now about 30 miles behind the front line troops, and I can envisage that ordeal only too clearly—a sopping jeep, bitter cold, no raincoat, ad infinitum.

Mail still scarce, but this is due to my severing of all relationships, except with my immediate family.

A bit of trouble with Major Kernan yesterday. Evidently the 415th Personnel is the "ugly duckling" of the 104th Rear Echelon.

A wet, dreary streambed
in the deserts of California
26 February 1944
<u>THREE YEARS IN THE ARMY TODAY</u>!

Again I say, three years in the Army today! Many of the things that have occurred are truly unbelievable. Others have been nice, and still others have changed beyond possible recall, old viewpoints, opinions. The somewhat turbulent course of my life has, without a doubt, been changed into utterly new channels, for the many things I have learned and observed have utterly destroyed about all of the former concepts and plans that I may have had prior to my entrance into the military. It is interesting to note that despite the many, many acquaintanceships and true friends that I have met, not once have I met a girl who possessed even partially any of the old-fashioned and sterling qualities that could convince me that the holy state of matrimony might have some redeeming qualities.

The first problem of the Corps maneuvers is over. We are now on a three-day break prior to the start of the second (and last) problem, which should end on about the 5th of March. The weather for the last two days has been utterly miserable with cold, driving rain; icy winds; and a slush composed of sand, mud, and rain.

My work here in the Personnel Section seems to be progressing satisfactorily. At least I have heard no complaints. But the accompanying outlook as to the future appears to be rather hopeless, especially in view of the fact that two more captains were assigned to our Regiment, and this addition places us actually two over our authorized strength. The "Camp Carson, Colorado, rumor" appears to be gaining in authenticity, and this I do not like. There are many other spots that appeal to me a great deal more than the frozen State of Colorado.

Not another word from "Sneaky ***" since he returned to Company A, although his anguish and pitiable moans were something to hear. I understood that he sought out Colonel Cochran and attempted to convince him that perhaps he had gone to school by a somewhat shady manner, but now that he had the training of that school, wouldn't it be best to utilize that training? In other words, give him the job of Personnel Officer. Sad to relate, Colonel Cochran turned on his heel and walked away.

I hope this 2nd problem goes fast, for I am only too anxious to leave this desolate terrain, and if our luck holds to return to civilization, if we go to an established camp such as Carson, the Personnel will be housed in a regular office building, which would be nice after the six-month session of tents and horrible climate that we have enjoyed.

What lies ahead of me in the coming 4th year of my life in the Army of the United States?

JOURNAL 4

VOLUME IV
MARCH 2, 1944 TO AUGUST 11, 1944
Ages 27–28

*WHY if my work is so good ... after all,
it IS a Captain's job that I am performing,
is any chance for advancement and promotion mollified
by some lousy little technicality in some half-forgotten circular?*

∼

*Now that we are definitely under orders
to go overseas, I feel actually relieved ...
all of my friends are overseas,
and I just feel that I should go.*

VOLUME IV
NOTES AND IMPRESSIONS
OF HAPPENINGS AND EVENTS,
WHICH OCCURRED DURING MY
FOURTH YEAR OF SERVICE IN
THE ARMY OF THE UNITED
STATES. NOTES RELATING
THE EXPERIENCES ENCOUNTERED
IN MY FIRST THREE YEARS
MAY BE FOUND IN PREVIOUS VOLUMES
FEBRUARY 26, 1944

Final days of California • Arizona Maneuver Area (CAMA) • Arrival at Camp Carson • Vivian marries • Decides to delay leave until promotion • Worries about health conditions • Personnel records inspections • Frustration and discouragement regarding politics and delay of promotion • Complimented for best Personnel Section in Division • Phyllis • Relationships with women • Dates with "Monty" restore faith in women • Departure for European Theater.

March 2, 1944
Camp Granite, Calif.
Much has happened since the last entry. One somewhat amusing, and at the same time, tragic, incident occurred. The "wet, dreary streambed" where we were encamped turned into an excellent funnel for tons of water rolling off the encircling hills, due to a series of torrential downpours.

The water came cascading into the tent where Mr. Lauck and I were sleeping, floating us and our bedrolls gently downstream. The men were harder hit than we—soaked blankets, clothing, and equipment. Fortunately, the next day, we learned that maneuvers were over for us, as all Personnel Sections were to move to Camp Granite to receive some 1300 new fillers for the Division. It was here that we learned that we were definitely going to Camp Carson, Colorado, upon the 15th of March.

It is evident that we will not be going overseas for a while, for most of these new men have never had basic training. I have been working day and night assigning these men to organizations and feel as though I were classifying cattle. For these men are all former ASTP men and are well educated, and yet they are assigned, for the most part, to the role of a basic infantryman.

I have been assigned (on paper) to Co. B (on SD with Sv. Co. as Personnel Officer.)

More later.

Camp Granite
March 5, 1944
More news. No more transfers to the Air Corps for either officers or EM of the Army Ground Forces. Still better news, however, is that the recent ban on officers' promotions has been lifted! I do not expect to be

promoted, however, as if Colonel Cochran even felt so inclined. This Regiment is now in excess <u>two</u> Captains, and no promotions can be effected while there is an excess.

Saw <u>Colonel Aaron</u> up at Division today, but he had nothing encouraging to offer as to my eventual return to S-3 work. Expect maneuvers to terminate within a couple of days.

Wonder what Colonel Cochran will have to say about the manner in which the Personnel Section has functioned, so far?

Received a letter from Bob, and he leaves tomorrow for the staging area in Kansas. Guess we will never get to see each other prior to overseas.

Guess my long silence has finally stifled all romantic thoughts in Margie, as I have received no more letters. Guess I am just a beast.

I'll bet it will be colder than the North Pole in Colorado. However, we are not far from Denver, and if we have barracks, it will not be too unbearable.

Thought I was coming down with the flu last night but fought it off.

On troop train (temporarily stopped in Gallup, N.M.)
en route to Colorado
9 March 1944

The final days spent in the California-Arizona Maneuver Area (CAMA) rushed by in a chaotic succession of events. As the 415th Personnel Officer, I was sent along with the advance party of the Division, and when we arrive at Camp Carson, I will have the job of classifying and placing some 4,000 new recruits. The rest of the outfit will not arrive in Colorado until about the end of the month. We passed through Needles, Calif; Flagstaff, Arizona, last night and this morning and observed quite a bit of snow in the vastness of upper Arizona. There will, without a doubt, be lots of snow in Carson, and it will be quite cold. Understand the General expects us to be at Camp Carson no longer than 3 months. And then?

It will seem wonderful to live in a barracks again. We have been living like animals for over 7 months now.

Lately, I have again become extremely melancholy and disconsolate, so much so, that I worry myself. But I have been battling my own principles and ideals for so long, in addition to the political bickerings and continual frustration within the Regiment that nothing seems to matter anymore— nothing! I have traveled much over these great United States, and the more of life I see, the more it sickens me.

Last night, lying in my lonely berth with the dreary, monotonous clicking of the wheels drumming in my ears, I thought of how different, how <u>normal</u>, my life <u>might</u> have been if one person had had the moral stamina, the courage, that is, perhaps given only by true love, to stand by the vows that I thought were among the more sacred things in life. After finally dozing off into fitful slumber, I had a most peculiar dream, but even dreams are not to be trusted. I, of all people, should realize that.

Tonight, as the dying rays of the sun bathe this lonely little town in New Mexico, I wonder--<u>how</u> I wonder—what lies in store for me in Colorado.

Troop Train En route
(temporarily stopped near Jansen, Colorado)
10 March 1944
1838

Spent all day traveling through the desolate, rugged, yet beautiful grandeur of New Mexico. Crossed into Colorado at about supper tonight. So far, much less snow is evident than I expected. We should arrive at our destination (Colorado Springs) sometime during the night or early morning.

We all piled off the train in Raton, New Mexico, and headed for a conveniently located bar. Due to the uncertainty of departure (10-minute stop at the most), it is, needless to say, that all imbibing was of a voracious nature.

I cannot help but dwell upon what may await me in Colorado. Will this, then, be the point in my pilgrimage where an iota of true happiness might befall me? Only God can answer that, however.

At any rate, events should start happening before long.

Camp Carson, Colorado
13 March 1944

Once again, after the rugged, rugged life of the past 7 months, I lie on a comfortable bed in my own room with a steam radiator nearby. We arrived early on the 11th, and to our delight, found Camp Carson a veritable country club with beautiful spring weather in addition. Much confusion at first, but we finally moved into our own area today.

Captain Smith is here, and I seem to get along very well with him. This is a huge camp with many Special Troops already here, including many WAC's, WAC officers, nurses, etc. These are the first WAC's we have seen.

Tonight, a 40-mile-an-hour wind is howling and yammering at the windows of the barracks, and it expresses quite adequately in its desolate voice, the loneliness and desolation that is in my soul.

I went into the town of Colorado Springs this Saturday past and found it the same as all Army towns. Cheap bars and cheaper women (but none for me, thank God!). I am not too enthused at the thought of going in again, and doubt if I will. I may go to Denver if the opportunity so affords and look up Colonel Smith's folks <u>or</u>, if possible, to Boise, Idaho, on a three-day leave and see Bob. <u>He is still there</u>!

Received a letter from Raff in Belfast, Ireland, and he tells me Vivian finally married a guy named Cooper. So another chapter in my life ends. She was a mighty fine person, and I hope to God she got a decent fellow. Good luck to you, Viv, and may God bless you.

No further word from Margie, so I guess that episode is over, too.

Physically I feel terrible (and also look), and I am determined to see the doc when the troops arrive and get to the bottom of the trouble.

I hereby resolve to turn over anew from here on out!

God willing—

CAMP CARSON, COLORADO
14 MARCH 1944

Another day done away with. Felt a bit better today, physically. Was busy, too, meeting at Div. HQ, laundry schedules, telegrams, etc. Tomorrow, I intend to move to my new personnel office and really fix it up. Have a lot of tables.

Pulled a terrible boner. Despite my known allergy to sulfa drugs of any kind, I bought some Barbasol shaving cream containing .1 of sulfathiazole and used it. Result? A face and neck looking like leprosy in its last stages. Remedied it tonight.

Phoned Bob long distance, but he was evidently flying, and I couldn't reach him. Will try again tomorrow.

Capt. Deane is going to be promoted to Major, evidently, which would cut down our Captains' quota by one, but whether it means anything, or not, remains to be seen.

I am still holding firm in my resolve to refurbish myself in all respects. One letter from Mother today.

CAMP CARSON, COLORADO
15 MARCH 1944
Felt much better today and accomplished quite a bit, too. I really have my new office looking nice. A little more work, and it will be deluxe! Bob phoned me about 1100 this morning, and we had a grand talk. He's such a swell kid. Maybe we can arrange a rendezvous yet. Everything seems to be going just swell, if only God can see fit to give me the proper guidance.

Getting along okay with all the work so far, and only the fillers remain to be met and classified.

I actually feel a bit happy tonight, but why I should, I don't know. Just good hard work into which I can sink my teeth. If they will only let me work without any of the damned political furor that usually upsets things.

I'm going to watch *** now, though, for sure.

CAMP CARSON, COLORADO
MARCH 18, 1944
Have been so busy of late that I haven't had time for the "old journal." My office is all complete now; only the floors remain to be oiled. Really looks nice. Tomorrow, the first of the fillers arrive. Must report to Div. HQ to assign them at 1030. 2nd Army inspects records on Monday. Bought 2 sets of sheets and pillowcases today, or rather, Capt. Smith's wife bought them for me. Good investment. Y'know, I can always use them when I get married (big laugh).

I sent all of my clothes to the cleaners, including my faithful sleeping bag.

Received a letter from the "Phoenix gal" today. Guess she can't be convinced. I sent a letter of congratulations to Vivian.

And finally, for tonight, am still determined to hold to my resolutions. I will!

CAMP CARSON, COLORADO
MARCH 19, 1944
I received and assigned 30 new men today. Came from my old hangout, Camp Callan. Tomorrow my records will be inspected by 2nd Army.

Oiled approximately half of the floors tonight. Still have half to go tomorrow. Most of the officers (single) have been going up to the station hospital to date the abundance of nurses on duty there. So far, I haven't felt particularly interested.

Have had the same disinterested attitude towards Colorado Springs but may change my mind when my clothes return from the cleaners.

Life, to me, is still drear and without meaning, a pointless existence, a mad millrace of fruitless aspirations.

As noted in recent entries, though, I am determined to improve myself, and this I <u>will</u> do, come what may.

Camp Carson, Colorado
March 20, 1944

2nd Army inspection over! Didn't touch any of my records, concentrating rather on the 414th Regiment. However, I realize that I have much, <u>very</u> much work to do if I am to successfully reorganize the Personnel Office of the 415th Infantry.

Face and neck about clear now of the recent "sulfa ravages" of late mention.

Captain Smith recently (today) dropped a hint as to my possible promotion at the end of my three months, i.e., May 1st; but this I doubt, as I don't see how there can be a vacancy unless they drop some of the "deadwood" captains now holding the rank.

I have made up my mind, though, that I will not take another leave unless I go home one grade higher.

From all information, Vivian married a Lt. (JG) Navy, and evidently, her folks were none too pleased, as he already had a family of three children and was somewhat of a boor.

A letter from Bob today, and that's all. Clothes returned from cleaners, so I <u>may</u> try Colorado Springs once more. It was horribly dull the last time, though.

A heavy snow covers the ground tonight. May be able to finish the Personnel Office tomorrow, if things work out okay.

Camp Carson, Colo.
March 21, 1944

The office is now completed except for one or two minor items. Worked like fiends all day. An intense blizzard has been raging all day and continues tonight. Snow piled in huge drifts, covering everything. A veritable gale, so intense it draws your breath, makes it nigh impossible to negotiate outside. As I lie on my cot tonight, the wind rages impotently outside my window, screeching like an irate banshee, matching somewhat the desolation and loneliness in my heart.

I may go to Colorado Springs with Lt. Leonard in a few days. I don't know. No mail at all today.

Not much more to note so far tonight. I may as well close.

CAMP CARSON, COLO.
MARCH 24, 1944
The rest of the Regiment moved in yesterday and today, and needless to say, I have been hectically busy. Looks like a lot of the higher-ups are going to C&G School. Some gossip—Captain *** relieved of his command (found by Colonel Cochran asleep in his tent at 1100).

Lt. Leonard and I went out last night. Made reservations for two at the Officers Club and met two Army nurses. Had quite a good time wining, dancing, and dining. My date's name was Lt. Gourck. Seemed nice and a phone number, but I dunno.

Received a letter from Margie dated March 10th.

Well, guess I'd best turn in. Lot of work tomorrow. May go out tomorrow night with Lt. Green and Leonard. No mail from home for quite a time.

CAMP CARSON, COLO.
MARCH 26, 1944
Decided against going out. Was sitting in my room reading (this, on a Saturday night, and not Duty Officer!) when Colonel Floyd called for me, the result being that I worked until 0100 this morning and from 0800 until 1200 today on some highly confidential work for Colonel Cochran (the reclassification proceedings against Captain ***). What a turn of fate. A few months ago, I thought I was hated by Cochran, and now one of his most highly trusted confidants, and administering oaths to him!

Personnel Office operating most satisfactorily, so far. No mail for some time.

Not feeling so good physically. Hope to goodness health improves before long. Still holding firm in my resolve to improve myself in every way.

Wonder if life will ever mean anything to me. Must say it appears rather hopeless at present.

Camp Carson, Colo.
March 29, 1944
A few hasty notes tonight.

Quite a mix-up on one of the general courts-martial, due to an inexcusable delay. Don't know what repercussions there will be, if any, but it worries me.

Felt sick and worried all day long. Physical health is terrible, and I wonder if fate will bludgeon me down once more, just when Providence had started to smile on me (excess Captains transferred, reclassified, etc.!). I suppose so—seems typical of my life.

Please, God, give me a decent break for once. God knows I've tried.

85 new men today. Worked till 1900 tonight. Tired, sick, worried, disgusted.

Camp Carson, Colo.
March 31, 1944
More hasty notes—12 officers shipped overseas including 3 Captains (French, Hitt, and Foster), which leaves a vacancy of some 2 or 3 Captains if the old man is ready to promote me, which things seem to indicate if I can conduct the Personnel as efficiently as I have for the past two months. But fate seems ready and poised tonight to bludgeon me down again. My physical condition is worse, and I have made up my mind to see Doc Leiser tomorrow.

Terrifically busy, but things working smoothly. Classified 109 men today. (Got up at 0500, went to bed at 2300, and as a result, am exhausted tonight.

No hope, God?

Camp Carson, Colo.
April 3, 1944
Working like a veritable fiend for the past week. Averaging about 18 hours a day of work. Finished assigning the last of the fillers today. Total—roughly 1,000.

Received another phone call from Bob. He is going overseas—was leaving Boise for a staging area when he phoned. Good luck, fella, and all of it, to a grand kid.

Promotion looks promising. Only 28 days, and I will be eligible, and the old man seems highly pleased with my work.

Physical condition still puzzles me, but I intend to settle it once and for all, soon.

If my promotion goes through, I will take a leave—home and Mother. Otherwise?

I pray the Lord tonight, as almost always, for guidance.

Still holding firm in my resolutions of some time ago!

Camp Carson, Colo.
April 4, 1944

Another hard day's work over and done with. Supposed to have been inspected by Division today as to condition of records, but they didn't appear. Probably tomorrow. Hope my records are okay, but it is hard to say--we have had so little time.

I hear that my "filler reception" report to Colonel Cochran was well received. Still hear that the old man is anxious to promote a few of us if we get our time in okay. Hope present luck stays with me.

Physical condition puzzles me. Sometimes feel swell, and at other times--.

No mail for some time.

If I get my promotion okay, I will take a leave, and what a glorious one it will be (and my last one too, no doubt).

God Above, please, please let everything work out okay this time. God be with me.

Camp Carson, Colo.
April 6, 1944

My physical condition still puzzles me. Today and yesterday I felt _swell_, and yet, well anyway, I am taking the day off tomorrow and shall get a complete check-over and shall settle things in my mind once and for all.

Have been working like a veritable fiend for the past few days, and if anything, the work grows more complex daily. However, to date, my work seems to satisfy the higher-ups, and if God only sees fit to let my present luck remain as it is, at present.

I have made a vow, though. No promotion, no leave.

Capt. Smith talking about a "get together" at the Officers Club with a blind date for me—a Nancy Conover. Don't know—maybe. My viewpoints will have to change a lot.

No mail at all for days. Something seems to be wrong in that direction.

CAMP CARSON, COLO.
APRIL 8, 1944

As I promised, recently, I obtained a VOCO and went to Colorado Springs and spent the day. Had a complete physical checkup with Dr. Corlett, and to my relief, and incidentally, surprise, found that I had nothing at all to worry about. As a matter of fact, he told me that was my biggest trouble—worrying too much. Said to forget my physical worries, and everything would be all right.

I spent quite a bit of money, as I bought an expanding wristwatch strap ($15) and a heavy sterling silver identification bracelet, complete with engraved name and serial number, which cost $25. I believe it was worth it, however, as God knows I haven't anything else to spend my money on and have wanted one for some time.

Eleven more officers are to be sent overseas. I imagine that the old man will continue his recent action of sending most of the useless deadwood-type over.

I had a total of two beers yesterday afternoon and was about to call a cab to take me home when I ran into Warrant Officer Lugo of Division HQ, and he talked me into remaining with him and going to the "Blue Spruce," a hangout for officers in that gala metropolis. We did and ran into a bunch of Army nurses. As usual, I got stuck with an introvert of the extreme type and was, for once, really glad that I was Duty Officer this weekend when the crowd started cooking up a party at the Officers Club for tonight. I felt sorry as hell for her, as she was convinced that I was giving her the "brush off." At the same time, however, I can't feel too sorry for a person like that, as 99% of the fault in a case like that is a woman's own fault. I mean, for one thing, bigness. Any woman can apply intelligent reducing measures if she so desires, and as for sloppy appearance, there is just no excuse for it.

The work gets more and more technical each day, and what with everyone from higher echelon on down madly inspecting records in order to meet POM requirements, the place is truly a madhouse.

Colonel Cochran called up today and seemed exceedingly wroth over some information that did not come out of this office. I told him the plain, blunt truth, but whether he was reconciled by this, or not, I do not know.

Feel swell today physically, and for once, my mind is somewhat free of worry. Wonder how long this unorthodox condition will last.

Still sweating out news of my pending promotion, but all I can do on that matter is to keep my fingers crossed.

CAMP CARSON, COLO.
APRIL 11, 1944
Still working like a madman. Didn't get through until midnight last night. 10 more officers were selected and sent overseas. Received a change-of-address card from Bob, and I guess he is on his way over, as his new address is an APO in New York.

Captain ***, the "deadwood" holding my present job (by virtue of rank) was transferred to Camp Wolters, so that obstacle is now out of the way. All in all, the entire promotion setup seems to be in a fair way, inasmuch as I hear that I am soon to be transferred to Sv Company from Co. B. Who knows? It <u>may</u> yet come to pass.

Feeling rather fine physically. Old Doc Corlett must have been right—mental worry seems to have a lot to do with the way you feel.

My identification chain came in the mail the other day, and it certainly is nice. Extremely sturdy, heavy--and a beautiful job of engraving was done on it. Might add, too, that the expanding bracelet for my watch certainly enhanced that investment.

Mail seems to have become a thing of the past, and I certainly miss the simple pleasure of carrying on a correspondence, as I am a gregarious individual by nature. No help for it, it seems, as loneliness seems to have become a part of my life.

CAMP CARSON, COLO.
APRIL 14, 1944
Steady, unrelentless, grueling work until midnight every night. The I.G. inspection is on, poring over my records like a group of sadists. So far, results have been somewhat encouraging. They told me that my records were the best of all inspected so far. However, this information, unfortunately, will never get down to the Colonel. All he will receive will be a report of a statistical inspection, and the errors, of course, when fully listed, will be limitless.

Only 16 days to go, and I will be eligible for promotion. From here on out it will be a race with destiny and time, for the almost insurmountable hurdles of Army red tape may delay it until too late to take a leave, and my vow—remember—is "no promotion, no leave."

Relations with all commanders seem to be on a high plane, now. I now have the additional duties of publishing all special orders and memorandums as well as complete power over the promotions and transfers of some 3,500 men.

CAMP CARSON, COLO.
APRIL 15, 1944
The inspection is still going on, and it bodes more and more ill. Wonder if it will affect my promotion in any way? If typical of my usual luck, I suppose so.

Don't know whether it's spring fever or not, but my mind is continually on leave, etc.

Was thinking of going to the dance tonight up at the Officers Club, but I dunno.

Futile, damned existence. This outfit is really "hot" now, as regards o'seas shipment. Will be moving before long, I think.

I just hope to God I get my Captaincy and they take my last farewell leave. After that, I won't give a damn, come what may.

CAMP CARSON, COLORADO
APRIL 16, 1944
Another horrible Saturday night over and done with. Worked until about 1900 last night and then had a thorough cleaning (shampoo, shower, shave, etc.), dressed in my best, and then went to the 104th Division Officers Club with Lt. Broome, Captain Luthi, where we met Lt. Cody, Captain Baker, and others. There was nothing to relieve the monotony of the evening except to drink bottle after bottle of beer. I absolutely don't touch the hard stuff anymore. Saw another example of the cheapness and sordidness of life. I think I have mentioned Lt. *** in this chronicle many times before. He is married to a very nice girl in San Diego, and his wife is expecting a new arrival within a very few months. She thinks there is no one like Lt. ***, and yet there he sat, up at the Club, with some gal whom he had undoubtedly hoodwinked into thinking that he was footloose and fancy free. Yet he has everything at home to which most men would hold true. Just another example of what is true in 99% of all cases of married life. He has the things in life for which

I would give almost any and everything to have, and yet he doesn't care or give a damn.

We received another Lt. Colonel in the Regiment by Division order yesterday, so that one factor complicated quite a few lives in this Regiment. By pushing one Major out in the cold, it means that Captain Baker must go back to the job of Motor Officer and that the silly blowhard and highly inefficient Major *** will take over the job of ***. In talking to G-1 last night (over a bottle of beer), I learned that we can also expect another large shipment of 1st and 2nd Lieutenants, which will mean that a lot of our old boys will be pushed back 2 and 3 deep. The thing that I expect now, in view of my usual run of luck, is a large shipment of Captains, which will fill up my job and knock my prospective promotion out the window and with only about 13 days to go, too. I have made up my mind that if that happens, I will submit a letter, through channels, asking for reclassification. As temperamental though it may sound, I am growing slightly tired of holding down a Captain's job (ever since I received my commission), getting a Superior rating on it, and not getting promoted, although I see on every side, crass blowhards, with inefficiency their chief characteristic, getting promoted. This may not happen, but as I say, taking into consideration my usual run of luck, it seems preordained.

As an incident hardly worth mentioning, Lt. *** (Sneaky) spent the day at the Personnel Office yesterday, drawing up a book on company punishment, which I can believe that he intends to use as a wedge and to impress the higher-ups as to his knowledge. However, the Sneak doesn't bother me at all, as he is quite thoroughly hated in this Regiment by almost everyone. His sneaky wife (one who is almost a direct facsimile of ***) was at the Club, and I imagine she feels ***'s lowered prestige even more than he does. For as a social climber, she is second to none.

Camp Carson, Col.
April 17, 1944
Here is trepidation indeed! Still sweating out the end of the month! For they moved in this new Colonel, and as previously mentioned, it caused a lot of changes.

However! The Chief of Staff (DeGraff) was down today and commented about the records of the 415th. Seems they're in pretty fair shape. <u>And</u> G-1, Colonel Rex complimented me on the same thing tonight. Good old Captain Smith is pulling away for me mighty hard, too; and if they don't ship in another load of captains, I may stand a chance. Who knows?

Still working like a bunch of fiends, though. Am going to see that my clerks get a 3-day pass if we pass this thing in fair shape.

CAMP CARSON, COLORADO
23 APRIL 1944

What a week! Truly, these are times that try men's souls. Due to interminable inspections and heavy shipments of men from this unit to stations all over the country, there has been much confusion in the Personnel Office. Despite the confusion and its attendant hardships, one thing of value was the result of it all. Major Kernan, one of the more hated higher-ups in Division, showed exactly where his cards were stacked. He is evidently out to get me, if and whenever I make the slightest error. This was shown only too plainly when my Sgt. Major and I, due to heavy pressure of work, slipped up on one of the shipments. The result of it all was, Colonel Cochran had to answer to the General by endorsement, Co. C's officers were restricted for a week, Co. H's officers were restricted for a week, and the Adjutant (Captain Smith) and the Personnel Adjutant (me) were restricted for a week. The only item that was blamed on Captain Smith and me was the failure of one of the shipped men to report for orders. However, Captain Smith, after a terrific argument with the Colonel, convinced him that the whole thing was based on Kernan's vindictiveness, and the fact that Kernan was out to "blacklist" me until he would have an excellent excuse to suggest the replacement of me with that of his pet and colleague, the erstwhile "Sneaky" Lt. ***, late of this Personnel Office and now of Company A. Very fortunately for me, however, earlier yesterday morning, Colonel Cochran received an OFFICIAL report from the Division that the personnel records of the Personnel Office, 415th Infantry, were in the best condition of any unit in the 104th Division, bar none. This, needless to say, made him extremely happy, and he lifted the restriction that pertained to Captain Smith and me. He also, at the weekly staff meeting yesterday, mentioned this report and termed it "an example of what can be done by the application of hard work and midnight oil when an officer is so inclined." This commendation, it is needless to say, undoubtedly caused Brother *** to writhe in agony.

As regards my pending promotion, if any, today is the 23rd of April, which leaves me just 7 days until my required servitude of 3 months in my present capacity is complete. However, what will happen at the completion of this time is a question, for Colonel Cochran leaves on Tuesday for the station hospital to have a major operation, and whether he will sign my promotion papers while in the hospital is a question. If he doesn't, it means that there will be a considerable delay in this major event, and I may as well give up all ideas of a leave. For I will not go home without the promotion, and it takes roughly a month for notification of the promotion to return from Washington once the papers have cleared Division, which is also another complication, which may have dire repercussions.

As regards my social life, there is none. Period. As regards my physical condition, there seems to be a slight improvement, but I am eternally tired, due to the late hours and continuous pressure.

As regards the future purchase of "a little white house with green shutters, lawns, cozy fireplace, etc.," I might report that my aggregate assets, figuring all War Bonds at full maturity value, now approach the astounding total of 1786 dollars and some-odd cents. With the increased pay for a Captaincy, and also for overseas duty, it is possible to say that at the conclusion of the war, this dream of such longstanding is now a definite possibility. If I don't come through the war, it will do the same thing for Mother, so on that score, I am at last happy. Quite a change from the unhappy, debt-ridden man who was once foolish enough to believe in the sacredness of marital vows.

Camp Carson, Colo.
April 24, 1944

A dreary, dreary weekend as Regimental Staff Duty Officer. Don't know whether I got myself in a jam or not. I left HQ to go to the BOQ and take a shower. In the interim, Colonel DeGraff, the Chief of Staff, phoned me and seemed very upset that I had left HQ for a few moments. Have heard no repercussion as yet.

Tremendous news! Colonel Cochran, as he left for the hospital this morning, told Captain Smith to put in my promotion at the end of the month. So, mayhap at last, my long-sought, worked-for promotion may come true. If there is no trouble, and it proceeds smoothly, I will also take a glorious leave.

God, please help me now in order that nothing may go wrong.

Camp Carson, Colorado
Tuesday, April 25, 1944

Looks as though I will need all of the help recently asked for. With only 5 days to go until the completion of my required tenure, they transferred in a Captain today from the 26th Infantry, which means that if they transfer in one more Captain, the T/O vacancies will be filled, and there will be no other opportunity for ultimate promotion. All that I can do for the remaining five days is to keep my fingers crossed.

With the arrival of the 2nd Army Inspector Generals in my office on this coming Thursday, I thought it expedient to organize a "Swing Shift" consisting of 10 men to do nothing but work on the errors noted in the recent inspection, in order to bring them up to date by that time.

I have the most terrific longing to travel home again and see everyone for the final time, but again I reiterate my vow, I will not go home in the grade of 1st Lt. If my promotion does not come through, it means no trip home. If the fact that I have held a Captain's job down since the time of my commission is not proof enough to the Army that I am capable of holding that rank, then some other steps will be taken, as far as I am concerned.

With all the nervous strain of the past period of time, I am almost determined that I am going into town with Lt. Broome, or by myself, if necessary, and blow off some steam, or else the results will be hard to foretell.

Colonel Cochran left for the hospital, as noted in earlier entries, and of course, this leaves the Regiment in a wild dither of rumors as to what his ultimate disposition may be. Return to the Regiment? Reclassification? Or what?

My mind seems utterly blank tonight, and I feel worn out physically, too, so may as well close and get to work for that is one thing that is plentiful around here.

Camp Carson, Colorado
Saturday Afternoon, 29 April 1944

My luck seems to be holding, for my promotion went up to Division yesterday, and Captain DeGroat phoned me and said that he would do everything he could to get it out of Division by the earliest practicable time on Monday, the 1st of May. So far, I have heard no reports of it bouncing. As a matter of fact, I caught a glimpse of it lying on G-1's desk when I was up there at an earlier meeting this morning, and the buck slip pertaining to it had all been verified and checked, so God willing, it may be on its way on Monday, and it shouldn't be too long a wait. Probably a little over a month until it goes through, it if does.

Meanwhile, the work appears to be piling in, in a never-diminishing amount, and I have to be on my toes all the time in order to keep up with it. Had an argument with Sneaky *** today, pertaining to the records kept up here; but I told him, frankly, I didn't give a good Goddamn what he did, wrote, or anything else. He appears none too happy at the present time, and this may be due to the current rumors regarding my pending promotion. Heartless as it may sound, however, I derive an inordinate amount of pleasure from this because of (see earlier excerpts regarding this gentleman).

Lt. Leonard and I may go out tonight, I am not sure. But I hope to goodness that my luck may have changed for once and that I can manage to have a fairly good time.

Colonel Cochran is still in the hospital, and I must admit that this new Lt. Colonel Kelleher is a mean son of a -----. However, to my intense pleasure, he really set the Desert Fox on his heels today in a staff meeting that was held. He told him off in so many words.

A letter from Raff today. He is still in Belfast, Ireland, and is serving under the notorious General Patton. He remarked that Vivian is living in Santa Barbara with the parents of the fellow she married. Good marital diplomacy?

Not much more to write about so may as well close. But needless to say, will be keeping my fingers crossed this entire weekend.

Camp Carson, Colorado
Regimental Headquarters (Duty Officer)
May 5, 1944

Again, much has happened since I last made an entry herein. First, and most important perhaps, is the fact that my promotion cleared Division Headquarters with a minimum of "bouncing." In fact, it didn't bounce at all. It cleared on May 2, 1944, so if all goes well, my promotion should be coming through around the first part of June. I want to take my leave (the last) as soon after the promotion, as possible, but don't know whether waiting for that event will eliminate me from a leave or not.

Received a letter from Bob, and he is now in Iceland, so the stinker beat me overseas but not by too long a time I hope, as we (the

104th Division) were placed in an A-2 priority today, which is the same as having one foot on the gangplank.

In preparation for my leave, I have bought a nice new woolen shirt and am hard at work in my spare time preparing my equipment and articles that I will take home. I think it is possible for me to obtain a Class 4 priority, and if so, I intend to fly home, which should prove to be quite an experience—flying over the Rockies. However, come what may, I shall take the train on the return trip, for the plane travel is too indefinite to risk returning late and automatically relegating myself to the doghouse thereby. Guess I will wire ahead for a hotel reservation in Oakland, for with Vivian now married to Cooper, I doubt if the same welcome will be imprinted on the Morgan doormat.

Work is still progressing at its terrific pace, and there were several unorthodox situations with the higher echelon at Division, but I think they worked themselves out satisfactorily. How it again impresses itself on my mind that I can never relax for a moment, I must be eternally on "the ball," for in the highly political job that I now hold, I have many enemies, and on the other hand, many friends. ***, I believe, heard the news of my promotion, and his face is now a complete study of wrath and frustration.

Leonard, Broome, and I went into Colorado Springs twice, and an exceedingly boring time was had by all concerned, and I might add, at the cost of quite a few shekels to me.

Camp Carson, Colorado
(PERSONNEL OFFICE)
Sunday, May 7, 1944

A quiet Sunday on the Post. I went to the Chapel yesterday afternoon and played the organ about all afternoon. Even though I cannot actually play the thing, I derive intense enjoyment from the mere act of muddling over the keys. Went to the show last night, then came home and showered, shaved, and shampooed and retired fairly early. I arose early enough to enjoy a nice breakfast this morning and must admit that such a weekend is far better than arising with the usual headache and gloomy outlook on life after a night of tearing around in town. I had my POM physical examination the other day, plus a vaccination for smallpox, and passed the examination without a hitch. All for the best, I might add, for it was disclosed to all officers that THE day has arrived. We entrain for points unknown on July 15, 1944. Which leaves me in a terrific sweat, FOR:

Will my promotion arrive in time for me to take my leave?
Will I be allowed to take a leave as late as June? ETC.

In the event that my leave is okayed, I have outlined the tentative procedure: to obtain a priority (air) of some kind, if possible, and FLY home; to wire ahead for some kind of hotel reservations in Oakland (for it is now impossible for me to take advantage of the former hospitality of the Morgans). As to whether I should rent a car to make the trip to Sonora or not, I do not know. It is much more convenient, but at the same time, it is so terrifically expensive. Wonder what Art Morgan's attitude will be now that things did not work out between Vivian and me as he had hoped? There really isn't much point in my going to Oakland at all, for there is no one there that means anything to me, outside of dropping by the plant and seeing the usual run of casual acquaintances. I suppose I will do that, however, for this is, without a single doubt, the last leave that I shall have here in the U.S. It is my personal opinion that we will not go directly into combat, but instead to some staging area here in the States, and then to another staging area perhaps in Ireland or England. I think we are more a "reserve" division than anything else, due to the fact that we have so many new green troops in our midst. I may be wrong on this, and we may be destined to provide a goodly supply of cannon fodder, but the former seems a more logical conclusion.

Bob is in Iceland, and I hope he remains there for the duration of the War. For if anyone is not to come back from this War from our family, I want it to be me. God knows that I have nothing to come back to after the War.

One thing that makes me superbly happy—if I don't come back, Mother is fixed for the rest of her life. For together with all my aggregate assets and the $10,000 insurance, she should be able to buy a nice little home and live in comfort for the balance of her declining years.

Camp Carson, Colo.
May 8, 1944

Bob is in England, so all I can do is hope and pray he comes through okay. So here is Godspeed to a grand guy.

Still sweating out my promotion—can only hope. It is a race against time now. Learned something interesting while working in Colonel Cochran's office today. Old Joe Blow had recommended Lt. Thomas for Captaincy. Too bad McKerney got it instead. The fair-haired boy is stuck for a time.

Have prepared some of my leave items but not too many, as it is still so indefinite.

Results of 2nd Army inspection came in and not so good! Must all be up to date by June 1st. So I started the night shift again. I hope to God everything turns out okay.

I sure hope we go overseas this time. I couldn't stand another session of maneuvers.

Finally located my cleaning I thought had been lost.

Received a letter for David Bertram down in the SW Pacific with the 147th Infantry. Another good guy.

Camp Carson, Colo.
May 10, 1944
Formulated plans to prepare all records. Clerks working until midnight every night. Classification section working on a 24-hour basis. Can only hope they will be okay by June 1st.

I am tired, both physically and mentally, but it must be done. Boots came back today. Have only admiration for my boys. They are really working and putting out at the sacrifice of their leisure time.

Went to the hospital today and saw Colonel Cochran. He approved my plan for "D-Day." Seemed pleasant enough. Wonder if result of the pending inspection will affect my leave in any way?

No news à la promotion, but then, it is still too early, and even then--.

Listened to an "inspiring" talk by General Allen tonight—"the certainty of combat," "the roles and duty of the junior officer," etc., etc., *ad infinitum*. I wish to God they would cut the bush-wah and eyewash and start soldiering.

May 11, 1944
I feel extraordinarily good today, in view of the late hours I have been working. I sent a wire to the Chief of Police, Sonora, requesting that he buy Mother five dollars' worth of red carnations and deliver them to Mother on Mother's Day. Reimbursement to follow, of course.

It is a beautiful spring day, and that in itself almost makes life worthwhile again.

Division came down and seemed satisfied with the progress of correction.

Still several things à la leave worrying me. Plane priority? Plane reservation? Promotion?

Received a letter from Mother today. She has been visiting Lola and Lena. Guess she had a good time, but it was, very evidently, unbearably hot weather.

This new Colonel Kelleher is quite a character. I think he is unduly blown up with his own importance. At least he manages to make quite an ass of himself by continually calling attention to his self-announced "pull" with General Allen.

Camp Carson, Colo.
May 12, 1944
Don't feel quite so good today, although work seems to be progressing quite satisfactorily. Possibly due to several minor clashes with various personalities. The beautiful spring weather continues.

Lt. Allwander's promotion to Captain came through today, and his papers left Division approximately a week before mine did, so IF I am lucky, mine should be coming through before long. If and when, Allwander and I shall go into town and celebrate appropriately. I hope to goodness nothing unforeseen comes up.

*** evidently definitely heard the news regarding mine, and he certainly looks happy. (?) Can't help but feel sorry for the darned fool, though. The other officers tend to ignore him, he eats alone, etc. However, he has no one but himself to blame. He stabbed so many in the back and slit so many throats in this Regiment that not too much sympathy for him is being dispensed.

Camp Carson, Colorado
14 May 1944
A beautiful day in May if there ever was one! I had thought of going into Colorado Springs yesterday, and possibly today, but just couldn't get enthused over the idea, so stayed home and saddle soaped a lot of leatherwork that needed it and cleaned up in general. Big News! Allwander's Captaincy came through, and as I have mentioned, his papers cleared Division only a week before mine did, so mine should be coming through about any time now. At least a pleasant sense of anticipation is now mine, and barring unforeseen difficulties, I should soon be wearing my "railroad tracks." I am taking quite a "kidding" over the whole matter but am happy to say that the large majority of my cohorts seem genuinely happy to hear of the impending event. I am still working on Colonel Floyd to give me the full fifteen days to

California, but knowing that crusty old gentleman as I do, it is entirely possible that he may cut it to 11 days (authorized) or may possibly give me 13 days in a sudden fit of generosity.

I suppose that, at the present time, I should feel completely happy in view of the progress of my work and of the impending events. But sad to relate, I do not feel so. My struggle for advancement and accomplishment is entirely meaningless. There is no point in it. I am not working for anybody or anything. It is more to satisfy some inner urge in me than anything else. With the corresponding increase in pay that a Captaincy brings, as well as the enhanced prestige, which may or may not mean something after the War is over, the possibility of satisfying one of my long-held dreams after the War is now almost assured; that is, of buying a home of my own. For I will certainly have enough to put down a very suitable down payment for the same. But it is truly ironic, that to me, to whom such things as a home, true domestic happiness, a family, and in short, the more simple joys of life mean everything, that they are denied. While to other men I know, whose chief joy in life seems to be in chasing, chiseling, cheating, and dissipating in a continual bacchanalian orgy, those things are offered to them on a silver platter, and they throw them away.

I hope that Chief of Police Hale followed my telegraphic request and bought Mother the carnations that I asked him to, for today is Mother's Day, and I certainly thought of Mother a lot. It takes a war, usually, to bring a true realization of just what a mother means.

From all reports and from certain words that have come to my ears, I seem to be doing all right in my new job, and I only hope that this will prove to be true in the trying days that are to come.

Camp Carson, Colo.
May 15, 1944
A rather discouraging day. The work seems to be getting more and more confusing due to a series of contradictory orders from Division. Smathers's promotion came through today—the only one. Still no news of mine. I wonder—if? Submitted my application for leave today. Wonder how much he will cut my leave down from the 15 days I asked for? Next thing to worry about is applying for a Class 4 priority <u>and</u> a reservation on the plane as well as a reservation at the hotel when I arrive in Oakland.

Have been working on equipment to wear home, but it is a somewhat monotonous task with everything so undecided.

Hope Mother received her flowers okay. I have been somewhat thoughtful, moody, and despondent in turn, lately.

Guess I will take off and shower and turn in.

CAMP CARSON, COLO.
MAY 16, 1944
Tuesday already! A lot of approved leaves came through this morning, but mine wasn't among them. I have no doubt that mine will be approved, but how much will the old man cut off? Still no news of the promotion, either. I should think it would be through Corps by now.

The General is reputed to have made the remark that, if all records do not pass the inspection in good shape, "not a damned Timberwolf will go out the Camp gate until they do." Which would fix my leave up nicely.

A very short letter from Mother today, and that was all. I guess my "women trouble" is now definitely over, for it has been months since I have heard from anyone except Mother, and I haven't been out with any nurses for weeks.

'Tis for the best methinks!
Need guidance and help on the
forthcoming inspection of records
!

[MAY 17, 1944]
Another hectic day. Had to lay the law down to the assembled clerks. Some of them were getting slipshod in their work. Still no news of the promotion, although I felt sure it would come through today.

Feel tired and discouraged. Medical inspection tonight, *ad infinitum*.

Colonel Cochran came back today, so imagine the hell will start soon.

Got some of my cleaning back and should soon be all ready to go on leave as far as personal effects are concerned, but no word as to whether my leave was approved or not, or for how long.

Colonel Hopelain and Major Cook were down today noting progress of corrections that had been made. Seemed somewhat satisfied, but if we don't pass the inspection, imagine the repercussions may be somewhat severe.

CAMP CARSON, COLO.
MAY 18, 1944
Another monotonous, soul-sickening day of hard, relentless work. 6 more officers to go overseas. This outfit seems to be rapidly developing into a replacement pool.

For the last two days I have been experiencing a steady, continuous stomachache of grinding intensity, of the same type that used to annoy me when at work at the plant in those happy, halcyon civilian days. In addition, I had a splitting headache of such intensity last night that I couldn't get to sleep until well after 1 a.m.

Still no news of my promotion and of my leave. (?)

Chaplain assures me I won't have too much trouble getting a reservation on a plane.

Cochran has been moderately quiet and self-effacing of late.

Rumors of more maneuvers. (Oh my God, No! I couldn't stand it—give me actual combat, please!)

CAMP CARSON, COLO.
MAY 19, 1944
Promotion came back today—<u>bounced</u>. Reason? "Not enough duty with troops," although I have as much duty with troops as Captain Buckley ever had. And I guess the fact that I served as Operations Officer of an infantry battalion all through two periods of maneuvers doesn't mean a thing, although I issued orders and manhandled troops into position all that time. In other words, hold down a Captain's job for 15 months, obtain Superior ratings all that time, and it doesn't mean a thing as far as the Army is concerned.

I am truly fed up. They can all go to <u>hell</u>. And they say "hard work" is recognized in the Army. What a laugh!

Well, it means one thing—no leave—for I will not take it under the present circumstances.

I had a talk with Colonel Cochran about it, and he was very nice, but of course, his hands were tied by 2nd Army. He said, quote: "I am sorry as hell about this. As you know, we submitted your recommendation as soon as you had filled the three months required, and that may have been a deterrent. We will wait a couple of months and resubmit it, and by that time, we may be under another administrative headquarters other than 2nd Army." All of which doesn't mean a damned thing.

It just doesn't seem fair. All of that hard work and merciless grinding for nothing.

God only knows what fate is in store for me now as a result of these events, for they will, without a doubt, fill us up to T/O strength with Captains before going overseas, and once overseas, "No promotion over the ocean."

Guess *** will be delighted to hear all this, as was Major Kernan, no doubt.

Again, as so often in the past, it is *KISMET!*

CAMP CARSON, COLO.
MAY 22, 1944
Another spiritually hopeless day drags its tortuous length along. Had quite a talk with Colonel Cochran Saturday. He stated that he was extremely satisfied and pleased with my work (incidentally, he gave me a superior rating for my work as Personnel Officer up to the time my promotion papers went through). He again reiterated the statement that he would put through my promotion again in a couple of months. I told him that I wanted to cancel my leave, and so I tore up my leave papers this morning. He also agreed that 2nd Army misinterpreted that paragraph in my case. Wonder what Captain Smith can or will do about his messed-up affair?

Old Major Kernan seems to be gunning for me, at least it appears that way, as a reprint of a '42 circular came out today that appears more or less directed at me.

I wonder, how I wonder, and I ask myself today, just what in hell have I to live for? No future, no present evidently, and nothing else. No incentive, no goal, no happiness.

Went into Colorado Springs, Saturday, with Capt. Allwander and CWO Ammons. Went to the Elks Club, drank beer, had a steak, and came home.

Allwander and I are going to try and join the Elks. I suppose, because that is something I want, it too will be impossible to attain.

We take to the field for an 8-day problem on about the 4th of June, again under the direct supervision of Major Kernan.

Oh God, when will this dreary, hopeless, pointless existence end? Will I never find a semblance of happiness, an iota of peace or contentment?

Today is truly the one day of my life when my cup of despair runneth over. I have truly, in the past few days, scraped the bitter dregs of the barrel of despair, and there seems no possible opening for a ray of the sunshine of life.

CAMP CARSON, COLO.
MAY 23, 1944
Still another day passes into oblivion. Things don't seem to be going any too smoothly—a certain undefinable amount of confusion. I hope and trust, however, that the big POM inspection on June 1st will pass without event. In view of certain political aspects, however, this may not be so.

Lt. McKerney's promotions came through today. He has one month more active duty than me and has never trained in any other job than company work, both deficiencies on which mine was turned down. The political subterfuge, which cancelled my promotion is only too obvious.

I felt rather good for a day or so but was mentally (and physically) exhausted this morning.

I filled out my application to join the Elks Lodge this afternoon, but I suppose it, too, will be rejected because of lack of sufficient prestige or political connections.

This coming POM inspection will be Kernan's big chance to crucify me. Wonder if he will take advantage of it? Probably so.

CAMP CARSON, COLO.
MAY 24, 1944
Another day drags by.

Captain Smith took my promotion papers up to G-1 and to the Chief of Staff to see what could be done, but I, frankly, expect no startling action to be taken.

I have determined (1) to keep my eyes and ears opened and my mouth shut, (2) to make my work as efficient and invaluable as I can, (3) to bide my time and see if Cochran follows through with his declaration of resubmitting the promotion "in a couple of months." If not, then will be the time to take some action, but to do so now would be "sticking my neck out," and without a doubt, just what Kernan and *** expect me to do.

To sum the whole bitter mess up, fate has again chosen to bludgeon me down, and it seems, just as the months and months of hard, unrelenting work seemed to have been not in vain after all.

There is nothing now to look forward to—no leave, no visit home, no ultimate promotion, no happiness, and most of all, no future. God help me now.

Camp Carson, Colorado
May 25, 1944
Captain Smith doesn't take my promotion papers up to the Chief of Staff for review until tomorrow, as the Regiment was involved in a CPX today, which fairly well tied everything up. From talking to Captain Smith this morning, however, I learned that he did take the matter up with G-1, who seemed of the opinion that the papers should again be forwarded to 2nd Army <u>without an endorsement</u>. It seems that I did have a somewhat legitimate "gripe" after all. Frankly, though, I didn't and still don't have any hopes of anything being effected by this, as once a higher HQ renders a decision on anything, it kills their soul to retract it.

Amazing things have been happening, though. Major Kernan came down to the unit last night and inspected us as to the progress of correcting these deficiencies, and such comments as, "What was once the worst Personnel Section in the Division is now the best," "the best organized plan for accomplishing these things," "better than the other two regiments," and "the best that the 415th has ever been," etc., etc., have been flooding into the office all day today. In fact, I was up at Division HQ this morning talking to Major Nau, and Kernan called me over and told me some of the above, and then remarked that he was going to inform the Colonel (Cochran) of the progress that had been made. I can't imagine what has called all that, but I certainly am not taking it at its face value; as usually (it has been my past experiences), just when the compliments are coming in the fastest, is about the time that the axe usually falls for good. However, the following fact still puzzles me: WHY if my work is so good and seems to be recognized as such, and after all, it IS a Captain's job that I am performing, is any chance for advancement and promotion mollified by some lousy little technicality in some half-forgotten circular?

No, on the contrary, I shall not let all this get me down in the least, but I shall work so damned hard and make them recognize my value in the present job until they will have to do something.

Something is radically wrong with my stomach. It has been aching something fierce for the last two or three days, and I am quite sure that it is not due to a sluggish system, either. It seems to strike immediately before and after a meal and, of course, this brings up the old bugaboo of ULCERS; but I do not see how that can be possible, as God knows I am far from a heavy drinker, although I do indulge in beer, occasionally. Well, I suppose time alone will tell on that matter. They do say, though, that worry has a lot to do with things of that sort, and I am somewhat of a chronic worrier.

??????????????????

Camp Carson, Colorado
May 26, 1944
Well, tomorrow is the day, as far as my future advancement in the Army is concerned (if any). It was finally decided that a big powwow would be held at Division HQ concerning the return of my recommendation. So tomorrow morning at 0800, Captain Smith will meet with the Chief of Staff, G-1, Major Kernan, and Lt. Christiansen of the Adjutant General's Dept. Must say that my future is certainly being decided by some big people, at least. Depending on how well Captain Smith is able to argue my case, something may happen. But in a way, I rather doubt that anything will come out of all this mess, so perhaps I had best resign myself to the fact that I am not going to be promoted, that hard work and earnest effort, in the Army at least, mean nothing.

Division inspectors were down again today and spot-checked some records from each company, and we were given a rating of superior. For about every error had been corrected, with the exception of Form 20 errors, which are being worked on tonight.

I received a letter from Mother today, and she is still expecting me to come home on leave, so I guess that she still hasn't received my letter in which I told her it would be impossible to do so. Much to my surprise and amazement, I also received a letter from Lena. Quite a newsy letter and interesting, but needless to say, under the circumstances, it would be difficult to write for quite a while at least.

At least tomorrow's meeting should clear the atmosphere as to just how I stand, and then about all that I can do is to wait and see if Colonel Cochran keeps his word about resubmitting the thing in another couple of months if and when we ever leave this damnable, confused, and bewildered 2nd Army.

So far, from all reports, our records and system of administration in this office is much better than those of the two adjacent units and sections, and if we can pass this big inspection "with flying colors," as it were, the old man may hesitate a long time about denying me a promotion or changing me to another job.

You know, things wouldn't be so bad about all these disappointments if I just had someone to confide in and to listen to all my plans and worries. But the way it is, it is hard to keep all of this bitterness and worry continually locked up inside of one. The truth of the whole matter is that I am bitterly and terribly LONELY, and I guess I always will be.

Another beautiful act of marital bliss, trust, and happiness displayed by Lt. *** in a little mess that is a little too sordid for even these pages. HOW BEAUTIFUL THE HOLY INSTITUTION OF MARRIAGE REALLY SEEMS TO BE!

Camp Carson, Colorado
May 28, 1944

Another dreary Sunday dragging its usual boring length along. I volunteered to take the Regimental Staff Duty Officer for Captain Baker. He's married and wanted to go to town quite badly. Went down and played the organ in the chapel for a couple of hours yesterday.

My stomach darned near tore me apart yesterday morning and last night, which just about decides me. As soon as this mess settles down somewhat, and the big inspection is over, I intend to see the medics and determine, once and for all, just what in hell the trouble is.

Well, Captain Smith had a big conference with Colonel DeGraff, Colonel Rex, etc., about the way in which my promotion was turned down. Both of them admitted that 2nd Army wasn't consistent at all in its verdicts, and the Chief of Staff (DeGraff) said that he would take it up with General Allen and see what could be done about it. Somehow, I don't expect anything to be done about it, for it doesn't seem to be the policy of this outfit to go to bat for its officers. Anyway, at the present time, General Allen is shivering in dread of the 2nd Army and its interminable inspections and ultimatums, for reliable rumor has it that his Division is on the verge of being broken up due to unsatisfactory ratings, etc. So it is already preordained that Allen is not going to stick his neck out by demanding that a lowly 1st Lt. be promoted, no matter how right it should be. At any rate, I should hear some sort of action that will be taken on the matter in the very near future anyway, and I will know just what basis to plan my action on from that. The big POM inspection is due this coming Thursday, and if I can only pass that in a very creditable manner, it may serve to enhance my present position in quite a few ways. On this, however, only the Good Lord will see fit to take what action he may desire.

About all that I can do is to continue to work hard, show them that I am deserving of a promotion, and who knows, some day ?????????????????

LONELY, as always, but there is no remedy for that, and I guess there never will be. What a helluva mess my life is in on this date.

Camp Carson, Colo.
May 29, 1944
1400

Stomach again tore me to pieces last night and again this morning. Work seems to be progressing smoothly enough, except for the matter of dog tags. We have received so many compliments and bouquets on our deficiency correcting that it will be somewhat embarrassing if we don't pass with a good score. A new Captain was assigned to the 415th today--from the 26th Infantry. (?)

Smith was talking to G-1 this morning about my "deal," and he said, "It looks as though we may be able to do some good." However, I doubt it very much, for reasons previously mentioned.

*** evidently endeavoring to obtain transfer by means of some sort of application.

May get teeth cleaned tonight. We hit the field again on next Monday.

Wrote a letter to Lena this weekend, the first in quite some time.

Mother still thinks I'm coming home.

Camp Carson, Colo.
May 30, 1944
"Decoration Day"

Last night was "Financial Night," held at the Recreation Hall for those who wished to adjust their finances prior to movement overseas. Colonel Cochran came down to see how I was getting along. Then Capt. Smith and I attended a USO show and witnessed a truly astounding exhibition of mass hypnotism.

Retired rather late (about 2400) and had a helluva time getting to sleep—body twitchings, nervousness, I guess, and my accursed stomach woke me early in the morning with its pulsating pain.

Am invited to a "Southern Fried Ham Dinner and Beer Bust" at Captain Smith's home sometime this week.

Lauck and all the boys say I should reapply for leave, but under the present miserable circumstances, that is impossible for me to do.

There seems to be no more joy in life for me. I feel, with a strong conviction, that I am steadily deteriorating, both mentally and physically. My dearest dreams of a home, a wife, and children I now view for what they are—impractical foolish dreams only—a farce.

CAMP CARSON, COLORADO
MAY 31, 1944
Today is one of the really beautiful days that causes me, at times, to think that I would like to live in Colorado after the termination (if any) of hostilities. However, that thought is immediately killed when I think of the winters and the monotonous rainstorms that this region is subject to.

Still no word from higher authority as to what action, if any, was taken on the possible resubmission of my recommendation. However, more developments, all tending to make me so damned disgusted and discouraged, have happened, that I just don't give a good damn anymore. I happened to be down at Regimental HQ yesterday afternoon, and Colonel Cochran came strolling out of his office, and blithely informed me that "he had to transfer me." Of course, I realize that he couldn't help it, as this new 26th Inf Captain (Beard) came in, so I was relieved of assignment to Sv Co and assigned to Company A (of all companies) and placed on SD with Sv Co. It is just one of those "paper shuffles," of course, but it tends to discourage one; and now, unless they postdate the resubmission of my promotion, it will really be impossible for me to ever get it, as we are once again filled up to T/O strength with Captains. I was Duty Officer last night and spent another rather horrible night—sleepless, nervous twitchings, and a series of kaleidoscopic dreams.

We are preparing for the forthcoming Division Test, which will be of some eight days' duration, and I can well imagine that it will be somewhat of a confused mess, what with the usually discordant motor movement, setting up in bivouac, trying to carry on the daily work, plus the fact that all administrative records will be inspected. As usual, I will very probably be Officer of the Guard and Officer of the Day and Sector Commander, which will do nothing to ease the perpetual state of confusion, which always exists in the rear echelon.

I received a nice long letter from Harold yesterday, and I spent last evening in answering it. He is certainly getting along fine in school, and all in all, is a great kid and a swell little brother.

Believe me, with my physical condition and mental outlook on life what it is, I have determined to relax a lot more upon our return from the field and to break away from this soul-destroying routine that has become so commonplace. I have got to, or else I will certainly be somewhat of a wreck, in all respects, upon my release from the Army.

It appears very much at this time that I can never look forward to any higher advancement in this "fair, nonpolitical, and absolutely unbiased" Army, and as a result, any ambition that I may once have had is now dying a natural death. All that I can look forward to now is my ultimate release.

CAMP CARSON, COLO.
JUNE 1, 1944
At low ebb again, today, although the cause was no shock for me. For my "papers" came back from G-1 with the notation, "inadvisable to resubmit, as they will press insufficient troop duty status." "Best to wait until approximately July 15th and resubmit when additional time in present capacity may counteract the mentioned deficiency."

Well, I expected this, for this confused, inefficient outfit is noted for not "going to bat" for its personnel.

So it is again the dull, dreary monotonous routine of waiting for endless days to pass with no incentive, no future, no <u>life</u>.

Stomach had stopped bothering me for a few days but had begun to twinge again today.

Had a row with several of the brass hats at Division, which, I suppose, didn't do much to increase my popularity in that quarter, <u>but</u> who gives a damn?

CAMP CARSON, COLORADO
JUNE 2, 1944
Friday already! We didn't work last night, so I took the occasion to

go over to the 2nd Bn Officers Club and imbibe in approximately six (6) bottles of beer. Had quite an interesting talk with one of the comparatively new officers and learned "that quite a few of the officers feel as badly as you do about the way in which you were deprived of promotion."

The day of the scheduled inspection draws near, and God help me if we don't pass with at least a fair rating. As usual, the various staff sections of Division are making these as tough and as complicated as they can with last-minute ultimatums and various and sundry changes.

Major Denisevich's promotion came through today, so mine was the only one that bounced out of them all. In the final analysis, the principal reason for mine being bounced was because I lacked 6 (six) days of the required amount of troop duty.

I may go into Colorado Springs with Captain Smith tomorrow and see what occurs (nothing, as usual, is expected).

Colonel Cochran was informed of G-1's decision as regarded my promotion and remarked that "we would resubmit it in another two months."

No mail at all recently, except that my application for membership in the Elk's Lodge was forwarded by the Colorado Springs Chapter of that organization.

CAMP CARSON, COLORADO
SUNDAY, 4TH OF JUNE, 1944

As expected, nothing spectacular came out of my trip to town. However, I had an extremely pleasant evening. Dressed and rode into Colorado Springs with Captain Smith. Purchased two ½ pints of a particularly horrible vintage whisky and went to Captain Smith's house and proceeded to enjoy several rounds of drinks in the company of Captain Smith, his wife, Captain Leiser and wife, and a medic from Division, Captain Brown. After a very nice supper with Captain Smith and family, we all went over to Lt. Woodman's house, and there was quite a nice crowd there, including Woodman, wife and baby, Lt. Pruitt's wife and baby (he is away at school). I certainly (and, as usual) was green with envy at the display of marital bliss and happiness, which seems to come so easily and naturally to some fellows. Had quite a few more drinks, and Captain Smith drove me back out to Camp. It was quite a struggle to get up this morning but finally made it and didn't feel too badly.

There will be a meeting of all personnel officers at the AG section at 1500 this afternoon. From all information obtainable at this time, it is apparent that we will move out tomorrow afternoon, sometime after 1700. As usual, when this Division takes to the field, or on outdoor problems of any kind, it has clouded up, and I imagine that we are in for a long session of some stormy weather. It will very probably be bitterly cold, and most of all, I can well imagine the confusion and discordance that will accompany the big Division inspection of records. On the latter, about all that I can do is to keep my fingers crossed and pray to God that we pass with a minimum of gigs, for if we don't, there have been many dire repercussions threatened.

For some reason or other, I have been thinking of Margie almost continuously, of late.

This damnable loneliness of mine seems to be getting worse and worse. It gnaws and gnaws. If I only had someone to work for, to plan for, and one who could lift, if even partially, this blanket of gloom, despondency, and despair that engulfs—and evidently will, forever.

GOD GUIDE AND LEAD ME IN THE TRYING DAYS AHEAD

CAMP CARSON, COLO.
JUNE 5, 1944

We are in the last stages of preparation for the "outing" tonight, which starts sometime after 1900. Understand we are moving a distance of some 29 miles out near Pueblo, Colorado.

This problem and inspection may well be a turning point in my "Army career," depending on how it comes out.

Am almost tempted to take a short leave of three or four days in Denver—if I knew someone in that city to visit. The above is only temporary, however, you may be sure.

I hope to goodness that we don't move all over creation on this problem, for it will be tough enough without that.

I may, and may not, have time to write in this chronicle out on the problem, but I am taking along some loose pages just in case.

I wish I could get Margie out of my mind. Such things as love and happiness are not for me.

CAMP CARSON, COLO.
JUNE 6, 1944

Major events are happening. News came this morning of the invasion of Europe. We were all sitting around last night awaiting orders to move out, when notice came that the problem had been cancelled for 24 hours. Reason? A confidential phone call from 2nd Army—we are now practically on an "alert" status. Furthermore, orders have been issued that this Division will receive priority on Arctic clothing. ----? The rear echelon will not move out until very early Wednesday morning, and the entire Division must be back in Camp by Friday night, so I certainly can't see the sense of it.

The Division I.G., in charge of a Captain Roy, has started inspecting our records for the POM inspection today. He seems like a nice chap, but if we don't pass this inspection, God help me.

It looks very much as though we are finally going overseas. I do hope this I true, for I am miserably tired of all this interminable training bush-wah that goes on at all times.

CAMP CARSON, COLO.
JUNE 9, 1944

Well, back in Camp already. We set up bivouac in an extremely picturesque location high in the rugged Rocky Mountains. Had the usual "perils" and mishaps. Narrowly avoided a bad smashup on a treacherous curve when the trailer of the truck in front of us overturned.

The situation was rigidly tactical at all times. We set up our own guard, all dug foxholes, and had a general defense plan outlined.

It rained violently both nights. The first night was accompanied by continuous thunder and lightning, and both nights, my sleeping bag absorbed copious amounts of water.

Killed three, 5-foot blacksnakes, and aside from the usual horrible maneuver food, that was the extent of the big problem. The I.G. inspected our records throughout, and sad to relate, is "gigging" them like a madman, mostly on minor errors, however. Don't know, yet, just how we will come out on the I.G. inspection as a whole, but I pray to God that we pass with a reasonably presentable score. Colonel Schnell (2nd Army Classification Officer) inspects our Form 20's tomorrow, and much will depend on his verdict, also; but I am somewhat pessimistic, as he is a b------ of the first water.

Lying in my bedroll of an evening, on the recent problem, I had occasion to go over my life in retrospect, and I'm damned if I can fathom any purpose, or even sense, in the present course, which seems to be outlined.

If utter despondency and disgust made any difference, there should be a big change, but all opportunity for advancement is nullified as long as we are under the jurisdiction of 2nd Army.

If we don't pass the coming inspections, God knows what my disposition will be; as unfortunately, I am held accountable for all of the errors and omissions of my 7 predecessors, and it is impossible to correct all of them in a period of two months.

Camp Carson, Colorado
June 11, 1944

The big inspection is still going on—not completed yet. I grew disgusted yesterday and decided to go into town and forget it all for a few hours, anyway. Much to my surprise, I had a good time. Went in with Lt. Woodman and Captain Smith. Ran into a bunch of the fellows at the Antlers Hotel and killed time there until about 2000. Then Captain McKerney and his date, Lt. Woodman and his wife, and I visited the Smith's for a while and then went out to the far-famed Broadmoor Hotel, an ultra-, ultra-resort, some miles out of town. Cost quite a bit of money but really had a fine time. Lt. Woodman surely has a nice wife. He's a lucky guy. While with the crowd at the Antlers, observed another example of marital fidelity and connubial bliss: The wife of some sap in the Army up in Idaho, chiseling around with one of our medical officers. All I could think of as I looked at her was, "You cheap little b----."

I was invited along with the Woodman's to attend a picnic out in the Garden of the Gods, but McKerney must have failed to get up, and as I didn't know the way out to the Woodman's home, I let it go. We didn't get home until about 0300, and I arose at 0909 and had a nice breakfast, then spent the morning reading the Sunday papers and current magazines, then had a nice dinner, and came over to the Personnel Office. Sure enough, dear Mother had written me another letter. By the way, Mother is now the only person who writes to me.

With the inspection about over and the Big Field problem finished, the way is now clear for me to take a leave if I so desire. But I made my vow, and I intend to stick to it—I could not bear the disgrace of going home in my present grade after the way that I have worked to earn a promotion. I have been toying with the idea of going to Denver or Chicago or some other large city to endeavor to get away from it all for a few days, but I can't seem to get enthused over the idea. I would very probably spend a lot of money, and it would be just another continuation of weekends here in Colorado—lonely, alone, thinking, thinking, and unhappiness engulfing me, as always.

I have determined to invest as high as $150, if necessary, in the purchase of a good camera and the necessary equipment for it. It is something I should get prior to going overseas, and I should be able to get many interesting pictures before my years of service in the Army terminate.

Not a single word from Bob, and this worries me, for he was, without a doubt, in the invasion.

CAMP CARSON, COLO.
JUNE 12, 1944
The Division inspectors finished up today, but goodness knows what our rating will be. I heard that the 414th Inf obtained a rating of excellent. We have an Army inspection coming up, then a Corps inspection, then an AGF inspection, and so on, *ad infinitum*.

Don't feel at all well today. My eyes seem to be bothering me considerably.

Must appear in court tonight, as a member of a Board of Officers re: the prosecution of 1st Sgt. ***.

Captain DeGroat has been here all day and now tells us our Form 20's are in bad shape, after telling us that they were excellent a week ago.

I am getting more and more disgusted with this present set-up. Hard work means absolutely nothing. The continual grinding sense of loneliness that haunts me always, remains an unbearable ache that disproves any theory that life might someday be worthwhile.

CAMP CARSON, COL.
JUNE 13, 1944
A crisis is fast approaching. Events are building up to something or other.

Our priority was changed today to a higher one, and it is evident that we can expect a movement order sometime in July. As a result, the annual Corps I.G. inspection of records will take place sometime this weekend. God only knows on that! The report of the Division I.G. will go to Colonel tomorrow--? In the interim, we have so much additional work to do that Division has adroitly crammed down our throats, that the present outlook appears hopeless.

It begins to appear that, at long last, we are headed overseas, and I only hope that it proves true, my only regret being that I won't get a final leave to see Mother and all. But I feel sure that she will understand, as she always has in the past.

Camp Carson, Colo.
June 14, 1944

Two items of major importance today. The report came in from the I.G. and not so good. We placed approximately 4th in the Division. We should have obtained a score of at least 45% and actually attained a score of 38.7. Don't know what repercussions there will be on this, but I know in my heart that we here in Personnel have put forth every effort, and as far as the last 6.3% is concerned, I attribute it directly to the mass of confused and conflicting directives issued from Division Headquarters.

We received a new Captain today—***—who is apparently an 8-ball from way back, at least according to his record—a series of U's, S's, and VS's—and from all indications, Cochran is going to railroad him. In about 30 days, proceedings should start. With his arrival, our quota of Captains is entirely filled up, and any chance for a promotion is forever blocked.

I believe that it is unnecessary for me to state that life means absolutely nothing to me anymore, and who gives a goddamn anyway?

Camp Carson, Colo.
June 15, 1944

Today is Infantry Day, and the 2nd bombing of Japan was announced today. There was a Division Review today (which we of Personnel did not attend, due to pressure of work), and the entire Division was given this afternoon off, except Personnel.

I had a meeting last night at which I laid down, once and for all, my policies as to the operation of the Personnel Office.

We are working day and night to get these records into shape, but it seems like batting your head against a stone wall. If we don't pass the Corps I.G. inspection in a highly satisfactory manner, I doubt if Colonel Cochran will be any too enthused about his Personnel Officer. On this, however, only fate will direct the outcome.

We worked until almost 0300 this morning, and needless to say, my eyes are burnt out as well as my mind.

I am also Duty Officer tonight and this weekend.

CAMP CARSON, COLO.
JUNE 16, 1944
The inspectors haven't arrived as yet. In view of the manner in which the men have worked for the past two days (and nights), I am turning them loose for tonight and the weekend. For God knows they'll certainly be restricted if we don't pass the inspection. Poor devils.

Gee! I haven't written Mother since about the 5th of June.

Needless to say, I am "sweating out" the inspection, to use Army terminology, for much depends on the outcome.

I hope to God Hubie is making out okay in the invasion. His outfit (2nd Division) is the one fighting around St. Lô, France, and the woods around Cerisy.

And Bob, too. Not one word from him since the invasion started (and sometime before).

I wish to hell I could get over there and get this miserable life over with. I, personally, am finished.

CAMP CARSON, COL.
JUNE 17, 1944
Accompanied the medics to the hospital last night and dated a nurse (Lt. Lucille DeMart). Went to the Officers Club and drank copious amounts of beer. The evening consisted of talking, for the most part, and to my amazement, evidently a few girls still find joy in the simpler things of life, i.e., hunting, fishing, your own home, etc. Probably a line, however.

Foolishly, I made a date for tonight before I remembered that I was Duty Officer, so I guess I will have to break it unless I can get a substitute, which is highly improbable.

Service Co. is throwing a huge beer bust tonight, and I would certainly like to go, but--.

No mail today.

Physically not too good.

CAMP CARSON, COLORADO
18 JUNE 1944
A particularly beautiful weekend in the Rockies! Spring is really here—a sunny, cloudless day, warm, and with a gentle zephyr caressing

the atmosphere. As usual, under such circumstances, I am Regimental Staff Duty Officer. I wanted, very badly, to go to the big party that Service Company was throwing in Manitou Springs last night, but do you think any of these so-called "officers and gentlemen" on the staff would take my Duty Officer for me? Hell no! Despite the fact that every one of them owed me a weekend or a weekday of duty. Just wait until one of them asks me again to take his duty for him. Assuredly the answer will be decidedly most negative.

Answer came back last night from the Elks Club in Oakland. It seems that their "Investigating Committee" will not pass on any applicant who cannot "appear before them personally." Well to hell with them. The Colorado Springs Lodge has invited me to join their particular lodge, so I will do that.

I wrote Mother a letter today, as I haven't written her since prior to the field problem. Also, I have received absolutely no mail from anyone for a decidedly long period of time. Haven't heard from Bob since long before the start of the invasion, and how I hope to God that he made out okay, for I figure he must have been in it, taking into consideration the total of 11,000 planes that was used. Not much additional news of Hubie or his outfit, the 2nd Division, which when last reported, was spearheading the attack around St. Lô, France.

The Colonel seems to be in a particularly jovial mood of late. As he was leaving yesterday, he said, quote: "*Harrumph*, you seem to be pulling most of the duty around here, Mac." I hope he is still as jovial after the results of the Corps I.G. inspection.

Several additional promotions went in a few days ago, but mine was not among them, as it is practically impossible to do anything about that until, when and if, we ever get out of the confused, defunct, and malodorous 2nd Army.

I hope to God we move overseas next month, as rumor has it at the present time, for I can't, for the life of me, stomach much more of this - - - -.

Camp Carson, Colo.
June 19, 1944
Another beautiful day. No inspectors have appeared, as yet, so we are still "sweating it out." I was Duty Officer all weekend. Arose in time for a ½ hour of calisthenics, and then, to work. Quite a bit of heavy work came in this morning, necessitating a Company Commanders Meeting.

Had a confidential talk with Colonel Cochran yesterday in which he asked my opinion of Major Herbert. I told him, frankly, that it wasn't very high and told him that I couldn't rate him truthfully with more than a VS rating. I don't know whether he figured me presumptuous or not, but he asked for a frank opinion and got it.

Was going out tonight, but they have a damned school on "defensive combat" scheduled, so no go, I guess.

Don't know whether to take a leave in Denver or some other large city, or not.

Camp Carson, Colo.
June 20, 1944
Did go out last night, after the school. Up to the Club again. Lt. Broome and I. We dated two nurses--mine named Lt. Mary McLoughlin. Had quite a nice time drinking beer and conversation, etc. Broome left early with his date, and I left so late that it was impossible to get a cab, so I had to walk the nurse back to the nurses quarters around the lake. All in all, it was a nice walk. A lovely, moonlit June night, soft breezes caressing the night, the silvery reflection of the Colorado stars glistening in the lake. But don't mistake me, no romance occurred. She asked if I would call again, and I said no.

Not for me—romance, love, and all its innocuous trappings are not for me.

Had some more vigorous calisthenics this morning, and I am stiffer than a board. Hope it leaves soon.

No inspectors, yet.

Camp Carson, Colo.
June 22, 1944
Usual boring routine. Stayed in the other night and retired fairly early. Went to the hospital again last night with Broome and Northington and then to the Officers Club with three more dates, mine being named Lt. Regina Russell, this time. Attractive, fairly so, but as silent and incommunicative as the Sphinx. Took them home at 2300 and retired.

Muscles still protesting violently at the calisthenics but are improving somewhat.

A letter from Bob, yesterday. He has been over France three times. I've got to write him a long letter, soon.

I was transferred from Co. A to Cn. Co. yesterday (still on SD with Sv Co).

Have determined to take a 7-day leave in Denver, Colo., effective 30th of this month. I hope the old man will approve it. Would like to go home, but under the present miserable circumstances, that is impossible.

CAMP CARSON, COLORADO
JUNE 23, 1944
Well, quite a bit is happening. We received news that the Personnel Office of the 415th Infantry would be tested and inspected by the Inspector General of the XVI Corps as to its administrative proficiency on this coming Monday (June 26, 1944). Well, I can only cross my fingers and hope from now on out.

I put myself on leave on yesterday's special order, as the old man had approved it in record time. It is from June 30, 1944, until July 7, 1944. I am only taking seven days, as I am only going up to Denver. I wired the Cosmopolitan Hotel in Denver today for reservations for that time. Strelnick, the Red Cross representative, obtained a reservation on the 1802 plane out of Colorado Springs, on the 29th of June, which means that I should be in Denver in about 40 minutes. Don't know whether these two reservations will hold up, and when I once get up to Denver, my leave will probably consist of sitting in some hotel and drinking immense quantities of beer, but at least it will be getting away from this miserable grind for a while, and I feel sure that Mother would understand why I couldn't come home under the present disgraceful conditions.

My application to join the Elks Lodge came back approved, and I am to appear before them on this coming Tuesday night to have the degree conferred upon me. I will have to go into town tomorrow evening in order to sign some of the necessary preliminary papers. Well, I don't think that I will have any cause to regret the above action, as the Elks is about the only fraternal organization that I would care to join.

Muscles are loosening up somewhat, and we have been playing from one to two tiresome and strenuous games of fast volleyball every day for the past few days.

We are definitely getting ready to go overseas, from all indications.

The Secretary of War will be here on this coming Tuesday. All furloughs and leaves are being cleared up, and we were told not to buy any more suntan clothing or tropical-worsted clothing, so from all indications, we must be going to a cold climate, but where in the hell could that be? It is a cinch that we won't go to Siberia, and I sure can't fancy us sitting on our posteriors up in Alaska for the duration of the War. Iceland? Norway? Where?

The work has been going along very nicely for the last few days, and all that I ask of life, right now, is that we pass the big inspection. I want this more than anything in view of the hard, grinding work that has been put in on these records in the past few months. On this, ONLY FATE CAN TELL.

CAMP CARSON, COLO.
JUNE 26, 1944
Today is the day. Colonel Booth, the Corps I.G., has not appeared, yet, and I hardly expect him before this afternoon. I hope to goodness that we pass all right.

I have the reservation on the Denver plane but was notified by wire that there were no vacancies at the Cosmopolitan Hotel so will have to work on that little detail.

Went in to Colorado Springs Saturday night and signed the preliminary papers at the Elks Club. We will be formally initiated into the Club tomorrow night.

Had a fairly good time over the weekend but spent a little more money than I had figured on.

I wonder how this crazy leave of mine will work out? Will it consist, as usual, of lonely nights sitting in some bar swilling beer? Perhaps I am crazy for wasting 7 days in such a manner, but I had to get away from here for a while, at least, and under the circumstances, I just couldn't go home.

CAMP CARSON, COLO.
JUNE 28, 1944
Many events have happened. The I.G. inspection is over and gone, and the inspector informed the Colonel that our records were in excellent condition. The Colonel, of course, was happy to hear this, and I might add myself. Went into Colorado Springs together with Capt. Allwander, Capt. Swann, Lt. McCarthy, Mr. Ammons, and was formally initiated

into the Benevolent and Protective Order of Elks. So I am, at last, a member of a fraternal organization, and I think, a pretty nice one.

The work at Personnel has become more and more tedious and difficult, what with the feverish activity caused by our pending departure for overseas service. For we are <u>definitely going</u> this time. The readiness date is August 15th, and we will go to a POE in either Boston or New York, so the presumption is, of course, the European Theater. Okay by me! I will be near Bob and Raff, anyway.

Life to me, recently, has ceased to mean anything at all. My loneliness has become a dreadful malady that taunts and burns. What, oh what, is wrong with me that I should be practically a leper as far as society, in general, is concerned? I am well liked by my fellow officers, I know. I have the reputation of being a hard worker, and yet--.

Tonight should be a happy night for me, for tomorrow night, I depart for Denver by plane on my leave. Yet it will not be enjoyable to me. I should be going home to see my Mother and family on what will be my last leave, and yet I can't. 2nd Army has seen to that. Foolish pride you say? But somehow I know Mother would understand.

And so, my last wondrous leave will be spent in Denver sitting in a hotel room doing nothing. And probably, as always, thinking of a past made sordid and unhappy by the unfaithfulness and cheapness of one woman—made a little happier and more bearable by two others—whom perhaps I hurt, but had to, because of inner convictions and circumstances that I could not help. Perhaps these pages will once more chronicle the events of a lonely (and last) leave.

CAMP CARSON, COLORADO
JULY 6, 1944

Well, here I am, back from leave. Had a fairly nice time. Spent quite a bit of money, but then I expected <u>that</u>.

Went out and had dinner with Colonel Smith's wife and family, and they certainly were fine people.

Believe me, I am fed up quite completely with "nightclubbing" and am sure it won't interest me for some time.

In the interim, I pray that the Good Lord will see fit to "keep an eye out for me," as it were, especially on a few of the worries that I have at the present time.

Thought of Mother a great deal on the leave and wished that I had gone home.

Looks as though we are getting into the final stages of POM preparations.

What new tomorrow?

Camp Carson, Colo.
July 7, 1944
Not too much a trying day. I was transferred to Reg'l HQ the other day, filling one of Liaison Officers T/O vacancies, now that Aronson has left the 104th Division—transferred overseas. According to the word we received, he was to have left AGF Replacement Depot #1 (Fort George Meade, Maryland), today. Well, here's all good luck to him. He was a grand guy.

Everything seems to be okay, so far, if the Good Lord above will only stand by my side for the next month or so. Guidance of the spiritual variety is needed once more, as badly as possible. Much will depend on events of the next few days, so I ask once more for all the spiritual guidance and help that is possible.

It seems about all I can do is to keep my fingers crossed, and that seems so futile that it is maddening.

Colonel Cochran rated me while I was gone and gave me a rating of "<u>Superior</u>" for my five months' work as Personnel Officer, which is something, I guess, inasmuch as I knew nothing of personnel work.

Camp Carson, Colo.
BOQ
July 8, 1944
I slept all afternoon today. Everything seems to be okay. No news from Denver. Phoned Phyllis this morning and stated it was impossible to assist in the financial jam. Don't know whether there will be any repercussions as to this, or not.

Still need spiritual assistance and guidance. Can only hope and pray on this. Am I worthy of such? Only God can help me on this, which I need more than anything in the world.

Work seems to be progressing satisfactorily at the office. Haven't written any letters since the latter part of June, nor have I <u>received</u> a great deal of mail, either.

Determined to get all of the sleep and rest that I possibly can.

Please God, give me thy guidance and succor this one time.

Camp Carson, Colo
BOQ
July 10, 1944

Just laid around all day, yesterday. Felt fairly good. Received a phone call from Phyllis. She still seems to be worried about the financial jam, but what beats me, if she was so worried, why did she fritter away the $25 she had to apply on the bill? Wants me to come up this coming weekend, but no thanks! "I think I will be stuck with Duty Officer, if I can."

Gave my soul some repose tonight and went down and played the Hammond Electric organ in the Chapel for a while. I received my lost gloves and a letter from Mrs. Smith today. Answered it and also wrote Mother a long letter.

Everything seems to be okay, so far, but am still wondering and more or less shaking in my "mental boots." Only God can divine and assist on this matter, however. So once more, as so often in the past, it is *Kismet*!

Europe seems to be the destination, from all rumors, and soon!

Camp Carson, Colorado
Personnel Office
July 11, 1944

Another day ticked away into oblivion. Today was a rather interesting day. WOJG Lauck is up for promotion to Chief Warrant Officer, and I hope he gets it. He is a nice fellow, works hard, keeps his mouth shut, and is really an A-1 assistant to have at my side. I wrote out a nice letter of recommendation for him and had Colonel Floyd sign it and then wrote out another one, which I signed myself.

Invited to a large steak fry and outing up at Captain Neilsen's cabin on this coming Friday night. Supposed to bring a girl along, but not me. I will stag it, as usual, I presume. Not a word from Phyllis up in Denver, and I hope that little episode is over. But on this, I can only keep my fingers crossed and hope. However, the break, will of necessity, have to be handled with extreme diplomacy, and therefore, I will have to phone her about tomorrow night and inquire as to the situation, as I told her I was coming up this weekend, and I will have to suddenly acquire the status of Duty Officer without too many repercussions, I hope.

Everything seems to be okay so far, but the whole situation, in general, lies in the lap of the Lord, and as fate decrees, such will be my fate. At this particular time, however, the entire situation is extremely delicate and ticklish, due to the many impending developments and changes, which are about to occur, so Lord BE WITH ME NOW, AS NEVER BEFORE.

Through the latest grapevine, we hear that the 91st Division, of which John Strahl's brother is a member, is now in England. Which reminds me, the Strahls must indeed think me a heel of the first water, for I have never written them since I closed correspondence with them late in January. Also, God knows what Margie thinks of me, severing all relationships as though cut clean with a knife, as I did. I feel sure, though, if they knew the circumstances that they would not think too hardly of me, but unfortunately, they will never know.

Had two terrifically rousing games of volleyball today, one of which was played in the midst of a terrific downpour of slashing rain and hail, and although soaked to the skin, it was fun. If I could only stop worrying, life would be so complete and full, that I feel I could actually start to enjoy it.

Now that we are definitely under orders to go overseas, I feel actually relieved. We have been fooling around here in the States for so long that I feel guilty; and all of my friends are overseas, and I just feel that I should go. It is somewhat of a puzzle to me as to how I am going to keep up this chronicle when we do go, for a record of this type is strictly against regulations.

Have got to pack all excess junk and equipment and send it home.

CAMP CARSON, COLO.
BOQ
JULY 12, 1944

Hard, hard work today. We are again being heckled by inspectors from Division. Had all 20's sent to units today to have them brought up to POM qualifications. Had to put on an additional crew of men to help—1 officer and 4 men.

Had three or four rousing games of volleyball today and won four bucks at it. Seems to enable me to sleep better. Actually beginning to feel fairly good physically. Oh my gosh, if my luck will only hold.

No word from Denver or Phyllis, as yet. Must phone tomorrow and beg off the weekend.

Have got to get organized on assembling and packing my stuff to send home.

Wonder how the staff and Colonel's party will work out this Friday night? It will probably rain as it has been doing for the past several days.

No mail at all today.

CAMP CARSON, COLO.
PERSONNEL OFFICE
JULY 13, 1944

A hectic day. Numerous difficulties occurred, which almost drove us frantic, plus the fact we are continually heckled by the ever-present inspectors.

Two more games of volleyball, which grow more and more vigorous, as each team grows more and more skilled. Doing me good, though, physically.

Wonder how the great Staff Party will turn out—steaks, rustic wooded atmosphere, liquor, and all the trimmings. But I shall stag it.

Phoned Phyllis tonight to beg off this coming weekend, but she was gone on an "overnight pass." (?)

Pruitt has returned from school and is his usual grand self—a good guy.

Guess I will write to Bob and Colonel Smith tonight. I owe them one, I think.

Must give a Company Commanders School tomorrow on the intricacies of the "Informational Roster."

CAMP CARSON, COLO.
BOQ
JULY 17, 1944

A hectic, hectic weekend. Friday night, the Regimental Staff Party. Much revelry, a good time in a sylvan setting. Much liquor consumed. Such incidents as the Colonel playing volleyball, stepping in the creek, etc. Saturday night, Clopton's wedding party. Big time at the Division Officers Club Sunday night. Pruitt invited me to his and Woodman's house. Quite a few drinks. Again, very envious of the scenes of domestic bliss, but such are not to be a part of my dreams methinks.

Much confusion and turmoil as to preparation for overseas. Packing, crating, who will go, etc. Rosters confused. Who will we lose? Who will we keep? The Colonel in a turmoil.

Vasilakes's promotion to Captain came in today (Brooklyn boy makes good).

Big argument at the Company Commanders Meeting this Saturday. Division seems to be unhappy at Personnel (415) again.

Felt like hell all today. Played volleyball (4 games), then to 2nd Bn BOQ Officers Club for 2 beers, playing the jukebox and then home. Shower, shave, shampoo.

Phyllis called from Denver (collect) and wants me to come up this weekend, <u>but</u> I think that can easily develop into somewhat of a bad deal.

The Personnel Office had its picture taken all in a group today. Hope it turns out okay.

I think I can be sure Mr. Lauck made CWO today; at least, I bought him a set of appropriate bars.

The CONFIDENTIAL movement order came in, and the readiness date is August 15th, and personally, I think we are going to England.

More tomorrow. Tired tonight and <u>need</u> the rest.

Bob? Rafferty?

Happiness?

CAMP CARSON, COLO.
BOQ
JULY 19, 1944

Forgot to mention it, but Bob made 1st Lt. on about June 24th, and nice going kid! Went to a picnic out in Stratton Park near the far-famed Broadmoor Resort. Had a boring time—all young punks. We danced the square dances, Virginia reel, etc., etc. Came back to Camp and went to the Officers Club and had a few beers. Some more examples of true marital fidelity, i.e., Capt. *** and Captain ***.

Work progressing a bit smoother. Big conference with the Chief of Staff and G-1 today. Advance party to leave on July 30th.

Played <u>six</u> games of volleyball today, and am I tired. Colonel Cochran played a game with us.

Received a letter from Phyllis today, but I still have trepidation about the deal.

Evidently God saw fit to answer my prayers, and I learned a great lesson, thereby.

Tired tonight.

<u>Got</u> to start working on my overseas packing of equipment.

Camp Carson, Colo.
July 21, 1944
Noon Hour—BOQ

Busy days again! Many men being shipped out (physically unfit, hospital cases, etc.). I don't feel quite so bad about my promotion. Three more bounced for the same reason. It's just this damned, lousy, <u>small</u> 2nd Army HQ.

Played two games of volleyball this noon and am exceedingly tired. Have to go down this noon for a physical exam—final overseas exam. Well, we are really going over this time, and now that it has finally come, I am glad—glad—and am sorry in only one respect. So many other of my fellow officers have something to come back to—a home, a family. Me? I have only bitter memories of what might have been and the ghastly present of cheap women and no one with a decent ideal. No one seems to want a home or a family.

So I guess I will board the transport with the realization that, for me, it doesn't matter at all whether I come back or not.

Kismet

Camp Carson, Colo.
BOQ
Sunday evening
July 23, 1944

Stayed home this weekend—worked yesterday afternoon. Went to the Club last night and met a nice nurse, Lt. Vivian Montagne. Nice kid, and I think I will take her to the "grand ball" of the 415th Regiment, which takes place this coming Friday night.

A letter from Phyllis today. Says she is going overseas again and wants me to be sure and come up. I don't know. Lt. Moen wants to have a last final fling in Denver, so I may do so.

Packed quite a few of the articles that I am going to send home—1 footlocker crammed full.

So much work up at Personnel, that we don't know which way to turn. All I can do, as so often in the past, is to rely on the Good Lord for guidance and help.

Feel pretty good physically.

May go fishing on this coming Tuesday.

Camp Carson, Colo.
BOQ
July 24, 1944
Worked late tonight and accomplished much today—I hope. More or less set on crates and am one jump ahead of them on rosters.

We received the C-O-N-F-I-D-E-N-T-I-A-L movement order today. We leave here August 15th for the Port of Embarkation (Camp Kilmer, New Jersey) and should take to the transports on about the 25th of August. So here we go, at last!

I have determined to go to Denver this weekend and will probably see Phyllis, I imagine. Will also attend the big Regimental dance this coming Friday. I am feeling in fairly good fettle physically, of late.

Big conference with Ol' Cochran, of late. He still seems to accept my decision and word in practically every matter of "state" that occurs.

Have got to ship my things home before long and get set in every respect.

Camp Carson, Colo.
BOQ
July 30, 1944
Much has happened since I last wrote. Have been working like a veritable demon. Not too much mail, however, with the mountainous series of confusing orders issuing from Div. HQ.

Met an awfully nice nurse about 5 nights ago and have seen her about three times in that period. She is _really_ nice. _Very_ attractive, blonde, pleasant personality, and all in all, a swell kid. Of course, it is typical of my luck that I meet such a person on about my last month in the States. Her name? Lt. Vivian Montagne, age 22.

Teeth have been bothering me to beat hell, but I think I am winning the battle.

A few complications with the clique at Division.

I must start shipping my things home and
Soon!

Camp Carson, Colo.
BOQ
Aug. 1, 1944
Montagne and I went to the show and then to the Club on Sunday. We have a date this Friday, and if all works out okay, we will go into

Colorado Springs and have dinner with Lt. and Mrs. Pruitt. Heard indirectly that she "likes me quite a bit." The feeling is certainly mutual. She really caused quite a bit of comment among my fellow officers, for frankly, she is one of the prettiest nurses I have ever seen. Beauty yes! But evidently <u>not</u> skin deep as in another instance. She doesn't drink, is a swell sport (imagine walking 3 miles to a dance!), and likes athletics and swimming. When I asked her ambition in life: "To lead a normal, happy life." And that is really nice.

Again, I reiterate, however, I would have to meet her during my last month in the States.

Kismet, I guess.

CAMP CARSON, COLO.
BOQ
AUGUST 6, 1944

Sap McCully. Sucker (again) McCully. <u>Fool</u> McCully. Why in <u>hell</u> was I born with a damnable idealistic nature, so fashioned that at the least provocation I commence building wild, sloppily romantic and sticky, sentimental daydreams? We have (Montagne and I) been going out almost continually, and last night at the dance, I casually asked her if she was engaged, and she replied in the affirmative. I rather expected that reply, but <u>why</u> couldn't she have been honest and aboveboard about the thing from the start? Why didn't she wear his ring if (as they are supposed to) it represents so much?

I had already dated her for swimming today, and so would not break it, of course, but after today, *Le affaire Femme* is *FINIS*.

Henceforth, for the remaining 12 days that we are at Carson, I shall not stir from this Camp, shall pack, and get all in readiness to leave here, and shall go on board the transport with the knowledge that life is a damnable farce, and I am one of the many to whom it means <u>nothing</u>.

CAMP CARSON, COLO.
BOQ
AUG. 7, 1944

A rather miserable day, typical blue Monday, I guess. We went to the Broadmoor yesterday and had a fairly good time but had still a better time when we left early and came back to the Division Club. Guess Monty is sincere all right. She felt quite badly about the fact that she hadn't told me sooner. It was really my fault, I guess. I rushed in like an impetuous fool and practically asked for it.

Miserably hot today—gig sheets, work, work, work—packing to worry about. It will be a relief to get on the boat. Guess I will be in New Jersey two weeks from now. And next month? A letter from Mom. She is going to spend some time in San Francisco. I wish she wouldn't; it wears her out so.

Funny thing, but I was quite happy for a little while. It seemed so good. I haven't been very happy since 1939.

CAMP CARSON, COLO.
BOQ
11:30 P.M., AUG. 8, 1944

Ten more days remaining in Colorado. Went to town tonight with Moen. The gals called up and invited us in. <u>They</u> paid for the dinner <u>and</u> the evening. Had a nice dinner and then returned to Camp and went to the Officers Club and danced. Had dinner at a spot in Manitou. Monty is really a wonderful girl. Guess I am just destined not to meet someone like her. If she wasn't already attached, it wouldn't be hard to go overboard.

Friday will be a holiday, so we hear, and I intend to pack and get set. Going to the dance tomorrow night with Monty. Moen will be on a night problem.

Things running fairly smooth at the office. Haven't heard much from the old man.

Haven't heard from Bob or Rafferty for a long, long time.

Guess Mom is in S.F.

We leave the 18th, and I hope we don't go to Europe. I hope it's Burma or Asia someplace.

CAMP CARSON, COLO.
BOQ (NOON HOUR)
AUG. 10, 1944

The place is a madhouse! We were suddenly alerted last night, and the date of departure has been moved up—Aug. 16th. I had borrowed Pruitt's car and took Monty to the show and then went to the dance at the Club, where Moen and Kay soon joined. Had still another wonderful evening, albeit a trifle sad at the knowledge that it was probably the last.

Knowing Monty has been a wonderful thing and has served somewhat to renew, a bit, my faith in womanhood.

A madhouse, particularly at the office, and if I ever manage to get on the boat, what a sign of relief will be forthcoming.

Moen and I had planned, if possible, to go to the Club again tonight, but unless I accomplish a helluva lot this afternoon, it may prove impossible.

Camp Carson, Colo.
August 11, 1944

"D-Day" has arrived. I am all packed and shall send home all my excess equipment this afternoon. Administration classes tomorrow at noon, and my train leaves at 1330 on August 16, 1944. So here I go at last, and it is with these thoughts that I close Volume III of my life in the Army. Whether a Volume IV is ever written, or not, depends on many things, for restrictions on diaries overseas are fierce. Then, too, circumstances and time may not permit, and even if it is written, the length of it will depend on fate.

If I return from over there, no one but my eyes will ever read again these pages, but if I do not return, I hope the person who reads them will not hold up to ridicule the thoughts of a somewhat lonely person. Fate hasn't been too kind in the last few years, and perhaps I am too prone to record only my worries and troubles, but writing in these books has given me a comfort and solace past understanding.

I thought for a while that fate would, at last, relent and give me someone with whom to plan a future life, someone to bring me home as it were, but life doesn't seem to hold such for me, so I go overseas with the deep conviction that it doesn't matter too much whether I come back or not.

[Remaining pages of the journal report personal financial status (e.g., assets, pay, disbursements, monetary gain, War Bonds purchased, loans to fellow soldiers, and notes) from January through August, 1944.]

[A map of the United States, marked with key locations, was pasted to the inside back cover of the journal.]

Photographs

*Ernie McCully: Outer Harbor,
Oakland, California, 1936*

*Ernie McCully (far right): "The gang" at Mother's Cakes.
Stag party, 1936*

Ernie McCully: On horseback near Wildcat Canyon, Richmond, California, circa 1935–1937

Ernie McCully: Lakeside Park, Oakland, California, 1937

Ernie McCully: Oregon or Washington, circa 1937–1938

Ernie McCully: Oregon or Washington, circa 1937–1938

Captain E.J. McCully:
Date and location unknown

Captain E.J. McCully:
European Theater circa 1944–1945

Captain E.J. McCully:
European Theater circa 1944–1945

Photographs   385

E.J. McCully:
Rank, date, and location unknown

Captain E.J. McCully:
Leipzig, Germany, circa June 1945

Demobilization Ceremonies of the 415th Regiment, San Luis Obispo, California, September 1945.
First Row: Lt. General Walter Krueger, Major General Terry Allen, Colonel John Cochran.
Second Row: Captain E. J. McCully, Unknown, Unknown.

"Mac" McCully: With future wife Emily, Phoenix, Arizona, circa 1946–1947

The six journals of E.J. McCully

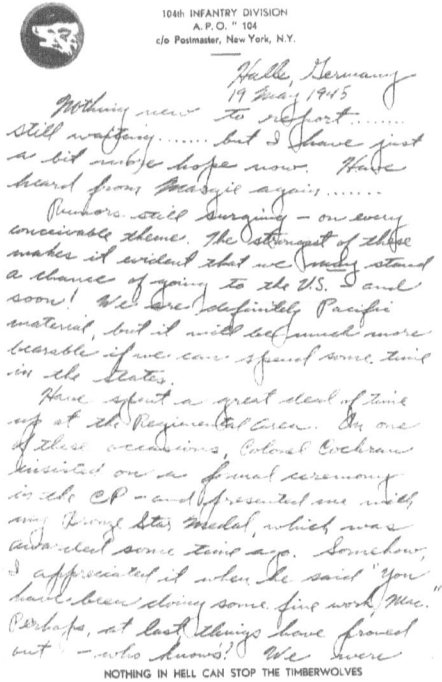

Warburg, Germany
14 April 1945

Another tortuous pilgrimage has been added to the list. Upon Mr. Lauck's return from the Rhine, I determined to try and catch up with regiment and, at the same time, shuttle a small advance party and a trailer load of equipment to the new location of the AG at Weende. We left at about 1030 the next morning, with a total of five men in the jeep, and an exceedingly fully trailer. For the trip forward we elected to use the route that we had discovered on the trip to Odelsheim, and after crossing the Weser, made our way down a miserable network of roads that had been literally torn to pieces by the continual pounding of our tanks. The engineers were endeavoring to repair them, but even so we were forced to travel in compound low range for a period of over seven miles, during which time I held my breath for fear that the trailer would overturn. About 1230 we arrived at the new location, at Gottingen. Without a doubt, but for the fact that it is still so far behind the regiments, it is the best location we have ever had. It is another military school, this time xx a German Cavalry OCS, and they left in such a hurry that there was no time to destroy anything, and therefore it is in excellent condition. Here, I dropped the trailer, and unloaded the two men who composed the Advance Party. The driver, Stansbury, and myself then immediately set out to find regiment. Again we battled the endless conveys and the stifling clouds of dust, for mile upon mile, passing village after village who now displayed the new National Flag of Germany - the white flag of surrender. At some points on the roads we passed columns of trucks heading back along the road and filled with captured German prisoners of war. Some of the more spirited burghers would display a bit of defiance and wave to the prisoners, who, of course, would wave back. I wonder how they like Blitzkrieg, now? I found the Division Command Post at Duderstadt, just in the process of moving out, but was fortunate in spotting Colonel Rex, the G-1, who showed me his Operations Map, and I was thus enabled to find the approximate location of the regiment. We immediately left and about 1630 entered Nordhausen, which had only been captured a few hours, and was still in a great state of confusion. The city had suffered heavily through our extensive artillery and bombing, and all of the principal streets and roads were practically impassable. We finally found the Regimental CP on the outskirts of Nordhausen, only to find them lined

Sample typewritten page from one of the six journals of E.J. McCully

Sample handwritten page from one of the six journals of E.J. McCully

"On the Bluffs at Callan." Sketch by E.J. McCully while at Camp Callan in the San Diego area. Found on the inside back cover of one of his journals.

War Department Identification Card for 1st Lieutenant Ernest J. McCully, July 7, 1944

Journal 5

VOLUME IV CONTINUED
September 3, 1944 to February 25, 1945
Ages 28–29

A beautiful sunny day,
the sky filled with lacy streamers of fluffy clouds,
birds in the trees, tinkling their melody of happiness
against the walls of this convent.
But down below, Man in his bestial ignorance
turns all his ingenuity and cunning,
acquired so laboriously through the centuries,
into more efficient devices
and means of killing one another.
The earth drips blood . . .

VOLUME IV (CONTINUED)

BEING A CONTINUATION OF THE RECORDING
OF HAPPENINGS AND EVENTS THAT OCCURRED DURING
THE COURSE OF MY FOURTH YEAR
IN THE ARMY OF THE UNITED STATES.

SEPTEMBER 3, 1944

LANDING AT UTAH BEACH IN NORMANDY • 13 AMERICAN SOLDIERS KILLED • ADMINISTRATIVE INSPECTION AND SCENES OF WAR • NIGHTLIFE • LIFEBLOOD OF MAIL • MARCHING AND RAIL TRANSPORT ACROSS FRANCE AND BELGIUM • SCENES OF DESTRUCTION AND IMPRESSIONS OF THE FRENCH • PROMOTION TO CAPTAIN • ENCOUNTER WITH BELGIAN MAQUIS • 415TH BATTLE CASUALTIES • MOVE TO HOLLAND • TRANSPORT OF REPLACEMENTS TO FRONT • FRUSTRATIONS WITH ARMY "EFFICIENCY" • DRIVING BLACKOUT OVER UNKNOWN ROADS • REFLECTIONS OVER PAST 5 YEARS • BIG PUSH • STRUGGLES WITH PERSONNEL WORK QUOTAS • VIVIAN GIVES BIRTH • REFLECTIONS ON MARRIAGE • FRIENDS KIA • COURTS-MARTIAL • OPINION OF 4-F CIVILIANS • GERMAN PROPAGANDA • AUTOBAHNEN • AIR RAIDS • CHRISTMAS 1944 • THOUGHTS ON EMPLOYMENT AFTER THE WAR • UPDATE ON THE WAR • MERITS OF THE U.S. ARMY • ANTICIPATION OF FINAL BREAKTHROUGH INTO GERMANY • MORE COURTS-MARTIAL • MORE THOUGHTS ON LIFE AFTER THE WAR • MAMA'S BOYS • GI BILL • CROSSING THE ROER RIVER

AT SEA—NORTH ATLANTIC
3 SEPTEMBER 1944

With this entry, Volume IV of the somewhat tedious happenings that have occurred since my entry into the Army continues. The last entry in Volume III was written on August 11, 1944, nearly a month ago, and it is with good reason, indeed, that there have been no entries in the interim. We left Carson on a troop train on August 16, 1944, and after a long, dirty, and very smoky trip through the Eastern States, arrived at Camp Kilmer, New Jersey (named in honor of the famous World War I poet, Joyce Kilmer), on the 19th of August. The night prior to leaving Camp Carson, Lt. Moen and I had our farewell dates with Montagne and Dorsey at the North Haven Officers Club in Camp Carson.

At Kilmer, I was driven frantic with the many sudden requests for rosters, inadequate supplies, and the stupid and inefficient manner of handling the final processing of our unit. At long last, however, we boarded the train at Kilmer on August 26th, and after a series of unfortunate accidents with that damnable "Val-Pak" of mine, which, weighing approximately 75 pounds, chose the time when I was stepping off the train to break its handle. Panting and cursing, I practically drug the damn thing down to the Hoboken Ferry, where fortunately, I obtained a piece of wire and a pair of pliers from a friendly crew-member and made some hasty repairs. We arrived at the pier at about

2200 hours (sped on our way up the gangplank by a somewhat tired-looking WAC band). We boarded the *USAT Cristobal* (a former Panama liner), which, being a comparatively modern boat (built in 1939), gave us some truly luxurious quarters, at least insofar as the officers were concerned. I think the average GI had quite a rough time of it down below, for a transport is very crowded and uncomfortable, at the best. We had only two days of what might be termed rough weather, and although a goodly portion of the personnel aboard ship became quite seasick, I managed to retain my sea legs. The days have been spent in interminable "abandon ship" and air raid drills, and while boring and very monotonous, are an ever-present necessity. We have been out approximately eight days now, and from what I can learn, we should reach our destination in about three days more. The most plausible rumor seems to have it that we will disembark at Cherbourg, France—so, in that event, it is a foregone conclusion that we will very probably go directly into combat . . .

Of course, I have received no mail since leaving New York, and only one letter was received there—from Mother, who had evidently received my WDAGO card informing her of my change of address. If we go directly to France, all chances of seeing Bob at any time are, of course, nullified. Rafferty, too, is in France, but as luck will have it, he will probably be in some distant sector of operations. I have spent quite some time at night, on deck, gazing at an enormous amber moon weaving a tracery of gold across the inky black waters and thinking, thinking, what my life could have been, but isn't. And all of the time so lonely, so unutterably lonely, that truly, from here on, as never before, my life becomes even more pointless and with absolutely no meaning.

BIVOUAC NEAR VALOGNES, FRANCE
12 SEPTEMBER 1944

We left the *USAT Cristobal* in a LCI (Landing Craft Infantry) on the evening of September 7, 1944, and were taken to one of the invasion beaches [Utah]. The landing craft ran aground on a sand bar, unfortunately, and we spent a wet, miserable, six hours in it until the tide rose sufficiently to free it. About midnight, we marched off on a partially submerged gangplank, loaded down with all of our equipment. My first step into France was a step into an oozy, black, quagmire of mud, and thus started a nightmare of rain, knee-deep mud, freezing cold, and continuous marching with unbearably heavy packs. We marched over these muddy roads until 0330 in the morning and then arrived in the area where trucks were supposed to pick us up. Due to poor planning, however, the trucks did not start until nearly 0700, and for that four hours, we sat and froze. At 0700 we were taken to another area in the trucks and were then directed to our bivouac (another march of 5 miles) where we arrived at about 1030.

At present, we are camped in a little meadow and nearby forest near the little French hamlet of Montagu. Valognes, the next largest town from here, is about 10 miles distant. This area is a particularly beautiful section of Normandy, but the utter desolation of war shows everywhere, as this area is where some of the hardest fighting took place during the invasion. The city of Montebourg, in particular, is a crumbling ruin, and its surrounding terrain is pitted with huge craters left by the shells of the 16-inch guns on the Allied battleships.

The French people in this area seem friendly enough, albeit a bit poverty stricken, for when the Germans left, they took everything. The natives will do anything for soap or American cigarettes.

The old man again submitted my promotion to higher headquarters, and if nothing unforeseen occurs, I may soon be a Captain. However, I certainly don't intend to get excited about it this time. Experiences are a lesson!

BIVOUAC NEAR VALOGNES, FRANCE
14 SEPTEMBER 1944
Still in the same locality, but we leave in a few days for an area near Barneville, France. It is only a short way from here and is still on the Cherbourg Peninsula. What we shall do there remains a mystery, as it is a "rest, recreation and rehabilitation area." However, it makes no difference to me, as the work of Personnel goes on regardless.

Received a letter from Bob, and he evidently thought I was in England, but there is no chance of seeing him, I know. He talked of returning to the U.S. before very long.

Still feel fine, physically, although today is a gloomy, dreary day.

BIVOUAC NEAR VALOGNES, FRANCE
15 SEPTEMBER 1944
Evidently, fall has arrived in France—with a vengeance. The sky is as black as ink, dead and fallen leaves are scurrying before a fitful, gusty wind, which carries a heavy portent of the coming rains. We are still

in bivouac, but I imagine we move soon, as the quartering party leaves this afternoon to lay out the new area. Was listening to several of the French and German radio stations this noon. The war news sounds good for the Allied cause, and it makes one wonder how long this damnable war will continue. Feel fairly good physically. My promotion has cleared division already—I wonder what the verdict will be from the CG, 9th Army.

Bivouac near Valognes, France
16 September 1944
Still in bivouac. There are several factors, which tend to cast a pall of apprehension over life in general, at present. For one thing, the situation concerning finances, pay, allotments, bonds, etc., is considerably confused, and I hope to goodness this is straightened out before very long. Popular rumor now has it that the 415th will be detached and sent on a special mission. In which case, what will be the disposition of Personnel? Rear echelon, or--? No mail at all, and I doubt if there is much point in anticipating any, at present. Played several games of rugged volleyball today and gave my men the afternoon off. No news at all of my pending promotion, but then it is a question as to how long it will take it to be processed through the administrative channels over here. I do not anticipate any approval—accustomed as I am. It grows steadily colder daily. More tomorrow.

Bivouac near Valognes, France
18 September 1944
A typically, rainy, OREGON day! It has been dark, cold, and gloomy throughout the day with intermittent heavy showers, and by tonight, I guess it has settled down to a continuous downpour. Tonight would be ideal for writing letters—if I had someone to write to. I have already written about four to Mother, however, and two or three to Bob and Harold, and those people are about the extent of my correspondents until fate decrees otherwise. I dread creeping into my bedroll tonight, for I know it will be clammy and damp not having had the opportunity to air and sun it properly. Much unhappiness on the part of the Company Commanders about the messed-up financial situation, but that is something that is out of my hands and cannot be helped. No word on promotion as yet . . .

BIVOUAC NEAR VALOGNES, FRANCE
19 SEPTEMBER 1944

It rained all last night, and was I miserable in that clammy "sack"! Cleared up around noon today, so I took the opportunity to air it out good. I sent a $100 money order to the bank today, for tomorrow is payday, and I could see no sense in packing around some 10,0000 francs, when it is almost impossible to spend even five of them. Besides, from now on, I am going to be in dead earnest in building up my bank account to a substantial figure so that I can buy the home that I always figured on having when this horrible mess is over with.

We move this coming Monday. The 415th will have the mission of guarding the line of communications, supply, power dams, reservoirs, gasoline pipeline that supplies the front and other such installations all over the Normandy Base Section. It means that the Regiment will be scattered all over Normandy, but the Headquarters (and Personnel) will be stationed at Valognes itself.

Still no mail as yet, and still no word on the promotions, except that mine was one of those that went forward from Division HQ on the 15th. Financial situation still in a mess, and higher headquarters don't seem able to clarify it any.

BIVOUAC NEAR VALOGNES, FRANCE
20 SEPTEMBER 1944

We were highly honored tonight and had as guests at the dinner table Major General Terry Allen, the Division Commander, and Brigadier General Moore, the Assistant Division Commander. At the conclusion of the dinner, General Allen gave a short talk of the variety, PEP, and the advisability of achieving well our present mission of guard duty in the southern sector of the Normandy Base Section.

Captain Smith went to Valognes today to lay out the new Regimental HQ, and from the tales he brought back, it must be quite a nice set-up. Cots will be available (off this damnable damp ground at last) and a building in which to house the personnel office. Will know better when I see it myself.

I for one will be extremely pleased to leave this bivouac, for showers will be available, and while the administrative procedure may prove to be a bit messed up due to the wide dispersion of the various elements of the Regiment, all in all, I think it will, in effect, prove to be a return to some semblance of civilization . . .

I sent home, today, money orders in the amount of $170 and a personal check for $15, so the old "home fund" is really building up, and another payday is due in about 10 or 12 days. I may as well do this, for I have absolutely no use for money over here; the only outstanding expense I have in mind being an officer's trench coat, complete with hood. Probably about $35—AND IT WILL BE WORTH IT.

The messed up financial condition is beginning to clear up, and I have hopes of obliterating it completely in a week or so . . .

Still no news on the promotion . . .

Bivouac near Valognes, France
22 September 1944

Another exceedingly busy day. Attended a meeting at Finance this morning, which took up the major part of the morning. Worked steadily all afternoon on Class E allotments and am happy to say that, for the most part, the financial mess is beginning to straighten itself out.

One point of interest—all of the promotions were returned to Division today, not approved, and not disapproved, but due to an administrative error on the part of Division, they will have to be resubmitted on the 1st of October.

Also found out that the reason many others and I have been receiving no mail is because of another "administrative error" committed by Division.

We received (that is, the Officers) another liquor ration allowance today—two large bottles of wine, which formerly were part of an old French chateau which had been plentifully stocked by the Germans and abandoned in the hasty retreat of the German Army. I don't particularly care for wine, although this is vintage of 1939, supposedly a very good year for wine. It didn't cost us a cent. On our previous allowance, we were allowed to purchase one fifth of Scotch (Dewar's White Label) and a pint of gin (Gordon's), both for the truly astounding price of $2.30. I always feel a trifle guilty at the time of the distribution of the liquor, for the enlisted men know it is being distributed, of course, and they are not given any. Guess I haven't reached a sufficiently hard degree of mental stamina.

Had a long talk with Captain Smith tonight, who had evidently had a long talk with Colonel Cochran earlier in the day, regarding the Personnel Office and its functions. From what I can gather, the Colonel is evidently highly satisfied with the operation of the Personnel Section, feels that it is now operating better than at any time since Camp Adair, is pleased with the attitude and industry of the clerks, and in general, thinks that we are doing a good job and now have it worked down into a system. This of course, is highly satisfying to me, although I myself am not satisfied with the actual operation of the office and do not feel that we have as good a system as can yet be effected.

We move soon (probably day after tomorrow, or at the latest, Monday), and I shall now be doubly glad to depart, for it is again raining violently, and I can again look forward to a night spent in a clammy bedroll. For I neglected to air the bedding this morning, when the sun managed to peep through the overcast for a few short hours.

More tomorrow . . .

IN QUARTERS, NEAR CHATEAU, FRANCE
26 SEPTEMBER 1944

We finally moved. And, for a change, an opportune time was selected in which to make it. It started to rain as we loaded the trucks and drizzled discouragingly throughout the trip, which took a little over an hour. We are truly fortunate participants of this war, at least so far. We are located in the precincts of an old French chateau and what formerly served as the Headquarters of the erstwhile "Desert Fox" Rommel while he was supreme commander of the German forces in this area prior to the invasion. We are billeted in what are termed "hutments" but, which to us, after the rigors of the soggy French meadows and dripping forests of recent date, seem like paradise. They are not bad at all—warm, dry, and quite spacious. Immediately upon arrival, the Personnel Section started to set up, and by the means of numerous foraging expeditions into property barracks of an adjoining outfit, enriched our equipment to the extent of three large field desks, suitable tables and chairs, and the like. This evidently, today, caused the adjoining outfit some mental anguish, but we, of course, were naturally unsympathetic and ignorant of the whereabouts of their property.

The chateau itself was evidently, at one time, one of the showplaces of France. The grounds are enormous with countless lush meadows, rolling green swards, and parkways. Although I have yet to see the building itself (which I intend to do tomorrow), I hear it is really palatial, and the cost of the statuary alone must have run into millions. What is more important at the moment, however, is the fact that showers were available to us today, and I treated myself to a thorough scrubbing, shampoo, shave, and a complete change of clothes, at the termination of which I felt like another man. It is wonderful what a little soap and water will do . . .

Disaster struck our Regiment today, and prior even to its actual entry into combat, which makes it seem all the more horrible. One of my close friends, Lt. Wood of the AT Company, had taken his platoon down to the beach near St. Marcouf to give them some training and to investigate some of the abandoned German pillboxes, which dot the beach. During the course of their investigating something went wrong, no one knows what. Whether it had been cleverly booby trapped, carelessness, as to just what the circumstances were, no one will ever know, but a tongue of flame some 200 feet long shot out of the pillbox, roasting alive some 13 members of the platoon, including Lt. Wood, and shortly thereafter, a tremendous explosion took place. Identification of the corpses was, of course, difficult. The ensuing paperwork, investigation, and red tape should keep me busy for weeks to come. I had seen, talked, and joked with Wood on the morning that the accident occurred, and it seems as though his last pleasantries still ring in my ears, for he was a likable chap.

IN QUARTERS, NEAR CHATEAU, FRANCE
29 SEPTEMBER 1944
I haven't written for some time, but my prediction concerning the administrative red tape connected with the deaths of the 14 men in the Anti-Tank Company came true—and how we have worked!

I have one gala event to record—I received a letter! From Mother, written on September 7, 1944, and she was not yet aware that I was in France. She sent word that Bob had received three oak leaf clusters to his Air Medal, and was expecting to return home soon. Believe me, there is a brother to be proud of!

We are certainly enjoying our present sojourn in semi-civilized surroundings, what with chicken two or three times a week, and steak at least twice. I wonder how long this will last? Seems to be a sort of stalemate at the front.

A group of our Staff Officers observed the fighting around Brest just before its capitulation, and I had an opportunity to see one of the operations maps used during that operation. The first symbol that smote my eyes was the CP symbol of the 38th Infantry—Hubie Rafferty's outfit.

Upon investigating a little further, I discovered that his outfit is now at Landerneau, France, which as near as I can figure out is near Brest and approximately 200 miles south of here. I can see no way of contacting him at the present time, and even if I could, I would not, until the disposition of my recommendation for promotion becomes known. Incidentally, I had an opportunity to view the one that was returned, and it had been approved all the way, and Terry Allen's sprawling signature was in the most prominent view. They are to be resubmitted on the day after tomorrow, so within one month I should know, one way or the other. How I hope that it goes through without a hitch, for it opens up at least 15 of my former correspondents with whom I ceased corresponding last January; and believe me, over here, mail is as important as blood plasma, and then some. On all of this, however, as so often in the past, only fate can decide, and no doubt will.

Physically, I have been feeling very well, and sleep comes more easily now, since yesterday I had an opportunity to completely sun and air my bedding. Rumors of a forthcoming party (complete with women and dancing) at the 68th General Hospital this coming Saturday night. This, however, I think is mostly rumor.

IN QUARTERS, NEAR CHATEAU, FRANCE
1 OCTOBER 1944

The first of October already! How time does fly! Other than one more letter from Mother, dated September 7th, and a statement from the bank, I have received utterly no mail of any kind. Had occasion to check on another lieutenant's promotion last night and find that all of the promotions have again been resubmitted, and by now, have probably cleared Division, so I should soon be hearing of the results, if any. It rained violently last night, the whole night through, but this morning dawned bright and clear, and it turned into a wondrous Indian summer day. Being Sunday, I relaxed for a change, finished two books, and played three or four violent games of volleyball with the medics. Was whipped to a "fare-you-weell," too, I might add. There are rumors of our being assigned to another Corps . . . which are supposed to definitely be Army of Occupation, which would mean at least another couple of years in the Army.

The endless red tape caused by the catastrophe in AT Company is more or less cleared and out of the way I hope, at least until the records started to be processed through ETOUSA.

I think I shall remake my bed tonight and turn in fairly early. I have been feeling quite fine physically but should get more rest.

I have quite a bit of work ahead of me tomorrow, and to be truthful, this present-wide dispersion of units of this command all over the Normandy Base Section complicates no end the prompt and efficient submission of reports...

In Quarters, near Chateau, France
3 October 1944

An interesting interlude has taken place. I decided to make an "Administrative Inspection" of our scattered units; and so yesterday, I obtained a jeep, provisioned it with emergency rations and gas, obtained a driver, and decided to take along a clerk of mine, who I knew would enjoy the trip. I obtained several clips of ammunition for my carbine (certain elements of the French population are none too friendly in the vicinity of St. Lô, and there is still considerable sabotage being carried on). We started out about 1300, passed through Valognes, St. Sauveur, La Haye Du Puits, Lessay, Coutances, Orval, Bréhal, Bréville, and ultimately arrived at our destination—Granville, where the old outfit of mine (Joe Blow's own) is stationed.

The pastoral beauty of the picturesque Norman countryside was beautiful to see, and in time of peace would have been breathtaking, but marred as it is by the destruction and utter chaos of war, scattered along the road were grim reminders of the death struggle that has but recently quieted in this area. Wrecked German "Tiger" tanks, with the swastika still glaring malevolently at the passerby, huge trucks burned and crumpled, a C-57 transport plane, which was a huge, charred, and battered hulk. We passed field after field of poles strung with wire, which the Germans had laboriously planted, to frustrate (in vain) the landings of our gliders. Wrecked Bren gun carriers, and here and there, remnants of American trucks. Huge craters from the heavy aerial bombardment yawned cavernously from every side of the road, and we passed group after group of the German prisoners of war toiling away, repairing the bridges, which they themselves, in all probability, had destroyed. The little town of Lessay, in particular, seemed to have been hard hit. Its streets were filled with mountainous piles of rubble, and not a house seemed to have been spared the merciless gunfire. Even so, the French people were living in these frameworks, trying to clear away the rubble, and endeavoring to pursue a somewhat normal, if scanty, existence.

We arrived in Granville about 1700 in the afternoon, and by the way, the town seems to have been spared the utter destruction that prevailed in all of the other towns. After inquiring of the military police, we drove to the Hotel Normandy, and as I stepped out of the jeep, who should I see but my old and hated enemy, JOE BLOW. He was all goody-goody, however, and I found that I would not have to go out to that unit's area, as Captain Hall was in town, and I could conclude my business with him. After seeing that the two enlisted men would be taken care of at the Grand Hotel, and that the jeep would be parked in the MP parking lot (under guard), I returned to the Normandy Hotel; and after assuring them that I was on official business (and showing them my identification card), I was allowed to register. This particular hotel must have been a tourist's paradise in its day, for it is a large, ornate, massive thing, placed directly on the English Channel. I was given a room on the fourth floor, and I was glad that I was only staying overnight, for I would have had legs developed like those of a mountain goat in a week's time. (The elevator was not functioning.) I collapsed on the bed (A REAL BED) and slept until about 1830, at which time I went down to the dining room for dinner. To my horror, I was trapped at the same table with Joe Blow, and that fact spoilt an otherwise pleasant meal. Had some difficulty with the French waitress but managed enough to get by, and escaped from Blow as soon as possible. I met Lt. Leonard and Lt. Green in the lobby, and we were intent on seeing as much of the nightlife as yet prevailed (the Officers Club in the Casino had been declared off limits only the night before my arrival) when Leonard was trapped by Joe Blow and his yawping mouth. Lt. Green and I forthwith deserted Leonard to his fate, and headed for town. We stopped in several of the local bistros but the most pleasing was one termed "Le Frigate" with the furnishing done with a marine motif. Whether this club was an imitation or an adaptation of an American nightclub, I don't know, but it was so tiny that the Yanks present had a difficult time, as their heads were continually banging the low-hanging chandeliers. The hostess was a huge blond, I would judge in her late thirties or early forties, and her long tresses were ensnared in a tremendous snood, which for all the world reminded me of the tail of a beaver. The only drinks available were Cidre (pronounced seeder) and a horrendous concoction known in this vicinity as Calvados, famed for its ability to blind the human eye and turn them into bestial roaring drunks. After about three drinks of this, I could see why. Of course, there had to be the usual drunken, soused, enlisted man, who seems to be present at every bar, who, upon the sight of the uniform of an officer, at once is stricken with an utmost sense of inferiority and must inevitably hang over your chair and elevate his pride by telling you about his brother who is a Captain (usually promoted to a Major General before the evening is over). This particular phenomenon is prevalent in the United States, too, for I noticed it every time that I had a leave. But I wander from the tale.

I made the mistake of ordering a sandwich from the hostess (through the aid of a French civilian, who acted as an interpreter), and to my utter dismay, I found that the Norman conception of a sandwich differs vastly from ours. She returned from the kitchen in a short time, with a loaf of hard French bread, the halves of which were lavishly spread with butter, and inserted between the halves were numerous slices of what looked like salami (or what is vulgarly termed in this Regiment, "swinging meat"), of which we had an overabundance while on maneuvers. I still do not know what this stupendous concoction cost, for it was Lt. Green's turn to foot the bill, and while he was trying to determine the number of francs that he owed, I slipped a little packet of tissue paper with the label, "WALDORF'S," in prominent view, onto his pile of franc notes. The result was that when Lt. Green invited the waitress to "pick out as much as she needed," she picked up the little packet with an extremely puzzled air. Needless to say, Green's confusion was something to behold.

We left Granville at about 0900 and nothing untoward happened until we approached Lessay, where a tremendous downpour drenched us until we approached the outskirts of Cherbourg. (I was to contact 3rd Bn HQ in this location, but as I had no idea where it was, some four hours were consumed in searching for it.) At long last, however, my business was completed, and we left Cherbourg and delivered ourselves to the God of Traffic that must surely preside over those souls who travel the Valognes-Cherbourg Road. It is a veritable madhouse with Negroes driving everything from a 2-1/2-ton truck to a 10-ton wrecker at well over 50 miles per hour (and believe me, these French roads would be termed <u>lanes</u> in the U.S.).

We arrived back at the area at about 1700, in time for supper. And so, tired and happy, tonight I look forward to a good night's rest. And I think the trip did me a lot of good.

IN QUARTERS, NEAR CHATEAU, FRANCE
6 OCTOBER 1944

Well, we leave our little paradise shortly, on about the 10th to be exact. The 415th Infantry has been relieved of its lowly guard duty and MP detail. We rejoin the Division in the area near Barneville, France, and from sources all my own, I understand that we will soon be traveling north, towards the front lines. Certainly okay by me. As long a time as this Division has been training, it is about time that we saw some action.

Received a letter from Mother and Harold today, and that little item served to boost my morale considerably. I wrote them a nice long reply, and I hope that this is only the beginning of a long series of letters yet to come. Still no answer to my three letters to Bob, and very probably, by now, he is on his way home. *C'est La Guerre*, I guess.

I took the ride to Barneville this morning to attend a meeting at Division Headquarters for all Personnel Officers and Regimental S-1's. Had dinner at the Division Officers Mess, and returned to the area about 1300. Not much to do today, but as soon as we arrive in the new area, I must present a school for all Company Commanders, 1st Sergeants, Bn S-1's, etc., on Battle Casualty Reporting. I acquired yet another tent for the Personnel Section today, namely, what is known as a "small wall tent." I figure that Lauck and I can use it as sleeping quarters when we get set up in rear echelon, for it will be very much more comfortable than a pup tent, especially in view of the fact that I intend to take my folding cot along with me, thus getting that damned sack of mine off the cold ground.

I think my promotion was submitted to Division on the 29th of September, and as today is the 6th of October, it should not be too long a time until I hear one way or the other on it, depending on how long it takes to process it through channels. I still don't anticipate its approval, as I have said before, due to my extensive experience along such lines before.

It has been raining almost continuously for the past week or so, marked by extremely high winds and bitterly cold weather. For tomorrow, however, I hope it dawns bright and clear, for it is Saturday, and we will have the afternoon off, and I intend to put out the tremendous stack of dirty laundry that has accumulated.

As for Mud! This French variety has a particular gooey, slimy, slippery quality all its own and is about ankle deep.

Work seems to be progressing satisfactorily, in general, and all of my equipment is now in good shape—all marked, boxed for convenient loading and unloading, etc. It seems my only big worry that I may have when we do get into a combat situation is Battle Casualty Reporting and possibly the matter of pay.

Bivouac, ¾ miles SW of Barneville
10 October 1944

Haven't written for some time—and with good reason—have been extremely busy getting set up in this new area and also in obtaining last-minute additional equipment.

We are encamped in another of the numberless French meadows, an old apple orchard to be exact, and it is not too bad. I exchanged our two pyramidal tents for one large "squad" tent, and it is a bit more roomy than the other arrangement. We also obtained a few more chairs, and did away with the numerous portable tables that we were going to use. I have our "small wall" tent set up as sleeping quarters and head office, and it is quite a comfortable arrangement inasmuch as I was able to bring along the cot that I had and am now off of the damp ground, albeit a bit cold, as the air comes up through the cot. However, I intend to remedy that situation tonight, by means of a few newspapers.

The advance party leaves in a few days, for _____, France, so we shall soon be on our way. I think that we are all ready to meet the situation but am a bit worried as to how my equipment and supplies will be transported—by truck or by rail—and as to whether we will go into rear echelon at once, or later on. I suppose these difficulties will iron themselves out, however.

I received another letter from Bob, yesterday, which I answered at once, and a letter tonight from Mother enclosing the $3 worth of airmail stamps that I had requested.

Still no word on my promotion, and no indication of it has been forthcoming.

I will have to conduct a "school" for all assembled Company Commanders, Surgeons, 1st Sergeants, S-1's, etc., on this coming Thursday at 1300, and I am just about prepared for it, except for running off a few essential forms.

I haven't been feeling any too terribly good of late, but I think a lot of rest will cure that situation. I had my hair cut to ¼-inch length recently, and together with my moustache, I imagine that I resemble an escaped convict.

I have a tremendous backlog of work but think that we will be able to keep up with it and the tremendous amount of work that, without a doubt, lies ahead of us.

More later.

BIVOUAC, ¾ MILES SW OF BARNEVILLE
11 OCTOBER 1944

A vicious, gusty storm sweeps the bivouac area today. Fortunately, all of our equipment is now under cover. The men are working industriously on installing a stove in the main tent, and if my arrangements for two additional stoves prove successful, I may have one put in this tent. Meanwhile, my feet feel like two sodden lumps of ice. With my usual (?) foresight, I sent my overshoes home, along with my overcoat, from Camp Carson. If worst comes to worst, my sole protection against the ravages of the elements will be to wear two or three pairs of sox, a set of l-o-n-g underwear, and my flight jacket, which leaves scanty protection from the waist down.

It rained violently all night, and breakfast and dinner today were eaten in a drizzling downpour. Work seems to be progressing smoothly enough, even though we received an influx of additional work.

It is dreary, somber days and nights such as these that drive me to think in retrospect.

I thought last night, my God, I will be 29 years old on the 30th of December. Surely that is too old to lay the foundations of a home and family, even in the remote event that the war terminated soon, and the even more remote possibility of finding a wife.

Providing that I come through this war all right, I will, in all probability, have a fair-sized nest egg with which to start life anew from the ash heap where Virginia left it. BUT—I have no trade, no profession, no outstanding ability, and have been schooled in nothing but the Arts of War, which most certainly, of all things, will be most useless when peace is declared. Where then, and in what direction will my life lead?

I know in my heart that my soul and nature is such that it could not stand a monotonous, soul-destroying job, such as the one I had prior to my entry into the Army—not now, at any rate. For if any benefit is connected with the Army, it is one of broadening one's former outlooks on life, furthering one's ambitions, opening new horizons of hopes and desires, and of climbing hitherto unattainable heights.

My somewhat unhappy childhood and fatherless upbringing, while no fault of a wonderful Mother, did preclude any possibility of a college education, and there must I return to a mode of life that is governed entirely by the amount of education one (or one's parents) has been able to afford?

Such thoughts of the always-unpredictable future haunt me as I struggle for sleep. For in this war, nothing is stable, nothing secure—and I, of all people, have nothing to cling to, nothing to look forward to, and most of all, nothing to return to or for.

IN BIVOUAC, ¾ MILE SW BARNEVILLE, FRANCE
15 OCTOBER 1944

I haven't written for a few days. Have received no personal mail at all for some time. A few periodicals and bank statements seem to come through with the utmost expediency but none of the yearned-for personal mail.

Well, we are definitely moving up to the front within a very few days. Mass church services will be held tomorrow to prepare us for the coming struggle and battle. From all indications, any mail will soon be headed "Somewhere in Belgium." Mr. Lauck, 7 men, and all of our equipment will proceed by truck, and the balance will travel by rail in the old familiar boxcars of World War I, I imagine. Upon arrival at the new area, we of Personnel will revert to rear echelon with all its strife, difficulties, and cliques.

Have an unpleasant situation in Personnel, at present, which I intend to remedy this afternoon. It seems that one of my boys has developed an inferiority complex along with a radical turn of mind. Either he will have to regain his sense of mental balance or will have to return to his unit in the grade of private. In view of the pending conditions, I can take no chances in having a temperamental prima donna jeopardizing the entire section—and I don't intend to.

The ill-famed weather of La Belle, France, has definitely come into its own. For the past few days, we have had nothing but rain and high winds. The roads have degenerated into slushing quagmires, the meadow in which we are at present bivouacked is somewhat similar to an evil-smelling swamp, and the profusion of cows and their resultant filth make this a truly "lovely" area.

We move about Tuesday, and I can well imagine the rigors of the forthcoming trip! Was paid today and received a little over $32. The balance goes home. Will have to straighten books today.

The promotions are evidently now at Corps Headquarters, for word came today on two of them—some administrative technicality on those two that were to be promoted to Field Grade. No word at all on mine; evidently still up there. Keep my fingers crossed I guess.

In Quarters, 10 miles N of Brussels, Belgium
20 October 1944

Without warning, we of Personnel were suddenly alerted and told that we were moving out at 0530 on the morning of the 16th. Accordingly, the men were alerted, and I spent the major portion of the evening preparing my equipment and getting in readiness for the trip by rail, with the remaining 18 men that were to accompany me. I had decided to go by rail, and Mr. Lauck was to travel by truck with all of our equipment and the balance of the men.

At 0400 the next morning, I arose and hastily rolled my bedroll, prepared my musette bag and duffle bag, and had an extremely early breakfast consisting of hotcakes and coffee. By 0530, the men were ready with packs rolled, and we fell into formation and moved out with Regimental Headquarters Company. Our destination was the little town of La Haye Du Puits, where we were to entrain. The march was a miserable experience—cold, dark, and of course, raining. We marched continuously for six hours, with a ten-minute "rest break" every hour. It was a hard, grueling march, particularly to we of Personnel, for we were very soft, due to the continuous indoor work. However, I was extremely proud of my men, for we out-marched many of the so-called "hardened" men in the column ahead of us. Not one of my men fell out. I must admit, however, that I was quite thankful when we finally reached the yards where we were to board our train.

What a shock awaited us, however, when we gazed upon the equipage that was to carry us to our next destination! Car No. 46—forever will that fateful number be emblazoned in my mind. A German boxcar of the vintage 1913—and it looked it. It had four wheels, not the luxurious eight-wheel type in common use in the U.S. Later, I held the firm conviction that at least three of these wheels were flat on one side. Fortunately, the sides and roof were in some semblance of repair. Ten men from Regimental Headquarters were assigned to ride in our car, making a total of 32 men who were to live, eat, and sleep in a boxcar that measured approximately 10 feet wide and 28 feet long! After cleaning a layer or so of refuse from the floor, left by the former occupants (horses), we stretched two collapsed tents across the floor, and used them for a carpet of a sort. The equipment of the men was hung on the walls. Four water cans were taken aboard, together with several cases of rations. It was interesting to note that the phrase, "*40 Hommes—8 Chevaux,*" used so often in World War I, was also painted on these cars. Still more interesting was an inscription, scribbled in chalk, in barely legible French: "In this car, a French soldier, Jean DuFarge, killed himself rather than go to the front." We managed to decipher it, after a bit.

Promptly at 1300, the train moved out, and from then until dusk, we were treated to a firsthand view of what the Germans must have undergone in their headlong retreat into Germany. On every hand was evidence of the terrific aerial warfare that had been meted out to them. For the most part, we rode on very recently repaired rails, bridges, and underpasses. On every hand was evidence of the utter horror of Modern War. Gaunt skeletons of wrecked and burned German rolling stock, destroyed yards, capsized engines, and cavernous bomb craters. As night fell, the scene of carnage was blotted out, and the problem of sleeping 32 men in the narrow confines of the boxcar presented itself. With such crowding, and strange men in the car, I had to rule them with an iron hand in order to maintain any sort of discipline. I finally decided on sleeping two rows of seven men each, across each end of the car, which would supposedly leave enough room in the center of the car, for the remaining four men. Much to my dismay, the men proved to be longer in stature than I had anticipated, with the result that we two officers (Lt. Miller and me) were forced to sit up the entire night. Fortunately, I had my heavy leather coat on, and was fairly warm, although the night turned bitterly cold. I curled up on top of my bed roll, which I didn't even bother to unroll, and by sleeping on one side of my body until it became numb, and then likewise the other, the long, long night eventually came to an end.

All the next day, we passed endless miles of the torn and tortured landscape, and as night approached, we were some forty kilometers from Paris. We retired early, and with a bit more scientific planning, I was able to lay my bedroll out and regain some of the sleep that I had lost the night before. We awoke the next morning in the heart of the Paris railway yards, and immediately, efforts were made to start the morning meal of C-rations. Hordes of penniless and destitute Parisians besieged the cars, begging for food, cigarettes—anything. We left Paris about 1030, and I had my first and last glimpse of the famed Eiffel Tower in the distance. As we passed through the suburbs of Paris, we noted a very noticeable change in the attitude of the French people towards the Americans. In Normandy, the local peasants maintained a more or less resentful air, for the Germans had gone out of their way to treat them kindly in order to boost their production of farm products, and naturally, when the invasion came, with its attendant destruction and horror, the average Norman failed to understand fully. About two in the afternoon, we passed through the little town of Compiegne, near which is the forest in which the railway car used for the signing of the armistice of World War I was placed at one time (later taken to Germany by Hitler, I believe). Again, there were endless miles of destruction in which the fury of total war was shown at its worst. About 1700 in the afternoon, we approached the town of Creil, France, where huge marshalling yards of the French Railway were evidently once centered. I say "once" with good reason. For a distance of about five miles on either side of Creil, the earth had been so utterly devastated and torn with all the monstrous effects of precision bombing, that it was unrecognizable as nothing more than mere wasteland. Tons and tons of track, cars, locomotives, cranes, foundries, embankments, hangars, and control towers were jumbled in a crazy mass of confusion and utter desolation. The Germans had evidently had a large ammunition depot placed here at one time, for there were huge caves in the sides of the surrounding hills, and enormous pillboxes were everywhere in evidence, though now cracked and gaping ominously. Creil was evidently a key point in the terrain, for the Allies had not left a space clear of shell and bomb craters for over five feet in all those miles— not without cost, however, judging from the many burned and crashed aircraft strewn over the area. In the city of Creil itself, we were besieged again by a tremendous mob of refugees of all nationalities—French, Russian, Poles, etc., all begging for whatever we would, or could, give them. We left Creil as dusk was falling (accompanied by fully 200 of the refugees riding between the cars). I bedded the men down with some little apprehension, for it was highly probable that many of these so-called "refugees" were part of the German Underground that are known to have been left throughout the liberated areas of Europe. Not only was sabotage a good cause for worry, but, too, a slit throat would mean nothing to some of the more unprincipled refugees, in order to obtain some of our food and equipment. I fell asleep, facing the door, and my sleep was disturbed by dreams of the most lurid type. I awoke once, with a start, and groped for my carbine and flashlight, but it was only one of my own men, restless, and stirring about the car.

On the night of October 19th, we crossed the Belgian Frontier and awoke in the rail yards of a sizable Belgian town. More devastation was much in evidence. These people we notice, however, are totally different than those in France. They seem to be much cleaner physically and are all wild with joy at the appearance of *Le Americans*. They hate the Boche with an undying hatred—usually signified by the expressive motion of a finger drawn across the throat, and with the word, "Boche!" hissed. The people are horribly in need in the outlying districts and towns. The arrival and passing of our train is invariably greeted with kisses blown by the hands, cheers, and continuous waving of hands and flags. We are, without a doubt, the first Americans to arrive in this vicinity, for our reception has been one of spontaneous warmth and friendliness.

After the dull, dreary episode of detraining, which it would be best to pass over, we were driven through one of the suburbs of Brussels in our motor trucks, and much to our confusion, the warm reception continued—crowds lined the streets and cheered, the children waving American flags and throwing apples and flowers. They formed spontaneous committees at the railway station to entertain us during the long wait, during the detraining process.

Upon arrival in our new Regimental Bivouac Area, I was met by Captain Smith who informed me that we would be quartered with Service Company. Accordingly, we pitched our tents, and I postponed setting up the office until the morrow, due to the lateness of the hour. I then retired to my little pup tent, to my thoughts, and to the incessant drumming of the rain on the tent.

I awoke at 0630 on the morning of October 20th, had breakfast, and had just started to set up the office when I was informed that word had come from Division that we were to join the Division Rear Echelon. Accordingly, we repacked, loaded our truck and trailer with its preposterous load of equipment AND men, piled in my jeep with Mr. Lauck, and set out on the extremely muddy road to Division. We arrived at about 0930, and much to my amazement, we are now quartered in a former Belgian millionaire's lakeside beach resort. It is extremely modern in all respects, with curved facades of paneled glass, modernistic chrome finishing, frosted glass windows, paneled walls in the natural finish, and even lavatories with indirect lighting! Our office is somewhat crowded, but at least it is indoors and dry. The men are sleeping in the squad tent, and we are using the small wall tent for supplies. Mr. Lauck and I are housed in one of the abandoned locker rooms, which is quite dry and comfortable. From what I can determine, we move from here in about three days. Also, it seems that we are now a part of the Canadian 1st Army, and as I surmised, are some of the first American troops in this area. I have news of our impending operations, but for security must forbear fully mentioning it at the present time. Had several of the British and Canadian officers at mess this noon. Interesting fellows.

Tomorrow I must go to Regiment and complete all final severing of the ties. I definitely must obtain some gasoline and clean some clothes, and also clear up once and for all, the large amount of laundry that awaits me.

No mail...

IN QUARTERS, 10 MILES N OF BRUSSELS, BELGIUM
21 OCTOBER 1944
O long months of bitter disappointment. O the dregs of the cup of despair. All the weary endless days of hard, hard, work—and now? O Red Letter Day! The dawn of a new future. A mind once more at peace with the world. For today, it happened! Example:

R E S T R I C T E D
HEADQUARTERS NINTH UNITED STATES ARMY
Office of the Commanding General

SPECIAL ORDERS)   APO 339
NUMBER   45)   E X T R A C T   16 October
1944
            *   *   *

    5.   Announcement is made of the temp promotion of the following named officers in the grade indicated in the AUS with rank fr date of this order:

<u>1ˢᵗ Lt to Capt</u>
Ernest J. McCully 01289287 Inf

So at last, the long weary days of waiting have come to an end. I am glad. For now, I can concentrate on more important matters, and also I have vindicated myself in my own eyes. Wonder what the great Joe Blow thinks. And his pet—the fair-haired boy—now locked in my old job, with the T/O vacancy filled by one of the leeches at Division HQ!

Wrote a lot of letters tonight, and intend to write more tomorrow. I washed my OD clothing (all of it) today, in gasoline, and tomorrow I have two very important things to do: (1) thoroughly clean and oil my carbine, and (2) wash <u>all</u> of my dirty laundry.

The CG made the announcement tonight that we go into action very soon with the Canadian 1st Army. From what I can determine, the rear echelon moves about Tuesday or Wednesday to about 15 miles from the city of Antwerp, which is still under attack by the flying robot bombs, and when finally established, we will be about 15 miles behind the front lines. So be it. Here we go, and I hope we get it over with soon.

IN QUARTERS, 10 MI N OF BRUSSELS, BELGIUM
22 OCTOBER 1944

We move either tomorrow or the day following. Some of the comforts that we had stored up will have to be disposed of, at least so orders from Division state. Oh well, we are still not too bad off.

At the present time, it seems probable that we will be housed in buildings most of the time that we are in rear echelon. As far as sleeping is concerned, once my air mattress arrives here (if it ever does), I will be as snug as a bug in a rug in my little pup tent, providing that I erect it properly.

One of the rocket bombs came over today, made a helluva racket, and exploded with a terrific earthshaking blast.

No mail at all today, but I should begin to receive quite a bit before very long, for I have written about 20 letters within the past two days. Managed to take a nice hot shower today, which is always an extraordinary treat in this type of life.

From all reports, Antwerp is really some town, and if at all possible, I would like to visit it, inasmuch as I only passed through Brussels and did not get to visit it. Well, time will tell on that matter.

The work has settled down into a routine, and all seems to be progressing very nicely. Our Morning Reports were the first in, all complete, after the long delay in same caused by the train trip, and I believe our payrolls will be among the first in.

Major Kernan (my one-time Arch Foe) is as ornery as ever, and I guess he is embittered because his promotion didn't go through. Wonder what stopped it?

I am exceedingly tired tonight, so I think I will make this a short chapter in this series of monotonous thoughts and close for tonight.

The Abbey De Westmalle
In Quarters near Antwerp, Belgium
24 October 1944

We moved today, and as a direct result, I find myself in one of the strangest places I have yet been in—a Trappist Monastery, "The Abbey De Westmalle," to be exact.

The trip itself took about two hours of moderate driving through several more Belgian towns of wildly cheering Belgians. It was noticeable, however, that the closer we got to the front, the less friendly the inhabitants became—still apprehensive of the Germans' return, I imagine.

The 104th Division was committed to action last night, and we are at the front at last. So far, have heard only rumors of our progress, but we are supposed to have made an advance of some 10 miles by tonight.

German "robot" bombs came over continuously, all day, and I had my first close view of one of them this morning. They travel at a terrifically high rate of speed, and the bomb itself seems to precede the sound. The motor, whatever type it is, has a peculiar guttural sound, and its heavy reverberations shake all nearby walls and windows. The motor will cut out suddenly, and then there will be an earthshaking blast.

To get back to the monastery, however, it is set in extremely picturesque surroundings, encircled by lush meadows, lowing herds of cattle and sheep, with here and there a few fine, healthy-looking horses. The major portions of the buildings were built in about 1934, for they are extremely modern. The grounds are meticulously neat and well tended, and it reminds one of a large university. They are extensive brewers of beer, which is made from the local crop of sugar beets and is very good and very potent (16% alcohol).

Men and officers were allowed to purchase the beer (the purchases of the men being under the supervision of an officer), and I told my men I didn't care how much they drank BUT to conduct themselves as soldiers, OR—.

A robot bomb just now came over and crashed in the general direction of Antwerp. I thought all the panes were coming out of these medieval-type, leaded window panes.

Our office itself is in the squad tent just outside the grounds, so I can look forward to a cold day's work tomorrow. However, <u>Captains</u> and above were assigned rooms in the Monastery, and it is quite interesting. The bed seems much shorter than the average American bed. Of course, the furnishings are of a predominantly religious nature. They include a linoleum floor with a throw rug beside the bed, a large writing table, an old-fashioned "dresser" with mirror, washbasin and a hot-and-cold water spigot (but no hot water), a towel rack, a night table (with enclosed chamber pot), and a crucifix stand for the evening devotions.

From what I can determine, we may stay here until our Division takes the Scheldt Estuary, our present objective.

No mail for days and days.

In Quarters, near Antwerp, Belgium
25 October 1944

Nothing very new to write about, so shall probably jabber on and on and fill this with inanities.

The troops move out in a dawn attack this AM, and the objective is a village considerably within the borders of Holland. At the present rate of advance, we shall probably be in Holland before too long a time.

The day was miserably cold today, and we were harassed by numerous petty administrative details. The food seems to grow progressively worse. Tomorrow I must have a couple of the lads make a reconnaissance of the nearby British units to try and swap red gas for white (unleaded) to use in our lanterns, as our lantern supply is running dangerously low.

About this coming Sunday evening I intend to throw a mild party for my section to celebrate, in some measure, the "wetting down" of my new bars, an old Army custom, and my boys evidently expect it of me. Probably cost ten or twenty dollars but it will be worth it—I have a good bunch of men.

In the past few days I have re-opened all of the former channels of correspondence that were closed to me because ----. As to what the reply from these sources may be, remains to be seen. I don't dare write to Margie. She was too deadly serious in a matrimonial way.

I have been doing some heavy auditing and bookkeeping of late, and it appears that I may come out of this Army with a nest egg of close to some five thousand dollars. Surely enough to pay for a moderate home, but after all, what is the sense of buying a home with no one to put in it and no future with which to hold it secure? Rather like putting the cart before the horse.

Another thing I have determined to do, if at all possible, before I leave the continent: I intend to visit Vienna, and if possible, Switzerland. Above all, however, Vienna! The home of my beloved Strauss waltzes, dreams of romantic terraces, swirling gowns and gallants, The Blue Danube, sparkling wines, and dinners. Vienna, literally the city of my dreams, although I hardly expect to find it the same, or nearly what I imagine it to be. Isn't it a paradox that one who possesses such a foolishly romantic nature, who knows all the lengthy love songs of a generation ago, who has such a capacity for love to give without question, my entire being, into the happy fulfillment of marital happiness, must be forever denied such fulfillment? It is only too apparent now that such things I will never know.

Perhaps 'tis as well, for I am glad that in my desperation to satisfy these longings, I have not rushed into a typical "War Marriage" with all its sordidness and attendant unhappiness and readjustment after the war, although I must admit that I have been tempted. Perhaps the reason that I did not succumb was due to the fact that my first experience left such a scar upon my soul, that I did not do so. Virginia! What a ghastly jest of fate, to have had a name meaning the acme of purity and virginity! The bitter ashes of "Love," "Honor," "Fidelity," and "Trust" of the supposedly sacred marital vows!

Nevertheless, have the house I will! And I shall have every comfort, convenience, and innovation of which I have dreamed for so long. I increase my allotment to $200 per month next month, and it is a rare civilian job where you can <u>save</u> that much per month!

KISMET!   AS FATE DECREES!

Abbey De Westmalle, near Antwerp, Belgium
27 October 1944

Much has happened in the past two days! For one thing, Mr. Lauck and I decided to go to the little town of Westmalle and sample the local beer. Accordingly, we started out last night, after work, and walked the two odd miles into town. We found it pitch black and deserted (blackout), but by chancing the cracks of light as they appeared, we found several cafes dispensing the local brew.

One place in particular was of interest. What passed for a "Juke-Box" in Belgium stood in one end of the café, and what a monstrosity! It was as big as the entire end of the café, was covered with ornate carving and lavish, if gaudy, tapestry from behind, which issued the most hideous cacophony of sound that I have yet to experience. The proprietress evidently suffered under the impression that we enjoyed the sound, for she continually pressed the button, which set it into action. We progressed to yet another bar and ran into two Belgian Maquis. As usual, with these Maquis, they were dressed in a hodge-podge of uniforms—Belgian berets, German blouse, English pants and boots, German cartridge belt and holster, and Belgian revolver. One of them had a .25-caliber Browning Automatic of Belgian make, but declined to sell it.

Their opening questions were of a suspicious nature—disposition of troops, progress, etc., but seeing that we did not "comprehend" the language when couched in those terms, we returned to a more normal conversation. When we left the café, they immediately followed us, and this set us on edge again, for these dark, blacked-out streets so near the front are highly dangerous, with German spies, collaborationists, and fifth columnists everywhere, and all highly active. Nothing came of the incident, however and after a few more beers we returned to the Monastery.

This morning, I determined to pay a visit to the front lines; and so loaded the jeep with two men who wanted to go for the sake of the trip, two cases of beer for some friends, and five gallons of white gas for their lanterns.

After quite a bit of searching, we finally found the Regimental CP, approximately one-half mile behind the front lines, an old chateau of past luxury and decayed grandeur. The boys were all glad to see me, and were most effusive with congratulations on the recent promotion. The 415th, particularly the 1st Battalion, has evidently had a bit of a rough go, quite a few casualties, including Captain McKerney, killed in action, Lt. Rutledge likewise, and many of the other officers were wounded. Company C, in particular, was hard hit AND my prediction concerning my old enemy Joe Blow came true. He messed up royally, and was wounded in the first five minutes of action. What a Buffoon! Horrible to think that *** for his Goddamned stupidity! Thank God, fate decreed that I was not to be S-3 of the 1st Battalion!

After a visit with the staff, collecting essential information, and a visit through the old Chateau, during which time I managed to collect a varied assortment of souvenirs. How in God's name I am going to get them home is a pressing matter indeed. One especially will mean much to me in the future. It is an old, old, piece of wood, nicely finished, and with the patina of age upon it, on which is mounted a thermometer (centigrade) and a delicate barometer, inscribed in French. It is truly lovely, and may yet adorn the walls of my own home.

ABBEY DE WESTMALLE, NEAR ANTWERP, BELGIUM
28 OCTOBER 1944

Probably a short note tonight—still no mail today—almost three weeks now, and not a single letter. It must really be messed up.

Didn't get up in time for breakfast this morning, and as a result felt punk the whole day. We received ten replacements and one officer replacement today, and I had to go up to the front again, to deliver them. There wasn't nearly as much activity up there today, as yesterday. When I arrived, the CP was in the process of moving, as a result, much confusion reigned. We arrived back in time for supper, and I had quite a talk with Kernan. Nothing definitely settled, though.

This present phase of our work is vitally important, and the various unit commanders are not cooperating any too well, not without good reason, I'll warrant. However, we seem to be "muddling through" fairly well, and I think our reports compare well with the other units. I hope to improve the procedure as fast as possible, but it will take time.

Robot bombs came over almost all day and are still coming over tonight. Our troops are making steady progress, and I believe our casualties were much lighter today.

I will have to go up front tomorrow, and if I am at all successful, I may be able to smooth some of the ruffled waters that, at present, surround us.

Abbey De Westmalle, near Antwerp, Belgium
29 October 1944

I have been out of communication with the Regimental CP all day today, and no reports have come in, so our reports are really falling behind, now. I was far too busy to go up front and hunt for the CP, as we received some 85 replacements, including 10 officers, and it took the majority of the day to assign them properly.

We move from here, early tomorrow morning, into Holland, and it is really going to be some convoy that I will be in charge of—all of the trucks that will carry our replacements, plus our regular section trucks which carry our men and equipment. I will have to turn the Personnel Section over to Mr. Lauck, and I will take charge of the replacement convoy. We will have to stop at the Forward Division CP and ascertain the location of the 415 CP, and I will deliver them to that point. The area into which we are going is exceedingly dangerous, as the town to which we are moving was under artillery fire all day, and all roads surrounding it are heavily mined. Which reminds me, my good friend Lt. Pruitt, appeared on the A&D sheet today. His jeep struck a mine, and he has a fractured skull, ruptured eardrums, and the lining surrounding the brain was also ruptured. Poor Kid! I hope he makes it OK, but I hear that he will be totally deaf from here on out. Also hear that Major Russi (of 3rd Bn) was killed today but [by] fire from a German 88.

Frankly, I am somewhat worried, for our carefully prepared procedure that was supposed to have functioned so smoothly in these cases is not operating as planned, mostly due to the fact that the unit commanders are not submitting information that is required of them. Only the future will tell what may happen to smooth this situation out. If the damned fools would give me a map set and sufficient codebooks for locating their CP, I would go up and get my information.

One thing of interest. Long ago, in my childhood, I remember reading a book, *The Belgian Twins,* and the locale was set during the First World War in the little town of Malines. Malines, or Mechelen, as it is called now, is only a few miles from here, and I think of that book every time I pass through it, for as I remember, the book mentioned that the city of Antwerp could be seen burning in the distance, and sure enough, Antwerp is only a few miles from here.

IN QUARTERS, ZUNDERT, HOLLAND
OCTOBER 31, 1944

What a day was yesterday! I had to take approximately 130 replacements, including 10 officers, up to the front lines, and so I started out about 1300 in the afternoon. I found the rear elements of the CP all right, but the command group had gone on forward by means of a march CP. I did not relish the thought of taking some 130-odd men clear up to enemy territory, as artillery and mortar fire were already bursting where we were, so I put the convoy in charge of a Captain replacement that we had received and told him to go back to our Service Company. Meanwhile, I went on forward and contacted the command group. Didn't have much time for a talk with Captain Smith, and it was continually interrupted by sniper fire, but I eventually finished my business with him and thought I would check at the rear CP again where they told me the trucks had turned around all right. So I headed for Service Company, where much to my amazement, I found that they had not appeared. Back to the rear CP again in hopes of catching them, but no soap. But finally, on my way back again, I found them lost on the road. I managed to get them into Service Company and called the roll, and happily, they were all present. So, my driver and I started back, as it was already growing dark, and we had some 25 miles of shell-torn, dangerous road to cover by blackout driving. We finally arrived back rather late and found the entire rear echelon in the process of moving out. As usual, the 415th was given the least number of trucks, and we didn't all close in the new area until 0230 in the morning. The present set-up is none too nice—a former Gestapo Headquarters of the Germans in the heart of town—but it will have to do.

Today was rather miserable. Our reports are not coming in satisfactorily at all. The pay situation is indeed messed up, but there is one encouraging note—I received about six letters today, all rather ancient, and I must get busy and answer them soon.

I must go up to the front again tomorrow, as I must contact 3rd Battalion and Regimental Headquarters. So intend to start out rather early. I imagine we will have some experiences, for the Jerries have been rather active with their landmines, snipers, and subversive elements.

One horrible note—my dear friend, Lt. George Moen, was caught in an artillery barrage and torn to pieces—he who was so happily married, so happy-go-lucky, and whose wife had just had a baby. Major Russi, Major Jeavons, Lt. Donley, and others have been killed in the murderous fighting, too.

IN QUARTERS, ZUNDERT, HOLLAND
1 NOVEMBER 1944

The work for the day is done, and I can think of no better way to relax than to write a few lines in this "Journal of War." I have some letters to answer but do not feel sufficiently inspired to do so tonight.

To the front again today, a repetition of yesterday's little jaunt, vain searching for the CP (due to lack of adequate maps and finally finding it). Shells whiffling overhead, the crump of mortar shells, and the incessant chatter of small arms fire. Our Regiment was hard hit on the river crossing last night. Casualties were heavy, particularly in the 1st Battalion. Of more, I cannot go into detail.

Still unable to obtain vital information from the unit commanders, and a lot of hell is being raised about it. Hope the reports improve so that I can catch up in the work.

Received a nice letter from Colonel Smith's wife, today, giving me his latest address (in India).

All civilians were ordered off the streets tonight, in preparation for the "Big Push," and the Dutch Underground is cooperating splendidly with us on this. Bands of the Underground, with rifles slung on their backs, patrol the streets and keep them indoors. Total blackout has been enforced.

Tomorrow I must go up front again, and it is quite a trip, as the CP will have moved forward during the night, and I must go through the whole miserable searching process again.

I managed to get my box of souvenirs boxed, tied, and off in the mail. Hope it gets through the censors okay, but I put the two required certificates inside, and one on the outside.

If time today, I intend to take my bedroll out into the sun and air it out as well as rearrange it, for it is so disarranged by now that it is highly uncomfortable to sleep in.

We are getting a lot of additional work now from the S-1 Section, for they are unable to handle it, at present. I don't, at this time, see how the pay situation will ever get itself straightened out. What with men killed, wounded, in hospitals, dropped from rolls, etc., it sure is hell.

I wrote another letter to the Morgans today, but I doubt if they have had time to receive my last one as yet. The mail situation is about cleared up by now. It finally caught up with us.

All of us wonder, how we wonder, when this miserable mess is going to be over with. How long will those bloody fools, the German

Boche, drag this thing out, expending more and more lives for the theory of the "Master Race"?

I shall probably have a big afternoon, for some 350 replacements are expected, and inasmuch as I have only a faint idea of how many are needed in each company (due to inadequate reports), it will be mostly a problem of pure guesswork.

IN QUARTERS, ZUNDERT, HOLLAND
5 NOVEMBER 1944

Again I take up my pen, for I don't know when I will have time to type this. We move tomorrow at 1300, and it will be a long trip. The mission of the Division has been accomplished. Canadian and Polish troops were enabled to effect a juncture. We are being withdrawn and will proceed to join the famed American 1st Army, commanded by Lt. General Courtney Hodges. It is rumored that we will go to a location near ruined Aachen, and will, in all probability, figure in the coming drive in that sector.

This presents a terrific problem to me. We had the highest casualties of any of the regiments, and we are still far behind in our reports of all kinds. Total and actual strength of the Regiment is still a confused issue. Grades and ratings likewise. Also, I made a major change in the Personnel procedure—changed the entire office over to the "Section System" in lieu of the individual clerk system. Of course, there are many necessary adjustments to be made, changes in office furniture, new files, etc. Of course, many of the lads were unhappy about this change, inasmuch as it takes away about 90% of the privacy they enjoyed heretofore. Rough! But we will make it work, or else.

I have contracted a beastly cold, and it is driving me crazy. Thought I had the flu last night, but I retired early and knocked it out.

My mail has been wonderful. A letter from Lola. One from Lena (!). Two from Colonel Smith. One from Mrs. Smith. None of them, however, are aware of the fact that I have been promoted as yet, so the age of the mail can be gauged.

Thank God we move in the daylight. Usually, we move at night, and it usually rains (it is now), and as a whole, I detest these night moves. Casualties have been heavy in this sector. One good piece of news—Lt. Pruitt returned to duty—apparently none the worse for his mishap with the German mine. The surgeon evidently reported his condition much worse than it actually was. He's a swell kid, one of my best friends.

The sector into which we are going is much colder than this, and being on the Siegfried Line, I imagine we will remain much more stationary than we have. I will be happy to leave the British and Canadians. They are none too cooperative.

Had a long talk with Captain Smith, today, at the culmination of my fourth trip to the front lines in as many days, and we both steamed up a bit, but finally parted on most amicable terms. I hope to God this administrative mess starts to straighten itself out within a few days.

In Quarters, near Aachen, Germany
7 November 1944

Another memorable experience to chalk up in the book. To begin with, someone got excited when the 1st Army order to move was first received. As a result (we found out later), we moved a day too soon, with the result that no guides were at the destination to meet us, no billeting had been arranged, etc. We left Zundert at about 1030 in the morning and drove all day through Holland and Belgium crossing and recrossing the Holland-Belgium border several times. We reached the city of Maastricht, Holland, at about 1730 in the afternoon and continued on towards our destination. We arrived at about 1930, but due to the fact that there were no guides, and were practically in enemy territory, the motor column was halted, and we sat for four solid hours in the most penetrating, freezing cold that I have ever experienced. The Jerries helped to pass the time by hurling a continuous series of robot bombs over our heads, none of which seemed destined for us. Finally, about midnight, we received word that we were going to billet in the town for the night, and the local Belgian folk, who seemed very friendly, took us in, bedded us down, and provided us with hot ersatz coffee. I slept fitfully, for I was half delirious, my cold having degenerated into what felt like an excellent case of double pneumonia. Awoke this morning, went to the little café in which we had received billeting instructions the night before, and proceeded to drink about sixteen cups of the coffee. This seemed to be all that kept me going.

Tonight our office is finally set up in an old, but tiny, theater. We are somewhat cramped for space but will get by, I hope. Complete blackout is in effect, and there are as yet many Germans in the town. Civilian refugees from nearby Aachen, and they wear yellow armbands. We are practically inside of Germany on the Belgian-German Frontier, and there is still much sabotage being committed by the German Underground.

I still feel none too good tonight, and I do hope that my cold does not get any worse, or it will be the Medics for me. No mail, of course, due to the move, and rumor now has it that we will move again tomorrow. I wonder just when this great confused unit, known as rear echelon, contemplates on us doing any work?

In Quarters, in a Convent, on the Belgian-German Frontier, near Aachen, Germany
12 November 1944
(First, an excerpt written on the 8th November 1944)

Tired tonight. Both physically and mentally. My cold seems to be diminishing, but slowly, as if reluctant to relax the excellent hold it had obtained. To top it all, today was one of the most confusing, disjointed, utterly demoralizing days that I have yet experienced. The so-called "efficiency" of the Army is a farce. Nothing but confused directives, undirected, misguided moves (and in the enemies' territory, too!), continuous requests for utterly useless information, and to top it all, prompt, accurate submission of vital reports is expected after a series of these ill-planned moves into inadequate working quarters!

OH WELL! They say the war can't last forever, but sometimes I wonder! We move tomorrow, back to the little town which we just left; and I hope to God we get more adequate working space. If I can get the accurate strength of the Regiment figured out, and get these BCR's figured out within this two-day "breathing spell," things may begin to straighten themselves out. At least I hope so.

I shall make a trip to the Forward CP tomorrow, which is well north of Aachen, and shall see Captain Smith and endeavor to get some of this information. But, in all, I imagine it will be a very confusing day; what with moving, going to the CP, taking 27 replacements and additional casuals and officer replacements forward (a total of two trips and a move).

How I wish this miserable mess was over, and I could once more enjoy a few of the dilatory pleasures of civilian life. One year ago today, I was boarding the troop train at La Pine, Oregon, preparatory to moving to the Desert Training Area; and shortly thereafter, I took my last leave, on 18 November 1943, to visit my home and friends.

12 November 1944
Today, being Sunday, I can afford to be lavish and spare a few moments

to write a few words herein. What mishaps have fallen upon my poor grey head.

I was forced to delay my trip forward for one day, because one of the AG lads took off with my jeep. When I finally did leave, with some 130-odd men in four trucks behind me, I had retained one of our Message Center boys to guide me forward, but I may as well have spared myself his company, for he proceeded to get lost 5 minutes after we hit the Aachen Highway. After cruising around the major portion of the day, much to the disgust of the men in the trucks, I finally located Service Company, and dropped them off. It was by then about 1900 at night, and dusk was falling rapidly; nevertheless, I determined to push on to the CP, and so set out driving blackout, over the unknown roads. After a series of eerie experiences, due to being directed into enemy territory by some stupid military police, I finally located the main Division Forward CP and from there phoned Smith, who sent one of his men over after me. We had a good evening in which we cleaned up a lot of the pending work, and as luck would have it, they had "obtained" three chickens from a nearby German farmhouse, and we had a feast of fried chicken. I slept sitting up in a chair all night but slept fairly well, although fitfully. In the morning, I took off again, for Service Company finished my business there, and then headed for the office again. This took the major portion of the morning due to one-way roads, messed-up MP's, and extremely muddy roads.

While at the Forward CP seeking directions the day prior, I ran into a meeting of the HIGH Brass and had a glimpse of Generals Eisenhower, Bradley, Hodges, and all the other big names.

I obtained another "souvenir," but if I will ever get it home remains to be seen. It is a German Schmeisser Automatic Machine Pistol. It would be nice to have at home, more as a trophy than anything else, but it is too heavy to mail, so I may have to lug it around until the conclusion of the war.

Battle Casualty Reporting seems to be the main bugaboo that it has always been. I am not getting the information that I need. Unit commanders are not very conscientious about complying.

IN QUARTERS, IN A CONVENT, NEAR AACHEN
15 NOVEMBER 1944
2040
Rapid have been the events and activities of the past few days. I have

made numerous trips through Aachen and the surrounding vicinity in an effort to satisfy the insatiable maw and appetite of the God of War. Truckload after truckload of replacements have I hauled to the front. Truly, these replacements are the "forgotten men" of this war. Some have entered the Army as late as May 1944. Their basic training completed, they go directly into combat. Shoved from one depot to another. Cold, wet, miserable most of the time, they have nothing but the cessation of hostilities to look forward to. What kind stroke of Providence must have been mine, to place me among the first of the "selectees," thus enabling me to take advantage of the many opportunities, which are no more—no matter how highly qualified. The Army is surfeit with officers.

Winter is definitely here on the Western Front. Slush, snow, sleet, and icy winds are prevalent at all times. Without my heavy jacket I would be lost.

The work has increased tremendously, and due to our recent heavy casualties, we are in a particularly sad mess on the records. I can only hope that we can "mull" through the situation as we have before in other problems. However, O Gloomy Thought, I have had several severe arguments with the Colonel and Captain Smith about all this.

As for my mail, it appears as though all friends and relations have deserted me in this my hour of need (that is, insofar as mail is concerned), with the exception of Mother and Harold.

Sometimes I begin to get moody because of the miserable conditions, principally (although I have it comparatively easy compared to other officers), but nevertheless, inadequate washing, laundry, and living quarters do make one a bit despondent. The front is certainly stalemated at the present time, and how I wonder, God, how I wonder, when this ceaseless, senseless, wanton slaughter will end.

I still have a miserable cold, which hangs on interminably, and my chest is wracked and tight upon arising daily. This could be caused from sleeping on cement floors, however. Well, who knows, perhaps someday spring will be here, and I can awake once more, free from the calls of the military, my own Lord and Master; but what will be my course in life then?

I was in a particularly reflective mood tonight on the drive back from Lichtenbusch. I thought of the past five years and what a perfect chaos they have been. Some wasted, yes, but most of them bitter lessons learned the hard way. I passed through the Siegfried Line with gaunt and burned-out pillboxes staring at me, their empty casemates like the eyes of a malignant skull. Rows and rows of the famed and pictured "Dragon's Teeth" painted a bilious green. "Quaint" farmhouses, in reality, almost invulnerable pillboxes, now broken and burned. As dusk fell, I found myself in the heart of the Wald Forest or in English, "Wild" Forest. Its sinister appearance gave the reason for the name as self-evident. I was forced to drive blackout, as enemy snipers and troops were prevalent in the area, and my anxiety was somewhat caused by the fact that I was following an illegible overlay, for they still refuse to issue me adequate maps, although I must make these trips. Made it okay, however, and arrived back at Moresnet in utter blackness . . . and so, another day.

In Quarters, in a Convent, near Aachen, Germany
16 November 1944
Mighty and many have been the messed-up situations in the past few days. I hope to goodness that things begin to adjust themselves shortly. However, I can expect none too much along that line; for today, the "Big Push" started, with an awesome prelude of 2500 four-engine bombers saturating the enemy lines at the given hour. This was followed by a terrific artillery bombardment lasting for hours, and the troops were scheduled to hit the line at a specified hour. As yet, we have heard no word of them back here, but tomorrow morning's reports should contain much.

 Still no mail today; I have almost given up hope along that line. I guess changing my address really messed things up. Like most soldiers, I guess, I think continuously of that happy day when I will head for home. How long, O Lord, how long? I wrote the firm from which I requested the air mattress (and which they never sent, despite the fact that I mailed them a check for $22) and asked them to do something about it. An air mattress would make this cement floor seem like heaven.

 Thanksgiving is reputed to be on next Thursday, which brings the thought that on exactly that date, one year ago, I was sitting at the festive board with Mother, Harold, and the others. Where, I wonder, will I be at this time next year?

 Another radical has turned up in the office, who continually bemoans what a hard life he is leading back here in the office. I intend to have a heart-to-heart talk with him tomorrow and convince him otherwise. The other chap with whom I had one of these talks saw the error of his ways and is a different person entirely now.

My cold still bothers me of a morning but is rapidly getting better, I believe. One joyous bit of news. Laundry is now available. I shall send out a huge bag of it tomorrow and hope to gosh that I get it all back. I wonder if that big box of souvenirs that I sent home ever arrived?

Had better cut this thing short of this banal chatter, as I don't even seem able to type tonight.

IN QUARTERS, IN CONVENT, NEAR AACHEN, GERMANY
19 NOVEMBER 1944

Sunday, the nineteenth of November, in the year of our Lord, nineteen hundred and forty-four! A beautiful sunny day, the sky filled with lacy streamers of fluffy clouds, birds in the trees, tinkling their melody of happiness against the walls of this convent. But down below, Man in his bestial ignorance, turns all his ingenuity and cunning, acquired so laboriously through the centuries, into more efficient devices and means of killing one another. The earth drips blood, the rumble of artillery is constant, and the continuous reverberating roar of robot bombs rattles the panes of the windows. What a mood in which to write! But, as is somewhat normal with me, I am depressed, morose, and a little bit lonely today.

An odd little jest of fate occurred today. One of my friends, 2nd Lt. Robert G. Donley, was buried in Henri Chapelle Cemetery #1 at exact 1100, 11 November 1944. Twenty-six years to the minute, since the signing of the armistice of the last war! The bitter irony of war.

The work increases daily, at a prodigious rate, and it seems futile to endeavor to keep up with it. It is like batting your head against a stone wall to try and cope with it. To tell the truth, I think I am getting just a little tired of the whole rotten stinking mess called war. On February 26th, I will have completed my fourth year in the Army. I might add, four of the best years of my life.

I am going to try and write some more letters to everyone today, which will be the second letter I have written to all of them, as my mail seems to have been cut off as though with a knife.

Nothing seems to be going right, anymore. No matter what it is, it seems that something always comes up to either complicate the work or to make it almost impossible. This tends to give one a sense of frustration that makes life almost unbearable at times.

The Regiment is in the thick of battle again, and the usual long, daily lists of casualties continue to pour in. I can expect more replacements in a few days, but I think the delivery of them will be much more simple, as Service Company is moving to Brand, Germany, which is simple to find. We ourselves are moving in the near future, supposedly to a location which gives us a little more room and more adequate working facilities.

I can only hope, as so often in the past, that things will soon begin to work themselves out.

In Quarters, in a Convent, near Aachen, Germany
22 November 1944

Some time since I have written, and the reason, as usual, is the tremendous overload of work. I have increased the strength of the Personnel Section to 35 men and plan on obtaining at least one more good man. Many are the trials and tribulations that occur daily.

We move from this abode shortly, further into Germany, for the recent "Big Push" was successful in a minor way. I have been extremely busy hauling replacements up to the front (some 170 in the last few days), and on one occasion, entered one side of Stolberg, Germany, while they were fighting like maniacs. Needless to say, I had an interesting time dodging sniper and mortar fire. Had several big talks with Smith, and we got quite a bit straightened out. However there are several aspects of the daily quota of work that still worry me. We had several unavoidable delinquent Battle Casualty Reports, and these the old man will have to answer by endorsement, over his own signature. It will indeed be interesting to see what the old man says. Whether I will have any repercussions out of the matter remains to be seen.

We leaped at an opportunity to purchase some hideous Christmas cards today, and I spent a busy hour or two tonight mailing them to every one of my correspondents. The mail situation is still on the rocks, as I have not received any mail since the 15th of October, and it seems something MUST be definitely wrong.

Our next residence is supposed to be far more roomy, and if it affords any degree of privacy, I intend to have some kind of a little party for the men

One of the Chaplains was killed today, Chaplain Stump, an awfully nice fellow. Stepped on a German S-mine, more popularly referred to as a "Bouncing Betty," a particularly vicious thing. When stepped upon, it leaps approximately five feet and explodes with a terrific shower of shrapnel.

Hitler's cohorts have been extremely busy all day, hurling their robot bombs back here. One landed in the field opposite us and shattered several of the huge panes of glass in the convent. One never knows when one goes to bed whether he will be in one piece or not upon arising.

Had a haircut and a shampoo today in a little Belgian town I stopped in. The enticing sign said, *Solon de Coiffure, pour hommes et dames.* My French (or Belgian) is getting pretty good when I can make that out.

Tomorrow is Thanksgiving, and it will certainly be a different Thanksgiving from the one that I spent last year. But I hope, with all the ardor of my soul, that on the next year, it will be spent with Mother and all the rest.

I surely hope that the lack of mail does not forebode any dire happening! That is the biggest worry about not receiving mail with any regularity.

IN QUARTERS, IN A CONVENT, NEAR AACHEN, GERMANY
THANKSGIVING DAY, 23 NOVEMBER 1944
O Day of Days. Truly a day of Thanksgiving in more ways than one, for I received two letters today. Actually, one from Rafferty, and to my surprise, one from Vivian. Rafferty is in a G.F.R.D awaiting reassignment. Didn't have much to say except to hurry and write, which I did, with great alacrity. Vivian's letter was much more newsy. She had just become the mother of a bouncing baby boy on November 3rd and wrote much of the happenings around Oakland. Eunice and Mutt getting a divorce, Charlotte and her husband splitting up. In fact, divorce, that great American pastime, seems to be all the rage around home. She begged me to write, but of course, I didn't. I prefer not to get entangled in a mess of that sort, and anyway, the kid has at last found the happiness that was denied her for so long, so far be it from me to cast any bolts into the machinery. Instead, I wrote her mother and dad a nice long letter, just as though I had never received Vivian's. At least the receipt of the two letters did much to boost my morale quite considerably.

We had quite a nice Thanksgiving Dinner, considering the fact that we are in combat. But the day brought me to stare into a sea of memories, for it was at just this date last year that I was home on leave with all the folks, and what a glorious leave it was.

The work continues to engulf us in ever-increasing amounts, and we strive vainly to keep our heads above water. Worked until one o'clock last night and until midnight for the three nights' prior, and still we can't keep up.

I must make a trip forward tomorrow to the new location, pick up some fillers and casuals, and take them on up to Stolberg to Sv Company.

Lt. Rehfus was killed today.

We are driving the bastards back, however. Understand the Regimental CP is now in Eschweiler, so we should soon be rolling well on the way to Cologne before very long. I hope to God big operations are on the way, for if we sit here on this line all winter, it will not be worth the price of lives that it will surely cost. Metz has fallen to the 3rd Army and, all in all, the entire Western Front is moving forward. There are indications that the Germans, in their desperation, are throwing green troops into the fray, for some prisoners we captured this morning said that most of the elements of their division were composed of ex-Naval personnel and Air Force ground crewmen. They are not too highly armed, either, a few Schmeisser Machine pistols and an MG34 per platoon.

There have been so many gripes, lately, that I have lost count of them but can only hope, as before, that we "muddle" through okay as we have in the past.

In Quarters, in a Convent, near Aachen, Germany
Saturday, 25 November 1944

This must certainly be my jinx month. Everything that is utterly possible has happened. Stifled and hampered in this entirely inadequate office, we try to do our work as efficiently as we can, but the snafued Army system of paperwork seems to defeat its purpose.

Today, someone stole my cherished "Schmeisser Pistol" from behind my desk where it usually hung. Well, it can't be helped, I guess.

Have a delinquent Battle Casualty Report hanging fire that will certainly cause me many a headache when it is reported. Am investigating the circumstances now but doubt if they will bear fruit.

No more mail since the surprise arrival of Hubie and Vivian's letters. As a result, the mail is rapidly proving to be a morale-lowering influence (or perhaps I should say the lack of it).

We move tomorrow at 1030. It will be quite a hectic move I imagine, but the new quarters should be entirely adequate. We have two rooms, each of moderately large size. From all reports, the intention must be to remain there for quite a while, for we are supposed to "store" our furniture and use the furniture, which is available in the place. It is an old German military school of some kind, with huge barracks, hallways, etc.

We have been working like fiends for the past few days with the result that I grow unbearably weary. Didn't get to bed last night until about 0130 and then had to get up at 0700. Tonight it will be the same thing, except that we must arise an hour earlier (0600).

This long silence from Mother is worrying me terribly, for she was always extremely prompt in replying and made it a point to write me every two or three days. I have not heard from her since the 1st of November, and the only circumstance that I can think of that might cause her to cease writing is either a physical mishap to herself or news of something happening to Bob. Neither of which possibilities, I hope to God, have happened.

I hope to goodness that I will have a different story to tell on the mail situation tonight, and I do hope that the general situation around here begins to improve before very long. I made one major change, put WOJG Lauck in complete charge of, and responsibility for, all morning reports, Battle Casualty Reports, and Strength Figures. Will see how this delegation of responsibility works out.

IN A MILITARY SCHOOL, BRAND, GERMANY
NOVEMBER 28, 1944

We moved, and while the quarters are not as roomy as we had anticipated, they are much better than any we have had yet. This was, until we captured it, a German military school. We have electric lights (although blackout regulations are very strict), a radio, heat, each man has a cot, and the officers have rooms. I am in with two chaplains so should not lack for spiritual uplift now and then. I have made several trips to the front and, incidentally, nearly got it the other day at the Forward CP when a German "88" bracketed in on us. The concussion knocked me down, which was fortunate, for the air was filled with shrapnel for a time. I obtained several more fairly interesting souvenirs, chief one being an old German powder horn, handsomely engraved, and evidently of great age.

I received two letters from Harold tonight and also a card and a short note from one of the girls who used to work at M.C.&C. Evidently, some of the mail is beginning to trickle through. Harold states that Bob is home, so that explains the long silence from him. He is to go to Santa Ana Army Air Base, California, at the conclusion of his leave. Went to the town of Eschweiler today, to Service Company, and passed through Stolberg on the way. It is most evident that the German civilians are not so enthused over the art of *blitzkrieg* at this time.

We have two "Delinquent" Battle Casualty Reports outstanding, but the old man knows about them, so God knows what the result is when they bounce. Can only hope on this.

The fact of Bob being at home might explain Mother's long silence, as she gets so excited, just like a little kid, when any of the kids are at home.

We seem to be advancing steadily, and the German resistance is somewhat sporadic. Evidently the cream of their army is being hoarded for the day when we face the Rhine River. Had an air alert last night, and Jerry dropped a few bombs in our immediate vicinity, but I, lackadaisical soul that I am, slept through it all. Buzz bomb activity has decreased noticeably. It has turned noticeably colder.

I dream constantly of the day when I shall again lead a normal, civilized life. Will I never know the simple pleasures of life, such as a wife to love, children, my home, etc.? On this puzzling thought, I shall retire for the night. For incidentally, I have been getting a bit more rest than usual, although one of the chaplains claimed I was tormented with nightmares last night.

In a Military School, Brand, Germany
30 November 1944

Today, the last day in November! God! How I wish this miserable, interminable war were over. Things seem to have taken this trend, and just will not come out of it. To top it all, this rundown physical feeling of mine had to occur, and today, too, I felt miserable. Despite that, I made a trip to Eschweiler today, to deliver some 20-odd men. I returned about 1300, and spent the balance of the afternoon in a mental fog. Saw a series of aerial battles on the way to and from the front. One crippled bomber had its crew bail out, almost directly overhead.

Received a couple of Christmas cards today, and that was all. Yesterday, at long last, I received a letter from Mother, postmarked

November 16th. Bob has evidently been at home for some time, and he reports to the Santa Ana Army Air Base on 2 December 1944. I am certainly glad he finished his tour of duty in the ETO safely and without mishap.

Certainly wish my mail would pick up. It is a bit disconcerting to see other fellows receiving 8 or 10 letters plus numerous Christmas packages. I received a great surprise the other day—a letter from my West Pointer friend, 1st Lt. Tom Furey. He is in Holland and seemed quite cheerful and satisfied. For a West Pointer, though, he has been buffeted around quite a bit; still a 1st Lt., when as a rule, they are pushed and coddled to the top, regardless of ability. In Tom's case, however, he is, without a doubt, the finest West Pointer I know and a very good friend.

I was still on leave exactly one year ago today, and I wonder just where I will be exactly one year from today? So very much has transpired in that one year that it seems almost inconceivable that as much could happen in the next one, but I know, as circumstances now are, that even more can happen. To me, at the age of 29, it seems a Herculean, if not impossible task, or should I say hope, to expect to establish a home and a family. So much of my life has been sacrificed to this War! I imagine other fellows are in the same fix, though, and if they can do it, I fail to see why I cannot.

IN A MILITARY SCHOOL, BRAND, GERMANY
1 DECEMBER 1944
The first of the month of December 1944.

My mail today consisted of one slightly ancient, and incidentally, wrongly addressed copy of "Time" Magazine. That was all, nothing more.

I felt a wee bit better today, but not a great deal. The work seems to be gradually straightening itself out, although there are still several loose strands lying about. I think that perhaps a hot shower, a change of clothes, and a general clean-up would make a new man of me, but as yet, shower facilities are still being arranged for. However, today we heard that within the next two days, they will be a possibility.

A Nazi dive bomber dropped a bomb in the near vicinity today but did no damage and was, in turn, shot down by our ANTI-AIRCRAFT gun crews stationed nearby.

I was paid today, and it is heartening indeed to see the strides that

I am making towards the purchase of my own home. Next month will see my resources mount well past the $3000 mark. How I wonder if all of this saving and planning will do me any good. Will I ever attain the goal for which I am striving?

Perhaps I have neglected to mention in recent entries the fact that I received news of the birth of a husky eight (8)-pound baby boy to Vivian Morgan, née [sic] Mrs. Vivian Cooper. I really hope that she has at last found happiness, but from certain aspects of her letter, I cannot help but note that already there are definite indications that all is not quite so rosy as it seems. Poor Kid! She was so desperately seeking a straw of happiness to cling to that she dared not look into the future. Despite the years of loneliness, yet I am happy that I did not plunge into another mess that would only cause additional years of heartache. When next I marry, if I ever do, it must be for once and for all; and both of us must be so terribly in love, so positive and sure, so certain--that nothing, nothing of whatsoever nature can ever shake our determination to make a complete and wonderful thing of our natures and of our marriage. Of course, I realize that I am very probably kidding myself when I think that such a thing is a remote possibility, but who knows? Such things have happened, even if most of the cases occurred in another age.

The trouble with the above outlook of mine is the fact that by the time this war is over, I will be so damned old that the only girls left with stars in their eyes, or with equal sentiments, will be desperate old maids and cast-offs, desperately seeking a husband to anchor to for the rest of life, and I am afraid that love or sentiment or high ideals will not enter into such a one's scheme of things.

To the above, however, as so often before, it is *KISMET*!

In a Military School, Brand, Germany
2 December 1944

At last, I am beginning to come out of this physical slump that has held me in its toils for the last several days. It has taken a long time to wear off.

Made another trip to Eschweiler today, took another truckload of replacements up. It was a miserable day, rainy roads slippery as glass. When I returned, my pants were a soaking mess, and the side of me exposed to the road was a mass of mud, so I took a good two hours this afternoon, washed thoroughly, shaved, and changed clothes. Needless to say, it made me feel like a new man.

The troops seem to have met a solid wall of resistance, at least there has been no action up front for some time. For the first time since we were committed to action, we had no casualties to report.

Much to my surprise, I received another letter from Vivian tonight, and she evidently is just as confused about the present situation she finds herself in, as before. She asked my advice, so I gave it to her, straight from the shoulder. I told her that in order to make any marriage work, it took a helluva lot of HARD WORK, on the part of the both.

Much of the work seems to have been cleared, at least all of the pressing reports, and other items seem to have been compiled and answered. There seems to have been a sudden increase of enemy air activity around here during the past two days, at least numerous bombs have been dropped in the near vicinity, and we are on a constant air alert. Today we were required by Corps to submit a Defense Plan to be used in the event that a battalion of enemy parachutists was dropped in our vicinity.

One of the Commanding Generals in the European Theater of Operations was reputed to have made the statement to the press the other day, to wit: "The majority of veterans from the ETO will be sent to the China-Burma-India Theater upon the successful conclusion of the war with Germany." Strange as it may sound, this meets with my hearty approval, for actually, have I anything to return to the United States for? I figure in this manner, I entered the Army long before we were actually at war, and I may as well stay in and see it through right to the end of Japan.

No other word from Mother since her letter of Nov. 16th, and as for Bob, I haven't heard from him for months. Hubie hasn't answered my letter yet, either, but then it was not too long ago that I wrote him, and the delivery of mail over in this theater is uncertain at best.

IN A MILITARY SCHOOL, BRAND, GERMANY
4 DECEMBER 1944

There is nothing of moment to write about. Life goes on in the accustomed, endless, dreary routine. We live from one day to the next, principally for the receipt of mail. Along that line, an interesting factor has occurred. A friend of Lola's wrote me a letter, probably at Lola's instigation. It was interesting to say the least. She mentioned the fact that she was "five feet ten, had black hair and large blue eyes, tall and slender, and was the same age" as me. I found the letter amusing and wrote an immediate reply just for the pure hell of it. God knows my receipt of mail is such that I clutch at each letter as a suffocating man gasps for air.

I treated myself to a nice birthday present (I'm sure I won't receive any other), a year's subscription to *Fortune*, a fine magazine. At quite a bargain rate, too, the ordinary subscription is $10 per annum, and the military rate was only $6. I feel sure that I will derive an immense amount of satisfaction from it, if and when it arrives.

Mail seems to be spasmodic at best; one letter will be postmarked fairly recently, and the next as much as two months overdue.

The situation up front still seems to be somewhat stalemated. The Germans are desperate now and are offering fanatical resistance now that at least seven Allied Armies are crouched on the Rhine ready to spring at the throat of Berlin. Nonetheless, each day sees them slowly and relentlessly pushed back, no matter how fanatically they resist. I fear, though, that this miserable war will not be over before August of 1945. The bloody fools, they know full well that they and their foul regime are doomed, and yet they continue the blood and slaughter.

A wild, tormented wind surged and howled around this abandoned school last night. I was restless and could not sleep. Shutters and doors banged interminably, so I arose, turned on the light, and read until fatigue brought sleep. The subject was Dickens's [A] *Tale of Two Cities*, which I read long ago as part of required reading in school. I find that I gain much more from the book at this time, possibly because it reflects a period of chaos and unrest similar in many respects to the present one.

IN A MILITARY SCHOOL, BRAND, GERMANY
6 DECEMBER 1944

December 6, 1944. Another dreary, gloomy day in the panorama of war, ticked away. Accomplished a good bit of work this day. Now that I have acquired a fairly intelligent driver, I am relieved of the troublesome chore of hauling every odd replacement up to Service Company. The driver does this for me as well as does odd chores and deliveries that may occur.

Many more of my friends have been killed in action—Carroll, Olsen, James R. McDonald, one of my former assistant clerks—T-5 Sammons—it seems as though the gory lists will never end. The

Division is getting quite a bit under strength, and there are no more replacements to be had. We are still advancing, though, have crossed the Inde River, and have taken the town of Inden in, as the *Stars and Stripes* terms it, some of the bloodiest fighting since Normandy.

I sat on my first court-martial today. It was a general court-martial, and the offense was violation of the 75th Article of War, "Misbehavior before the Enemy," or in other words, cowardice. In secret ballot, the sentence was to be dishonorably discharged from the service, to forfeit all pay and allowances due or to become due, and to serve at hard labor for the rest of his natural life. Severe as this sentence was, the man narrowly missed the maximum sentence, "to be shot to death by musketry." Needless to say, the thing was quite an ordeal to me, for I had never sat on one of the proceedings before, and I could scarcely enjoy my supper after the court was adjourned. The man was guilty beyond all doubt and had endangered the lives of the rest of the men in his squad by his actions.

During the past few days, my mail has been wonderful. I received almost a letter daily. Of course, I answered them all faithfully. I sent Mother a $50 money order and told her to buy all of the family some Christmas presents. It is the only practical thing to do over here. There is nothing to buy, and it is so much red tape and bother to send anything home. Along the mail situation, only one puzzling factor remains—not a word from the Strahls in Los Angeles. Perhaps they are really and truly miffed at me this time for my sudden cessation of writing, but I feel sure if they knew the true circumstances, they would understand perhaps.

Have begun to feel a little the worse for wear, physically. Perhaps it is because we do not get outside enough. The weather has turned a bit for the better. A few days of clear weather occurred, enabling our bombers to get through for a while, and even that short period of time helped tremendously.

At this writing, the end of the war appears to be just as far off, just as far in the future, and just as hopeless in all aspects.

IN A MILITARY SCHOOL, BRAND, GERMANY
7 DECEMBER 1944
Thursday, the 7th of December 1944—the anniversary of Pearl Harbor. Three years ago on this date, it was a peaceful Sunday afternoon, and I was lying on my bunk in the barracks at Camp Callan gazing out over

the azure blue waters of the Pacific. Then the radio changed suddenly from the lilt of music, an announcer's voice broke in with the fateful announcement that held, for me, such ominous portent.

Today, I am deep into Germany, the very heart of this sore that festers the heart of the world, the spawning ground of foul Nazidom. And the great people of the United States? Those great patriots, the civilians, yes, they are indeed doing their part. Yes, their part of shirking their bit of striking, lying down on the job. Now they must coddle them even more, or they "won't play." What a laugh, what beastly irony, that on one side of the world they are coddled, praised, and petted for accepting wages that are grossly unfair and overpaid, and on this side of the world, a poor little kid is sentenced to life imprisonment because, scared to death, he chose to run away from battle. BUT HOW ABOUT THE BASTARDS WHO STRIKE? IS THERE ANY DIFFERENCE? The result is indirectly the same; our guns are rationed as to the amount of rounds they can fire each day, due to the shortage of ammunition CAUSED BY THESE WONDERFUL 4-F CIVILIANS. You must lie and crouch ever deeper in your foxhole, and see your friends blown to pieces because we haven't the ammunition to retaliate. Enough.

No mail today. I wrote Mother and Lola another letter. We have at last been taken off of the "SECRET" list and can now reveal that we are in the famed 1st Army. This may help the folks, some, to trace our progress. Two more of my friends were seriously wounded today and evacuated to the rear.

Still feeling pretty much the worse for wear, physically. Probably a good deal of this is due to the fact that not enough change in routine takes place. The same old boring routine, day after day. All that we can do is live, almost continually, in the future. A future which we can never be sure of.

Why one generation should have to fight and struggle for its existence will always be one of the unexplainable mysteries to me. Others seemed to have lived and died in eras of peace and well-being. But I am in too reflective a mood tonight. Perhaps I had best close this puerile attempt, and go to bed. Although I dread the thought. With the blackout curtains all in place, the room is terribly close and stuffy, and for some reason or other, I have been bothered somewhat with dreams and nightmares of a weird character, lately.

The news reports were the usual run of the mill--the German reports boding ill for the Allies; the Allied reports boding ill for the Germans.

IN A MILITARY SCHOOL, BRAND, GERMANY
8 DECEMBER 1944
Tonight, with the radio playing softly such a memory-laden tune as "Smoke Gets in Your Eyes," I cannot help but be in a reminiscent mood.

Have had no mail for the past four days, and out of some 26-odd correspondents, it seems that surely some would appear. I understand seven truckloads came in tonight, however, so perhaps tomorrow?

Two more of my friends seriously wounded. One was good old Captain Gregory. I liked him especially. Hope he will be all right.

Physical well-being still below par. Not only that, but I can't seem to get to sleep of nights. Needless to say, it impairs my efficiency.

One of the depressing aftereffects of processing these Battle Casualty Reports is beginning to make itself evident; many of the wives and mothers of the casualties are writing me for more details, and heartless though it seems, all I can do is to refer them to either the Quartermaster General or Adjutant General in Washington, D.C., as I am not allowed to divulge casualty information of any kind. Night after night, as I sign the seemingly countless records with the ominous terms "KIA" or "MIA" on them, I think, "How long, O God, how long?"

It is odd, indeed, that I have not heard from the Strahls, for I wrote them on, I believe, October 22nd, and unless they have moved in the interim, I cannot account for the long silence. Some ground was gained this morning in an early morning attack, but the Germans are still resisting desperately, and it is slow going, what with the mud making advance impossible for the tanks to give much support, and the cloudy skies overhead deriving us of adequate air support.

My mind seems to be absolutely void of anything to record in these annals tonight, so perhaps I had just as well close for tonight and go to my dank and cheerless room, and again, as usual, fight for sleep.

IN A MILITARY SCHOOL, BRAND, GERMANY
9 DECEMBER 1944
Quite an eventful day! Captain Smith came down and paid us a visit. The mail situation improved tremendously! Received a letter from Hubie's mother, and one from Lola, a package from Mother, A N D my AIR mattress arrived from Ohio! Needless to say, the arrival of all this was quite a happy event for me. I wrote replies to the letters immediately and thanked Mother for the package. I shall try out the air mattress and feel sure that it will be a welcome relief to my weary bones.

Work seems to be progressing so smoothly that I am almost afraid it is building up to a climax of some sort of other. Rumor has it that Colonel Floyd will be relieved soon of his duties as Regimental Executive Officer.

The situation is again more or less stalemated at the front, and I believe that we are storing up supplies and energy for a "Big Push" in the near future. I hope so; every damned mile that we travel on the road to Berlin takes us that much closer to home.

I think that I shall take a trip up to the Regimental CP in the near future.

I have another nice souvenir—will have to see if I can hang on to this one longer than I did the Schmeisser! It is a nice leather riding crop, the top of which is handsomely capped in sterling silver, taken from a German Colonel who was captured by our Regiment.

I am going to make a determined effort to find the whereabouts of the 2nd Division and see if I can locate Hubie Rafferty. I feel pretty sure that he is in this sector someplace, but just where I do not know.

Health seems none too sparkling and vivacious as yet, but I do think there is a definite sign of improvement. For one thing, I slept like a log last night.

Am listening to this sickening German propaganda, and it is enough to nauseate one—the fools, the bloody fools. Not only must they bathe the world in blood and gore for almost six years, but they must prolong the agony until the last possible minute.

IN A MILITARY SCHOOL, BRAND, GERMANY
12 DECEMBER 1944

Nothing of major importance to write about—life goes on, and that is about all. The Germans have evidently had time to move the launching ramps for the V-1's and V-2's back to more stabilized locations, for after a considerable respite from rocket activity, they have again started to send them over in ceaseless flight. One landed so close last night, it nearly threw me out of bed, and another this morning shattered windows downstairs. I wouldn't be surprised if some of these Nazi civilians aren't acting as "rearward" observers and radioing the location of the bursts, so that they correct the directional propensities of them. They are far more accurate than they were formerly.

Mail has been somewhat spasmodic—received a card from the

Raffertys and from Melanie, John Strahl's mother, and a few of my long-delayed magazines.

The daily work has devolved into so much of a system and has slacked off to such an extent that I am truly amazed. For the first time since the hectic days of Camp Carson, we have a bit of spare time in which to write or take care of personal necessities.

In the *Stars and Stripes,* this date, appeared an article noting that the Navy thought, from all indications, that the war with Japan would be terminated in 1949. Such articles certainly aren't conducive to a high state of morale. Not that I feel "nervous in the service," but four years of this is beginning to pall on me, and like every other GI, I am only too anxious to start a home of my own, for God knows the 4-F's back home certainly have a head start on us when it comes to the better jobs, etc. Then too, the 30th of this month sees the dawn of my 29th birthday, and I can well remember the time when I thought that was a helluva old age. So much for postwar thoughts.

My friend, Captain Gregory, died. I liked him, too, although we used to argue like cats and dogs. It was so senseless; he was up on the front lines trying to pay his men off when an 88 shell burst behind him. The shrapnel penetrated to the left of his spine and came out his stomach. The money bag he had drawn was No. 13. He was happily married, and his wife had just had a baby prior to his embarking for overseas.

My physical condition still abnormal. But there is nothing I can do about that but wait for improvement. I don't consider it of sufficient importance to go to the Medics.

Still no reply from Hubie, but I am sure that he is very probably in a transient state at the present time and will not have the time to write for quite a while. Sure hope he gets back to the 2nd Division okay.

In a Military School, Brand, Germany
14 December 1944
Again, nothing of major importance to write about, but I shall at least make an endeavor. At long last, my laundry returned today, so I promptly hied myself to the dispensary and made suitable arrangements for a HOT TUB BATH, which glorious event, shall take place tomorrow morning at 1000. I have decreed that the entire Personnel Section shall participate in a half hour of calisthenics daily, from now on. Most of these men are sitting at their desks for an average of 12 hours per day

with no physical activity to speak of, so I think it well, not only for them, but for me, too.

I think I mentioned the fact (or did I?) that my damnable air mattress sprung a leak, and deflated rapidly the other night, so I am trying vainly to patch it with a cold patch. Hope it works all right. My curses on the K&W Rubber Company!

I received a letter from Mother, which I answered this date. Also received a bank statement, together with a book of blank checks to be used if and when I ever get out of this vile Nazi land of iniquity. Glad to see that the bank's figures and mine coincide to within a matter of a very few dollars.

Seems to be quite a bit of the old political strife and struggling up at the Regiment. Even a war, it seems, as well as the realities of actual combat, cannot end the petty strife and smallness of some men. Thank God I am more or less isolated from that mess. Quite a bit of gossip from that section, also.

In about an hour, I shall go over to the mess hall and see a world premiere of *Saratoga Trunk* with Gary Cooper and the much publicized Ingrid Bergman. It will be the first picture show that I have seen since leaving Camp Carson.

I saw Major Melloh, the fine old doc we have serving us here, and he prescribed some paregoric emulsion to see if it cannot alleviate, to some extent the ailment, which has struck me down.

I wish to goodness some more mail would arrive soon and at least some of the long-awaited packages could arrive.

Our little captured German radio is proving a great source of comfort. At the present time it is merrily sending forth the strains of polkas and other lively music, redolent of happier days and still happier memories of . . .

In a Military School, Brand, Germany
15 December 1944
Received two ancient letters today—November 11th—one from Mother and one from Harold. Both of them were past history, due to the fact that I had received letters as late as November 28th only recently. However, they made for enjoyable reading. Also a card from Marcella, one of the girls who used to work at the plant. I sent my A I R mattress back today, together with a letter telling them that it had arrived in a defective condition and that if they did not care to repair or replace it,

to keep it, as I would have neither the time nor the facilities for doing so.

I had a most wonderful experience today—a HOT TUB BATH! And do I feel fresh and clean tonight! I scrubbed and scrubbed and scrubbed and then soaked some more. It was wonderful!

I think that I shall go up to the Regimental CP tomorrow and try to get some things straightened out with Smith. It will be quite a long trip, for they have moved up a considerable distance, and I am not sure exactly where but can probably find out in Service Company.

We have been issued our monthly "ration" of Scotch and gin, PLUS (paid for, of course), PLUS an extra ration this month for Christmas. What in the world I will ever do with all that liquor, I don't know, for I hardly ever drink the stuff, and usually end up giving it away.

The work still seems to be progressing smoothly, and it still amazes me that things could have smoothed out to such an extent. We had our first period of calisthenics today, and it went very well with wholehearted cooperation from most everyone concerned.

Hitler's buzz bomb activity has increased again as well as his long-range artillery from 210-mm guns. The whole area shook and shivered last night from the continual impact of these missiles. I didn't lose too much sleep, though. If they hit, they hit, that's all.

My reception of mail has picked up wonderfully as far as magazines are concerned, but am not doing too good as far as personal (and more interesting) mail is concerned.

Mother enclosed a clipping about Bob, which evidently appeared in one of the Sonora papers. He certainly has done SWELL. He really is a grand kid and one to be proud of. I hope that he gets a decent break at Santa Ana.

Feeling much better, physically.

In a Military School, Brand, Germany
16 December 1944
Went to the front today, the Regimental CP. The same horror and desolation of war presented itself—ruined villages and towns (happily <u>German</u>), dead horses lining the roadway where they were caught by one of our artillery barrages, gutted pillboxes, empty (and significant) foxholes, and slit trenches. Demolished bridges were much in evidence today. The Germans had madly blown every bridge in the path of our advance in an effort to stop us (to no avail, as

our engineers hastily replaced them with Bailey Bridges and Hasty Bridges).

I can say that I have driven quite a few miles on Hitler's *Autobahnen* or Super-Highway. It really is an excellent highway and reminded me greatly of some of the four-lane highways to which I was accustomed in California. Arrived back here at approximately 1500 and immediately was called to the Office of the Inspector General of the Division. Seems they are conducting an investigation of the poor manner in which the records of the replacements of the Division reach the Personnel Sections. I gave them my views on the matter, which I may add, were quite vehement.

I received another letter from Mother even more ancient than the ones I received the other night (dated November 6th), and so I took the time tonight to answer all three of the old ones.

Had quite another "discussion" with my Sgt. Major, in which I told him flatly that some of the men of this section could either get over some of their temperamentality and prima donna attitudes or would be welcome to try a change. They act like a bunch of high school boys rather than men, at times.

I have been bothered recently with a determined inability to get to sleep. For the first time since we have been receiving our "liquor ration," I indulged in drinking some of the Scotch with some friends last night and enjoyed a blissful night's slumber for the first time in weeks. Didn't drink enough to be called "drunk" by any means, but enough to bring sleep in good haste.

Some German bombers just flew over, and our antiaircraft guns opened with a tremendous roar and clatter. It didn't last very long, however, and they evidently flew away in quite a disorganized manner.

Had quite a long talk with Captain Smith today and ironed out a few of the difficulties that have pressed the section of late. These visits to the front always pay off in that respect. There is so much you can accomplish personally that you cannot do over the phone or by courier.

Haven't heard from my old friend, Pruitt, lately, but he evidently is doing fine and going strong. He certainly is a grand kid and doing a great job.

IN A MILITARY SCHOOL, BRAND, GERMANY
18 DECEMBER 1944
Same old dull, dreary routine of war. We were kept awake most of the night by the worst air raid we have yet experienced. The Jerries came over singly and in small waves of two or three planes. They dropped many flares and fragmentation bombs as well as what sounded like a few 500 pounders. The noise from our own answering *ack-ack* was terrific and a sight to behold—red tracers stabbing into the inky blackness, the *ka-rump, ka-rump* of our 90- and 120-mm AA guns. All in all, it was quite a show. The raid itself did no damage to U.S. facilities that I could ascertain, but this morning, the German radio was bleating of its stupendous successes. Some 1600 parachutists WERE dropped in the 1st Army area but were quickly rounded up.

Happened across an interesting article that has to do with zodiacal forecasts, and in a way, it hits so close to home, and is so amusingly accurate, that I reprint it for my later amusement:

Sun in Capricorn:

Self-preservation aggressively carried into ambition and aspiration is the key to Capricorn activity. Not content with keeping body and soul together, Capricorn must amount to something, must have some accomplishment to point to, some property to take care of, some obligation to fulfill. His mind is subtly balanced between defense and attack; he will rarely risk either, but will pyramid his life by stepping from one to the other. Since he will never voluntarily step backward, he first shoves his security a little above his ambition, and then his ambition a little ahead of his security, till finally, he is top of the heap and has taken no risks at all. He is worldly and careful; selfish, but capable of great devotion if he thinks it is merited; a stickler for the proprieties. He drives a hard bargain, but not an unjust one, and he asks no mercy from anyone. He has plenty of suspicion, and figures that anyone who can "Put one over" on him has earned what he gets. Not the most ardent of signs in personal relations, Capricorn's love is still a much-to-be-desired thing, stable and steady, able to put up with a good deal for the sake of loyalty if not indeed for affection. He will rarely marry beneath his station and frequently marries above it. He understands "Thee shouldst marry for love, but thou canst just as well love where there is money." He is an excellent executive and will not long remain subordinate. He rules by instinct and sometimes makes those he rules quite angry. He has little interest in seeing their point of view or answering their questions, and believes that "orders is orders": he took 'em once, and now it's someone else's turn. When the main chance requires it, Capricorn can be mild and meek as a lamb, but he'll snap off the foreman's job if he gets a chance. Once arrived, however, he can be lavishly charitable. He loves the sense of importance it gives him, the feeling that he has made the world give to him, and now he can afford to give something back to it. Underlying all his virtues and faults is the primary instinct to vindicate himself with power, to preserve himself materially in the highest structure he can build; and if some affliction in his life sphere doesn't undermine his judgment (which it often does) and cause him to overplay his hand at some critical point, he generally emerges with the world or some considerable portion of it at his feet."

All in all, an interesting essay. Just now received quite a bit of mail (4 letters) so will proceed to devour their contents.

IN A MILITARY SCHOOL, BRAND, GERMANY
19 DECEMBER 1944

Another general court-martial today, but as I had drawn up the charges on this particular man and had further knowledge of past discrepancies, I was challenged, and therefore, excused. (Thank God.)

The recent heavy counterattack of the Germans is still progressing. They have thrust a spearhead some 20 miles deep into Belgium. This puts elements of the German Forces some distance to the east, AND behind us. Numerous parachutists have been dropped, and tonight a "SECRET" alert reached us that 30 captured American jeeps were in the 1st Army area, manned by Germans in American uniforms. As a result, the guard was doubled, and breakfast hours were boosted to 0530. We must be prepared to move out of here on two hours' notice. The present offensive of the enemy is evidently quite powerful and well planned, made from carefully hoarded stores of supplies of tanks and planes.

I hit the "jackpot" on mail yesterday—some six letters, including one real long one from Lena. I answered that one last night and tonight answered one from one of the fellows that I used to work with. Several of Mother's arrived, and they were all of rather ancient date. She acknowledged the receipt of the $50 dollar money order that I mailed to her on November 15th, and she had also made an actual count of the number of War Bonds on hand. I find that I actually had one more $50 war bond than I had figured.

Today was another of those dull, dreary, boring days composed solely of attending to the routine administrative procedures of an infantry regiment—allotments, insurance, discharging, commissioning, complying with this, complying with that, and in addition, all of the additional work of seeing that my own Personnel Section was adequately informed, cared for, and advised.

One good stroke of fortune recently—one of the fellows was going back into Belgium on some business, and I asked him to purchase me the best field coat he could find. He did, and it is a honey, so heavy, thick, and comfortable that I feel sure that I will be able to use it, if and when I return to civilian life, by the simple expedient of having it dyed an appropriate color.

Finis for tonight.

IN A MILITARY SCHOOL, BRAND, GERMANY
23 DECEMBER 1944

I have been retiring fairly early, of late, in an effort to store up some reserve strength for the events that are sure to come. Things are none too stable here in our particular sector of the Western Front, since the big German breakthrough or counteroffensive, which started a week ago today. So far, all that we can determine is that one spearhead has penetrated into Belgium to a depth of some 40 miles. This spearhead is directly to our rear and east of us, so we feel none too secure or comfortable. We have been on a continuous alert since the thing started and had a series of air raids when the thing first started with Jerry dropping flares, bombs, etc. There has been a regrouping of the forces on the Western Front in order to cope with the situation, and I have a hunch that we will soon be with the Ninth U.S. Army instead of the 1st.

I received a letter from Colonel Smith, who is still in India, and he had quite a bit to say. Certainly is a great old gentleman, and I hope that I will have the opportunity of seeing him again, upon the conclusion of the war.

Today's radio edition of *Combat Diary* was quite optimistic, and the fierce German Drive seems to be halted on the flanks, but the center is still fluid. I have received another letter from Claude and Effie, and they tell me that Hubie returned to the hospital from the Replacement Depot where he was located. This, without a doubt, accounts for the long silence from him; and in a way, I am glad, for at least he is out of this muck--and worse--for the time being.

The German propaganda was going full blast last night. About all you could get on the radio was the German station, and they were in a rare state of jubilation, chortling about their great victory, and how it was too bad that we had all planned to be home by Christmas; but instead, they would be celebrating New Year's in Paris, once more. Sickening. However, we all got a big laugh out of the broadcasts.

It is becoming evident that we may be forced to move to another location, presumably without buildings, but hope that this is not true. For if I have to squeeze two tons of equipment plus 38 men into a squad tent, it is going to bring on an unpleasant situation. Guess we will survive it, though; we always have in other pressing predicaments.

IN A MILITARY SCHOOL, BRAND, GERMANY
CHRISTMAS DAY, 25 DECEMBER 1944
Christmas Day in foul Nazidom! Events have been moving swiftly since the start of [Von] Rundstedt's offensive. Since I last wrote, we have had endless air activity and placed on an alert status. So far, we have had no close enemy action, with the exception of the daily and nightly air raids, but no damage has been caused by these. True to my prediction, we are now in the Ninth U.S. Army. I am inclined to agree with Eisenhower and all of the higher brass that this is the enemy's last desperate thrust, and if all goes according to plan, it may well end in the final "knock-down-and-drag-out" battle, which will terminate the war.

Last night brought many memories of past Christmas Eves, and we celebrated it by having a few drinks of Scotch. But even this palled on me after a while, and I retired at the decidedly Christian hour of 2045.

Due to our change in armies (again), the mail is again messed up, as always, and I have only received two letters, both from my dear friend, Colonel Smith, in India.

Despite the tension of the present delicate tactical situation, we are going to have a gala Xmas dinner, complete with table wine for all concerned. This festive meal will not take place until 1530 this afternoon, and so I must curb my hunger until that time. My boys had their Christmas party last night, and from what I observed when I paid them a little visit, they evidently had a good time. Very probably, they will have another celebration on New Year's Eve, for I doubt if they managed to do away with the huge stock of liquor they managed to accumulate.

The past two days have been ideal for the operation of our Air Force. Clear, cloudless skies and balmy weather, albeit a bit cold.

I managed to shave, wash, and clean up in general this morning, but I think I will hit the Medics up again at an early date and arrange for another soul-restoring "tub bath."

Oh yes! I have a sidearm at last! A German P-38 pistol. It has a sentimental value, too, for it was formerly the property of Lt. Moen, my good friend who was killed in Holland. The financial cost of it was sent to help his wife out. I have cleaned it thoroughly and managed to obtain some new grips for it, as the original grips were the only bad feature of the gun.

Enough for now.

IN A MILITARY SCHOOL NEAR BRAND, GERMANY
27 DECEMBER 1944

Life goes on in its dull, dreary, soul-destroying routine. The daily procedure of work has been organized into such a state of precision that we find ourselves with more spare time on our hands then we have ever had before. Due to the administrative change effected when we were placed under the jurisdiction of the Ninth U.S. Army, our receipt of mail has again been disrupted. I have received nothing but a few ancient magazines and a letter or two from Mother that managed to slip through.

The German counteroffensive to the south of us is still shrouded under a pall of secrecy, although reports as late as forty-eight hours ago had it brought to a standstill, and we seem to be holding on all flanks. A radio report this morning indicated, however, that the Germans were only four miles from the Meuse, so we hardly know whether to assume an air of optimism or not. Needless to say, our little group feels much more comfortable with the recent arrival of additional troops in the immediate vicinity.

It is a beautiful day, almost like spring. There is not a cloud in the sky, and the sun is bathing the surrounding terrain in its rays, even though the air is brisk and nippy. The little country lane, which lies directly outside my window, reminds me much of similar, though far more peaceful, country lanes in California. Who could possibly believe that a few short miles away men are dying violent deaths in the preliminary prelude to the final and deciding battle that is sure to come?

Went to a show last night and saw an ancient picture, *It Started with Eve*, with Deanna Durbin. Nevertheless, it was enjoyable, chiefly due to the splendid singing, as far as I was concerned. I didn't get to bed until about 0020, and as a result, felt none too good this morning but am determined to retire a little early tonight to make up for it.

In a Military School, Brand, Germany
28 December 1944

Indeed a change from yesterday! Today the sky is overcast and clouds hang low. The ground is covered with a thin blanket of snow, and it is bitterly cold. This is ideal weather for the Germans to again resort to their infamous "sneak" tactics.

We were alerted again last night. Reports indicated that a large force of parachutists was expected. I imbibed to a moderate extent last night. Had intended to retire early but found myself exceedingly nervous and restless—paced the floor in my room and then joined some friends across the hall.

I have been doing much thinking recently, and that is NOT good, for under the present conditions and circumstances, "those who stop to think are lost." Thinking again of what may take place at the termination of the war, again I reiterate: I do not desire to return to my former employment, and yet employment may well prove to be scarce at that time. Eleven million other veterans will be searching for other jobs due to the same motives that will compel me to do so--changed viewpoints, fully matured minds, higher ambitions, goals, and ideals. Indeed, I MAY have enough funds put aside by that time to purchase a modest little home, but why purchase something as permanent and conclusive as that if I will not have the means to maintain it? Another factor—all employment will very probably be highly specialized, or have very high educational requirements, and my educational qualifications are mediocre, to say the least. And still another—age. I may well be over 30 years of age by the time this holocaust ends, an age incidentally, when other men are well started on their professions and have driven deep roots into their community life. Will the learning and advancement that I have managed to acquire in the military mean anything at all, outside of the anticipated veterans benefits and/or the "GI Bill of Rights?" My dear wish to have a home and family—how can that ever be accomplished at such a late period in my life? What possible thing have I to offer any woman, except myself?

Such a sea of unanswerable questions seems to engulf me, and no possible solution to any of them seems evident. At the present time and place, however, it seems foolish to worry about the future. Managing to exist and come through the mess with a whole skin will be an accomplishment in itself. Perhaps it is best to figuratively shrug my shoulders and say, "So be it, come what may."

IN A MILITARY SCHOOL, BRAND, GERMANY
29 DECEMBER 1944

The present time is one of tension and uncertainty, to say the least. From all available G-2 sources, it can be assumed that a large German drive, in quite strong force, can be expected on our immediate front. This would be quite logical, for with the present breakthrough somewhat stalemated, another breakthrough, particularly in our sector, would provide the Germans with a diversionary feint, not only relieving the pressure on their present thrust, but forming the needed "claw" to form a pincer of gigantic proportions around not only Aachen but Liège and its surrounding terrain as well. We must be prepared to move on short notice and will, in the event the expected breakthrough happens, have to abandon all of our equipment with the exception of Form 20's, service records, and master payrolls. All other papers will be burned including, I presume, this beloved copy of thoughts and impressions.

Good old Captain Martin came through today and brought me a nice leather shoulder holster for my P-38. This relieves the necessity of packing the damned thing in that cumbersome German holster, which stuck out from my hip like a sore thumb. I shall continue to pack the automatic, even though it is sure death to do so, in the event of capture by the Germans. It is much more convenient than packing that cumbersome carbine around.

The mail situation improved somewhat today—three overdue Christmas cards, a letter from Mother, one from Lola, and one from Fred Strahl down in Italy. Have hopes of some more (much more current mail coming in tomorrow). I have determined to go up to the Regimental CP tomorrow, in connection with a special report.

Things seem to be going exceptionally smoothly of late, in fact, almost too good to be true. The weather is still heavily overcast, and the thin blanket of snow remains with us, replenished slightly each night. Had a number of visitors down to see me today but managed to handle all of the business problems in short order with the exception of one bad case, snafued MAC recommendations.

I have instructed my jeep driver to maintain the jeep in a condition of instant readiness—completely gassed and oiled and ready to load essential equipment at a moment's notice. He is a likable chap and seems quite thorough and conscientious in his work. He is a Pfc named Henry Bresser, and his association with us resulted when he came back through here on his return from the hospital. A recipient of the Purple Heart, incidentally.

IN A MILITARY SCHOOL, BRAND, GERMANY
30 DECEMBER 1944

My birthday—29 years old. T-w-e-n-t-y N-i-n-e years old! My God! I'm a doddering old man! The mere thought of having reached such an antiquated age and having accomplished so little, horrifies me. It brings to mind as always, the ever-present, unanswerable enigma, "What in the hell will I do after the culmination of the war?" Today I received a package from my old employers, M.C.&C. Co., in which was enclosed a booklet, which outlined the benefits, rules, and regulations of those who worked at that organization. Truly, the place has prospered and progressed mightily since my departure some four years ago. But even so, my determination never to return to that mode of life and living was only heightened by the receipt of the booklet. What then? Where? In what direction lies my future happiness? These I cannot answer. Only the dull, hopeless knowledge of how much the Army has changed me remains with me, but as to what direction my destiny will lead me from this birth date on, only fate will decide, in her inscrutable manner.

In the interim, things do not seem entirely in our favor here on the Western Front. Certain knowledge that I acquired today bears this out, but I must refrain from mentioning it here. I made a trip to the front today to Lamersdorf, Germany. Artillery fire was quite intense, but fortunately, the CP was located in a series of underground air raid shelters recently wrested from the foul Hun. Had quite a talk with the

Colonel (and incidentally, sampled his Scotch while in the process). I gather that he is quite pleased with the smooth progress of my particular section.

Tomorrow will be payday again, and I shall again have the $200 allotment coming from my pay. Good! The more I can put aside for the ultimate purchase of my home, the safer and more secure I will feel. For I VOW THAT I WILL HAVE THAT HOME SOMEDAY, COME WHAT MAY!

Arrived back today from the front, in time for the daily meeting of our section; and to my surprise, the men surprised me mightily by spontaneously bursting into a rendition of "Happy Birthday to You." For the most part, they are a fine bunch of kids, but they are just like a bunch of kids, fighting and squabbling, and I am forced to be the Father Confessor to them all. What an assortment!

The men are planning a small party in celebration of New Year's, as a small liquor ration was authorized for them, and I must attend on orders of the AG to see that it is properly supervised.

In a Military School, Brand, Germany
31 December 1944

On this last day of 1944, I must pause, at least momentarily, and take stock of myself. A moderately heavy snow blankets the area. Our particular sector has been ominously quiet for the past few weeks. The counteroffensive seems to be securely bottled up at this writing, but certain knowledge indicates that the Germans will make at least one more supreme effort to break out of the "West Wall" to save their humbled prestige, if nothing else. So much for tactics.

A magazine and one ancient letter from Lola arrived today, but nothing else. Outside of that, nothing of moment occurred today. The proficiency of Battle Casualty Reporting was graded today, and my section was graded 100%, or first in the entire Division. We have been alerted to evacuate the premises upon a moment's notice in the event of a successful German penetration in our sector.

How I wonder what the year 1945 holds for me! Will it be as momentous (and as soul destroying) as this past year? Or will it see the successful culmination of this ghastly war and perhaps the materialization of a few of my hopes and dreams? On one thing I am determined. I shall utilize every resource of willpower and determination to improve my body and my mind. For when I leave the Army to return to civilian life, I intend to be in the best possible condition mentally, physically, financially, and in every other way.

I hardly look for 1945 to see my return to civilian life, but I hope it soon thereafter, as I have so much to do, so much to strive for, so much to regain. Strangely, I do not count the years in the Army a loss, for I have gained in every way during the course of those years. But the years I do consider a loss are those that I spent married to that "Monument of Purity," and the ensuing year spent paying off her debts. These I vow that I shall regain with interest in the years that are to come.

And so, at the end of this excerpt, and of this year, I again close with a query: What lies ahead of me, and in what direction will destiny see fit to guide my steps in the trying days that lie ahead? *KISMET*!

In a Military School, Brand, Germany
5 January 1945

I haven't written for some time. Certainly don't feel "in the pink" of condition today. Lt. Tufts and I absorbed two full bottles of champagne last night, celebrating his return from the hospital, and contrary to popular belief, that particular beverage DOES leave a hangover of lasting and potent effect.

Since the last tremendous receipt of mail, which came all on one day, I have had utterly none. Could certainly use a few letters today.

Lt. Pruitt distinguished himself mightily the other night on a patrol action and has been recommended for the Distinguished Service Cross. I certainly hope he gets it. He is well on the way to being the most decorated man in this Regiment, and I for one am damned proud of him. Another indication of how wrong that buffoon, JOE BLOW, was. He always said Pruitt was no S-2 and wanted to railroad him to a rifle company at the same time he was trying to railroad me.

Thus, the war goes on in its dreary way. The action seems to have become stalemated again, although our outfit is prepared for any sudden flare-up on the part of the Germans. A heavy snow has covered the ground for the last few days, and it has been bitterly cold, with the roads covered with a heavy film of ice daily.

Had to attend another general court-martial the other day, but was excused again because the man was from the Regiment, and I had drawn up the charges on him. Charge? Violation of the 86th Article of War, a sentry deserting his post. Maximum sentence for this offense is death, and so I imagine he will receive a severe sentence. The last two violations of similar nature received life imprisonment at hard labor.

Melanie's recent letter was very interesting. She has a manner of writing that is inimitable. According to her, Margie was certainly having her share of trouble. Poor kid—it always seems that the decent and fine people in this world are the ones who have an entirely disproportionate share of trouble and worry. I hope she comes out of it okay.

Rafferty's latest letter stated that he expected to go to Paris on some kind of a service command assignment—court-martial work of some kind or other. I hope so. He was wounded quite badly, and it is still giving him trouble, evidently.

In a Military School, Brand, Germany
10 January 1945
I have been sicker than a dog for the past two days, my semiannual bout with Old Man Flu, I guess. It surely knocked me for a loop. I retired to my cold, dank, dismal room where my fellow roommates (the chaplains) nigh to have killed me with well-meant expressions of brotherly love. The doc brought over various pills, and these seemed to do the trick, inasmuch as I crawled from my couch, shaky and drawn, and made my way back to the salt mines.

I have received no mail at all since Mother's letter, which she had written on Christmas Day. Bob was evidently able to make it home in time for Christmas. I wrote her a letter tonight and requested that she send me a 5-pound box of assorted cheeses, pickles, olives, sardines, anchovies, chicken, tuna, salami, crackers, and other such tidbits with which to concoct cracker sandwiches. Such material will go well around here after supper, especially on those evenings when we have the delectable C-rations for supper. UGH!

Correspondence from all other sources seems to have ceased as though cut off with a knife. Possibly due to the fouled-up mail situation again but not in all cases, surely.

Another of my old friends, and a buddy of mine, was killed today, Captain Luthi, married and with two lovely children. The hell of it was, he was in the bunch that was killed by the bombs of our own Air Force that fell short of the enemy lines. He sure was a grand little guy, and thank God I said that about him <u>before</u> he was killed.

While I was deathly sick and more or less tossing in a half-delirious state, I sure did a helluva lot of thinking. The more I think, however, the more hopeless it all seems about any sort of life after the war, I mean. What in hell will I find to do? How will I be able to accomplish everything that I want to do in so short a time? How in the world can I ever lay the foundations for a home and family if I have no means of sustaining one, much less founding one? As usual, though, there seems to be no solution for these as well as for so many other questions. As in the last war, at present, nothing is too good for the soldier, but wait until six months after the armistice and see what the reaction will be, despite all of the protestations to the contrary.

IN A MILITARY SCHOOL, BRAND, GERMANY
13 JANUARY 1944

Saturday already! The week has fairly flown by, although we have not been overly busy. A thick carpet of snow has blanketed the area all this time, for it has been quite cold. If this were not a war and conditions were not as they are, it would be a beautiful and picturesque sight—winter in the Old World!

I have discovered a new means of passing the evenings. The Red Cross Field Director has a record player and a large and varied assortment of fine music. In this manner, I have spent many recent evenings, and enjoyable they were, too.

Insomnia seems to have returned to me, for I find it impossible to get to sleep; and all the while, my tired mind is filled with an interminable galaxy of the most depressing thoughts of the hopelessness of the present and the still more hopeless future. I relive past instances in my life, the good as well as the bad, the mistakes as well as the accomplishments. It is bad to brood in this manner, that I know, but such is my accursed nature, I guess.

The daily work continues to function in a smooth manner, and we are, at present, preparing for another I.G. inspection from which I do not anticipate too much trouble; although, without a doubt, the condition of records will not be judged as satisfactory. For it would be an impossible task to bring the records up to date or to the state of excellence attained while we were at Carson, what with the fact that 80% of our records are now replaced with those of reinforcements, and the balance being constantly shifted to and from the various hospitals.

A situation arose the other day, which tends to disconcert me somewhat. Margie wrote me a letter on my birthday wishing me well, and I felt obligated to send her a reply out of common decency, if nothing else. I concluded it in a "final" tone and hope that she sees fit to reply no further. For if she does, I will have to be most diplomatic and tactful in order to avoid any further entanglements or repercussions.

Mail has been extremely scanty of late, and I imagine this is due, in good part, to the heavy fighting to the south of us where most of the transportation is tied up hauling supplies. Such is as it should be, of course.

IN A MILITARY SCHOOL, BRAND, GERMANY
17 JANUARY 1945
1910

Practically nothing of interest has occurred that merits writing about. One or two strafing attacks by the *Luftwaffe*, an alert against parachutists (which proved to a be a false alarm). The situation at the front, in this particular sector at least, has become very static. Aside from the usual harassing artillery fire, sporadic combat patrols and clashes, the situation is calm, and the troops are, for the most part, gaining a well-earned rest. It appears that the nefarious counteroffensive of Von Rundstedt's has dwindled away into nothing. The "Bulge' has practically been eliminated, and he is withdrawing his forces. Daily G-2 reports maintain that indications point to a swift counter-drive in our immediate area with Aachen as the immediate objective. I do not think this too probable, however.

Mail has again dwindled to nothing, and even the receipt of magazines, which had been good for a while, has ceased. I have not felt particularly good since my recovery from an attack of the "flu." Had a few sociable drinks of Scotch last night with the other two Regimental Personnel Officers, Captain Mallalieu and Captain Hurst. Turned in about 2300.

I intend to leave early tomorrow morning for an all-day visit at the Regimental CP in which I shall endeavor to get some of the complicated and tangled business of the Regiment straightened out.

The news tells us that the Russians have attacked in force on a new winter offensive, and I certainly hope this is true, for this stalemate that confronts us at present is soul destroying in its monotony. Also heard that the British on the north end of the line have started a small-scale offensive in Holland. American units, in the meantime, are cleaning up the remnants of the "Bulge" and holding the German offensive on the south end of the line in the Saar area.

I shall retire early tonight and endeavor to get a good night's rest in preparation for a hard day tomorrow. Sleep does not seem to come easily to me, of late, and I have to struggle to gain it. A few of the boys are getting passes to Brussels and Paris, but I have no hopes of one myself. I await the receipt of mail with the utmost anticipation and interest. It's all we have to look forward to.

IN A MILITARY SCHOOL, BRAND, GERMANY
20 JANUARY 1945

I spent two days and a night at the Regimental CP. Straightened out a lot of miscellaneous business and had a good visit with all the lads. Things are certainly quiet on the front. Smith and I went out to a makeshift range that had been constructed for the training of the reinforcements, and I fired about three clips from my P-38. A nice firing gun, accurate and true, with an exceptionally fine balance.

Things are just as dull and boring around here as ever. Same deadly, monotonous routine, day in and and day out. At lunch today, I was seated next to Brigadier General Woodward, stiff and formal introductions, etc.

All mail since the first of the year has ceased, with the exception of a letter and a package from Lola. To my surprise, I learn that <u>my</u> mail is not being forwarded promptly, either. According to Lola, Mother was somewhat worried because she had not heard from me for so long. This, despite the fact that I have written at least every two days since the start of the German counteroffensive!

The lack of mail, as in other people, tends to have a depressing influence on me. My thoughts and reflections then have too much time to gaze in retrospect on things that have been and things that are to come. The latter, in particular, have been the cause of much thought of late, on my part. So many seemingly impossible things to accomplish or find. So much of life to be lived, and yet, so many handicaps and difficulties to be overcome before life will again regain a semblance of normalcy. I know the Pollyannas will say, "But look at all the good things you may have—look at the brighter side of the ledger." Very true! For instance, I have accomplished much since my entry into the Army, and the resultant experience and training should count for something. The Army has replaced, with confidence and aggressiveness, what formerly was a somewhat timid and reticent nature. It has brought out abilities and resourcefulness that not even

I suspected. There is the suggestion in a recent magazine article that such men as I, having proved and found themselves, should remain in the Army even after the war. This, while it may seem to have merit on the surface, is not such an ideal solution as it first appears. For instance, such things as a certain reduction in rank will be almost inevitable as well as the none-to-desirable nomadic and abnormal aspects of a military life. Then, too, the requisite entrance requirements would very probably prove to be quite rigid, and although I feel sure that I would not have too much trouble in successfully passing them, my lack of the necessary string of diplomas and degrees would probably not prove an attractive feature to the government. I have thought, too, of the many governmental agencies that will necessarily be created to maintain our newly acquired bases and lands throughout the world, but especially in the Pacific, and thought that this might be a good thing to keep my eye on, but again, my lack of a formal education is bound to hamper me in that respect.

Inasmuch as I know such subjects prove incapable of solution at the present time, it is futile to think of them, and yet indeed, they provide interesting food for thought!

I think that I will retire early tonight, for I am abominably tired and have felt so for the past few weeks. It is a struggle to gain the blessedness of sleep, and yet it is even more of a struggle to get out of bed the following morning.

And so, to bed!

IN A MILITARY SCHOOL, BRAND, GERMANY
22 JANUARY 1945
Truly, this has been an interesting and eventful day. Arose at 0645 as planned, and together with Lt. Colonel Kernan and the other two Regimental Personnel O's, departed for the Division Command Post at Weisweiler. We arrived at approximately 0830, and I met Captain Smith and my Regimental Commander, and we then proceeded to the General's mess for a big "powwow" on the matter of excess grades and ratings. The meeting was very interesting, chiefly because of two factors: the presence of Terry Allen, the CG, and the odd facets of his personality. During the course of the meeting, a communication was read, which (essentially) stressed the dire need of utilizing all available manpower. It was suggested that all excess personnel be eliminated, administrative staffs be cut to a minimum, and where possible, to

replace administrative staffs with limited service personnel. This, of course, vitally affects me, and it is still to be determined into just how high an echelon of command this procedure will be carried. There are certain aspects of the thing that are depressing. For instance, if this is carried out, this will be the second time that the Army and its "efficient" higher brass have wasted months of training and placed me in a job of which I know nothing. One: I was trained for over 18 months as a Battalion S-3, a job which I knew well and was perfectly happy in, and without warning, my CO appointed me the Personnel Adjutant of this Regiment, a job of which I was totally ignorant of even the basic principles. By hard study, diligent work, and perseverance, I have at last reached a state of proficiency that the Regimental Commander himself grades as "Superior." Now if this plan is carried out to its ultimate conclusion, I will very probably be placed in the role of either a company commander or a staff position commensurate with the grade of Captain. The latter would not be too bad, for I have done nothing but staff work since my graduation as an officer. But as for the job of a company commander, it would be manifestly unfair to both me and to the men under me, for I have never had a bit of that particular training. Further directives on this matter are pending, and it will be interesting to see just how far they intend to carry this matter. Whatever the decision, I shall abide by it and do my best. My principles and creed will not allow me to do otherwise. *KISMET*!

I received a total of five letters in the mail today, which served immeasurably to increase my morale. I shall answer them all in the near future. Also am happy to report that my state of health seems to be improving, for I felt a thousand times better this day!

IN A MILITARY SCHOOL, BRAND, GERMANY
29 JANUARY 1945
I have felt terribly fatigued of late—cannot seem to obtain enough sleep—and yet when I retire early, it is almost necessary to fight for sleep. That is, with one exception. Last night, I fell into bed exhausted and, for once, fell asleep instantly.

We have been very busy recently—general courts-martial, special courts-martial, summary courts-martial, reclassifications, efficiency reports, and even the resignation of an officer under the odious AR 605-275. Seem to be accomplishing it, however, and the mess concerning the "illegal" grades and ratings seems to have become calm and serene.

Smith went to Brussels for three days in connection with some GCM charges. I could go to the Falkenburg "Rest Camp" if I so desired, but I cannot seem to attain any enthusiasm for the idea, try as I will.

I have been trying for two days, now, to finish this entry but seem to be getting nowhere. Work has been piling up at a tremendous rate, but we managed to accomplish it with some semblance of efficiency.

There is really nothing to remark on. Dull and boring are these days of "manning the Western Front." I recommended five of my boys for the Combat Infantryman Badge, and wonder of wonders, the old man approved. I plan on getting it for all of them eventually.

Again, my mail has slowed to a mere trickle, and this, of course, does not lead to a high state of morale. Anyone can note that I long ago ceased mentioning the fervent wish that I had someone to whom I could write and pour out my heart and soul with plans of the future, my dreams, my likes and dislikes. Such is not to be, however, and I, for one, am able to recognize that fact, for when I am eventually discharged from the Army, I will certainly be too old to start building and planning anew. What then in life is left for me? Like a doleful dirge of these Aachen church bells, the answer is—nothing.

The interesting speculation that I mentioned in a recent excerpt has been answered in a somewhat satisfactory manner by none other than Lt. General Ben Lear in these words: "Technicians and other highly trained personnel will not be taken." I, myself, certainly come into that category, and on second thought, being in an actual combat outfit, there is not much chance of a shift in personnel.

This month has flown by in an amazingly fast manner, and yet there has been no substantial change in the tactical situation, with the sole exception of the amazing Russian drive on the Eastern Front and the elimination of Von Rundstedt's "Bulge." Believe me, just one month ago today, things were none too stable, secure, or certain around here. What next month?

IN A MILITARY SCHOOL, BRAND, GERMANY
4 FEBRUARY 1945
Time has again flicked a few more days from the calendar since I last wrote. In the interim, an amazing influx of mail has cascaded across my desk. Letters from Mother, Lola, Lena, Bob, Melanie, Fred Strahl, Mamie, Harold, Roger Rebman (who I thought was dead), and even the K&W Rubber Corporation. I have spent several happy evenings

answering this and can expect more, for another large batch of it came in today.

I participated with three unhappy souls recently in a drinking bout of no mean proportions. Two of the officers, Captain Hall and Captain Thomas, were up for reclassification, and the third, Chaplain Vick, was being transferred to another outfit. Three full quarts of champagne, two of Scotch, and one of cognac were consumed, much to the detriment of my poor aching head the following morning. Needless to say, I have arrived at the happy conclusion that I am definitely <u>not</u> a drinking man. Thank God, the stuff has no definite appeal for me. I can go for months without touching the stuff and, in fact, I have to practically force the damned stuff down my throat. Probably the only reason that I do drink occasionally is because of the fact that the monotony of the present situation is enough to drive a man crazy.

I went up to the Regimental CP the other day and spent two days and an evening up there. Had a good visit and managed to clear up a lot of business. All is extremely quiet on the Western Front, but recently, what with the slackening of the vicious Russian offensive, there has been an ominous pause, and I personally believe that things are once more building up to a smashing, and we hope, final breakthrough into Germany. Even the prospect of an early cessation to hostilities does not serve to cheer us up too much, for we, of this particular outfit, are doomed to one or two ultimate possibilities, either the Army of Occupation or immediate transfer to the China-Burma-India Theater of Operations.

One of the semiannual efficiency reports was turned in recently, and on my own, Colonel Cochran had graded me as "Superior" (the highest obtainable) on some ten leading factors. It is evident from this that he is highly satisfied with my present work, and for this I am glad, for such a rating may well have its value in the postwar years. With this thought in mind, I have made a true copy of this report and inserted it in the back of this little "manual."

Received a somewhat interesting letter from Lena in which she mentioned the fact that a friend of hers, a Miss Dorothy Keiser, was writing me. I assured her I would be glad to answer her and give her a synopsis of "life on the Western Front." Sounds like a very interesting person.

Enough for tonight.

In a Military School, Brand, Germany
8 February 1945

Again, my physical condition is at a low par. Nothing serious, just feel generally run down and at a low ebb, in general. We have been extremely busy of late with a flood of the inevitable administrative work that always arises when the troops are not busy and find the time to get into every kind of mischief. We had two general courts-martial today. One man received a life sentence for desertion, and the other two men at a common trial were sentenced to "be shot to death by musketry." It is evident that the High Command is starting to crack down on the crime of desertion. A recent survey in the ETO revealed that a total of some 8000 men were A.W.O.L. in this theater, almost enough to form a full-fledged fighting division. The two men sentenced to death were from my Regiment, and I had prepared the cases against them. In doing so, I naturally became cognizant of many facts and was thus able to claim that I was prejudiced when the court was called to order, and thus, will be able to sleep with a clear mind tonight. I had to sit on the court, which sentenced the other man to life imprisonment, however.

I received a very nice letter from Miss Dorothy Keiser and a very interesting one at that. It is evident that she is well educated and has the ability to carry on an extremely interesting discourse. I answered promptly and endeavored to make it as interesting as possible. Strange to say, since the time that my sister mentioned the possibility that she might write me, I have been very interested. Hers is a peculiar case, at least to me. She is 24 years old, and yet despite the usual trend in these times, is still single. She has worked as the secretary to the Chief of Police of Richmond, California, for the past two years, no mean achievement in these times. At any rate, I shall continue to write her if she sees fit to reply, and then, too, it gives me something to do. The Incurable Romantic! I guess I'll never learn. As often as I have reiterated to my fellow males that "all women are base and foul," it seems that I will never finally learn that they really ARE!

Foul rumors have been making themselves evident of late that we may soon be "ranked" out of our happy home here at Brand. It seems they are thinking of turning this extremely commodious and lavish school into a General Hospital. However, I do not think this will be for some time yet, at least until the front lines are moved up a bit further. This will not discourage me too much, unless we are forced to take to our field tents, as it is an utter impossibility to crowd 38 men into one tent with over two tons of necessary equipment.

Enough for tonight—my mind is an utter vacuum!

In a Military School, Brand, Germany
10 February 1945

Only the dictates of long habit enable me to make an entry in my journal this night. I am tired, unbearably so, both physically and mentally. I have been wrestling interminably with more of the reclassification cases that our Regiment is rapidly becoming noted for. In fact, these cases have reached such a peak that there is now a current saying sweeping the Division, and I quote, "In the 415th, it's either the Silver Star or else reclassification." In a measure, this saying is indicative of the nature of Colonel Cochran, for he is an extremely strict disciplinarian, and his concept of the "duty responsibility" of an officer borders, at times, on the icily inhuman side.

Orders and circumstances have indicated today that we will move shortly to a new location. Rumor has it that it will be the bombed-out factory, once used as a Division Command Post at Weisweiler, Germany.

Colonel Cochran arrived back from his week-long "leave" in London and officially assumed command of the Regiment again on February 8th.

The Canadians have attacked on our left flank, and at this date, have advanced some five miles and are inside the Reich. Soon, perhaps, our own sector shall burst forth in the old familiar threnody of Carnage and Death. Tonight, the noise of the nearby front lines is unusually clear. The deep bark of the long-range 240-mm guns shakes the panes of the windows periodically while the more indistinct rumble of the 105-mm guns is almost continuous. Much air activity today, both enemy and our own, but whether this presages possible coming events, I cannot say.

Received a letter from June yesterday, which I answered last night. Also one from Rebman, one from Bertram, two more from Mother, and a surprise one, from Lyle. I answered them all, and it was late last night when I went to bed. I have been reading Bram Stoker's, *Dracula*, recently, and found it even more absorbing than it was the first time. Unhappily, I became so absorbed in the thing that I read until late last night and that may, in some measure, account for my extreme lethargy tonight.

Prior to the time that we move from this area, I have about a million things that must be done. Chief among these, or at the least, shortly after the move is completed, is the tremendous bag of laundry that I must get out of the way. However, the more pressing items, such as rearranging my bedroll, packing all of my personal equipment, and getting my desk in order, must be somehow accomplished.

IN A MILITARY SCHOOL, BRAND, GERMANY
SUNDAY, 11 FEBRUARY 1945
Today, for a change, the grim, murky weather so common in this foul land has made an abrupt change for the better. It is a beautiful day, almost like spring. The clear blue sky is predominate, with scattered patches of fluffy white clouds floating lazily about. Of course, our Air Force is unusually active as a result of this good fortune, and hundreds of vapor trails are interlocked across the sky while the steady drone of their motors continually reverberates against the windowpanes. The artillery, too, is more active than usual (due to good observation, I presume), and the deep, hacking cough of the larger guns is very distinct.

Today is Sunday, and I think I shall endeavor to accomplish many of the little tasks that await me. If this were Sunday back in the halcyon civilian days, I would no doubt be preparing my car for a trip to Sonora, or no doubt a picnic or an outing of some kind, perhaps in the lush, verdant sweeps of Redwood Canyon in the foothills of Oakland. Perhaps, too, if that fancy were but real, there would be a companion by my side, and life and love would be rich with all its meaning. Even as I write, however, the grim roar of hundreds of bombers laden with their cargo of death and the *ka-rumph* of heavy shells bring back to sharp reality the task that yet lies before us that must somehow be accomplished before we again pick up the tangled skeins of our lives.

In this connection, what a confusing problem will present itself on the day when I am ultimately discharged. From that day forth, I go forward into—what? Other men will have former trades and professions to turn to, but as for me, the five years that I will have given to the service of my country will be as naught. In effect, they will be as utterly wasted years, five of the most potentially fruitful years of my life. Even my oft-repeated vow that I shall purchase my own home immediately upon release will mean nothing. For what could be more foolish than to drive a stake of permanency, something other men do only after the most careful consideration of their lucrative assets, the steadiness of their employment, etc. What then? Obtain a loan through my past record as a veteran, add to it my assets, and establish a business? No! Hundreds and thousands of other erstwhile Army men will be doing the same thing and will very probably all become bankrupt at the very same time. Return to my old job, which by law must be held open to me for forty days? Definitely, finally, and irrevocably NO! Remain in the Army? This has possibilities, but final acceptance would hinge on many factors, i.e., reduction in rank, and if so, how much? Pay? Would the old "Regular Army Politics and Prejudice" again hold full sway? Only after a thorough survey and the utmost consideration would I accept this outlet. Federal Administration? A possibility, but it depends. Would the old, customary educational barriers remain in effect? God knows I certainly do not relish the thought of becoming a menial government clerk!

From all this mass of questions, possibilities, and suppositions, there must be some happy solution, and if so, what can possibly direct me to the proper solution? I think and think of the above, until I can think no more, but there seems to be no possible answer to the problem.

I save diligently for my home (and, in truth, that is not too difficult over here, for there is no place to spend money) but to what avail? Under the conditions previously mentioned, it would be foolish to buy one, and then too, logically speaking, of what use a home, if there be no one to put in it? For all my bitterness and prejudice against women, I realize I am human and that the true happiness of man is based largely on a home, a wife, and a family. Certainly at the age of 29, it is too late to lay the foundations of such things unless, in desperation, I grasp at anyone or anything to achieve it and ultimately find myself in that soul-sickening, heartrending mere existence that I have seen (and have been nauseated by) in countless cases of the like. A marriage in name only, a mutual existence, endured only for what pitiful benefits each can derive!

What a discourse this has been! But it had been on my mind for several days, and now I feel much better.

IN A MILITARY SCHOOL, BRAND, GERMANY
13 FEBRUARY 1945
An extremely busy day! Normal distribution this morning, through Message Center, and then I was appointed Investigating Officer in the

case of a self-inflicted wound, and the necessary gathering of facts and evidence took up the major part of the day. It was obviously a case of deliberate malingering and was most obviously self-inflicted. I termed it "not in line of duty" and "due to his own misconduct." We learn something new every day!

Tomorrow is evidently Court-Martial Day again, for I received notice tonight that there would be two of them—both general courts-martial, one at 0930 and another in the afternoon at 1330.

I have been busy acquiring as much rest as I possibly can in an effort to overcome this lethargy that seems to affect me daily and am happy to state that it is evidently improving the condition. I feel better tonight than I have for quite some time.

Spoke to Captain Martin the other day about acquiring an additional field jacket. Much to my surprise, he sent one down today, which is of the latest current Army style, what is most popularly referred to as a combat jacket. It certainly is nice, and as soon as he sends down five pairs of shorts and another pair of wool O.D. trousers, my wardrobe will be somewhat in shape once more. The horrible fact that I have approximately fifty pounds of laundry awaiting my physical handling haunts me like a bad dream.

Mail has again taken a turn for the worse, but then I cannot expect a whole sheaf every day. All in all, it has been very good. The other day I received a letter from Bob, one from Mother, another letter from June, a valentine from Mother, and the outstanding fact was that the majority of these letters had been mailed from the West Coast on February 5th, and I received them on the 12th—exactly one week!

I sent back a bunch of the efficiency reports today, including Colonel Cochran's for correction, and I rather expect he was not too happy about it. I'll be able to tell better upon their return again.

The weather for the past two days has been delightful, almost like spring. I imagine the "Big Push" would have started if it were not for the fact that the damned Nazis had blown the big Schwammenauel Dam at the headwaters of the Roer River, and had so flooded all of the area in the present sector that any kind of operations are necessarily disrupted for now. This condition should not last for too long a time, however.

I have been wondering, with quite some interest of late, just what kind of a reply I will receive in answer to my letter from Miss Dorothy Keiser.

Enough for tonight, before I succumb to drivel and make this journal even more monotonous than it already is!

IN A MILITARY SCHOOL, BRAND, GERMANY
15 FEBRUARY 1945
In truth, I hardly know what to write about tonight, and if I deemed this journal worthy of the effort, I would abstain from writing and not clutter up the pages with the usual monotonous claptrap that I am accustomed to enter herein! I received three letters from Lola tonight, along with one from my old friend, Melanie, and one from Margie. I answered Lola and Melanie, but abstained from writing to Margie for reasons already known.

Poor Lola! The poor kid has certainly been buffeted about by an unkind fate, until it seems absolutely unfair. I wonder if it will be possible for life in some mysterious manner to mete her out a small measure of happiness. I hope so. She has suffered many trials and tribulations, due in no small part to ***. There, in capital letters, is one reason why liquor will never have too great an attraction for me (and I do NOT say it with a smirk of self-satisfaction!)

And Melanie! What a unique and strange friendship is ours! John's Mother, almost 80 years of age, and yet what a noble soul has she! She loves music—good music I mean—and being the Mother of three sons, she understands men and their problems. She takes an interest in life and all about her. A native of Vienna, her letters are filled with quaint utterances, calm outlooks on life, and optimistic assurances for the future. May the gods be good to her—there are few of her stature today.

Was busy on the courts-martial cases all day yesterday. The men were sentenced to 25 years at hard labor. Indeed, war is not a gentle mistress with miscreants. Work seems to be progressing satisfactorily— no outstanding troubles or major difficulties. The front is still static-- both we and the enemy waiting for the rushing floodwaters of the Roer River to subside so that once again the bloody carnage can commence.

The words of that haunting song, "Mine Alone," from the *Gypsy Baron* by Strauss, had been haunting me for nearly a week, so last night, I availed myself of the opportunity and managed to transcribe them from the record.

My investigation of the case of the self-inflicted wound was successful. At least Colonel Cochran signed it without any question, and it was immediately forwarded out through the Adjutant General's Office.

For tonight, then, this shall be all, for a blank page is always better than a volume of utter inanity!

IN A MILITARY SCHOOL, BRAND, GERMANY
17 FEBRUARY 1945
Saturday again, bringing with it nostalgic thoughts of what I would be doing on this selfsame night, if in civilian life. The past seven days have passed rapidly, as do all days over here. Nine days from today, I complete my fourth year in the Army. Little did I think, that memorable morning in the National Guard Armory in San Francisco, February 26th, 1941, when I raised my right arm and took the oath of allegiance, how many miles I would travel, how many foreign ports I would enter, what momentous decisions I would be forced to make. The chaotic tempo of these times has, without a doubt, altered the course of my life in many respects and, even now, I cannot foresee in the slightest what may yet take place <u>after</u> the Army. For the most part, I can state flatly that I have benefited in the extreme by my association with the military. My outlook on life has broadened, experience has given me a confidence I never before possessed, and as a final summary, if fate so decides, I may yet terminate my military service far better equipped to face life mentally, physically, and financially with a healthier mental attitude, with more poise and self-assurance, and with a deep appreciation for all the finer things in life.

All about me I see men who have deliberately allowed the Army to ruin them in all of the above-listed factors. To them, the time served in the Army is identical with a prison sentence, a period of time to be served, a thing to be forgotten, a period to let the mind stagnate, to shrink the delicate sensitivities of America's Mama's Boys. For the large majority of the great U.S. Army is that: Mama's Boys, all alone and lost, crying to go home and return to Mama's apron strings. Very seldom do you see men who can grin and bear it, take the horrible difficulties as they come, slap life in the face, and challenge it for more. No more of that breed are left; of that, I am convinced. Pampered, praised, and petted, the modern U.S. soldier is a ghastly and sickening spectacle. They cannot stand discipline, though without it, an army cannot function. Whining and sniveling, I give you--the modern GI in his true colors.

Perhaps I sound radical tonight, but I see it all about me, especially here in my present location. The very sound of their pitiful mewing makes my gorge rise.

IN A MILITARY SCHOOL, BRAND, GERMANY
19 FEBRUARY 1945

Monday again and the start of another week of work, although in reality, there is no cessation in the never-ending flow of administrative details.

The past two or three days have been without mail of any kind. The weather, however, has been delightful, exactly like spring, and much warmer than has been normal for quite some time.

The tactical situation has not changed. We, encamped on one side of the Roer River, and the Germans on the other, with both participants waiting for the subsiding of the turbulent waters. For the river remains badly swollen, even though it has been a week since the destruction of the locks of the Schwammenauel Dam by the enemy.

I imagine that the day of action is not far off, however. Our strength has again been built up to a normal state with reinforcements, mostly from adjacent units.

My physical condition puzzles me greatly, although I realize that, due to a nervous temperament by nature, I do not obtain a sufficient amount of rest in comparison to the number of hours that I work daily. In an effort to alleviate this condition, I am determined to retire at an extremely early hour tonight, although just as sure as I do, it will be impossible for me to go to sleep. Very probably, all that I will do is to roll and toss, until from sheer mental exhaustion, I drop off to a blessed but fitful sleep.

The Regimental Command Post moved up to the town of Merken, Germany, today, so that means that when next I visit the front, it will be an extremely long and arduous trip.

Was greatly disappointed today in that I failed to receive a single letter, although a huge shipment of mail came through, and the majority of men received copious amounts of same. Well, there is nothing I can do about it but wait and see who will be good enough to write me.

The war news in the *Stars and Stripes* today seemed very heartening, indeed, but I maintain that the fanatical Germans will fight until the bitter bloody end, and it will only be with the greatest of good fortune that we see the termination of the war with Germany by midsummer. When the Japs will choose to capitulate is another story, for they are even more fanatical than the Germans, if that is at all possible.

IN A MILITARY SCHOOL, BRAND, GERMANY
21 FEBRUARY 1945
Tonight I am mad. Mad at myself and at the world in general. Most of all, however, I am mad at myself. For the past two or three days, I have been extremely depressed and moody. I have read various articles and short stories, the majority of which were of a depressing nature—of poverty, old age, and the bestiality of man in general. These always have an unsound effect on me, as it starts me thinking and wondering, and in the present life that I find myself ensnared, that is decidedly unwise. I know this, but I seem unable to do anything about it. With the approach of my fourth anniversary in the Army, the feeling of hopelessness, of wasted years of knowledge acquired too late in life, beset me in continuous waves. Any discussion of postwar life always worries me. Under the famed GI Bill of Rights, I do not stand to benefit from the clause entitling one to pursue an education, chiefly because I came in the Army just two months after my 25th birthday. The lack of a formal education will, without doubt, bar me from all of the more established trades and professions. As far as a trade is concerned, I am too old; for the years which I could have spent in learning one, have been spent in the Army. Civil service? I know only too well the usual trend in that direction. It is chiefly "who you know" or the amount of political "drag" that determines whether or not you can get into that type of a career. Then, too, administrative work, which has been my principal forte in the Army, demands its price—in this particular case, a none-too-rugged state of health. It would take quite a long period of time to put me back in the physical condition that I enjoyed, say at the time of my graduation from O.C.S.. Well, enough! Bleating about the situation will certainly do no good, and come what may, I intend to make something out of my life; and God willing, I will someday have a wife, a home, and children.

No mail at all for several days, and I certainly hunger for news from home. What little I have had has been so outdated that it was valueless.

In view of my black state of mind, and what to me seems to be the depressing years that yet lie ahead, the only thing for me to do is to put my foot down, finally, once and for all. To resolve firmly to let nothing swerve me from my intentions, to improve myself in every way possible from this date forward, to become a better man, to live a life that will mean something. I am convinced that if I search for happiness long enough, and hard enough, that sooner or later, it must come.

In a Military School, Brand, Germany
23 February 1945

Big news! We jumped off last night at 0330. So far this morning, the crossing of the Roer River has been very successful, and we are advancing steadily against only moderate resistance. The crossing was preceded by an intensive artillery barrage that lasted for approximately 45 minutes. Finally then, the interminable situation has ended. We had become stalemated at this side of the River Roer, and here we had stopped for some two months. I pray that this may be it, the final drive, which in coordination with the Russians, may crush the last spark of resistance from these filthy beasts and so end this interminable phase of the war.

The receipt of mail has dwindled to nothing except for a communication from the K&W Rubber Company regarding my air mattress, which they evidently repaired and shipped to me on the 22nd day of last month. That, and a few ancient magazines have been the total sum of my mail for the past week or so. Needless to say, the above situation is not helpful to morale.

Had a long talk with Smith over the telephone, yesterday, and it seems the old man was quite pleased with my recent memorandum on Battle Casualty Reporting, and what he evidently termed my foresight in forwarding it. The work, in general, seems to be progressing at a fine rate, but I daresay that from this date forward we will be much busier than we have been in recent weeks. I only hope that we do not again find ourselves in the same dilemma that confronted us at the time the unit first went into action in Holland. I hardly think this probable, however, in that we had to learn the hard way on many of the details, and these problems have all become a matter of Standard Operating Procedures since that time.

The Air Corps seems to be out in force today and is most evidently giving the maximum amount of support to the present drive. The air is filled with the roar of planes, and a highly spectacular dogfight took place last night about 1700, which ended, I am happy to say, in the demise of the *Heinie* pilot.

Physically, I feel a bit better today than I have for some time past, and I have the hope that this condition will continue.

It is my prediction that we will soon leave our present set-up (depending on the rate of advance of our present drive), and needless to say, it is highly doubtful that we will be successful in finding another set-up with the ideal conditions that existed at this one. This will present many difficulties, for we have acquired additional equipment and impediments, and the problem of adequately housing and caring for some 38-odd men is no minor one. This, I venture to say, is in the hands of the gods.

IN A MILITARY SCHOOL, BRAND, GERMANY
25 FEBRUARY 1945

The advance continues. Losses, though very light, considering the nature of the operation, are bad enough. Partially complete reports received thus far indicate twenty-one men as killed in action yesterday, plus the usual average of missing in action.

Hitler gave a speech last night in which he said, "Final Victory will be Germany's this year," or words to that effect. General Eisenhower also gave his first press conference in some time and said in part, "Our intention is to destroy every German west of the Rhine!" So . . . ?

Things seem to be functioning in a highly satisfactory manner and without the extreme confusion that existed during the last period of action.

Only one letter yesterday, from Fred Strahl, in Italy. Much appreciated, but I do wish some of the other mail that is, without a doubt, in transit would arrive.

Have begun to feel just a wee bit better physically, but it will no doubt be some time before I regain the fresh bloom of unbounded health.

Much air activity today: bombing, strafing, dogfights. A jet-propelled Nazi plane was shot down not far from us this morning. The steady *kaaa-rumph* of heavy bombs continually shakes the windowpanes.

I believe the rumors of an impending move have finally come to a head, and we will move very shortly. It seems this location is wanted for a general hospital and also by 12th Army Group. Just where we will move remains a question. Most of the towns en route forward are a mass of rubble--Stolberg, Eschweiler, Weisweiler, Lucherberg—and they are still fighting in Düren and Huchem-Stammeln. I hope to God it isn't tents, but it may very possibly be just that, and what a hopeless mass of confusion that will be!

My eyes have been bothering me considerably during the past two days, and I suppose I could very easily rectify this condition by wearing my glasses, but when I wear them, they bother me so much, I just cannot seem to get used to the feeling that I am behind a glass wall.

If we move, all chances of getting that tremendous sack of laundry done is, of course, nullified. I am beginning to realize that very soon, and at the first opportunity, I shall be forced to turn washerwoman. If there is one job that I thoroughly detest, it is laundering in all its forms and aspects.

In reading over some new aspects of the famed GI Bill of Rights yesterday, I came across the startling change announcing that EVERY veteran of the war will be entitled to at least one year of education in whatever field he may choose. This is indeed hopeful, and I may yet take advantage of this clause, for certainly a year of say, business school, could do me no harm.

(CONCLUDING ENTRY IN VOLUME IV)

JOURNAL 5

VOLUME V
FEBRUARY 26, 1945 TO JUNE 16, 1945
Age 29

We passed through Schöneberg,
meaning literally, "Beautiful Village,"
and what a ghastly parody its name now stood for—
buildings blasted, gutted, and torn;
doors and windows hanging by splinters of wood,
burnt windows showed clearly that
the interior of a house was completely burnt and ruined.

-/-

VOLUME V

-/-   -/-

BEING A RECORDING OF HAPPENINGS
AND EVENTS THAT OCCURRED
DURING THE COURSE OF MY FIFTH YEAR
OF SERVICE IN THE ARMY OF THE UNITED STATES.

-/-

February 26, 1945

CHANGES DUE TO LOSS OF OFFICERS • INVESTIGATION OF SELF-INFLICTED WOUND • BOMBING ATTACK BY THE BOCHE • TRANSPORT OF REINFORCEMENTS • SCENES OF DEVASTATION • SOUVENIRS • MAIL • MORE COURTS-MARTIAL • NINE MEN DROWN • DREAMS OF POSTWAR LIFE • SCENES OF GERMAN COUNTRYSIDE • FINAL DRIVE OF WAR • PRISONER OF WAR ENCLOSURE • SCENES OF DEVASTATION • SIGNS OF LIBERATION AND GERMAN SURRENDER • INTERROGATION OF ENEMIES • NORDHAUSEN CONCENTRATION CAMP • CONCERNS ABOUT POSTWAR JOB • BRONZE STAR MEDAL • LAST LETTER TO VIVIAN • TRAVEL ON AUTOBAHNEN TO VISIT REGIMENT • END OF WAR • LETTER TO MARGIE NIXING IDEAS OF MARRIAGE • PREPARATION FOR LEAVE IN U.S. • TRIP BY BOXCAR THROUGH CENTRAL EUROPE • STAGING AREA

FOUR YEARS IN THE ARMY TODAY

IN A MILITARY SCHOOL, BRAND, GERMANY
26 FEBRUARY 1945

With this entry, I start the <u>fifth</u>, and I hope it will be the last, volume of my experiences in the Army. So filled have the preceding volumes been with the excerpts of the past four years, that I can scarcely recall the golden days of civilian life. I feel, at the present time, as though it will take me years to readjust myself to the normal life with its slower tempo and peaceful pursuits.

The drive continues! The Timberwolf Division certainly distinguished itself in this one. We captured more prisoners in the past two days than the entire 9th Army. Reports have it that the 3rd Armored is now only ten miles from Cologne. We (the 104th) had a tremendous write-up in the daily edition of the *Stars and Stripes*. Too, casualties have been extremely light.

We move about day after tomorrow. From all indications, it will be to the newly captured town of Düren, and most appropriately, into the local insane asylum. I will be very glad to get up there, for the line of communications between Regiment and me has been overlong for sometime past, now. This will not only remedy that situation but will make for a more efficient distribution through Message Center, at the same time.

Much to my relief, I was enabled to get my huge bag of laundry off to Belgium this date where, no doubt, some good Belgian *hausfrau* will proceed to knock herself out in restoring it to a snowy white condition.

Not without appropriate remuneration in francs, however, and they usually manage to gouge you quite nicely.

The dearth of mail continues, and I am beginning to wonder just what can be wrong in that direction, although I have had this scarcity exist before. However, I really believe that this has been the longest period of time I have yet had to endure.

Inasmuch as it is my sincere wish that this shall prove to be my final year in the Army, I intend to make it just as progressive and fruitful for myself as I possibly can. In this respect, I intend to take advantage of every opportunity to improve myself, both physically and mentally, and to continue to save, as assiduously as I can, for the ultimate purchase of my own home. I am certainly happy that I had the foresight to start saving, if not for the home, then for any eventuality that may take place after my discharge, for conditions are certain to be unsettled for quite a period of time after the cessation of hostilities, and it is quite manifest to me, at this time, that I be prepared to make the best of every possible opportunity that may afford itself at that time. Perhaps the future years will determine just how wise I have been in this respect.

In a Military School, Brand, Germany
27 February 1945

In the midst of preliminary plans for moving, discarding superfluous equipment and odd luxuries that we have accumulated during the course of our stay, some three months now, in these quarters. I have sent two men ahead to the new location to "acquire" and make ready for occupancy our new site. The driver, Bresser, took them up in order to familiarize himself with the route and is to return at once. I have found, from past experience, that such preparatory planning usually pays in the long run. Fortunately, insofar as my personal equipment is concerned, I am quite well off now that I have rid myself of that tremendous bag of laundry.

I felt sure that some mail would come in yesterday, or at least late last night, but was miserably disappointed. It has, indeed, been a long time since I have heard from anyone. I will no doubt receive a batch of five or possibly ten letters, and then again, there will be a complete cessation.

Düren, from all reports, is as well bombed and gutted as the now famous St. Lô. It was here that the enemy offered the most fanatical resistance and fought most bitterly, for Düren is the second largest German city yet captured on the Western Front and was, at one time, a very rich municipality with a population well in excess of 30,000 people. Unconfirmed reports last night had the spearheads of our units already at the famed Erft Canal (the next sizeable water barrier, and the last, next to the Rhine itself).

Transportation difficulties are predominate today, so I must make this only a partial entry for today.

Düren, Germany
1 March 1945

At last, the hectic process of moving is over and done with once more. This time we are in the "Düren Health and Welfare Institution," the local asylum for aged, infirm, and insane. It is badly battered and shell torn, and evidently the fighting was fierce and bloody in this particular portion of the city. Artillery bursts still blanket the air, and occasionally, a near miss will knock plaster from the ceilings. The windows were all blown out, but fortunately, we were able to locate some large pieces of glass and cut them down to the proper size so that the room is fairly windproof. The room itself is large. For once, we have adequate room for all sections. We erected the two stoves, and as a huge coal pile is conveniently near, we should not lack for heat. All in all, the place is not nearly as convenient or luxurious as the school, but certainly, we can't complain at all.

The prima donnas of the section are again in action, so in accordance with what I told the assembled group at my last meeting of the sort, I am taking action in the matter—two transfers, and one man returns to his unit. I'm through talking; a little action may have more positive results.

A little unpleasantness occurred while loading trucks prior to the move with one of AG's cohorts. I expect no untoward results, but if there are, I have appropriate answer to the situation.

We are now shelling Cologne, and the drive had crossed the Erft Canal this morning. 9th Army seems to be keeping pace with us on our flank. Happily, the 415th Regiment is finally in reserve. We had been in the firing lines a total of 116 days out of 128. As a result of this, our casualties have, of course, subsided to some extent.

Düren is a city of the dead--shell-wracked, gutted, and torn. When will the senseless fools ever realize that their defeat is inevitable?

The preceding paragraphs were written last night, but I shall add a few more tonight, for today was hectic in more ways than one. The Regimental Commander of the 414th Regiment was killed, along with a whole tent full of other brass, and the resultant changes have caused quite a few repercussions in our own Regiment. Many transfers and changes. Along with this, I have had to assign some 170-odd reinforcements to companies and attend to a multitude of other details. I was appointed investigating officer for another self-inflicted wound, and this kept me quite busy throughout the day. The man had been drunk at the time he shot himself in the hand, and so my findings, naturally enough, were "Not in line of duty, due to his own misconduct."

A bit of mail came through tonight, including one from Margaret, which somehow I feel I must answer, although I shouldn't.

Düren, Germany
4 March 1945
Sunday again. The commotion and confusion of moving has finally subsided, and we are comfortably established with a great profusion of tables in addition to such conveniences as electric lights, stoves, and even a radio. The first night spent in this location was exceptionally sleepless. We suffered a full-scale bombing attack by the Boche in a last desperate effort to vindicate himself somewhat in the recent dilemma in which he now finds himself. The continuous blast and concussion of the heavy bombs shook the building as though it were made of cardboard. At the same time, the incessant cough of our 90-mm *ack-ack*, in addition to the 40-mm Bofors guns, and scores of 50-calibre machine guns, made the night a nightmare of sound. It finally subsided about 0600 the next morning.

Received a letter from Mother, Lola, my old friend Colonel Smith, and one from Margie. The latter is a peculiar case with me. I felt obligated to answer and did but so worded it that I feel sure no unpleasant entanglement will result. She is such a fine person. Extremely intelligent, sensitive, and yet life has not offered her a great deal of happiness. If we both find mutual pleasure in corresponding, however, I can see no harm in doing so.

We are now four miles from Cologne, and it is rumored that the 9th Army has a bridgehead across the Rhine. The German radio admits that the whole sector along the Canadian Army front has been abandoned. It is to be hoped that the final phase of the war with

Germany is here at last, but it is to be expected that the fanatical devils will fight until the last drop of blood is wrung from an anguished world.

True to my promise, I had several drastic changes in the section, and as a result, there has been a noticeable improvement in many attitudes. I was tempted to relent on one of the culprits, but I have found that having once made a decision, it is best to stick to it, and later events proved that it was well that I did so.

I think I will endeavor to catch up on a few letters this afternoon. I am also looking forward with some anticipation to the receipt of *Fortune Magazine*, some information I requested from "The Gramophone Shop" in New York, and four books that I ordered from Grosset and Dunlap. When they will arrive will be a question.

Enough for today—my mind is an utter vacuum.

DÜREN, GERMANY
5 MARCH 1945
Resistance has been so light that it almost makes one wonder what diabolical trick the Germans can have up their sleeve now. We are now two miles from Cologne, and their (the Germans) resistance appears to be nil. The Regimental CP is now in Brauweiler, Germany. About the only resistance being offered is by the AA guns that the Jerries have turned around and are firing with depressed muzzles. They had thousands of these in and around Cologne, which was one of the best-protected cities in Europe, insofar as anti-aircraft artillery was concerned. It remains a mute question as to whether the Germans will put up a strong defense of Cologne, or whether they will abandon the city to its fate.

I am truly hungry for some mail today, but there seems to be no indication that we are going to receive any. I wrote to the Raffertys yesterday. It seems that Hubie is on his way back to the U.S. Still having trouble with the wound that he received shortly after D-Day. Also wrote a letter to Lola yesterday.

Things seem to be running extraordinarily smooth insofar as the work in the office is concerned. Every task is performed in a perfunctory manner and is smoothly and quietly accomplished.

It rained violently yesterday, and upon investigation, I discovered that my room on the upper floor of this dilapidated building had turned into a fine imitation of a modern shower. The room had been exceedingly dank, dismal, and uncomfortable anyway, so I determined to move my bed down to the office and to keep it rolled up during the day. I found the arrangement much more satisfactory, as it is warmer, much more convenient, and I find it much easier to arise in the mornings.

Due to the rapid advance of the Regiment, I have found it almost impossible to maintain contact with them by telephone (in fact, I have been out of communications with them for two days now), and I am determined to visit the CP tomorrow. In addition to that fact, my chief worry now lies in the difficulty of acquiring a sufficient number of trucks to transport the large number of reinforcements that we are continually processing. I sent my driver to Service Company, about 1030 this morning, in an effort to obtain one truck, and as yet, he has failed to return, which would indicate that Service Company has probably moved.

I am still bothered by periodic pangs of thought whenever I occasion to dwell on just what I will do in the postwar world, and it all seems so hopeless and confused that I really can arrive at no solution. Very probably, however, the entire situation will work itself out, for as an example, I might say that my life in the Army appeared very confusing for some time, but things eventually worked themselves out.

More, anon.

DÜREN, GERMANY
6 MARCH 1945

A very interesting day. At about 1000, I set out for the Regimental CP, which was located in Lövenich, Germany. It was a long, tortuous trip, for the roads were bomb scarred and pitted with the recent heavy fighting; and the rainy weather, which has been prevalent for the past two days, had turned all roads into rutted, muddy trails. We stopped at Service Company, which was located in Sindorf, Germany, and dropped off a casual that we were returning to duty. A sandwich, then onto Lövenich. The ghastly horrors of modern warfare were evident everywhere. Abandoned enemy gun positions, what once were busy villages, were now hollow, gutted, burnt-out shells. Huge craters, the result of pattern bombing, were everywhere. A huge factory, torn and desolate, with enormous piles of coal and sawdust still burning violently. Hulks of downed aircraft, everywhere ruin and desolation, and the stench of death. At length, we came to the famed Erft Canal, from which the Germans had expected to make a last-ditch stand.

However, our onslaught was too violent and rapid to be stopped by such a barrier. We crossed on a temporary engineer[ed] Bailey Bridge, and here the power of our Army was most highly evident. Enormous pillboxes with walls of cement, some 20-feet thick, were tossed and split open as though by a giant's hand, and the blackened fringes surrounding the casemates made it evident that flame throwers had been used to oust the original occupants.

Finally arrived at the CP in Lövenich to find Colonel Denisevich in the midst of an argument with a German civilian who had been ousted from her home when it was chosen to be used for the Regimental CP. It seems that she wanted to return and pick up a few articles. The Colonel wasn't progressing too well in the argument until I offered the services of my driver, Bresser, who soon straightened the matter out. Captain Smith had gone forward to Cologne to pick out a new CP, and as the rear CP was just then displacing forward, I decided to go along. Just prior to this, however, Colonel Cochran came in and seemed to be in an exceedingly cheerful frame of mind, for we had quite a discussion regarding my work (incidentally, he seemed quite pleased) and discussed the present advance, which had surprised us all by its exceedingly light toll of casualties.

We arrived in Cologne in a matter of minutes, as it is only three or four miles from Lövenich. Fighting is still going on in the streets of Cologne. The new CP location was one aptly chosen—the former *Gauleiter* Headquarters, formerly occupied by a German General. Luxurious hardly describes the place. Bombproof basements, an officers lounge, plenty of office space. Here I acquired some truly fine souvenirs, valuable even more so because of their acquisition under enemy fire—shelling from 88-mm guns was still going on, and the surrounding area was truly resounding with the sharp *s-p-a-n-g* from the rifles of enemy snipers. One of the souvenirs was a lovely dress sword, evidently from a former storm trooper, for the scabbard is ebony black. It is practically new in appearance, and I intend to mail it home as soon as possible. Another is a massive desk ornament, which surmounted the old general's desk. It is of solid chromium steel and is in three parts, a solid base about three inches square and nicely beveled, a pyramidal upper base cut with a groove into which a Nazi swastika, approximately six inches square, fits nicely. The whole thing is highly polished and is exceedingly heavy. It must weigh in the neighborhood of at least 12 pounds. At the same time, I brought back a beautiful German radio and intended it for the use of the boys in the office. It was complete with all modern attachments, including a very expensive crystal Telefunken microphone. Unfortunately, I did not investigate properly before bringing it back, and upon arrival at the office, discovered that some unprincipled German had removed the tubes, out of sheer orneriness I guess. Nevertheless, I intend to keep the microphone, and sooner or later, I will acquire a good radio for the office. I doubt if I will be able to ship the microphone home legally, so I shall keep it stored away in my effects until such time as I go home, for I intend to use it with the home recording set that I intend to have.

I arrived back in time for chow and found that work had been progressing smoothly, which all leads to peace of mind. We move shortly to a new location near Cologne, so I must lay preparatory plans for that event.

Enough for tonight.

Hospital, Brauweiler, Germany
12 March 1945

I haven't had time for entries recently, and with good reason--we moved; and prior to that, I paid another visit to the CP and during the course of the visit, managed to acquire a really good radio for the Section.

As usual, the move was quite messed up. Alerted at 0600, and the trucks didn't arrive until 1500 in the afternoon. "Hurry up and wait," typical of the Army. It was quite a jump for us, but I was thankful for it. My communications had bogged down.

We are firmly established in quite the nicest set-up we have yet had. It is a rather old conglomeration of buildings. The chapel, which is annexed to the buildings, dated back to the 11th century. Our room is approximately 40 feet square, a former ward in the hospital. Eight large windows overlook a courtyard. The electricity is plentiful, 250 volts, furnished by the city power supply, for Brauweiler was largely bypassed in the fighting and was not badly damaged. There are approximately 1500 civilians left in the town, which includes several hundred French, Poles, and Russians that the *Herrenvolk* had been using as slave labor. At any rate, we have a profusion of electric lights hung all over the office. I have a large fluorescent desk lamp, the radio, and a large auxiliary speaker mounted on the wall pours forth a tremendous volume of music. (The latter was already installed for the benefit of the former inmates of the ward, but we saw fit to utilize it for our own enjoyment.)

My desk certainly gives cause for amusement. A large, ornate thing, it must be fully ten feet by five. I have a large, immaculate green blotter directly in front of me. To the right is the radio, surmounted by the aforementioned *Gauleiter* swastika. To my front, an array of necessary desk accessories, i.e., letter opener, stylus, pencils, pen holder and pen, memo cards, clips, a small steel mirror I use to sign stencils on, ink, and the large tray separated into three compartments labeled respectively, "IN," "OUT," and "HOLD," over which the administrative work of the Regiment flows in an endless stream. To my left, easily within reach, is a huge ashtray (German), a field telephone, and a convenient switch for cutting the radio when phoning. Truly such luxury we have never had before, even at Carson, and we revel in it, for God only knows what lies in store for us on the next move. So far, I can say that we have been truly fortunate in our various locations

I mailed my souvenir storm trooper dress sword home yesterday, first class mail, and I hope it arrives safely and on time. This morning I shall endeavor to mail home my highly prized swastika, but due to its weight, I shall be forced to mail it via parcel post.

There is quite a spread of typhus and typhoid fever in Cologne and Aachen, and the Army is taking the necessary precautions.

Hospital, Brauweiler, Germany
13 March 1945

I felt rather "off key," physically today. We are still in our sumptuous location and have been too busy to do anything else but work since I last wrote. I intend to go up to the CP tomorrow morning and also to go down to Charlie Company and pay old Tufts a visit.

Had quite a session last night with the old man regarding the grades and rating situation. Still don't know whether he was miffed about it or not, but such things don't worry me a helluva lot anymore. Spent all last evening writing Margie a tremendous letter, six full pages, on some of that huge Nazi stationery that is on hand here. Discussed about everything under the sun but managed to keep it as impersonal as possible.

Received a tremendous influx of mail today, about six letters, but three of them were Easter cards and so were not as enjoyable as letters would have been. I have always detested cards in any form, birthday, holiday, or what have you.

Sometimes the war news is very optimistic in feeling, and at other times, I don't see how the mess can finally end before another year. It certainly keeps one up in the air. The Old Timberwolf Division is gaining such notoriety and a reputation that it is almost certain that we will head for the CBI upon the conclusion of the fighting over here. Well, it will at least mean that we MIGHT get a three-weeks leave, at home, before we take off for the Pacific. How long, O Lord, how long will this go on, before I can again take up the normal pursuits of life and living?

Courts-martial are pouring into the office. What with a populous number of German civilians left in Cologne, among which are many young girls, plus a plentiful supply of captured liquor, the men are running wild. They are tried mostly on "fraternization" charges, and also on charges of insubordination (caused mostly by the influence of liquor). Truly, we have LESS work when the actual fighting is going on.

None of Mother's packages that she mailed sometime in January have arrived yet, nor those that Lola mailed. I understand that the boat, which was delayed for so long (still holding mail that was mailed from home during the first two weeks of December), has finally docked in France, and perhaps that is where all of my Christmas packages are.

I certainly hope that the two nice souvenirs that I mailed home, recently, arrive home in good shape, and soon. The sword should be there within a month at least, as I mailed it first class. The swastika will undoubtedly take much longer, as it was sent by fourth-class mail.

CWO AMMONS, my brother Elk here in the Regiment, phoned me tonight and told me that he had finally acquired a battle flag (Nazi) for me. Promised to send it down through Message Center. We shall see what we shall see.

Hospital, Brauweiler, Germany
16 March 1945

Another day ticked away. Work has increased, and there are several imperfections in the system that I want to iron out. I interviewed two of the new replacements, and I think in time, they will work out satisfactorily. One of them is exceedingly young (19), and the other did not impress me too highly regarding his mental capabilities but am hopeful that they will prove themselves.

Attended a fairly good show tonight, *My Reputation*, with George Brent and Barbara Stanwyck. As usual, it brought many nostalgic memories of what used to be.

The front has again settled down into a stalemate of temporary nature. Each side is presumably rebuilding and reorganizing for the final battle that is to come.

Mr. Lauck leaves tomorrow for a three-day pass to Paris. I may soon obtain a pass myself, if I so desire, but I have no desire to go to Paris. If anywhere, I think I will choose the City of Brussels.

I have had no mail, recently, with the exception of a letter from Leo Cook in Calcutta.

A laundry service has been established here in Brauweiler, and I took a chance and sent my sleeping bag. God knows it certainly needs a good cleaning.

My mind is not very fruitful tonight, and perhaps it would be best to abstain from entering such trivia as this.

Saw a great deal of the City of Cologne yesterday. Went up to the front lines stretched along the banks of the Rhine and from which some of the enemy positions were clearly visible. Went through the Cologne Opera House (Co. F CP) and it must have been a beautiful structure at one time, although now it is a ghastly mess of ruined rubble. I obtained a small 35-mm slide showing the interior of the place when it was in its heyday, and it is most beautiful. Have passed by the beautiful and ancient Dom Cathedral and have seen the remnants of the ancient gates and walls that used to encircle the original city. Several sections are remarkably well preserved, considering the merciless attacks that have been the fate of Cologne. Also visited a huge underground air-raid shelter, formerly the headquarters of the *Gauleiter* of the Aachen-Cologne District. This is where the aforementioned dress sword and chrome swastika came from.

The radio is pulsating with the vibrant sweetness of "Souvenir," and of course, I am drinking it in avidly. Music here in Europe is so much finer than that on the radio at home. Not so much of the discordant blasphemy of "swing."

Nine of our men were drowned last night in a rehearsal of assault boat landings. An unavoidable accident, but the resultant investigation and administrative details will cost me a pretty headache, and I have one tonight, too!

Ammons's flag came, and a nice one it is!

Brauweiler, Germany
18 March 1945

Sunday in Germany again. The sky gives promise of a beautiful day of spring. The sun is shining, trees are in bud, and there is great activity among the birds and animals in the area. It is ironic that only man remains bestial and ugly.

I wrote Lola two long letters yesterday. She writes very regularly now, and so much more of her is revealed in her letters than when speaking to her. I think I am beginning to know and understand my sister much better. Also wrote Melanie, but I was definitely not up to par on this one.

The Regimental CP and service elements have again moved to new locations in Cologne, and our troops are widely dispersed in various sectors of the city. I do not anticipate any trouble in locating them, however. The 3rd Army, on our right flank, is attacking the diamond-shaped palatinate of the Saar, and it is evident that if Patton and Patch of the 7th Army can bring into play an enormous pincers movement on this area, the whole of the Saar and of German soil up to the Rhine in that area will be ours. General Eisenhower has warned the citizens of Frankfurt and surrounding communities that they will be subjected to a merciless bombardment and to start evacuating the community immediately. But enough of tactics and the plans of war!

I have not heard from Mother for a deuce of a long time, or so it seems. She had mentioned in previous letters that she was going to San Francisco to pay Lola another visit. I do hope that she won't tire herself unnecessarily and wear herself out. That is what ordinarily happens. She is getting too advanced in years for that sort of thing.

Today being Sunday, I cannot look forward to the receipt of any mail, for ordinarily, no deliveries are made on that day.

A particularly fine rendition of Rimsky-Korsakov's, *Scheherazade*, is now emanating from the radio, and it is soothing and particularly delightful this morning. I wonder if the time will ever come when there will be a warm, sunny Sunday morning when I can awake in a clean, comfortable bed; dress most leisurely; go downstairs to a piping hot breakfast of ham and eggs, hot buttered toast, coffee, and fruit juice; then retire to the living room, the radio, and Sunday papers. Utter relaxation and contentment. Possibly, in the afternoon a drive, a picnic or an outing of some sort, in which worries and troubles do not enter, and life itself could take on a new meaning. Then home to a nice dinner and an evening's relaxation by the fire, listening to my favorite recordings and programs, or reading. In this description of my Utopia, there is no mention of another person, and with excellent logic. The memory of the first horrible hell of matrimony precludes the acquiring of another.

BRAUWEILER, GERMANY
19 MARCH 1945
Just finished a two-day siege of the flu. I can't recall another like period when I felt so absolutely terrible—fever, chills, muscles aching. Took some sleeping pills last night and retired about 1900, but the effects wore off about 2200, and from then on, it was cursed wakefulness helped to a considerable degree by the sound effects of a raucous drinking party in the adjacent sleeping quarters. After breakfast, I again retired and slept until lunch when I felt much better. Tonight, I believe I have the thing licked and hope there will be no recurrence.

Again, a dearth of mail. Seems no one bothers to write anymore. I seem to be hounded and thwarted by loneliness at every turn.

Attended another show tonight: *Janie*. Light and gay, but a bit fantastic. Such features are to me distasteful, if only for the reason that the inevitable return to reality comes as a completely physical shock.

Mother's latest letter, dated 5th of March, was quite cheerful, and it is evident that she knows our present location. It is increasingly evident that the "Timberwolves" have received a great deal of publicity and notoriety back in the U.S.A.

From the lack of interesting news, I shall have to close tonight and finish this another day.

* * * * * *

BRAUWEILER
21 MARCH 1945
I take up the well-worn Remington again. Just about fully recovered from the disastrous attack of flu at this writing. I had a nice, hot shower and change of clothing, so at the present time, I feel like a million dollars.

Mr. Lauck just phoned from Service Company. Seems he just returned from a three-day pass to Paris and desired transportation back to here. Well, I hope the pass did him some good. Gosh knows he earned it, and then some.

Big events in the offing, but security reasons preclude any mention of them.

No mail as yet today, but I have hopes.

BRAUWEILER, GERMANY
24 MARCH 1945
This beastly aftermath of the flu, now plaguing me in the form of a chest cold, simply refuses to leave.

This morning, due to insufficient reports from Regiment, I determined to visit the Command Post, up forward. Accordingly, I dressed warmly, loaded carbine and gas mask into the jeep, and took off. We had to cut through the suburbs of Cologne in order to reach the road paralleling the banks of the Rhine, but after a bit of question asking, we reached the road and headed east along that river. All of the reputed scenic and historic beauty of the ancient Rhine has been well founded. A beautiful, picturesque, pastoral countryside. On the far side of the Rhine, mountains rise abruptly from the river's edge, and the crumbling towers and bastions of feudal castles, and the strongholds of the legendary robber barons, stand stark against the sky. All of the mythological stories of the fabled, "Rhein," are brought to mind, and the sight of a jewel-like island, with its crown of crumbling ancient ruins, brought to mind the tales of Wagner, the Rhinemaidens, *Die Walküre*, the "Magic Fire Music," the *Twilight of the Gods*, and *Götterdämerung*. Needless to say, I drank it all in, avidly.

The area in and around Bad Godesberg (where Hitler met with Chamberlain in 1939) was most evidently famous as a wealthy resort district. Luxurious hotels, pavilions, and boathouses lined the banks of the river. The cities in this district appear quite prosperous, but the newly conquered inhabitants appeared much more surly and unhappy about the present turn of events than those we had met previously.

The 1st Army now has three pontoon bridges across the Rhine, and we crossed to the eastern bank on the one located at Königswinter. Across the river, the more verdant beauty of the countryside is at once apparent. Due to the enormous activity and traffic, however, the roads were choked with dust. I finally located Service Company in the little town of Honnef, bivouacked in a field. I enjoyed a nice dinner consisting of steak, potatoes, puree of tomatoes, and fresh onions. After straightening out a few difficulties here (and acquiring a new pair of pants), I ascertained the location of the enemy and proceeded on to the front lines. The CP was located in the little village of Quirrenbach, which we reached after a tortuous journey through the heavily wooded mountains. Their beauty now defiled by burnt and splintered foliage, gaping shell craters, the hastily erected, but futile tank traps and roadblocks of the enemy, burnt and gaping pillboxes, crushed and burnt-out enemy tanks, acres of deactivated mines, and all of the other garish, and monstrous destruction of war.

Eventually arrived at the Command Post and had a long consultation with Smith and arranged for a mutual meeting point for our two drivers in order that distribution of administrative dispatches might be more quickly effected.

About 1530, I headed back, and this time, recrossed the Rhine at the Bonn crossing. It was a more difficult trip on the return, for the roads were even more choked and unbearably dusty. By the time I reached my Headquarters, my eyes were raw and inflamed and smarted terribly. I retired about 2300, and so ended another day on the Western Front.

Brauweiler, Germany
(Sunday) 25 March 1945

I take up the pen to write tonight, for it may be some time until another opportunity affords itself. We move tomorrow. My outfit will move on the second shuttle, about 1230. As stated before, we move to Honnef, which incidentally, according to late new reports, was being counterattacked by the Germans tonight. Our new set-up will be half again less roomy than the present one and with very crowded sleeping quarters. When we move from Honnef, that is according to all indications, it will be back to the rugged life for us in tents. God knows how we will surmount this difficulty, for we have insufficient tentage, and if the weather should turn bad, it would be catastrophic. The weather, on the other hand, has been absolutely delightful for the past week, but I doubt if it will last.

A bit of mail has trickled in—two letters from Lola, one from Dorothy, and a very complete bank statement. Cashier Doyle, in Sonora, is really on the ball. Dorothy writes a very interesting letter, and I answered in some length. She also enclosed a couple of snapshots of herself.

Oh! Have I not mentioned the fact that my AIR mattress (brand new) arrived, and the package included a much needed and wished-for little air pillow? Heaven bless the K&W Rubber Co.!

From all reports, the Regiment is having one helluva time of it today, and I only hope that the situation eases off a little soon.

I had to send my driver up to the Command Post, this afternoon, with some important dispatches, and I am a little worried about him, for he has not returned yet, and blackout driving can be fierce, I know. I sent two of the other boys along with him, however, so that eases my mind a little.

I must write Lola tonight. She has been so perfectly swell about writing, lately. It seems Don has finally returned home, and so she is not so distraught as she was for a time. He had been gallivanting about the countryside. Reminded me of the time I became disgusted with the Depression immediately after my graduation from high school when I could find no employment and took a little pilgrimage up to Oregon and Washington. Part of the process of growing up, I guess. I am glad now that I had continually reassured her in my letters to her.

My eyes are still bothering me terribly, and I am determined, that if conditions permit in the next area, I shall do nothing but acquire as much rest as I can. For I have not had over five hours sleep per night for over a month now, and I feel quite sure that has a great deal to do with my eye trouble.

Honnef, Germany
28 March 1945

We moved two days ago and again, as a result, we are somewhat behind in our work, but I think we will regain this lost "momentum" without any trouble. Contrary to our pessimistic expectations, it was not tents, but a schoolhouse. While not as fine or as roomy as our past locations, it is not too bad, and at least we have a roof over our heads.

Honnef is a picturesque, typically German village, perched on the undulating bluffs, which line the east bank of the Rhine. It is about 10 miles upstream from the fairly large (95,000) university city of Bonn. Two large bluffs dominate the village. They are called the "Drachenfels" and atop of each are perched the ruins of two ancient, medieval castles, one much older than the other, dating back to the 6th century. What I wouldn't give to have the time and the opportunity to explore them! The local population, but newly conquered, and who had felt so safe and secure behind their Rhine "barrier," are much more resentful of our presence than the Germans we have met heretofore. We have had an endless amount of trouble with them over the billeting of our troops (for when a house is selected for our men, the civilians move out). All of this wailing and gnashing of teeth. At last they know how the Belgians, the French, the Poles, and the Norwegians felt.

Already the front lines are some 50 miles away, and we are preparing to move again within a day or two. I have been receiving a bit more mail—some magazines, a package from Mom containing food tidbits, and a letter from Bob. For the past two nights, I have made it a point to retire fairly early (about 1000 p.m.) and, as a result, my eyes feel somewhat better. However, the detestable chest cold continues to annoy me.

Good news! The 3rd Army is now 50 miles on the other side of the Rhine and has captured Frankfurt. The 9th Army and the British Canadian units are making good progress. I saw General Eisenhower the other day while driving through Bad Godesberg.

All communications with Regiment, of course, have been out for several days, and I am using the Service Company shuttle system for the necessary pick-up and delivery of daily dispatches.

It appears very much from PW interrogation reports and other sources, that this is the final drive of the war with the Nazis. Optimism is high, and I do hope there is no setback of the type that we experienced in December. Even with an early termination of the struggle, however, I do not feel that I will be discharged for at least a full year, as there are too many factors standing in the way of such a happening, all of which I have gone over too many times, to bear repeating. I hope that we move soon, because this lack of communications tends to worry me a great deal, and our reports are not as efficiently tendered as they could be.

HONNEF, GERMANY
(BOB'S BIRTHDAY) 30 MARCH 1945
There is a good show tonight, *Meet Me in St. Louis*, but my eyes are bothering me too much to go. Of course, typing is not exactly comforting to the eyes either, but there is nothing else to do, and one must keep the brain well occupied or risk mental stagnation in war. Perhaps this is a poor escape, but I enjoy it, and it may well be that in later years I may relive these poorly written passages with some pleasure.

Yesterday, I went on an odyssey that will long remain in my memory. Communications had been steadily deteriorating for some time, because of the extreme rapidity of our unit's advance into Germany. I determined to visit the Command Post and, accordingly, alerted the driver to have the jeep well gassed and oiled and ready for the trip. We left at about 0700 and took the winding mountain road that leads out of Honnef. The road was quite familiar until we reached the town of Asbach; the same vista of destruction, burnt out "Tigers," and gaping bomb craters that I have described in earlier pages. At Asbach, which was only partially demolished, was located one of the large PW enclosures (Prisoner of War). Inside the barbed wire, some 200 members of the touted "Master Race" were milling around, dejected and beaten, utter defeat showing in their very stance. On we went, and it was after passing Asbach that the inexorable, relentless, utter power of the current drive revealed itself. I received the distinct impression that I was following in the path of a mammoth auger boring ruthlessly forward, all obstructions of whatever nature twisted and flung violently aside. Pure destruction lined the sides of the roads for mile upon mile. We passed through Schöneberg, meaning literally, "Beautiful Village," and what a ghastly parody its name now stood for—buildings blasted, gutted, and torn; doors and windows hanging by splinters of wood. Burnt windows showed clearly that the interior of a house was completely burnt and ruined. The streets were littered with all of the grim debris of war—dead horses, paper, rubble, glass, smashed vehicles, broken guns. At length, we reached the extremely modern *Autobahn*, one of Hitler's superhighways, which we crossed, and continued up a smaller but more direct road. It was evident that the Air Force had trapped innumerable German columns of vehicles, both motor driven and horse drawn, for both sides of the roads, for miles, were festooned with large trucks, small trucks, carts, wagons, dead horses, dead Germans, knocked-out anti-tank guns turned drunkenly on their sides, the famed 88-mm Flak guns, scores of them now lying with their ugly snouts buried deep in the mud of the Vaterland. Clearly, the columns of vehicles had been caught without air protection of any kind, and in the greatest state of confusion.

    At length, we arrived in the town of Geilenkirchen. Here the enemy had evidently decided to dispute possession of the town, and the results were most decisive. Other towns had been, in comparison, but mildly shelled and bombed. In Geilenkirchen, however, the full force of a mighty Air Force and the destructive power of American artillery and heavy mortars had been unleashed. About the best way to describe conditions in Geilenkirchen, about the time that I passed through, is to say that American bulldozers were engaged in shoveling one side of the main street to the other in order that the never-ending stream of Army vehicles could get through with the least amount of delay.

Approximately some twenty miles up the road, we passed a German landing field that had been run down in the swift advance, and the destruction at this location was even worse than in Geilenkirchen, if that could be possible. In the short space of time that it took to pass the field, I counted at least twelve planes: Stuka dive bombers, JU-88's, four-motored bombers, two-motored bombers—all burnt and twisted with motors hanging drunkenly from their mounts, gaping holes blown in their wings and fuselage.

We passed fuel dumps that had been overrun—intact—with all supplies secure. Not even demolition had been possible. Ammunition dumps the same. The hurried flight of the Germans was shown by the countless piles of German uniforms, rifles, helmets, gas masks, and boxes of perfectly usable ammunition that lined the ditches of the roads. Here and there, the German dead, stretched in grotesque and awkward postures of death, lay in mute and bloody clumps.

In the little town of Lauterbach, we finally caught up with Service Company of our Regiment, and I went in and had a few moments' conversation with Major Herbert, Clopton, and the rest. It was here that we ascertained the approximate location of the CP and continued on, mile after mile deeper into Germany. At length, we reached Rabenscheid, which was to be the next location of Service Company, and from here on, the advance had been so swift that no opportunity to clear the roads of mines had been possible. We continued on through the little town of Alsdorf, where a column of horse-drawn vehicles had been trapped. Fully forty dead horses lined the streets of this picturesque little village in the awkward positions of death and with the mutilation that only high explosive can cause. On and on, finally coming out on a road that rapidly degenerated into little more than a trail, until we came to the little hamlet of Dillbach, where the Command Post was presently located. After looking around, I finally spotted a CP sign and soon located Smith. We accomplished our business with some dispatch, for I had come some 74 miles from the Rhine, and needless to say, the task of bucking the long lines of traffic would put me back in Honnef at a late hour.

I left the CP at about 1530 and, using slightly different routes, passed even more tragic examples of the horror that is war. Long lines of freed Allied prisoners, slave labor, and liberated French, Belgian, and Dutch. Here and there, scattered groups of German soldiers were marching back to the rear areas to surrender, for they were surrendering in such droves that it was impossible to find guards for them all. Endless lines of German refugees, moving from their bombed-out villages and towns, with all their worldly possessions piled about them in crude carts and wagons. Some were expressionless and displayed no emotion, their faces reflecting only the dull despair that is universal to a people entrapped in the cruel, chaotic confusion of an advancing army. Others displayed their dislike for their present role by gestures and shouted words. Despite a tug at the heartstrings at the sight of the little children and the old people thus forced into the ignominious role of refugees, I can feel no pity for the German people. When the situation was reversed, most of them cared not a whit about the fates of the French, the Belgians, or the Dutch and sat back and enjoyed the subsequent sacking and looting of Europe and filled their fat German bellies with all of the food of Europe while millions of fellow human beings met starvation and worse. No, I say it is just retribution for the German people. Let them straggle along every road from here to Berlin and further.

On every front our armies are sweeping forward. The Germans retreated in mad confusion; the civilians hang out white flags with the utmost alacrity and beg only for the artillery to stop. Can this be it, then? Can this finally be the end of five years of mass murder and slaughter? Or will the demented fools continue on? Will they make a last desperate stand? And if, in a few more weeks it be the end, what then? Will it be the China-Burma-India Theater for us? Or the Army of Occupation? Will I at least be enabled to see my family before we depart for the Orient?

All of those questions, I am afraid, remain in the dim, unpredictable future, and whither leads the karma of McCully, no man can say.

There was no mail today.

Honnef, Germany
2 April 1945
I am afraid any excerpt I write tonight may prove to be somewhat

incoherent and a worthless attempt, but nevertheless, I have to the urge to write, so . . .

It appears probable that we may move within a day or so. At last, the priority on trucks has been relinquished; at least enough of them will be allocated for us to make the move. I am much relieved at this move, for we are well nigh 100 miles behind our forward elements, and the ensuing difficulties of communication are truly insuperable.

I received no mail today, with the exception of one from Bob, but I wrote three or four. Recently, in answer to my letter written some time ago to Davidson and Licht Jewelers, requesting them to fashion a bracelet from my souvenir coins, I received a reply containing their estimate, $37.50. I am hardly that affluent, at least for something I could fashion myself in a few hours, and when I thought of the pleasurable recordings or furnishings for my home that the sum would buy, my decision was NO, and I wrote them accordingly.

Until today, we were all quite delirious at the continuous announcements of advances and good news, but today all news seemed to point to the fact that the Germans are beginning to organize, and their defenses are stiffening. Perhaps I am unduly pessimistic, but it was pitiable to see the hope that was mirrored in the faces of my men, the unspoken hope that was felt—HOWEVER! As though to refute my pessimism, the radio just announced that the Ruhr has been completely encircled! The 1st and 9th Armies have linked up in the little village of Lippstadt.

HONNEF, GERMANY
APRIL 4, 1945

This shall be a continuation of the preceding excerpt, as events arose the other night, which forced me to cease its composition.

It became evident that I had to somehow contact Headquarters again. The next morning, about 1030, we departed, fully loaded and armed. I took one of the lads, Sergeant Ross, along with me, for it is extremely dangerous to travel alone, and one man is needed to watch the roadside with a fully loaded carbine. Again we passed the familiar vista of carnage previously described in earlier excerpts and continued on, deep into the vitals of Nazi Germany, for as events later proved, Headquarters was a full 170 miles into the heart of Germany, much of it through desolate, uninhabited, and lonely terrain. It is to be remembered that the advance of our armor was so swift that many pockets of enemy resistance were simply bypassed, and it is estimated that up to 150,000 amply armed Germans have been trapped in the encircled area. They are continually probing the ring about them for weak spots in an attempt to escape the trap, and it is this factor that makes travel so very dangerous. It was a factor that we were not cognizant of at the time we left on the journey, and as events later proved, ignorance must have been bliss.

We passed through utterly devastated Altenkirchen, which had suffered the consequences of being the headquarters of one of the German armies, for it was practically obliterated from the earth. On and on, through Harburg, Dillenburg, and finally to Marburg, then north to Wetter, Frankenberg, and late in the afternoon, we arrived at Korbach. Most of the trip forward consisted of battling heavy traffic— huge convoys hauling gas, rations, ammunition, mammoth prime movers hauling tanks, 240-mm guns and carriages, columns of tanks, tank destroyers, steam shovels, bulldozers, road scrapers, earth movers, troops moving to the front in endless streams of 2-1/2-ton trucks. We passed one convoy whose total length was 69 miles bumper to bumper. In the many, many villages where the people had surrendered without resistance and had hung out the white flags of surrender, hardly any damage was done, and it was a beautiful and scenic journey through old Germany and its Rhineland. Pastoral fields with healthy livestock, cool and verdant forests with sylvan streams tinkling and babbling away into the cool depths. I had not realized before how very heavily Germany was forested. The only thing that brought the realization of war to mind was the endless procession of refugees, freed slave labor, and newly liberated Allied prisoners of war, all making their way to the rear areas of our army.

At Korbach, I grew a bit worried, for it became evident that we still had a great distance to travel, and it was, even then, getting dark rapidly. I was not filled with rapture at the thought of wandering through those heavily forested areas in the dead of night. We made all the speed we possibly could over the war-torn roads, but it was quite dusk when we reached the town of Niedermarsberg where the Division Headquarters was located. I had a distinct premonition that the outfit had moved again, so I went into the G-3 section and looked at the operations map. Sure enough, Service Company was now located in the little town of some ten miles on down the road. My good friend, Major Lilienstern, admonished me to make all haste, for it would soon be dark. It seemed to me that the road to Adorf was particularly deserted, for not a vehicle did we see the entire trip. As it turned out later, several parties had already been ambushed on the road, and it had been under continual enemy observation all day. In Adorf, we had to spend another twenty minutes of futile searching for the Service Company, as they had neglected to place their signs in an easily distinguishable place, and the narrow, medieval streets did not simplify the task. At length, however, we found Captain Martin and his cohorts ensconced in a comfortable German dwelling, much to the discomfort of the *hausfrau* who owned it. I had intended to go on to the Command Post but changed my mind, and it was indeed a fortunate thing that I did so, for a nine-man enemy patrol was captured on the same road we had just traveled not an hour before. Chow had been over with for some time, so we had to make out with K-rations and a bit of cherry brandy. We decided to interrogate three of the prisoners that had been taken. In they came, and never have I seen sorrier spectacles than these so-called "Supermen" presented. Average age about forty-five, they claimed to have deserted, as they knew *Deutschland Kaput* (they all say this). Stupid in appearance, with their typically square heads, they reminded me of nothing so much as a swine standing on its haunches.

    I was treated like a royal guest and was given the signal honor of occupying a huge German featherbed. It was appreciated, too, for I was dog-tired after some ten hours of merciless bouncing and jolting in the jeep. I awoke about 0730, and it was a dreary morning with a heavily overcast sky through which a steady drizzle poured. Happily, we had FRESH eggs for breakfast, and this put me in an exceedingly happy mood. Again we loaded up, picked up the distribution, and obtaining approximate directions, headed for the Command Post. It seems we had to go back to Korbach, and then head for a different range of mountains, as Regiment was now located in the little hamlet of Dillinghausen. Through deserted, muddy roads, and with some apprehension, too, for at every little village and cluster of houses, you could see the Germans inside, peering out from their curtains. There is much hate in the attitude of these people, for their sudden drop from power was not to the liking of many of them, and their sons and men have been fed into the maw of war, too. At length, however, we arrived at the Regimental CP where I accomplished my business with as much dispatch as possible, for already it was almost afternoon, and I now knew how far the return trip was.

About 1330, after lunch, we started the return journey, and due to the fact that we did not have to buck the continuous lines of trucks, we made much better time. We only stopped once at an abandoned German ammunition dump to pick up three ammunition boxes—watertight— that I intended to use in the handling of all our dispatches. The roads had been literally shredded to bits by the continual pounding of the tanks and prime movers, so that by the time I arrived back at Honnef, I felt as though I had been beaten over the back with a two-by-four. We had heard, the night previously, while at the Division Command Post, that our outfit was moving out, but much to my surprise, everyone was still here upon my return and, O Happy Day, a lot of mail had come in for me, which I spent today answering (in my spare time, that is). According to the radio, the Germans have now organized a guerrilla army in our rear, who call themselves the "Werewolves," and it is their sworn intention to kill each and every Yank. I'm not too damned worried about it. The end is near, and they know it, but the miserable fools will prolong it until the bitter end.

Enough for now—a good night's rest awaits.

HONNEF, GERMANY
5 APRIL 1945

We leave at 0545 in the morning. The move was announced at Officers Call this noon. It is to a location southeast of Paderborn, evidently in the proximity of Niedermarsberg. Late this afternoon, we started loading and finished shortly after the evening meal. At the present time, everything is stowed away in a shipshape manner, and the truck containing the office equipment was covered with our canvas tent, for the sky was ominously dark, and a high wind foretold a stormy night. The journey will be one of the longest and most arduous that we have yet made, some 165 miles east of the Rhine, and to the very perimeter of the present 1st Army breakthrough. Inasmuch as neither of the two allotted trucks have tops, it will be a particularly miserable trip for all of us if it rains. Discomforting as the trip may be, I welcome it, for again, we will have some semblance of contact with the Regiment, even though I anticipate four days of extremely hard work before we will once again be current on all phases of work.

So we leave beautiful Honnef-on-the-Rhine, lying at the foot of the "Drachenfels," or in English, "Dragon's Rock," which is, according to Teutonic mythology, the exact spot where Siegfried slew the fabulous dragon, "Fafnir." I think I have already described the crumbling ruins that surmount the peak, which overlook the smooth, green expanse of the Rhine.

Tonight the news is exceptionally good; our spearheads are thrusting ever deeper into the vitals of Nazi Germany. Also good food for thought is the dramatic announcement of Russia's denunciation of her neutrality pact with Japan.

Mr. Lauck found a huge box of stamps of all nations and gave it to me. I shall send them to June, for she is an inveterate stamp collector, and she'll probably get a lot of fun out of sorting them over.

Warburg, Germany
7 April 1945
We moved out, but a little later than was anticipated, and for the most part, the journey was quite uneventful. It drizzled off and on, but fortunately, it was not a heavy downpour, and the men were quite comfortable under their raincoats. The roads, though, were churned into a viscous mass of mud, and by the time we reached our destination, everyone and everything was well splattered. At a point about six miles this side of Niedermarsberg, a good many of the vehicles ran out of gasoline, fortunately, directly in front of a gasoline dump, and it took us a half hour or so to refuel. When I stopped in Niedermarsberg to inquire from one of the guards just where the new location was now situated, I assumed, naturally enough, that I was now alone and was leading only my own two trucks. Much to my surprise, though, when in the process of turning around, I discovered that I had the remainder of the column behind me, some 20 trucks and 200 men. Evidently Captain Hurst, who was originally in command of the column, had become separated from us. I was not exactly overjoyed at this news, for the only map I had was a German service station map of the vicinity. At any rate, we started out, and sure enough, we were well on our way to Hannover and enemy territory when I had an extremely strong "hunch" that we were on the wrong road. Accordingly, I turned around, much to the griping of the entire column, and headed back some 10 miles. Sure enough, we found the crossroads where an MP had given us the wrong directions and were soon on the way to Warburg. We arrived at almost dusk and found the new location not exactly a choice one—an old school of which we were allotted one room. Making the best of the situation, though, we cleaned it out thoroughly, moved in,

and were soon set up. I had sent my driver back to Service Company (we were now located <u>ahead</u> of our Service Company) to pick up the long-delayed collection of distribution, and I then spent a major portion of the evening sorting it out. Coffee and C-rations were served at about 2200, and after piecing it out a bit with a few of the "snacks" that Mother and Lola have been sending me, I retired to the blessed oblivion of sleep. Praise be again to the makers of that wonderful air mattress. I only hope that it stays whole and free from defects for the remainder of the war.

Warburg, Germany
7 April 1945

I awoke this morning feeling just as I must have looked--dirty, unkempt, unshaven. Breakfast was served at a little house down the street, and after breakfast, I apportioned out the work and then heated a goodly amount of water. After a thorough scrubbing and a good shave, I felt immensely better and was soon ready to depart for my trip to the Regimental CP. Bresser and I started out about 1130, which actually was rather late in the day for such a trip, and after a ride of about 15 miles over extremely rough roads, arrived in the little town of Duisburg. Here I found that Captain Smith had gone on forward to set up a new CP. Nevertheless, we delivered our distribution, stopped long enough to have a good hot meal—the first real meal in two days—and then set out in search of Smith. I neglected to mention that I found two excellent 12-inch records in this CP and packed them carefully, for I shall take them with me in the hope of eventually getting them home. One is "Naila" (Delibes) with Dvorak's "Humoresque" on the opposite side. The other is Schubert's famed "Ave Maria," with the "Waltz from Faust" on the opposite side.

We continued on up the road, which was unusually interesting, for the continual procession of little villages had just been overrun by our troops. No particular damage had been done, for most of them now choose the white flag of surrender, rather than the horror of our artillery. At length, in the little village of Hümme, we finally found them, only to discover that they were displacing forward to another town, which had not yet been completely cleared of the enemy. As I stepped out of the jeep, I ran into none other than Colonel Cochran, who gave me an extremely hearty greeting, and almost immediately afterwards, discovered Smith standing on the steps of a little schoolhouse. He waved a cheery greeting, and inasmuch as his jeep was gone, we decided to use my jeep for the advance party. We started out and traveled some 20-odd miles to the little village of Beberbeck, which, as near as I could see, consisted solely of a large hospital, which had been maintained by the German government for the care of the pregnant wives and women of the German soldiers, and five or six enormous stables with a small number of necessary administration buildings. Here the usual process of setting up a CP in a Nazi village was brought into play—notifying the local burgermeister to have all guns, weapons, and cameras collected and brought to a central point, the acquisition of several houses in which the various elements of the command group would be located, and the notification of such persons who would thus be displaced. After meeting several officers whom I had not seen in a long while and straightening out several pressing matters with Smith, I decided to return to Warburg. We arrived back about 1530, had supper, and called it a rather complete day.

WARBURG, GERMANY
10 APRIL 1945
But a short entry tonight, although it has been an eventful interim. It became necessary that some 28 men be brought back to Personnel for various reasons, and one of the surest ways of getting them back was to get them myself. I will not again describe the journey forward, as it was the same route we followed a few days ago to Beberbeck, only we continued on and crossed the Weser River, traveled south along the river until we located Service Company in Ödelsheim, and then proceeded five miles still further south and found the CP in the little village of Bursfelde. Smith had gone forward, so I finished my business with Sgt. McGinnis, had dinner with the Colonel, Major General Terry Allen, and Major General Milligan of the 3rd Armored Division. The Colonel was again quite cordial and affable. I then returned to Ödelsheim and started rounding up the men. About 1400, we started back, and although we made a speedy trip of it, it was dusk when we returned. I found that things had been going well in my absence, and now that we have the men here, we can get that much out of the way—men to be naturalized, to go to the O.C.S. at Paris, and going home on the "rotation" policy.

Recently, we received a new ¼-ton trailer, and I feel sure that it will alleviate our transportation difficulties immensely.

I managed to get caught up on the news again after a lapse of four days and find the war progressing nicely on all fronts. Gave cause for optimism, in fact, until I read the article describing the utmost haste that will be called for in shipping ETO troops to the Japanese Theater. "No furloughs or leaves home," was stated flatly and bluntly.

Today I had to send Mr. Lauck back to the Rhine to place a court-martial prisoner in confinement and expect him back about 1000 tomorrow. If he does arrive then, I shall leave immediately for the CP and may as well plan to make a two-day trip of it, for the advances have been prodigious. Then, too, it is going to be no simple matter to find them this time, although for a change, I have some good maps. I may as well take my bedroll along.

I have received no mail at all for a long, long, time, and in one situation, at least, it is quite puzzling. The two long letters that I wrote to Margie, well over a month ago, have never been answered. I have a letter from Vivian that I should have answered long ago, but in thinking it over, I feel that I should not carry on the correspondence any longer. After all, she is married now, and it is best to let the whole thing end there. She is following her destiny, and I shall have to follow mine. But to be truthful, the course of the path of my destiny certainly puzzles me at times. I feel that I will be so damned ancient by the time that I eventually get out of the Army that there will be no point at all in trying to organize my life into some kind of a planned existence. To bed—I'll need all reserves of energy, tomorrow.

Warburg, Germany
11 April 1945
A hectic day. Mr. Lauck was unaccountably delayed and didn't return until 1700 today. Meanwhile, the problem of getting six men their naturalization papers had grown into a problem of immense proportions. It seems some trivial certificate was required, and it meant a round trip of some 300 miles for me to deliver them to Army Rear. About 1600, I obtained the load of the medics' jeep, which meant I would have to travel unarmed (under the Geneva Red Cross, which is flamboyantly painted on all medic vehicles). When I looked at the map, I discovered Army Rear was located in a particularly inaccessible spot and along a most dangerous route. Inasmuch as dusk would see me about in the center of a heavily forested area, I then and there decided to leave at daybreak tomorrow. This decision caused much

anguish and gnashing of teeth among the higher ups, but I remained steadfast, and as it turned out, it was fortunate that I did so; otherwise I would have had the trip for nothing. At supper, Mr. Lauck casually mentioned the fact that he had delivered the necessary certificates on his return journey!

Woodman "came through" in noble fashion this morning when Message Center made its delivery. It seems the first battalion had captured an entire carload of SS 7.65-mm automatic pistols, and he was thoughtful enough to send Lauck and I one apiece. It was still in the original packing box with Cosmoline still covering the gun, an extra clip, a cleaning rod, and even a wad of silk floss for cleaning! No ammunition of that particular caliber was available, but by an odd stroke of fate, I remembered that we had thrown out a case of 7.65 ammunition when we first moved here. I dug it up, and sure enough, albeit a bit water-soaked and rusty. I spent an hour or so removing the rust and oiling the cartridges and soon had ten boxes of ammunition stored away in my desk (250 rounds plus two full clips). I am really delighted with the gun.

The general situation is getting so confusing that it really isn't funny anymore. Regiment is now some 150 miles away from me, and Message Center cannot deliver that distance. Kernan is still back on the Rhine but will soon displace forward to a new location some 50 miles away across the Weser. Casual Company is set up in a field someplace, and we will have to move by "organic transportation," which in my case means my jeep and ¼-ton trailer to move two tons of equipment and 38 men! If we do not move, I intend to go up to Regiment tomorrow, which will be a two-day trip, and so I had best take my bedroll along (although I don't think I will). I shall endeavor to work out some sort of liaison with Smith so that I can get the dispatches back here, but the Service Company shuttle has proved impractical in the past, due to the fact that Service Company inevitably loses most of the reports.

Ah well! Surely the war cannot last forever.

WARBURG, GERMANY
14 APRIL 1945

Another tortuous pilgrimage has been added to the list. Upon Mr. Lauck's return from the Rhine, I determined to try and catch up with the Regiment and, at the same time, shuttle a small advance party and a trailer load of equipment to the new location of the AG at Weende.

We left at about 1030 the next morning with a total of five men in the jeep and an exceedingly full trailer. For the trip forward, we elected to use the route that we had discovered on the trip to Ödelsheim, and after crossing the Weser, made our way down a miserable network of roads that had been literally torn to pieces by the continual pounding of our tanks. The engineers were endeavoring to repair them, but even so, we were forced to travel in compound low range for a period of over seven miles, during which time I held my breath for fear that the trailer would overturn. About 1230, we arrived at the new location at Göttingen. Without a doubt, but for the fact that it is still so far behind the regiments, it is the best location we have ever had. It is another military school, this time a German Cavalry O.C.S., and they left in such a hurry that there was no time to destroy anything, and therefore, it is in excellent condition. Here I dropped the trailer and unloaded the two men who composed the advance party. The driver, Stansbury, and I then immediately set out to find Regiment. Again, we battled the endless convoys and the stifling clouds of dust for mile upon mile, passing village after village that now displayed the new national flag of Germany, the white flag of surrender. At some points on the roads, we passed columns of trucks heading back along the road and filled with captured German prisoners of war. Some of the more spirited burghers would display a bit of defiance and wave to the prisoners who, of course, would wave back. I wonder how they like *blitzkrieg*, now? I found the Division Command Post at Duderstadt just in the process of moving out but was fortunate in spotting Colonel Rex, the G-1, who showed me his operations map, and I was thus enabled to find the approximate location of the Regiment. We immediately left and about 1630 entered Nordhausen, which had only been captured a few hours and was still in a great state of confusion. The city had suffered heavily through our extensive artillery and bombing, and all of the principal streets and roads were practically impassable. We finally found the Regimental CP on the outskirts of Nordhausen, only to find them lined up in convoy formation in readiness to proceed to their new location at Brücken, 84 miles from Berlin as the crow flies. I spotted the jeep belonging to the S-1 Section and immediately pulled into line behind it. Due to the fact that the main highway was again jammed with the endless miles of supply convoys, we took a route running parallel to the highway but some miles back in the nearby hills. Most of it was extremely dusty, country roads and little-used "trails." It was almost dusk when we finally arrived at the new Command Post, and the first persons I saw were Captain Smith and the Colonel. The latter seemed quite surprised at my appearance and greeted me quite heartily. I remained overnight, and during the course of the evening, we had fresh eggs and bacon (cooked by the terrified *fraulein* who occupied the house) and then about 2200, the regular cooks prepared a sumptuous steak dinner. I slept on a makeshift bed composed of German mattresses, sheets, and an enormous feather comforter, which seems to be the vogue in this part of Germany.

The next morning, about 1000, we left on the return journey, and due to the fact that we did not have to fight the interminable convoys, and also, we were considerably more familiar with the route. We had heard rumors of the concentration camp that had been overrun at Nordhausen, and I determined to pay a visit to it. On the outskirts of Nordhausen, I asked an MP as to its location and found that it was not far off—just at the city's edge. The area had been particularly hard hit by our bombers, and we picked our way carefully over the debris in the jeep until we came to a massive enclosure surrounded by barbed wire, the only entrance to which was an ornate iron gate decorated with the crossed sheaves of lightning denoting the SS troops. There was a sizable crowd of American soldiers, military government, Red Cross, and other personnel milling about. I picked my way through the crowd and ran across a VII Corps Chaplain that I had become acquainted with on the road and asked him where the bodies were. He pointed down one of the squares, which was surrounded by huge barn-like structures. Walking about 100 yards down the street, I came across a scene that will live forever in my memory. The camp had held thousands of Polish slave labor, whom the Germans used in manufacturing parts for the nefarious V-1 and V-2. These unfortunate Poles had been systematically starved to death over a period of months, and although many of them had died from the effects of our bombing of the V-1 plants, as the Germans claimed, practically all of them had died from malnutrition or outright starvation. None of the bodies was over four days old, and the large majority of them had not been scratched by the bombing. Just prior to the time they had died, they must have looked like living skeletons, for only the bones, tendons, and sinews jutted from the human frame, a frame with skin stretched over it. Imagine if you can, a hot, dusty enclosure, surrounded by enormous barracks. Down this length of enclosure lay row upon row of dead Poles in all postures—some face up with their heads thrown back, their mouths snarling in the last bitter paroxysm of death—others face down, with their heads resting upon forearms, as though sleeping. Most of them were utterly naked, their bodies showing the marks of previous beatings and the sadistic tortures of the SS troops. Others had clothing resembling the material that awnings are made from. I saw one old man, evidently a Jew, whose face, even in death, maintained a kind of peaceful dignity, as if at least in death, he had found the peace which had been denied him so long. Row upon row of the dead—blonde men, brunettes, men with Slavic features, here and there a woman and little children five and six years old—all emaciated beyond description. The bodies had started to putrefy in the sun, and the American Military Government had rounded up all able-bodied Germans and had put them to the task of carrying the dead from the surrounding buildings. Across the highway, our bulldozers were leveling a turnip field, and the commandeered Germans, dressed in excellent topcoats and grey fedora hats, presented an incongruous sight busily preparing a mass grave in which to bury the unfortunate Poles. My driver and I investigated one of the barracks and here was the ultimate horror—many of the slaves had died in bed, too weak to run for the air raid shelters, if the Germans had provided any. They had slept on crude, wooden, double-decker bunks with straw mattresses and must have been forced to live like animals, for the quarters were the epitome of filth. Human heads, arms, legs, and torsos were scattered about. I saw one torso so charred and burnt that it was scarcely recognizable. Two men had died side by side with their arms still flung protectively about each other. By this time, nausea was sweeping over me, and we left the compound filled with a bitter, burning hate for the entire German race. What filthy, slimy beasts the entire race must be. You cannot tell me that a city the size of Nordhausen did not know what the SS troops were doing at this camp. I used to have a bit of compassion in my heart, if for nothing more but humanity's sake, at least for the little children and the aged. But no more. Every time that I look at a fat, healthy, well-dressed German Swine, I think of those poor, forsaken people in that compound. Surely God will bring just retribution upon a people such as the Germans.

    The balance of the return journey was a hard, dusty trip, and we arrived back just in time for the evening meal. Some elements of the outfit have moved to Göttingen already, and today just the 415th, the 413th, and a few of the smaller sections remain. I sent Mr. Lauck and three more men up to prepare the new quarters, and if my driver returns in time today, I shall send yet another shuttle this afternoon. In the meantime, there is not too much to do but wait for sufficient transportation to move the rest of us.

I have another trophy of some value, a new Agfa Kodak, which happily takes size-120 film and had a very good lens with a time attachment enabling me to take pictures of myself, too. I hope to obtain some film before long and take some pictures.

Have a delicate political situation to iron out with Kernan, but I do not anticipate any trouble, for I have already seen the G-1 about it.

Our troops had bypassed Leipzig today, and the 2nd Armored Division was at Magdeburg two days ago, so Berlin should be in sight before very long. How I hope that this mess will soon end!

Göttingen, Germany
17 April 1945
Mail has arrived in an unprecedented flood, so many in fact, that I will have difficulty in answering them all promptly. I received four from Margie alone. She writes such a fine letter. Others from Grosset and Dunlap, Mother, Dorothy, Social Security Board, etc.

We finally moved, and almost entirely by our own jeep and trailer, a feat that can best be gauged when it is realized that almost two tons of equipment and 38 men had to be moved in a vehicle the size of a small coupe. We are still over 100 miles behind, and already an advance party is looking for a new location. We are presently located in an immense cantonment, somewhat similar to the military school at Brand, for in fact that is what this is, in this case, an SS Cavalry School. The infamous insignia of the SS troops is on everything. We have an unusually large amount of room—3 rooms—more than we actually need, so we are using one room for storage. We have the additional speaker connected to the radio so that it plays in the other room. Mr. Lauck is in one room, and I in the other. I have a large, ornate desk, though not so large as the one I had at Brauweiler. Very probably, not over 28 hours ago, some Nazi *Hauptmann* sat where I am sitting and barked his guttural orders.

In Mother's letters, she had made another check of the War Bonds, and I am happy to state that my original estimation of the total number was correct: thirteen $25 bonds and seventeen $50 bonds, including the one she purchased during the first part of April, or a grand total of $1175 in bonds. I only intend to buy $1500 worth, as I figure that is enough, and I don't intend to have all of my eggs in one basket.

I am certainly pleased with my new Kodak and am looking forward to the receipt of the film, which I have requested so that I can take some pictures. Was investigating the case today, when out fell one of the little plunger devices so that the shutter can be operated without jarring the camera.

I have ordered four more books, but as to just when they will arrive, I cannot say. They are: *Desk Copy of the Common English Errors, Expressive English, Roget's Thesaurus,* and *Mental Tests for Civil Service Examinations.* A little studying will not hurt me at all. The music books that I ordered are evidently on the way but cannot say when they will arrive. Margie is loaning me one of her books, too.

My mind is not very fruitful tonight, so I had best close and turn my efforts to answering some of my mail. The work seems to be quite well caught up.

GÖTTINGEN, GERMANY
18 APRIL 1945

Quite a row today over the decreased efficiency shown in Battle Casualty Reporting. Primarily, this had been caused by the unsatisfactory locations of this echelon. I have always maintained that this outfit could be located much closer to the units than it usually is. I was not hesitant in expressing my views, either. Nevertheless, I am going up to the Regimental CP tomorrow to forestall any letter that my dear colleague, Kernan, may have the General sign. It will also be an ideal opportunity to straighten out many other matters.

Word came today that Magdeburg had fallen. However, fighting is still going on in Halle, which is the present location of the Regimental CP. It will certainly be an extensive trip, for it is some 350 miles round trip.

I finally managed to get all caught up on my mail and now have received absolutely none for two days. That is the way it usually is, though. Gobs will arrive in one day and then an absolute dearth of mail for weeks; a most unsatisfactory arrangement, but there is nothing I can do about it. I have requested people in the U.S. to send me some 25 rolls of film for my new Kodak, and I certainly hope that they are able to buy some of it, for that means that I will be able to take many pictures here and in other foreign lands, especially in view of the fact that the Kodak has one of the little time-release devices that enable one to take self-portraits.

It is rumored that we may move from here in just a few days, and I hope this is true, for I hate this being so far behind. It hinders the work no end and causes countless other difficulties. The Germans still resist as fanatically as ever, and it is evident that we have much bitter fighting yet to do before the fanatical fools can be convinced that Fascism is a lost cause.

I have been so busy of late that I have not had time to think or worry about the postwar problem, and to me it IS a problem, for I cannot fathom HOW in the world fate or destiny is going to solve this little problem. I have only one consolation, and that is the fact that, if all goes well, and barring unforeseen difficulties, I should come out of this war with a sizable little nest egg. I have previously mentioned the fact that I made an inquiry to the Social Security Board, and it seems that earnings from Army pay do not apply to the old age insurance. However, I discovered that it is necessary to have 40 "quarters" of Social Security coverage before you are fully covered under the benefits of Social Security, and they informed me that I had earned, so far, some 17 quarters, which is not too bad—almost half. They also mentioned the fact that both the President and Congress had recommended that Army earnings be applied against old age insurance.

GERMAN MILITARY AIRPORT—HALLE, GERMANY
25 APRIL 1945
Oh so very much has happened! We moved—sufficient trucks were provided for a change. I have been up to Regiment several times in the interim. The work has been particularly heavy of late, what with two months' payrolls, thousands of money order requests, and the usual reports and work—and impending administrative inspections hang over our head.

Word came tonight that Berlin was surrounded by the Russians, and Hitler's Berchtesgaden had been bombed by the RAF with 12-1/2- and 5-1/2-ton bombs. I do not see how the fanatical fools can resist much longer. All of their principal cities are being slowly pounded to bits. In fact, in our particular sector, we have been doing little more than holding a line on the Moldau River, a tributary of the Elbe. For when the Russians and the Americans join, we of the 1st Army will be "pinched out" and will have no further work, at least in this immediate area.

It was reliably rumored today that the general had announced that the 104th would soon go into a concentration area and then leave for an area near Le Havre, France, where we would undergo two months of intensive training, together with countless inspections (including administrative), and at the end of that period, would leave for the China-Burma-India Theater—direct—and with no possibility of a 3-week leave in the U.S. This information did not serve to raise the spirits of the men any noticeable degree, of course. Time alone will prove whether it is a rumor or not.

I received a bit of mail tonight, plus some that I had not had time to answer during the past few days, and spent this evening answering them. Vivian had written me two, and her statement telling me that all was now fine with her and her husband, resolved me not to interfere with her life further, and I wrote her accordingly, telling her that tonight's letter would be my last.

I have boxed up another three boxes of souvenirs and shall mail them tomorrow but cannot say when they will arrive home, for those I mailed in Brauweiler have not arrived home, even yet.

On 20 April 1945, on General Order No. 113, I was awarded the Bronze Star Medal. The citation reads:

"Captain ERNEST J. MCCULLY, (Army Serial Number 01289287), Infantry, Service Company, 415th Infantry, United States Army, for meritorious service in connection with military operations in Belgium, Holland, and Germany from 25 October 1944 to 21 March 1945. Entered military service from Sonora, California." Well, so be it, then. It may mean a few additional points when discharge time comes, if it ever does.

Tonight, I am disconsolate and depressed. It is late, and soon I must grope my way through the blackout over to my quarters, which are cold and dismal. Our present location is truly the most luxurious we have yet had and only 30 kilometers from the CP. We have two large rooms to serve as offices, plus a smaller room used for storage and supply in what was, until recently, the Fort Monmouth of the German Army, a communications school with millions of dollars' worth of equipment in it. The buildings are of the ultramodernistic type—glass facades, ornate columns, huge parade grounds, chromium steel stairways (Germany—the "have not" nation!), modernistic light fixtures. Acres and acres of grounds all carefully landscaped and camouflaged. A huge *Luftwaffe* school is part of the set-up. I have a German flying suit I intend to take home with me. Here I sit in my office tonight, a square room about 35 feet square, cream-colored walls, and a light blue ceiling. Huge ceiling-to-floor windows, now covered by built-in blackout curtains, and some truly luxurious blue drapes, easily 20 feet in length. I have the most massive desk I have yet had—modern, and a beautiful piece of furniture. At my right hand, a German field telephone; at my left, a German field radio. I am writing on a desk piece, a beautiful mirror, about a foot by a foot-and-a-half square. I have a marble and plastic fountain pen holder and an intricately designed little saber about six inches long, used as a letter opener, which in fact, is what it was.

The room itself was once a classroom, and four, six-foot stairs rise to the rear of the room. On these, the various sections of my office are set up, and I sit at the bottom in front of the blackboard in a truly commanding position. On the rear wall, printed in the ugly German script, is a German quotation from *Mein Kampf*, signed by Hitler, which says, "To obtain your ideals, you must be willing to die for them." Well, they are dying, and in great numbers. But will they obtain their "ideals"? God forbid! And I somehow doubt that they will.

Well, enough! To bed. Tomorrow I intend to arise early and take some pictures of the area, for I now have 72 rolls of 120 film and shall indeed have a goodly supply of snapshots to take home with me if there is any conclusion to this thing.

MILITARY AIRPORT—HALLE, GERMANY
3 MAY 1945
I have been neglecting my journal dreadfully during the past few days. I have made numerous trips to the Regimental CP at Bitterfeld, have been inordinately busy, and today I sped down miles of Hitler's *Autobahnen* or Superhighways and visited Regiment at its new location of Puchau; and shortly after my arrival, we moved an additional five miles to the village of Machern near the Elbe River and south of Leipzig.

Momentous have been the happenings during this interlude. Himmler's offer of surrender to the U.S. and Britain, but not the Russians, and its subsequent rejection. Mussolini's capture and immediate trial and execution by Italian patriots. The collapse of the Italian Front and its recent unconditional surrender. The merging of the Russian and American armies, not far from our present location.

In truth, it appears that the end of the war, at least with Germany, is near. We expect the news momentarily.

I have received a great deal of mail, lately, but for some reason or other I have lost all enthusiasm for letter writing. Smith and I went on a couple of parties in Bitterfeld in which I certainly did not use my head, particularly on the one that occurred on April 28th. An end to such experiences! There will be no more! I have spoken!

My four little books on music that I had ordered in Brand, Germany, finally arrived today. I shall peruse them and then send them on home. Mother writes that the chrome swastika arrived home in excellent shape. I wonder when the rest of my things will arrive? I sent home two German Army field telephones recently. Planning to use them as garage-house-rumpus room communications on some happy future date. I plan to send home three more—a total of five should prepare me for almost any contingency. As an interesting aside, an excerpt in today's *S and S* stated that U.S. Army field telephones were being sold to civilians for the same purpose I have in mind for $39.95 per pair. I estimate that these I send home cost me approximately $2 apiece for postage, and they are a superior phone. (!).

I have had no mail for the past two days. Melanie has stopped writing, for what reason I don't know. I am about ready to drop the June correspondence. As seems to be usual, it is developing past the friendly stage, and certainly, I can't have that.

More later.

AT A GERMANY MILITARY AIRPORT—HALLE, GERMANY
7 MAY 1945
I really believe the great day is almost here! Tonight the radio announced that an announcement by Prime Minister Winston Churchill could be expected within the next few days concerning the news of the end of the war in Europe. The only fighting in Europe today was in Czechoslovakia. So at last it is here (or almost, at any rate)! What is next in the twisted and confused destiny of McCully? Clearly, there are but three logical dispositions possible. They are: (1) Assignment as part of the Army of Occupation, (2) Immediate transfer to the Pacific Theater, and (3) Home. I doubt the latter eventuality very much, however.

A deep and melancholy mood has possessed me for the past week. I cannot fathom the <u>purpose</u> of this fruitless existence. I have absolutely nothing to live for. There seems to be no discernible goal in life for me, and yet, some inner fire, some fierce compulsion, drives me on in a relentless desire to continually improve myself, to advance, but to WHAT?

In addition to the above troubles, I have been extremely worried about my physical condition of late, and only time can tell if my worries have any basis. At any rate, I have been getting the maximum amount of sleep possible under the circumstance, and that fact has helped considerably.

With the approach of the end of the war, the necessity for all administrative records to be in an excellent condition is becoming of paramount importance, and the various echelons of command are, of course, putting on the necessary pressure, until at the present time, conditions are nearly the same as at Carson, when we were preparing for the POE. Somehow, the situation doesn't galvanize me into the same furor that existed then. We shall do our best, and that is all that we can do.

Discovered an interesting fact today. As a veteran of this war, my wife, any minor children (if any), and I are entitled, at death, to burial in one of the national cemeteries maintained by the U.S. Government for its veterans.

No mail has filtered in for quite some time, although I have been quite busy answering some that I had been forced to neglect for a time. I mailed home the three additional German field telephones that I wanted for my home, today.

As to the brain-chilling, unfathomable problem as to what my future is upon the conclusion of the war in its entirety, I cannot venture tonight. Perhaps I dare not.

I may go to Regiment tomorrow, providing the weather permits (it has been raining miserably for the past two or three days). If so, perhaps a few pertinent matters can be rectified at that time.

I feel perfectly marvelous this morning—had a wonderful night's sleep, but of course, my tendency to worry horribly at the slightest cause does not give exact peace of mind.

AT A GERMAN MILITARY AIRPORT—HALLE, GERMANY
9 MAY 1945
My worries as to my physical condition have increased. I have determined to settle the matter once and for all, and by tomorrow at

the latest, I shall know definitely whether it is my accursed overactive imagination, or whether I am the world's biggest fool. At this auspicious moment then, when all the world is celebrating Victory in Europe Day, has fate chosen once more to bludgeon me to my knees?

Oh My Good Father in Heaven, I pray not. It seems always that, at just the precise moment when I have the most to look forward to, when I am filled with the utmost of determination and new resolve, that fate must choose that moment to belabor me with blasted hopes and the bitter price of folly.

I received a most enjoyable letter from Colonel Smith. He is at the Command and General Staff School in China. The letter was filled with appreciated fatherly advice and was, in general, a splendid letter from a splendid man.

The war was officially over at 0001 this morning, and just now, the radio announced the surrender of all German troops in Norway, the capture of Quisling, and of Hermann Goering.

Our future disposition is unknown and will probably remain so for some time.

I have one more box of souvenirs to send home, and that will be the last one, I think. It contains a .22-caliber Mauser, almost new; an old, but well-conditioned 16-gauge shotgun; and a pearl-handled German dress saber.

The next pressing question will be how to bring home my collection of pistols and miscellaneous trophies that I have in my field desk. Official rumors hint that 21-day furloughs may be granted prior to fighting the Japs, but whether this will hold true for officers in my capacity remains to be seen. And then, too, much depends on tomorrow.

AT A GERMAN MILITARY AIRPORT—HALLE, GERMANY
11 MAY 1945

No news to report as yet. Soon, however. The point system for discharge was announced last night, and although I have plenty of points on longevity and decorations, the fact that I have no dependents or children makes it seem probably that I will not be discharged until after the Japs are licked. However, that plan was only for enlisted men. The plan for the discharge of officers has yet to be announced.

I bought an "Eisenhower" Jacket today (dress), which is certainly nice and only cost me $14. I am taking vitamin pills twice a day now, and that, in conjunction with lots of sleep, has made me feel like a new man for the last two days.

No more for now. All I can do is to await developments.

[*The following entries were handwritten on Timberwolf stationery.*]

AT A GERMAN MILITARY AIRPORT—HALLE, GERMANY
15 MAY 1945
Results still pending.

Work, administrative red tape, senseless directives, etc., continue to engulf us in a ceaseless flood. Although not too distraught, we are very near it. From now until the time I entrain for home, at the start of a short leave, if we are fortunate enough to go to Japan via the U.S., I can look forward to nothing but endless days of hard, unrelenting work.

Although nothing definite on the discharge of officers has been disseminated, it is quite clear that the release of officers will be based upon four things:

    a. The same point values that apply to EM
    b. Military necessity or essentiality
    c. Efficiency
    d. The individual officer's desire

Inasmuch as I am 10 points below the minimum (85), am in a highly essential position, and all efficiency ratings have been "superior," my desire will not count for much, so I may as well gird myself for the Pacific fray. As usual, in the Army, the inefficient, worthless individuals will get the best breaks.

HALLE, GERMANY
19 MAY 1945
Nothing new to report, still waiting, but I have just a bit more hope now. Have heard from Margie again.

Rumors still surging on every conceivable theme. The strongest of these makes it evident that we <u>may</u> stand a chance of going to the U.S., and soon! We are definitely Pacific material, but it will be much more bearable if we can spend some time in the States.

Have spent a great deal of time up at the Regimental area. On one of these occasions, Colonel Cochran insisted on a formal ceremony in the CP and presented me with my Bronze Star Medal, which was awarded some time ago. Somehow, I appreciated it when he said, "You have been doing some fine work, Mac." Perhaps at last, things have proved out. Who knows? We were required to state on our ASR cards "yes" or "no" as to whether we desired to be retained in the service until the end of the war with Japan. I said <u>yes</u>, for what have I to return to in the U.S.? Somehow, I feel that my destiny lies in the Army. Whether this shall prove true or not remains to be seen. Foolish as it may be, I wouldn't feel true to myself if I quit now, with the war only half over.

Work is going well.

HALLE, GERMANY
21 MAY 1945

The latest rumor? <u>Direct</u> to the Pacific Theater. Went up to Regiment yesterday and accomplished quite a bit (drank a lot of beer, too).

Picked up a beautiful radio while there, and I intend to take it to the CBI with us, but I shall first have to get a little work done on it and how successful that may be is doubtful.

Am in a terrible mood tonight, although I received some mail.

No more for now.

HALLE, GERMANY
22 MAY 1945

At a low ebb again, mentally. Have received very little mail, and the work is mounting steadily.

From all indications, we will leave here about June 15th for Le Havre, France, but whether the boat will head for the U.S. or China, no one seems to know. However, I am inclined to think it will be the U.S.

Physically, I feel far below par and hope that this situation solves itself in short order.

At the present time, about all we have to look forward to is a series of interminable inspections, POM preparation crating, and more inspections. The Corps Inspection will take place tomorrow, and after that, even more. How we shall make out on all these remains to be seen, and all we can do is our best. At any rate, I do not intend to get upset about it, as I did at Camp Carson.

I cannot help but dwell upon the possibility of a leave of some sort if we do go to the U.S. It would be joy past all understanding to see Mother and all the folks once more, and I certainly hope that such an event comes to pass.

Regiment has now moved to the northern limits of Halle, and as a result, I can accomplish much more readily all of the multitude of things that must be done.

HALLE, GERMANY
27 MAY 1945
As usual, there is a tendency for me to neglect the journal when worries cease for me. In fact, this book seems to be a refuge for me when worries beset me. All is well as far as my physical condition is concerned, and my mind is at ease.

Events have crystallized, and it is quite definite: We are going to the U.S. and will receive a leave of as yet unknown duration. Then, additional training and off for Japan. We leave soon, some say as soon as June 3rd, for Le Havre, France. As usual, under such pressing circumstances, we were swamped under a staggering flood of administrative detail. I guess we will "muddle through" as we always have before.

Another situation now presents itself. Many of the officers will be released (those who have 85 points, possibly) and among these will be Smith. This makes me almost a certain candidate for the position of adjutant, a job for which I have no great enthusiasm, living under the thumb of the "old man" as it were. Whatever happens, though, I intend to do my best.

Have felt absolutely no inclination to write anyone for over a week, and to tell the truth, haven't really had the time.

Had quite a beer drinking party at the CP last night after a two-hour session of sculling on the River Saale. Had a lot of fun with the fellows. Good bunch.

HALLE, GERMANY
3 JUNE 1945
Again, as so often in the past, we are so swamped with work that I often wonder if we will ever accomplish it all. No sense in going into detail about it, it's the same old pre-POE line we were handed at Carson.

Other complications, though. Margie has suddenly developed a matrimonial complex, and I had to answer her letter and explain as tactfully and diplomatically as I could why I could never marry. Am awaiting the results of this letter. I hated to do it. She's such a swell girl, but there are two or three impossible barriers that forever preclude such a venture, and so it had to be.

Naturally, I am anticipating a nice leave in the U.S., but so much must be done before that occurs!

I wonder if I must again leave the U.S. with nothing to return to, or for, and a vacant, barren future staring me in the face!

HALLE, GERMANY
5 JUNE 1945
Here it is, well into June, and we sit twiddling our thumbs, awaiting movement orders. Politics and intra-regimental political intrigue are in full sway. I will have a Company Commanders Meeting at 1500 today in an effort to straighten out the surplus personnel problem.

I have been drinking lots of beer recently, but it doesn't seem to affect my weight in any appreciable manner. No word from Margie in answer to my last letter, but I expect catastrophic results. I guess it is futile for me to expect her to understand, or for that matter, to ever expect to plan on any happiness.

I have been feeling very well physically and received my copy of the "Final Type Physical Examination" recently, with excellent results. However, I do need more rest than I have been getting.

Now that we know definitely that we are going home, it is quite trying to endure the endless miles of red tape and administrative bunk that are so prevalent in Army channels.

Mail has fallen off terribly, and I do not have too much hope of it improving prior to the time we leave here.

HALLE, GERMANY
7 JUNE 1945
The Company Commanders Meeting came off smoothly enough, but as I had foreseen, nothing was really accomplished in it. So yesterday, I did what I had originally planned to do, went around and had a personal talk with each unit commander. Results were most gratifying. Came home last night, dog-tired (I had covered some 200 miles), to find that no mail had arrived. I felt particularly despondent last night. In fact, for the past few days, I have been feeling as though there was for me, of a certainty, absolutely no point in living. Why do I strive so

hard to improve myself to advance, to make something out of myself? I certainly can't answer that question. What a foul mess my life seems to be in. Perhaps, is it possible that the ghastly mess caused by Virginia and the divorce left some hidden psychological reaction that is not evident even to me that shall blight the remainder of my life? Ah well! I daresay the fighting in the Pacific Theater may well settle that question once and for all.

The latest foul rumor now circulating states that we shall remain in this theater for another 60 days. God forbid!

Political intrigue still sways the Regiment, and an interesting situation has arisen regarding the disposition of Captain Fox and Captain Vasilake.

St. Valery, France (near Le Havre)
16 June 1945
Haven't written for several days, and with good reason—we moved. Again a long, tortuous trip "by boxcar," with all the misery that phrase means. We passed through much of the scenic and pastoral beauty of Central Europe—Leipzig, crossed the Rhine at Frankfurt, on into the Saar, through well-demolished Saarbrücken, and on into France, still bearing the scars of two separate waves of destruction. Thirty-six men to a tiny boxcar posed a major problem insofar as sleeping the men was concerned, but we mastered it by packing them together à la sardine can, 18 to a side. Messing, and its attendant difficulties, was eliminated by means of "kitchen cars" spaced equitably the length of the train. The trip was long, slow, dirty, and extremely tiring, but we arrived, eventually, after an interval of four horrid days. We "enjoyed" a brisk march of 5 miles to the Staging Area, "Camp Lucky Strike," and here the pure, unadulterated hell of administrative confusion continued. Conflicting decisions, unconfirmed information, authorities totally ignorant, contradictory orders and ultimatums, needless and senseless work. It goes on even now and will no doubt continue, even though senseless, until I leave the reception center for home.

I write tonight because of the extreme sense of confusion my mind is in. Moreover, this may well be the last entry in my journal until my return from a leave of unknown duration. Some say 30 days at home, others 21, but no one really knows. At this time, it appears as though we will be sent home in battalion formation. Probably by Liberty Ship. At the Port of Debarkation on the East Coast, we will be sent directly to a reception center near our homes—in my case, Camp Beale, California, near Sacramento, I believe.

So many problems are in my mind, I feel almost at my wit's end. The tremendous responsibility of preparing the administration of 3,500 men and getting them accounted for aboard ship is a job of no mean proportions. All of the junk that I want to get home and how and when I can get it home. The problem of Margaret, and I have received no reply to the three letters I have written, and due to our movements, I doubt whether I will receive them until after I return to Camp. My uniforms are in a deplorable state. I shall have to purchase many new items, and many of the items are now quite difficult to purchase.

I suppose all of the above items will be worked out, they usually are, but it is quite hectic at present.

And so, for a short time at least, I shall again see my family and friends prior to departure for a new and more terrible war. Perhaps succeeding entries in this journal shall indicate a mind more at peace with itself, a small bit of happiness flung my way. Or shall it be merely a continuation of trials and tribulations, insignificant when shown against the present background of history and grandiose events, but to me, so terribly vital and important?

[*Remaining pages of the journal report personal financial status (e.g., assets, pay, disbursements, monetary gain, War Bonds purchased, loans to fellow soldiers, and notes) from August 1944 through June 1945.*]

[*A small remnant from a handwritten letter was found inside the journal with the following inscription:*]

"The Best Captain In the Whole Damn Army" (My Brother!)

[*The journal also contained the following magazine clippings:*]

1. A picture of a husband arriving home from work while his wife watches for him out the kitchen window. She is pouring two glasses of beer as he walks up the path to their home. The picture is labeled in ink: "BROKEN IDEALS."
2. A picture of a modern kitchen in a $6,000 home.
3. A picture of a couple reading the day's mail together. The husband is wearing a suit and tie with wine glass in hand; the wife is dressed in

a blouse and skirt, her arm around him. A carafe of wine, an extra glass, and a tray of crackers sit on the table beside them. The picture is labeled in ink: THE DREAM.

4. *A picture of a helmeted soldier kissing a woman in the clouds under a starry night. A printed caption is stapled to the picture: "Tonight I leaned across 10,000 miles and kissed you!"*

Journal 6

The Postwar Years
May 1, 1946 to August 16, 1949
Ages 30–33

*I was placed in the cherished position of
a Contact Representative for the VA . . .
it includes a very bright and shiny future
and is very pleasant work.*

∼

*Hard as it is to believe, it has happened at last.
I have fallen in love so deeply that it isn't even funny.
Try as I may (and I have really tried), I cannot find a flaw in the girl.*

DISCHARGE FROM ARMY • SECURES VA JOB IN PHOENIX AS CONTACT
REPRESENTATIVE • RESUMES DATING AND SOCIALIZING WITH FRIENDS •
REVELATION OF MARGARET *** • LOUISE AND THE STARLIT CONCERT •
BOB MARRIES • ITINERANT WORK IN ARIZONA • FALLS IN LOVE WITH EMILY
• ENGAGEMENT TO EMILY • BECOMES ITINERANT REPRESENTATIVE FOR
ENTIRE STATE • CONCERNS RELATED TO JOB SECURITY • MARRIAGE TO EMILY
• GRANTED SERVICE CONNECTION RATING DUE TO SKIN DISABILITY • PASSES
CIVIL SERVICE TEST • MISTRUST OF WOMEN ERADICATED BECAUSE OF EMILY •
GRANTED SERVICE CONNECTION RATING DUE TO STOMACH ULCER • PURCHASES
NEW CAR AND A HOME

PHOENIX, ARIZONA
407 N. 10TH ST.
MAY 1, 1946

One hundred and seventy-four days have elapsed since my discharge from the Army, eventful days you may be sure. Days of boundless joy at the spectacle of my good fortune, days of wonderment, days of puzzlement, and as always in my tumultuous existence, days of bewilderment and despair at the extreme irony of fate—lavish with good fortune on one hand, and so seemingly unjustly cruel on the other.

To begin with, I received my discharge from the Army on November 7, 1945, at Camp San Luis Obispo, California, and instead of hurrying home for a well-earned rest after five arduous years in the Army; I sped to the City of Phoenix in search of employment. My good friend, Smith, had preceded me by approximately one month and had written that opportunities were excellent in the particular field we had chosen (Civil Service with the Veterans Administration). It was well that I had chosen to exercise sound judgment in this matter, for later events proved that veterans were having a particularly difficult time in becoming readjusted to civilian life, and especially in the matter of reemployment. I, for one, had definitely made up my mind that I should never return to the fruitless empty toil of my former employer. As later events developed, I was only out of work for approximately 13 days. You may be certain my familiar pessimistic nature asserted itself during those entire 13 days! Imagine my enjoyment and utter disbelief, when after preliminary skirmishing and interviews, I was placed in the cherished position of a Contact Representative for the VA at a salary, which with overtime, averages approximately $3600 per year. Even better, though, it includes a bright and shiny future and is very pleasant work. My own desk—the work is interesting and gives one a feeling of accomplishment.

My first assignment of a week's duration was at Davis-Monthan Air Base, just outside of Tucson, Arizona, where I worked in the company of Mr. Lynn B. Willoughby, an old hand at the game.

The next assignment was as Contact Representative at the Separation Center of Fort Huachuca, near the Mexican border. A total of two weeks was spent here, and the work was so similar in nature to what I had been doing in the Army that it was amazing. Too, I lived at the "Lakeside Officers Club," ate at the Officers Mess, so all in all, my conversion to civilian life was a slow, painless problem. Ninth Corps Area received orders to close all Separation "Points," so my stay at Fort Huachuca was terminated after only 15 days. I then returned to the Regional Office at Phoenix, Arizona, and though filled with trepidation at first, events happened so rapidly, and the work appealed to me to such an extent, that in the days that followed, I could scarcely believe my good fortune in finding a type of work that gave me so much enjoyment.

Events followed rapid order—my daily work, talks at Luke Field, a 2-1/2-hour lecture before the State Service Officers School conducted at the American Legion hall, talks before other organizations.

On February 8, 1946, I met Margaret ***, the daughter of the State Adjutant of the American Legion. At first, I thought that perhaps here at last was what I had been seeking for so long, and although I knew in my heart that I was not in love, I thought that perhaps I could never fall in love again, and that if I desired matrimony and the things that a home means, I might as well take the plunge. After a tumultuous two-and-a-half months, however, I discovered that I would have been the world's biggest fool if I had allowed myself to become ensnared. Once again, that little inner voice gave me due warning, and I almost didn't heed it. On Easter Sunday, Margaret told me that she was four months with child . . . Needless to say, in my perhaps ruthless manner, I severed all relationship. A good deal of bitterness and hard feeling ensued, and I suppose there will eventually be even more.

Smith and I finally managed a trip to Los Angeles, where, in my own particular case at least, nothing more was accomplished than the drinking of a tremendous amount of hard liquor, a restless night's sleep, and a terribly tiresome return trip. Furthermore, *** . . .

Stedwell, my boss, and I just completed an organizational survey in several communities in the eastern portion of the State, for an itinerant service for that area is planned for the near future, and I am to be the one who serves the communities. We had quite an interesting trip, covering some 300 miles.

PHOENIX, ARIZONA
407 N. 10TH ST.
MAY 12, 1946
9:20 P.M.

The past weekend was ghastly. My old friend, Loneliness, was at his horrid best. Like a lost soul, I wandered the thoroughfares and byways in what I sincerely believe is the most unfriendly city in the world. I finished work at noon, Saturday, and hurried to my dismal room; and hot and uncomfortable as it was, managed to sleep about three hours. About 5 p.m., I arose, bathed, shaved, and dressed meticulously in my grey suit. Stopped by the Stedwells for a few moments, then sallied forth to the American Legion, where I consumed a quantity of beer. Left the slightly boring confines of that institution and proceeded to a nightspot that had only recently opened, "The Silver Spur," filled with rows of (smug) vacuous dupes only too anxious to pay the exorbitant demands for a highly watered drink. I left in disgust almost as soon as I arrived, stopped at a drive-in on the way home, ordered a hamburger and coffee, and retired a little after midnight—a completely wasted evening.

I arose about noon, dressed in slacks and sport shirt, and spent a fruitless two hours searching for a restaurant that was open. Finally located one (of the greasy spoon type) and had lunch.

Proceeded to the Stedwells again, and Sted and I consumed a number of excellent bourbon highballs. About 4 p.m., Anne prepared an excellent repast of fried chicken, after which Sted and I went over to the home of Guy Gaston and had a pleasant hour or two of conversation. Mr. Gaston promised to rent me one of his apartments. It will be much better than the one that I have for it has a private bath, a garage, a bedroom, AND a living room. Also, the Gaston's have a lovely backyard complete with lawn, lawn chairs, and cool shade. I feel sure that I will feel much more settled when I move, for I shall be enabled to purchase little things, and to have company in a place of which I am not ashamed.

Forgot to mention the fact that, when in Globe recently, I purchased (or rather ordered) a 1946 Packard Clipper, and its subsequent delivery is supposed to be effected within 90 days. All Contact Representatives are supposed to attend a three-weeks' school at the Branch office in San Francisco, and I hope that I can so arrange mine that I attend the school for the prescribed three weeks, and immediately thereafter, start my 15-day vacation. It should be a real vacation, the first in five years, and yet in view of all my good fortune, it should be an extremely happy one, even though, as usual, I will be by my usual lonely self.

Phoenix, Arizona
407 N. 10th Street
May 15, 1946
9:10 p.m.

The last few days have been busy ones filled with the usual press and rush of the day's work. However, I dread for the quitting hour to arrive, for I know that I am doomed to an evening of loneliness, boredom, and wakefulness. It is impossible for me to fall asleep until long after the hour of midnight has come and gone. I received three letters tonight—one from Mother, one from Bob, and one from Marilynn in Los Angeles. She and I had a trip planned for the coming weekend, but she hedged and simpered in such a sickening manner that I wrote her tonight and told her off in no uncertain terms. Stated that it would be unnecessary for her to correspond further.

Last night, I gave a talk to the assembled ladies of the Hazel Morton Post of the American Legion. Subject: "Your National Service Life Insurance." Can't see why they don't assign Palmer to those things. He gets 4300 per year as the insurance expert of the Regional Office. At any rate, the talk came off in great shape. I gain more and more poise and confidence each time I speak and am actually enjoying it.

What I shall do this weekend is beginning to worry me already. One consolation, I will work Saturday afternoon, and that will help to pass a lot of the time. I will only have Saturday night and Sunday in which to go insane. I can hardly wait until I can move into the new apartment. It will give me much to do, and when I return from my vacation, I intend to return with many of the little possessions and belongings that serve to make life a busy, interesting adventure.

My work seems to be progressing satisfactorily. A new man was hired the other day—fellow by the name of Birdsall. Imagine

Smitty and I will be swamped with work before too long a time—Greiger goes to Tucson, Bray to Flagstaff, Clark and Davila to school in San Francisco, and Stedwell leaves on his vacation. That leaves Smith, Birdsall, and I. Birdsall won't be very much help for about a month. Oh well, Smitty and I have had some big assignments before.

Think I will shower and shave and (try) to get a little sleep.

PHOENIX, ARIZONA
407 N. 10TH ST.
MAY 30, 1946
(MEMORIAL DAY)
No work today (holiday) and, of course, I practically went insane for wont of something to do. Arose about noon—bathed, dressed comfortably, had dinner at a downtown restaurant, went to the Smith's for a short visit, then went to a matinee at "The Palms." Cruised about for a time, then had dinner at a "joint," then a beer at Hubbard's, then home.

Have had two separate dates recently. Mary *** (one date was sufficient). Nice, but too many potential complications. I dropped it like a hot potato after one date, which act undoubtedly puzzled her no end. At any rate, she has been quite frank in her hints for another date, even suggesting a picnic for today. The other date really had me in a quandary for a time—a cute, little blonde named Louise. After about four dates, however, exact attributes formerly possessed by the great Virginia made themselves evident. My sudden severance evidently puzzled her. No more for me, however.

It is clearly evident to me that I must find some work or hobby to occupy my mind, or else I'll drive myself mad in this solitude.

PHOENIX, ARIZONA
711-1/2 E. MCDOWELL
(SUNDAY) JUNE 16, 1946
Managed to achieve some much-needed rest this weekend. Bought an album of tangos downtown yesterday afternoon, then came home to the apartment and rested most of the afternoon. Had a perfectly horrible supper at the "drive-in" and then back to the apartment with the Sunday papers. Played records and read until about 11 p.m. Awoke this morning about 11 a.m., had bacon and eggs at the drive-in (few cooks can murder so simple a dish as that) and then drove the car up

on the lawn in the backyard and washed it. Poor old car—the paint on it is really getting chipped. It still looks pretty good, though. Must take it to the mechanic tomorrow and have the generator and the miss in the motor corrected. Wrote some letters this afternoon, played some more records, finished my book, *The March of the Barbarians*, one of Harold Lamb's factional histories. A bit dry in spots and certainly not his usual style.

This evening, I really gave the old body a complete wash and polish—spent fully two hours in the tub and bath. I really feel good, at present. There has been an ominous silence from home, both on Bob's part and Mother's, so I guess the kid really did take the plunge and get married. Well, I certainly wish him all of the luck in the world.

I forgot to mention that I recanted on my original determination and have seen Louise several times since my first date with her. There is something fascinating about the girl. She is certainly very intelligent, definitely a good girl, practical. However, her attitude puzzles me. She gives an impression of utter coldness. There is an unemotional quality that is hard to fathom. She seems to be most definitely "set" in many of her ways and yet, at times, she can be a wonderful companion. One gathers a definite impression that Louise is all for Louise and could be utterly merciless and cool if her way was not always hers. Frankly, at this stage of the game, I am not particularly interested, one way or the other.

It is rumored that Margaret's pregnancy is far advanced by this time, and she will soon be going away to achieve the event. I only thank God that I was not the responsible one and that my eyes were opened before I had committed myself too far. When I think what a miserable existence would have been mine, chained to that—MY GOD—are there no decent women left in this forsaken world?

I should have mentioned, I presume, that I finally moved to my new apartment, and it is really nice. I feel sure, that in time, I can fix it up and have a small semblance of the home that I have always yearned for.

Work is progressing nicely, but I have the old ghost of the Civil Service priority eternally haunting me. Even though I have been reassured time and time again by Appling and Stedwell that I have nothing to worry about, it irks me. For a permanent status on Civil Service can never be achieved except with the 10-point preference granted a disabled veteran. My claim on this matter has been back in Central Office for some time, but no word as yet. I feel sure that although service connection in certain of the listed disabilities may be granted, certainly they will not meet the required 10 percent. The only action I can take in the interim is to write certain affidavits and obtain a statement from Doc Marcus. Stedwell constantly assures me that Appling thinks that I am the best of the Contact Representatives hired so far and that with Stedwell's promotion to another job, I may well be the Contact Officer within a year or so. This is just a little too optimistic for me, and I am certainly not banking on it. In addition, reports reach us that the required three-week school in San Francisco is a mean school of the first water, and three days of solid examination are in order. How about that? I wonder if I will FEEL like taking a vacation after that?'

As always, though, some inner voice compels me to keep on and do my best, for as always, what will be, will be—*OM MANI PADME HUM!*

711-1/2 E. McDowell
Phoenix, Arizona
June 19, 1946

Quite a number of unusual events since I last wrote. First, and perhaps of paramount importance, *l'affaire* Louise is finished. Odd, how our natures seemed to be at continual sword points. One might almost think that there is a basis for the study of horoscopes. Her birthday was December 29th; mine December 30th. I am very cognizant of the fact that I am perhaps somewhat intolerant of womankind in general, due to a series of unfortunate experiences with them. But I can truthfully state that I was far more tolerant with Louise than I have been with any woman since the great V., as there is no doubting the fact that Louise had all of my respect. She was entirely decent and clean. BUT, she was also one of the most selfish persons I have ever met, as well as entirely too cold and merciless. She was the epitome of the demanding, domineering harpy that so many men are literally chained to. Her own desires and conveniences were all that mattered; other people's were secondary. It all came about in an interesting manner. I had invited her over to a "Starlit Concert" in the Gaston's backyard. I put a great deal of preparation into the event—arranging the event, hauling phonograph and records to the backyard, preparing the champagne bucket and the necessary equipment for cold drinks, rigging up extension cords, taking her home from work, calling for her after dinner, etc., etc., ad infinitum. She responded nobly by being late a full half hour when I called for her and then insisted on leaving approximately an hour after her arrival. Naturally I acquiesced politely enough, but when she made her haste so obvious by continually looking at her watch, I remarked (perhaps sarcastically), "I realize it is late, but I shall hurry with the dismantling," and strode off with an armful of records. The thing that utterly sickened me (shades of Virginia) was her reply, hissed in the usual snide way that women have, "Oh, you make me sick—you have to spoil every evening." That was enough. I do not have to take that sort of thing anymore. As she entered the car for the return trip, she said, "You are going to have to act differently if you expect to see more of me." After a long silence, I replied, "You know, somehow I don't think you will have to worry about that." Not another word was spoken on the trip home. I escorted her to the door, and while she hunted for her key, I thanked her for a wonderful evening and walked off. I have not contacted her since and certainly don't intend to.

The days at work have been very busy. I have already answered 169 letters this month and have advised over 500 veterans. I have a new workmate in the office—the new prosthetic appliance Contact Representative—a nice fellow by the name of Ahearn. He has two legs off below the knee. Also, a sickening fop by the name of *** transferred down from the Denver office with 20 months of the highly valued seniority (he made this factor well recognized soon after his arrival). Ahh well, I am becoming so skeptical of the merits and principles of the highly touted Civil Service that nothing shocks me anymore.

I have managed to achieve quite a bit of badly needed sleep recently, and consequently, feel much better than I have for some time.

I am planning another concert for Friday night for lack of anything better to do and have invited Alma Best and Ruth Smith over. Both are of the motherly, matronly type, but they appreciate music, and it should be a friendly evening.

Finally heard from Mother. Bob was married on the 8th of June. *** God forbid that he go through the searing flames that I did, however.

PHOENIX, ARIZONA
711-1/2 E. MCDOWELL RD.
JUNE 24, 1946
Had quite a rugged weekend and spent a bit of money in the process. I

do feel, however, that it was worth it, for I had been growing increasingly restless and ill at ease for some time, and this episode served to release a bit of steam, as it were. Had my first date with a divorcee named Emily Peach. She is a Louisiana girl and has a scintillating personality. Quite attractive physically, but her fun-loving disposition is definitely her biggest asset. Not that I am particularly attracted or smitten, and I shall probably see her a few more times, but it is refreshing to meet someone who can make you laugh.

Work grows busier by the day, or so it seems . . . I now have the twice weekly trek to Papago Park Veterans Hospital (Tuesdays and Fridays), and Appling called me in this morning and informed me that I had been designated to open the new office in Globe. I am to prepare a two-day itinerary tomorrow. THAT shall definitely prove a relief to me—two days out of town. The joy of working hard, new experiences, and who knows, perhaps a bit of fun. People say, occasionally, that I do not laugh enough, and mayhap they are right.

Had an opportunity to peruse the proposed curricula for the forthcoming school at Branch 12 in San Francisco. It does not appear to be too rugged, nothing that I cannot master if it is adequately presented. I presume that I shall go sometime in September, that is, unless plans change. I do hope that the delivery of the Packard can be effected by that time.

Another letter from Mother tonight. She is all "adither" over her forthcoming trip to Long Beach. I am so glad that she is enabled to engage in the many little activities in which she is so interested at the present time.

It is odd, but I seem to have a certain temperament, which allows me utterly no rest. I am never completely satisfied with myself. I have the recurrent feeling that I am accomplishing nothing, that I am getting nowhere. And so it is at the present time, I have a definite, powerful urge to improve myself, to make myself a better man by means of the most careful, meticulous planning. I have most certainly determined that I shall take up valued courses this fall at the Phoenix Junior College, courses that will prove of value and assistance to me in my work. But the thing that beats upon my mind, with the insistent repetition of dripping water, is the question WHY-WHY-WHY do I strive so mightily? For what reason? I, who have utterly no reason to do so, nothing to strive FOR, no incentive, WHY? And yet, it was the same in the Army—there was something that would not let me remain a buck private. Amid the saurian slash of competition at the VA, however, it may well prove to be another story.

Phoenix, Arizona
711-1/2 E. McDowell
July 5, 1946

The Globe trip was quite a success in many ways. At least I had no particular trouble, finished the trip on schedule, and turned in a fairly comprehensive report. Not too much in the way of a reply came from the front office, but I assume it was satisfactory, at any rate. It seemed almost at once after my return that I was again given the task of drawing up plans for the new Contact Office and the new Loan Guarantee Office.

Yesterday was the 4th of July, and Peachy and I rode up to Globe, just for the ride, and took two rolls of pictures. She seems to be a wonderful girl, but of course, one can never tell about women, and it may be some time before I can figure her (and me) out. I have rushed into the situation in my usual impetuous manner, but so far, I have not committed myself definitely. I almost believe, however, that I am in love with her, if such a thing can be possible in the short time that I have known her. She SEEMS to be loving, kind, considerate, a pleasant person, and one who believes and likes the same things I do. But who knows?

Another amazing incident—I received a book in the mail, and naturally, I assumed that it was from Fred Strahl. He delights in sending little things of that nature. But what was my amazement upon opening the card encased inside, to find the following message:

Dear Mac:
 I hope that you will enjoy this book as much as I did.
 I thought of you when I read it because it seemed to
 express all the things that are deep in our hearts.
  Louise

As I noted in an earlier entry, I terminated most abruptly, and with the utmost finality, my association with Louise following the episode on the night of the Starlight Concert. Just what this means I don't know, but at any rate, I am forced to thank her for the book.

Too tired tonight to write much more. Am supposed to have a weekend with Peachy.

PHOENIX, ARIZONA
711-1/2 E. McDOWELL
AUGUST 12, 1946

I note that well over a month has passed since my last entry. Much has happened since then. I have been going out almost continually with Peachy since I first met her about the middle of June—only missed one or two nights, as a matter of fact.

Hard as it is to believe, it has happened at last. I have fallen in love so deeply that it isn't even funny. Try as I may (and I have really tried), I cannot find a flaw in the girl. She is cheerful, loving, and entirely optimistic. She is devoted to me and has the greatest trust in me. She is very pretty, and above all, is clean, decent, and just downright good. Still, I am not rushing into the thing, and I intend to observe very closely. If she lives up to my expectations, and I have no reason to think otherwise, I shall marry her as soon as her divorce is final in April 1947. I have already purchased an engagement ring, but I have it laid aside until about December of this year. I do hope that she proves to be what she so evidently is—a good, clean, woman. I love her dearly, and she gives every indication that she loves me from the bottom of her heart. It's funny, she is the first woman in all this time who has been able to understand me. She understands me in all my blackest moods. She is so tiny and fragile that it makes me want to do my utmost to please her. She is so kind and considerate. She wants no more out of life than I do—just security, a home, a family, and—most of all—a little happiness.

Work and its problems are another story. The old, pressing worry of the 10-point Civil Service Preference has come to the fore again, and it seems as though I must present definite proof to Central Office of some sort of disability. I am working diligently on this by means of affidavits from several people and a physical examination, but only the Good Lord above can tell what the results will be.

Matters seem to be pressing in on me from all sides. The new car definitely will not be available by the end of August, so I intend to keep the Chevy, and if so, I must have a few essential repairs made and plan to keep it for a few more years. The vacation is looming up, and I must purchase a few things for that. The Contact School in S.F. will, in all probability, open in September, and I must prepare for that.

On top of all that, I do not feel too good physically—tired all of the time—and of course, there is a reason for that—too much night life and not enough rest, although I have not been drinking any to speak of.

A bath tonight, and then to bed, and perhaps all of the troubles and worries will soon begin to dissipate.

711-1/2 E. McDowell
Phoenix, Arizona
August 22, 1946

I left at 8 a.m. this morning for the State Penitentiary at Florence. Had some business to transact there, but as I had previously surmised, the totally inefficient staff of clerical help at this institution proved to be utterly valueless, so the statistics that I required will be mailed to me in approximately one week. I could have informed the VA of precisely what would happen, but if they choose to spend some odd 11 dollars to send me down there, I guess I shouldn't howl. I visited Casa Grande on the return and arrived back in Phoenix approximately 2 p.m.

Peachtree was sick at her stomach all day—a touch of ptomaine poisoning, she thought. She felt better by dinner, though.

I began to check over my finances last night and was quite dismayed at the enormous outgo—am determined to cut down and so informed Peach.

Went to the Grunow Clinic and had complete physical to support the various affidavits I intend to send in with my claim. On this matter, only the Good Lord above knows what the outcome will be, but I am certainly hoping, at any rate.

I think the Packard deal is definitely off—at least I wrote the dealer and told him so—and to refund my $100 deposit.

711-1/2 E. McDowell Road
Phoenix, Arizona
August 26, 1946

Home early tonight. Wrote a letter to Mother. Sted and Anne came over and brought me some "T" Shirts and a white shirt that Anne had purchased for me back East. Sorely needed they were, too. All is well with Peach and I. I am more in love with her every day. Sometimes I am awfully impatient and mean with her, caused mostly by my nervousness, I think. She, God bless her, always seems to understand, however. She is the calmest person I have ever met. The only thing that upsets her is when I get in one of my black moods and tell her that it would be best if we parted. She invariably talks me out of it, however. God, how I pray that I have not been fooled once more, that this understanding nature of hers is not a transient, fleeting thing, that it is not something that she utilizes temporarily until we are married. I should know full well by next April, however. She is really undergoing a minute scrutiny, albeit she is standing up well under it.

Work is a veritable holocaust—work, work, work, and more work. The Papago Park detail has developed into a full-time job. On Wednesday, I must speak before the assembled soldiers of Ajo Army Air Base, and on the following Friday, before 2600 soldiers at Williams Field. Subject: "The Activities of the Veterans Administration and How They Affect You."

Sted came out with the portentous news tonight that he may be promoted to the Adjudication Division sometime next month. If so, it is my assumption that Phil Clark will take over the job of Contact Officer; rightfully so, inasmuch as he has seniority to a large degree over the rest of us.

I wrote the Packard Dealer and put my cards on the table—either to get a new car down here—or to return my $100 deposit (to be used to repair the Chevrolet). No reply as yet.

I cannot take my vacation until I hear one way or the other on that matter. I fully expect to leave sometime in September, however. I rather hope the Packard will prove unavailable, for it will undoubtedly prove quite expensive in view of the recent price increases.

711-1/2 E. McDowell Road
Phoenix, Arizona
October 15, 1946

As always, I turn only to "the book" when things are the blackest, and again, as always, after much has taken place. Most important, I am engaged. Yes, on September 6th, 1946, I made what is perhaps the most important decision of my life. I gave Emily her engagement ring. I was convinced, deep in my heart, that I loved her very deeply, else I would never had given it to her. However, if I needed yet more convincing proof, it was furnished me on my vacation for which I departed the next day. I discovered, almost immediately after departure, that I missed her so much that it was almost intolerable. Not a particle of benefit did I gain from the vacation. I did not relax for a moment, hurried from one destination to another, felt tense and hurried during my entire stay, and the longing for Emily was so very intense I could scarce stand it. I returned, bringing Mother with me for a week's stay, but to my dismay, found myself so nervous and irritable that I am yet afraid that I was a miserable host to her. Seemingly, she enjoyed herself, however, and I sent her home on the train. Emily had, prior to my return, flown to Louisiana to visit her Mother who was critically ill with pneumonia, hence she returned only a day or so before Mother's departure. They met, however, and Mother fell in love with Emily. Oddly enough, they have the same birth date—August 13th. O Shades of Astrology! When Emily stepped off the plane on her return, I felt as though life could start anew once more. Our meeting and subsequent courtship has always been so strange; we have both commented on it. Rather than a case of meeting someone and becoming acquainted, it has always been as though two old friends were meeting again after a long absence. I felt as though I were home at last after a long, long absence. God help me now, if anything should ever mar our love, for I am so hopelessly lost it is almost dismaying to me. I fair worship her, and truly, it is the way I have always dreamed of feeling about the girl who would eventually be my wife. I know now, as never before, that the miserable affair that was Virginia was nothing—sordid, cheap, physical, a lesson that had been carved for me on the wheel of fate. Emily is all that is clean and decent, true and faithful, honest, and wondrously trusting. I love her so . . .

After the vacation and the hectic week that followed, I plunged into my work with a vengeance. Much travel ensued, and here came the first hint of trouble. Trouble began to develop with the car—first the tires, then the alignment of the wheels, then the water pump, then the generator, and now the entire motor must be completely overhauled. The upshot of it all was that I have, at the present time, been out some $300 to get the thing in presentable running order.

However, a more sinister development made itself evident. Clark (in charge during Stedwell's absence) informed me of a pending assignment. With a sense of foreboding, I knew for a certainty just what it was—to head the operation of the first Mobile Unit in Arizona. I had been vainly hoping that I would not receive this assignment, for with the hiring of many new representatives, I had hoped to be relieved of some of my itinerant duties. However, willy-nilly, the assignment was mine with insipid excuse, of course, that I was the only "capable man qualified to do it." Eyewash! I caused a considerable commotion about it, and in doing so, uncovered some unpleasant factors. Had some unpleasant words with my old friend, Smith, who took it upon himself to explain the status of my job to me. A bit presumptuous, I thought, in view of the fact that we have identical jobs. However, the reason became clearer, even though Smith and I had a friendly discussion and subsequent understanding. Today, Stedwell, although he didn't have to, informed me that due to the fact that I would be away on the Mobile Unit run, it would be impossible to send me to the two, six-week schools in L.A. and S.F., the Primary and Advanced Schools, without which eventual promotion is impossible. Stedwell informed me that this was not so, but Clark inadvertently showed me the circular previously, which clearly stated the schools were a prerequisite. A very beautiful display of "politics," and as we used to say in the Army, "apple polishing," and by individuals whom I counted as good and true friends. PFAH! Rather stinking and little, *n'est ce pas?*

Tonight, I was rather low ebb, and due principally to the fact that I have a hideous chest cold and am all torn up physically, I determined to stay home on the morrow. Of one thing I am certain, though. I will not allow this sordid mess to discourage me. I shall perform to the best of my ability and give the job everything I have, but the questions that are tearing at my mind tonight are (1) If I lose my job, what is the fate of Emily and I and the life we planned together? (2) When will expenses cease to mount, so that I can save for my home instead of depleting my savings, as at present?

Truly, tonight, rolling back through the years, I hear once more the unanswerable question, "What is it—what is to be? *KISMET*?

711-1/2 E. McDowell
Phoenix, Arizona
December 16, 1946

The showdown is here! Things have been progressing quite smoothly. I was made Itinerant Representative for the State of Arizona and placed in charge of all itinerant operations in this State. I have traveled much during the past two months and have accomplished much in the line of work. However, just the other day was received word that all nonprobationary, nonpermanent representatives would be required to take a standard Civil Service Test in order to retain their positions. Well this is it. Either I pass it, or I don't. In one sense of the word, it is a relief. At least after the test is over, I either will be, or I won't. All I can do in this circumstance is to hope and pray that the test will not prove to be one of those horrendous "anagrams," quite impossible to pass, similar to the ones we have already had, albeit I managed to pass those, so far. The ten-point preference evidently will not mean too much, other than an additional ten points on the exam.

In this emergency, Peach is proving herself to be the loyal, wonderful person that she is. Nothing dismays the girl, and she wants to continue with our marital plans, regardless. Somehow that woman can build me up to the point where I have the utmost confidence in myself. God grant that I merit a woman such as her and always appreciate her for the lovable person she is. I love her.

711-1/2 E. McDowell Rd.
Phoenix, Arizona
December 26, 1946

A bit more of the morass has cleared. I was promoted to a CAF-8 ($3773 per annum salary), and technically, under such a rating, I would not have to take the feared examination. However, I would be required to take it at a later date, and so I feel that I might just as well take it and get it out of the way. Smith's rating finally came through. He was awarded 20%. No word on mine yet, and I doubt that there ever will be any action, at least of the positive type, on it.

The thing that is bothering me at this time, though, is Stedwell's extremely antagonistic attitude. It may be my imagination as Peach says, but I rather think it is a case of my friend, Smith, getting in a good case of old-fashioned politics. Stedwell acts extremely formal and aloof, and compared to his former warm friendliness, the change is rather noticeable. All I can do is to perform my work to the best of my ability.

Peach is as wonderful as ever, and it will only be 3-1/2 months now until we are married. I bought a 12-tube Zenith console radio--$412 for it, but I do think it was worthwhile.

711-1/2 E. McDowell Rd.
Phoenix, Arizona
January 2, 1947

Well! The first entry for the new year. Which all brings to mind, how I wonder just what kind of a year it will be? Undoubtedly eventful—all of mine seem to be. Will there never be peace of mind for me, and a feeling, or at least some semblance of security? Most people, I presume, would tell me to examine my head, what with fortune practically breaking out into a toothsome grin soon after my discharge from the service, and the resultant smooth conversion to civilian life, a wonderful job, a raise in less than a year to a professional salary, and most of all, my meeting with the most wonderful girl in the world—the finest, cleanest, sweetest, inherently good and decent girl in the world—my Peach. However, as usual, there are two sides to every story. Primarily, Civil Service, and its attendant evils, politics and its disgusting subservience to the powers that be. For a time, I had calmed down a bit at the thought of the coming Civil Service Examination, but I visited Smith tonight while Janie and Peach went to the show, and he managed to throw me into the doldrums quite nicely. If the truth were known, Smith is a bit of a smooth politician himself, much more adept than I myself, I might add; and while he is extremely goodhearted and has been a good friend to me, he is not to be trusted, and when it comes to the saurian slash of competition, wields a mean knife in the back.

Peach, as usual, managed to talk me back into a semblance of confidence, and I can face the coming day with a bit more mental fortitude than would be normal under such circumstances. Her never-failing common sense, faith in me, and the love that I seem to know she has for me, never fail to amaze me. She has the ability to make me see everything in a different light, and the realization of what a wonderful person she is makes me realize how truly fortunate I am to have found a person like her in this sordid, mercenary day and age. I could get down on my knees every night and thank the Good Lord for the wonderful day when I met her. I know full well that I shall always love her with all my soul, that I shall never violate her faith in me, and that I shall always treasure what the Lord has seen fit to grant me—the answer to all of my lonely dreams in Europe—and before.

Forward then! To hell with the bitter blows of life, and I shall cram all adversities back into the pits of hell, from whence they came. With Peach beside me, I can take anything.

711-1/2 E. McDowell Rd.
Phoenix, Arizona
January 4, 1947
There is absolutely no sense in kidding myself—I am worried as hell about my job. It just seems as though one little thing will start an

avalanche of others. Roughly, it breaks down into about three separate worries:
   a. The Civil Service angle
   b. Smith's treachery (I seem to sense this)
   c. Stedwell's attitude

While I know it would be best to take the entire situation in good spirits, as other individuals do, the questions that pulsate in my mind interminably and far into the night are WHY? Just as I seem to have arrived at a position, found a girl, and in general, the vista of a beautiful future seems to be unfolding, WHY must a situation of this type arise? Other humans in situations of these kinds have always, it seems, "an ace in the hole" upon which to rely. I—not I—and have never had. Which way to turn then? It is a maddening feeling, one of utter helplessness, a trapped feeling, as though the entire universe were descending, and there is no path leading out. Guess I will have to grin and bear it, however. Thank God, a semblance of Mother's indomitable pioneer courage seems to be in me, and if worse comes to worse, I feel that I will make it somehow. Thank God for Peach, and please God, let her be what I think she is.

711-1/2 E. McDowell Road
Phoenix, Arizona
January 26, 1947
THE DAY IS HERE! By nightfall, tomorrow, I shall know my fate. On one hand, a marriage to the girl I love in only a matter of 78 days, a lovely honeymoon, and the subsequent return to a job that I love. On the other hand, dismissal, and a poverty stricken existence, the subsequent degeneration of our love to a sordid existence caused by poverty and its attendant evils. The saying, "When poverty comes in the door loves flies out the window," I believe to be inherently true. Tomorrow morning at 8:30 a.m. at Bishop Atwood Hall in the Trinity Cathedral, I take the Civil Service Examination, which will determine whether I retain my job or not. I can only deliver myself into the hands of the Lord on this, for if it is a test similar to the Junior and Professional Test given some time ago, I do not anticipate too much difficulty. However, if the powers that be throw in undue amounts of higher calculus and mathematics, then I am sunk before I even start. Tomorrow night, then, I shall enter in here just what fate has decided for me, and until then, I must be of good hope. Forward then! For

Peach and I! For truly, she is the most wonderful woman in the world, and I love her with all my heart and soul.

711-1/2 East McDowell Road
Phoenix, Arizona
January 27, 1947

Well, I THINK I passed the test! To the best of my knowledge, I only had difficulty on about 6 of the 80-some-odd questions. It was a test similar to the Junior and Professional Examination. Of course, it is impossible to ascertain my exact score on the thing, but I do believe that it will be at least the passing grade—70. In talking to Charlie Appling today, he quoted the following interesting statement: "Well, Mac, if worse comes to worse, we can always demote you to a TRAINEE Contact Representative at your present salary." All in all then, the picture does not look too dark. At the completion of the test, I felt as though a load weighing many tons had been lifted from my shoulders. I can only hope and pray that my total score will be above average, and how I hope it is, for I do so want to make good in this vocation. Notice came through today that another mobile unit must be run in early March. It is still questionable whether it will be (1) by bus, (2) by Buick, or (3) coordinated by the planned routes from the regional office, but at any rate, Appling is leaving the thing entirely in my hands, to run as I see fit.

I took Gaston and Anne and Peach to dinner tonight and had a wonderful time.

711-1/2 East McDowell Rd.
Phoenix, Arizona
February 1, 1947

Life, to me, for the past few days, has become unbearable. I feel that I am cracking up physically. I am so tired all of the time, and of late especially, my stomach has a chronic, gnawing ache that is terrible. I really think it is due to the fact that my system became deranged on the last trip that I was on, but the symptoms are so close to those of ulcers that it has me worried. A large part of my nervousness is due to the uncertain status of the Civil Service Examination, for no word has been heard from that thing, and then too, I don't know whether it is just me or not, but the attitudes of STED, Clark, and Smith bother me a lot. Of course, since Smith *** managed to get himself a permanent rating, thus getting out of the examination, he has become unbearable in his attitude. More and more responsibility is thrown on me, and well, why go on? Today, I feel almost as if I were licked. Peach and I haven't been getting along too well, either, due principally, I think, to my physical condition and its attendant nervousness. This thing has got to break sometime, and I hope to God it is soon. I want to know the worst as soon as possible, and if the Lord sees fit, I guess all my dreams can end.

711-1/2 E. McDowell Road
Phoenix, Arizona
February 13, 1947

Tumultuous days, and events by the score. First, I couldn't stand the stomachache any longer, and finally had a gastrointestinal examination. Diagnosis—duodenal ulcer. Evidently not too serious, but enough to restrict my diet and eating habits for some time to come. Second, a letter from 6th Army asking me if I would like to report back to active duty for a period of three months. In a few months from now, such offer might prove very attractive, but at the present time, I would certainly not profit, so I declined with a letter of thanks. Third, a letter from 6th Army, advising me that sometime in February or March I would be required to report to Williams Field to take examination for my application for a Regular Army Commission. Fourth, a talk with Appling regarding my claim and possible Civil Service Status. He was very gracious, as always, but not too much encouragement on either the claim or the Civil Service Register, which is due to be published about April 1st. Sted and Smith went fishing this past weekend. Upon his return, I note Sted still possesses his old attitude to a certain degree. Can't figure out what is wrong with my work or my attitude. I have certainly tried to work my head off but have the feeling Sted doesn't think it satisfactory or something.

711-1/2 E. McDowell Road
Phoenix, Arizona
March 13, 1947

Typical McCully luck! With my impending marriage only 38 days away, I returned from a grueling four-day itinerant tour through Central Arizona tonight, to find an ominous stack of mail awaiting me. First, a notice of my noneligibility for the hallowed 10-point preference from the Central Office in Washington (only 13 months to make this drastic decision). The decision had not taken into consideration the recent diagnosis of ulcer that was sent in. Second, a notice to report for Regular Army Integration at Williams Field on March 11th. Of course, it was impossible for me to comply, so I sent a reply requesting an alternative date.

On all this, as usual, I can only resign myself to fate and await the outcome of the Good Lord's decision. It seems, somehow so very damnably bitter. A man is penalized because he has the guts to get out and get himself a job without waiting for his terminal leave to expire, and when he gets it—on his own initiative—it is taken away because of some asinine technicality.

Truly, what a miserable farce life is.

711-1/2 E. McDowell Road
Phoenix, Arizona
March 20, 1947

Today was the first day of the Regular Army Integration Procedure. I received the notice this morning by registered mail. I informed Sted that I would have to take three days of annual leave in order to complete all of the tests. Nothing was accomplished today but the physical examination, and this is a laugh. According to the Army doctors, I am in perfect health, with the exception of being four pounds underweight, which all goes to show ...

Peach was not too happy about my taking the tests, but I finally convinced her that it was merely to be used as an "ace in the hole." I don't know what, if any, repercussions this may have on my job, but I can only hope that they see and understand my reasons. I hope the determination on the Civil Service exams comes through before the Army tests are finished.

The way I feel, however, I've got to get established in something that will offer a little security inasmuch as I am getting married one month from today.

To me, Emily is all that I have ever dreamed of in a woman. She has proven herself loyal, unselfish, loving, and well, just the most wonderful woman in the world. All I desire is the privilege of taking care of her in an adequate fashion for the rest of our lives.

711-1/2 E. McDowell Road
Phoenix, Arizona
April 1, 1947

At the rate I have been writing in this booklet, I may well be married by the time I make another entry. The Regular Army Integration Tests were a snap. I passed them all with no trouble, however, I imagine it will be some six months before I hear anything regarding the matter. Work has been progressing on the same plane—lots of work, with the exception that my relations with Stedwell, and for that matter, about all of them, have improved. It is evident, now, that most of my nervousness and trouble were caused by the stomach ulcer. The treatment has helped considerably. Still no word as to the results of the Civil Service Examination. I have applied for 10 days annual leave which will make a full two weeks' honeymoon. In preparation for the great event, I ordered a new suit ($75) and bought the necessary accessories to go with it—shirts, ties, socks, etc. Well, no one can say that I have splurged heavily on clothes in the past, so I guess it is not to be regretted. The Chevy, however, is another story—nothing but trouble. I am going to do something about it, but I don't know what. A new one is far too expensive, and the used ones? M'God. Things will just have to work out, I guess. They seem to for everyone else. Why not me?

711-1/2 E. McDowell
Phoenix, Ariz.
July 24, 1947

As usual, a long lapse, and many events.

Peach has proven herself to be a most wonderful wife in every respect. I was granted the 10-point preference for Civil Service by means of a 0% service-connected rating for the old skin disability acquired in Hoff General Hospital. As a result, I passed the Civil Service Test with a total score of 90, including the 10 points granted. On April 11, 1947, I received an adverse decision as to my claim for service connection for the duodenal ulcer. Today, I appealed that decision before a Central Office Rating Board and should know their reaction within two or three days. I do not feel optimistic about any decision they may reach.

As usual, Civil Service is still messed up. The register has not yet been compiled, and hence, I do not know if I will be granted a permanent appointment as yet. In the interim, Congress, by madly slashing all budget appropriations, has caused a general reduction in all positions. This affected our office by the transfer of several training officers to positions of trainee Contact Representatives. This means that they will ultimately be required to take the exam, and it may result in some of the older contact men (such as I) being shoved out (unless I get the permanent appointment).

We bought a 1947 Studebaker Commander on May 22nd, and it has apparently solved all of our garage bills and mechanical expenses, but the payments are quite high. It isn't that we haven't the money to pay the thing off in cash, but doing so would put a ruinous hole in the savings we have accumulated for the purchase of a home (IF I could ever get a permanent rating). The whole situation, in general, tends to worry me terribly, for living expenses are terribly expensive, eating out all the time; and if anything happens to the job, just what in hell would I do to take care of Peach?

Peach developed a fistula and is now in the hospital for its removal. Everything is okay now, though she was operated on this morning and should be home in a few days, thank God.

Once more, as regards everything in general, all I can do is to place myself in the hands of the Lord and let what must happen, HAPPEN.

711-1/2 E. McDowell Rd.
Phoenix, Ariz.
August 12, 1947
A few events of interest, in order to keep the old tome up to date. Still no word on the blasted Civil Service rating, or even of the publication of the hallowed roster (register). In the interim, the reduction of personnel continues, due to the niggardly budget appropriations of the past Congress. The last reduction (still pending at this time) will mean the severance of some 8,000 VA personnel by September 1st. It is nationwide in scope, however, and I do not think the cut will be too drastic in our own office. Certainly, some contact men are going to be eliminated, but in talking to the Assistant Manager today, he indicated that such cuts would remove the training officers recently shifted to contact on a "paper" transfer. As usual, I had quite a bad day of it when I first heard of the cuts, but that wonderful wife of mine talked me out of it. With her, I have the firm conviction that I can face anything. She is undoubtedly the most wonderful person that God ever put breath into. She gives all and asks nothing in return—only for me to love her

and for we two to live our lives together. I, thank God, find all the old mistrust and callousness I formerly had towards all women completely eradicated. I love her more than life itself, for she is all and more that I have always dreamed of finding in a woman.

She returned to the hospital today for the second phase of her operation. I do not think this phase will be quite so serious, for it is merely cauterization of the incision. She has been so very wonderful about the entire ordeal that I almost feel humble about it.

Somehow or other, I am not worrying about the job, for I have the conviction, somehow, that as long as I perform my work efficiently, they are not going to release me, at least not without a struggle.

Our financial situation is a bit critical at this time, but it is understandable with such tremendously high car payments. I will certainly be thankful when the thing is paid for.

OCTOBER 1, 1947
711-1/2 E. McDOWELL
PHOENIX, ARIZ.

Virtually a deluge of water over the dam this time! First, we paid off the balance due on the Studebaker, and so it is now all ours. Secondly, we have purchased a home. I do not think it is too bad a bargain in view of the current trend in prices--$9100. However, I purchased it FHA and paid $1750 down, so the remaining balance is not too bad when spread over the next few years. It is a three-bedroom home with attached garage. It took almost all of our resources to accomplish these two deals, and although very probably the first two months may prove to be quite rough sledding, I believe that, eventually, we will come out all right in the end. How could things go wrong with the wonderful wife that I have? Thirdly, and a source of great satisfaction to me, my appeal to Washington was successful, and I was granted service connection on the duodenal ulcer. With all of these happenings occurring in such rapid succession, my head is practically in a whirl, but I intend to keep my head and more or less tread cautiously in the coming months, for I certainly don't want to go head over heels in debt because of a sudden run of extreme good fortune. Will write more later.

July 15, 1948
950 West Roma Ave.
Phoenix, Arizona

Truly, the swift rush of events since last I wrote in this book has prevented any frequent recording of same. Much has been accomplished. It was necessary to buy the essential furnishings needed to start housekeeping, and so it was necessary to go into debt to a certain extent. Since we moved into the home, however, we have paid very assiduously on such debts and have now depleted them by almost 1,000 dollars. The remaining balance does not look discouraging at all. Truly, I have a most wonderful wife. She is working like a little trouper to help us get the initial increment of furniture, and that is the only thing that is worrying me at present. She is working so hard that she is getting a little nervous and is easily irritated. As for me, I have so much work to do around the house now, and my job to keep up with, that I seem to be chronically tired and easily irritated and upset over the smallest thing. This situation, of course, leads to crankiness and a few minor quarrels, but so far, my marriage has been so perfect, and I have been so happy with my Emily, that I do not want even such little quarrels as we have to appear. I do hope the situation clears itself in time, but I really think the only final solution will be for her to stop work and stay home and be a regular wife and mother. I find myself thinking more and more of how nice it would be to come home to a house sparkling clean and with a nice hot meal waiting AND to be met by a wife who was pleasant and soothing. Then, too, the thought of children seems to gnaw at me of late, for after all, Emily and I are not getting any younger, and even if it means a bit of privation and possible sacrifice, I believe we should plan on a family soon.

Work is progressing satisfactorily, and since my worries about permanent status were stopped, I find that I am able to work with much peace of mind.

I still believe my Emily to be all that I thought she was. I love her dearly and would never knowingly do anything to hurt her. She is such a sweet little person and is truly all that a wife can be.

[*Over one year later.*]

Phoenix, Arizona
950 W. Roma Ave.
Aug. 16, 1949

Well, over a year since the last entry! Again, a veritable deluge of water over the dam.

Congress seems bent on trimming the VA each year, and it seems that each fiscal year means a period of mental agony until the number of personnel to be cut is known.

We were practically forced to buy a new car, a Mercury, by virtue of the fact that the Studebaker turned out to be a first-class lemon. If all goes well, we will have it paid for by Christmas.

The fact that we are again in debt, though, is somewhat depressing, in view of the uncertainty of tenure of employment.

Then, too, politics has reared its head again. ***, it is apparent, is no friend of mine and neither is ***—one that can be trusted, that is.

On the above situation, however, all that one can do is to wait and see what fate decides.

Perhaps the next entry will reveal the solution to what appears to be the unknown at this time.

?

Appendix A: Glossary of Terms

22-5 Manual. Basic Field Manual of Infantry Drill Regulations.
3.2 Beer. Low-alcohol beer.
3R Schools. School for illiterates.
40 Hommes et 8 Chevaux. French for 40 men or 8 horses.
4-F. Registrant not acceptable for military service.
500 pounders. General-purpose bombs that weigh 500 pounds.
66-1. *See* WD AGO Form 66-1.
75th Article of War. Misbehavior before the enemy.
86th Article of War. Misbehavior of sentinel.
A&D sheet. Admissions and Dispositions (medical).
A.W.O.L. Absent Without Leave.
A-2 priority. Assigned to units sent overseas.
AAF. Army Air Force.
Activation Day. Formal activation of the 104th Infantry Division.
Advance Party. A group sent ahead of a military force to perform reconnaissance.
Advanced Service Rating Score (ASR). Determined which soldiers were eligible to be repatriated to the United States for discharge from military service.
AG. Army Ground.
AGF. Army Ground Forces.
AGO. Adjutant General's Office.
Aiming circle. Instrument used to determine gunnery data and laying guns in artillery surveying.
alidade. A sighting device for determining directions or measuring angles, and used in surveying.
American Legion. A wartime veterans' organization chartered by Congress in 1919.
antiaircraft guns. *See* flak guns.
AR 345-415. Army Regulation for sick not in the line of duty.

AR 605-275. Army Regulation for resignation in lieu of trial by court-martial.
Army of Occupation. Army sent to occupy and control the territory of a conquered enemy.
ASR. *See* Advanced Service Rating Score.
ASTP. Army Specialized Training Program.
AT. Antitank.
autobahn. German word for a major high-speed road.
B.A.R. Browning Automatic Rifle.
bacchanalian orgy. Partying involving alcohol and uncontrolled behavior.
Bailey Bridge. A portable, prefabricated truss bridge.
banshee. Female spirit whose wailing foreshadows death.
Battalion Commander's Scope (BC Scope). A tripod-mounted telescope, range finder, and direction finder.
Battle of the Bulge (Bulge). A battle during WWII in December 1944 in which von Rundstedt launched a powerful counteroffensive in the forest at Ardennes and caught the Allies by surprise.
BC Scope. *See* Battalion Commander's Scope.
BCR. Battle Casualty Replacement.
Belgian Maquis. Rural guerilla bands of the Belgian Resistance.
Berchtesgaden. Town where Hitler's "Eagle's Nest" retreat was located.
Big Push. Troop surge that was supposed to bring the war to victory.
billeting. Lodging for troops.
bivouac. A temporary encampment.
blackout. Driving with no lights.
blitzkrieg. German for "lightning war." A swift, intensive military attack designed to defeat the opposition quickly.
boche. Disparaging term for a German.
Bofors gun. A type of light antiaircraft gun.
Bombay. Khaki uniform.
BOQ. Bachelor Officers Quarters.
Bouncing Betty (S-Mine). Hidden underground mine that launches into the air at waist height and then explodes in shrapnel.
Bren gun carriers. Small armored vehicles equipped with Bren guns--lightweight, quick-firing machine guns.
Bulge. *See* Battle of the Bulge.
Bunk fatigue. Sleeping or resting in bed, especially during the daytime.

buzz bomb (robot bomb; V-1 flying bomb). An unguided jet-propelled missile used by the Germans during WWII, characterized by a buzzing sound.
C&G. Command and General Staff School.
C.A. Coast Artillery.
C.M.S. Compulsory Military Service.
Cadre. A nucleus of military personnel.
CAF. Classification for civil service jobs: Clerical-Administrative-Fiscal.
Calvados. Apple brandy.
CAMA. California-Arizona Maneuver Area.
Camels. Cigarettes.
Casual Company. Soldiers who have been grouped together for administrative holding purposes.
casual. A soldier temporarily attached to a unit while awaiting permanent assignment.
CBI. China-Burma-Indian Theater.
C'est la guerre. French phrase of resignation: "It's the war."
CG. Commanding General.
Charge of Quarters. A member of the armed forces who handles administrative matters in a unit, particularly after duty hours.
Chesterfield. Sofa.
CIB. See Combat Infantryman Badge.
Cidre. French cider.
Class 4 priority. Air transportation space available for personnel on leave.
Class E allotments. Portions of pay that soldiers authorize to be paid to other persons or institutions.
CO. Commanding Officer.
Combat Infantryman Badge (CIB). Awarded to soldiers who participate in active ground combat.
command car. Armored vehicle used by military staff and for reconnaissance.
concentration area. An area where troops are assembled before beginning active operations.
Contact School. School for Veterans Administration Contact Representatives.
conventional signs. Various features shown on a map.
Cosmoline. A brand of rust preventative.

CP. Command Post.
CPX. Command Post Exercise.
C-rations. Individual canned, pre-cooked, and prepared wet rations issued to U.S. military when standard food is impractical or unavailable.
D Series maneuvers. Abbreviation for Divisional Maneuver Training (extended maneuvers to test capabilities).
D&C. Drill and Command.
DB. Duty Bulletin.
Decoration Day. Original name of Memorial Day.
Defilade. Protection from exposure to enemy fire.
DEML. Detached Enlisted Men's List.
dermatitis. Inflammation of the skin.
Deutschland Kaput. Reference to the 3rd Reich being broken or finished or dead.
dispensary. A place where medical care and medicines are dispensed.
Dragon's teeth. Square-pyramidal fortifications of reinforced concrete used during WWII to impede the movement of tanks and mechanized infantry.
DS. Detached Service.
Dutch Resistance. *See* Dutch Underground.
Dutch Underground (Dutch Resistance). A resistance group outraged at their country's invasion and their revulsion at what happened to the Dutch Jews.
Duty Officer. Individual charged with responsibility for a military unit.
Eastern Front. A theatre of conflict between the European Axis powers and Finland against the Soviet Union, Poland, and other allies.
efficiency report. Performance report.
Eisenhower jacket. A waist-length military jacket worn on its own or as an insulating layer beneath a field jacket.
Elks (Elks Club, Elks Lodge). Benevolent and Protective Order of Elks (BPOE). An American fraternal order and social club.
Elks Club. *See* Elks.
Elks Lodge. *See* Elks.
EM. Enlisted Men.
ETO. European Theater of Operations.
ETOUSA. European Theater of Operations United States Army.
Fafnir. Dragon slain by Siegfried.

Fascism. A government ruled by a dictator who controls the lives of the people and in which people are not allowed to disagree with the government.
fever therapy. A treatment of disease by fever induced by various artificial means.
flak guns (antiaircraft guns). Artillery designed to shoot upward at airplanes.
FO. Field Order.
Form 20. Qualification record for enlisted personnel.
Forward CP. A base which is set up out in the field.
fragmentation bomb. Aerial bomb that scatters shrapnel upon explosion.
fraternization. Prohibition from personally associating outside of professional duties and orders.
Free Mail. During WWII, mail that was postage free if the word "free" was written in the upper right-hand corner of the envelope.
funny papers. Comic section of the newspaper.
G. T. Graded Test.
G.I. Government Issue.
Garand M1. Semiautomatic rifle.
Garden of the Gods. Area with unique rock formations in Colorado Springs.
Gauleiter. Nazi political leader.
GCM. *See* General Court-Martial.
General Court-Martial (GCM). Consists of not less than five members and a military judge.
German 88. German 88-mm antiaircraft gun.
GI Bill of Rights (Servicemen's Readjustment Act of 1944). Provided college or vocational education for returning WWII veterans as well as one year of unemployment compensation. It also provided loans to buy homes and start businesses.
gig. Demerit.
Grahams. Automobiles manufactured by Graham-Paige.
Guard Mount. Installing the new guard and relieving the old one.
Hasty Bridge. Constructed with inflatable bridging sections, such as pontoons.
Hauptmann. German for "head man," usually translated as captain when it is used as an officer's rank.
Heinie. A derogatory term used for a German soldier.

Hell. "Oh Hell" card game.
Herrenvolk. Master race.
hoosegow. Jail.
horse operas. Westerns.
Hun. Disparaging word for a German soldier.
hutment. Camp of military huts.
I.D.R. Infantry Drill Regulation.
I.G. Inspector General.
Infantry Day. Anniversary of the day (June 15) that George Washington was named commander in chief of the Revolutionary Army.
infantry. Soldiers who fight on foot.
IV Corps. The IV Corps Observation Group was formed for the purpose of operations in the forthcoming American offensives of First Army.
Jerries. Nickname given to Germans during WWII by Allied soldiers and civilians.
JU-88. The Junkers JU-88 was a WWII Luftwaffe twin-engineer, multi-role aircraft.
K.P. Kitchen Police or Kitchen Patrol.
karma. Destiny or fate, following as effect from cause.
KIA. Killed in action.
kismet. Destiny; fate.
K-rations. Individual daily combat food rations, which provided three separately boxed meal units: breakfast, lunch, and dinner.
L&N Railroad. Louisville and Nashville Railroad.
L. rumor. Latrine rumor.
L.M.G. Light Machine Gun.
Latrine. A communal toilet in a camp or barracks.
LCI. Landing Craft Infantry.
liberty ship. Cargo ships built in the United States during WWII.
Luftwaffe. Official name for the Nazi air force.
Luke Field. Arizona air base.
M.C.&C. Mother's Cakes and Cookies.
M.G. Machine Gun.
Manning table. A list of positions and/or workers.
Maquis. *See* Belgian Maquis.
Mauser. A make of firearm, especially a repeating rifle.
Mein Kampf. Adolf Hitler's autobiographical manifesto.

meningitis. Inflammation of the membranes surrounding the brain and spinal cord.
MG34. Maschinengewehr 34: A German machine gun.
MIA. Missing in action.
mortar. A short, smoothbore gun for firing shells (bombs) at high angles.
MOS. Military Occupation Specialty.
MP. Military Police.
MTP. Master Training Plan.
musette bag. A small knapsack.
NCO School. Noncommissioned Officer School.
n'est-ce pas. French phrase added to the end of a question in expectation of an affirmative response.
Nippon. Another name for Japan.
Nips. During WWII, a derogatory term for a Japanese person.
Non-Com. Noncommissioned Officer.
O.C.S. Officer Candidate School.
O.D. Officer of the Day.
O.D. Olive Drab.
O.S.C. Oregon State College
Officer and a gentleman. Expression taken from Article 133, of the United States Uniform Code of Military Justice.
Om mani padme hum. Buddhist mantra.
Orderly Room. A room in the barracks for administrative use.
P&P. Police and Prison.
P&T Office. Plans and Training Office.
Pacific Theater. A major theater of World War II between the Allies and Japan.
palatinate. A federal state in Germany
paregoric. A medicine for the relief of diarrhea and intestinal pain; also used as a cough expectorant.
PEP. Pep talk.
pillbox. A concrete structure for guns and weapons.
POM. Preparation for Overseas Movement.
Port of Debarkation (POD). The geographic point at which cargo or personnel are discharged.
Port of Embarkment (POE). The geographic port from which cargo or personnel depart.
ptomaine. Food poisoning caused by bacteria or bacterial products.

Pullman. A train car with extra comfort such as a sleeping berth.
PW. Prisoner of War.
PX. Post Exchange; an Army post.
pyramidal tent. A canvas shelter shaped like a pyramid, capable of holding six or more persons.
QM. Quartermaster.
Queen of Battles. Napoleon's term for the Infantry.
R.O.T.C. Reserve Officer Training Corps.
RAF. Royal Air Force.
rangefinder. Measures distance from the observer to a target.
RCT. Regimental Combat Team.
rear echelon. The section of an army concerned with administrative and supply duties.
reception center. A place where military recruits are assembled and processed.
reconnaissance patrols. Patrols whose primary mission is to gather information.
reconnaissance. Gathering information about an enemy before taking action.
red gas. Leaded gas.
Remington. Typewriter.
robot bomb. *See* buzz bomb.
rocket bomb. An aerial bomb equipped with a rocket for added velocity after being dropped from an aircraft.
rolling stock. Typically, vehicles that move on a railway; may include vehicles on roadways.
rum go. Surprising happening or unforeseen turn of events.
S&G. Schwartz & Grodin clothier.
S.P. Commissary. Southern Pacific Commissary.
Sam Browne belt. A wide, leather belt supported by a narrow, diagonal strap.
Schmeisser Machine pistols. German automatic weapons, especially submachine guns.
SD. Special Duty.
Servicemen's Readjustment Act of 1944. *See* GI Bill of Rights.
Siegfried Line (West Wall). A series of fortifications along the western frontier of Germany.
small wall tent. A tent with four perpendicular sides, usually larger and with more headroom than most pyramid-shaped tents.

S-mine. *See* Bouncing Betty.
smoker. Barbecue.
spearhead. To lead an attack.
Special Court-Martial. Consists of not less than three members and a military judge.
special order(s). Instructions from headquarters.
squad tent. A tent that accommodates a military squad.
staging area. A place where troops or equipment in transit are assembled or processed.
Station Complement. A base with people assigned to do the routine, everyday tasks necessary to keep the center operating properly.
Stuka dive bomber. The classic blitzkrieg dive bomber of WWII.
Summary Court-Martial. Consists of one commissioned officer.
T/O. Tactical Operations.
Telefunken. A German radio and television company.
Teletype. An electro-mechanical typewriter used to communicate typed messages from point to point through an electrical communications channel.
Third Reich. The German "empire" during the Nazi regime (1933–1945).
trench mouth (Vincent's disease). A severe form of gingivitis.
Trichophytosis. Fungi infection.
typhus. An infectious disease caused by rickettsiae bacteria.
USO. United Service Organizations. Provides programs, services, and entertainment to U.S. troops.
V-1 (V-1 flying bomb). *See* buzz bomb.
V-2 (V-2 rocket). A liquid-fueled ballistic missile and long-range artillery weapon designed for strategic bombing during World War II.
VA. Veterans Administration.
Val-Pak. A type of suitcase.
Victory in Europe Day (V-E Day). Holiday celebrated on 8 May 1945 to mark the formal acceptance by WWII Allies of the unconditional surrender of Nazi Germany and the end of WWII in Europe.
VII Corps. The 104th Infantry Division was the left-flank member of the U.S. VII Corps, which fell under the command of the First Army.
Vincent's Disease. *See* trench mouth.
V-mail (Victory Mail). During WWII, a secure method to correspond with soldiers stationed abroad. A V-mail letter would be censored, copied to film, and printed back to paper upon arrival at its destination.

VOCO. Verbal Orders of Commanding Officer.

WAC. Women's Army Corps.

Wasserman Test. A test for syphilis.

WD AGO 66-1. Officers' and Warrant Officers' Qualification Card. Contains information such as officer's family history, education, civilian experience, qualifications in military specialties, and performance ratings.

WD AGO. War Department Adjutant General's Office.

WD. War Department.

Werewolves (Werwölfe). Members of a Nazi plan to create a resistance force which would operate behind enemy lines as the Allies advanced through Germany. The propaganda far outweighed its actual achievements.

Western Front (WWII). European Theater area encompassing the United Kingdom, France, Belgium, the Netherlands, Luxembourg, Norway, and Denmark.

West Wall. *See* Siegfried Line.

wetting down. A boisterous ceremony for newly promoted officers.

white gas. Camping fuel for lanterns.

XVI Corps. Part of the Ninth United States Army.

Appendix B: Maps

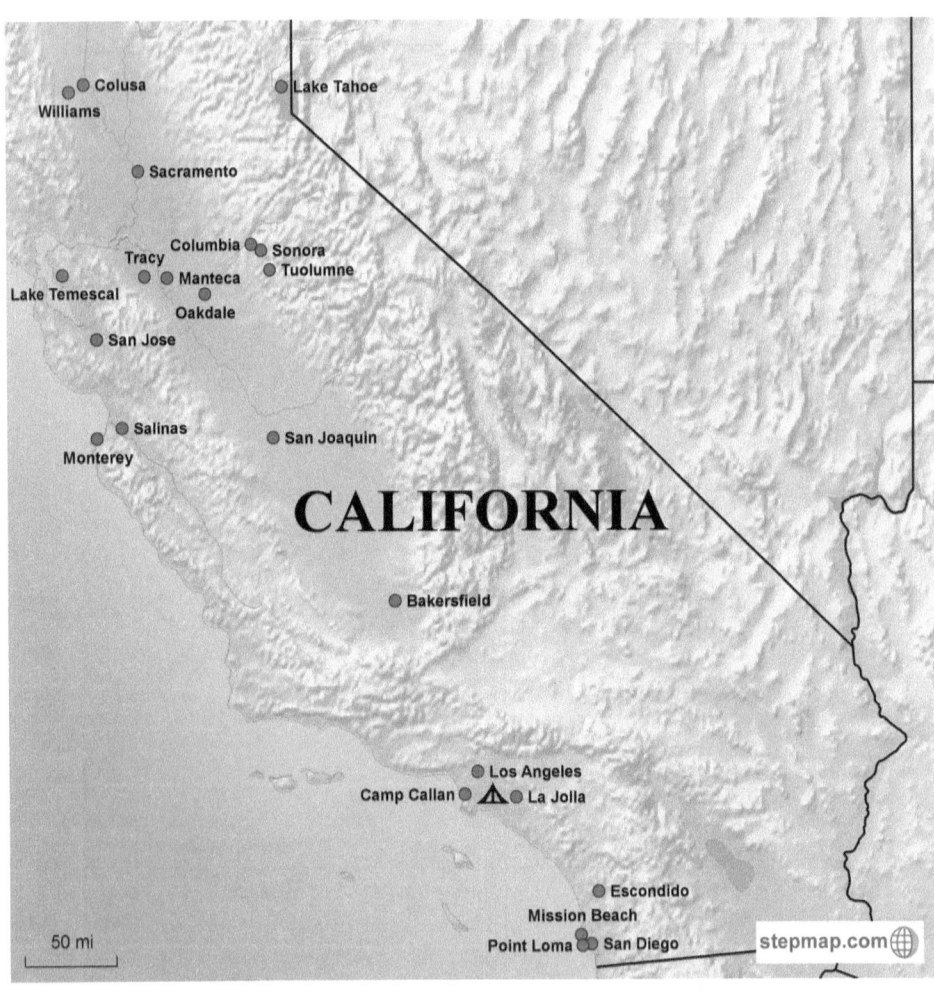

Appendix B: Maps 569

Appendix B: Maps 571

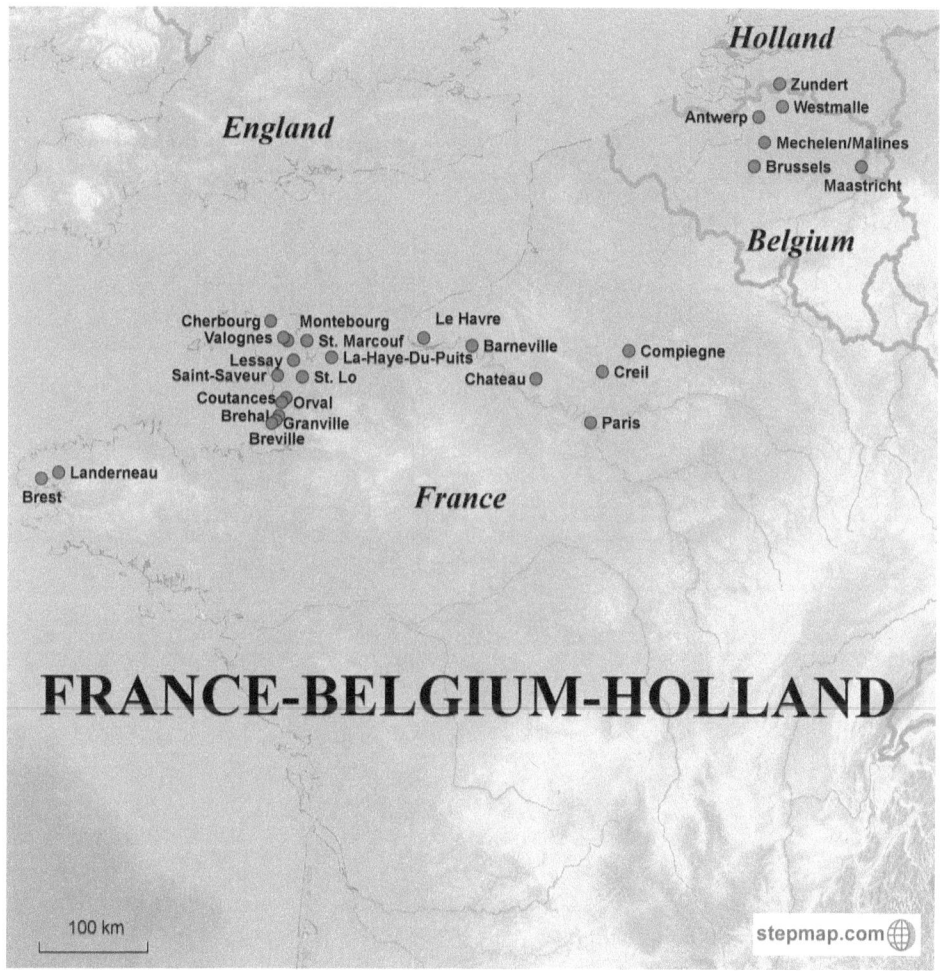

DUREN-COLOGNE AREA GERMANY

Appendix c: Military Awards and Commendations

HEADQUARTERS
104TH *(Timberwolf)* INFANTRY DIVISION

BRONZE STAR MEDAL CITATION

Captain ERNEST J. McCULLY, (Army Serial Number O1289287), Infantry, Service Company, 415th Infantry, United States Army, is awarded the Bronze Star Medal for meritorious service in connection with military operations in Belgium, Holland, and Germany from 25 October 1944 to 21 March 1945. During this period of combat, Captain McCully performed the duties of regimental personnel officer in a superior manner. Because of his great organizing ability, initiative, and loyalty to duty, Captain McCully's regiment is at the top of the list in accuracy and promptness of battle casualty reporting as well as all other phases of administrative work that comes under his supervision. Captain McCully's untiring work and unprecedented devotion to duty is an inspiration to his men and reflects great credit upon himself and the military service. Entered military service from Sonora, California.

SEAL   BY COMMAND OF THE DIVISION COMMANDER

GENERAL ORDERS No. 113 - 1945

Appendix C: Military Awards and Commendations 575

THE PRESIDENT OF THE UNITED STATES OF AMERICA

To all who shall see these presents, greeting:

Know Ye, that reposing special trust and confidence in the patriotism, valor, fidelity and abilities of _____ ERNEST JOHN McCULLY _____ I do appoint him _____ CAPTAIN, INFANTRY _____ in the

Army of the United States

such appointment to date from the _____ SEVENTH _____ day of _____ NOVEMBER _____, nineteen hundred and _____ FORTY-FIVE _____. He is therefore carefully and diligently to discharge the duty of the office to which he is appointed by doing and performing all manner of things thereunto belonging.

He will enter upon active duty under this commission only when specifically ordered to such active duty by competent authority.

And I do strictly charge and require all Officers and Soldiers under his command when he shall be employed on active duty, to be obedient to his orders as an officer of his grade and position. And he is to observe and follow such orders and directions, from time to time, as he shall receive from me, or the future President of the United States of America, or the General or other Superior Officers set over him, according to the rules and discipline of War.

This commission evidences an appointment in the Army of the United States, under the provisions of Section 37, National Defense Act, as amended, and is to continue in force for a period of five years from the date above specified, and during the pleasure of the President of the United States, for the time being.

Done at the City of Washington, this _____ EIGHTH _____ day of _____ MAY _____, in the year of our Lord one thousand nine hundred and _____ FORTY-SIX _____, and of the Independence of the United States of America the one hundred and _____ SEVENTIETH _____.

By the President:

Adjutant General.

W. D., A. G. O. FORM No. 0650 C.
AUGUST 1, 1938

R-E-S-T-R-I-C-T-E-D

HEADQUARTERS, 415TH INFANTRY
APO 104 UNITED STATES ARMY

NS)
44)

9 April 1945

	Section
PURPLE HEART--Awards	I
COMBAT INFANTRYMAN BADGE--Deletion	II
COMBAT INFANTRYMAN BADGE--Awards	III

I. PURPLE HEART--Awards: By direction of the President, under the provisions of AR 600-45, 22 September 1943, as amended, and pursuant to the authority contained in Par 5, Sec I, Cir. No. 2, Hq First United States Army, 4 January 1945, the Purple Heart is awarded to the following EM:

Private First Class Edward W. Davis, (Army Serial Number 13170418) Infantry, Hq Co 1st Bn, 415th Infantry, United States Army, for wounds received as a result of enemy action on 2 April 1945, in Germany.

Sergeant Harry W. English, Jr., (Army Serial Number 38034816) Infantry, Hq Co 1st Bn, 415th Infantry, United States Army, for wounds received as a result of enemy action on 2 April 1945, in Germany.

Private Parven M. Goings, (Army Serial Number 34987312) Infantry, Hq Co 1st Bn, 415th Infantry, United States Army, for wounds received as a result of enemy action on 2 April 1945, in Germany.

Private First Class John B. Smith, (Army Serial Number 33380582) Infantry, Company F, 415th Infantry, United States Army, for wounds received as a result of enemy action on 2 April 1945, in Germany.

Staff Sergeant Neils F. Youngblood, (Army Serial Number 39324272) Infantry, Company F, 415th Infantry, United States Army, for wounds received as a result of enemy action on 2 April 1945, in Germany.

Private First Class Donald W. Hanson, (Army Serial Number 42002125) Infantry, Company I, 415th Infantry, United States Army, for wounds received as a result of enemy action on 2 April 1945, in Germany.

Private First Class Jerome M. Loveland, (Army Serial Number 39323187) Infantry, Company M, 415th Infantry, United States Army, for wounds received as a result of enemy action on 2 April 1945, in Germany.

II. COMBAT INFANTRYMAN BADGE--Deletion: So much of Par. 1, General Orders 14, Hq 415th Inf, dated 29 November 1944, as pertains to Pfc Juan G. Garcia, Jr., 38361300, Co L, is deleted.

III. COMBAT INFANTRYMAN BADGE--Awards: Pursuant to authority contained in Sec I, Par. 2, b, WD Cir. 408, 1944, the Combat Infantryman Badge is awarded to the following named O and EM for satisfactory performance of duty in ground combat against the enemy:

Grade	Name	ASN
Capt	ERNEST J. McCULLY	01289287

SERVICE COMPANY, 415TH INFANTRY

Grade	Name	ASN
Pfc	Gearld W. Bibb	38323152

SERVICE COMPANY, 415TH INFANTRY, CONT'D

Grade	Name	ASN
Pfc	Lee M. Brown	7005150
Pfc	Alexander C. Gitcho	36679538
Pfc	Charles J. Hons	42127844
Pvt	Alvorn Howard	38654346
Pvt	Kendle C. Pestle	35560688
Tec 5	Samuel Singer	32652230

-1- (Over)

R-E-S-T-R-I-C-T-E-D

General Orders # 44, Hq 415th Inf, 9 April 1945, Cont'd:

By order of Colonel COCHRAN:

OFFICIAL:

E. J. McCULLY,
Captain, Infantry
Ass't Adjutant

E. J. McCULLY,
Captain, Infantry
Ass't Adjutant

R-E-S-T-R-I-C-T-E-D

Appendix C: Military Awards and Commendations

RECORDS SECTION
C.A.S.C. UNIT No. 1930
PRESIDIO OF MONTEREY
CALIFORNIA — March 1, 1942
(Reception Center)   (Date)

This is to advise you that

Pvt. Ernest John McCully   39002909
(Name and Army Serial No.)

has this date been assigned to C.A.S.C. 1953, Station Complement, Camp Callan
(Organization, Replacement Center, or other installation) California

His post office address is: As above

This card to be filled out for each man at Reception Center, upon assignment. He will be required to address the card and mail it to his nearest relative.

W. D., A. G. O. Form No. 203
November 1, 1940

HEADQUARTERS 104TH INFANTRY DIVISION
Camp San Luis Obispo, California

24 September 1945

To Whom It May Concern:

    I have known Captain Ernest J. McCully, 415th Infantry Regiment since February 1st, 1944, through intimate contact with him in his duties as Regimental Personnel Officer.

    His duties consist of the personnel administration of over 3000 men including classification and assignment.

    I know Captain McCully to be a man of excellent character and high personal ideals. I consider him exceptionally well qualified in all personnel procedures.

CYRIL T. NAU
Major, AGD
Asst Adjutant General.

**HEADQUARTERS
ARMY GROUND FORCES
OFFICE OF THE COMMANDING GENERAL
WASHINGTON 25, D. C.**

5 January 1946

Captain Ernest J. McCully
206 Shepherd Street
Sonora, California

Dear Captain McCully:

    Your recent return to the civilian pursuits which you left at our country's call, prompts me to express my sincere appreciation for the service you have rendered the Army Ground Forces.

    Our victory would not have been possible without your aid and the aid of other citizens who, like you, left their homes and families to defend our principles of freedom.

    The responsibilities of members of a citizen army have not ceased with the termination of hostilities. I know that you realize your duties to your Government as a private citizen all the more as a result of your military experience.

    I know too, that you will always remember, with pleasure and just pride, the friendships you have made, your experiences with the finest Army in the world and the sincere gratitude of our Nation.

                                          Sincerely,

                                          JACOB L. DEVERS
                                          General, USA
                                          Commanding

HEADQUARTERS, 415TH INFANTRY
CAMP SAN LUIS OBISPO, CALIFORNIA

3 November 1945

Captain Ernest J. McCully
415th Infantry
Camp San Luis Obispo,
California

Dear Captain McCully:

    At this time I desire to express my sincere appreciation for the loyal support you have rendered me and the "Old Faithful" Regiment for the entire period you served with it. Your work was instrumental in making it the outstanding Regiment that it is.

    My very best wishes go to you for continued success in civilian life.

                    Sincerely,

                    JOHN H. COCHRAN
                    Colonel, 415th Infantry
                    Commanding

Lt. Col. Melvin M. Kernan, A.G.D., Adjutant General. / Major Cyril T. Nau, A.G.D., Chief of Personnel Division.
Captain Henry E. Christiansen, A.G.D., Chief of Miscellaneous Division.
Captain Thomas E. Harrington, A.G.D., Postal Officer. / First Lieut. James L. Ryburn, A.G.D., Chief Clerk

HEADQUARTERS 104TH INFANTRY DIVISION
Office of the Adjutant General
APO NO. 104

Camp San Luis Obispo, California

28 September 1945

To Whom It May Concern:

 Captain Ernest J. McCully, O1289287, Infantry, Headquarters, 415th Infantry has been Unit Personnel Officer of the 415th Infantry under both direct and indirect supervision by my office from February 1, 1944 to date and has performed his duties under my close personal observation during all of the above period in a superior manner.

 Captain McCully is well qualified in all classification, job assignment, and personnel procedures and has shown unusual aptitude and insight in the problems involving personnel administration while directly responsible for the entire personnel administration of over 3,000 men and officers in the 415th Infantry Regiment.

 In addition to his thorough knowledge of office management, and personnel procedures, he has indicated superior ability to work long and arduous hours and to get the job done under harassing conditions, including six months of arduous combat in the European Theater of Operations.

 I would highly recommend Captain McCully for assignment to any civilian administrative position involving personnel management.

MELVIN M. KERNAN,
Lt. Col., A.G.D.,
Adjutant General.

HEADQUARTERS 104TH INFANTRY DIVISION
Office of the Commanding General
Camp San Luis Obispo, California

12 October 1945

SUBJECT: Recommendation of Captain ERNEST J. McCULLY, O-1289287, Headquarters 415th Infantry, 104th Infantry Division, for Permanent Commission in the Regular Army.

TO: The Adjutant General, Washington 25, D. C.

1. I have known Captain McCully since 15 October 1943. Since that time, he has served as Personnel Officer, 415th Infantry and in that capacity his work has been known to me by reports and by my own personal observation.

2. Captain McCully is an officer of excellent character, of good judgment, intelligence, and furthermore has a great deal of common sense. He is thoroughly dependable, is very attentive to his duties and is meticulously careful in handling the details of his work. The functioning of the Personnel Section in the 415th Infantry has been most outstanding in this division. I attribute this to the careful supervision and direction of Captain McCully.

3. Captain McCully would be very valuable in the Regular Army, particularly if he continues to operate as a Personnel Officer. He could be used to good advantage in the G-1 Section of a Division General Staff or as a Regimental Personnel Officer. I would be particularly glad to have him continue to serve under me in that capacity. As a Regimental Personnel Officer I would rate him number two of twenty such officers that I know. As a line officer in the infantry in his grade, I am not too familiar with his capabilities, but I would give him a general rating of seven or eight out of twenty such officers.

Terry Allen

TERRY ALLEN
Maj. Gen., U. S. Army
Commanding

SEPARATION QUALIFICATION RECORD
SAVE THIS FORM. IT WILL NOT BE REPLACED IF LOST

This record of job assignments and special training received in the Army is furnished to the soldier when he leaves the service. In its preparation, information is taken from available Army records and supplemented by personal interview. The information about civilian education and work experience is based on the individual's own statements. The veteran may present this document to former employers, prospective employers, representatives of schools or colleges, or use it in any other way that may prove beneficial to him.

1. LAST NAME—FIRST NAME—MIDDLE INITIAL				MILITARY OCCUPATIONAL ASSIGNMENTS		
McCULLY ERNEST J.				10. MONTHS	11. GRADE	12. MILITARY OCCUPATIONAL SPECIALTY
2. ARMY SERIAL NO.	3. GRADE	4. SOCIAL SECURITY NO.		3	2nd Lt	Platoon Leader 1542-9
01 289 287	CAPT	Unknown		14	1st Lt	Battalion Operations Officer 2162-5
5. PERMANENT MAILING ADDRESS (Street, City, County, State)				21	Capt	Personnel Officer 2200
Post Office Box 635 Tuolumne County 204 Shepherd Street Sonora, California						
6. DATE OF ENTRY INTO ACTIVE SERVICE	7. DATE OF SEPARATION	8. DATE OF BIRTH				
4 Aug 42	16 Jan 46	30 Dec 1915				
9. PLACE OF SEPARATION						
Camp San Luis Obispo, California						

SUMMARY OF MILITARY OCCUPATIONS

13. TITLE—DESCRIPTION—RELATED CIVILIAN OCCUPATION

BATTALION OPERATIONS OFFICER: Directed and coordinated functions of staff relative to organization and training and combat operations. Prepared plans for movements of organization for the purpose of tactical training and disposition of troops. Supervised the activities pertaining to mobilization, organization and training of unit. Prepared and coordinated yearly and monthly training directives to conform with those of higher authorities. Kept Battalion Commander informed in current projects, changes orders and directives pertaining to operations and training. Issued operational orders, rules and regulations.
RELATED CIVILIAN CONVERSION: 1. Manager, Office   2. Junior Executive

PERSONNEL OFFICER: Directed and supervised activities relating to unit personnel in the European Theater of Operations. Supervised the preparations and maintenance of records, rosters, correspondence and reports pertaining to personnel matters. Maintained service records of military personnel and requisitions personnel according to qualifications, and handled matters pertaining to transfers and promotions. Supervised preparation of payroll and other reports relative to pay.
RELATED CIVILIAN CONVERSION: 1. Personnel Manager   2. Contact Representative
3. Employment Interviewer

```
                    THE   CHAPEL   NEWS
Chaplain Bratcher - Editor              Chaplain Vick - Co-Editor
Vol. 1 - Issue 3        415th Infantry Regiment     November 13, 1942
```

PLANS MADE TO BEAUTIFY CHAPEL - FUNDS NEEDED!

| THIS AND THAT - HERE AND THERE. Joe Blow. | NOT DEFEATISTS! by Ch. Talbot | Voluntary Gifts Sought!! |

THIS AND THAT - HERE AND THERE. Joe Blow.

Joe wonders why no EM is willing to tell anything on another EM. May be that there is too much known and blackmail is being accepted. Orchids to Co. I this week. Have you seen the orderly room?..Strange to this QQ that Lt. Lepore should receive telephone calls at just any hotel where he is.. Did we say strange!.Two new officers have joined us: Lt. Thomas of Iowa C Co. and Lt. Orndorff of Ill. L Co.Hope you like us..Lt. Voso, the Ju Jitsu expert, had difficulty this morning when in the midst of his antics his pants refused to stay up. Maybe they thought he was doing a rumba..Notice of warning given:Herewith is given official notice that all men valuing their lives should stay clear of Lt. Rochester and his knife..We sincerely hope that Capt.

NOT DEFEATISTS! by Ch. Talbot

We're not licked before we start! We're not afraid of life. We're convinced religion will work. We've listened to the enemies of Christianity decry it so long that you'd think it had failed. While communists believed in communism and tried to put it into the whole of life - while the nazi believes in nazism and has fought this fierce world war to put it into the whole world, we havent failed to try to put Christianity into the Army, business and politics.We're not beaten before we begin, nor are we defeated. We're sure that we can win. We have real faith in our faith. We've hope in Christs promises.
St. Augustine was no soldier, but he was no defeatist.He believed the Christian cause could win and would win. Three years after Aleric sacked Rome he wrote "The City of God".The whole Roman empire had crashed, and with ruin all around him he wrote a book to show how Christianity could save the world.
In the words of the President, this war "is not only a struggle to save democracy.It is also a struggle to preserve our heritage of freedom of conscience.Our enemies have sneered at Christianity as a decadent myth. They are learning that the militant

Voluntary Gifts Sought!!

Have you seen the large jars in Bn. & Hq. bldgs. labeled "Chaplains Fund"? If so you may have wondered if the Chaplains were broke or were trying to collect enough to retire. But as Lt. Eroza would say "At Ease Men". These funds are to make Your Chapel the 'beauty spot' of our Regiment. Ch. Vick with the aid of Lt. McCully and his gang have done 'fine job outside and now we want to do as much inside. We want the Chapel to be a place all men will be happy to worship in. Our first goal is that of purchasing a $100.00 runner,for it is the one way to keep the floors. Other goals are in mind, but this is the most important one.
So brudder, how about a donation? Lets make Our Chapel a Beautiful Chapel!

Information from Remarks section of Form 66-1

Departed for Overseas service 27 Aug 1944, POE NYNY
Arrived overseas - 7 September 1944
Port of Debarkation - Normandy, France. Left Le Havre, France for the US on 2 July 1945 arrived POE NYNY on 11 July 1945

Combat Infantry Badge awarded per General Order 44, Hq 415th Inf Regt, dtd 4/9/45
Bronze Star Medal awarded per General Order 113, Hq 104 Inf Div dtd 4/29/45
Bronze Battle Star - Campaign Northern France - per Ltr Hq ETOUSA, AG 200.6, OPGA dtd 31 Jan 45
Bronze Battle Star - Campaign Rhineland - per ltr 2nd Ind, Hq ETOUSA 14 June 45 to Ltr Hq ETOUSA AG 200.6 11 June 45.
Bronze Battle Star - Campaign Central Europe - per Ltr Hq ETOUSA AG 200.6 OPGA dtd 25 June 45.
EAME THEATHER RIBBON - WD Circular 62, 1944
American Defense Service Medal - WD Circular 44, 1942

Served in France - 7 Sept to 17 Oct 1944
Served in Belgium - 18 Oct to 26 Oct 1944
Served in Holland - 27 Oct to 6 November 1944
Served in Germany - 7 Nov to 17 June 1945
Served in France - 18 June to 2 July 1945

Combat Infantryman Badge presented in Honnef Germany on 9 April 1945
Bronze Star Medal presented in Kothen Germany on 16 May 1945

Appendix D: Curriculum Vitae of E.J. McCully

VITAL STATISTICS

NAME: Ernest John McCully

DATE OF BIRTH: December 30, 1915

PLACE OF BIRTH: La Grande, Oregon

PHYSICAL CONDITION: Excellent

DEPENDENTS:

    WIFE: Emily Virginia - ***

    DAUGHTERS: Anne Denise - ***
        Susan Laurie - ***
        Vicki Lynne - ***

PRESENT ADDRESS: 7250 East Villa Way
Scottsdale, Arizona 85257

TELEPHONE: 946-5623

EDUCATION

GRAMMAR SCHOOL: Attended various grammar schools in McMinnville, Oregon, and in Oakland, California, 1922-1930.

HIGH SCHOOL: Attended Castlemont High School; Oakland, California, 1930-1932. Transferred to and graduated from Roosevelt High School; Oakland, California, in June 1934.

CHRONOLOGICAL STATEMENT OF WORK HISTORY

JUNE 1934-MAY 1935
Following graduation from high school in June 1934, in the depths of the Depression, there followed a period of almost a year of unemployment. Jobs were almost unavailable despite considerable travel in an attempt to locate employment.

MAY 1935-FEBRUARY 1941
In May, 1935, was offered a job as stock clerk at a large wholesale baking concern [Mother's Cakes and Cookies]. Beginning wage was $16 per week (40 cents per hour). By February 1941, had progressed to the position of Stock Control Supervisor with seven employees under my direct supervision. In charge of storage of completed manufactured products, proper rotation thereof, and the ordering of all supplies required in the packing, handling, storing, and shipping of finished products. By the end of this period, had progressed to a monthly wage of $180.

FEBRUARY 26, 1941-JANUARY 16, 1946
Entered service in U.S. Army under the provisions of the Selective Service Act of 1940. Entered service on February 26, 1941, in rank of Private. Monthly pay, $21 per month.

After classification procedures at Presidio of Monterey, California, was ordered to Camp Callan; San Diego, California, where I was placed on duty with the Station Complement in the Plans and Training (Operations) Division at Camp Headquarters. Was in this position for approximately 14 months, during which time I became familiar with all phases of the training operations of a Coast Artillery Replacement Training Center. Acted as Secretary to the head of the Operations Division, Lt. Colonel E. R. Crowell;

responsible for the publication of training schedules; headed the offshore target boat detail during firing practice of 155-mm Coast Artillery Weapons. Was promoted to Noncommissioned Officer rank, and volunteered for Infantry Officer Candidate School.

In May 1942, was ordered to the Infantry School, Fort Benning, Georgia, as an Officer Candidate, and was graduated therefrom in the rank of Second Lieutenant on August 1942. Ordered to duty with the 104th Infantry Division at Camp Adair, Oregon, with a ten-day delay en route. Assigned to Company B, 415th Infantry as a platoon leader. Two weeks later, was assigned as Regimental Police and Prison Officer and held this position until November 2, 1942, when I was appointed to the position of Battalion S-3 (Staff Operations Officer.) In this position, I was responsible for the basic, advanced, tactical, and field training of a full-strength Infantry Battalion of approximately 1,000 men.

In November 1943, was transferred to Headquarters 104th Infantry Division and assigned position of S-3, Special Troops. Was charged with the responsibility of training all Divisional Headquarters Special Troops in a special training program for rear area troops, with emphasis on rear area demolitions and counteroffensive warfare.

Continued in the position of Staff Operations Officer (S-3) with responsibility for basic and advanced field training until a chaotic administrative condition then existing in Regimental Headquarters occasioned my transfer to HQ 415th Infantry Regiment as Adjutant.

During this period of active service as Adjutant, I was responsible for the entire administration of a Regiment of over 3,500 men. This involved all phases of supply, messing, administration recordkeeping, battle casualty reporting, courts-martial, personnel administration, and recordkeeping. Pay, allotments, and allied fiscal matters for over 3,000 men were my distinct responsibility during this phase of activity. I was a member of the Board of both summary and special Courts-Martial and participated as a board member of a general courts-martial involving the death penalty. Participation in these disciplinary and punishment phases of my work necessarily required rather extensive knowledge of military jurisprudence.

The 415th Infantry Regiment landed on Utah Beach in Normandy and fought in France, Holland, Belgium, Luxembourg, and Germany. The Regiment crossed the Rhine at the Remagen Bridgehead, and ended battle on the Elbe River, 44 miles from Berlin, Germany, in May 1945.

In June 1945, the organization was returned to the continental United States and was subsequently deactivated at Camp San Luis Obispo, California.

On November 7, 1945, I was released from active service and placed on terminal leave until January 6, 1946, which ended almost five years of active duty with the U.S. Army, including six consecutive months of frontline infantry combat. During this period of extended active duty, I was subject to the standard efficiency rating procedure then in use. Under this system, every officer is graded once per year, or upon changing assignment, under a scale of ratings ranging from the lowest to the highest in the following order: Unsatisfactory, Satisfactory, Very Good, Excellent, and Superior. These ratings are accompanied by a written documentary relative to the rated officer's abilities and character. During my entire period of active service, I never received less than a Superior rating. I had served under five different rating officers.

I was discharged in the rank of Captain and had been awarded the Combat Infantryman Badge, the Bronze Star with oak leaf cluster, the EAME Theatre Ribbon with three battle stars, the American Theatre Ribbon, and the American Defense Medal. Both Colonel John H. Cochran, my Regimental Commander, and Major General Terry Allen, commanding the 104th Infantry Division, recommended that I be given a Regular Army Commission. ***

NOVEMBER 7, 1945-SEPTEMBER 30, 1954
EMPLOYMENT WITH THE U.S. VETERANS ADMINISTRATION

On November 7, 1945, upon discharge at Camp San Luis Obispo, California, I entrained for Phoenix, Arizona. I had heard that there was a possibility of employment in the Phoenix area. On November 21, 1945, two weeks after arrival, I was employed by the U.S. Veterans Administration Regional Office as a Contact Representative at a beginning salary of $2,980 per annum.

My duties as a Contact Representative are efficiently illustrated in the following excerpts from the Official Veterans Administration "Job Description."

"Duties and Responsibilities:

***

By the early spring of 1949, the Veterans Benefits Program, as promulgated by Congress, had burgeoned to such an extent that the local Regional Office had been forced to designate five additional "Contact" offices in the State of Arizona. Personnel at these offices were then required to service various adjacent communities on an itinerant basis. In effect, this allowed complete coverage for all major communities in Arizona. In July 1949, I was promoted one grade and given the position of Chief, Field Service, for the Veterans Administration in Arizona. The duties and responsibilities of this position are again best described in the official agency "Job Description."

"Duties:

***

In 1952, there was a return to austerity in all Government agencies, and the Veterans Administration was no exception. The position of Chief, Field Services, was abolished, and all outlying offices were closed, with the exception of those Contact Offices in the three major V.A. Hospitals at Phoenix, Tucson, and Prescott. I was retained at the same salary and appointed to the position of Chief, Interviewing Unit, at the Regional Office in Phoenix. As such, I had ten subordinates under my direct supervision and was responsible for their daily activities and personnel administration. In the absence of the Contact Officer, I acted in his place and assumed his responsibilities. I was also held responsible for a continuing program of instruction and education for all Contact Representatives in the State. This included twice yearly seminars and other conference-type periods of formal instruction, with regard to the latest legislative changes.

In approximately 1950, I had met Mr. Hayden C. Hayden

while we were both engaged in U.S. Army Reserve activities. In 1953, he suggested that I leave the Veterans Administration and accept a position with the Hayden Flour Mills. I was reluctant to do so at first, due to the length of time I had incurred in the Federal Service. By the summer of 1954, the ever-recurring office politics of a government office, coupled with the fact that I had practically reached a dead-end street promotion-wise in the Contact Division, impelled me to accept this offer from private industry, and on October 1, 1954, I started to work as Office Manager of the Phoenix office of Hayden Flour Mills. My concluding salary with the Veterans Administration was $6,200 per annum. ***

OCTOBER 1, 1954-MAY 1959

During this period, the Phoenix office of Hayden Flour Mills was moved three times, each time to a more modern location. The full gamut of the administrative functions of a separate office was observed, including posting of receivables and the supervision of a sales force of four salesmen. I had the opportunity to learn every phase of sales, marketing, merchandising, and routine administrative functions. To a degree, this separate office specialized highly in the bakery sales aspect, more so than the other offices.

MAY 1959-TO DATE

In May 1959, I was transferred to the home office in Tempe, Arizona, and given two newly created positions, those of Purchasing Agent and Credit Manager. The company was 87 years old at the time and had never operated these departments as operational entities prior to that time. It was necessary to literally start from zero in both areas. There was no clearly defined credit policy, and operations in this important area were simply chaotic. As for Purchasing, this function had been parceled out to as many as five different people. Duplications, inefficiency, and losses were rampant.

Credit Operations: A general, detailed description of the formation and operation of the Credit Department at Hayden Flour Mills is manifestly too technical to describe here, but perhaps can best be illustrated by referring to my initial Credit Report and the Report for the Fiscal Year ending in April 1967. The enormity of the credit problem facing this corporation in 1959 can clearly be contrasted with the 1967 report, which indicated a corporate loss of only 1/10 of 1%! ***

Purchasing Operations: Hayden Flour Mills, with its diversified activities, purchases enormous amounts of materials and products. As an example, for the bean packaging operation alone, approximately 4,000,000 pounds of various dried beans (15 varieties) are purchased annually. As jobbers for General Mills Bakery Flours, it is my responsibility to contract and purchase 4 to 5,000,000 pounds of such flour yearly. As jobbers for Rust Bakery Products, I purchase from a complete line of 300 manufactured products and over 3,000 jobbed items. The Candy Department utilizes over 41 different types of candy in its rebagging operation.

In addition to the basic materials for these operations, I am also responsible for all other sundry and miscellaneous purchases, such as polyfilm roll stock, enormous amounts of paper and cotton flour bags (91 different types), fibreboard cases, and other packing/shipping requirements.

All of these items are maintained and controlled on a daily perpetual inventory system I devised to best control purchasing in the interest of conservation of working capital.

Among other duties for which I am responsible are those of editor of the company newspaper, published once a month, and for most of the correspondence pertaining to customer relations.

I investigated and checked the possibilities and potential of the addition of the Rustco line to our activities, and after a trip to Denver, recommended its acquisition, even though it meant the construction of a new "cold room" and refrigerated trucks. The addition has since proven an unqualified success.

I participated to a great degree in the organization and setting up of the Hayden Brokerage, flying to Washington, D.C., to aid in this task.

At the present time, I am deeply engaged in a complete redesign and overhaul of our leading brand flour bags.

Responsible for all phases of Federal Government contracting, including submission of bids, negotiation, general administration necessary liaison with subagencies, and other governmental units. As an example, during one seven-month period of 1968, we bid, contracted, and milled in excess of 3,200,000 pounds of all-purpose flour for the Surplus Commodity Program. The entire administration of this program from the original bid to final payment was my responsibility.

In November 1967, I was appointed to the Board of Directors of Hayden Flour Mills and Hayden Brokerage and given the post of Secretary-Treasurer of these organizations.

Ernest J. McCully

CREDIT DEPARTMENT OPERATIONS [Report to H. C. Hayden]

***

<u>APRIL 10, 1950-MAY 31, 1966</u>
During this period of time, which was concurrent with my employment in the Veterans Administration and Hayden Flour Mills, I was active in the organized U.S. Army Reserve. In April 1950, I was appointed Adjutant of the 59th Armored Infantry Battalion, serving under Lieutenant Colonel Donald C. Allen. I attended the usual summer two-week encampments each year in this organization, and as a Staff Officer, it was necessary to devote considerable extracurricular time at staff meetings, conferences, and specialized schooling. In April 1951, I attended a ten-day refresher course for Armored Officers at Ft. Knox, Kentucky. Later in 1951, the organization was changed to the 59th Infantry Regiment, and I was designated Adjutant of the First Battalion of this Regiment.

In April 1952, I attended a refresher course for Field Grade Officers given in a 30-day course at Fort Benning, Georgia.

Early in 1953, I was appointed Regimental Supply Officer for the 59th Infantry Regiment and was in this position until November of that year, when I was promoted to Major and transferred to the position of Regimental Adjutant. I continued in this position, attending the usual summer encampments, etc., until the early spring of 1956, at which time I was appointed to the position of Battalion Commander. During this phase of my activities, I was under the command of Colonel Burton S. Barr.

I was promoted to Lieutenant Colonel in June 1956, and served in this capacity until March of 1958, at which time the unit was again reorganized and designated the First Battle Group of the 59th Infantry. Under this reorganization, I was given the post of Deputy Battle Group Commander, serving under Colonel William F. Campbell.

In approximately 1962, the Battle Group designation was done away with, and the unit was again reorganized into the First Battalion, 59th Infantry of the 191st Infantry Brigade. I was then appointed Commanding Officer of this organization. Vigorous training ensued during the months that followed, and in March of 1963, my organization, by then the largest Reserve organization in Arizona, was ordered to attend the regular Army Maneuver known as "Operation Desert Strike." This took place along the Arizona-California state line, adjacent to the Colorado River.

Routine activities in the Reserve field continued during the next two years, until finally, after twenty-five years of active and reserve duty, I requested a release to inactive duty.

At a ceremony almost a year later, the Department of Defense awarded me the Army Commendation Medal for the conduct of training of my Battalion during these years, and in particular, for the manner in which my Battalion acquitted itself on "Operation Desert Strike." I was informed that the awarding of this medal was unprecedented, as it was the first Commendation Medal ever issued to a Reservist for reserve activities. ***

[The preceding Curriculum Vitae was created by Ernest J. McCully in 1968 at age 53 and was lightly edited by Anne McCully Dorre.]

Appendix E: Timberwolf Resources and Additoinal Reading

104th Infantry Division
http://www.104infdiv.org/

Baker, John H. (2005). *Camp Adair: The Story of a World War II Cantonment* (5th ed.). Newport, OR: John H. Baker.

Hoegh, Leo A., & Doyle, Howard J. (1946). *Timberwolf Tracks* (2004 ed.). Washington, DC: Infantry Journal, Inc.

National Timberwolf Pups Association
http://www.timberwolf104inf.org/

United States Holocaust Memorial Museum (The 104th Infantry Division)
https://www.ushmm.org/wlc/en/article.php?ModuleId=10006155

Wiegand, Brandon T. (2004). *Index to the General Orders: 104th Infantry Division* (1st ed.). Creighton, PA: D-Day Militaria.

Index

104th Division
104th Infantry Division
104th Rear Echelon
1st Army (American)
1st Army (Canadian)
1st Battalion
2nd Army
3rd Army
414th Infantry Regiment
415th Infantry Regiment
9th Army
Aachen (Germany)
Aaron, Thomas
Abbey De Westmalle (monastery)
Adams, Lt. Col.
Adorf (Germany)
Agua Caliente (resort)
Ahearn, John
Ajo Army Air Base
Alaska
Albany (Oregon)
Allen, Donald
Allen, Terry de la Mesa
Allwander, Charles
Alsdorf (Germany)
Altenkirchen (Germany)
American Legion
Ammons, Emmett
Anderson, Lucille
Ann S. *See* Simpson, Ann.
Annabelle. *See* Simpson, Ann.
Annie (social circle)

Antlers Hotel
Antwerp (Belgium)
Applegate (OCS candidate)
Appling, Charlie
Ardell (potential date)
Arizona
Arleen (blind date)
Arline (social circle)
Armory (National Guard)
Aronson, Lt.
Asbach (Germany)
Asia
Atlantic, North
Australia
Aztec (Arizona)
Bad Godesburg (Germany)
Baker, Edward
Balboa Park
Bank of America
Barbara (dance partner)
Barnes, G. C.
Barneville
Barr, Burton
Barurby (soldier)
Beard, William
Beatrice (date)
Beberbeck (Germany)
Bee (social circle)
Behr (OCS candidate)
Beistel, Maj.
Belfast (Ireland)
Belgian Frontier

Belgian(s)
Belgian-German frontier
Belgium
Ben (social circle)
Bend (Oregon)
Benjamin, Bob
Berchtesgaden (Germany)
Bergman, Ingrid
Berkeley (California)
Berlin (Germany)
Bernice (social circle)
Bertram, David
Bessie (social circle)
Best Yet
Best, Alma
Betty (date)
Betty Lee (potential date)
Beverly (date)
Bill F. See Ferguson, Bill.
Bill. See Ferguson, Bill.
Bill. See Meder, Bill.
Bill. See Vaughn, Bill.
Birdsall (co-worker)
Bishop Atwood Hall
Bitterfeld (Germany)
Blanche F. (date)
Blow, Joe. See Elliott, John.
Blue Spruce
Blythe (California)
Blytheville
Bob. See Gilbert, Bob.
Bob. See Westrem, John Robert.
Bochterle (soldier)
Boise (Idaho)
Bonds, Emily. See Peach, Emily.
Bonn (Germany)
Booth, Col.
BOQ (Bachelor Officers Quarters)
Boston
Boulder Dam

Bourke, Ned
Bradley, Omar Nelson
Brand (Germany)
Brauheim (Germany)
Braun, Col.
Brauweiler (Germany)
Bray (co-worker)
Brechbiel (person)
Bréhal (France)
Brent, George
Bresser, Henry
Brest (France)
Bréville (France)
Broadmoor Hotel
Brooks
Broome, Lt.
Brothers (Oregon)
Brown, Ernest
Brownie (social circle)
Brücken (Germany)
Brussels (Belgium)
Buchanan Range
Buckley, William
Bud (social circle)
Bulge (Battle of the)
Burma
Bursfelde (Germany)
Butch (social circle)
Calcutta
California Hotel
California-Arizona Maneuver Area
CAMA. See California-Arizona Maneuver Area.
Camille (social circle)
Camp Abbott
Camp Adair
Camp Beale
Camp Callan
Camp Carson
Camp Granite

Camp Horn
Camp Ibis
Camp Kilmer
Camp Lucky Strike
Camp Robinson
Camp San Luis Obispo
Camp Seely
Camp White
Camp Wolters
Campbell, William
Canifax (social circle)
Cantor, Eddie
Capitol Theatre
Carey, Hugh
Carol (social acquaintance)
Carroll, Ralph
Casa de Mañana
Casa Grande (Arizona)
Castro (social circle)
Cecil's Tavern
Cerisy (France)
Chabot, Lake
Chamberlain, Neville
Chambles, H. E.
Charlie. *See* Schwab, Charlie.
Charlotte (married social acquaintance)
Charlotte (unmarried social acquaintance)
Chattanooga (railroad)
Cherbourg (France)
Cherbourg Peninsula
Cheyenne (Wyoming)
Chicago
Chief of Police. *See* Hale, Chief of Police.
Christiansen, Henry
Chuck (social circle)
Churchill, Winston
Cigar Box (dining establishment)
Civic Center playground
Clark, Phil
Claude. *See* Rafferty, Claude.
Clear Lake (California)
Cliff (social acquaintance)
Clopton, Thomas
Co. D (Company D)
Co. F (Company F)
Coast Artillery Replacement Training Center
Cochran, John
Cody, Lt.
Coffin Butte
Colby, T. B.
Collins, Dean
Cologne
Cologne Opera House
Colorado River
Colorado Springs
Columbia (California)
Columbus (Georgia)
Colusa (California)
Combat Diary
Command Post (CP)
Company 12
Company 20
Company A
Company B
Company C
Company D (Co. D)
Company F (Co. F)
Compiegne (France)
concentration camp
Conover, Nancy
Contact Officer (Arizona VA)
Cook (friend)
Cook, Leo (Camp Adair)
Cook, Maj. (Camp Carson)
Cook, Maj. Gen. (Camp Adair)
Cook, Staff Sgt. (Camp Callan)
Cooley, L. I.
Coon (social circle)

Cooper, Gary
Cooper, LTJG
Cooper, Vivian. *See* Morgan, Vivian.
Corcey, Col.
Corine (social circle)
Corlett, Dr.
Corvallis
Cosmopolitan Hotel
Coutances (France)
Cox, Lt./Capt.
Crane, Capt.
Creil (France)
Crooks (dining establishment)
Crowell, E. R.
Crutchfield, Betty
Curly (work supervisor)
Curti, Ray
Curwood, James Oliver
Czechoslovakia
Dateland (Arizona)
Dave. *See* Davis, David.
Dave's Café
Davidson and Licht (Jewelers)
Davidson, Al
Davila, Lou
Davis, David
Davis-Monthan Airbase
Daylight Limited (railroad)
Deane, John
Deetz, Lt.
DeGraff, Bartholomew
DeGroat, Capt.
Della (social circle)
DeMart, Lucille
Denisevich, Peter
Denver
Deschutes River
Desert Fox. *See* Fox, Ernest.
Desert Fox. *See* Rommel, Erwin.
DeTennencourt, Ted

Diamond (California)
Dillbach (Germany)
Dillenburg (Germany)
Dillinghausen (Germany)
Dom Cathedral
Donley, Robert
Doris (Joe's niece)
Doris (Virginia's sister)
Dorsey (Lt. Moen's date)
Dot (social circle)
Doyle (cashier)
Drachenfels
Dragon's Rock
Drosman, Lt.
Dublin (California)
Duderstadt (Germany)
DuFarge, John
Dugans
Duisburg (Germany)
Dunkel, Gen.
Dupont, Walter Mr. and Mrs.
Durbin, Deanna
Düren (Germany)
Düren Health and Welfare Institution
Dyer, Jack (social circle)
Eastern Front
Eckert, Capt.
Ed E. *See* Erickson, Ed.
Ed. *See* Erickson, Ed.
Eddy, May
Effie. *See* Rafferty, Effie.
Eiffel Tower
Eisenhower, Dwight D.
El Adobe
El Cortez Hotel
Elbe River
Elks Club. *See* Elks Lodge.
Elks Lodge
Elliot, Lt.
Elliott, John

Elwood. *See* Read, Wilbur Elwood.
England
English Channel
Ereza, Lt.
Erft Canal
Erickson, Ed
Erickson, Jean
Erickson, Veryl
Ernest. *See* Leurquin, Ernest.
Ernie. *See* McCully, Ernest John.
Eschweiler (Germany)
Eugene (Oregon)
Eunice (Vivian's sister)
Fairfax (theater)
Fair-Haired Boy. *See* Thomas, Capt.
Falkenburg Rest Camp
Farrington, Capt.
Ferguson, Bill
Flagstaff (Arizona)
Floyd, Col.
Fort Benning
Fort Bragg
Fort Devens
Fort George Meade
Fort Huachuca
Fort Knox (Kentucky)
Fort Leavenworth School
Fort Leonard Wood
Fort Meade. *See* Fort George Meade.
Fort Monmouth
Fort Monroe
Foster, Capt.
Fox Oakland (theater)
Fox, Ernest
Fox, Sneaky. *See* Fox, Ernest.
France
Frank (social circle)
Frankenburg (Germany)
Frankfurt (Germany)
Fred (Vivian's friend)

Fred, Uncle. *See* Read, Fred.
Fred. *See* Strahl, Fred.
Freddy. *See* Strahl, Fred.
Freeland, Capt.
French, Capt.
Frey Ridge
Fruitvale (California)
Furey, Tom
G-1 (Asst Chief of Staff Personnel)
G-2 (Asst Chief of Staff Intelligence)
G-3 (Asst Chief of Staff Operations)
Galloway Range
Gallup (New Mexico)
Garden of the Gods
Gaston, Guy
Geilenkirchen (Germany)
Geneva (social circle)
George (social circle)
Georgia (state)
Georgia, Aunt
German House (Oakland)
Germany
Gilbert family
Gilbert, Bob
Gillingham (person)
Gilmore Oil
Ginny (social circle)
Gladys (social circle)
Glendale (California)
Globe (Arizona)
Goering, Hermann
Göttingen
Gourck, Lt.
Gramophone Shop, The
Grand Canyon
Grand Hotel
Granville
Green, Lt.
Gregory, Forrest
Greiger (co-worker)

Grunow Clinic
Guadalcanal
Guy (social circle)
Haggard, "Pipsqueak"
Hale, Chief of Police
Hall, Harold
Halle (Germany)
Hampton (Oregon)
Hannover (Germany)
Hap. *See* Happy.
Happy (social circle)
Harburg (Harborg)
Harmony Holler
Harold. *See* Westrem, Harold.
Hartman (soldier)
Harvey, Louis [Lewis]
Harvey, Martha Read
Harvey, Wavel [Waval]
Hawaii
Hawkins, Lt. Col.
Hayward, Virginia. *See* Rafferty, Virginia.
Hazel Morton Post (American Legion)
Helen (date)
Helen (social circle)
Henri Chapelle Cemetery
Herbert, Victor
Herbert, William
Himmler, Heinrich
Hiner, Richard
Hines, Shirley
Hitler, Adolph
Hitt, Capt.
Hoboken Ferry
Hodges, Courtney
Hoegh, Leo
Hoff General Hospital
Holder, Master Sgt.
Holland
Holzmann (soldier)

Honnef (Germany)
Hopelain, Richard
Hopkins (in California)
Hopkins District (California)
Hopkins, Mrs.
Horse Ridge
Hotel Alameda
Hotel Corvallis
Hotel Leamington
Hotel Multonomah
Hotel Normandy
Hotel Oakland
Houston
Howard, Lt. Col.
Howell Studio
Hu. *See* Rafferty, Hubert.
Hubbard's
Hubert. *See* Rafferty, Hubert.
Hubie. *See* Rafferty, Hubert.
Huchem-Stammeln
Hümme
Hungary
Hurst, Howard
Hutchings (new recruit)
Hyder
Iceland
Ila. *See* Vaughn, Ila.
Inde River
Inden
Indiantown Gap (Pennsylvania)
Indio (California)
Italy
Jack (Vivian's love interest)
Jack. *See* Dyer, Jack.
Janie (Mrs. John G. Smith, Jr.)
Jansen (Colorado)
Japan
Jeavons, John
Jessen, Capt.
Jessie (social circle)

Jessie H. *See* Jessie.
Jim (husband of Virginia's sister Doris)
Jo (social circle)
Joe (social circle)
Joe Blow
Joe Blow. *See* John Elliott.
Joe. *See* Elliott, John.
John, Uncle. *See* Read, John.
Joyce. *See* Rafferty, Joyce.
June (mail correspondent)
Jingletown
Kansas City
Kaup (soldier)
Kay (Lt. Moen's date)
Kay (social circle)
Keiser [Kaiser], Dorothy
Kelleher, Gerald
Kernan, Melvin
Kilmer, Joyce
King, Maj.
Knape, Col.
Knut. See Westrem, Knut.
Königswinter (Germany)
Koonrod, Lt.
Korbach (Germany)
Kramer, Brig. Gen.
Krauser, Laura (social acquaintance)
Kreitz, Sgt.
Kyne, Peter B.
L&N Railroad
L.A. (Los Angeles)
L.P. (social acquaintance)
La Belle (France)
La Haye Du Puits (France)
La Jolla (California)
La Jolla Shores Beach
La Pine (Oregon)
Lakeside Officers Club
Lakeside Park
Lambert (work foreman)

Lamersdorf (Germany)
Landerneau (France)
Landing Craft Infantry
Lauck, Marvin
Lauterbach (Germany)
LCI (Landing Craft Infantry)
Le Frigate
Le Havre
Lear, Ben
Leipzig (Germany)
Leiser, Doc
Lena. *See* Schwab, Lena (McCully).
Leonard, Lt.
Les ***
Lessay (France)
Leurquin, Ernest
Lewises (landlords)
Lichtenbusch (Germany)
Liège (Belgium)
Lilienstern, Charles
Lippstadt (Germany)
Local Loan
Lola. *See* Sainsbury, Lola (McCully).
Long Beach
Long Butte (Oregon)
Lonnie (blind date)
Lorraine (social circle)
Los Angeles
Losey, Lt.
Louie, Uncle. *See* Harvey, Louis.
Louise (date)
Louis-Godoy fight
Louisiana
Lövenich (Germany)
Lt. Thomas (fair-haired boy, Major's pet)
Lucherburg [Lucherberg] (Germany)
Lucky 13
Luftwaffe
Lugo, Adolf
Luke Field

Luthi, Adolph
Lyle (former best friend)
M.C.&C. (Mother's Cakes and Cookies)
Maaschrict (Holland)
Mac. See McCully, Ernest John.
Machern (Germany)
Magdeburg (Germany)
Major Elliott
Malines. See Mechelen.
Mallalieu, Charles
Mamie (mail correspondent)
Manitou Springs (Colorado)
Manteca (California)
Marburg (Germany)
Marcella (former co-worker)
Marcus, Doc
Margaret ***
Margaret. See Margie.
Margaret. See Read, Margaret.
Marge (social circle)
Margie (love interest)
Marilynn (mail correspondent)
Martin, George
Mary ***
Maryann (social circle)
Maryl (social circle)
Mattie, Aunt. See Harvey, Martha Read.
Maud (co-worker)
Max (acquaintance of mother)
Maxine (date)
Maxine (social circle)
May (social circle)
McCarthy, Lt.
McCully, Emily. See Peach, Emily.
McCully, Ernest John
McCully, Nettie. See Westrem, Nettie.
McDonald, James
McGinnis, James
McKerney, Bernard
McLaughlin [McLoughlin], Comerford

McLoughlin, Mary
McMinnville (Oregon)
McRaff (social circle)
Mechelen (Belgium)
Meder, Bill
Mel (social circle)
Melloh, Maj.
Merken (Germany)
Metz (France)
Meudes (social circle)
Meuse, The (river)
Mexico
Mike (social circle)
Miller, Lt.
Milligan, Maj. Gen.
Mills, A. K.
Mission Beach (California)
Mittelbau-Dora Concentration Camp
Moen, George
Moldau, The (river)
Monmouth (Oregon)
Monohan (debtee)
Montagne, Vivian
Montagu (France)
Montebourg (France)
Monterey Bay (California)
Monterey Station
Monterey, Presidio of
Monterey, Reception Center at
Monty. See Montagne, Vivian.
Moore, Bryant
Moraga (California)
Moresnet
Morgan, Art
Morgan, Mrs.
Morgan, Vivian
Mother. See Read, Nettie.
Mother's (Mother's Cakes and Cookies)
Mother's Cakes and Cookies
Mulcahy, Col.

Mussolini, Benito
Mutt (husband of Vivian's sister Eunice)
Myrtle (date)
Naas, Sgt.
Nadine (second cousin)
Nashville
National Guard Armory
Nau, Cyril
Needham, Fred
Needles (California)
Neill, Robert
Neilsen, Capt.
New Mexico
New Orleans
New York
Nicky (Margie's brother)
Niedermarsberg (Germany)
Niles Canyon
Nippon
Nordhausen (concentration camp)
Nordhausen (Germany)
Normandy
North Haven Officers Club
Northington, Harold
Norway
O.C.S. (Officer Candidate School)
O.S.C. (Oregon State College)
Oahu
Oakdale (California)
Oakland (California)
Odelsheim (Germany)
Officer Candidate School
Oglesbee, Roscoe
Olive (John Strahl's girlfriend)
Olsen, John
Oregon State (College)
Orval (France)
P&T Office (Plans & Training Office)
Pacific Limited (railroad)
Pacific Square

Paderborn (Germany)
Palladium
Palmer (co-worker)
Pam (social circle)
Papago Park Veterans Hospital
Paramount (theater)
Paris
Park Boulevard
Pat (social circle)
Patch, Alexander
Patton, George S.
Paul's Inn
Peach, Emily
Peachtree. *See* Peach, Emily.
Peachy. *See* Peach, Emily.
Pearl Harbor
Peggy (social circle)
Pennington (soldier)
Petersen, Captain
Phil (fellow soldier)
Philippines
Phoenix (Arizona)
Phoenix Junior College
Phyllis (date)
Piemonte's
Plans and Training Office
POD (Port of Debarkation)
POE (Port of Embarkment)
Point Loma (California)
Portland (Oregon)
Post Engineer's Office
Post Theatre
Powell, Maj.
Power, Tyrone
Prevics, Martin
Pruitt, Lt.
Puchau (Germany)
Pueblo (Colorado)
Que Tal (nightspot)
Quirrenbach (Germany)

Quisling, Vidjun
Rabenscheid (Germany)
Raff. *See* Rafferty, Hubert.
Rafferty, Claude
Rafferty, Effie
Rafferty, Hubert
Rafferty, Joyce
Rafferty, Virginia
Rasmussen, Bob
Raton (New Mexico)
Read, Fred
Read, John
Read, Major. *See* Read, Wilbur Elwood.
Read, Margaret
Read, Nettie. *See* Nettie Westrem.
Read, Ruth
Read, Wilbur Elwood
Rebman, Roger
Redding (Vivian's fiancé)
Redwood Canyon
Rehfus, John
Reno (Nevada)
Rhine River
Rices, The
Richmond (California)
Richmond Baths
Richmond Plunge
Richton, Lt.
Riggs (co-worker)
Rita (social circle)
Ritz
Robbins, Lt.
Robbins, Maj.
Robertses (landlords)
Robinson, Maj.
Rockefeller, Winthrop
Rocky Mountains
Roer River
Rommel, Erwin
Ross, Sgt.

Round-up
Roxie
Roxie
Roy, Capt.
Ruby (social circle)
Ruhr (Germany)
Russell, Regina
Russi, Robert
Russians (Russian Army)
Ruth (date)
Ruth, Aunt. *See* Read, Ruth.
Rutledge, Carl, Jr.
S.F. (San Francisco)
S.P. Commissary (Southern Pacific Commissary)
S-1 (Personnel Staff Officer)
S-2 (Intelligence Staff Officer)
S-3 (Operations Staff Officer)
S-4 (Logistics Staff Officer)
Saale, River
Saar
Saarbrücken
Sackett, Miss
Sacramento (California)
Sainsbury, Lola (McCully)
Sainsbury, Walt
Salem (Oregon)
Salerno, Margaret
Salinas (California)
Salt Lake City
Sam (co-worker)
Sammons, Cecil
Sam's Log Cabin
San Diego
San Francisco
San Francisco Bay
San Joaquin (river)
San Joaquin Valley
San Jose (California)
Santa Ana Army Air Base

Santa Barbara (California)
Santa Fe Streamliner (railroad)
Santa Monica (California)
Scheldt Estuary
Schnell, Col.
Schöneburg (Germany)
Schwab, Charlie
Schwab, Lena McCully
Schwammenauel Dam
Scrugham, John
Seaman (social circle)
Secretary of War (Stimson)
See Huy Low's (Chinese restaurant)
Sentinel (Arizona)
Service Company
Sheppard Field (Texas)
Sherman's (dining establishment)
Siberia
Siegfried Line. See West Wall.
Silver Lake (Oregon)
Simpson, Ann
Skipper
Slichter, Vernon
Smathers, Don
Smerz, William
Smith, Capt. See Smith, John, Jr.
Smith, John, Jr.
Smith, Lt. (regiment)
Smith, Lt. Colonel
Smith, Lucille (date)
Smith, Mrs. (Colonel's wife)
Smith, Ruth
Smitty. See Smith, John, Jr.
Sonora (California)
Sorrwine (social circle)
South America
South Pacific
Southern (fellow soldier)
Spud (social circle)
St. Lo (France)

St. Louis (Missouri)
St. Marcouf (France)
St. Sauveur
St. Valery
Stambaugh, Clinton
Stanley (social circle)
Stansbury (driver)
Stanwyck, Barbara
Sted. See Stedwell, Hermon.
Stedwell, Anne
Stedwell, Hermon
Stefanski, Ted
Stevenson, "Sneaky." See Major Stevenson.
Stevenson, Maj.
Stolberg (Germany)
Stone, Vivian
Storm (draftsman)
Strahl, Fred
Strahl, John
Strahl, Melanie
Stratton Park
Strauss, Johann
Strauss, Johann, Jr.
Strelnick, Danny
Stump, Clarence
Sucey (fellow soldier)
Sullivan's Plunge
Sulphur Springs
Sunset Cliffs Road
Suttle Lake
Swann, Capt.
Switzerland
Sylvia (date)
T&D (theater)
Tahoe, Lake
Taliaferro, Lt. Col.
Temescal (California)
Temescal, Lake
Texas

The Beaver (railroad)
The Owl (railroad)
The Palms (theater)
The Silver Spur (nightspot)
Thibodeaux (OCS candidate)
Thomas, Lt.
Thomas, Russell (Capt.)
Three Sisters (mountains)
Timberwolf
Timberwolf Division
Timberwolf Regiment
Timberwolves
Tommy (social circle)
Toni (social circle)
Toots (social circle)
Tower Bowl (bowling)
Tracy (California)
Trappist Monastery
Treasure Island (San Francisco)
Trinity Cathedral
Tucson
Tufts, William
Tuolumne (California)
U.S. Grant Hotel
Upham, Lt.
USAT Cristobal (ship)
Utah Beach (Normandy)
VA (Veterans Administration)
Valerie (secretary)
Valognes (France)
Valognes-Cherbourg Road
Vancouver (Washington)
Vasilake, John, Jr.
Vaughn, Bill
Vaughn, Ila
Venita [Vineta] (Vivian's daughter)
Veryl. *See* Erickson, Veryl.
Veterans Administration
Vic (social circle)
Vick, Capt. *See* Vick, Thomas.

Vick, Thomas (chaplain)
Vienna
Virginia. *See* Rafferty, Virginia.
von Runstedt, Gerd
Vrick, Pvt.
Wagner, Richard (composer)
Wald Forest
Wally (social circle)
Walt (social circle)
Walt. *See* Sainsbury, Walt.
Warburg (Germany)
Washington (D.C.)
Washington (state)
Washington Park
Wavel [Waval]. *See* Harvey, Wavel.
Wee Willies
Weende (Germany)
Weisweiler (Germany)
Wellton (Arizona)
Weser River
West Point(er)
West Wall. *See* Siegfried Line.
Western Front
Westmalle, Abbey de
Westrem, Harold
Westrem, John Robert
Westrem, Knut
Westrem, Nettie.
Wetter (Germany)
Willamette
Williams (California)
Williams Field
Williams, Maxine
Willoughby, Lynn
Wingenbach, Lt.
Wood, James
Woodward, William
Yakima (Washington)
Young, Sterling
Yuma (Arizona)

Zane, Pvt.
Zundert (Holland)